THE DE HAVILLAND
DRAGON / RAPIDE FAMILY

An AIR-BRITAIN Publication

DH.90 Dragonfly VP-YAX of Rhodesia & Nyasaland Airways shows its smooth lines on a pre-delivery flight   *[via C N Dodds]*

THE DE HAVILLAND
DRAGON / RAPIDE FAMILY

John F Hamlin

An AIR-BRITAIN Publication

Published in the United Kingdom by:

Air-Britain (Historians) Ltd.,
12 Lonsdale Gardens,
Tunbridge Wells, Kent TN1 1PA

Sales Dept:
41 Penshurst Road, Leigh,
Tonbridge, Kent TN11 8HL

Correspondence to:
John F Hamlin, 26 Chivers Road,
Haverhill, Suffolk CB9 9DS
and not to the Tunbridge Wells address

ISBN 0 85130 344 7

Printed in the United Kingdom by:
The Cromwell Press Ltd,
Aintree Avenue,
White Horse Business Park,
Trowbridge, Wiltshire BA14 0XB

Origination by: Steve Partington,
                 Nailsworth, Gloucestershire

Colour illustrations by: Peter Coker

Front cover photograph:
  Beautifully restored Dragon Rapide G-AEML "Proteus", c/n 6337, over water.   *[via C N Dodds]*

Rear cover illustrations:
  Top: *After a period of use by Hillman's Airways, G-ACAO, c/n 6001, became the Dragon demonstrator before returning to Hillman's.*
  Centre: *Originally G-ADEA, c/n 2323 of Hillman's Airways, DH.86 Express A31-7 was used as an air ambulance in the Middle East.*
  Bottom: *G-ADAJ, c/n 6276, one of Hillman's Airways' Dragon Rapides, later spent time in Madagascar as F-BEDY before going to Indo-China.*

Contents

Foreword

I never cease to be surprised, whenever the Dragon Rapide is mentioned in conversation, how many people say to me *"Oh yes, I remember that old aircraft – it was the first aircraft I ever flew in"*. Without exception, those people then happily recall affectionate memories of the old girl – a rare and unusual feeling in relation to any aircraft, but one regularly expressed about Dragons.

In this book, John Hamlin and the Air-Britain team have created, through years of considerable knowledge and research, the definitive record of this aircraft and its close relatives; its younger sister the DH.84 Dragon, its senior sister the DH.86 Express Air Liner (or 'Double Dragon' as *The Aeroplane* dubbed it), and the lightweight DH.90 Dragonfly, so that all those pleasant memories can be recalled in detail. These four types were all conceived and built by the enterprising de Havilland company within the remarkably short period of two and a half years, and yet, nearly seventy years later, reasonable numbers of all but the Express Air Liner remain extant throughout the world. This fascinating book and its forthcoming second volume provide the most detailed information ever available in one place, and tell us all about these delightful old aircraft, who used them, and where to find the survivors.

As one who has flown all but the Express Air Liner, I find the superbly researched histories and the fascinating photographs totally absorbing, and suggest that the book has an essential place on the bookshelf of everyone who has an interest in the de Havilland enterprise and its illustrious place in our aviation heritage.

Colin Dodds.

Acknowledgements

Lennart Andersson
Phil Butler
A Chivers
Peter Coker for the colour drawings
Paul Crellin for information on the Israeli Rapides
P J Cummins
John Davis
Colin Dodds for the Foreword and for his ready help
Carlos Dufriche for his help with aircraft on the Brazilian register
David Duxbury
Malcolm Fillmore for his invaluable support
Peter H T Green for the loan of many photographs
James J Halley MBE
John King
Michael Magnusson for his help with aircraft on the Argentinian register
Ray C Sturtivant ISO for his unstinting help and loan of photographs
N D Welch

We must also mention that Air-Britain stalwart, the late Dennis Fox, who sadly died early in 2003. When his estate was being settled, a large box of Dragon Rapide photographs came to light, suggesting that he, too, intended at one time to compile a history of the type. We are grateful to his widow for making the photographs available and, in part, dedicate this book to his memory.

Introduction

Apart from the ubiquitous Dakota, few transport aircraft have made such a significant contribution to the development of airline travel, particularly in the United Kingdom and Australasia, as the four members of the de Havilland Dragon family, the DH.84 Dragon, DH.86 Express Air Liner, DH.89 Dragon Rapide and the DH.90 Dragonfly. By 1936, almost every scheduled airline service within the UK was being flown by one or more of the types which are the subject of this book.

When the Dragon first took to the air in 1932 in response to requests from existing de Havilland customers, the design team cannot, surely, have envisaged the long-term effects on civil and military aviation that their new design would have. The Dragon appeared at a time when airline services in the United Kingdom were just becoming viable, and there were few suitable aircraft on the market outside the United States. The design therefore soon established an excellent reputation among many new airline companies which appreciated its economy of operation and its reliability.

It must, therefore, have given the de Havilland team great satisfaction to be asked to produce drawings for a four-engined development, the DH.86 Express Air Liner, principally for use in part of the new Empire Air Route to Australia. However, as will be seen, the design process of the prototype was rushed, which led to a stability problem which had to be dealt with after the first few aircraft had entered service. Eventually the problem was resolved by de Havilland, but it is doubtful whether the DH.86 reached its full potential before production ended in 1937.

After the Dragon had been in production for less than two years a development of the design, the DH.89 Dragon Six (soon renamed Dragon Rapide) appeared. A more efficient development, this was the type that became best-known and respected throughout the world. It was a winner from the outset, and nearly 200 had been built for civilian use before the outbreak of the Second World War. They entered service with a host of airlines and air charter companies at home and overseas, as Appendix 4 demonstrates, and were remarkably reliable.

Finally, the DH.90 Dragonfly was designed, more as a smaller development of the Dragon Rapide for private owners than as an airliner, although several were used as such. There was a restricted market for an aircraft of this type, the 'executive' aircraft of its day, and only 67 had been built by the time production ended in 1938.

For British military purposes, all four types were accepted, albeit belatedly. Before the war, the DH.89 was submitted to the Air Ministry as a potential coastal reconnaissance aircraft, but the contract was awarded to the Avro Anson. A few DH.89s were acquired for use in Radio Schools and for short-distance VIP transport, but when war broke out, substantial orders were placed for the design, to be known by the RAF as the Dominie, for communications work and for use as navigation and radio trainers. Further examples were impressed from their civilian owners. Production continued throughout the war and beyond, latterly by Brush Coachworks Ltd at Loughborough. The RAF withdrew the Dominie from service soon after the war, but the Fleet Air Arm, which had acquired a substantial number of the type, continued to use them until 1961. On a smaller scale, impressed DH.84s were found useful by the RAF for a relatively short time early in the war. No DH.84s were built specifically for military use in the UK, but in Australia 87 were constructed for the RAAF for communications and navigation and radio training. A few DH.86s were acquired second-hand by the Air Ministry for the RAF before the war to carry VIPs on tours of inspection and more were impressed later, as were a few DH.90s. Likewise, examples of all four types were used by the air forces of Australia, New Zealand, South Africa and Canada, as well as Lithuania, Iraq, Iran and other countries.

To operate important internal air services during the Second World War, the Associated Airways Joint Committee was set up and used DH.89s and some DH.84s and DH.86s. Reliability in those days of shortage of spares and fuel was paramount, and the de Havilland types seldom let their crews down.

When the war ended, few examples of the Dragon, Express or Dragonfly remained in service in the UK, but the Dragon Rapide was a very different matter. Aircraft at the end of the Brush Coachworks production run of Dominies, not used for military purposes before being converted for civilian use, found ready customers anxious to start operating a variety of small-scale air services in many parts of the world, for which the type was seen to be eminently suitable. In the UK, the AAJC developed into British European Airways, which became the largest owner (though not necessarily operator) of Rapides. Many former RAF Dominies of older vintage also found their way onto the post-war civilian market, again eagerly acquired by small airlines, many of which unfortunately did not survive long.

Inevitably, use of the Rapide declined as more modern types were introduced, and gradually the type was withdrawn, firstly from scheduled services and later from charter work. Since then, several Rapides have been rebuilt in various parts of the world and are flying in first-class condition, though not doing anything more arduous than giving pleasure flights. Likewise, a few Dragons and Dragonflies still exist, though unfortunately no DH.86 Express Air Liner has been seen in the air since 1958.

The DH.92 Dolphin, of which only one was built and flown, should not be forgotten, although its excessive weight would not have allowed it to become a success. An updated DH.89, it carried two pilots and had a retractable undercarriage, and is said to be the only de Havilland product not to have been photographed in the air.

This volume, the first of two, provides the reader with information on the development and use of each member of the Dragon family, a detailed history of each aircraft, brief technical notes, and information about the many UK airlines and charter companies which have used them. A companion volume will include much more detailed operational and anecdotal material, and although there may be some overlap of information between the two publications it is intended that together they will provide the complete, comprehensive story of this fascinating family of aircraft.

In this volume an attempt has been made to provide as much information on individual aircraft as space allows. Of necessity, a certain amount of 'shorthand' is involved, particularly where military units are concerned. Designations of such units are readily accessible through the Abbreviations list, while code markings are shown between square brackets. To conserve space, categories of damage sustained in accidents are generally not mentioned. Inevitably, the fates of a relatively small number of aircraft cannot be traced, often because official records in some countries no longer exist. If readers are able to provide the missing information it will be gratefully received.

John F Hamlin

July 2003

The precursor of a large family; prototype DH.84 Dragon c/n 6000 as E.9 at Stag Lane in November 1932

Part 1: The DH.84 Dragon

Background

Aware of the success that use of the single-engined DH.83 Fox Moth biplane was bringing him on his route from Clacton to Ramsgate via Essex Airport (Maylands), Edward Hillman of Hillman's Airways & Saloon Coaches Ltd lost no time in urging de Havilland to produce a larger, twin-engined version offering the same economy of operation. One of his criteria was that the initial cost must not be more than £500 per revenue-earning seat. Coincidentally, the Iraqi government had already made a request for a similar design, although earning capacity did not enter their equation! De Havilland's designer, A E Hagg, quickly set about producing working drawings for a wire-braced two-bay biplane with a fixed undercarriage, designed to carry up to six passengers to Paris, for example, on no more than 4.5 gallons of fuel per passenger, each with 45 pounds of baggage, an economy that had never been accomplished before.

After just four months in the design and construction stage, the prototype DH.84 Dragon, registered E.9, took to the air at Stag Lane on 24th November 1932 in the hands of H S Broad. It was to sell for £2900 ex works, for which money a fully-furnished cabin, tools, and covers were included. The disposable load equivalent was 82% of its operating weight, and simplicity was the keynote. It could be maintained by one mechanic and a labourer, who had access to all control cable runs via a zip fastener that ran the length of the underside of the fuselage. The airframe was extremely strong but light, a major contributory factor to the Dragon's economy in use.

Hillman's Airways took delivery of the prototype, re-registered G-ACAN, in December 1932, enabling Hillman to open his route to Paris from Romford (Maylands/Essex Airport) in April 1933. With a fare structure which reflected the Dragon's economical operation, this service became an immediate success, and three more Dragons were delivered in May to allow expansion. All four were modified to contain eight seats after the rear luggage compartment had been removed.

At the end of April 1933 a two-week promotional tour of the United Kingdom was undertaken by Dragon G-ACCE *Pathfinder* of Brian Lewis & Co Ltd, which had just received its Certificate of Airworthiness. The itinerary for the trip was as follows:

30th April	Heston – Southend (probably Ashingdon) – Norwich (Mousehold)
1st May	Norwich – Cambridge (Fen Ditton) – Nottingham (Tollerton)
2nd May	Nottingham – Manchester (Barton) – Liverpool (Speke) – Blackpool (Squires Gate) – Blackpool (Stanley Park)
4th May	Blackpool – Hull (Hedon) – Newcastle (Cramlington)
5th May	Newcastle – Glasgow (Renfrew)
6th May	Glasgow – Edinburgh (Turnhouse) – Belfast (Sydenham)
8th May	Belfast – Dublin (Baldonnel) – Hooton Park
9th May	Hooton Park – Birmingham (Castle Bromwich) – Coventry (Whitley) – Bristol (Whitchurch)
10th May	Bristol – Cardiff (Pengam Moors) – Plymouth (Roborough)
12th May	Plymouth – High Post – Portsmouth
13th May	Portsmouth – Shoreham – Eastbourne (either Frowd's Field or Wilmington)

Further military authorities soon began to take an interest in the Dragon after the first was delivered, on 13th May 1933, to the Iraqi Air Force. Known as the DH.84M, these aircraft were to be involved in the quelling of local disturbances and for patrol work, and could carry sixteen 20lb bombs. In addition, a mid-upper gun position, lower fuselage and nose guns were provided. A long curved dorsal fin was a feature of the DH.84M. Other DH.84Ms included two for the Danish Army Air Force delivered in March 1934 and three from the end of the production line in 1937 for the Portuguese Air Force.

Dragons began to replace Fox Moths on routes operated by Midland & Scottish Air Ferries and Scottish Motor Traction Co. in 1933. Established with one Dragon as its fleet, Northern & Scottish Airways flew scheduled services between Glasgow (Renfrew), Campbeltown, Islay and the outer Hebrides, while Aberdeen Airways operated three Dragons on routes from Kintore (later from Dyce). Also flying out of Aberdeen was Highland Airways, which operated four Dragons on the Orkney Islands route to Kirkwall.

The Dragon proved popular in export markets, largely due to its economy and simplicity of operation. Examples were soon delivered to Spain for Automobiles Fernandez, Canada for Canadian Airways, Iraq for Iraq Petroleum Transport Co to replace DH.50s on pipeline patrols, to India for Indian National Airways, and many to African operators. These included two operated by Wilson Airways on a route from Nairobi to Mombasa, Zanzibar and Dar-es-Salaam. Dragons were frequently employed by small airlines and charter companies and for photographic and survey work, particularly in Australia and New Guinea.

Some Dragons were owned by private individuals, including the Prince of Wales, who used a suitably equipped four-seat aircraft, G-ACGG. Dragon G-ACCV *Seafarer* was modified to have extra fuel capacity and a stronger undercarriage for an attempt on the world long-distance record by Jim and Amy Mollison, but on taxying out at Croydon on 8th June 1933 the undercarriage gave way, delaying the departure. After repair, the aircraft took off from Pendine Sands and arrived at Bridgeport, Connecticut, 39 hours later, only to turn over on landing. The engines and tankage were retrieved and used in a second Dragon, G-ACJM *Seafarer II*, which was used for an abortive second attempt at the record. However, in the hands of J R Ayling and L Reid this aircraft did create a record for the first non-stop flight from the Canadian mainland to Great Britain in August 1934.

An improved version known as the Dragon 2 entered production at the 63rd aircraft, and boasted faired-in undercarriage struts and separately- framed windows. One of the pioneer British airlines was Jersey Airways, which took delivery of its first aircraft, six-seat Dragon G-ACMJ, at Stag Lane on 15th December 1933. Seven more Dragons entered service with Jersey Airways within the next few months, carrying thousands of passengers safely, proving the technical features of the design and its economy in operation. Another major user of the Dragon was Railway Air Services, which used them on its network of scheduled services.

During the Second World War, eighteen British-registered Dragons were impressed into the RAF for use with Anti-Aircraft Co-operation Units and other support units. Of these, only one survived to be restored to the civilian register, the others all being Struck Off Charge after short but intensive service lives. Other examples were retained to fly the few very important civilian services maintained throughout the war by the AAJC, and G-ACPY was shot down by a Luftwaffe aircraft in the course of such a flight to the Scilly Isles.

In Australia, seven Dragons Mk.1 and four Mk.2 were impressed by the RAAF between January 1940 and March 1941. This number did not, however, satisfy the expanding demand for radio and navigation training aircraft, and so an order was placed with de Havilland Aircraft Pty Ltd at Bankstown for eighty-seven Dragons with enlarged windows, to be built on jigs sent out from

Hatfield. The first of these, A34-12, was flown on 29th September 1942. Several examples were used as communications aircraft and in the air ambulance role. At the end of the war 46 of the RAAF Dragons were sold to civilian operators and saw service with airlines and charter operators in Australia for several years.

From the individual aircraft histories, it will be seen that several examples of the DH.84 still exist in the UK or Australia, either airworthy, in museums or derelict.

Technical specifications

Designed to carry six passengers, each with 45 lbs (20.45 kg) of luggage, the fuselage of the DH.84 was of spruce and plywood construction with a high proportion of glazing. The single pilot reached his cockpit through a door in the cabin bulkhead and when seated enjoyed an excellent field of vision. The two engines were housed in nacelles on the lower mainplane, beyond which were standard Gipsy Moth high aspect ratio outer wing panels which folded for ease of hangarage. A rear luggage compartment was sometimes removed to allow two extra seats to be installed for short-range journeys. The Dragon's cruising speed, 109 mph (175 kph) required the consumption of only 13 gallons (23.11 litres) of fuel per hour, giving the economy of operation demanded by the type's early operators.

Engines:	Two 130 hp de Havilland Gipsy Major 1	
Dimensions (from maker's original manuals):		
Span	47 ft 4 in (14.43 m)	
Length	34 ft 6 in (10.52 m)	
	[2 ft 0 in (0.61 m) longer in floatplane version]	
Height	10 ft 1 in (3.07 m)	
Wing area	376 sq ft (34.94 sq m)	
Weights:		
Tare	2285 lbs (1039 kg)	[Dragon 1]
	2510 lbs (1141 kg)	[Dragon 2 landplane]
	2910 lbs (1323 kg)	[Dragon 2 floatplane]
Max. perm.	4200 lbs (1909 kg)	[Dragon 1]
	4500 lbs (2045 kg)	[Dragon 2]
Maximum speed:	128 mph (206 kph)	[Dragon 1]
	134 mph (216 kph)	[Dragon 2 landplane]
	120 mph (193 kph)	[Dragon 2 floatplane]
Cruising speed:	109 mph (175 kph)	[Dragon 1]
	114 mph (184 kph)	[Dragon 2 landplane]
	95 mph (153 kph)	[Dragon 2 floatplane]
Initial climb:	612 ft/min (186 m/min)	[Dragon 1]
	565 ft/min (172 m/min)	[Dragon 2 landplane]
	500 ft/min (152 m/min)	[Dragon 2 floatplane]
Service ceiling:	12,500 ft (3811 m)	[Dragon 1]
	14,500 ft (4420 m)	[Dragon 2]
Range (still air):	500 mls (805 km)	[Dragon 1]
	570 mls (918 km)	[Dragon 2]

Australian-built DH.84 A34-13, c/n 2002, in RAAF service   *[P H T Green collection]*

Production

6000 – 6061	DH.84 Dragon I
	(except 6003 – 6008, 6012, 6013 DH.84M)
6062 – 6114	DH.84 Dragon II
2001 – 2087	DH.84A Dragon III

Individual Aircraft Histories

6000   The prototype DH.84, originally regd as **E.9** and first flown by Capt Hubert Broad at Stag Lane 24.11.32; regd **G-ACAN** (CoR 4018) 16.11.32 to Hillman's Saloon Coaches & Airways Ltd (t/a Hillman's Airways Ltd), Maylands (fleet number 7); first CoA issued 16.12.32; named *Maylands* by Amy Johnson 20.12.32; transferred to new company Hillman's Airways Ltd 11.33; to Aberdeen Airways Ltd, Dyce,16.8.34 and regd (CoR 5359) 17.9.34, replacing G-ACRH; named *The Starling* after the company's chief pilot, Eric Allen Starling; leased to Olley Air Service Ltd, Croydon, 21.8.35 and returned; company renamed Allied Airways (Gandar Dower) Ltd by its owner, Eric Leslie Gandar Dower, 13.2.37; on 21.5.41 Harry Reed agreed to fly two company employees and three passengers at very short notice from Dyce to Kirkwall after the grounding of a DH.89 Rapide with engine problems; due to an error the machine had not been refuelled, and both engines stopped over the Moray Firth; by jettisoning equipment the pilot managed to glide over the cliffs and force-land in a field on Hilltown Farm, near Dunbeath, Caithness, the aircraft running through a stone wall which crushed the nose; Harry Reed was seriously injured, and died nine days later, but all other occupants were unhurt.

6001   Regd **G-ACAO** (CoR 4019) 16.11.32 to Hillman's Saloon Coaches & Airways Ltd (t/a Hillman's Airways Ltd), Maylands, named *Goodmayes*; regd (CoR 4122) 11.1.33 to de Havilland Aircraft Co Ltd, Stag Lane for use as demonstrator; first CoA (3742) issued 3.2.33; regd (CoR 4304) to Hillman's Saloon Coaches & Airways Ltd 31.3.33 (fleet no 8); to new company Hillman's Airways Ltd 11.33; possibly to Portsmouth, Southsea & Isle of Wight Aviation Ltd, Portsmouth; to Norman Edgar (Western Airways) Ltd, Weston-super-Mare, 6.35 and regd (CoR 6405) to director and nominee Lady V E M Apsley, Badminton, 15.10.35; regd (CoR 8617) 8.7.38 to Norman Edgar (Western Airways) Ltd (Western Airways Ltd from 18.10.38); impressed into RAF with civilian registration; 6 AACU, Ringway, 4.4.40; 7 AACU, Castle Bromwich, 3.5.40. allocated serial **X9398** 10.5.40; while flying from Church Fenton to Usworth 21.10.40 pilot lost his bearings in poor visibility and aircraft force-landed at Parliament Oak, Clipstone, Ollerton, Notts, colliding with a hedge and suffering undercarriage collapse and damage to the port wing-tip and both starboard mainplanes; to DH RU, Witney, for repair 24.10.40, but SOC 21.2.41.

6002   Regd **G-ACAP** (CoR 4020) 16.11.32 to Hillman's Saloon Coaches & Airways Ltd (t/a Hillman's Airways Ltd), Maylands; first CoA (3743) issued 9.2.33; del 25.2.33, named *Romford* and given fleet no 9; to new company Hillman's Airways Ltd 11.33; crashed at Stapleford Tawney 23.6.35 and repaired; taken over by British Airways 10.35; sold via Airwork Ltd 12.35 and regd (CoR 6717) 8.2.36 to Commercial Air Hire Ltd, Croydon; crashed at Stoney Cross, nr Lyndhurst, Hants 26.3.36 during night Army co-operation flight; five killed including pilot F J Birmingham.

Prototype DH.84 G-ACAN at Stag Lane in late 1932, carrying out engine runs before delivery to Hillman's Airways   *[via C N Dodds]*

Seven of eight DH.84M aircraft for the Iraqi Air Force just before delivery from Hatfield on 5th May1933. They were fitted to carry a gun in the nose, lower fuselage and mid-upper position, plus twelve 20lb (9 kg) bombs   *[via C N Dodds]*

6003   First CoA (3858) issued 7.4.33 for Iraqi Ministry of Defence as **16**; left Hatfield 5.5.33; no further trace (NFT).

Two of the Iraqi Air Force DH.84Ms in flight   [Keystone B8479]

One of the Iraqi Air Force DH.84M Dragons, serialled 19, after crashing at Mosul in August 1943   [MAP via P H T Green]

6004   First CoA (3871) issued 20.4.33 for Iraqi Ministry of Defence as **17**; left Hatfield 5.5.33; NFT.

6005   First CoA (3854) issued 8.4.33 for Iraqi Ministry of Defence as **18**; left Hatfield 5.5.33; NFT.

6006   First CoA (3855) issued 8.4.33 for Iraqi Ministry of Defence as **19**; left Hatfield 5.5.33; crashed on take-off from Mosul 8.33 when undercarriage failed; probably repaired; NFT.

6007   First CoA (3879) issued 25.4.33 for Iraqi Ministry of Defence as **20**;left Hatfield 5.5.33; NFT.

6008   First CoA (3880) issued 25.3.33 for Iraqi Ministry of Defence as **21**; left Hatfield 5.5.33; NFT.

6009   Regd **G-ACBW** (CoR 4065) 13.1.33 to Hillman's Saloon Coaches & Airways Ltd, Maylands (later Hillman's Airways Ltd), named *Gidea Park*, fleet number 10; first CoA (3856) issued 13.4.33 and del same day; to new company Hillman's Airways Ltd 11.33; regd (CoR 5319) 25.8.34 to Flt Lt H Thomas and W J Byrne for operation by Provincial Airways Ltd, Croydon (later Plymouth (Roborough)); company ceased trading 9.35; named *Neptune*; converted by Airwork Ltd as air ambulance for Air Dispatch Ltd, Croydon; nominal sale to Union Founders Trust Ltd 3.9.36 and thence to Federation Populaire des Sports Aeronautiques, Paris but not delivered; sold 19.10.36 to Joseph Hermann, Paris, on behalf of Cie Air Taxi, Vienna (a non-existent company) but detained at Croydon; regd (CoR 7548) 15.12.36 to Union Founders Trust Ltd, Croydon; bought back by Air Dispatch Ltd 26.1.37 and regd (CoR 7732) 5.3.37 to Mutual Finance Ltd, Croydon; regd (CoR 8409) to (associate) Advance Air Lines Ltd, Croydon; regd (CoR 8468) 22.4.38 to Anglo European Airways Ltd, Croydon; operated in 1.39 by Air Dispatch Ltd and sold but not regd 28.2.39; regd 11.12.39 to (associate) Commercial Air Hire Ltd, Cardiff; impressed into RAF 27.10.40 as **BS816**; 6 AACU, Ringway, 2.11.40; to DH RU, Witney, for inspection 6.9.41; SOC 22.10.41; became GI airframe **2780M** at 115 ATC Sqn, Peterborough, 29.10.41.

6010   Regd **G-ACCE** (CoR 4073) 24.3.33 to Hon. Brian Lewis, t/a Brian Lewis & Co Ltd, Heston; used for demonstration tour, named *Pathfinder*; first CoA (3864) issued 21.4.33; loaned to Highland Airways 14-19.7.33; loaned to Jersey Airways Ltd, Portsmouth, wef 18.12.33; sold (but not regd) to Highland Airways Ltd, Inverness (Longman) 24.4.34, named *Caithness*; operated first-ever British internal air mail service, to Kirkwall, 26.5.34; written off 29.8.34 when it failed to take off from Kirkwall (Wideford) after a downpour and hit a stone wall; pilot and seven passengers were not badly hurt; broken up for spares at Inverness; regn cld 9.34.

The last of the eight DH.84Ms delivered to the Iraqi Air Force, c/n 6013, was serialled 23. Its mid-upper gun mounting can be seen clearly
[MAP via P H T Green]

6011   Regd **G-ACCR** (CoR 4085) 28.2.33 to W. A. Rollason for Rollason Aviation Co Ltd, Croydon; regd to R T Boyd, also of Rollason Aviation; first CoA (3846) issued 3.4.33; operated wef 10.33 by Barnstaple & North Devon Air Services, Heanton Court, Barnstaple (formed by Boyd); damaged on third landing on Lundy Island 3.6.34; rebuilt and sold 8.34 to Maurice Goodley, t/a Commercial Air Hire Ltd, Croydon; hired to Jersey Airways; regd (CoR 5497) 13.12.34; converted to air ambulance 8.35; struck by lightning during night flight from Le Bourget to Croydon 22.1.36 and force-landed off beach near Ault lighthouse, Le Treport and wrecked by tide; regn cld 1.36

6012   First CoA (3885) issued 1.5.33 for Iraqi Ministry of Defence as **22**; left Hatfield 5.5.33; NFT.

6013   First CoA (3886) issued 1.5.33 for Iraqi Ministry of Defence as **23**; left Hatfield 5.5.33; NFT.

6014   Specially-built for long range record flight, with 600-gall fuel tanks and other modifications; regd **G-ACCV** (CoR 4089) 7.3.33 to Mrs J A Mollison (Amy Johnson), Stag Lane, named *Seafarer*; first CoA (3925) issued 4.3.33; positioned to Croydon on 8.6.33 for non-stop flight to New York as part of record flight to Baghdad; due to the heavy weight of the aircraft, it was positioned at the extreme end of the airfield to allow the maximum take-off run, but it ran over rough ground, which caused the undercarriage to collapse; damage repaired and the aircraft flew to Pendine Sands, South Wales, for another attempt; departed 22.7.33 on first westward transatlantic flight; arrived Bridgeport, CT, 24.7.33 after 39 hours but wrecked on overshooting at night, Jim Mollison and Amy Johnson being slightly injured; airframe was badly damaged and was abandoned, but engines and fuel tanks were salvaged and used in replacement aircraft G-ACJM (c/n 6049).

6015   Regd **G-ACCZ** (CoR 4093) to Midland & Scottish Air Ferries Ltd, Renfrew; first CoA (3872) issued 11.5.33; modified to allow carriage of stretcher in place of normal eight seats; flew first ever Scottish air ambulance flight on day after delivery; damaged in accident at Antrim due to engine failure 14.9.33, but returned to Glasgow by sea and was repaired, flying again on 14.12.33; M&SAF ceased trading 9.34 and aircraft sold to unnamed dealer; regd (CoR 5874) 15.5.35 to Crilly Airways Ltd, Doncaster and Leicester (Braunstone); receiver appointed 9.9.36 and aircraft seized in Portugal; sold 10.36 to H Welch of General Motor & Tyre Co, Hammersmith but still in Portugal 1.37; CoA lapsed 29.6.37; regd (CoR 8224) 16.11.37 to Aircraft Facilities Ltd, Witney; possibly used by Western Airways Ltd in 1938; regd (CoR 8450) 12.4.38 to Flt Lt E Noddings and operated by Air Dispatch Ltd, Croydon; CoA renewed 23.5.38; regd 22.1.40 to Air Dispatch Ltd, Cardiff (Pengam Moors); impressed into RAF 7.40 as **AW154**; SF Ringway 6.7.40; 8 AACU, Weston Zoyland, 10.8.40; loaned to 7 AACU, Castle Bromwich, 16.9.40 to 5.10.40; 7 AACU 13.1.41; SOC 10.11.41; became GI airframe **2820M** at ATC 635 Sqn, West Hartlepool; 3.12.41; SOC 20.12.42.

6016   Regd **G-ACDL** (CoR 4166) 21.4.33 to Midland & Scottish Air Ferries Ltd, Renfrew; first CoA (3873) issued 12.5.33; regd (CoR 5361) 19.9.34 to Hon Mrs Victor Bruce; operated by Commercial Air Hire Ltd, Croydon; sold 1.35 and regd (CoR 5701) 16.3.35 to Provincial Airways Ltd, Croydon, named *Juno*; company in liquidation 12.35; regd (CoR 6984) 2.5.36 to Luxury Air Tours Ltd, Croydon; sold (but not regd) 8.36 to Union Founders Trust Ltd; purchased by Cdte Pastor Krauel (Senior Spanish Air Force Officer); left Croydon for Barcelona 15.8.36 on delivery to Republicans; transferred from Prat de Llobregat (Barcelona) to Sarinena near Zaragoza in Aragón 18.8.36 to be fitted with rudimentary armament and be incorporated into Alas Rojas (Red Wings) Squadron until unit disbanded 10.36; possibly survived until 1937 when issued type code 'LD' and relegated to Escuela de Polimótores (Multi-engine Flying School) at Totana, Murcia; NFT.

6017   Regd **G-ACDM** (CoR 4167) 21.4.33 to Scottish Motor Traction Co Ltd, Edinburgh; first CoA (3905) issued 18.5.33; reported as used by Midland & Scottish Air Ferries Ltd, Renfrew; regn cld 11.33 and CoA renewed 19.1.34; regd in South Africa as **ZS-AEI** (CoR 113) 23.3.34 to Aircraft Operating Co; impressed into SAAF at Zwartkop 2.8.40 as **1570**; School of Photography / 67 AS 11.10.40; became GI airframe **IS13** at 70 AS 4.42; SOC .43.

6018   Regd **G-ACDN** (CoR 4168) 21.4.33 to Scottish Motor Traction Co Ltd, Edinburgh; first CoA (3907) issued 29.5.33; regd (CoR 4812) 12.33 to Midland & Scottish Air Ferries Ltd, Renfrew; based at Hooton Park wef 5.34; M&SAF ceased trading 9.34; sold

to unnamed dealer; regd (CoR 5846) 2.5.35 to Crilly Airways Ltd, Doncaster and Leicester (Braunstone); nominally sold to Spanish Republicans but not delivered; Crilly in receivership 9.9.36; sold to H Welch of General Motor & Tyre Co, Hammersmith; regd (CoR 7886) 21.5.37 to Commercial Air Hire Ltd, Croydon; impressed into RAF at Ringway 7.7.40 as **AW170**; 8 AACU, Weston Zoyland (later Old Sarum), 10.8.40; dived into ground near Trewithen Farm, St Wenn, Cornwall, while flying from St Eval to Exeter, 27.11.40.

6019   Regd **G-ACEK** (CoR 4216) 2.5.33 to W L Everard MP, Ratcliffe, named *The Leicestershire Vixen II;* first CoA (3890) issued 11.5.33; regd (CoR 7143) 23.6.36 to Olley Air Services Ltd, Croydon; sold 8.36 and regd (CoR 7316) 3.9.36 to Cecil H Stave (perhaps pseudonym for Leonard H Stace of Air Commerce), Croydon; sold 9.36 to Union Founders Trust Ltd and on to Fédération Populaire des Sports Aéronautiques, Paris, for Spanish Republicans but not delivered; sold to Joseph Hermann, Paris, 19.10.36 on behalf of Cie Air Taxi, Vienna (a non-existent company) but detained at Croydon; regd (CoR 7549) 15.12.36 to Union Founders Trust Ltd, Croydon; sold to Air Dispatch Ltd, Croydon, 26.1.37; regd (CoR 7733) 5.3.37 to Mutual Finance Ltd, Croydon; regd (CoR 8410) 23.3.38 to (associate) Advance Airlines Ltd, Croydon; sold 1.5.39 and del 8.39 to (associate) Commercial Air Hire Ltd, Cardiff; regd to Commercial Air Hire Ltd 22.1.40; impressed into RAF as **AX867** at Ringway 21.7.40; 7 AACU, Castle Bromwich 23.8.40 but to DH RU, Witney, same day for major inspection; allotted to 110 (AAC) Wg, Ringway 8.9.40 but returned to 7 AACU; DH RU 15.7.41 and SOC 21.7.41

6020   First CoA (3928) issued 29.5.33; ferried to Spain as **EC-W14**; regd as **EC-TAT** 9.33 to Automobiles Fernandez SA, Barcelona, for operation by Airotaxi (or Air Taxi) SA, Palma and Barcelona; requisitioned 7.36 by Cdte Díaz Sandino of Catalan Air Force at Prat de Llobregat Airport, Barcelona for use in Spanish Civil War; possibly damaged by night fighters over Aragón front 19.10.36.

6021   Regd **G-ACET** (CoR 4228) 21.4.33 to Scottish Motor Traction Co Ltd, Edinburgh (later Renfrew); fleet no 22; first CoA (3922) issued 3.6.33; loaned to Jersey Airways Ltd, Portsmouth, wef 18.12.33; to Midland & Scottish Air Ferries Ltd, Renfrew (later Hooton Park) 15.2.34 and regd (CoR 4925) 3.34; del 27.9.34 and entered service 23.10.34; regd (CoR 5931) 31.5.35 to Highland Airways Ltd, Dyce, named *Kirkwall*; to de Havilland Aircraft Co Ltd, Hatfield, 25.6.37 in part-exchange for Rapide G-AEWL; regd (CoR 8128) 8.10.37 to Flt Lt Eric Noddings for operation by Air Dispatch Ltd, Croydon; regd 22.1.40 to Air Dispatch Ltd, Cardiff; impressed into RAF as **AW171** at Ringway 6.7.40; 6 AACU, Ringway, 13.7.40; to DH RU, Witney, for major inspection 6.9.41 but SOC 22.10.41; became GI airframe as **2779M** at ATC 328 Sqn, Kingston-on-Thames, 29.10.41; some parts, including wing panels, tailplane, fin and rudder, acquired by Capt. Mike Russell late 1984 and held by EMK Aeroplanes; regd 10.1.89 to M C Russell, t/a Russavia Collection, for restoration to airworthy condition; for sale 12.92; regd 31.7.95 to M D Souch, Southampton; extant.

6022   Regd **G-ACEU** (CoR 4229) 24.3.33 to Hillman's Saloon Coaches & Airways Ltd, t/a Hillman's Airways Ltd), Maylands (later Stapleford Tawney), named *Brentwood*, fleet number 11; first CoA (3887) issued 10.5.33; to new company Hillman's Airways Ltd 11.33; regd (CoR 6290) 13.9.35 to Hillman's Airways Ltd, Stapleford Tawney; taken over by British Airways Ltd 10.35; regd (CoR 6634) 13.1.36 to Airwork Ltd, Heston; flown to Barcelona direct from Croydon 15.8.36, probably for use in Spanish Civil War; NFT.

C/n 6017, ZS-AEI of the Aircraft Operating Co (South Africa) Pty Ltd, who used it from March 1934 to August 1940, when it was taken over by the SAAF
[via K Smy]

The Prince of Wales' Dragon G-ACGG, c/n 6025, seen in September 1934, when it was based at RAF Hendon in the care of 24 Squadron   *[via C N Dodds]*

6023   Regd **G-ACEV** (CoR 4230) 8.5.33 to Hillman's Saloon Coaches & Airways Ltd, t/a Hillman's Airways Ltd), Maylands (later Stapleford Tawney), named *Ilford*, fleet number 12; first CoA (3900) issued 12.6.33; del 7.7.33; to new company Hillman's Airways Ltd 11.33; achieved notoriety when Elizabeth and Jane Dubois committed suicide by jumping from aircraft on London to Paris service over Upminster 21.2.35; regd (CoR 6514) to Hillman's Airways Ltd, Stapleford Tawney; taken over by British Airways 10.35; sold 12.35 and regd (CoR 6665) to Airwork Ltd, Heston; left Croydon 13.8.36 with new CoA for delivery to Spanish Republicans and regn cld as sold; detained at Le Bourget and returned to Croydon but left again 15.8.36, arriving 17.8.36; transferred from Prat de Llobregat (Barcelona) to Sarinena near Zaragoza in Aragón 18.8.36 to be fitted with rudimentary armament and to be incorporated into Alas Rojas (Red Wings) Squadron until unit disbanded 10.36; possibly survived until 1937 when issued type code 'LD' and relegated to Escuela de Polimótores (Multi-engine Flying School) at Totana, Murcia; NFT.

6024   First CoA (3878) issued 26.5.33; to de Havilland Aircraft Co., Canada; regd **CF-APJ** (CoR 1288) 13.5.33 to Canadian Airways Ltd, Montreal; merged into Canadian Pacific Airlines 1.42; reduced to spares 10.42 for rebuild of CF-AVD.

6025   Regd (CoR 4335) 3.5.33 **G-ACGG** to Flt Lt Edward Fielden for Edward, Prince of Wales; first CoA (3892) issued 6.6.33 and based at Hendon under the care of 24 Sqn; regd (CoR 5618) 14.2.35 to Richard O Shuttleworth, Heston, for operation by Aeronautical Advertising Co Ltd with underwing neon signs, but this scheme abandoned; regd (CoR 6100) 22.7.35 to C J Donada, Hanworth; regd (CoR 6960) 29.4.36 to L H Stace, MD of and nominee of Air Commerce Ltd, Heston; regn cld as sold abroad 9.12.37; regd **VH-AAC** (CoR 690) 18.2.38 to W R Carpenter & Co Ltd, Salamaua, NG; to Mandated Airlines of Australia; impressed into RAAF 17.4.41 as **A34-10**; 3 EFTS, Parafield; 2 AOS, Mount Gambier, 19.8.41 to 20.11.41; School of Photography, Canberra, 5.11.43; suffered engine failure and crashed in forced landing 4.1.44; not repaired and remains transferred to Department of Civil Aviation; regd to Aircraft Pty Ltd, Brisbane, as **VH-AAC** 29.8.44; regd 4.11.44 to Mandated Airlines, NG; to J Taylor, operating as Taylor's Air Transport, NG; taken over by Guinea Air Traders 3.49; returned to Mandated Airlines 4.50 when previous company failed; thought to have been leased to Wewak Air Transport from 5.50 to

11.50; crashed on approach to the notorious Slate Creek airstrip, NG, 29.1.51; remains stored at Lae pending a possible rebuild until being sold to Territory Airlines, Goroka, NG, in 1952, but the rebuild never took place; parts used in the rebuild of VH-AIA (2086).

6026   First CoA (3921) issued 26.5.33 to de Havilland Aircraft Co of South Africa Ltd; del 30.6.33; regd **ZS-AEF** (CoR 110) 28.7.33 to The Aircraft Operating Co of South Africa Pty Ltd, Johannesburg, for use on 20,000 sq ml air route survey of Northern Rhodesia; crashed after steep turn during take-off from Baragwanath 26.9.33, killing Maj W J C Kennedy-Cochran-Patrick, founder and MD of The Aircraft Operating Co, and Sir Michael Oppenheimer.

6027   Regd **G-ACFG** (CoR 4260) 3.5.33 to de Havilland Aircraft Co Ltd; first CoA (3891) issued 26.6.33; entered by Lord Wakefield in King's Cup Air Race 7.33 and flown to fifth place by Capt Hubert Broad; sold 28.9.33 to R H Beverton as nominee for an Italian Count for tour to Vienna, Belgrade, Bucharest and Constantinople; regd (CoR 5316) 22.8.34 to G Nicholson, t/a Northern Airways, Cramlington; regd (CoR 5495) to Northern & Scottish Airways Ltd, Cramlington (later Renfrew) regn cld as sold 2.37; regd **VH-UZG** 19.4.37 to North Queensland Airways Pty Ltd, Cairns; crashed 2.5 mls N of Cairns 7.5.37 on delivery flight; regn not officially taken up.

6028   First CoA (3939) issued 14.6.33; del from Heston 16.6.33 to Misr Airwork Ltd as **SU-ABH**; retd to UK 20.7.36; regd **G-AEKZ** (CoR 7081) 7.36 to Airwork Ltd, Heston; regd (CoR 7295) 25.8.36 to L. H. Stace, Hounslow as MD and nominee for Air Commerce Ltd, Heston; operated 2.38 by Channel Air Ferries; sold 16.2.39 and regd 19.4.39 to Hon. Mrs Victor Bruce, operating as Air Dispatch Ltd, Croydon; impressed into RAF 30.6.40 as **AW163**; 110 (AAC) Wg CF, Ringway, 22.7.40; 7 AACU, Castle Bromwich, 23.8.40; overshot landing at Castle Bromwich 18.11.40 and ran into wire fence; to DH RU, Witney, for repair 19.1.41, but SOC 4.2.41.

6029   First CoA (3937) issued 13.6.33; regd **VH-URE** (CoR 465) 29.8.33 to West Australian Airways Ltd, Perth; taken over by ANA 1.7.36 and regd 4.8.36 to Adelaide Airways Ltd, regd 25.11.36 to ANA, named *Yannana*; regd 26.2.38 to Airlines of Australia Ltd, Mascot; regd 9.2.40 to NSW Section of Australian

Aerial Medical Services, Sydney, and named *L M Pattinson;* regd 23.7.42 to NSW Flying Doctor Service, Broken Hill; re-regd **VH-FDB** 30.9.48 to The Flying Doctor Service of Australia (NSW Section), Sydney; re-regd **VH-DMA** 1.11.56 to Muir Aviation, Darwin, for agricultural use; crashed 4 mls S of Katherine, NT, 11.12.57 when engine failed; regn cld 5.58.

6030   First CoA (3942) issued 17.6.33 to de Havilland Aircraft Co of South Africa Ltd; regd **ZS-AEG** (CoR 111) 28.7.33 to Hon John Stuart, Bechuanaland; to Aircraft Operating Co Ltd; to African Air Transport; to de Havilland Aircraft Co of South Africa and leased to Rhodesia & Nyasaland Airways; regn cld 9.9.38; regd in Southern Rhodesia as **VP-YBY** (CoR 58) 18.6.38 to Rhodesia & Nyasaland Airways, Salisbury; impressed into Southern Rhodesia Air Services 1.10.39 as **260**; written off .44 after accident.

6031   First CoA (3947) issued 21.6.33 del from Heston to Misr Airwork Ltd as **SU-ABI**; crashed 10 mls W of El Arish 15.3.35 during a sandstorm which caused engine failure; pilot Capt Spooner, Chief Pilot of Misr, and two passengers were killed.

6032   First CoA (3960) issued 27.6.33; regd **G-ACIE** (CoR 4403) 28.6.33 to Victor A Schmidt, nominee for Bata Shoe Co, Zlin, Czechoslovakia; initially based at Stag Lane; regd in Czechoslovakia as **OK-ATO** 4.10.33 to Bata AS, Zlin; del to Zlin 11.5.34; believed regd **G-ACIE** (CoR 5207) for unknown operator 12.34, but regn cld as sold abroad; regd **OK-ATO** 1935 to Zlinska Letecka, Bayov-Napajedla; returned to UK and regd **G-ACIE** (CoR 8527) 28.5.38 to Airwork Ltd; used by School of Air Navigation, Shoreham (fleet no 4); sold to Misr Airwork 11.9.38 and UK regn cld 3.39; regd **SU-ABZ** 3.39; broken up for spares at Almaza 12.46.

6033   Regd **G-ACGK** (CoR 4357) 1.6.33 to E C G England, manager and nominee for Vacuum Oil Co Ltd, Hanworth; first CoA (3968) issued 30.6.33; del 3.7.33 and flown to Java on tour 11.33; flown on survey from UK to Australia 12.33 to 1.34 (56 days and 340 flying hours), by sales manager H J White; regd (CoR 5227) to Highland Airways Ltd, Inverness, 11.7.34, named *Loch Ness*; written off 8.1.35 when aircraft ditched about 20 yds offshore after taking off from Inverness (Longman), coming to rest on the sea-bed with the top wing just clear of the surface; later salvaged, but was scrapped because of the effects of sea water; cause of accident was carburettor and airframe icing; pilot Eric Coleman.

6034   Regd **G-ACGU** (CoR 4368) 1.6.33 to Blackpool & West Coast Air Services Ltd, Squires Gate; first CoA (3962) issued 28.6.33; sold to British-American Air Services Ltd, Heston, 5.35 but not regd; crashed and burnt on take-off from Heston 16.7.35 when on charter flight to Spithead; two passengers killed and pilot, S Fines, and four passengers injured, .

6035   Regd **G-ACHV** (CoR 4394) 14.6.33 to Anglo-Persian Oil Co Ltd, Heston (renamed Anglo-Iranian Oil Co Ltd 3.35); first

CoA (3972) issued 4.7.33; regd (CoR 5942) 5.6.35 to Airwork Ltd, Heston; regd (CoR 6155) 6.8.35 to Railway Air Services Ltd, Croydon (based Barton); sold to Rollason Aircraft Services Ltd, Croydon, 15.8.36; sold to de Havilland Aircraft Co Ltd 19.8.36; regd (CoR 6925) 25.8.36 to J Morris, London and Hanworth; official register shows that CoR 6925 had already been allotted to Hendy Heck G-AEGK 4.36 but had not been taken up; entries in registers of the day show firstly that G-ACHV carried CoR 6925 but secondly that G-AEGK carried that number; the DH.84 was duly painted as G-AEGK 5.9.36 for export to Spain and use in Spanish Civil War, but sale prohibited by British Government and aircraft never left the country; regd G-ACHV (CoR 7550) 15.12.36 to Union Founders Trust Ltd, Croydon; sold 26.1.37 to Air Dispatch Ltd, Croydon; regd (CoR 7734) 5.3.37 to Mutual Finance Ltd, Croydon; regd (CoR 8411) 23.3.38 to Advance Air Lines Ltd, Croydon; regd (CoR 8466) 22.4.38 to Anglo-European Airways Ltd, Croydon; regd (CoR 8944) 10.12.38 to Air Taxis Ltd, Croydon; impressed into RAF 31.3.40 as **X9379**; 6 AACU, Ringway, 4.4.40; 7 AACU, Castle Bromwich, 3.5.40; to DH RU, Witney, for major inspection 29.5.40; SOC 7.8.40.

6036   Regd **G-ACHX** (CoR 4396) 7.7.33 to R. V. Wrightson, t/a Wrightson & Pearce, Heston, named *Lucretius*; first CoA (3975) issued 11.7.33; initially bought for long-distance flight to Cape Town but project abandoned; damaged in fatal take-off crash at Doncaster (Armthorpe) 15.9.33 but repaired; transferred to Wrightways Ltd, Croydon, 17.12.34; regd (CoR 6034) 3.7.35 to Wrightways Ltd; crashed at Woodcote Lane, Purley, Surrey, 25.4.38, while on approach to Croydon; pilot killed.

6037   First CoA (3974) issued 3.7.33; regd **VH-URD** (CoR 466) for de Havilland Aircraft Pty Ltd for Tasmanian Aerial Services Pty Ltd, named *Miss Launceston;* reformed as Holyman's Airways Pty Ltd late 1933 and so regd 7.34; taken over by Australian National Airways Pty Ltd 1.7.36 and so regd 25.11.36; based Parafield, named *Yoorana;* operated by Australian Aerial Medical Service 1939; damaged in forced landing Raglan Hill, NSW, 19.1.40 but repaired; impressed into RAAF 31.8.40 at 1 AD as **A34-7**; 1 AOS, Cootamundra, 3.2.41; 2 AOS, Mt Gambier, 1.4.41; damaged in forced landing at Casterton, Vic, 14.10.41 but repaired; converted to air ambulance 4.42; 33 Sqn, Townsville, 9.5.42 to 27.10.42; 1 WAGS, Ballarat, 30.8.43; transferred to DCA 5.10.44 and regd **VH-URD** to Aircraft Pty Ltd, Archerfield; to RC Mission of the Holy Ghost, Alexishafen, NG, 8.48; to QANTAS 3.5.50; crashed in Tauri River valley 24.12.51 when on charter to the NG Administration, carrying mail and freight to outpost at Menyamya.

6038   Regd **G-ACIW** (CoR 4420) 28.7.33 to William McEwan, Stag Lane; first CoA (3993) issued 29.7.33; regn cld 2.7.34 as sold; regd in France as **F-ANGE** 18.9.34 to Jacques Germain, Mouzainville, Algeria; regn cld after .39.

G-ACIT, c/n 6039, at Yeadon on 11th May 1956, when it was owned by Air Navigation & Trading Co Ltd and operated by Border Flying Club   [R C Sturtivant]

G-ACIT at Wroughton on 25th June 1986, in the hands of the Science Museum after fifty years of service [R C Sturtivant]

6039 Regd **G-ACIT** (CoR 4417) 24.7.33 to Highland Airways Ltd, Inverness; first CoA (3991) issued 29.7.33; named *Aberdeen* at ceremony 7.5.34; used to inaugurate Highland Airways services; transferred to Scottish Airways Ltd, Renfrew, 12.8.37 and so regd (CoR 8559) 16.6.38; renamed *Orcadian* 1939; to NAC, later AAJC, 27.6.40; regd to BEA 1.2.47; CoA lapsed 2.2.49; regd 10.3.49 to Speedbird Flying Club Ltd, Denham, which became Airways Aero Association Ltd 19.4.49; regd as such 2.11.49; sold to Air Navigation & Trading Co Ltd, Squires Gate, 11.10.51 and so regd 10.11.51; operated by Border Flying Club, Carlisle; regd 30.1.62 to British Executive & General Aviation Ltd, Kidlington (Beagle Aircraft) and used as personal aircraft by Sir Peter Masefield; sold to R L Whyham, Squires Gate 29.6.64 but not so regd; regd to J Beaty, Kettering, 3.9.69; loaned to Historic Aircraft Museum, Southend, 19.9.71; CoA lapsed 25.5.74; regn cld 19.8.81; sold to Science Museum, Wroughton, for £28,000 by auction 10.5.83 and so regd 26.5.83; del 8.83; refurbished by Skysport .93 and painted in Highland Airways livery as *Aberdeen;* extant.

6040 Regd **G-ACJH** (CoR 4431) 9.8.33 to S T Weedon, Stag Lane; first CoA (4010) issued 23.8.33; regn cld as sold 11.33; regd in France as **F-AMTM** (CoR 3631) 4.12.33 to André Garric, Agen-Leyrac; destroyed in fatal crash at Fontet, nr La Reole, Gironde, 3.11.38, killing Garric and five of his family; regn cld 11.38.

6041 Regd **G-ACIU** (CoR 4418) 25.7.33 to Marmaduke, Rt Hon Viscount Furness, Stag Lane, in VIP fit; first CoA (3995) issued 5.8.33; regd (CoR 5489) 7.12.34 to Hon Brian Lewis, t/a Brian Lewis & Co Ltd, Heston; loaned to Whitney Straight for flight with Richard Seaman and Michael Straight from Heston to South Africa, which left 10.12.34; to Maddox Airways Ltd, Brooklands, 4.35; regd (CoR 6022) to Surrey Flying Services Ltd, Croydon, 29.6.35, named *Blue Mist;* impressed into RAF 2.4.40; 24 Sqn, Hendon 3.4.40; damaged on take-off from Mourmelon, France, 29.4.40 and burnt on ground on evacuation 9.5.40; serial **X9395** allocated but never carried; SOC 28.5.40.

6042 Regd **G-ACJS** (CoR 4441) 2.8.33 to Midland & Scottish Air Ferries Ltd, Renfrew and used as John Cuthill Sword's personal aircraft (note appropriate registration), fitted with toilet and radio; first CoA (3996) issued 4.8.33; remained at Renfrew after M&SAF ceased trading; regd (CoR 5529) 8.1.35 to Northern & Scottish Airways Ltd, Renfrew; regn cld 11.36; possibly sold for use in Spanish Civil War.

6043 Regd **G-ACJT** (CoR 4442) 24.8.33 to Norman W G Edgar, Whitchurch and operated by Norman Edgar (Western Airways) Ltd after formation on 7.9.33; first CoA (4011) issued 26.8.33; regd (CoR 5876) 16.5.35 to Norman Edgar (Western Airways) Ltd; moved to Weston-super-Mare 5.36; name changed to Western Airways Ltd 18.10.38; regd to Southern Airways Ltd, Weston-super-Mare, 14.2.39 but continued to be operated by Western Airways; loaned to RAF 24 Sqn, Hendon, 7.10.39 to 11.11.39; crashed on take-off from Weston-super-Mare 20.12.39, killing pilot, L I Arnott, one of the original directors of the company.

6044 Regd **YI-AAC** 9.33 to Airwork Ltd for operation in Iraq; first CoA (4019) issued 5.9.33; left Heston for Bombay 17.9.33, piloted by T N Stack and carrying surgeon, anaesthetist and nurse for urgent operation on relative of Maharaja of Nepal and arrived 26.9.33; retd to UK 22.10.33, not having been delivered to Iraq; regd **G-ACLE** (CoR 4478) to Airwork Ltd, Heston, 31.10.33; to Crilly Airways Ltd, Leicester, 9.35; CoA lapsed 25.4.36 and receiver appointed 9.9.36; sold c.10.36 to Aircraft Facilities Ltd and/or H Welch; regd (CoR 7645) 2.2.37 to North Eastern Airways Ltd, Croydon; regd (CoR 8258) 7.12.37 to Allied Airways (Gandar Dower) Ltd, Dyce, named *Old Bill;* badly damaged on hitting stone wall on take-off from St Margaret's Hope (Berridale) in early 1939; returned by sea to Dyce for rebuilding before sale; regd 18.5.39 to Western Airways Ltd, Weston-super-Mare; impressed into RAF 2.4.40; 6 AACU, Ringway, 2.4.40; 7 AACU, Castle Bromwich, 5.5.40; allocated serial **X9397** 10.5.40; DH 24.2.41; struck by runaway bowser at Odiham 8.4.41; to DH RU, Witney, 24.4.41 for inspection, but SOC 12.5.41.

6045 First CoA (4036) issued 3.9.33; regd **VH-URF** (CoR 471) 15.12.33 to Western Mining Corp Ltd, Perth, named *Gay Prospector;* regd 27.11.34 to MacRobertson Miller Aviation Co Pty Ltd, Maylands; impressed into RAAF 15.5.41 as **A34-9;** 3 EFTS, Parafield, 5.5.41; 2 AOS, Mount Gambier, 16.8.41; converted to air ambulance 1.42; 34 Sqn, Darwin, 25.2.42; destroyed by incendiary bomb at Darwin and SOC 16.3.42.

6046 First CoA (4037) issued 3.10.33; regd **VH-URG** (CoR 470) 9.12.33 to Western Mining Corp Ltd, Perth, named *Golden West;* regd 14.12.34 to Holyman's Airways Pty Ltd, Western Junction; taken over by Australian National Airways Pty Ltd 1.7.36 and based at Parafield; so regd 25.11.36 and renamed *Yuptana;* regd 20.6.39 to Airlines of Australia Ltd, Sydney; crashed and DBF at Wenlock, Qld, 4.2.42; regn cld 18.2.42.

6047 First CoA (4014) issued 1.9.33; regd **VP-KAW** 9.33 to Wilson Airways Ltd, Nairobi; crashed on take-off from Kilindini, Kenya, 8.12.33, following engine failure.

6048 First CoA (4063) issued 20.10.33; left Heston 2.11.33; regd **VT-AEL** (CoR 190) 29.1.34 to Indian National Airways Ltd, Dum Dum, Calcutta; named *Emerald* by Lady Willingdon 20.11.33; crashed 40 mls from Lahore 26.8.39 during mail flight, two killed.

6049 Regd **G-ACJM** (CoR 4436) to Mrs J. A. Mollison (Amy Johnson); first CoA (4018) issued 6.9.33; incorporated parts of c/n 6014; this was the replacement aircraft for G-ACCV; named *Seafarer II* for proposed transatlantic flight to Baghdad; shipped to Canada on SS Duchess of York 9.33; damaged undercarriage on attempted take-off from Wasaga Beach, Georgian Bay, nr Toronto 3.10.33 and flight abandoned; retd to UK by sea as the first aircraft to carry out double Atlantic crossing on board ship!; to DH for repair; regd (CoR 5072) 15.5.34 to Captain L G Reid, named *Trail of the Caribou* for further record attempt; shipped back to Canada 18.6.34; flown by Reid and J R Ayling from Wasaga Beach to Heston 8/9.8.34 in 30 hrs 50 mins; hit fence on landing at Hamble 12.8.34; not badly damaged but not repaired; CoA expired 5.9.34; wreckage survived until 9.39 when it was surveyed at Hatfield.

6050 First CoA (4064) issued 21.10.33; left Heston 2.11.33; regd **VT-AEK** (CoR 189) 29.1.34 to Indian National Airways Ltd, Dum Dum, Calcutta; named *Ruby;* regn cld 6.5.37.

6051 First CoA (4062) issued 21.10.33; left Heston 27.10.33; regd **SU-ABJ** to Misr Airwork Ltd, named *El Barak;* DBF at Almaza, 22.6.38, when signal rockets exploded inside aircraft after night-flying exercise with Army.

6052 Regd **G-ACKD** (CoR 4452) to Hon. Brian Lewis, t/a Brian Lewis & Co Ltd, Heston; first CoA (4026) issued 15.9.33; Lewis was nominee for Vicomte de Sibour who left 9.33 on 17,500 mile tour of Far East, returning to Paris 2.34; regd (CoR 5239) 16.7.34 to Flt Lt H Thomas & W J Byrne; operated by Provincial Airways Ltd, Croydon, named *Saturn;* converted by Airwork (Croydon) Ltd into air ambulance for League of Nations Union, to whom regd (CoR 6598) 14.12.35; flown from UK to Addis Ababa, arriving 21.1.36 for presentation to Ethiopian Red Cross; crashed on take-off from Akaki and DBF 23.3.36.

6053 Prototype Mk.II; regd **G-ACMC** (CoR 4732) 11.33 to de Havilland Aircraft Co Ltd; first CoA (4096) issued 24.11.33; to Walter L Thurgood, t/a Jersey Airways Ltd, 29.12.33, named *St Brelade's Bay;* to United Airways Ltd, Blackpool (Stanley Park) 4.35; regd (CoR 5917) 28.5.35 to Jersey Airways Ltd, based at Heston; loaned to Northern & Scottish Airways Ltd, Renfrew, 15.8.35; transferred to British Airways Ltd 1.10.35; regd (CoR 6666) 23.1.36 to Airwork Ltd, Heston; regn cld as sold 8.36, nominally sold to agents of Spanish Republicans but not delivered; regd in Australia as **VH-UXK** 10.10.36 to North Queensland Airways Pty Ltd, named *Cairns;* stalled and crashed in sugar cane field on approach to Innisfail (Mindoo) airfield, Qld, while on scheduled flight from Townsville to Cairns, 29.8.38; pilot B Gordon and four passengers killed, four injured; wreck to Airlines of Australia Ltd, Sydney, for spares 20.2.39.

6054 First CoA (4058) issued 19.10.33; left Heston 26.10.33; regd **ZS-AEH** 21.11.33 to Aircraft Operating Co. Ltd; to African Air Transport; to Stewarts & Lloyds of South Africa Ltd, named *Corby;* impressed into SAAF 1940 as **1414**; NFT.

6055 Regd **G-ACKB** (CoR 4450) 9.33 to Iraq Petroleum Transport Co. Ltd and operated on their behalf by Imperial Airways; first CoA (4074) issued 6.11.33; left for Iraq 10.11.33 and retd 8.11.35; regn cld as sold early .36; to Air Dispatch Ltd, Croydon; purchased by Cdte Carlos Pastor Krauel (Senior Spanish Air Force Officer) acting through Union Founders Trust Ltd, for use by Republicans in Spanish Civil War, but sale prohibited by British Government on 19.8.36 and aircraft never left the country; bought by Hon Mrs Victor Bruce; regd (CoR 7321) 3.9.36 to Commercial Air Hire Ltd, Croydon; impressed into RAF 7.7.40 as **AX863**; SF Ringway 13.7.40; 6 AACU, Ringway, 13.7.40; to DH RU, Witney, 15.1.41 for major inspection, but SOC 1.2.41.

6056 Regd **G-ACKC** (CoR 4451) 9.33 to Iraq Petroleum Transport Co Ltd and operated on their behalf by Imperial Airways; first CoA (4082) issued 9.11.33; left for Iraq and retd 8.11.35; regd (CoR 6950) 27.4.36 to Commercial Air Hire Ltd, Croydon; purchased by Cdte Carlos Pastor Krauel (Senior Spanish Air Force Officer) acting through Union Founders Trust Ltd 8.36 for use by Republicans in Spanish Civil War; left Croydon 15.8.36 for Barcelona, piloted by A D Jaffe; transferred from Prat de Llobregat (Barcelona) to Sarinena near Zaragoza in Aragón 18.8.36 to be fitted with rudimentary armament and to be incorporated into Alas Rojas (Red Wings) Squadron until unit disbanded 10.36; possibly survived until 1937 when issued type code LD and relegated to Escuela de Polimótores (Multi-engine Flying School) at Totana, Murcia; NFT.

6057 Regd **G-ACLP** (CoR 4720) 7.11.33 to W S Ordway, Hatfield; first CoA (4075) issued 6.11.33; regn cld 11.33 as sold to G Descampes, France; regd **F-AMTR** (CoR 3658) 26.1.34 to Robert Germain, t/a Lignes Aériennes Nord-Africaines (LANA), Algiers; LANA ceased trading late .36 and aircraft taken over by Etat Français (French Government) by 3.37 and operated by Régie Air Afrique; possibly used in Spanish Civil War; regd 10.37 to Etat Français; destroyed 2.38.

6058 Regd **G-ACMJ** (CoR 4739) 12.33 to Walter L Thurgood, t/a Jersey Airways, named *St Aubin's Bay*; first CoA (4105) issued 7.12.33; single-engined tests at Martlesham Heath 14.3.34; crashed at Heston 12.9.34 but repaired; leased to United Airways Ltd, Blackpool (Stanley Park); regd (CoR 5918) 28.5.35 to Jersey Airways Ltd, based at Heston; transferred to British Airways Ltd 1.10.35; regd (CoR 6668) 25.1.36 to Airwork Ltd, Heston; sold 7.36 to Norman Edgar (Western Airways) Ltd, Weston-super-Mare but regd (CoR 7204) 22.7.36 to director and nominee K Machonochie; regd (CoR 8601) 1.7.38 to Norman Edgar (Western

Airways) Ltd; name changed 18.10.38 to Western Airways Ltd; impressed into RAF 2.4.40; 24 Sqn, Hendon, 3.4.40; allocated serial **X9396** 10.5.40; 1 Cam. Unit, Hendon, 26.7.41; to DH RU, Witney, for major inspection 3.11.41, but SOC 12.11.41.

6059 First CoA (4123) issued 12.12.33; regd **VP-KBA** to Wilson Airways Ltd, Nairobi; impressed into KAAU 9.39 as **K15**; NFT.

6060 First CoA (4176) issued 12.12.33; to Danish Army Air Force as **S-21**, delivered 27.2.34 by C C Larsen; crashed near Ringsted, Isle of Sjælland,Denmark, 24.2.36 when engaged on a search for an aircraft in difficulties in a snow-storm; Lt C O P Schack, the pilot, Lt V P Steengaard and Lt N Klinky-Peterson, observers/passengers, were all killed.

6061 First CoA (4177) issued 12.2.34; to Danish Army Air Force as **S-22**; delivered 24.3.34 by C C Larsen; crashed on take-off from Vaerlose 9.8.39 following engine failure; Lt A H Axelsen, the pilot, one instructor and five pupils injured (killed ?).

6062 First production Dragon Rapide Mk.II; regd **G-ACMO** (CoR 4744) 12.33 to W L Thurgood, t/a Jersey Airways, named *St Ouen's Bay*; first CoA (4164) issued 31.1.34; regd 1.34 to Jersey Airways Ltd; swung into sea wall on take-off from St Aubin's Bay, 25.8.34, killing 10-year old Dennis Dust; regd (CoR 6043) 4.7.35 to Northern & Scottish Airways Ltd, Renfrew; regn cld as sold 3.38; regd **VH-ABK** (CoR 722) 27.10.38 to South Queensland Airways Ltd, Archerfield, named *City of Toowoomba;* impressed into RAAF 4.7.40 as **A34-4**; 3 EFTS, Parafield; 1 AOS, Cootamundra, 9.12.40; 2 AOS, Mount Gambier, 19.2.41; converted to air ambulance 2.42; 35 Sqn, Maylands, 16.4.42; loaned to MacRobertson Miller Aviation Pty Ltd, Perth, 7.5.43 and restored as **VH-ABK** 21.5.43; retd to RAAF 31.8.43 as **A34-4**; 35 Sqn, Pearce, 2.9.43; 7 CU, Pearce, 10.11.43; to storage 30.3.44; SOC 12.9.44; being rebuilt 1999 by G and N Challinor of Mothcare at Murwillumbah for J Sinclair; extant.

Dragon 1414, c/n 6054, of the SAAF was previously ZS-AEH of Stewarts & Lloyds of South Africa Ltd   *[via K Smy]*

Dragon G-ACKB, c/n 6055, being inspected by a group of interested personnel at RAF Hal Far, Malta, while on delivery to Iraq Petroleum Transport Co Ltd
[via author]

6063 Regd **G-ACMP** (CoR 4745) 12.33 to W L Thurgood, t/a Jersey Airways, named *St Clements Bay*; regd (CoR 4842) 31.1.34 to Jersey Airways Ltd; first CoA (4184) issued 20.2.34; leased to Norman Edgar (Western Airways) Ltd 5.35; crashed on mudflats on Splott foreshore near Cardiff, 22.7.35, killing pilot J G Mansfield and two passengers.

6064 First CoA (4188) issued 22.2.34 to G Descampes, France; regd as **F-AMUZ** (CoR 3691) 5.3.34 to Henri Germain, t/a LANA, Algiers; LANA ceased trading late 1936, aircraft taken over by French Government 3.37 and operated by Régie Air Afrique; regd to French Government (Etat Français) 10.37; crashed in fog at El Aria, 45 mls from Constantine, Algeria, 13.6.38; pilot and five passengers injured; regn cld 7.38.

6065 First CoA (4217) issued 17.3.34; regd **VT-AES** (CoR 225) to Indian National Airways Ltd, Dum Dum, Calcutta, named *Sapphire*; regn cld 6.4.40; sold to Australia and regd **VH-UZF** 19.7.40 to Qantas Empire Airways Ltd, Brisbane; impressed into RAAF 16.8.40 as **A34-8**; 3 EFTS, Parafield; 1 AOS, Cootamundra, 3.2.41; 2 AOS, Mount Gambier, 11.3.41; converted to air ambulance 2.42; 33 Sqn, Townsville, 30.3.42; badly damaged in forced landing 8.6.42 when engine failed; to DH, Sydney, 3.7.42; SOC 11.9.42.

6066 Regd **G-ACKU** (CoR 4468) 10.33 to de Havilland Aircraft Co Ltd, Hatfield, as second prototype Mk.II; built to luxury standard; first CoA (4094) issued 24.11.33; loaned to W L Everard MP, Ratcliffe, 11.33 for International Oasis Meeting, Cairo; flown by W D Macpherson and winner of Circuit of the Oases and the Oases Trophy; sold 2.34 to Wrightson & Pearce, Heston and operated by British Air Navigation Co Ltd (BANCO), Heston, named *Vagrant*; regd (CoR 6024) 1.7.35 to Wrightways Ltd, Croydon; sold 12.8.36 to C P W Stebbing (agent for Mrs Victor Bruce); purchased by Cdte Pastor Krauel (Senior Spanish Air Force Officer) acting through Union Founders Trust Ltd; left Croydon 15.8.36 for Barcelona for Republican side in the Spanish Civil War; seen by RN cruiser monitoring the blockades; returned to Croydon and impounded 18.8.36 (ostensibly because its long-range tanks were leaking), having failed to reach Barcelona; regd (CoR 7551) 15.12.36 to Union Founders Trust Ltd, Croydon; sold to Air Dispatch Ltd, Croydon, 26.1.37; regd (CoR 7735) 5.3.37 to Mutual Finance Ltd, Croydon; regd (CoR 8412) 23.3.38 to Advance Air Lines Ltd, Croydon; regd (CoR 8465) 22.4.38 to Anglo-European Airways Ltd, Croydon; sold 1.5.39 to unconfirmed owner; badly damaged in force landing at Little Hungerford, Berks, when engine failed; regd 18.1.40 to Commercial Air Hire Ltd, Cardiff; impressed into RAF 7.7.40 as **AW172**; 110 (AAC) Wg, Ringway, 7.7.40; 7 AACU, Castle Bromwich, 15.11.40; dived into ground at Hanney Fields, Wantage, 10.2.41, when port engine failed while on Army Co-operation duties over Shrivenham; remains to DH RU, Witney; SOC 26.2.41.

6067 Regd **G-ACNA** (CoR 4755) 25.1.34 to Olley Air Service Ltd, Croydon; first CoA (4194) issued 28.2.34; damaged on landing at Old Field, Kings Acre, Hereford, 9.11.34 but repaired; purchased by Cdte Pastor Krauel (Senior Spanish Air Force Officer) acting through Union Founders Trust Ltd; left Croydon 15.8.36 for Spanish Republicans at Barcelona; transferred from Prat de Llobregat (Barcelona) to Sarinena near Zaragoza in Aragón 18.8.36 to be fitted with rudimentary armament and to be incorporated into Alas Rojas (Red Wings) Squadron until unit disbanded 10.36; survived until at least 1937, when issued type code LD and relegated to Escuela de Polimotóres (Multi-engine Flying School) at Totana, Murcia; NFT.

6068 First CoA (4209) issued 10.3.34; regd **VH-URO** 21.4.34 to Western Australian Airways Ltd, Perth; regd 28.12.34 to W R Carpenter & Co Ltd, arriving Salamaua, NG 26.1.35; failed to arrive at Mau while on a supply flight from Salamaua in the Black Cat mining area, 30.9.35; the aircraft was found in Black Cat Creek, wedged in trees 30 feet above the ground; pilot, Colin Ferguson, was thrown from the aircraft, but died on the way to hospital at Lae before receiving medical help.

6069 Regd **G-ACNG** (CoR 4761) 2.34 to Jersey Airways Ltd, named *Portelet Bay*; first CoA (4223) issued 23.3.34; regd (CoR 5985) 27.6.35 to Spartan Airlines Ltd, Cowes (Somerton); transferred to British Airways Ltd 1.10.35; regd to them (CoR 6790) 2.3.36; regd (CoR 7608) 19.1.37 to Northern & Scottish Airways Ltd, Renfrew (officially transferred 17.2.37); regd (CoR 8177) 29.10.37 to British Airways Ltd, Renfrew; regd (CoR 8552) 14.6.38 to Scottish Airways Ltd, Renfrew; crashed at Hatston 19.4.40; regn cld 7.5.40.

6070 Regd **G-ACNH** (CoR 4762) 2.34 to Jersey Airways Ltd, named *Bouley Bay*; first CoA (4231) issued 26.3.34; sold 1.6.35 and regd (CoR 6042) 4.7.35 to Northern & Scottish Airways Ltd, Renfrew; presumed to have suffered serious accident after last CoA renewal 13.8.36; regn cld 1.37.

6071 Regd **G-ACNI** (CoR 4763) 2.34 to Jersey Airways Ltd, named *Plemont Bay*, later *Bonne Nuit Bay*; first CoA (4234) issued 28.3.34; transferred to United Airways Ltd 4.35; leased to Railway Air Services Ltd mid.35; operated by Spartan Air Lines Ltd, Heston 8.35 to 9.35; merged into British Airways Ltd 1.10.35; regd to them (CoR 6701) 5.2.36; sold 8.36 and regd (CoR 7571) to Airwork Ltd, Heston, 31.12.36; converted to DH.84M with bomb-racks etc by Airwork Ltd at Heston 1.37; del to Irish Air Corps as **DH.18** 16.3.37 (but did not carry letters DH); operated by 1 Reconnaissance & Medium Bombing Sqn, Baldonnel, as target tug; crashed on take-off from Baldonnel 16.2.41 when ground locking devices had not been removed.

The Irish Air Corps' only DH.84 was c/n 6071, serial 18, seen at Baldonnel (Casement) with two Walruses and an Anson in the background. Note the four-bladed mahogany propeller attached to the starboard side of the fuselage, behind the wings, to drive the drogue target-towing winch mechanism. A landing light is in the nose, and an aerial survey camera was installed in the fuselage.
[P J Cummins]

6072 Regd **G-ACNJ** (CoR 4764) 2.34 to Jersey Airways Ltd, named *Rozel Bay*; first CoA (4235) issued 27.3.34; possibly not delivered until 8.6.34; regd (CoR 7879) 18.5.37 to A C Pearson, Heston; sold 19.11.37 and regd (CoR 8252) 6.12.37 to Allied Airways (Gandar Dower) Ltd, Dyce, named *Sir Rowland* in honour of Sir Rowland Hill, founder of the Post Office; operated until CoA lapsed 28.5.43; regd to Air Taxis Ltd, Kenley and Croydon, 29.6.45, probably for spare parts; broken up at Dyce 1946; regn cld 9.4.47.

6073 Regd **G-ACOR** to G McKinnon, Penshurst, 4.34, named *Fiona* (McKinnon possibly nominee for Viscount Furness); first CoA (4292) issued 19.5.34; regd (CoR 6419) 21.10.35 to British Continental Airways Ltd, Croydon, named *St. Christopher*; transferred to British Airways Ltd 1.8.36 and regd to them 3.37; regd (CoR 7743) 8.3.37 to Northern & Scottish Airways Ltd, Renfrew, to whom del 24.4.37; merged into Scottish Airways Ltd 12.8.37; regn cld as sold abroad 23.2.38; regd in Australia as **VH-AEA** (CoR 707) 23.6.38 to K Parer, t/a Wewak Air Transport, Wewak, New Guinea; damaged in NG 11.38 but repaired; company renamed Parer's Air Transport, Salamaua, 9.39; owner was in cockpit awaiting take-off from Salamaua 21.1.42 when Japanese aircraft attacked; he was trapped in burning aircraft until rescued by W E Clarke but was killed in another strafing run; Clarke awarded George Medal.

6074 Regd **VT-AFF** 14.4.34 to J Roy, Dacca, but not del and regn cld 5.34; first CoA (4315) issued 29.5.34; regd **VH-USA** (CoR 481) 27.7.34 to W R Carpenter and Co Ltd, Salamaua, NG, named *Grace;* del 3.8.34; regn cld 26.7.35 but regd to same owner 28.8.36; regd 6.10.36 to Mandated Airlines Ltd, Salamaua; destroyed 21.1.42 in same Japanese air raid as 6073; regn cld 11.3.42.

6075 Regd **G-ACPX** 4.34 to Railway Air Services Ltd, Croydon; first CoA (4272) issued 26.4.34; del 3.5.34; regd (CoR 5427) 2.11.34 to W L Hope for operation by Air Taxis Ltd, Croydon; regd 24.7.35 to Brian Allen Aviation Ltd, Croydon; regd (7333) 29.1.36 to The British Aviation Insurance Co Ltd, Bristol; regd 8.9.36 to H Crook as Director of Norman Edgar (Western Airways) Ltd. Weston-super-Mare; regd (CoR 8652) 23.7.38 to Norman Edgar (Western Airways) Ltd 23.7.38; name changed 18.10.38 to Western Airways Ltd; impressed into RAF 4.4.40; 6 AACU, Ringway, 4.4.40; loaned to 7 AACU 4.40; suffered engine failure on take-off from Castle Bromwich 22.4.40 while on Army Co-operation flying; pilot Sgt C A L Brown turned downwind and aircraft stalled vertically into the ground, killing him and AC2 C Parking; serial **X9399** allocated but never applied; SOC 7.5.40.

6076 Regd **G-ACPY** 4.34 to Railway Air Services Ltd, Croydon; first CoA (4286) issued 10.5.34; del 11.5.34 to Olley Air Service Ltd, Croydon; regd (CoR 5648) 28.2.35 to Blackpool & West Coast Air Services Ltd, Speke; regn cld as sold abroad 5.36; regd **EI-ABI** (CoR 38) to Aer Lingus Teoranta, Baldonnel, named *Iolar*, for lease and initially t/a Irish Sea Airways; operated Aer Lingus' first flight; restored to British register as **G-ACPY** (CoR 8371) 1.3.38 to Olley Air Service Ltd, Croydon, and operated by subsidiary Channel Air Ferries Ltd, Land's End (St Just); taken over by Great Western & Southern Airlines Ltd, Land's End, 12.38 and regd to them 15.3.39; shot down 3.6.41 by Luftwaffe aircraft, believed to be a Ju88, while on service from Scilly Isles (St Mary's) to Land's End (St Just); pilot Capt W D Anderson and five passengers killed; regn cld 11.6.41.

6077 Regd **G-ACRF** (CoR 4489) 30.4.34 to Portsmouth, Southsea & Isle of Wight Aviation Ltd, Portsmouth; first CoA (4291) issued 18.5.34; regn cld as sold abroad 2.36; regd in Australia as **VH-UXG** (CoR 582) 27.4.36 to Aircraft (Pty) Ltd, Archerfield, named *Riama*; regd 30.11.48 to Queensland Flying Services, Brisbane; regd 24.1.53 to S J Porter, Tingalpa, Qld; crashed and DBF 19.4.54 when engine failed on take-off from Archerfield.

6078 Regd **G-ACRH** (CoR 4995) 16.6.34 to Aberdeen Airways Ltd, Dyce, named *Aberdonian*; first CoA (4349) issued 21.6.34; crashed on take-off from Dyce 13.7.34 due to brake binding, hit culvert and DBF (two passengers injured); regn cld 7.34.

6079 Regd **G-ACRO** (CoR 5007) 3.5.34 to de Havilland Aircraft Co. Ltd, Hatfield; first CoA (4281) issued 4.5.34; del 7.5.34 to Mrs F K Wilson, t/a Wilson Airways, Nairobi; regn cld as sold 10.34 and UK CoA renewed 2.11.34; regd in Kenya as **VP-KBG** 23.11.34 to Wilson Airways Ltd, Nairobi; crashed on take-off from Nairobi 14.4.37.

6080 First CoA (4363) issued 4.7.34; DH Australia Pty; regd **VH-URW** (CoR 487) 31.8.34 to MacRobertson Miller Aviation Co Ltd, Maylands, named *Pilbara*; regd 22.3.39 to Mandated Airlines, Salamaua, NG; crashed on landing at Little Wau Creek, Wau, NG, 30.1.40; killing three, including pilot R Doyle; parts used on VH-AEA (c/n 6073)

6081 First CoA (4387) issued 13.7.34; DH Australia Pty; regd **VH-URX** (CoR 488) 11.9.34 to MacRobertson Miller Aviation Co Ltd, Maylands, named *Gascoyne*; impressed into RAAF 8.1.40 as **A34-1**; 1 ATS, Cressy, 26.1.40 to 7.8.40; 2 AOS, Mount Gambier, 20.2.41; converted to air ambulance 2.42; 35 Sqn, Pearce (later Maylands), 25.2.42; ditched 18 mls from Dongarra 14.6.42 after engine failed; SOC 21.6.42.

6082 First CoA (4388) issued 13.7.34 to DH Australia Pty; regd **VH-URY** (CoR 489) 11.9.34 to MacRobertson Miller Aviation Co Ltd, Maylands, named *Murchison;* sold 13.8.38 and regd 27.8.38 to Airlines (WA) Ltd, Perth; impressed into RAAF 22.7.40 as **A34-6**; 3 EFTS, Parafield; 2 AOS, Mount Gambier, 12.7.41; sold 24.5.43 to Royal Flying Doctor Service, Cloncurry, Qld; restored as **VH-URY** 14.6.43 to Qantas Empire Airways Ltd for Flying Doctor Service, named *John Flynn;* badly damaged on landing at Cloncurry 4.10.43 and repaired; regd 2.4.49 to ANA for operation by Trans Australian Airways on behalf of RFDS, Queensland Divn; del 24.7.49; crashed at Boulia, Qld, 19.4.50 and repaired; crashed on take-off from Cheviot Hills Station, Qld, 20.10.53, killing pilot M Garrett and one other and injuring three; regn cld 22.10.53

6083 First CoA (4350) issued 21.6.34 to Roger Levy, France; regd **F-ANES** (CoR 3851) 25.7.34 to Roger Levy; regd 5.35 to Roger Seligman, Neuilly; regd 1.36 to Henri Germain, t/a LANA, Algiers; ceased trading late .36 and aircraft taken over by French Government 3.37 and operated by Régie Air Afrique; regd 10.37 to Etat Français (French Govt); regd 4.40 to Sté Algérienne de Transports Tropicaux, Algiers; regd 5.48 to G Descamps, Ben Aknoun, Casablanca; regd 26.8.55 to J Vidillac, Casablanca; regn cld .57.

6084 Regd **G-ACVD** (5183) to Railway Air Services Ltd, Croydon, named *Star of Cheshire*; first CoA (4408) issued 24.7.34; on hire from DH until 10.34; regd (CoR 6123) to de Havilland Aircraft Co Ltd, Hatfield; regd (CoR 7285) 19.8.36 to Railway Air Services Ltd, Croydon; sold back to DH .37; regn cld as sold abroad 9.37 and UK CoA renewed 6.10.37; regd in Australia as **VH-UZX** to E MacArthur, Onslow; overhauled at Croydon by Air Dispatch Ltd for Air Travel & Survey Ltd, Sydney; destroyed in crash half mile west of Waddon station, Beddington, while on approach to Croydon 26.2.38; aircraft was on test flight before delivery and carried Australian registration although regn was officially cld as NTU; Capt P Bailey and two passengers injured.

6085 First CoA (4443) issued 30.7.34; regd **PP-SPC** 22.9.34 to Viação Aerea Sao Paulo SA (VASP) and del 11.34, named *VASP III*; regn cld 29.6.39 when del to Govt of State of Sao Paulo; donated to Naval Aviation 5.40 to be used in mail service from Santos to small coastal towns to north and south; serialled **D4H-178**; reported to have crashed at Cananea, State of Sao Paulo, 28.12.40, without casualties.

The crash of VP-KBG, c/n 6079, of Wilson Airways on 14th April 1937 at Nairobi　　　　　　　*[via D Hallen and P H T Green]*

Floatplane CF-AVD, c/n 6086, the second DH.84 in Canada, converted by DH Canada for Quebec Airways in 1934. Note the wooden propellors and a wind-driven generator on the port lower wing *[via C N Dodds]*

6086 To DH Canada without CoA; fitted with floats and regd **CF-AVD** 24.1.35 to de Havilland Aircraft of Canada Ltd, Toronto; regd 1.2.35 to Quebec Airways Ltd, Montreal; regd 24.8.35 to Canadian Airways Ltd, Winnipeg; merged into Canadian Pacific Air Lines Ltd 2.42; crashed in gusty crosswind take-off from Baie Comeau, PQ, 26.5.44.

6087 Regd **G-ACXI** (CoR 5285) 16.8.34 to Railway Air Services Ltd, Croydon, on hire from DH; first CoA (4465) issued 18.8.34; regd (CoR 5401) 20.10.34 to de Havilland Aircraft Co Ltd, Hatfield; demonstrated to Turkish Air Force 9.11.34; sold to them 12.34.

6088 First CoA (4489) issued 4.9.34 to DH Australia; regd **VH-URU** (CoR 495) 9.11.34 to Butler Air Transport Co Ltd, Mascot / Cootamundra, named *Charleville;* impressed into RAAF 8.1.40 as **A34-2**; 1 ATS, Cressy; 1 AOS, Cootamundra, 7.10.40; stalled and spun in 2 mls SW of Cootamundra 11.11.40 and DBF.

6089 First CoA (4488) issued 5.9.34 to DH Australia; regd **VH-URV** (CoR 496) 9.11.34 to Butler Air Transport Co Ltd, Mascot / Cootamundra, named *Cootamundra;* regd 26.5.49 to Qantas Empire Airways Ltd, Brisbane; crashed on landing at Yarramunda, NG, 13.12.51; pilot S Peebles and two passengers killed.

6090 First CoA (4664) issued 22.1.35 to East Coast Airways Ltd, Gisborne, New Zealand; regd **ZK-ADR** 15.4.35 to East Coast Airways Ltd, named *Huia;* re-regd **ZK-AER** 30.12.37 when it was realised that ADR was a prohibited registration; regd (CoR 129) 7.7.38 to Union Airways of NZ Ltd, Wellington; impressed into RNZAF 25.10.39 as **NZ551**; E&W Flt, Wigram, early .40 – mid-.42; force-landed, damaging undercarriage and propellers, 21.2.40; 2 EFTS, Ashburton; Comm Flt, Rongotai, 10.42; broke back on landing at Rongotai 10.11.43 but repaired; regd 24.3.44 to Air Travel (NZ) Ltd as **ZK-AHT**; crashed at Mount Hope, nr Nelson, 30.6.44; the aircraft had left Westport, Greymouth and Hokitika

with six passengers, and was heard to circle over the Glendale area in rain at about 13.30, but nothing more was known until 22.15, when one passenger made his way to a road to find help. The aircraft had crashed into trees, the nose section breaking off and catapulting several of the passengers out; injured survivors and the bodies of Capt J C 'Bert' Mercer, founder of Air Travel, and M Dawe, company secretary were recovered; an inquiry found that while crossing a ridge against strong headwinds the machine had been caught in an updraught and the pilot had lost control.

6091 First CoA (4667) issued 23.1.35 to East Coast Airways Ltd, Gisborne, New Zealand; regd **ZK-ADS** 15.4.35 to East Coast Airways Ltd, named *Tui;* regd (CoR 128) 7.7.38 to Union Airways of NZ Ltd, Wellington; impressed into RNZAF 13.10.39 as **NZ550**; E&W Flt, Wigram; Fiji Communications Flight, Nausori, 9.42; SOC 4.7.43 due to deterioration of airframe.

6092 Regd **G-ADCP** (CoR 5606) 6.3.35 to Blackpool & West Coast Air Services Ltd, Squires Gate; first CoA (4723) issued 30.3.35; regd (CoR 8153) 19.10.37 to Isle of Man Air Services Ltd, Ronaldsway; impressed into RAF 4.4.40 as **X9440**; 6 AACU, Ringway, 5.4.40; 7 AACU, Castle Bromwich, 3.5.40; 18 MU, Dumfries, 10.11.40; Limavady 20.4.41; to Short Bros & Harland Ltd 15.12.41 and SOC for scrap.

6093 To DH Canada without CoA; first CoA issued 2.11.34; regd **CF-AVI** (CoR 1624) 2.10.35 to Consolidated Mining & Smelting Co Ltd, Trail, BC; operated on floats; sold to DH Canada 10.11.37; regd (CoR 2144/A.136) 6.12.37 to Howard Watt, Toronto; regd 30.11.38 to North Shore Airways Ltd, Toronto, 12.37; swept from moorings and over dam at Godbout, PQ, 13.1.41, while on floats.

6094 Regd **G-ADCR** (CoR 5607) 6.3.35 to Blackpool & West Coast Air Services Ltd, Squires Gate; first CoA (4717) issued 6.4.35; transferred 9.37 to Isle of Man Air Services Ltd and operated by associate Channel Air Ferries Ltd, Land's End (St Just); crashed on landing in fog at St Just 25.6.38; pilot Flt Lt D L Dustin killed, four injured; regn cld 1.1.39.

6095 Regd **G-ADCT** (CoR 5613) 21.3.35 to Highland Airways Ltd, Inverness, named *Orcadian*; first CoA (4747) issued 28.5.35; crashed into trees on landing at Westness, Rousay Island, Orkneys, 6.9.35 but ferried by rowing boat to Kirkwall and repaired; reflown 10.11.35; transferred to Scottish Airways Ltd 12.8.37 and regd to them (CoR 8557) 16.6.38; crashed at Inverness (Longman) 14.12.39 and repaired; crashed Inverness (Longman) 14.2.40; regn cld 7.5.40.

A somewhat weatherbeaten G-ADDI, c/n 6096 *[R C Sturtivant]*

"City of Plymouth", c/n 6097, G-ADDJ of Railway Air Services was first registered in March 1935 and subsequently had a chequered civil and military career in Australia

[C F Scandrett via A S Thomas and P H T Green]

6096   Regd **G-ADDI** (CoR 5655) 18.3.35 to Railway Air Services Ltd, Croydon, named *City of Cardiff*; first CoA (4836) issued 18.5.35; renamed *Island Maid* 3.38 for joint operation with PS&IoW Aviation; transferred 9.8.38 to Channel Air Ferries Ltd, Land's End (St Just); sold 5.12.38 to Great Western & Southern Air Lines Ltd, Land's End; hit hedge on take-off from Land's End (St. Just) 17.12.38 but repaired and re-entered service; impressed into RAF 24.9.39 but no serial issued; 24 Sqn, Hendon; to NAC, later AAJC and operated by GW&SAL from St Just 6.40 to 7.43; at DH RU, Witney, 3.41; regd to W S Shackleton Ltd 15.7.43; regd to Vickers-Armstrongs Ltd, Castle Bromwich (later Wisley); CoA lapsed 25.2.46; regd to G A Phelps 23.5.46; sold 3.47 to Air Charter Ltd, Croydon and regd to them 22.8.47; regd 8.3.51 to Air Navigation & Trading Co Ltd, Squires Gate, for pleasure flights around Blackpool tower; sold 11.62 to Aero Enterprises (JHS) Ltd, Ramsgate (later Sywell) and regd to them 26.4.63, operated by Chrisair; named *Liftmaster*; CoA lapsed 25.5.68; regn cld 18.11.70 as sold in USA; flown from Headcorn to Rotterdam as **N34DH** 21.2.71 for shipment by sea to Perlitch Transportation Museum, Morgan Hills, CA; on display at South County Aviation Museum, CA, .80; to M J Kimbrell, Oakville, WA, 5.81 and rebuilt; painted in Chrisair colours and named *Sir Geoffrey de Havilland*; extant.

6097   Regd **G-ADDJ** (CoR 5656) 18.3.35 to Railway Air Services Ltd, Croydon, named *City of Plymouth*; first CoA (4847) issued 25.5.35; operated in winter of .36/.37 by PS&IoW Aviation Ltd; sold to de Havilland .37; regn cld as sold in Australia 3.37; regd **VH-UZZ** (CoR 644) 21.6.37 to Aircraft Pty Ltd, Archerfield, named *Riada*; impressed into RAAF 11.1.40 as **A34-3**; 1 FTS, Point Cook, 26.1.40; CFS, Camden, 12.8.40; 1 AOS, Cootamundra, 10.40; 2 AOS, Mount Gambier, 6.4.41; converted to air ambulance 2.42; 35 Sqn, Pearce (later Maylands) 5.3.42; 33 Sqn, Townsville, 3.5.42; 36 Sqn, Essendon, 2.9.42; WFU 30.10.42; BER 11.10.43; sold to Airlines (Western Australia) Ltd, Perth, 29.6.45, presumably for spares.

6098   Regd **G-ADED** (CoR 5682) 13.4.35 to Railway Air Services Ltd, Croydon; operated on Manx Airways services; first CoA (4848) issued 27.5.35; crashed on take off from Ronaldsway 1.7.35. Capt. R Pierce, the pilot on 11.50 service from Ronaldsway to Blackpool, Liverpool and Manchester with six passengers on board; the aircraft took off to the north, with a run of 700 yards available, but never became airborne, hit the hedge and a stone dyke; although all escaped, the pilot and two passengers were slightly injured, and the aircraft was DBF.

An unnamed DH.84 of Railway Air Services was G-ADED, c/n 6098, which met its end when it crashed at Ronaldsway on 1st July 1935

[E J Riding via P H T Green]

6099   Regd **G-ADEE** (CoR 5683) 15.4.35 to Railway Air Services Ltd, Croydon; operated on Manx Airways services; first CoA (4849) issued 13.6.35; crashed 1550 feet up Fairsnape Fell, nr Garstang, 19 mls ENE of Blackpool, 26.10.35; pilot C Crow and sole passenger killed and aircraft DBF.

6100   Regd **G-ADFI** (CoR 5731) 5.9.35 to Aberdeen Airways Ltd, named *The Silver Ghost*; first CoA (5058) issued 4.9.35; del 14.10.35; name changed 13.2.37 to Allied Airways (Gandar Dower) Ltd; failed to become airborne from Thurso (Claredon) 3.7.37 when it struck a stone boundary wall and burst into flames; pilot H Hinkley and all seven occupants survived.

6101   First CoA (4956) issued 10.7.35; regd **OE-FKD** 7.35 to Osterreichischen Aero Club, Vienna; issued serial **64** for use by Austrian Army Air Force; NFT.

6102   First CoA (5185) issued 29.10.35; regd **VH-UVB** (CoR 573) 24.2.36 to W R Carpenter & Co Ltd, t/a Mandated Airlines, named *Helen;* name changed to Mandated Airlines Ltd 9.36 and regd to them 6.10.36; WFU at Salamaua, NG, 24.6.41 but re-regd to same owner 27.11.41; destroyed in Japanese air raid 21.1.42; regn cld 11.3.42.

6103   First flown by de Havilland as **E.4**; first CoA (5060) issued 3.9.35; tested at A&AEE 9.35; regd **G-ADOS** (CoR 6206) 21.10.35 to S Smith & Sons (Motor Accessories) Ltd for use as flying showroom and laboratory by Smith's Aircraft Instruments, Heston, after fitting out by Airwork Ltd; CoA lapsed 12.6.40; impressed into RAF 6.6.42 as **HM569**; 3 SoGR, Squires Gate, 6.6.42; undershot on landing at Squires Gate 24.6.42 and hit low bank; to DH RU, Witney, but SOC 7.8.42.

6104   To Air Board, Commonwealth of Australia, without CoA; regd **VH-UTX** (CoR 583) 17.4.36 to W R Carpenter & Co Ltd, Salamaua, NG, t/a Mandated Airlines, named *Hope;* name changed to Mandated Airlines Ltd 9.36 and regd to them 6.10.36; impressed into RAAF 25.3.41 (9.4.41 ?) as **A34-11**; 2 AOS, Mount Gambier, 23.6.41; converted to air ambulance 1.42; 34 Sqn, Darwin, 25.2.42; 36 Sqn, Essendon, 17.7.42; undercarriage collapsed on landing at Alice Springs 17.10.42 but repaired; 34 Sqn, Parafield, 13.2.43; destroyed in gale at Oodnadatta whilst on delivery flight 15.2.43; SOC 26.3.43.

Repainted temporarily as EI-ABI "Iolar" of Aer Lingus in 1957, this DH.84 was in reality EI-AFK, c/n 6105   *[Air-Britain]*

6105   Regd **G-AECZ** (CoR 6753) 11.3.36 to Air Cruises Ltd, Hatfield; first CoA (5394) issued 18.4.36; regd (CoR 7638) 1.2.37 to Straight Corpn Ltd, Ramsgate; regd (CoR 8215) 15.11.37 to Ramsgate Airport Ltd; operated by associate Norman Edgar (Western Airways) Ltd, Whitchurch; name changed to Western Airways Ltd 10.38; regd 14.2.39 to Southern Airways Ltd, Ramsgate, but still operated by Western Airways Ltd, Weston-super-Mare; impressed into RAF; 24 Sqn, Hendon, 11.10.39; regn cld 8.5.40; 110 (AAC) Wg, Ringway, 12.5.40 and allocated serial **AV982**; 7 AACU, Castle Bromwich, 16.5.40; badly damaged on landing at Castle Bromwich 22.9.40; to DH RU, Witney, for storage; 18 MU, Dumfries, 30.6.41 and rebuilt; to English Electric 13.10.41 for use by MoAP overseer; damaged at Castle Bromwich 4.11.41; 5 MU, Kemble, 31.8.44; sold to Air Taxis (Croydon) Ltd, Kenley, 3.4.46; regd **G-AECZ** 18.6.46; regd 18.3.47 to Air Taxis Ltd, Croydon (which ceased trading early .48); regd 13.1.48 to F T Bingham, Lockerby, Hants; regd 30.4.48 to Wiltshire School of Flying Ltd, High Post; regn cld 24.2.50 as sold abroad; regd **EI-AFK** 16.3.50 to J Cleary, Mullingar; regd 1.8.50 to Weston Ltd, Weston; repainted temporarily as 'EI-ABI' for Aer Lingus 5.57 but reverted to EI-AFK by 9.57; regn cld 11.3.66 as WFU; stored Weston .59; sold to Aer Lingus .67 and flown to Dublin Airport 1.9.67 for preservation as 'EI-ABI'; used to greet Aer Lingus' first Boeing 747 on arrival at Dublin 6.3.71; placed on display in terminal building 5.76; removed .85 and regd **EI-ABI (2)** 12.8.85 to Aer Lingus, named *Iolar;* reflown 10.4.86 after rebuild; CoA renewed 18.4.86; preserved in flying condition.

6106   Regd **G-AEFX** (CoR 6904) 23.4.36 to W S Shackleton Ltd, Hanworth; first CoA (5448) issued 5.5.36; regn cld 5.36 as sold abroad; regd **VH-UVN** (CoR 597) 10.7.36 to MacRobertson Miller Aviation Co Ltd, Maylands; operated by Australian Aerial Medical Service from 8.38, named *Dunbar Hooper II;* crashed at Broome, WA, 7.1.42, and DBF; regn cld 19.1.42.

6107   Regd **G-AEIS** (CoR 7018) 14.5.36 to de Havilland Aircraft Co Ltd, Hatfield; first CoA (5498) issued 13.6.36; after conversion to semi-military standard, sold 12.36 to Ministry of National Defence, Ankara, Turkey, for Turkish Air Force; NFT.

6108   Regd **G-AEIT** (CoR 7019) 14.5.36 to de Havilland Aircraft Co Ltd, Hatfield; first CoA (5499) issued 9.6.36; after conversion to semi-military standard, sold 12.36 to Ministry of National Defence, Ankara, Turkey, for Turkish Air Force; NFT.

6109   Regd **G-AEIU** (CoR 7020) 14.5.36 to de Havilland Aircraft Co Ltd, Hatfield; first CoA (5500) issued 18.6.36; after conversion to semi-military standard, sold 12.36 to Ministry of National Defence, Ankara, Turkey, for Turkish Air Force; NFT.

6110   Regd **G-AEMI** (CoR 7250) 14.8.36 to Union Founders Trust Ltd, Heston; purchased by Cdte Carlos Pastor Krauel (Senior Spanish Air Force Officer) for use in Spanish Civil War, but sale prohibited by British Government 19.8.36 and aircraft never left Hatfield; regd (CoR 7315) 2.9.36 to Commercial Air Hire Ltd, Croydon; first CoA (5624) issued 5.9.36; operated by Air Dispatch Ltd, Croydon; impressed into RAF 6.7.40; 110 (AAC) Wg,

As G-AECZ of Air Taxis (Croydon) Ltd, c/n 6105 awaits joy-riding customers at an early postwar air show   *[MAP via P H T Green]*

C/n 6110, G-AEMI of Air Dispatch Ltd, Croydon, was occasionally used for Army co-operation work in the late 1930s before being impressed into the RAF as AW173   *[via A Chivers]*

Ringway, 6.7.40; serial **AW173** allocated but not used; 7 AACU, Castle Bromwich, 19.8.40; stalled and crashed during attempted forced landing on Fosse Way near Bury Farm, Pillerton Hersey, Warwickshire, 14.12.40, after engine failure; Plt Off T Walczak and Sgt T Tubis killed; SOC 5.2.41.

6111   Regd **G-AEMJ** (CoR 7251) 14.8.36 to Union Founders Trust Ltd, Heston; purchased by Cdte Carlos Pastor Krauel (Senior Spanish Air Force Officer) for use in Spanish Civil War, but sale prohibited by British Government 19.8.36 and aircraft never left Hatfield; regn cld as sold 1.37; first CoA (5870) issued 13.4.37; to Portuguese Air Force as **504**, later **2304**; still airworthy at Sintra in .53; NFT.

6112   Regd **G-AEMK** (CoR 7252) 14.8.36 to Union Founders Trust Ltd, Heston; purchased by Cdte Carlos Pastor Krauel (Senior Spanish Air Force Officer) for use in Spanish Civil War, but sale prohibited by British Government 19.8.36 and aircraft never left Hatfield; regd (CoR 7313) 1.9.36 to Union Founders Trust Ltd, Heston; first CoA (5642) issued 3.9.36; regd (CoR 7552) 15.12.36 to Union Founders Trust Ltd, Croydon; sold 26.1.37 to Air Dispatch Ltd, Croydon; regd (CoR 7736) 5.3.37 to Mutual Finance Ltd, Croydon; export licence issued 11.5.38 to Tozer Kemsley & Milbourn Ltd as agents for Air Travel & Survey Pty Ltd, Sydney and fitted out for survey work by Rollason Aircraft Services Ltd, Croydon; left Croydon 11.9.38, arrived Darwin 19.10.38, flown by E McA Onslow; not regd as **VH-AAO** until 15.2.40; impressed into RAAF 15.7.40 as **A34-5**; Survey Flight, Canberra, 1.10.40; 34 Sqn; loaned to Guinea Airways 28.1.43; del to Butler Air Transport Pty Ltd, Mascot, 25.7.43; restored as **VH-AAO** 30.7.43 and sold to them 22.10.43; wrecked at Coonamble, NSW, 20/21.12.47, when a severe storm blew it into Castlereagh River.

6113   First CoA (5912) issued 10.5.37; to Portuguese Air Force as **505**, later **2305**; crashed, details unknown.

6114   First CoA (5919) issued 20.5.37; to Portuguese Air Force as **506**, later **2306**; WFU c.50

Australian DH.84 Production

2001   RAAF serial **A34-12**; first flight 29.9.42; TOC at 2 AD, Bankstown, 21.2.43; 33 Sqn, Port Moresby, 13.3.43 to 26.10.43; 9 CU, Port Moresby, 4.11.43; crashed on landing when blown into drainage ditch at Berry Strip, NG, 9.12.43 and DBR; 15 ARD for spares; SOC 30.5.44.

2002   RAAF serial **A34-13**; TOC at 2 AD, Bankstown, 12.10.42; to ANA at Essendon for conversion to air ambulance; 6 CF/CU, Batchelor, NT, 30.5.43 (2.43 ?); overhauled by DH at Mascot .45 and stored at Evans Head; sold 24.5.46 for £50 and converted to civil standard; regd **VH-ASK** 19.8.46 to Commonwealth of Australia (Department of Health); operated by Northern Territory Aerial Medical Service, Darwin; regn cld 4.1.54 as WFU; regd **VH-SNB** 2.58 to J G & G Schulz, Prairie, Qld (later Camden, NSW); regd to L G Nixon for Les Nixon Evangelistic Mission, Bexley, NSW, named *White Wings*; regn cld 8.66 and restored 10.66; regn cld 10.67; stored Camden for six years before sale to Sir William Roberts and the Strathallan Collection in the UK, to whom del 4.75; superficially rebuilt; sold at auction to Museum of Flight, East Fortune, for £7000 and del late .81 for static display; extant.

A34-13 was civilianised in August 1946 as VH-ASK; later re-registered VH-SNB, it eventually found its way to the Strathallan Collection, where this photograph was taken, and finally to the Scottish Museum of Flight at East Fortune
[D Richardson]

2003 RAAF serial **A34-14**; TOC at 2 AD, Bankstown, 12.10.42; 1 R&C Flt, Port Moresby, 25.10.42; crashed at Popindedda, NG, 17.1.43; SOC 11.2.43.

2004 RAAF serial **A34-15**; TOC at 2 AD, Bankstown, 25.10.42; 33 Sqn, Townsville (later Port Moresby), 23.11.42; undercarriage collapsed on take-off from Terapo 19.6.43; SOC 30.5.44.

2005 RAAF serial **A34-16**; TOC at 2 AD, Bankstown, 28.10.42; 33 Sqn, Townsville (later Port Moresby), 14.11.42; 1 R&C Flt, Goodenough Island, 28.10.43; 9 CU, Port Moresby, 4.11.43; deemed no longer fit for tropical service 4.44 and SOC 14.6.44.

2006 RAAF serial **A34-17**; TOC at 2 AD, Bankstown, 5.11.42; 1 R&C Flt, Port Moresby, 23.11.42; damaged 5.12.42 and repaired; 35 Sqn, Pearce, 3.11.43; 7 CU, Pearce, 10.11.43; converted to civil standard; sold 24.1.46 to W R Carpenter Pty Ltd, Sydney, and del 5.2.46; regd **VH-AOS** 29.4.46 to Mandated Airlines Ltd; took off from Lae, NG, 29.1.47 with a load of freight bound for Kerowagi, and in poor weather crashed into Mount Kerigomna, killing the pilot.

2007 RAAF serial **A34-18**; TOC at 2 AD, Bankstown, 10.10.42; 1 R&C Flt, Port Moresby, 7.12.42; damaged 14.2.43 but repaired; 6 CF, Batchelor, 4.10.43; damaged in storm at Katherine Strip 1.11.43; SOC 22.11.43.

2008 RAAF serial **A34-19**; TOC at 2 AD, Bankstown, 11.11.42; 35 Sqn, Maylands, 19.11.42 (or 24.11.42); converted to air ambulance by ANA 2.43; 3 CF, Mascot, 10.3.43 (or 14.3.43); 2 AAU, Kingaroy, 3.6.43; crash-landed at Toogoolawah, Qld, 17.9.43 after hitting tree in bad weather; Flg Off A F Thorley killed; SOC 23.10.43.

2009 RAAF serial **A34-20**; TOC at 2 AD, Bankstown, 16.11.42; 1 CF, Laverton, 30.11.42; 6 CF, Batchelor, 11.8.43; engine failed, stalled on approach to forced landing at Marami Station 25.8.43 and DBR; SOC 14.9.43.

2010 RAAF serial **A34-21**; TOC at 2 AD, Bankstown, 16.11.42 and converted to air ambulance; 2 AAU 17.12.42 to 14.11.44; converted to civil standard and sold 24.1.46 to W R Carpenter Pty Ltd, Sydney for £400; del 30.1.46; regd **VH-AOP** 14.3.46 for Mandated Airlines Ltd, Lae, NG; brakes failed on take-off from Heyfield, NG, 9.8.54, forcing the aircraft to swing into a deep ditch, bursting into flames; all eight occupants uninjured, but aircraft DBF.

2011 RAAF serial **A34-22**; TOC at 2 AD, Bankstown, 22.11.42 and converted to air ambulance; 2 AAU 19.12.42 to 14.11.44; converted to civil standard and sold 24.1.46 to W R

Carpenter Pty Ltd, Sydney, for £400; del 31.1.46; regd **VH-AOQ** 15.3.46 to Mandated Airlines Ltd, Lae, NG; regn cld as WFU 12.9.60.

2012 RAAF serial **A34-23**; TOC at 2 AD, Bankstown, 22.11.42; 34 Sqn 29.11.42; 6 CF, Manibulloo (later Batchelor), 9.1.43 to 11.9.43; 6 CU, Batchelor, 17.12.43 to 27.6.44 and 24.9.45 to 5.3.46; Darwin 5.3.46; undercarriage collapsed on take-off from Darwin 21.3.46; sold as spares to Department of Health, Canberra, for £25 29.5.46.

2013 RAAF serial **A34-24**; TOC at 2 AD, Bankstown, 25.11.42; 5 CF, Garbutt, 18.12.42; missing on flight between Cairns and Mareeba 7.3.43; remains found five days later at Freshwater Gorge, on mountainside 2 mls above Crystal Cascade, nr Cairns, Qld.

2014 RAAF serial **A34-25**; TOC at 2 AD, Bankstown, 26.11.42; 3 CF, Mascot, 4.1.43 for exclusive use of US Army Services of Supply Horse Purchasing Board; 5 CF, Garbutt, 6.6.43 for use by Base Section 2 US Army, Townsville; crashed at Croydon, Qld, 6.12.43, while carrying radar equipment from Garbutt to Mornington Island; SOC 20.12.43; remains to Dept of Health .46 for spares.

2015 RAAF serial **A34-26**; TOC at 2 AD, Bankstown, 3.12.42; 36 Sqn, Townsville, 16.12.42; damaged at Oodnadatta 15.2.43 and repaired; 6 CF 14.12.43; force-landed on beach at Merets Island 16.1.44, but could not take off due to soft sand, so abandoned; SOC 22.10.44.

2016 RAAF serial **A34-27**; TOC at 2 AD, Bankstown, 30.11.42; 6 CF, Manibulloo (later Batchelor), 16.12.42 to 14.9.43; 6 CU, Batchelor, 12.4.44; swung and crashed on take-off from Darwin civil airport 2.12.44 and DBR; SOC 19.3.45.

2017 RAAF serial **A34-28**; TOC at 2 AD, Bankstown, 2.12.42; 5 CF, Garbutt, 16.12.42 to 13.9.43 and 1.12.43 to 5.3.44; converted to civil standard and sold 24.9.45 to Rev. T Jones for Church Aid Society for Australia & Tasmania, Brisbane for £750 and del 4.10.45; regd **VH-AGI** 15.3.46 to Bush Church Aid Society for Australia & Tasmania, Sydney, for use as aerial ambulance; crashed at Batemans Bay, NSW, 1.10.61.

2018 RAAF serial **A34-29**; TOC at 2 AD, Bankstown, 6.12.42; 33 Sqn, Port Moresby, 9.1.43; swung into drainage ditch on landing at Terapo 11.9.43 and undercarriage broke; SOC 12.1.45 at 15 ARD, Port Moresby.

2019 RAAF serial **A34-30**; TOC at 2 AD, Bankstown, 14.12.42; modified as air ambulance; 2 AAU 31.12.42 to 5.8.43; converted to civil standard and sold 27.5.46 to Queensland Ambulance Transport Brigade for £50; regd **VH-AON** 11.6.46; to

C/n 2017, VH-AGI of the Bush Church Aid Society outside the hangar of Kingsford-Smith Flying Service. Note the separately-framed cabin windows in this example
[via A Chivers]

VH-AON, c/n 2019, is seen here marked clearly as being operated by Air Surveys Australia, but this owner does not appear in the aircraft's recorded history!
[via A Chivers]

QANTAS 26.3.47; damaged in NG 11.4.47 when carrying freight to Kainantu strip; pilot touched down late, believing the end of the strip was boggy, but due to gusting winds was forced to overshoot; the port engine did not respond, so he was forced to land two-thirds the way down the strip; when the brakes did not stop the aircraft on the wet surface the aircraft ran off the end of the runway into a creek, damaging the nose, undercarriage, lower mainplanes and engine nacelles; rebuilt and sold 20.11.52; regd .55 to Territory Airlines, Goroka, NG; regd to H J & E Z Hughes, Talwood, Qld; regd to Aircraft Engine Overhauls, Moorabbin; regn cld as WFU 12.7.72; ferried to Joe Drage of Woodonga 24.12.72 and regd to him 21.1.77; WFU and regn cld 24.6.81; ferried to Drage Aero World, Wangaratta City, 27.1.85, named *Puff The Magic Dragon*; regd 17.8.87 to City of Wangaratta; extant.

2020   RAAF serial **A34-31**; TOC at 2 AD, Bankstown, 14.12.42; 36 Sqn, Essendon (later Townsville), 16.12.42; damaged in crash at Tennant's Creek (when ?); 34 Sqn, Darwin, 1.2.43; 6 CF, Batchelor, 22.6.43 to 8.10.43; 6 CU, Batchelor, 24.9.45; RAAF Darwin 5.3.46; del to Dept of Health, Canberra, 5.6.46 and sold to them for £50 14.6.46; converted to civil standard and regd **VH-ASL** 22.11.46 to Dept of Health, for operation by Northern Territory Aerial Medical Service, Darwin; crashed on take-off from Brunette Downs, NT, 7.5.50 and repaired; regd 27.5.55 to L A Wall, t/a Air Charter Services, Townsville, Qld; regd **VH-SJW** 19.11.56 to same owner; crashed 12 mls E of Bulliwallah, Bundaroo Station, nr Charters Towers, Qld, 16.8.57; pilot W Seckold killed.

2021   RAAF serial **A34-32**; TOC at 2 AD, Bankstown, 14.12.42; 33 Sqn, Port Moresby, 24.12.42; 9 CU, Port Moresby, 4.11.43; swung on landing at Bulldog airstrip 17.1.44 and DBR; SOC at 15 ARD, Port Moresby, 14.2.44.

2022   RAAF serial **A34-33**; TOC at 2 AD, Bankstown, 16.12.42; PTU, Tocumwal (later Richmond), 20.12.42; 4 CU, Archerfield, 4.4.44 to 27.8.44; sold 22.2.46 to K Virtue, Yeronghilly, Qld, for £50 and del 9.4.46; converted to civil standard; regd **VH-ALL** 23.5.47 to QANTAS; regd 5.5.50 to ANA, t/a Trans-Australian Airways Ltd and operated for Royal Flying Doctor Service, named *John Flynn*; crashed into tree on take-off from Moothandilla Station, nr Windora, Qld, 6.2.51.

2023   RAAF serial **A34-34**; TOC at 2 AD, Bankstown, 17.12.42; converted to air ambulance; 2 AAU 1.1.43 to 14.11.44; sold to Queensland Ambulance Transport Brigade, Brisbane, 10.10.45 for £670 and del 17.10.45; converted to civil standard; regd **VH-AMB** 28.11.45 to Queensland Air Transport Brigade, Cairns; struck trees on take-off from Palmerville Station (150 mls north of Cairns) 23.2.49 and destroyed, but occupants unhurt.

2024   RAAF serial **A34-35**; TOC at 2 AD, Bankstown, 17.12.42; 1 CF, Laverton, 20.12.42; 6 CF, Batchelor, 2.8.43 to 15.12.43; sold to Bridgewater Amplavox Sound Systems, Sydney, 8.10.45 for £750 and del 22.11.45; converted to civil standard; regd **VH-AFK** 7.3.46 to Shark Patrol Service; to Taylors Air Transport; crashed at Bena Bena, NG, 7.9.48.

2025   RAAF serial **A34-36**; TOC at 2 AD, Bankstown, 22.12.42; 1 R&CS, Port Moresby, 24.12.42; damaged at Goodenough Island 31.3.43 but repaired; 5 CU, Garbutt, 12.3.44; engine cut after take-off, crashed in swamp at Higgins Strip 13.5.44; SOC 12.6.44.

2026   RAAF serial **A34-37**; TOC at 2 AD, Bankstown, 26.12.42; PTU, Tocumwal (later Richmond), 26.12.42; crashed into forest on survey flight 4 mls north of Lime Burner Creek 14.10.43; SOC 15.11.43 at DH.

2027   RAAF serial **A34-38**; TOC at 2 AD, Bankstown, 4.1.43 (27.12.42 ?); 34 Sqn, Darwin, 6.1.43; 3 CF, Mascot, 14.6.43; 5 OTU, Forest Hill (later Tocumwal), 23.8.43; 3 CU, Mascot, 21.11.43; 6 CU, Batchelor, 26.8.44 to 22.1.45; sold 15.3.46 to R T Knight & A J McCarthy, Brisbane, for £480 and del 9.4.46; converted to civil standard; regd **VH-BAF** to QANTAS 28.5.47; on 14.7.47 pilot R Crabbe left Lae, NG, with a load of freight and two passengers bound for Wau; his instructions were to 'follow the road', and he was so intent on doing so that he failed to notice the lowering cloudbase and rising valley floor; the valley became narrower and steeper, forcing the aircraft into a position where the pilot could not turn or climb over the hills, so was forced to 'land' in tree-tops near Zenang; he was catapulted from the aircraft but was not seriously injured, although the passengers were hurt and trapped in the wreckage; they were found later by native hunters who had heard the accident and gone for help; the passengers were freed 21 hours after the accident, and a day later aircraft and tree fell to the ground.

2028   RAAF serial **A34-39**; TOC at 2 AD, Bankstown, 4.1.43; PTU, Tocumwal (later Richmond), 15.1.43; 2 CU, Wagga, 29.11.43; 7 SFTS, Deniliquin, 3.4.44; 6 CU, Batchelor, 10.10.44 to 9.11.44; sold to W R Carpenter Pty Ltd 12.2.46 for £50 and del 8.4.46; converted to civil standard; regd **VH-ARI** 29.7.46 to Mandated Airlines Ltd, NG; when pilot R Burrt and five passengers took off on 31.8.46 from Wewak for Lae, the starboard engine started to misfire, losing power rapidly; the pilot attempted to reach a nearby beach, but was forced down early into a clearing in a swamp; the starboard wing hit a palm tree, slewing the aircraft around, and it caught fire; all occupants escaped; the aircraft had flown only 78 hours since delivery from Sydney and it was thought that the problem had been caused by water contamination.

2029   RAAF serial **A34-40**; TOC at 2 AD, Bankstown, 3.1.43; 1 R&C Flt, Port Moresby, 16.2.43; hit a ridge in a down-draught north-east of KB Mission, Milne Bay, NG, 16.6.43 (the day that the unit moved to Milne Bay); SOC 26.6.43.

2030   RAAF serial **A34-41**; TOC at 2 AD, Bankstown, 10.1.43; converted to air ambulance; 33 Sqn, Port Moresby, 28.2.43; DBR when swung on landing and undercarriage collapsed at 30 Mile Strip, Papua, 3.7.43; 15 ARD 11.7.43; SOC 4.8.44

2031   RAAF serial **A34-42**; TOC at 2 AD, Bankstown, 8.1.43; 35 Sqn, Maylands (later Pearce), 4.2.43; 7 CU, Pearce, 10.11.43 to 22.8.44; sold to Royal Queensland Aero Club, Brisbane, 26.2.46 for £50 and del 8.4.46; converted to civil standard; sold to QANTAS 9.46; regd **VH-AYM** 1.11.46 to Qantas Empire Airways, named *Norman Bourke*; DBF at Canobie Station, Qld, 24.11.48 during engine start-up.

2032   RAAF serial **A34-43**; TOC at 2 AD, Bankstown, 10.1.43; 33 Sqn, Port Moresby, 1.2.43; undercarriage collapsed on landing at Terapo, NG, 12.7.43; 15 ARD, Port Moresby, 18.7.43; SOC 4.8.44 (24.5.44 ?).

2033   RAAF serial **A34-44**; TOC at 2 AD, Bankstown, 15.1.43; converted to air ambulance; 34 Sqn, Darwin, 28.3.43; loaned to Royal Flying Doctor Service; 1 R&C Flt, Port Moresby (later Milne Bay), 24.5.43; crashed on take-off from Berry Strip 26.7.43.

2034   RAAF serial **A34-45**; TOC at 2 AD, Bankstown, 17.1.43; 34 Sqn [J], Darwin, 15.2.43; carried radio c/s VHCSL for Adelaide to Darwin courier service; crashed and DBF 35 miles north of Tennants Creek, NT, 1.4.43, after a propeller detached; SOC 5.5.43.

2035   RAAF serial **A34-46**; TOC at 2 AD, Bankstown, 17.1.43; converted to air ambulance; 1 R&C Flt, Port Moresby, 8.4.43; crashed at Hope Island, Coomera, Qld, 13.4.43 when engine lost power (but alternative source gives crash after engine failure on take-off from Wedau 27.7.43); SOC 18.8.43.

2036   RAAF serial **A34-47**; TOC at 2 AD, Bankstown, 19.1.43; converted to air ambulance; 34 Sqn, Darwin, 24.2.43; disappeared during flight from Sydney (Mascot) to Melbourne, 17.4.43; last seen near Prospect Reservoir, Parramatta and may be submerged under waters of Warragamba Dam, in Burragorang Valley, NSW; Sgt D B Doyle (pilot), Flg Off G H Lester, Sgt F J Doyle, Lt Umstead USMC and Lt Teague USMC posted missing; SOC 4.5.43.

2037   RAAF serial **A34-48**; TOC at 2 AD, Bankstown, 22.1.43; 34 Sqn, Darwin, 26.1.43; crashed Parafield, SA, 11.3.43 after stalling on approach; SOC 4.4.43.

2038   RAAF serial **A34-49**; TOC at 2 AD, Bankstown, 29.1.43; 4 CF, Archerfield, 14.2.43 for GOC 1st Army; crashed into trees in cloudy valley 3 mls E of Toowoomba, Qld, 2.3.43 and DBF; SOC 15.3.43.

2039   RAAF serial **A34-50**; TOC at 2 AD, Bankstown, 29.1.43; 5 CF, Garbutt, 14.2.43 to 11.3.44 for GOC 5th Division; 3 CU, Mascot, 4.1.45 to 18.7.45; sold 27.5.46 to Flying Doctor Service, Perth, for £50 and del 26.6.46; regd **VH-ASN** but NTU; ferried Mascot to Maylands .46 for spares; sold .51 to D Craig, Carnarvon, WA and rebuilt at Maylands; regd **VH-ASX** 9.4.52 to D J Craig, Marron Station, Carnarvon, WA; regd to Territory Airlines, Goroka, NG; last flight 28.8.54; WFU at Lae, NG; regd 14.9.54 to Mandated Airlines Ltd, Lae, for spares; regn cld 1.11.56.

2040   RAAF serial **A34-51**; TOC at 2 AD, Bankstown, 29.1.43; converted to air ambulance; 6 CF, Batchelor, 28.2.43; crashed into sea 15 mls SW of Goulbourn Island 31.5.43 after hitting a tree while overflying beach; SOC 19.6.43.

2041   RAAF serial **A34-52**; TOC at 2 AD, Bankstown, 4.2.43; converted to air ambulance; 6 CF/CU, Batchelor, 3.4.43; crashed into sea off Mindil Beach, Darwin, NT, 3.9.44, after engine failure; SOC 11.9.44.

2042   RAAF serial **A34-53**; TOC at 2 AD, Bankstown, 4.2.43; converted to air ambulance; 2 AAU 24.3.43 to 2.4.44; sold to W R Carpenter Pty Ltd 24.1.46 for £400 and del 5.2.46; converted to civil standard; regd **VH-AOR** 30.8.46 to R L Farquharson; to QANTAS 30.8.47 until 9.3.53; to A L McLachlan, t/a Air Express Co, Archerfield 2.54; damaged in forced landing in swamp nr Bajool, Qld, 27.2.54 and repaired; to S J Porter; hit tree and crashed on landing at Doboy Creek, Wynnum, Tingalpa, Qld, 23.10.54, killing S J Porter and his son.

2043   RAAF serial **A34-54**; TOC at 2 AD, Bankstown, 4.2.43; converted to air ambulance; 2 AAU 27.3.43 to 14.11.44; sold 12.2.46 to Sydney Aero Club, Mascot, for £50 for spares and del 9.4.46; NFT.

2044   RAAF serial **A34-55**; TOC at 2 AD, Bankstown, 7.2.43; converted to air ambulance; 35 Sqn, Maylands (later Pearce), 28.3.43 for use by GOC 3rd Australian Corps; 7 CU, Pearce, 10.11.43 to 11.9.44; sold 26.2.46 to Aircraft Pty Ltd, Archerfield, for £50 and del 4.3.46; converted to civil standard; regd **VH-BJH** 28.9.48 [with c/n DG.44]; regn cld as WFU 6.8.51; regd 2.12.54 to A Earle, Dalby, Qld; regd to C R Laver, Mackay, Qld; regn cld as WFU 11.9.60.

2045   RAAF serial **A34-56**; TOC at 2 AD, Bankstown, 11.2.43; converted to air ambulance; 6 CF, Batchelor, 8.4.43 to 17.4.44; 2 AAU ?; sold 27.5.46 to RFDS, Qld, and del 26.6.46; converted to civil standard; regd **VH-ASO** 10.3.47 to RFDS (WA Section); regd **VH-FDA** 30.9.48 to Broken Hill Flying Doctor Service; sold .54; regd **VH-AGC** 7.8.56 to Adastra Airways Pty Ltd, Mascot; regd to R S & S P Macdonald, Clermont, Qld; regd .63 to

VH-AGC of Adastra Airways, c/n 2045, decorated for the 1958 Smith's Mobilgas Trials   *[via A Chivers]*

VH-AQU of Marshall Airways charter service, Bankstown, had started life as RAAF A34-59 and saw a good deal of service before being sold in December 1945. C/n 2048, it is now in the UK for restoration and operation by the Norman Aeroplane Trust   *[Air-Britain]*

Queensland Airplanters Pty Ltd, Bundaberg; regd .66 to Newcastle Parachute Club, Tighes Hill, NSW; badly damaged on take-off from Newcastle; regn cld as WFU 20.7.62; restored 28.11.63; ground-looped on landing at Maitland, NSW, 1.12.68 and regn cld same day; stored at Maitland and Geelong; remains sold .72 to J O'Connell, Melbourne and rebuilt at Point Cook, Vic; regd to him 12.4.76; stalled and crashed on take-off from Point Cook 13.12.79 and DBF; O'Connell killed; regn cld 17.1.83.

2046   RAAF serial **A34-57**; TOC at 2 AD, Bankstown, 11.2.43; converted to air ambulance; 1 R&CF, Port Moresby (later Milne Bay), 16.5.43; 8 CU, Goodenough Island, 5.11.43; 9 CU, Port Moresby, 23.11.43; 2 AAU 21.3.44 to 30.3.44; sold 24.9.45 to Royal Flying Doctor Service, Perth, WA for £750 and del 11.10.45; converted to civil standard; regd **VH-AGJ** 15.10.45 to RFDS (WA Section); regn cld as WFU 14.6.51.

2047   RAAF serial **A34-58**; TOC at 2 AD, Bankstown, 2.3.43; 5 OTU, Forest Hill (later Tocumwal), 6.4.43; 4 CU, Archerfield, 2.12.43; crashed into fence while overshooting at Toowoomba, Qld, 20.3.44, killing four and DBF; SOC 19.4.44.

2048   RAAF serial **A34-59**; TOC at 2 AD, Bankstown, 3.3.43; 5 OTU, Forest Hill (later Tocumwal), 6.4.43; 4 CU, Archerfield, 28.12.43; 5 SFTS, Uranquinty, 17.3.44; 6 CU, Batchelor, 14.9.44 to 1.12.44; sold 13.12.45 to D S Marshall, Rochdale, NSW; converted to civil standard; regd **VH-AQU** 27.9.46 to S Marshall, Bankstown; regn cld as WFU 28.9.48; restored 14.4.49; regn cld as WFU 11.1.55; regd 10.9.57 to Marshall Airways, Bankstown; regn cld 30.9.70; stored at Bankstown; regd 14.11.79 to R J Fox, Henley Beach, SA; regn cld 12.3.82; regd 18.11.83 to R St John, Henley Beach, SA; regd 15.5.85 to Hawker de Havilland Ltd, Bankstown; repainted .86 in RAAF colours as A34-59 [XJ:A]; regd **VH-DHX** 22.12.86 (or 19.11.86) to same owner; allocated to Power House Museum, Sydney, .93; regd .96 to N Challinor, Murwillumbah, NSW; regn cld as sold to UK 28.12.00; regd **G-ECAN** 11.1.01 to T P A Norman, Rendcomb, for rebuild by Hants Light Plane Services Ltd, Chilbolton; regd 29.11.01 to A J Norman, t/a Norman Aeroplane Trust, Rendcomb; first flown after rebuild 28.5.03 and new CoA issued 26.6.03.

2049   RAAF serial **A34-60**; TOC at 2 AD, Bankstown, 5.3.43; 5 OTU, Forest Hill (later Tocumwal), 6.4.43; 5 CF/CU, Garbutt, 17.10.43 to 3.9.44; sold 20.12.45 to D S Marshall for £50 and del 4.3.46; converted to civil standard; regd **VH-GAU** but NTU; regd **VH-BMX** 24.2.49 to Guinea Air Traders; crashed at Atemble Mission, NG, 14.2.50; regn cld 23.2.50.

2050   RAAF serial **A34-61**; TOC at 2 AD, Bankstown, 9.3.43; 1 W&GS, Ballarat, for trial installation modification of W/T for air gunners' use; 3 W&GS, Maryborough, 16.8.43; sold 24.1.46 to H K Morris, Rose Bay, NSW for £570 and del 25.1.46; converted to civil standard; regd **VH-AOT** 21.3.46 to H K Morris; to QANTAS 2.1.49; regd 10.52 to Qantas Empire Airways Ltd; regd .55 to B Passlow, t/a Riverlea Market Gardens Ltd, Madang, NG; when flying from Madang to the Seventh Day Adventist Hanseside colony at

Togoba, NG, on 2.8.55 with a full load of freight and passengers the aircraft crashed into the side of a mountain gorge near Togoba, killing the pilot, W E Passlow.

2051   RAAF serial **A34-62**; TOC at 2 AD, Bankstown, 21.3.43; 5 SFTS, Uranquinty, 29.3.43; 6 CU, Batchelor, 4.10.44 to 15.11.44; sold 15.2.46 to W R Carpenter Pty Ltd for £50 and del 9.4.46; converted to civil standard; regd **VH-APL** 29.4.46 to Mandated Airlines Ltd; regd 9.52 to J A W Gray and operated by Territory Airlines Ltd, Goroka, NG; pilot J Rose and two passengers took off from Madang, NG, on 23.9.52 with a load of Government supplies, the aircraft being at maximum all-up weight; pilot overshot landing at Chimbu due to a tailwind and up-draughts, tried to go around again, but was restricted by the turning area and heavy aircraft; close to stalling speed, the aircraft hit the side of a hill, badly injuring the pilot.

2052   RAAF serial **A34-63**; TOC at 2 AD, Bankstown, 15.3.43; 7 SFTS, Deniliquin, 26.3.43; 6 CU, Batchelor, 10.10.44; crash-landed on beach on Bathurst Island, off Darwin, NT, 12.3.45, after engine cut after take-off; submerged by tide; SOC 21.3.45.

2053   RAAF serial **A34-64**; TOC at 2 AD, Bankstown, 16.3.43; 4 CF/CU, Archerfield, 12.4.43 to 28.8.44 for use with 1st Australian Army; sold to K Virtue, Yerongpilly, Brisbane, 14.2.46 for £50 and del 9.4.46; converted to civil standard; regd **VH-AYZ** 1.11.46; regd to Edward D Hill and Co, Wyandra, Qld, 3.56; regd to H W Baldwin & T Beverley-Smith, Sydney; regd .62 to Aerial Work Co, Temora, NSW; crashed at Bega, NSW, 24.11.62 but repaired; regd .63 to North Queensland Air Transport Co, Mareeba; regn cld as WFU 22.6.64.

2054   RAAF serial **A34-65**; TOC at 2 AD, Bankstown, 19.4.43; modified for W/T fitment; 5 OTU, Forest Hill (later Tocumwal), 25.6.43 to 26.5.44; 6 CF, Batchelor, for exclusive use of Allied Works Council; 5 CU, Garbutt; crashed in forced landing on ferry flight between Plumbton and Mount Druit, NSW, 5.1.45; SOC 23.1.45.

2055   RAAF serial **A34-66**; TOC at 2 AD, Bankstown, 28.3.43; modified for W/T fitment; 3 W&GS, Maryborough, 9.8.43 to 17.9.44; sold 24.5.46 to Namoi-Walgett District Ambulance Service, Narrabri, NSW for £50 and del 26.6.46; converted to civil standard; regd **VH-BAH** 23.5.47; to QANTAS 1.6.48 to 13.5.49; regd 2.4.49 to ANA (t/a Trans Australian Airlines) for operation by Queensland Aerial Ambulance and Taxi Service Pty Ltd; sold 11.55 to Royal Newcastle Aero Club; crashed on take-off from Brewarrina, NSW, 1.7.56, and DBF; pilot R M (or M D?) Hart killed.

2056   RAAF serial **A34-67**; TOC at 2 AD, Bankstown, 23.3.43 (28.3.43 ?); modified for W/T fitment; 1 W&GS, Ballarat; 3 WAGS, Maryborough, 15.12.43 to 17.9.44; sold 23.11.45 to Newcastle Aero Club, Broadmeadow, NSW for £590 and del 9.4.46; converted to civil standard; regd **VH-AOK** 4.7.46; to QANTAS 6.4.50 to 19.9.50; WFU 6.8.51.

VH-AYZ, c/n 2053, wearing the name "Rosevale", its owner at the time not known   *[Air-Britain]*

2057   RAAF serial **A34-68**; TOC at 2 AD, Bankstown, 24.3.43; modified for W/T fitment; 1 W&GS, Ballarat, 2.8.43 to 16.8.43 and 3.8.44 to 30.10.44; sold 20.2.45 to Butler Air Transport Pty and del 21.2.45; converted to civil standard; regd **VH-AEF** 29.4.45 to Butler Air Transport Co Ltd; regd 18.6.48 to QANTAS and delivered 29.6.48 to New Guinea; chartered to Trans Australia Airlines 9.52; sold 14.5.53 to Fawcett Aviation Pty Ltd, Bankstown; regd in New Zealand as **ZK-AXI** 14.7.53 to Rolvin Airways Ltd, Palmerston North; regd 17.5.54 to Nelson Aero Club and used as ambulance and for supply-dropping; WFU 4.63; sold 7.63 to A J Bradshaw, Nelson, named *Puff*; sold 10.4.67 to Auckland Flying School Ltd (E Cox and J Bergman); badly damaged at Ardmore 23.4.67 when during take-off with six parachutists on board faiure of port engine caused the pilot to force-land in a field, the aircraft hitting a fence post and tipping onto its nose; remains donated to Museum of Transport & Technology, Auckland, by NZ Insurance and stored; sold 5.83 to G S Smith, Dairy Flat, Auckland, for rebuilding (in exchange for DH.83C ZK-APT); regd 3.3.97 to G S and G A Smith, Dairy Flat; rolled out 8.3.97 and named *Taniwha*; flown 22.4.97; extant.

2058   RAAF serial **A34-69**; TOC at 2 AD, Bankstown, 24.3.43 (8.4.43 ?); modified for W/T fitment; 1 W&GS, Ballarat, 27.7.43 to 30.10.44; sold 13.12.45 to S D Marshall, Rockdale, NSW for £300 and del 3.1.46; converted to civil standard; regd **VH-AOE** 5.3.46 to

S D Marshall; regd .55 to Madang Air Charters, Madang, NG; regd 10.55 to Madang Air Services Ltd; crashed into Madang harbour on take-off from Madang 29.10.55; no casualties; salvaged but not repaired; regn cld 25.7.57.

2059   RAAF serial **A34-70**; TOC at 2 AD, Bankstown, 8.4.43; modified for W/T fitment; DH, Mascot, 5.43; 1 W&GS, Ballarat, 2.8.43; to 5 AD, Wagga, for storage 30.10.44; sold 25.10.45 to K Virtue, Yerongpilly, Qld, for £480 and del 24.11.45; converted to civil standard; registered **VH-AMN** 4.12.45 to Capt K Virtue, Brisbane; regd 31.7.46 to QANTAS; damaged at Cloncurry 21.11.48 when blown 100 yards in a gale but repaired; regd 2.4.49 to ANA, t/a Trans-Australian Airlines, Cloncurry (later Charleville), and operated on behalf of the Flying Doctor Service, named *John Flynn*, later *Norman Burke*; regd 14.12.55 to Schutt Airfarmers Pty Ltd, Moorabbin, Vic, for crop-dressing use after conversion; regd 7.12.59 to Bob Couper & Co, Cunderdin, WA; regd 5.6.60 to Ross International Fisheries Pty Ltd, Perth, for use by Blaxell & Grummel, Perth, to carry crayfish; ground-looped at Jurien Bay airstrip, WA, 12.11.60 due to an attempted landing in strong crosswinds; the pilot, who had only two hours on the type, was uninjured, but aircraft was DBR; regn cld 25.7.61.

2060   RAAF serial **A34-71**; TOC at 2 AD, Bankstown, 8.4.43; modified for W/T fitment; 1 W&GS, Ballarat, 2.8.43; flew into a hill 12 mls SW of Daylesford, Vic., 21.7.44; SOC 21.8.44.

2061   RAAF serial **A34-72**; TOC at 2 AD, Bankstown, 8.4.43; modified for W/T fitment; 35 Sqn, Maylands (later Pearce), 24.7.43; 7 CU, Pearce, 10.11.43 to 11.9.44; sold 15.2.46 to W R Carpenter & Co Pty for £50 and del 21.2.46; converted to civil standard; regd **VH-AKX** 24.3.47 to Mandated Airlines of NG; left Lae, NG, 11.5.48 for Sydney for major CoA overhaul, stopping overnight at Daru; left Daru early next day on the over-water leg to Horne Island; halfway across the Torres Strait the pilot (J Spiers) encountered a bad storm, which forced him to lose sight of the surface of the sea, so he turned back for Daru; the aircraft was almost

VH-AMN, c/n 2059, of Schutt Airfarmers Pty of Moorabbin, Victoria, was used as a crop-dresser   *[via A Chivers]*

VH-PSZ, c/n 2064, of the Royal Aero Club of New South Wales crashed in June 1961 *[via A Chivers]*

at sea level when a small island, Turnagain Island, was sighted ahead; Spicrs attempted a landing but crashed in the process; the tide was out but the pilot had no food, water, weapon or radio; he was found six days later and had been forced to climb on top of the aircraft remains to escape the rising water; a RAAF Catalina was sent to rescue him, but another storm blew up, forcing the Catalina to leave behind its engineer; both airmen were eventually rescued by a pearling lugger.

2062 RAAF serial **A34-73**; TOC at 2 AD, Bankstown, 8.4.43; modified for W/T fitment; 3 W&GS, Maryborough, 13.9.43; crashed and DBF at Maryborough 19.9.43 when it hit up-draught on take-off and stalled; SOC 14.10.43.

2063 RAAF serial **A34-74**; TOC at 2 AD, Bankstown, 8.4.43; modified for W/T fitment; 2 W&GS, Parkes, 16.8.43; 3 W&GS, Maryborough, 6.1.44 to 17.9.44; sold 21.2.46 to W R Carpenter Pty Ltd for £50 and del 7.3.46; converted to civil standard; regd **VH-BDB** 20.5.47 to Mandated Airlines of NG; crashed on take-off from Kerowagi airstrip in the highlands of NG 3.4.51; pilot, L Jenkins, and two of the eight passengers were seriously injured; investigations proved that the aircraft was more than 18kg over-weight, it was carrying 8 instead of the maximum 6 passengers, only four seat belts were provided, the freight was not secured behind the passengers, the pilot failed to carry a load sheet to compute the centre of gravity, the tailwind exceeded the maximum for take-off and the pilot failed to adjust the mixture controls for maximum take-off power.

2064 RAAF serial **A34-75**; TOC at 2 AD, Bankstown, 11.4.43; modified for W/T fitment; 2 W&GS, Parkes, 30.8.43; 3 W&GS, Maryborough, 6.1.44 to 17.9.44; sold 12.2.46 to Royal Aero Club of NSW for £50 and del 9.4.46; converted to civil standard; regd **VH-APJ** 28.10.47 to Royal Aero Club of NSW, Bankstown; re-regd **VH-RSZ** 12.6.57; re-regd **VH-PSZ** 9.58; crashed at Maitland, NSW, 10.6.61.

2065 RAAF serial **A34-76**; TOC at 2 AD, Bankstown, 15.4.43; modified for W/T fitment; 2 W&GS, Parkes, 16.8.43; 3 W&GS, Maryborough, 6.1.44 to 17.9.44; sold 21.2.46 to W R Carpenter Pty Ltd for £50 and del 9.4.46; converted to civil standard; regd **VH-AYB** 21.2.47 to Mandated Airlines of NG; port engine failed just after take-off from Lae, NG, for Kokoda and Popondetta 20.8.47, forcing the machine to ditch, but all occupants were rescued by fishermen.

2066 RAAF serial **A34-77**; TOC at 2 AD, Bankstown,15.4.43; modified for W/T fitment; 1 W&GS, Ballarat, 30.8.43 to 20.10.44; sold 7.11.45 to K Virtue, Yerongpilly, Qld for £520 and del 29.11.45; converted to civil standard; regd **VH-AOM** 28.2.46 to R T Knight and A J McCartney; crashed at MacKay, Qld, 20.7.46, killing pilot R T Knight plus one, five injured.

2067 RAAF serial **A34-78**; TOC at 2 AD, Bankstown, 20.4.43; modified for W/T fitment; 5CF/CU, Garbutt, 18.5.43 to 20.9.44; sold 15.10.45 to N H Blackman, Brisbane for £520; converted to civil standard; regd **VH-AMO** 23.12.45 to T H McDonald; to Catholic Mission of the Holy Ghost, Alexishafen, NG, 1.47; pilot, Father J Glover, killed when the aircraft crashed on landing and was destroyed by fire at Mingende, NG, 31.12.48.

2068 RAAF serial **A34-79**; TOC at 2 AD, Bankstown, 20.4.43; modified for W/T fitment; 2 CF, Wagga, 28.6.43; damaged 9.11.43 but repaired; 6 CU, Batchelor, 14.7.44 to 9.11.44; sold 15.10.45 to Zinc Corporation Ltd, Melbourne for £750 and del 25.2.46; converted to civil standard; regd **VH-AQW** to them 1.7.46; to QANTAS 7.3.49 until 23.4.53; to Madang Air Charters, NG, .55; to Madang Air Services Ltd .56; regn cld 19.6.61.

2069 RAAF serial **A34-80**; TOC at 2 AD, Bankstown, 22.4.43; modified for W/T fitment; 5 CF, Garbutt, 16.7.43; crashed in forced landing at Wentlock airstrip, 21.9.43 when lost on delivery flight to 1 RSU; SOC 22.11.43.

2070 RAAF serial **A34-81**; TOC at 2 AD, Bankstown, 26.4.43; modified for W/T fitment; 1 R&C Flt, Milne Bay (later Goodenough Island), 23.8.43; 8 CU, Goodenough Island, 5.11.43; 9 CU, Port Moresby, 24.11.43; 2 AAU 12.43; engine failed on take-off, hit trees 3 mls N of Vivigani, Goodenough Island, 22.12.43; SOC 7.1.44.

2071 RAAF serial **A34-82**; TOC at 2 AD, Bankstown, 28.4.43; 5 CF, Garbutt, 16.7.43; damaged 3.8.44 but repaired; 6 CU, Batchelor, 19.9.45; SF Darwin 5.3.46; sold 14.6.46 to RFDS, SA for £50 and del 5.8.46; converted to civil standard; regd **VH-AXL** 1.9.46; to QANTAS 9.5.47; pilot, F G Barlogie, took off from Lae, NG, 21.9.51 with a load of freight for Wabang; visibility in the highlands was poor due to smoke haze and low cloud; aircraft crashed into a ridge 5 km NE of Koranka airstrip; Barlogie, who was believed to be flying on instruments, was killed.

2072 RAAF serial **A34-83**; TOC at 2 AD, Bankstown, 28.4.43; modified for W/T fitment; 5 CF/CU, Garbutt, 16.7.43 to 25.10.44; sold 9.4.46 to Shark Patrol Service, Sydney for £50 and del same day; converted to civil standard; regd **VH-APP** 6.7.46 to New England Airways; re-regd **VH-CPP** 1.9.49; to Brown and Dureau Pty Ltd, Melbourne, .55; re-regd **VH-DMB** 7.57 to D C Muir, t/a Muir Aviation, Darwin; crashed at Darwin 27.2.59.

2073 RAAF serial **A34-84**; TOC at 2 AD, Bankstown, 1.5.43; modified for W/T fitment; 5 CF/CU, Garbutt, [KF:Q] 16.7.43 to 3.7.44; 3 CU, Mascot, 29.3.45 to 8.6.45; sold 8.10.45 to Bridgewater Amplavox Sound Systems, Sydney for £750 and del 30.11.45; converted to civil standard; regd **VH-AHY** 24.5.46 to Shark Patrol Service; to Taylors Air Transport 7.47; crashed at Hope Creek, NG, 20.5.48.

2074   RAAF serial **A34-85**; TOC at 2 AD, Bankstown, 7.5.43; modified for W/T fitment; 6 CF, Batchelor, 3.11.43 to 14.11.44; sold 21.2.46 to Butler Air Transport Pty for £50 and del same day; converted to civil standard; regd **VH-AVU** 21.11.46; regn cld as WFU 23.5.51.

2075   RAAF serial **A34-86**; TOC at 2 AD, Bankstown, 17.5.43; modified for W/T fitment; 6 CF, Batchelor, 3.11.43 to 18.10.44; sold 22.2.46 to Queensland Ambulance Transport Brigade, Brisbane for £50 and del 9.4.46 for use as spares source.

2076   RAAF serial **A34-87**; TOC at 2 AD, Bankstown, 17.5.43; 6 CF, Batchelor, 24.11.43 to 1.12.44; sold 21.2.46 to W R Carpenter Pty Ltd, t/a Mandated Airlines of NG, for £50 and del 4.3.46 for use as spares source.

2077   RAAF serial **A34-88**; TOC at 2 AD, Bankstown, 13.5.43; 5 CU, Garbutt, 22.12.43; struck overhead wires on take-off from Coffs Harbour, NSW, 23.12.43 while on ferry flight; SOC 7.1.44 at 3 AD, Amberley.

2078   RAAF serial **A34-89**; TOC at 2 AD, Bankstown, 20.5.43; 7 CU, Pearce, 2.2.44; 6 CU, Batchelor, 1.7.44; suffered power loss on take-off and crashed 1 ml NE of Batchelor, NT, 3.2.45; SOC 27.2.45.

2079   RAAF serial **A34-90**; TOC at 2 AD, Bankstown, 20.5.43; 33 Sqn, Port Moresby, 7.6.43; 9 CU, Port Moresby, 4.11.43; 8 CU, Goodenough Island, 19.5.44 to 14.10.44; sold 21.2.46 to W R Carpenter Pty Ltd for £50 and del 7.3.46; converted to civil standard; regd **VH-ASU** 27.9.46; to QANTAS; regn cld as WFU 19.12.47, restored 11.6.48; regd 13.5.49 to ANA for Royal Flying Doctor Service; sold 11.55 (to A V Browning ?); regd 12.55 to Schutt Airfarmers Pty Ltd, Moorabbin; regd **VH-APK** 3.5.60 to Queensland Air Planters Pty Ltd, Childers; regn cld as WFU 9.10.64.

2080   RAAF serial **A34-91**; TOC at 2 AD, Bankstown, 25.5.43; 6 CU, Batchelor, 24.1.44 to 9.11.44; sold 12.2.46 to W R Carpenter Pty Ltd and collected 11.3.46; converted to civil standard; regd **VH-ARJ** 18.7.46; regd 5.53 to Mandated Airlines of NG; damaged on landing at Wewak, NG, 8.1.54; regn cld as WFU 1.9.60.

2081   RAAF serial **A34-92**; TOC at 2 AD, Bankstown, 30.5.43; 5 CF, Garbutt, 25.12.43 to 3.9.44; sold 15.2.46 to W R Carpenter Pty Ltd for £50 and del 9.4.46; converted to civil standard; regn **G-AJKF** reserved for Butlins Ltd 28.3.47 but cld 19.8.48 ; regd **VH-BDS** to QANTAS 28.4.48; sold 14.11.52 to Wagga Flying School Pty Ltd; regd 19.8.54 to N R Thompson, t/a North Australian Flying Service, Darwin; regd 17.6.59 to South Australian Air Taxis Ltd, Adelaide; regd 9.11.62 to Rostrevor Building Co, Rostrevor, SA; re-regd **VH-AML** 19.9.63 to Bob Couper and Co, Cunderdin, WA; regd .68 to N J Hyder, Busselton,

WA; regd .69/70 to H W Hockin, Capel, WA; regd 1.7.85 to Mrs M C Hockin, Nedlands, WA (later Williamstown, Vic); to RAAF Museum, Point Cook in airworthy condition as **A34-92**; extant.

2082   RAAF serial **A34-93**; TOC at 2 AD, Bankstown, 30.5.43; School of Photography, Canberra, 13.2.44 to 25.8.44; sold 25.9.45 to RFDS, NSW for £750 and del 4.10.45; converted to civil standard; regd **VH-AGM** 7.12.45 (but seen with this regn 12.10.45); regn cld as WFU 31.7.46

2083   RAAF serial **A34-94**; TOC at 2 AD, Bankstown, 10.6.43; 9 CU, Port Moresby (later Lae), 29.11.43 to 26.9.44; sold 15.2.46 to W R Carpenter Pty Ltd for £50 and del 9.4.46; converted to civil standard; regd **VH-BDC** 13.6.47; regd 4.51 to Mandated Airlines of NG; regd .55 to Territory Airlines Ltd, Goroka, NG; regn cld as WFU 11.7.57.

2084   RAAF serial **A34-95**; TOC at 2 AD, Bankstown, 11.6.43; 1 CU, Laverton, 6.3.44 to 23.8.44; 9 CU, Lae; sold 20.12.45 to Newcastle Aero Club, Broadmeadow for £80 and del 9.4.46; converted to civil standard; regd **VH-AOL** 3.7.47; owner renamed Royal Newcastle Aero Club 2.53; crashed on take-off from Orange, NSW, 10.5.53 and DBF.

2085   RAAF serial **A34-96**; TOC at 2 AD, Bankstown, 20.6.43; 1 CU, Laverton, 16.1.44; 9 CU, Port Moresby (later Lae), 23.4.44 to 26.9.44; sold 31.10.45 to J L Reid, Sydney for £690 and del same day; converted to civil standard; regd **VH-AFH** 12.12.45 to A T Reid; regd .55/.56 to Northern Australian Aviation Services Pty Ltd, Darwin; operated 8.56 by North Australian Uranium Corpn, Darwin; crashed on take-off from Sleisbeck, NT, 31.8.56; regn cld 22.9.59.

2086   RAAF serial **A34-97**; TOC at 2 AD, Bankstown, 24.6.43; 9 CU, Port Moresby (later Lae), 1.4.44 to 26.9.44; sold 3.9.45 to Aircraft Pty Ltd, Archerfield for £1000 and del 17.9.45; converted to civil standard; regd **VH-AIA** 31.10.45; regd 21.8.47 to Butler Air Transport; regd 7.48 to QANTAS; regn cld 6.10.48; regd 23.6.50 to QANTAS; sold 16.3.53; regd 12.53 to Territory Airlines Ltd, Goroka, NG; damaged in accident 24.4.55 when pilot A Chadim took off from Lae for the Bona airstrip, where on landing the port wingtip touched the grass, causing a swing to develop into a ground-loop and the tail to break off; a replacement tail from VH-AAC was carried on a three-day overland journey to Bona; within a week repairs were made and the aircraft was returned to service; regd .55/.56 to Mitchell Aerial Services Pty Ltd, Cairns; regd .57 to Queensland Air Planters Pty Ltd, Childers; regn cld as WFU 2.9.63.

2087   RAAF serial **A34-98**; TOC at 2 AD, Bankstown, 23.6.43; 9 CU, Port Moresby (later Lae), 22.7.44; crashed on take-off 27.9.44 when engine cut during flight to 5 AD, Forest Hill (Wagga Wagga).

VH-AML was the 1963 registration of the former VH-BDS, c/n 2081, and as such passed through several private owners' hands   *[Air-Britain]*

Prototype single-pilot DH.86 E.2 in the air early in 1934, before registration as G-ACPL   *[via R C Sturtivant]*

Part 2: The DH.86 Express Air Liner

Background

Known officially as the Express Air Liner, the DH.86 was a logical development of the DH.84. It came about in 1933 when a specification was issued for an aircraft required by Qantas Empire Airways to operate the Singapore to Brisbane sector of the proposed Empire Air Route from London to Australia. High performance and safety were the main criteria, to meet which de Havilland designed a scaled-up version of the DH.84, powered by four 200hp Gipsy Six engines.

In the hands of Hubert Broad, the DH.86 prototype, E.2, flew at Stag Lane on 14th January 1934. Very rapid acceptance trials at A&AEE, Martlesham Heath, were then carried out, and the Certificate of Airworthiness was issued on 30th January, meeting by one day a time limit set by the Australian authorities. Further flight tests followed, after which E.2 was furnished and painted in the colours of Railway Air Services and on 21st August 1934 inaugurated a new route from Croydon to Castle Bromwich, Manchester (Barton), Belfast and Glasgow (Renfrew). The first four aircraft were designed for operation by one pilot, but as QEA changed its specification for a captain and first officer in side-by-side seating the prototype quickly returned to Stag Lane for modification, involving an elongated nose section which became the pattern for all further DH.86 production. It then became one of the six examples operated by QEA but registered to Imperial Airways.

Other early operators of the DH.86 included Holyman's Airways, which used VH-URN, the fourth single-pilot aircraft, on a service from Melbourne to Hobart until it disappeared in the Bass Strait on 19th October 1934. A replacement two-pilot DH.86, VH-URT, was also lost when it came down off Flinders Island a year later. Of the six QANTAS aircraft, VH-USG was written off in a crash at Longreach on 15th November 1934, after which QANTAS cabled de Havilland to request urgent trials at A&AEE, Martlesham Heath, to determine the causes of these incidents. Meanwhile the airline grounded its other DH.86s, as did Imperial Airways its single-pilot models. Preparation for the inauguration by QANTAS of the Singapore to Brisbane sector of the Empire Air Route was suspended but arrangements were made with Imperial Airways to operate between Singapore and Darwin temporarily using AW.15s while

QANTAS would fly DH.86s between Darwin and Brisbane. A conference in London on 13th December between interested parties failed to discover any defects, but QANTAS found that poor rigging of the fin bias adjustment mechanism could cause damage to the forward fin attachment. When de Havilland refused to modify this QANTAS did the work, resulting in much better stability. It was now decided that DH.86s could be flown after modification, although not carrying fare-paying passengers for the first three months.

However, all was still not well, as QANTAS discovered when VH-ASF arrived at Darwin on its delivery flight on 21st January 1935 and was found to have the same problem as before. This prompted a vehement complaint from QANTAS but before long they had re-rigged the fin bias adjustment mechanism, and on 26th February 1935 VH-USC *Canberra* left Darwin on its way to Koepang on the route to Singapore, inaugurating Australia's first regular outbound overseas airmail service. Passenger-carrying began on 17th April 1935, with Lady Louis Mountbatten and Maj H Phillips among the travellers.

Two airlines that had pioneered the use of the DH.84, Jersey Airways and Hillman's Airways, were quick to order the DH.86 to meet increasing passenger numbers. In anticipation of the new Jersey airport and certainly in the firm belief of continued growth, Jersey Airways placed a £50,000 order on 10th November 1934 for six DH.86s, which could fly from Heston in less than ninety minutes. Hillman's Airways ordered three DH.86s, which were delivered in June and July 1935 and put into service on the route from Essex Airport (Stapleford Tawney) to Paris (Le Bourget). In Egypt, four DH.86s entered service with Misr Airwork on routes connecting Cairo, Alexandria, Baghdad, Cyprus and Haifa, again replacing the smaller Dragon and taking advantage of increasing numbers of passengers. Late in 1935, three DH.86s were shipped to New Zealand for use by Union Airways on its service between Palmerston North, Blenheim, Christchurch and Dunedin. Later, these were impressed for service with the RNZAF.

Towards the end of 1935 a modified version of the DH.86 with pneumatic undercarriage legs, more efficient brakes, a metal rudder and a steeper windscreen was developed. Known as the DH.86A, the prototype flew in January 1936 and was delivered to Imperial

G-ADUF, c/n 2334 "Dido" of Imperial Airways was taken over by BOAC, survived the war and remained active until 1952. The most obvious feature of conversion to DH.86B was the addition of end plates to the tailplane.   [R C Sturtivant]

Airways as G-ADFF. This and eleven others were put into service on Imperial Airways' European routes and on a route from Khartoum in the Sudan to Accra which opened on 13th February 1936. On 23rd March 1936 G-ADCN, an earlier DH.86, inaugurated Imperial Airways' service from Penang in Malaya to Hong Kong via Saigon.

In 1936 Hillman's Airways was taken over by British Airways, thus adding the three DH.86s to their fleet, which operated from Gatwick to the Continent, carrying passengers by day and mail at night. Two eighteen-seat examples were used by Blackpool & West Coast Air Services on a route to the Isle of Man, one later being acquired by Aer Lingus for services from Dublin (Baldonnel) to the Isle of Man and Liverpool and to Bristol and Croydon.

The loss of British Airways' G-ADYF at Gatwick in September 1936 prompted an A&AEE report which criticised rudder and aileron control on the DH.86. This problem was overcome by the addition of end-plates to the tailplane of all DH.86As, which were then reclassified as DH.86Bs. Ten more aircraft were built to DH.86B standard, with tailplanes given increased chord at the tips and ailerons with higher gearing. The first of these was G-AENR, which underwent testing at Martlesham Heath in February 1937. Among the production DH.86Bs were examples for Railway Air Services, Allied Airways (for use on a service from Newcastle to Stavanger in Norway) and Western Airways, which used one on its short route from Weston-super-Mare to Cardiff (Pengam Moors), later extended to Swansea (Jersey Marine). Four went to the Turkish airline Devlet Hava Yollari for use on its Istanbul–Ankara–Izmir and Ankara–Adana routes, and the last three were put into service on the 3000-mile route between Sydney and Rabaul (New Britain) via Townsville and Thursday Island operated by W. R. Carpenter & Co. Ltd.

Production of the DH.86 came to an end in October 1937 after 62 had been built. Additional routes opened on 31st May 1937 by Jersey Airways were to Shoreham, using DH.86s five times per week, and to Exeter, while on 28th February 1938 the Portsmouth route was reopened, also using DH.86s. A route to Dinard in France was added

from 9th August 1938, operated jointly by Jersey Airways with DH.86s and Air France with Wibault Tri-Motor aircraft, each airline providing two flights per week. Sadly, on 4th November 1938, DH.86 G-ACZN *St. Catherine's Bay* crashed on take-off from Jersey for Southampton and was destroyed by fire, killing fourteen people.

To expand the activities of 24 Squadron, the Air Ministry placed an order under Contract 670941/37 for one DH.86A aircraft, which was allocated serial number L7596 and delivered to Hendon on 9th October 1937 to be allocated to the squadron's 'C' Flight. This was the first four-engined aircraft acquired by the RAF, and must have seemed enormous on Hendon's restricted landing area. The first major task given to L7596 was the incredible one of transporting three senior officers of the fledgling Luftwaffe and their staffs from Mildenhall to Cranwell on a tour of inspection on 19th October, a job for which the squadron borrowed another DH.86, G-AENR, from de Havilland for the day! A much more extensive mission came about during the spring of 1938, when the Secretary of State for War was carried to Malta. Leaving Hendon on 14th April, L7596 flew to Paris and Marseille, on the next day to Pisa and Naples and thence via Catania to Malta on 16th April. The return journey began on 22nd April via Catania to Rome, where two days were spent before continuing to Marseille and Paris and arrival at Hendon on 25th April.

This solitary DH.86 continued to fly VIPs of various nationalities wherever the occasion demanded, among them members of a French mission who visited Hullavington, Marham, Cranwell and Halton over a three-day period at the end of May 1938. One of several unlikely places at which the DH.86 landed was Orfordness, a First World War airfield on a shingle spit off the coast of Suffolk, to which it brought the Chief of the Air Staff on 10th June 1938. Another was Flimston Down in Pembrokeshire, where there was a gunnery range requiring inspection by high-ranking Army officers.

In August 1938 another DH.86, B-model N6246, was taken on charge by 24 Squadron, and almost at once was put to use on a tour of the Middle East and east Africa as far south as Nairobi, calling at Cairo and Malta among many other RAF outposts. Such trips, though seldom as protracted, provided work for the two DH.86s over the next few months. More mundane was the carriage of ammunition from Geneva to Hendon by N6246 on 30th March 1939. A trip in L7596 to Guernsey by the Secretary of State for Air (Sir Kingsley Wood) and Sir E Campbell on 5th May was for the opening of the island's new airport; little could he have envisaged that a year later the Luftwaffe would be in residence! Unfortunately L7596 was written off on 28th July in a crash in Cumberland, but N6246 soldiered on, flying senior officers and mail to and from France after the outbreak of war. It was joined on 5th May 1940 by G-ADYI and G-AEJM but was destroyed in a hangar fire at Hendon in May 1942.

DH.86 N6246, c/n 2343, at RNAS Hal Far, Malta, while carrying VIPs on a long overseas tour   [National War Museum Association, Malta; neg 4673]

Soon after hostilities began, several DH.86s were impressed for military service with the RAF and Fleet Air Arm, the RAAF and the RNZAF. Overseas, 117 Squadron, a transport unit based at Bilbeis in Egypt, used impressed DH.86s for about three months early in 1942, but then surrendered them in favour of more modern American aircraft. Another organisation with DH.86s was 1 Air Ambulance Unit, a RAAF unit which used a mixture of RAAF and RAF aircraft.

Three DH.86s which remained on the civil register were camouflaged and operated by National Air Communications on priority military services, mainly to and from France before that country was over-run.

Post-war, several survivors began a new lease of life, albeit a short one. The last airworthy example of the DH.86 was G-ACZP, originally owned by Jersey Airways, which was overhauled by Vivian Bellamy at the Hampshire Aero Club. Sadly, after twenty-three years of hard service, this pioneer aircraft was written off near Madrid in September 1958 when its undercarriage collapsed.

Technical specification

Of normal de Havilland construction, the DH.86 had a plywood and spruce box fabric-covered fuselage clear of internal obstructions. Highly tapered high aspect ratio mainplanes of two-spar wooden construction were firmly braced, and the lower one carried the four engines in faired nacelles. The fixed undercarriage was mounted on the inboard nacelles and covered in streamlined downward extensions often referred to as 'trousers', and in the same units were two 57-gallon (101-litre) fuel tanks. Ten passengers, their luggage and a quantity of mail were accommodated in the soundproofed cabin. The first few aircraft were built for operation by one pilot, but the Australian authorities then demanded side-by-side seating for two pilots and incorporation of auxiliary fuel tanks giving a capacity of 191 gallons (340 litres). Split trailing edge flaps were also soon added to the specification.

Following the early loss of DH.86 VH-URN in service with Holyman's Airways Pty Ltd in Australia and very soon after that the crash of the fifth QANTAS aircraft, VH-USG, trials were staged immediately at Martlesham Heath and Hatfield to identify any problems. No structural deficiencies were found, but to be on the safe side the fin was strengthened, the rudder servo tab was removed and the space filled.

An improved version, the DH.86A, appeared in late 1935 and featured larger brakes, pneumatic undercarriage legs, a differently-shaped windscreen and a more substantial tailwheel. This model was marketed with the option of Gipsy Six I engines driving two-bladed wooden or alloy propellers or with Gipsy Six II engines driving de Havilland variable-pitch propellers, although in fact only one of the latter type was built, and that reverted to the Six I format before delivery to Misr Airwork.

Engines:	Four 200 hp de Havilland Gipsy Six I or 205 hp Gipsy Six II	
Dimensions:		
Span	64 ft 6 in (19.66 m)	
Length	46 ft 1 in (14.05 m)	[two-pilot type]
	43 ft 11 in (13.39 m)	[single-pilot type]
Height	13 ft 0 in (3.96 m)	
Wing area	641 sq ft (59.57 sq m)	
Weights:		
Tare	5520 lbs (2509 kg)	[single-pilot type]
	6303 lbs (2865 kg)	[DH.86 two-pilot type]
	6140 lbs (2791 kg)	[DH.86A Srs.I]
	6430 lbs (2922 kg)	[DH.86A Srs.II engines]
	6560 lbs (2978 kg)	[DH.86B]
Total all-up	10,000 lbs (4545 kg)	[DH.86 two-pilot type]
	10,250 lbs (4659 kg)	[DH.86A Srs.I]
	11,000 lbs (4994 kg)	[DH.86A Srs.II engines and DH.86B]
Maximum speed:	170 mph (273 kph)	[DH.86 two-pilot type]
	166 mph (267 kph)	[DH.86A Srs.I and DH.86B]
	150 mph (241 kph)	[DH.86A Srs.II engines]
Cruising speed:	145 mph (233 kph)	[DH.86 two-pilot type]
	142 mph (229 kph)	[DH.86A Srs.I]
	152 mph (245 kph)	[DH.86A Srs.II engines and DH.86B]
Initial climb:	1200 ft/min (366 m/min)	[DH.86 two-pilot type]
	925 ft/min (282 m/min)	[DH.86A Srs.I and DH.86B]
	1050 ft/min (320 m/min)	[DH.86A Srs.II engines]
Rate of climb at sea level:		
	1050 ft/min (320 m/min)	[DH.86B]
Service ceiling:	18,500 ft (5640m)	[DH.86B]
Maximum range:	760 mls (1223 km)	[DH.86 two-pilot type and DH.86A Srs.I]
	726 mls (1169 km)	[DH.86A Srs.II engines and DH.86B]

The term Series (eg Srs.1) refers to the airscrews, which were either fixed pitch (Srs.1) or controllable-pitch (Srs.2).

Protoype DH.86 E.2 at Stag Lane in January 1934. Note the original shape of undercarriage leg fairing   *[via C N Dodds]*

The first DH.86, G-ACPL, at Hatfield before being painted in Imperial Airways colours   *[via C N Dodds]*

Production

2300–2303:   DH.86 Express airliner for single pilot operation; short nose, but 2300 modified to have long nose, 2302 to DH.86A and later DH.86B standard and 2303 modified to DH.86B standard

2304–2327:   DH.86 Express for two-pilot operation

2328:   DH.86A

2329–2332:   DH.86 Express for two-pilot operation

2333–2351:   DH.86A (converted to DH.86B in 1937)

2352–2361:   DH.86B (carried auxiliary fins)

Individual Aircraft Histories

2300   Prototype DH.86, for single pilot operation; first flown 14.1.34 by Herbert Broad as **E.2**; first CoA (4162) issued 30.1.34; regd **G-ACPL** (CoR 4954) 23.4.34 to Imperial Airways Ltd, Croydon; delivered to Croydon 19.5.34 in Railway Air Services livery, named *Diana*; repainted in IAL colours 6.34 and named *Delphinius;* converted to two crew operation 8.34; operated by RAS 17.8.34 to 18.12.34; departed on transfer to Karachi 15.2.36; to Penang 12.7.36; damaged on overshooting in rain at Haiphong, Indo-China, 8.3.38 and repaired; to Bangkok 22.8.38; transferred to BOAC 1.4.40 at Bangkok; to Cairo 10.40 following closure of Bangkok route; impressed into RAF 13.12.41 as **HK844**; 117 Sqn, Bilbeis, by 4.3.42; 1 AAU, RAAF; suffered undercarriage collapse at Maaten Bagush landing ground (LG14) 10.4.42 when both starboard engines cut and aircraft swung; SOC 1.12.42.

2301   First CoA (4407) issued 25.7.34 to Tasmanian Aerial Services Pty Ltd; regd **VH-URN** 27.9.34 to Holyman's Airways Pty Ltd; assembled and tested at RAAF Laverton and del to Launceston (Western Junction) 1.10.34; named *Miss Hobart* 2.10.34; first scheduled flight 3.10.34; crashed into Bass Strait near Rodondo Island, off Tasmania, 19.10.34; wreckage found three days later; all twelve on board, including chief pilot Capt Victor Holyman (acting as radio operator) and pilot G E M Jenkins, lost their lives; a dangerous exchange of position between Holyman and Jenkins may have been the cause.

2302   Regd **G-ACVY** (CoR 5234) 21.7.34 to Railway Air Services Ltd, Croydon, named *Mercury*; first CoA (4464) issued 15.8.34; modified to DH.86B standard; involved in accident near Renfrew 16.1.39 but repaired; operated by AAJC during WW2; WFU following in-flight main spar failure before 8.46; regd to Skytravel Ltd, Speke 22.10.46 (presumably for spares); to Langley; regn cld 5.11.48.

2303   Regd **G-ACVZ** (CoR 5235) 21.7.34 to Railway Air Services Ltd, Croydon, named *Jupiter*; first CoA (4600) issued 7.12.34; badly damaged on hitting tree while landing at Renfrew 12.12.35; moved to Heston by road for rebuild by Airwork 1.36 and modified for two-crew operation 3.36; leased to Imperial Airways 21.1.37; crashed at Elsdorf, 20 mls W of Cologne, Germany, during night of 15/16.3.37 while on flight from Croydon; pilot Flt Lt George Holmes, C F Wolley Dod (European Manager of IAL) and C E Langmann of IAL killed; regn cld 4.37.

G-ACWC, c/n 2304, "Delia" of Imperial Airways saw service in the Middle East and Far East and was eventually taken over by BOAC   *[R C Sturtivant]*

VH-UUA, c/n 2306, "Adelaide" spent three years with Qantas Empire Airways before being sold to Tata Airlines in India   [MAP via P H T Green]

G-ACWD, c/n 2305, seen from an unusual viewpoint at Hong Kong (Kai Tak)
[via C N Dodds]

After being impressed into the RAF in 1942 as HX789, this aircraft spent a few months with Coast Defence Flights in India before being written off
[G J Cruikshank]

2304 Regd **G-ACWC** (CoR 5241) 29.1.35 to Imperial Airways Ltd, Croydon, named *Delia*; first CoA (4713) issued 5.3.35; transferred to Khartoum 23.3.36; to Bangkok 15.6.38; damaged on take-off from Bangkok 23.5.39 and repaired; transferred to BOAC at Bangkok 1.4.40; transferred to Cairo 15.10.40 on closure of Bangkok route; ran out of fuel and crashed at Minna, Nigeria, 17.6.41; to RAF for spares 17.9.41.

2305 Regd **G-ACWD** (CoR 5242) 29.1.35 to Imperial Airways Ltd, Croydon, named *Dorado*; first CoA (4706) issued 28.2.35; delivered 4.3.35; to Penang 30.9.35; to Bangkok 30.3.38; damaged by engine fire at Hong Kong 3.6.38 and repaired; transferred to BOAC .4.40 at Bangkok; transferred to Cairo 15.10.40; impressed into RAF as **HK829** 22.11.41; to 216 Sqn 12.41; to 117 Sqn, Bilbeis, 4.3.4229.5.42; 1 AAU, RAAF, Heliopolis, 11.7.42; DBR at Nefatia North 17.3.43 when undercarriage collapsed; SOC 28.3.43.

2306 Regd **G-ACWE** (CoR 5243) 1.35 for Imperial Airways Ltd, Croydon, named *Daphne* but diverted to Qantas Empire Airways Ltd, Brisbane; regd **VH-UUA** 22.1.35 to them, named *RMA Adelaide*; CoA (4676) issued 14.2.35; left Croydon on delivery 22.2.35; sold to Tata Airlines, Juhu, 12.9.38; regd **VT-AKM** 17.9.38; impressed into RAF as **HX789** 13.1.42; 2 Coast Defence Flt (IAF), Juhu; 5 Coast Defence Flt (IAF), Cochin (redesignated 105 Flt 6.42); DBR at Cochin 15.9.42 when undercarriage collapsed on take-off; SOC 2.7.43.

2307 Regd **VH-USC** (CoR 483) 1.9.34 to Qantas Empire Airways Ltd, Brisbane, named *RMA Canberra*; first CoA (4499) issued 13.9.34; left Croydon on delivery 24.9.34, the flight taking 16 days, 17 hours 27 minutes; damaged on landing at Seletar 11.1.36 and repaired; sold to MacRobertson-Miller Aviation Co Ltd, Maylands, 22.7.38; impressed into RAAF as **A31-5** 24.9.40 and

TOC 30.9.40; 1 AOS, Cootamundra, 13.1.41; returned to QANTAS as **VH-USC** on loan 27.3.42; tail damaged in collision with eagle hawk 1.10.43; starboard undercarriage collapsed at Brisbane 13.10.43 during a violent swing for which the pilot was blamed; fatal ground accident 23.10.43 when apprentice engineer was struck and killed by a propeller during engine start-up at Longreach; during crosswind landing at Darwin, NT, 9.10.44 aircraft swung off runway into ditch, causing severe damage to undercarriage and breaking lower main spar; SOC 6.1.45 and burnt.

2308 First CoA (4511) issued 24.9.34 for Qantas Empire Airways Ltd; shipped to Australia on SS *Bendigo*, arriving 12.11.34; regd **VH-USD** (CoR 504) 22.1.35, named *RMA Brisbane*; sold to MacRobertson-Miller Aviation Co Ltd, Maylands, 28.7.38; sold to Tata Airlines, Juhu, 26.2.39; regd **VT-AKZ** (CoR 371) 17.3.39; impressed into RAF as **AX800** 21.6.40; possibly used by 1 SFTS, Ambala; 2 Coast Defence Flt (IAF), Juhu, 4.41 for fitting with anti-submarine bombs; 5 Coast Defence Flt (IAF), Cochin (redes 105 Flt 6.42); crashed on take-off from Ahmadabad on ferry flight to Bombay 18.12.41 when an uncontrollable swing developed, causing port undercarriage to collapse; remains transferred to DCA 1.9.43; restored to Tata Airlines as **VT-AKZ**; regn cld 20.11.44.

After landing at Singapore (Seletar) on 11th January 1936, DH.86 VH-USC, c/n 2307, "Canberra" of Qantas suffered an undercarriage collapse, but was repaired to fly again
[via P Arnold and P H T Green]

VH-USE , c/n 2309, "RMA Sydney" of Qantas ready for delivery from Hatfield [via C N Dodds]

2309 First CoA (4522) issued 2.10.34 for Qantas Empire Airways Ltd; shipped to Brisbane, arriving 1.12.34; regd **VH-USE** (CoR 504) 22.1.35, named *RMA Sydney;* crashed on slopes of Mount Pirie, near Belmont, on outskirts of Brisbane, 20.2.42, shortly after take-off for Darwin, killing the two crew (inc Capt C H Swaffield) and seven passengers; it is thought that in low cloud the accident occurred either due to instrument failure or to the inability of the pilot to fly on instruments; wreckage said to have been burnt deliberately before accident inspectors could reach site; regn cld 31.3.42.

2310 First CoA (4630) issued 27.12.34 for Qantas Empire Airways Ltd (after tests at Hatfield and possibly at A&AEE following accidents); left Croydon for Australia 7.1.35 with an Imperial Airways crew, Capt A B H 'Jimmy' Youell, 1st Off Allen, engineer T Wilson and WOp Bill Cash; after total flying time of 69 hrs 58 mins, grounded on arrival at Darwin on 23.1.35 due to recent DH.86 accidents but later released; regd **VH-USF** (CoR 505) 22.1 35, named *RMA Melbourne;* impressed into RAAF 28.9.40 as **A31-6** and TOC 5.10.40; 1 AOS, Cootamundra, 20.1.41; loaned to Qantas Empire Airways Ltd as **VH-USF** 27.3.42; ground-looped on take-off from Roma, collapsing undercarriage and breaking lower starboard main spar; similar incident 9.7.44 when port outer engine failed on take-off from Blackall, Qld, causing a violent swing and collapsing starboard undercarriage; wreckage to 3 CRD, Amberley, for salvage; sold to MacRobertson-Miller Aviation Ltd by

War Disposal Commission 2.2.45 and restored to civil register as **VH-USF** 22.5.45; crashed at Geraldton, WA, 24.6.45, killing the pilot and one of nine passengers.

2311 First CoA (4549) issued 18.10.34 for Qantas Empire Airways Ltd; left UK 2.11.34; allocated registration **VH-USG** 11.34; crashed 15.11.34 at end of delivery flight from the UK and before registration formally issued; soon after leaving Longreach the aircraft began a slow flat turn to the right which tightened up, causing it to enter a flat spin before crashing in open country on Barsdale Station, 15 mls SE of Longreach; pilot (Flt Lt Prendergast), co-pilot (1st Off W V Creetes) and engineer (F R Charlton) killed instantly, the only other occupant, E Broadfoot of Shell Oil Co, died soon after; position of bodies in wreckage showed that Prendergast and Charlton had changed places soon after take-off, which could have caused crash; alternatively, damage may have been sustained during an unscheduled landing at Alroy Downs, between Darwin and Longreach.

2312 First CoA (4572) issued 8.11.34; regd **VH-URT** 29.1.35 to Holyman's Airways Pty Ltd, Launceston, Tas, named *Loina;* del 9.35; crashed on Blue Rocks, Flinders Island, 2.10.35 on flight from Melbourne to Launceston with loss of crew (pilot A N Evans, second pilot M Brown, engineer E Best) and passengers; there was evidence of a small fire in the cabin.

Jersey Airways' G-ACYF, c/n 2313, "Giffard Bay" at Southampton (Eastleigh) in 1937 [via A S Thomas]

2313 Regd **G-ACYF** (CoR 5351) 7.12.34 to Jersey Airways Ltd, named *Giffard Bay;* first CoA (4668) issued 6.2.35; loaned to British Airways 12.36; to Wearnes Air Services Ltd, Singapore, as **VR-SBD** 6.38, named *Governor Murchison;* ferried Jersey to Hatfield 28.6.38 and left Heston 7.7.38; ferried to Australia 26.4.40; regd **VH-ADN** 24.6.40 for W R Carpenter and Co Ltd (t/a WRC Airlines, Sydney); arrived Sydney 3.5.40; used on first New Guinea service 6.6.40; to South Queensland Airways; impressed into RAAF 9.7.40 as **A31-2**; 1 AOS, Cootamundra, 15.11.40; 1 SFTS, Point Cook, 13.3.42; 36 Sqn, Essendon, 21.9.42; 5 AD for repairs 4.12.42; DH, Mascot, for repairs, 4.1.43; 34 Sqn, Parafield, 3.4.43; 35 Sqn, Maylands, 30.5.43; to MacRobertson-Miller for conversion to air ambulance 1.9.43 but not undertaken; ran out of fuel and damaged in subsequent forced landing 1 ml NW of Maryborough 1.5.44 when on way to 1 AAU for ambulance modifications; salvaged 9.5.44; 3 CRD 30.5.44 but not repaired; SOC 9.10.44.

2314 CoR (5352) issued 7.12.34 as **G-ACYG** to Jersey Airways Ltd, named *Grouville Bay;* first CoA (4722) issued 8.3.35; loaned to Imperial Airways 5.11.35 to 26.1.36; impressed into FAA 21.7.40, originally as **BD105** but altered to **AX840**; 782 Sqn, Donibristle, 7.40 to 12.40; at DH RU, Witney, 5.41; 783 Sqn, Arbroath, [6] 6.41; hit by gunfire from RN minesweeper near Bell Rock 8.7.42; damaged in crash-landing 19.7.43; 782 Sqn 1.44; DH RU, Witney, for repair 25.9.44 but SOC; scrapped 4.3.45.

2315 First CoA (4716) issued 6.3.35; regd **VH-USW** (CoR 521) 13.5.35 for Holyman's Airways Pty Ltd, Launceston, Tas, named *Lepena*; force-landed on uninhabited Hunter Island, 30 mls off Tasmania, 13.12.35 after interplane strut believed to have failed (in fact, problem was a loose fairing); salvaged, repaired at Essendon and returned to service after three months; to Australian National Airways Pty Ltd 1.7.36 and regd to them 25.11.36; damaged on landing at Wagga, NSW, 29.12.37 while avoiding cattle; repaired but undercarriage collapsed again 6.1.38 and roaded to Melbourne for repairs; impressed into RAAF 13.9.40 as **A31-4**; 1 AD 19.12.40; 1 AOS, Cootamundra, 16.4.41; loaned to Qantas Empire Airways 27.3.42 to 4.5.42 as **VH-USW**; returned to RAAF as **A31-4** and converted to air ambulance at 1 AD; 1 AAU (or 2 AAU ?), New Guinea, 3.7.42; to Civil Aviation Dept, Archerfield, 7.9.44; 3 AD 28.9.44 'in crashed condition'; sold 'as is' to MacRobertson-Miller Airways Co Ltd, Perth, WA, 14.2.45; regd **VH-USW** 3.5.45; sold to Universal Flying Services, Kidlington, UK, 19.11.46; damaged at Allahabad, India, 26.12.46 during delivery flight and abandoned due to alleged unsafe condition; parts reported as extant 1977 and said to have been sent to Australia for possible rebuild.

2316 Regd **G-ACZN** (CoR 5439) 7.12.34 to Jersey Airways Ltd, named *St Catherine's Bay;* first CoA (4752) issued 22.3.35; del 26.3.35; leased to Imperial Airways Ltd, Croydon, 8.11.35 to

Seen in service with 783 Sqn at Arbroath is AX840, the former G-ACYG was c/n 2314   *[via G M Simons and P H T Green]*

22.1.36 (CoR 6532); returned to Jersey Airways Ltd 31.1.36 (CoR 6695); crashed and DBF on take-off from Jersey Airport 4.11.38; loss of control in low cloud caused aircraft to sideslip into ground, killing all 13 on board (pilot 1st Off A G Carey) and one on ground; regn cld 7.1.39.

2317 Regd **G-ADCM** (CoR 5603) 15.2.35 to Imperial Airways Ltd, Croydon, named *Draco;* first CoA (4764) issued 30.3.35; DBR when force-landed through icing at Zwettl, Austria, 22.10.35; two injured (pilot N J Capper); regn cld 12.35.

2318 Regd **G-ACZO** (CoR 5440) 7.12.34 to Jersey Airways Ltd, named *Ouaine Bay;* first CoA (4771) issued 9.4.35; damaged on landing at St. Aubin's Beach, Jersey, 17.8.35 and shipped to England for repairs; impressed into FAA 7.40 as **BD106**, altered to **AX841**, but destroyed on ground by enemy aircraft at Lee-on-Solent 16.7.40 before entering service.

2319 Regd **G-ADCN** (CoR 5604) 15.2.35 to Imperial Airways Ltd, Croydon, named *Daedalus;* first CoA (4783) issued 15.4.35; del 17.4.35; flown to Khartoum 26.1.36–1.2.36 for survey flights of West Africa; crashed on landing at El Geteina, Sudan, 5.4.37 but repaired; transferred to Bangkok 11.37; DBF during engine tests at Donmuang 3.12.38.

2320 First CoA (4865) issued 27.5.35; regd **SU-ABN** for Misr Airwork Ltd, Cairo, named *Khartoum;* left Hatfield 10.6.35; damaged in forced landing 45 mls E of Rutbah Wells, Iraq, 11.1.39; presumed repaired as reported as damaged on landing at Lydda, Palestine, 23.4.42; NFT.

2321 Regd **G-ACZP** (CoR 5441) 7.12.34 to Jersey Airways Ltd, Portsmouth, named *Belcroute Bay;* first CoA (4830) issued 11.5.35 and del 15.5.35; loaned to British Airways Ltd 12.36;

VH-USW, c/n 2315, was operated by Australian National Airways until it was impressed into the RAAF as A31-4   *[F G Swanborough via P H T Green]*

DH.86 G-ACZP, c/n 2321, "Belcroute Bay" of Jersey Airways at Heston during that airport's heyday. This aircraft lasted until being written off near Madrid in 1958   *[Hounslow Libraries]*

allocated for impressment into FAA as **AX843** 21.7.40, but restored to civil register as **G-ACZP** 29.8.40 and released to Railway Air Services Ltd; reopened service from Croydon to Liverpool and Belfast 13.11.44; to Skytravel Ltd, Speke, 4.10.46; CoA lapsed 18.4.47; auctioned 9.12.47 following liquidation of company; CoA test flight 18.2.48 but CoA not issued and aircraft believed stored at Prestwick; regd to finance company Bowmaker Ltd 2.7.48; stored at Squires Gate until purchased by Lancashire Aircraft Corp Ltd 20.4.51; CoA renewed 25.5.51; to British Aviation Services Group, parent company of Silver City Airways Ltd, Eastleigh, 28.10.57; to V H Bellamy, Eastleigh, 21.2.58 for Hampshire Aeroplane Club; DBR on landing at Barajas, Madrid, 21.9.58, when undercarriage collapsed after tyre burst; remains stored behind hangar at Barajas until at least 8.63 but later burnt.

2322 Regd **G-ACZR** (CoR 5442) 7.12.34 to Jersey Airways Ltd, Portsmouth, named *La Saline Bay;* first CoA (4879) issued 29.5.35; del 31.5.35; leased to Imperial Airways Ltd, Croydon, 11.11.35 to 18.12.35 (CoR 6533); retd to Jersey Airways (CoR 6669) 27.1.36; damaged at Jersey Airport 27.12.38 but repaired; impressed into FAA 21.7.40 as **BD104**, altered to **AX844**; 782 Sqn, Donibristle, 7.40; crashed on take-off from Donibristle 31.3.43, when aircraft made a steep right hand turn, stalled and spun in, killing pilot (PO F Parr) and five of six passengers.

2323 Regd **G-ADEA** (CoR 5679) 18.5.35 to Hillman's Airways Ltd, Stapleford Tawney; named *Drake* by Lady Cunliffe-Lister 20.6.35; first CoA (4844) issued 5.6.35; taken over by British Airways Ltd 11.12.35 and regd (CoR 6898) 9.4.36; badly damaged in lightning strike 11.36; to Airwork Ltd, Heston, 11.10.37 (CoR 8132); regn cld as sold 6.38; left Heston for Singapore 7.7.38, arriving 14.7.38; regd **VR-SBC** to Wearnes Air Services Ltd, Singapore, named *Governor Ibbetson;* ferried to Australia 13.6.40; regd **VH-UZX** to W R Carpenter and Co Ltd (t/a WRC Airlines) 17.7.40; impressed into RAAF 2.1.41 (27.12.40 ?) as **A31-7;** modified to air ambulance by ANA; 1 AAU 25.3.41; shipped from Laverton to Middle East 30.4.41, arriving Cairo 3.7.41; to Gaza 22.7.41; damaged on ground at Mersah Matruh by enemy action 31.1.42 but repaired at Heliopolis and flown 24.4.42; WFU 9.43 due to lack of 77-octane fuel; to British Aircraft Repair Unit, Heliopolis, 2.44 for disposal; probably scrapped there; SOC 22.10.48.

2324 Regd **G-ADEB** (CoR 5680) 18.5.35 to Hillman's Airways Ltd, Stapleford Tawney; first CoA (4845) issued 20.6.35; taken over by British Airways Ltd 11.12.35 and regd (CoR 6851) 24.3.36; crashed into mountains near Altenkirchen, Germany, (35 mls SE of Cologne) 12.8.36 due to suspected icing while on Hanover to Gatwick mail service; Capt C G Gill and WOp K J Bayliss killed; regn cld 12.36.

2325 Regd **G-ADEC** (CoR 5681) 18.5.35 to Hillman's Airways Ltd, Stapleford Tawney; first CoA (4846) issued 1.7.35; taken over by British Airways Ltd 11.12.35 and regd (CoR 6627) 10.1.36; to Airwork Ltd, Heston 2.9.37 (CoR 8100) and stored pending sale; to Cia Primeras Líneas Uruguayas de Navegación Aérea (PLUNA), Montevideo, 10.38 as **CX-AAH**, named *Santa Rosa de Lima;* DBR on landing at Artigas 22.10.45 but still on register .50.

2326 First CoA (4960) issued 15.7.35; regd **VH-UUB** to Holyman's Airways Pty Ltd, Launceston, Tas, 27.9.35 (CoR 542), named *Loila;* taken over by Australian National Airways Pty Ltd, Essendon, 1.7.36; regd 25.11.36; damaged in forced landing at Seymour, Vic, 3.12.36 but repaired; impressed into RAAF 13.9.40 as **A31-3;** 1 AOS, Cootamundra, 10.11.40; 1 AD 14.2.41; converted to air ambulance; 1 AAU 24.4.41; shipped from Laverton 30.4.41, arriving Cairo 3.7.41; to Gaza 9.9.41; after major overhaul at Heliopolis, the aircraft was parked awaiting redelivery to 1 AAU on 19.4.42 when it was hit by Beaufighter X7804, which swerved when an engine failed on take-off; DBF.

2327 Allocated to Wrightways Ltd, Croydon, but NTU; regd **G-ADMY** (CoR 6126) 9.8.35 to British Continental Airways Ltd, Croydon, named *St George;* first CoA (5003) issued 26.8.35 and del 28.8.35; taken over by British Airways Ltd 1.8.36 and regd (CoR 7668) 17.2.37; to Airwork Ltd, Heston, 14.10.37 (CoR 8136); to Mrs L H Falk 25.6.38 (CoR 8587) for operation by British-American Air Services Ltd, Heston; regd to LHG Ltd, Heston (parent company of BAAS) 2.12.38 (CoR 8928); operated by Imperial Airways Ltd 4.12.38 to 22.12.38; to British-American Air Services Ltd, Heston, 26.6.39; impressed into RAF 10.5.40 as **X9442** and intended for 24 Sqn as an ambulance but in poor condition; DH RU, Witney 6.40; 9 MU, Cosford, 29.11.40; transferred to FAA; 782 Sqn, Donibristle, 28.2.41; damaged, but repaired by DH 14.2.42, and again 30.12.42; returned to 782 Sqn 1.4.43; SOC 4.4.44 (but reported as still in use 12.44!).

2328 Regd **G-ADFF** (CoR 5728) 7.11.35 to Imperial Airways Ltd, Croydon, named *Dione;* first CoA (5303) issued 13.1.36 and del 15.1.36; transferred to Khartoum c36/37; converted to DH.86B 4/5.37; taken over by BOAC 1.4.40 and regd 22.8.40; transferred to Alexandria 5.40; impressed into RAF 15.8.41 as **AX760**; Lydda Comm Flt; undercarriage collapsed while taxying for take-off from Lydda 26.11.41; SOC 30.7.42.

2329 First CoA (5068) issued 10.9.35 as **SU-ABO** for Misr Airwork Ltd, Cairo, named *Al Fostat*, later *Beyrouth;* regn cld postwar, aircraft believed scrapped.

2330 First CoA (5115) issued 23.9.35 to Union Steamship Co Ltd; regd **ZK-AEF** (CoR 43) 10.12.35 to Union Airways of New

A fine airborne study of DH.86 G-ADMY, c/n 2327   *[P H T Green collection]*

Seen keeping company with DH.84 SU-ABZ, c/n 6032, is DH.86 SU-ABO, c/n 2329, "Al Fostat" of Misr Airlines   *[P H T Green collection]*

Ready to go! Union Airways' DH.86 ZK-AEG, c/n 2331   *[via author]*

The former ZK-AEG in RNZAF service as NZ553, coded '2'
[MAP via P H T Green]

C/n 2331 became ZK-AHW of Union Airways after return from wartime service in the RNZAF   *[via C N Dodds]*

Zealand Ltd, Wellington, named *Kotuku*; despatched by sea aboard SS *Waipawa*, arriving Lyttelton 20.11.35; first flight in New Zealand 2.1.36; impressed into RNZAF 17.9.39 as **NZ552**; AG&AOS, Ohakea, [1] 14.11.39 and converted to military standard; 3 SFTS, Ohakea, [1] 20.10.40; 2 GR Sqn, Nelson, 1.41; Detached Flt Fiji, Nandi, 13.3.41; to 4 GR Sqn 8.10.41; to CF Nausori 26.5.42; DBR while taxying at Nausori 7.12.43; spares and all salvageable items returned to New Zealand and used in rebuild of NZ553; remains SOC 12.7.44.

2331   First CoA (5163) issued 8.10.35 to Union Steamship Co Ltd; regd **ZK-AEG** (CoR 44) 10.12.35 to Union Airways of New Zealand Ltd, Wellington, named *Karoro*; despatched by sea aboard SS *Waipawa*, arriving Lyttelton 20.11.35; first flight in New Zealand 8.12.35; impressed into RNZAF 13.10.39 as **NZ553**; AG & AOS, Ohakea, [2] 14.11.39 and converted to military standard; Detached Flt Fiji, Nandi, 13.3.41; to Union Airways for overhaul 8.41; 1 SFTS, Wigram, for E&WS use 12.41; CF Nausori 8.42; damaged on take-off from Nandi 19.12.42; to DH, Rongotai, for rebuild, involving components of NZ552 and NZ554; flown 10.11.44; returned to RNZAF for storage at Woodbourne; loaned to Union Airways as **ZK-AHW** 28.2.45, and regd to them 9.3.45, named *Korimako*; taken over by NZNAC 1.8.46; returned to RNZAF for spares 8.10.46 and broken up at Palmerston North 11.46; regn cld 21.10.46.

2332   First CoA (5191) issued 31.10.35 to Union Steamship Co Ltd; regd **ZK-AEH** (CoR 47) 17.12.35 to Union Airways of New Zealand Ltd, named *Korimako*; despatched by sea aboard SS *Port Wyndham*, arriving Lyttelton 12.35; first flight in New Zealand 6.1.36; impressed into RNZAF 25.10.39 as **NZ554**; AG&AOS, Ohakea [3] 14.11.39 and converted to military standard; 3 SFTS, Ohakea [2] 28.10.40; during down-wind take-off from Ohakea on 13.11.40, the aircraft, fully fuelled and loaded with two 250lb and four 20lb bombs for an operational patrol, passed through a fence and line of trees before coming to rest; crew suffered minor injuries but aircraft was SOC and remains used as spares for NZ553.

2333   Regd **G-ADUE** (CoR 6344) 19.12.35 to Imperial Airways Ltd, Croydon, named *Dardanus*; first CoA (5309) issued 20.1.36 and del 21.1.36; converted to DH.86B Srs.1 4/5.37; operated by British-American Air Services Ltd, Croydon, 5.39; to Bangkok 20.6.39; forced down on Waichow Island by Japanese seaplanes 8.11.39 when flying from Hong Kong to Bangkok; landed safely and flown to Fort Bayard 13.12.39; three passengers were released, but pilot J Wilson and WOp held for questioning until 20.12.39, when released with the aircraft; to Hong Kong 20.12.39 and Singapore for repair 30.12.39; returned to service 16.1.40; to BOAC, Khartoum, 1.4.40 and regd 22.8.40; impressed into RAF 20.9.41 as **AX762**, but marked **AX672** in error; 216 Sqn,

G-ADUE, c/n 2333, "Dardanus" of Imperial Airways while it was in use by British Airways in the Western Desert   *[MAP via P H T Green]*

EI-ABK, c/n 2338, "Eire" of Aer Lingus lasted until 1952 in the hands of several owners   *[P H T Green collection]*

El Khanka; 117 Sqn, Bilbeis, 4.3.42–29.5.42; 1 AAU, RAAF, Heliopolis, 18.6.42; DBR when undercarriage collapsed on landing in soft sand at Siwa 24.6.42 and SOC.

2334   Regd **G-ADUF** (CoR 6345) 19.12.35 to Imperial Airways Ltd, Croydon, named *Dido*; first CoA (5314) issued 25.1.36 and del 27.1.36; converted to DH.86B Srs.1, 1.4.37; to West Africa 8.39; to BOAC 1.4.40 and regd 27.8.40; impressed into RAF as **HK828** 5.11.41 but released to Misr Airwork Ltd almost immediately; sold to Misr Airwork Ltd 11.41 as **SU-ACR**, named *Beirut*; probably sold to L Azzopardi 6.47 for operation by Peacock Air Charter, Alexandria; damaged on landing at Croydon 13.7.47; restored as **G-ADUF** 24.5.48 for Field Aircraft Services Ltd, Croydon; to J A W Hill, Jersey, 3.6.49; to Air Navigation & Trading Co Ltd, Squires Gate, 28.12.50; to Gulf Aviation Ltd, Bahrain, 17.10.51; WFU upon CoA expiry 3.5.52 and broken up; regn cld 17.6.52.

2335   Regd **G-ADUG** (CoR 6346) 19.12.35 to Imperial Airways Ltd, Croydon, named *Danae*; first CoA (5321) issued 7.2.36; delivered 12.3.36; converted to DH.86B Srs.1 4/5.37; to West Africa 5.11.38; to BOAC 1.4.40 and regd 22.8.40; impressed into RAF as **HK831** 5.11.41; 216 Sqn, El Khanka 12.41; shot down between 21.12.41 and 31.12.41; SOC 15.2.42.

2336   Regd **G-ADUH** (CoR 6347) 19.12.35 to Imperial Airways Ltd, Croydon, named *Dryad*; first CoA (5381) issued 9.3.36; port undercarriage collapsed at Croydon 15.7.36 but repaired; converted to DH.86B Srs.1 4/5.37; sold to Aer Lingus Teoranta and regd **EI-ABT** 14.10.38, named *Sasana*; restored to British register as **G-ADUH** 26.11.46 for D L Steiner, Speke and CoA renewed 9.12.46; regd 24.1.47 to C Treen and H D Collins Free (t/a Union Air Services Ltd), Gatwick; regd 11.10.47 to Bond Air Services Ltd, Gatwick; CoA lapsed 8.12.47, not renewed until 8.6.50; regd 30.1.51 to Aerocontacts Ltd, Gatwick; regd 3.4.51 to Gulf Aviation Co Ltd, Bahrain; written off in collision with Auster G-AIBO at Bahrain (Muharraq) 22.5.51; regn cld 13.8.51.

2337   Regd **G-ADUI** (CoR 6348) 19.12.35 to Imperial Airways Ltd, Croydon, named *Denebola*; first CoA (5329) issued 18.2.36 and del 21.2.36; converted to DH.86B Srs.1 4/5.37; to Bangkok, arrived 31.12.38; to BOAC 1.4.40 and regd 22.8.40; to Lagos 8.41; impressed into RAF as **HK830** 5.11.41; 216 Sqn, El Khanka; 117 Sqn, Bilbeis, 4.3.42; DBR at Bilbeis 11.3.42 when port tyre burst; SOC 31.12.42.

2338   Regd **G-ADVJ** (CoR 6396) 4.2.36 to Blackpool & West Coast Air Services Ltd, Squires Gate, named *Ronaldsway*; first CoA (5430) issued 8.4.36 and del 22.4.36; sold to Aer Lingus Teoranta and regd **EI-ABK** 16.9.36, named *Eire*; originally operated by Irish Sea Airways; converted to DH.86B Srs.1 12.37; restored to British register as **G-ADVJ** 30.10.46 for Bond Air Services Ltd, Gatwick, named *County of Sussex;* regd 30.1.51 to Aerocontacts Ltd, Gatwick; regd 1.8.51 to Gulf Aviation Co Ltd, Bahrain (although apparently went into service 25.7.50); regn cld 18.3.52; derelict at Bahrain 8.52.

2339   Regd **G-ADVK** (CoR 6397) 4.2.36 to Blackpool & West Coast Air Services Ltd, Squires Gate, named *Spirit of Liverpool*; first CoA (5318) issued 21.4.36; converted to DH.86B Srs.1 standard; regd (CoR 8146) 19.10.37 to Isle of Man Air Services Ltd, named *Ronaldsway;* damaged 14.9.38 about 30 minutes after take-off from Liverpool (Speke); at 4,000ft there was a loud bang, followed by vibration; after climbing to 9,000ft for safety, pilot throttled back engines; starboard inner had shed a propeller blade, which had lodged in side of fuselage; a safe three-engined landing was made at Ronaldsway; regd (CoR 8950) 21.12.38 to Jersey Airways Ltd, Jersey; badly damaged in collision with fence and floodlight on landing at Jersey 31.12.38 but repaired; regd 22.4.39 to Guernsey Airways Ltd, Jersey; abandoned at Jersey Airport late 6.40 when undergoing CoA renewal; regn cancelled 22.8.40; may have been put into service by Germans after the invasion of the Channel Islands, from photographic evidence of a DH.86 in Luftwaffe markings in France.

2340   Regd **G-ADYC** (CoR 6524) 29.2.36 to British Continental Airways Ltd, Croydon, named *St Columba*; first CoA (5502) issued 14.5.36; taken over by British Airways Ltd, Gatwick, 1.8.36 and regd (CoR 7665) 16.2.37; converted to DH.86B 6.37; sold to Airwork Ltd, Heston, 8.37 but regn not transferred and cld 11.37; converted to radio trainer for Air Ministry by Airwork; sold to RAF as **L8037** (Contract No. 686051/37); E&WS, Cranwell, 18.7.38, named *The Citadel IV*; damaged Cat B 22.2.42; ROS by DH; 24 Sqn, Hendon, 2.7.42; transferred to FAA; 782 Sqn, Donibristle, 26.6.43; SOC after 2.45.

2341   Regd **G-ADYD** (CoR 6525) 29.2.36 to British Continental Airways Ltd, Croydon; first CoA (5512) issued 19.5.36; taken over by British Airways Ltd, Gatwick, 1.8.36 and regd (CoR 7666) 16.2.37; converted to DH.86B .37; sold to Airwork Ltd, Heston, 8.37 but regn not transferred and cld 11.37; converted to radio trainer for Air Ministry by Airwork; sold to RAF as **L8040** (Contract No 686051/37); E&WS, Cranwell, 11.8.38; damaged 10.3.39 when it swung on take off and suffered port undercarriage collapse; 24 Sqn, Hendon, 20.2.42; to DH RU, Witney, 8.6.42; to 3 SoGR, Squires Gate, 9.9.42; transferred to FAA; to 782 Sqn, Donibristle, 1.10.42, named *Merlin IX*; starboard undercarriage collapsed during marshalling at Hatston, 22.1.44; SOC 5.2.45.

DH.86B L8037, c/n 2340, of 24 Squadron was formerly G-ADYC of British Airways

In wartime service with 782 Sqn at Donibristle, DH.86B L8040, c/n 2341, "Merlin IX" suffered an undercarriage collapse while being marshalled at Hatston on 22nd January 1944   [G Lamb via R C Sturtivant]

2342   First flown as **E.2** with small inset fins, but modified with 'Zulu shield' end-plate fins as prototype DH.86B Srs.1; regd **SU-ABV** to Misr Airwork Ltd, named *Al Mahroussa;* to A&AEE, Martlesham Heath, 12.36 for handling trials with Gipsy Queen 2 engines (later removed); first CoA(5743) issued 1.1.37; to UK register 8.4.47 as **G-AJNB** to L Azzopardi and Albert Horsting de Pauw (t/a Peacock Air Charter), Alexandria, named *Peacock* and then *Paul;* CoA renewed 9.5.47 and lapsed 8.5.48; WFU at Wadi Halfa, Sudan; seized by High Court of Khartoum in legal action between Shell Co of Sudan and A H de Pauw; offered for sale 'as is' 9.48; regn cld 2.8.49 when derelict at Wadi Halfa.

2343   Regd **G-ADYG** (CoR 6528) 21.5.36 for British Airways Ltd, Gatwick; first CoA (5563) issued 30.6.36; converted to DH.86B .37; regn cld 6.38; sold to RAF as **N6246** 27.8.38 (Contract No 773287/38); 24 Sqn, Hendon; carried SoS for Air and CAS on tour Biggin Hill – Linton-on-Ouse – Church Fenton – Waddington – Hucknall – Castle Bromwich – Biggin Hill – Hendon 20.5.39;

Probably photographed at Heston (with Sidney Cotton's Lockheed 12A in the background), DH.86B SU-ABV, c/n 2342, had just returned from Egypt before being placed on the British register in April 1947. It was already wearing Peacock Air Charter titles and then had the name "Peacock"   [E J Riding via P H T Green]

G-ADYH, c/n 2344, of British Airways was at A&AEE, Martlesham Heath for tests on 21st October 1936   *[RTB 8250B via P H T Green]*

carried CIGS Hendon – Thornaby – Peterborough 25.7.39; damaged in flying accident 20.2.42, ROS by DH by 11.3.42; DBF in hangar 68 at Hendon 21.4.42; SOC 5.5.42.

2344 Regd **G-ADYH** (CoR 6529) 21.5.36 to British Airways Ltd, Gatwick; first CoA (5599) issued 21.7.36; to A&AEE, Martlesham Heath, 10.36, for trials following Australian accidents to DH.86s; converted to DH.86B Srs.1 .37; to Airwork Ltd, Heston, 8.37 but regn not transferred; regd (CoR 8261) 13.12.37 to West Coast Air Services Ltd, Speke; operated by AAJC during WW2; regd 22.10.46 to Skytravel Ltd, Speke; regd 27.10.47 to H W G Penney for operation by Intercontinental Air Lines (Pty) Ltd, named *Denebola;* flown to Darwin 11.47; regn cld 13.4.48 and not regd in Australia; sold 4.48 to Frank J Grigware (an American) who delivered the aircraft to Singapore; left there 19.5.48 ostensibly to return to UK but abandoned at Penang and appropriated by Indonesian rebels; operated by AURI, initially as G-ADYH and then as **RI-008**; captured by Dutch at Maguwo 12.12.48 and broken up at Bandoeng .49.

2345 Regd **G-ADYI** (CoR 6530) 21.5.36 to British Airways Ltd, Gatwick; first CoA (5631) issued 26.8.36; converted .37 to DH.86B Srs.1; to Airwork Ltd, Heston 8.37 but regn not transferred; regd (CoR 8292) 5.1.38 to Wrightways Ltd, Croydon; impressed into RAF 5.40, retaining civil regn; serial **AX795** allocated 5.40; 24 Sqn, Hendon, 5.5.40; 1 SS, Cranwell, 14.10.40; RAE, Farnborough, 22.11.40 for fitment of unspecified equipment; returned to 1 SS 31.3.41; SF Halton 10.6.42; loaned to FAA for 2 months from 27.10.42; SOC 27.5.43;

2346 Regd **G-ADYE** (CoR 6526) 29.2.36 to British Continental Airways Ltd, Croydon, named *St Chad;* first CoA (5605) issued 28.7.36; taken over by British Airways Ltd, Gatwick, 1.8.36 and regd (CoR 7667) 16.2.37; converted to DH.86B .37; to Airwork Ltd, Heston, 8.37 but regn not transferred; regn cld 11.37; regd **CX-ABG** to PLUNA, named *San Felipe y Santiago;* WFU and scrapped .49.

2347 Regd **G-ADYF** (CoR 6527) 29.1.36 to British Continental Airways Ltd, Croydon but taken over by British Airways 1.8.36 before delivery; first CoA (5647) issued 2.9.36; crashed at Rowley Farm 15.9.36 shortly after take-off from Gatwick on night mail service to Hamburg; three crew killed included Capt W F Anderson, chief pilot of BA; regn cld 4.37.

2348 Regd **G-ADYJ** (CoR 6531) 15.5.36 to British Airways Ltd, Gatwick; first CoA (5515) issued 19.5.36; converted to DH.86B; to Airwork Ltd, Heston, 8.37 but regn not transferred; regn cld 10.37; refurbished by DH at Hatfield; sold to RAF as **L7596** (Contract No 670941/37) 10.37; 24 Sqn, Hendon, 9.10.37; crashed in forced landing on hill at Kirby-in-Furness, nr Ulverston, Lancs, 28.6.39 when engine failed; was flying from Biggin Hill to Belfast, piloted by Wg Cdr D F Anderson, with passengers Sir Kingsley Wood (SoS for Air) and AVM Sir Sholto Douglas (DCAS) to open new Belfast Airport.

2349 Regd **G-AEAP** (CoR 6645) 27.1.36 to Imperial Airways Ltd, Croydon, named *Demeter,* first CoA (5408) issued 17.3.36; converted to DH.86B Srs.1 4/5.37; to West Africa .37; taken over by BOAC 1.4.40 and regd 22.8.40; to Cairo 24.2.41; impressed into RAF as **HK843** 22.10.41; 117 Sqn, Bilbeis, 4.3.42; 1 AAU 6.42; DBF while evacuating patients at Pachino, Sicily, 23.7.43, when Verey pistol fired.

2350 Regd **G-AEFH** (CoR 6865) 15.4.36 to Railway Air Services Ltd, Croydon, named *Neptune;* first CoA (5437) issued 10.8.36; converted to DH.86B Srs.1 4.37; flown from Exeter to Bordeaux 17.6.40 and abandoned there next day on evacuation.

2351 Regd **G-AEJM** (CoR 7044) 6.7.36 to Wrightways Ltd, Croydon. first CoA (5669) issue 24.9.36 and del 7.10.36; converted to DH.86B Srs.1 .36; impressed into RAF 4.40; 24 Sqn, Hendon, 12.4.40; allocated serial **X9441** and painted as such 1.41, named *The Cathedral;* at DH RU, Witney, 2.42; DBF at Hendon 17.2.43 when starboard engine caught fire; fitter LAC A Nixon killed when struck by propeller while fighting fire; SOC 31.3.43.

Impressed for service with 1 AAU of the RAAF, HK843 (c/n 2349, formerly G-AEAP) is seen in the Western Desert

An unusual piece of nose-art on a weatherbeaten DH.86 of 117 Sqn, either HK829 or HK843, seen at an oasis landing strip in May 1942. Unfortunately, it is not possible to read the inscription on the white band below the cockpit
[T Armstrong via A S Thomas]

2352 Regd **G-AENR** (CoR 7346) 30.9.36 to Blackpool & West Coast Air Services Ltd, Squires Gate, named *Ronaldsway*; to A&AEE, Martlesham Heath, c1.37 for handling trials; first CoA (5787) issued 8.2.37; loaned by DH to 24 Sqn, Hendon, 19.10.37, probably for one day; regd (CoR 8147) 19.10.37 to Isle of Man Air Services Ltd; damaged on hitting wall when landing at Ronaldsway 9.5.38; to DH for repair; regd 21.3.39 to Guernsey Airways Ltd, Jersey; allocated for impressment into FAA as **AX842** 21.7.40 but NTU; regd as **G-AENR** 29.8.40 to Railway Air Services Ltd, Speke, with whom it operated throughout WW2; hit by AA fire from merchant ship off Holyhead 18.10.41 while flying from Manchester to Dublin but landed safely; CoA lapsed 21.7.46; regd 22.10.46 to Skytravel Ltd, Speke; company in liquidation 9.47; presumed sold for spares and scrapped at Langley 11.48; regn cld 5.11.48.

2353 Regd **G-AETM** (CoR 7650) 6.4.37 to Allied Airways (Gandar Dower) Ltd, Dyce, named *The Norseman* for opening of route from Newcastle (Woolsington) to Stavanger; first CoA issued 29.6.37; sold 4.39 to satisfy court order; regd 18.5.39 to Western Airways Ltd, Weston-super-Mare; probably sold to Finland as **OH-SLA** 12.39 but NTU; at Airwork Ltd, Gatwick, 10.1.40 to 27.1.40 for conversion to air ambulance; regd 1.2.40 to H McGrady-Bell, Gatwick, on behalf of The Finnish Fund, named *Silver Star;* left Heston for Turku 15.2.40; regn cld 20.2.40; regd **OH-IPA** 26.2.40 to Finnish Govt; intended for transfer to Finnish Naval Coastguard Service as **DH-1** but serial NTU; badly damaged on ground at Helsinki/Malmi 2.5.40 when struck by Brewster 239 BW-394; rebuild by Aero O/Y abandoned and aircraft scrapped; regn cld 5.40.

2354 Regd **G-AEWR** (CoR 7780) 7.5.37 to Railway Air Services Ltd, Croydon, named *Venus*; first CoA (5900) issued 29.6.37; flown from Exeter to Bordeaux 17.6.40 and abandoned there 18.6.40 on evacuation.

2355 Regd **G-AFAJ** (CoR 8011) 22.7.37 to de Havilland Aircraft Co Ltd, Hatfield; first CoA (6018) issued 18.8.37; to Devlet Hava Yollari (DHY) as **TC-ERK**, fleet no 7; to Hurkus Airlines, Ankara, 5.59; regn cld .67.

2356 Regd **G-AFAK** (CoR 8012) 22.7.37 to de Havilland Aircraft Co Ltd, Hatfield; first CoA (6043) issued 8.9.37; regn cld as sold 9.37; to DHY as **TC-FER**, fleet no 8; NFT.

2357 Regd **G-AFAL** (CoR 8013) 22.7.37 to de Havilland Aircraft Co Ltd, Hatfield; first CoA (6068) issued 30.9.37; regn cld as sold 12.37; to DHY as **TC-GEN**, fleet no 9; NFT.

2358 Regd **G-AFAM** (CoR 8014) 22.7.37 to de Havilland Aircraft Co Ltd, Hatfield; first CoA (6109) issued 29.10.37; regn cld as sold 12.37; to DHY as **TC-HEP**, fleet no 10; to Hurkus Airlines, Ankara, .58; NFT.

2359 First CoA (6141) issued 30.11.37; regd **VH-UYU** (CoR 696) 10.3.38 to W R Carpenter & Co Ltd, Sydney (t/a WRC Airlines), named *RMA Carmania;* impressed into RAAF 20.6.41 as **A31-8**; 1 AD for conversion to air ambulance 22.8.41; to Middle East; 1 AAU, Fuka Main (LG17) 10.11.41; shot down by Bf110 of III/ZG26 2 mls S of LG138 8.12.41 (no casualties).

2360 First CoA (6167) issued 18.12.37; regd **VH-UYV** (CoR 698) 12.4.38 to W R Carpenter & Co Ltd, Sydney (t/a WRC Airlines), named *RMA Caronia;* impressed into RAAF 11.12.39 as **A31-1**; 1 FTS, Point Cook, 11.12.39; 36 Sqn, Essendon, 16.9.42; 34 Sqn, Parafield, 2.1.43; 35 Sqn, Maylands, 24.5.43; converted to air ambulance by ANA 1.44; 2 AAU, New Guinea, 19.1.44; DBR 15.8.44 when tyre burst on take-off and main wing spar broke; 6 AD 23.8.44; SOC 12.9.44.

2361 First CoA (6172) issued 30.12.37; regd **VH-UYW** (703) 9.5.38 for W R Carpenter & Co Ltd, Sydney (t/a WRC Airlines), named *RMA Carinthia;* crashed in bad weather off New Guinea 15.3.40 when it ran out of fuel and ditched near Kavieng, New Ireland, but remained afloat allowing passengers, mail and freight to be carried ashore; eventually sank in 110ft of water and was abandoned by its owners and insurers; later recovered by F Saunders of Kavieng, but found to be beyond repair due to water damage.

DH.86B G-AEWR, c/n 2354, "Venus" of Railway Air Services seen at Stoke-on-Trent (Meir) during a request stop. This aircraft was lost in the fall of France
[R Lycett-Smith]

Hillman's Airways was the first customer for the DH.89 and here their fifth example, the apparently brand new G-ADAH, c/n 6278, is seen at Renfrew in 1935. It was transferred to British Airways in December of that year   *[Denis Fox collection]*

Part 3: The DH.89 Dragon Rapide

Background

Following the introduction of the four-engined DH.86 Express Air Liner, the de Havilland Aircraft Co began the design of a twin-engined version, the DH.89, towards the end of 1933. Originally referred to as the Dragon Six, the aircraft was technically similar to the DH.86, using the same fuselage construction method, with tapered mainplanes, nacelles and undercarriage. The prototype, carrying the registration E.4, flew at Hatfield on 17th April 1934 with H S Broad at the controls, and before long the type's name was altered to Dragon Rapide.

Confident of the new design's benefits, the first customer was Hillman's Airways Ltd, which took delivery of three in the summer of 1934 and four more later. Railway Air Services and Jersey Airways, both already operating the DH.84, soon followed suit. Hillman's first aircraft, G-ACPM, was flown in the King's Cup Air

Race at Hatfield on 13th July 1934, averaging 158 mph until hail damage forced the pilot, again H S Broad, to land. Railway Air Services put their new DH.89s into service on the routes from Croydon to Liverpool, Glasgow and Belfast and between Liverpool, Bristol, Southampton and Shoreham. Other early operators were Olley Air Service, Northern & Scottish Airways and British Continental Airways, but of the first hundred Rapides built, forty-one were delivered to overseas users. Oil companies in the Middle East found the design very suitable for pipeline patrols and general transport use, often as a replacement for earlier types.

Production of the Dragon Rapide continued, modifications such as a landing light in the nose and heating in the cabin being added in 1936. In 1937 the design was modified again when small trailing-edge flaps were incorporated under the lower inboard mainplane, this variety being designated DH.89A. Many earlier aircraft were modified similarly as they became due for major overhaul.

An interesting scene at Croydon in 1939, with Rapides G-AERN and G-AEPF, Dragon G-ACHV and another, several more civil aircraft and two Vickers Wellesleys of the RAF   *[MAP via P H T Green]*

By the beginning of the Second World War in 1939, Dragon Rapides had been placed in service by a huge variety of airlines, charter operators and private owners in every continent. Details of British airline and charter operators are provided in Appendix 1, and it can be claimed that without the economic and simple operation of the Rapide many such organisations would not have been established when they were. The last delivery to an airline before the outbreak of war was the 205th aircraft, VT-ALO of Tata Airlines Ltd in India.

When all airline operations in the UK were suspended on the outbreak of war Rapides were among the types of aircraft put under the control of National Air Communications for use by the Services. Other Rapides escaped this fate by being returned to service to operate priority routes under the auspices of the Associated Airways Joint Committee, an example being the Land's End to Scilly Isles service, which was maintained throughout the war.

British military use

Interested in the DH.89 for communications purposes, the Air Ministry placed Contract 362793/34 with de Havilland for one example, which was allocated serial K5070. It was delivered to the RAF's premier communications unit, 24 Squadron, at Hendon on 29th March 1935 and entered VIP service on 10th April, when it carried the Prime Minister (J Ramsay Macdonald) and the Foreign Secretary (Sir John Simon) to Paris, returning five days later. The Under Secretary of State for Air, Sir Phillip Sassoon, made use of the aircraft on 30th April, when he flew from Hendon to Blackpool (Stanley Park) and return. Many similar flights were made over the next three years, notable passengers being the Minister of Defence for South Africa, Mr Pirow, who flew to Portsmouth and back on 17th June 1936 and to Boscombe Down and Filton next day, and the Swedish Minister of Defence, Field Marshal Mannerheim, who flew to Filton and back on 24th September 1936. However, K5070 left 24 Squadron in August 1937 and was not replaced until February 1939, when P1764 and P1765 arrived. One of the first trips made by P1764 was to fly staff officers on a tour to St Athan, Weston-super-Mare, Hullavington, Kemble, Aston Down, Yatesbury, Little Rissington, Brize Norton and back to Hendon.

When RAF Coastal Command required a new general reconnaissance aircraft, Specification G18/35 was issued and tenders invited. The de Havilland Aircraft Co submitted a militarised version of the Dragon Rapide known as the DH.89M, and a prototype, K4772, was constructed. Similar in profile apart from the addition of a curved extension to the fin, this aircraft was equipped with a Vickers Mk.V gun on the nose, a Lewis Mk.III gun in the upper fuselage and a bomb bay for two 100 lb (45 kg) and four 20 lb (9 kg) bombs. There was a crew of three: pilot, navigator/bomber and wireless operator/gunner. Although the design failed to win the contest against the Avro Anson, valuable

experience was gained and several of the type were built later for foreign air forces, among them the Spanish Government, which acquired three in December 1935 for patrol duties in Morocco, and the Lithuanian Government.

Three DH.89s intended for use at Electrical & Wireless Schools, R2485-2487, were purchased by the RAF in 1938, the first of hundreds which would be constructed over the next few years.

On the outbreak of war in September 1939, 24 Squadron experienced a major expansion of activity, particularly involving flights to and from France, where RAF squadrons had been posted to await events. To enlarge the fleet civilian Rapides, complete with civilian crews, began to arrive for service with the squadron. First to turn up at Hendon were two from Isle of Man Air Services on 4th September, followed by three from Great Western & Southern Airlines two weeks later. Western Airways contributed two on 30th September, and the early arrivals joined in mail-carrying sorties under the fledgling Air Delivery Letter Service, as well as VIP flights. The ADLS was reorganised on 18th September, when one DH.89 was based at Le Mans to operate to Le Havre, Rouen (Boos) and Paris (Le Bourget) and another at Reims to fly the Coulommiers and Le Bourget sector. Other aircraft delivered the mail from Hendon to Le Bourget for onward movement. This activity continued through the 'phoney war' of late 1939, but on 18th January 1940 a detachment of 24 Squadron was established at Vitry-les-Reims. Two of the DH.89s, still civil-registered as G-ADNH and G-AEAM, were sent there, and carried out a variety of useful tasks. G-AEAM was replaced by G-ADSV on 23rd February, but both aircraft were abandoned when the personnel of the detachment were withdrawn to Le Bourget on 16th May. All flights to France ceased on 17th June 1940.

As the quantity of impressed Dragon Rapides was not nearly sufficient for the RAF's rapidly-expanding needs, the Air Ministry awarded Contract No B104582/40 for 149 aircraft to de Havilland, who increased production of the type at Hatfield. The aircraft was designated by the RAF as the DH.89B Dominie Mk.I navigation and radio trainer, which was equipped with a visible DF loop, or the Mk.II communications aircraft. By 1942 de Havilland's facilities at Hatfield had reached saturation, yet space was needed badly for production of Mosquitos. The Dominie contract was therefore subcontracted to Brush Coachworks Ltd at Loughborough, where 346 aircraft were built between 1943 and 1946. Users of the Dominie were many and varied, but prominent among them were the Air Transport Auxiliary, who used Dominies for crew delivery and retrieval, Air Observer & Navigator Schools, Radio Schools and Station Flights. The Fleet Air Arm also used the Dominie in some numbers, mostly from late production batches, until at least 1961. In all, the RAF took delivery of 528 new DH.89s, all of which are dealt with in some detail in the individual aircraft listings section that begins on page 50.

K4772, c/n 6271, was the first DH.89 for the RAF as a DH.89M – note the machine-gun in the nose   *[G M Simons collection]*

The Spanish Civil War

Before the outbreak of civil war in Spain, examples of the DH.89 had been supplied to state airline LAPE and to the military authorities. LAPE had taken delivery of c/n 6262 in late 1934 as EC-AZZ, and in the following year the Aviación Militar (Spanish Air Force) began to look for a replacement for its elderly Fokker F.VIIb3m aircraft. To help the service decide on the best aircraft, competitive tests were held between the Airspeed Envoy and the DH.89, after which a military version of the latter, the DH.89M, was selected. This choice reflected the perceived greater reliability of the DH.89s Gipsy Six engines and its fixed undercarriage, major factors in the proposed use of the aircraft in the western Sahara desert.

Three DH.89Ms were supplied to the Spanish Air Force (c/n 6310 to 6312) and arrived at Cuatro Vientos, Madrid, in January 1936. Given serial numbers 22-1 to 22-3, they featured the extended dorsal fins of DH.89Ms already delivered to Iraq, an arrangement designed to counter the aerodynamic problem created by a dorsal gun position. Firing through a hatch in the fuselage floor was a Vickers F machine gun, and racks carrying twelve 12kg bombs were installed. Another Vickers F gun, firing forward, was installed in the port side of the nose for the pilot's use. The bomb-aimer/rear gunner had the use of a Marconi wireless set, and cameras could be mounted vertically in the fuselage. Easy conversions to troop transports or ambulances were possible.

Soon after arrival of the Dragons (as they were known locally) a Popular Front government was elected in Spain. As a military coup d'état was seen as a distinct possibility, Gen Nuñez de Prado, the Director General de Aeronáutica, decided to base the DH.89Ms near Madrid rather than in the Sahara, so they were sent to the Escuela de Vuelo y Combate (Air Combat Training School) at Alacalá de Henares. However, it was soon found that senior officers there were potential trouble-makers, and the DH.89Ms were transferred to Getafe.

At the start of the civil war Dragon Rapides featured in a number of crucial events. Prominent was G-ACYR of Olley Air Services, which was chartered on 11th July 1936 to fly journalist Luis Bolín and three spurious holidaymakers, Maj Hugh Pollard, his daughter Diana and her friend Dorothy Watson, from Croydon to Gandó airfield on Las Palmas in the Canary Islands. The object was to provide Gen Franco with an aircraft to fly him to Tetuán in Spanish Morocco, where he would take command of the Spanish Army and begin a rebellion in earnest. Capt C W R Bebb was the pilot, with Mr Bryers as flight mechanic and with an unnamed radio operator. After delivery of Gen Franco at Tetuán, the Rapide flew Bolín to France via Lisbon and then returned to Croydon. After a long and busy life, G-ACYR was restored and presented to the Spanish government, who placed it on display at the Museo Aire at Cuatro Vientos.

Gen Nuñez de Prado was ordered by the Premier, Casares Quiroga, to fly to Zaragoza on 18th July 1936 to persuade the local commander, Gen Cabanellas, to remain loyal to the Republic. He and his adjutant used DH.89M 22-3, but on landing at Zaragoza were arrested with the pilot and a few days later all were shot and their bodies displayed as a deterrent to Republican sympathisers. The aircraft was then taken over by the Nationalist side. On 20th July LAPE's Rapide EC-AZZ carried two officers to Paris to attempt to buy military aircraft there, while at the same time a Rapide of British Airways piloted by R H McIntosh ('All-weather Mac') flew three well-known British journalists to Burgos to interview the rebel leader, Gen Mola.

One of three DH.89M aircraft for the Spanish Air Force in December 1935. Eight bombs were carried under the fuselage and there is a machine-gun in the nose
[via C N Dodds]

In England, Airwork Ltd at Heston had purchased four DH.89s which were then resold to Juan de la Cierva and Tom Campbell-Black on behalf of the Nationalists. On 1st August the first one, G-ADCL, left Heston, piloted by Lord Malcolm Douglas-Hamilton with Richard L'Estrange Malone as navigator. Five-gallon fuel containers almost filled the fuselage, and spurious registrations were applied. On arrival at Burgos, 'DCL was converted into a fighter-bomber, a forward-firing Vickers gun being fitted beside the pilot and a hole cut in the fuselage floor through which bombs could be shoved by a bombardier! Three days later, the second Rapide, G-ADFY, previously owned by King's Cup winner C E Gardner, was flown from Heston to Burgos by A Rowley. On 13th August the other two aircraft, G-ADAO and G-ACPN, left Heston for Burgos. These four aircraft were allocated serial numbers 40-1 to 40-4, while the DH.89M captured at Zaragoza became 40-5. Apart from 40-1, which became a transport aircraft, they were absorbed into the Fokker-Dragon Group at Olmedo, from where intensive operations began on 20th August 1936. Six days later, 40-5 was accidentally shot down by 'friendly' He.51s near Segovia, its occupants, Capitáns Pouzo and Vela, losing their lives. Afterwards, their names were painted on the noses of 40-1 and 40-2. The Group disbanded in December 1936, and 40-2 became the personal mount of Gen J-A Ansaldo, while the other three aircraft were relegated to training or transport duties.

Republican forces, meanwhile, were also acquiring aircraft, among them DH.89s. On 30th July 1936 DH.89M 22-2 was flown from Madrid to Barcelona and on 5th August from there to Sariñena to operate as an escort fighter for the Alas Rojas Group. Resplendent in black, it was known unofficially as El Avión Negus. It was shot down on 19th October when its pilot, Luis Aguilera Cullell, attacked a formation of He.51s to draw them away from two aircraft that he was escorting. Its sister aircraft, 22-1, was sent to the Basque front and was destroyed at Albericia airfield, Santander, by Nationalist bombers on 6th April 1937. Republicans also took possession of Italian-registered Rapide I-DRAG via W A Rollason Ltd of Croydon in August 1936. From Le Bourget it was flown to Barcelona on 14th August but before long was apparently destroyed in a taxying accident.

Three more Dragon Rapides were bought in England by agents for the Republican cause in the autumn of 1936, but despite great efforts were prevented from reaching their destination. One, G-ADAK, had been bought by C H Stone from British Continental Airways and resold to Union Founders Trust in August 1936. At the end of that month it passed to Le Fédération Populaire des Sports Aéronautiques, but on 5th September an attempt was made by a group of Frenchmen to steal it from a guarded hangar at Croydon. Another was G-AEMH, which was purchased from de Havilland but the order was cancelled before delivery. The others were G-ADWZ of Personal Airways and G-ACTU of Lord Douglas Forbes, both of which were kept in the Personal Airways hangar at Croydon. G-ADWZ was flown to Paris and re-registered F-APES but then returned to Croydon and the sales of both were aborted. Two more Rapides are thought to have reached the Republicans: G-ADDF, sold by Airwork Ltd to Lejeune Aviation in September 1937 and another, probably OO-JFN, recorded as being sold in France on 25th April 1937 but which then disappeared without trace.

At the end of 1937 and during 1938 ten DH.89A Dragon Rapides were bought direct from de Havilland by a group of Frenchmen, Paul Legastelois, Dr Réné Arbeltier and A Rodier. As they were delivered, these men sold them to SFTA, who in turn arranged delivery of nine of them to the Republicans in Spain. De Havilland construction numbers of the ten were: 6382, 6383, 6393, 6395, 6396, 6420, 6424, 6425, 6427 and 6428. It is now almost impossible to trace the histories of the Rapides from this point on; several are known to have served at the Republican Escuela de Polimótores at Totana in Murcia in 1938/39 but most of these would have arrived too late to see much service in the civil war.

Other military users

Examples of the DH.89 were used by the Royal Australian Air Force, which impressed nine from civilian operators; the Royal New Zealand Air Force, to whom nine Dominies were diverted from RAF stocks and who impressed a further five older aircraft; and the South African Air Force, who took delivery of fourteen diverted Dominies and impressed three civiian aircraft.

After the war

Too late to be needed for military purposes, the last hundred Brush-built Dominies were delivered to the de Havilland Repair Unit at Witney and converted for civilian use as Dragon Rapides. Many of them formed the initial post-war equipment of such airlines as KLM, Jersey Airways and Iraqi Airways, and other airlines in almost every part of the world which saw the type as an economical way of establishing scheduled services. Rapides were also supplied to the constituent airlines of AAJC in order to expand their operations. At the same time, scores of surplus airworthy Dominies that had seen

Ex-RAF Dominies being converted to Dragon Rapides by de Havilland at Witney soon after the end of the Second World War   [*P H T Green collection*]

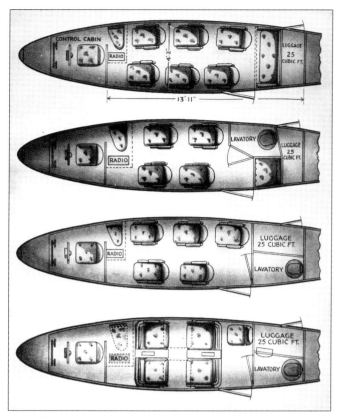

Four different cabin layouts offered for the DH.89   [G M Simons collection]

military service flooded the civilian market and were snapped up by minor airlines in the UK and overseas. A few found their way to air forces such as the Belgian Air Force, the Royal Netherlands Air Force and the Israeli Air Force. When British European Airways was formed in 1947 it inherited a large number of them and used many for several years on their routes in the Scottish Highlands and islands until they were replaced by more modern types.

After refurbishment many were put to use by a plethora of charter operators, who found the Rapide an ideal aircraft for carrying holidaymakers from the Midlands and north of England and Scotland to such destinations as the Isle of Wight, the Isle of Man, the Channel Islands and a little further afield, and also as a fast method of taking jockeys and trainers to race meetings. Sport parachutists made full use of the Rapide as a jumping-off platform for many years, and several were employed on aerial survey work or as basic 'executive' aircraft. Pleasure flying at air shows and other events was another useful source of income for Rapide operators.

In the early nineteen-fifties, however, the Rapide began to become a victim of its own success. More and more people wanted to fly to their holiday destinations, and slow eight-seat Rapides could no longer handle the volume of traffic, for which faster ex-RAF Dakotas with twenty seats were more appropriate. Furthermore, modern aircraft such as the DH.104 Dove and DH.114 Heron were becoming available for shorter routes, offering a higher speed and better standard of comfort. In addition, the wooden Rapide was becoming more difficult to maintain to Certificate of Airworthiness standards, and use of the Rapide began a gradual decline. The type has not been used on scheduled services since the 1960s, but today significant numbers are still used for pleasure flying or are in museums.

Nearly sixty years after DH.89 production ended, a full-size model was built by Michael Davy and volunteers from the North West Aviation Heritage Museum Group at Hooton Park, Merseyside. It has been placed at the entrance to the Liverpool Marriott Hotel, which is in the original terminal building at Liverpool Airport. Painted as G-AEAJ of Railway Air Services, it bears the name *Neptune* for Neptune Developments, who were responsible for refurbishing the old building. Construction of the two-ton model from steel tubes and plywood took 4000 man-hours.

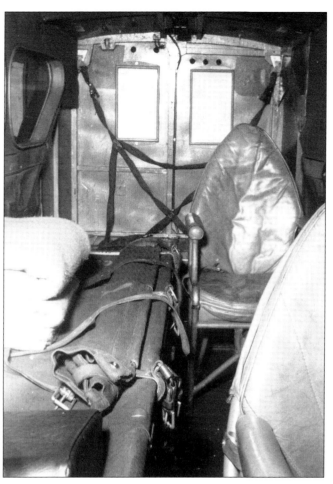

Interior view of an ambulance-configured DH.89, with seats 7 and 8 on the right, a stretcher, blankets and stowage   [G M Simons collection]

A stretcher being loaded onto a Dominie of the ATA; note the invasion stripes under the fuselage   [G M Simons collection]

Technical specification

Designed as an eight- to ten-seat biplane airliner, the DH.89 was powered by two 200 hp de Havilland Gipsy Six air-cooled inline engines, superceded in the DH.89A by Gipsy Queens of the same horsepower. Construction was of wood, the fuselage being a box structure with spruce longerons and struts covered with plywood. The upper mainplane was built up from two spars and girder ribs, braced by wire and covered with fabric. The lower mainplane wing stubs as far as the engine positions incorporated tubular steel spars, and had outer panels similar to the upper mainplane. Wings were braced by parallel struts. Split trailing-edge flaps and mass-balanced ailerons were provided. The tail unit was wooden construction covered by fabric, with a balanced rudder, and was braced externally. A fixed, faired, cantilever-type undercarriage incorporated Dowty shock absorbers and Bendix brakes.

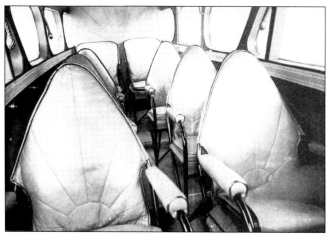

The standard DH.89 eight-seat interior   *[G M Simons collection]*

Although seldom used in practice, additional Mark numbers were allocated to modified aircraft, for instance the Mk.2 being the wartime Mk.II, Mk.3 covering a version for eight passengers, Mk.4 using Gipsy Queen 2 engines, Mk.5 incorporating manually-operated variable-pitch propellers and Mk.6 using Fairey fixed-pitch metal propellers.

The following information is from the maker's manuals:

Dimensions:

Span	48 ft 0 in (14.63 m)	
Length	34 ft 6 in (10.52 m)	
Height	10 ft 3 in (3.12 m)	
Wing area	340 sq ft (31.6 sq m)	

Weights:

Tare	3100 lbs (1409 kg)	[DH.89]
	3276 lbs (1489 kg)	[DH.89A and DH.89B]
	3230 lbs (1468 kg)	[DH.89A Mk.4 & Mk.6]
	3368 lbs (1531 kg)	[DH.89M]
	3400 lbs (1545 kg)	[DH.89A floatplane]
All-up	5500 lbs (2500 kg)	[DH.89, DH.89A, DH.89B and DH.89A floatplane]
	6000 lbs (2727 kg)	[DH.89A Mk.4 & Mk.6]
	5750 lbs (2614 kg)	[DH.89A Mk.5]
	5372 lbs (2442 kg)	[DH.89M]

Maximum speed:	157 mph (253 kph)	[DH.89, DH.89A and DH.89B]
	156 mph (251 kph)	[DH 89M and DH.89A Mk.4 and Mk.6]
	145 mph (233 kph)	[DH.89A floatplane and DH.89A Mk.5]
Cruising speed:	132 mph (212 kph)	[DH.89, DH.89A and DH.89B]
	125 mph (201 kph)	[DH.89M]
	123 mph (198 kph)	[DH.89A floatplane]
Initial climb:	1000 ft/min (305 m/min)	[DH.89]
	867 ft/min (264 m/min)	[DH.89A and DH.89B]
	1200 ft/min (366 m/min)	[DH.89A Mk.4 & Mk.6]
	890 ft/min (271 m/min)	[DH.89M]
	700 ft/min (213 m/ min)	[DH.89A float plane]
Range:	578 mls (930 km)	[DH.89, DH.89A and DH.89B]
	573 mls (923 km)	[DH.89A Mk.4 & Mk.6]
	550 mls (885 km)	[DH.89M]
	530 mls (853 km)	[DH.89A floatplane]

Production

6250 – 6341	DH.89 (including some DH.89M)
6342 – 6399	DH.89A
6400	DH.92 Dolphin
6401 – 6456	DH.89A
6457 – 6978	DH.89B Dominie
	(civil conversions became DH.89A)

Individual Aircraft Histories

6250   Prototype Dragon Six; first flew at Hatfield 17.4.34 in Class B marks as **E.4**; CoA (4306) issued 10.5.34; regd **CH-287** 19.7.34 to Osterschweiz Aero Gesellschaft, Altenrhein; re-regd **HB-ARA** 1.35 to same owner; carried St Gallen titles in 3.35 for St Gallen - Zurich - Berne service; regd 20.3.37 to Swissair AG, Zurich (Dubendorf); regd **HB-APA** 6.37 to same owner; to Farner-Werke AG .54 and on overhaul; reported sale to Spain .54 abandoned; regd .55 to Farner-Werke AG, Grenchen; regd .55 to Motorfluggruppe Zurich, Aero Club de Suisse, Kloten; aircraft in use on joy-riding flights until 1961, fitted with non-standard windscreen and a longer rear window; regn cld 10.5.61, when aircraft was WFU and stored at Kloten; despite efforts to preserve it this machine was broken up and burnt by Zurich Airport Fire Service 8.64.

Dragon Rapide prototype, c/n 6250, HB-APA at St Moritz, at the time the highest airfield in Europe at 6000 feet (1830 metres) above sea level. The occasion was the arrival of the first non-stop Swissair flight from Croydon, made by the DC-2 in the background   *[via R C Sturtivant]*

Painted blue overall, G-ACPP c/n 6254, was seen at Kidlington on 25th April 1959, just after registration to Aviation Traders Ltd　　　　　*[P H Butler]*

6251　　Regd **G-ACPM** (CoR 4955) 7.6.34 to Hillman's Airways Ltd, Stapleford Tawney; CoA (4365) issued 5.7.34; entered by Lord Wakefield in King's Cup Air Race 13.7.34, flown by Capt Hubert Broad but withdrawn after hail damage over Waddington; crashed in sea 4 mls off Folkestone when inbound from Paris 2.10.34 in heavy mist, killing all seven on board, including Capt W R Bannister; regn cld 10.34.

6252　　Regd **G-ACPN** (CoR 4956) 12.8.34 (error for 12.7.34 ?) to Hillman's Airways Ltd, Stapleford Tawney; CoA (4389) issued 2.8.34; transferred to British Airways Ltd 12.35 but not used by them; regd to them (CoR 6890) 8.4.36; but in fact to Airwork Ltd, Heston, 1.36 for disposal; leased to Highland Airways Ltd, Inverness, 19.4.36 to 9.8.36; regn cld 9.36 as sold; bought by Juan de la Cierva and Louis Bolin for the Nationalist side in Spanish Civil War; left Heston, flown by Tom Campbell-Black, 13.8.36; probably allocated serial **40-4**; either shot down 27.8.36 or DBF at Aragón 13.9.36.

6253　　Regd **G-ACPO** (CoR 4957) 12.7.34 to Hillman's Airways Ltd, Stapleford Tawney; CoA (4390) issued 4.9.34; regd .34 to unknown party, probably DH for demonstration to Highland Airways Ltd; regd (CoR 5480) to Hillman's Airways Ltd; badly damaged in gale at Ronaldsway 26.1.35 but repaired; transferred to British Airways Ltd 12.35 but not used by them; regd to them (CoR 6850) 24.3.36 but in fact to Airwork Ltd, Heston 1.36 for disposal; regn cld 1.36 as sold abroad; CoA renewed 12.6.36 and flown to Australia; regd **VH-UBN** (CoR 602) 17.8.36 to Rockhampton Aerial Services Ltd, Rockhampton, Qld; regd 1.10.36 to Airlines of Australia Ltd, Sydney; impressed into RAAF 9.8.40 as **A33-5**; 3 EFTS, Essendon, 12.8.40; 1 AOS, Cootamundra, 11.12.40; to Department of Civil Aviation 16.4.42 and restored to civil register as **VH-UBN** for use by Guinea Airways

Ltd., Adelaide, SA; crashed at Mount Kitchener 20.7.44 while flying from Broken Hill to Adelaide in poor weather, killing the pilot, Capt F Gill, and six passengers.

6254　　Regd **G-ACPP** (CoR 4958) 20.2.35 to Railway Air Services Ltd, Croydon, named *City of Bristol*; CoA (4730) issued 12.3.35; del 4.4.35; sold 5.12.38 and regd 31.1.39 to Great Western & Southern Airlines Ltd, Shoreham 31.1.39, named *Volunteer;* impressed temporarily into RAF 17.9.39 and used by 24 Sqn, Hendon; retd to Great Western & Southern Airlines under AAJC 6.40; to Scottish Airways Ltd, Renfrew, 22.2.41; retd to AAJC, Speke, 26.6.41; to Scottish Airways Ltd, Renfrew, 2.1.42; retd to AAJC 16.9.42; regd 1.2.47 to British European Airways Ltd, Northolt; regd 16.4.48 to Aircraft & Engineering Services Ltd, Croydon; regd 16.6.48 to Kenneth Nalson and Aircraft & Engineering Services Ltd, Croydon; regd 22.6.48 to Yellow Air Taxis Ltd, Elmdon; CoA lapsed 16.3.51; regd 4.9.51 to Air Couriers (Properties) Ltd, Croydon; regd 7.5.52 to Hawker Aircraft Ltd, Langley, and CoA renewed; CoA lapsed 21.9.57; regd 3.1.58 to W H Wetton t/a 600 (City of London) Sqn Flying Club, Biggin Hill; CoA renewed 5.9.58; regd 23.4.59 to Aviation Traders Ltd, Stansted; CoA lapsed 4.9.59; sold 11.3.60 to Air Navigation & Trading Co Ltd, Squires Gate and regd to them 29.11.60; regn cld 19.5.61 as sold to Canada and delivered in crates to North Air Services Ltd 6.61; plan to operate aircraft as a floatplane from Lake L'Orange abandoned; sold to Dr McLean and stored at Toronto Airport .62; sold to J R Bowdery .63; overhauled and regd **CF-PTK** 2.3.64 to J R Bowdery, Sept Iles, PQ; CoA lapsed 2.3.65; regd 10.12.97 to K M Bowdery, Barrie, Ont, and believed to be under rebuild at St John, Newfoundland; regd 30.1.01 to M Bowdery, Cookstown, Ont; for sale in dismantled condition .01; to Reynolds Aviation Museum, Wetaskiwin, Alb .01 and regd 3.1.02 to Reynolds Aviation Preservation Foundation; extant.

ZS-AES, c/n 6256, of African Air Transport Ltd, Germiston, wearing the name "Mau-Hea-Tom"　　　　　*[via K Smy]*

6255   Regd **G-ACPR** (CoR 4959) 20.2.35 to Railway Air Services Ltd, Croydon, named *City of Birmingham;* CoA (4743) issued 18.3.35; del 30.3.35; sold 5.12.38 and regd 31.1.39 to Great Western & Southern Airlines Ltd, Shoreham, named *Valkyrie;* impressed temporarily into RAF and used by 24 Sqn, Hendon, 17.9.39 to 7.12.39; crashed at Burford 19.2.40.

6256   CoA (4602) issued 10.12.34 as **ZS-AES** to Cyril Hull (although sold new to African Air Transport via Jack Barclay Ltd); left Hatfield 29.12.34, piloted by H N Hawker, in London to Cape Town race; regd **ZS-AES** 31.1.35 to African Air Transport Ltd, Germiston, named *Mau-Hea-Tom;* regn cld 30.6.38 as sold in Southern Rhodesia; regd **VP-YBZ** (CoR 59) 6.38 to Rhodesia & Nyasaland Airways, Salisbury; taken over by Southern Rhodesia Air Services 9.39 as **302**; restored as **VP-YBZ** 4.42; crashed 11.43.

6257   Regd **G-ACTT** (CoR 5120) 6.34 to Anglo-American Oil Co Ltd, Heston; CoA (4475) issued 20.10.34; not delivered and replaced by G-ADCL; ownership reverted to de Havilland at Hatfield 7.1.35 and fitted with luxury interior for HRH Prince of Wales; regd (CoR 5644) 25.2.35 to Flt Lt E H Fielden AFC on behalf of HRH Prince of Wales; del to Hendon 27.4.35 and maintained by 24 Sqn, but little used; offered for sale 10.35; sold 13.3.36 to Olley Air Service Ltd, Croydon and regd to them (CoR 6872) 30.3.36; regn cld as sold 9.2.40; impressed into RAF; 24 Sqn, Hendon, 9.2.40; allocated serial **X8509** 31.3.40; damaged 14.7.41; to DH RU, Witney, for repair 27.7.41 but SOC 29.8.41.

6258   Regd **G-ACTU** (CoR 5121) 3.9.34 to C R Anson, Hanworth; CoA (4477) issued 24.9.34; del 11.34; regd (CoR 7193) 17.7.36 to Rt Hon Viscount A P H Forbes and operated by Personal Airways Ltd, Croydon; Republican agents attempted to purchase this aircraft for use in Spanish Civil War, but sale was blocked by British Government; regd (CoR 7426) 2.11.36 to Rt Hon Viscount Forbes; regd (CoR 7994) 14.7.37 to The Channel Trust Ltd and operated by Norman Edgar (Western Airways) Ltd, Weston-super-Mare; regd (CoR 8445) 9.4.38 to Weston Airport Ltd and operated by Western Airways Ltd; regd (CoR 8854) 1.11.38 to Western Airways Ltd, Weston-super-Mare; impressed into RAF 30.9.39; 24 Sqn, Hendon, 30.9.39; detached to Le Bourget 8.11.39; retd to Western Airways 5.40; regn cld as sold 4.6.40; 8 AACU, Filton, 10.6.40 (later Weston Zoyland and Pengam Moors); allocated serial **AW115** 25.7.40; stalled on take-off from Pengam Moors 15.2.41 and DBF; 3 injured; SOC 28.2.41.

6259   Regd **ZK-ACO** 8.10.34 to NZ Melbourne Centenary Air Race Committee, Mangere, named *Tainui;* CoA (4535) issued 9.10.34; flown by Sqn Ldr J D Hewett, F Stewart and C E Kay, it finished fifth in the MacRobertson Race, taking an elapsed time of 13 days 18 hrs 51 mins and flying time of 106 hrs 51 mins; made forced landing at Boulogne and also suffered slight wing damage at Cloncurry, Qld, 28.10.34; arrived Essendon, Melbourne, Vic., 3.11.34, the first DH.89 seen in Australia; the first twin-engined aircraft to cross the Tasman Sea, it flew to New Zealand on 14.11.34 for resale, but due to depressed local economy was shipped back to Australia on *Wanganella,* arriving Sydney 27.5.35; tail was damaged during unloading when it struck the wharf; trucked to Melbourne; erected and flown at Essendon 5.6.35; regd in Australia as **VH-UUO** (CoR 528) 10.6.35 to West Australian Airways Ltd, Perth, WA; regd 1.7.36 to Adelaide Airways, Parafield, (which on same day became Australian National Airways); severely damaged on landing at Mt Gambier, SA, 30.9.36, but repaired and put back into service 3.37; meanwhile regd 25.11.36 to Australian National Airways Pty Ltd, Essendon; based at Parafield and named *Malonga*; regd 8.8.39 to Guinea Airways Ltd, Adelaide, SA, named *Lae*; impressed into RAAF 2.7.40 as **A33-1**; regn cld 8.7.40; 1 EFTS, Parafield, 2.7.40; 1 AOS, Cootamundra, 26.8.40; to Department of Civil Aviation 15.4.42; restored to register as **VH-UUO** 21.4.42 to Airlines of Australia Ltd, Sydney; to Allied Works Council, Qld, early 1943?; regd 26.6.43 to Australian National Airways Pty Ltd, Melbourne, named *Yuptana;* leased to Queensland Airlines Ltd pre-.50; regd 7.2.50 to Butler Air Transport Pty Ltd, Sydney (Mascot); crashed and DBF in wooded area on Warrumbungle Mountain, 11 mls north of Tooraweenah, NSW, 23.5.52, when inbound from Barradine in bad weather; pilot and four passengers injured; regn cld 8.9.52.

6260   CoA (4633) issued 27.12.34; regd **I-DRAG** 29.1.35 to Ala Littoria SA, Rome (based at Littorio); regd 5.8.36 to F Mazzotti Biancinelli, Milan; regn cld as WFU 3.9.36; purchased in France by Spanish Republicans through W A Rollason Ltd and flown to Barcelona 14.8.36 by Corniglion-Molinier; reportedly wrecked in ground collision with captured Fiat C.R.32, date unknown.

6261   Regd **G-ACYR** (CoR 5375) 15.10.34 to Olley Air Service Ltd, Croydon; CoA (4534) issued 2.2.35; chartered from Olley to fly Gen Franco from Canary Islands to Morocco at start of Spanish Civil War 7.36; operated by Olley/AAJC, Speke, early WW2; at DH RU, Witney, 15.7.40; to Scottish Airways Ltd, Renfrew, 4.3.41; retd to AAJC 25.4.42; at DH RU, Witney, 14.10.44; regd 6.4.45 to Miles Aircraft Ltd, Woodley; regd 15.8.46 to Reid & Sigrist Ltd, Desford; CoA lapsed 23.8.47 and stored at Desford; sold to Air Couriers Ltd, Croydon, 7.53 and del by road; presented to Gen. Franco by Air Couriers .54; regn cld 18.3.59; restored to static display for preservation in Museo del Aire, Cuatro Vientos, Madrid; extant.

6262   CoA (4577) issued 27.11.34; del to Spain 8.12.34 as **EC-W27** (ferry marks); regd to Líneas Aérea Postales Españolas (LAPE); re-regd **EC-AZZ** on arrival and given fleet no 20; used during Spanish Civil War and restored to Iberia Airlines afterwards; known to have been in service until at least .41, possibly as **EC-AGO** or **EC-AGP.**

G-ACTU, c/n 6258, was one of several Rapides destined for service in the Spanish Civil War but prevented from leaving by the British government

[Denis Fox collection]

6263 Regd **G-ADAL** (CoR 5487) 30.1.35 to Hillman's Airways Ltd, Stapleford Tawney; CoA (4715) issued 2.3.35; transferred to British Airways 11.12.35 and regd to them (CoR 6788) 2.3.36 but not used; to Airwork Ltd., Heston, 1.36 for sale; regd (CoR 7109) 4.6.36 to Wrightways Ltd, Croydon; impressed into RAF 14.4.40 as **X9448**; 6 AACU, Ringway, 9.4.40; 7 AACU, Castle Bromwich, 6.7.40; to Wrightways Ltd for repairs 20.7.40; 9 MU, Cosford, 26.8.40; 3 FPP, Hawarden, 2.11.40; to Wrightways/Air Taxis, believed for repair, 21.11.40; SF Andover 30.11.40; 7 FPP, Sherburn-in-Elmet, 5.2.41; force-landed near Standish, Wigan, due to fuel starvation on a flight from Kemble to Dumfries 25.3.41; to DH RU, Witney, 10.4.41 for repair, but SOC as BER 21.4.41.

6264 Regd **G-ACZE** (CoR 5407) 20.11.34 to Anglo-Persian Oil Co Ltd, Abadan (later Anglo-Iranian Oil Co Ltd); CoA (4612) issued 15.12.34; del to Almaza 25.12.34; retd to Heston 24.11.38; regn cld 1.1.39; regd 17.3.39 to Airwork Ltd, Heston; operated by 7 CANS, Perth; unit became 7 AONS 1.11.39; 6 AONS, Staverton, 23.5.40; to DH for conversion to ambulance aircraft 22.8.40; 48 MU, Hawarden, 18.9.40; allocated RAF serial **Z7266**; 3 FPP, Hawarden, 8.12.40; to Allied Airways (Gandar Dower) Ltd, Dyce, 21.9.41 for rebuild; regd **G-ACZE** 7.2.42 to Eric L Gandar Dower and operated by Allied Airways (Gandar Dower) Ltd, Dyce; CoA renewed 11.3.42; regd 20.6.42 to Allied Airways (Gandar Dower) Ltd, named *The Dawn;* 5 MU, Kemble, for repair 29.11.43; crashed at Grimsetter 27.12.45; to DH RU, Witney, .46; SOC by RAF 21.6.47; completely rebuilt with c/n W1001 (q.v.).

6265 CoA (4648) issued 8.1.35 to Asiatic Petroleum Co Ltd (a Shell company); regd **VH-UVS** 31.3.35 to Shell Co. of Australia Ltd, Melbourne, Vic, named *The Spirit of Shell;* test flown 27.3.35 at Sydney (Mascot), fitted with long range tanks; leased to Airlines of Australia early .37; DBF 12.5.37 at Mascot during engine start-up while on regular Brisbane service; regn cld same day.

6266 Regd **G-ADAG** (CoR 5482) 30.1.35 to Hillman's Airways Ltd, Stapleford Tawney; CoA (4675) issued 6.2.35; transferred to British Airways 11.12.35 and regd to them (CoR 6696) 31.1.36; based at Eastleigh; regd (CoR 7274) to Northern & Scottish Airways Ltd, Renfrew; regd (CoR 8099) 2.9.37 to Airwork Ltd., Heston, and eventually operated by 6 CANS, Shoreham; unit became 6 AONS 1.11.39; damaged in landing at Okehampton 24.11.39; allocated serial **Z7264** 15.7.40; HQ ATA, White Waltham, 29.3.41; HQ FPP, Kemble, 19.6.41; damaged Cat AC/FA at Prestwick; to DH RU, Witney, 10.1.42; to DH RU, Witney, for repair 20.8.43, but SOC 13.9.43.

6267 RAF serial **K5070**; TOC 29.3.35; 24 Sqn, Hendon, 29.3.35 for use by the Air Council as VIP transport; DH 19.8.37; CoA (6098) issued 22.10.37; supplied to Imperial Airways 26.10.37 on loan under contract 635715/37; regd **VP-KCK** (CoR 62) 4.11.37 to Wilson Airways Ltd, Nairobi; impressed into Kenya Air Auxiliary Unit 9.39 as either **K11** or **K16** (probably the former); purchased from British Govt 7.10.40; broken up for spares at Nairobi .46.

VH-UVS, c/n 6265, "The Spirit of Shell" being handed over to the Shell Company of Australia at Hatfield in January 1935 [G M Simons collection]

6268 Regd **G-ACZF** (CoR 5408) 20.11.34 to Anglo-Persian Oil Co Ltd, Abadan (later Anglo Iranian Oil Co Ltd); CoA (4684) issued 11.2.35; retd to UK 24.11.38; regn cld 1.1.39; regd 17.3.39 to Airwork Ltd, Heston; regd 16.5.39 to Allied Airways (Gandar Dower) Ltd, Dyce, named *Carina;* taken over by British European Airways Ltd 12.4.47 and regd to them 24.10.47; CoA lapsed 18.5.47; regn cld 20.8.48; scrapped at DH, Witney, 8.48.

6269 Regd **G-ACYM** (CoR 5368) 10.1.35 to Olley Air Service Ltd, Croydon; CoA (4649) issued 6.3.35; regd 6.4.39 to Great Western & Southern Airlines Ltd, Shoreham, named *Vanguard;* impressed into the RAF 17.9.39; 24 Sqn, Hendon; serial **X9320** allocated 31.3.40 but not used; force-landed at Moyenville, France, when lost in snowstorm, 12.2.40 and remains destroyed in evacuation; SOC 4.4.40.

Rapides VP-KCK c/n 6267, and another, with Dragonfly VP-KCS, all of Wilson's Airways, basking in the sunshine at Dodoma   *[Denis Fox collection]*

Originally A33-1, c/n 6270 became A33-3 of the RAAF, here displaying its radio call-sign VHCRP   *[G M Simons collection]*

6270   CoA issued 7.7.35 as **A3-1** for RAAF (Air Board Order 451); CoA (4935) issued 2.7.35; TOC 2.7.35 and shipped to Australia 9.7.35 on *Port Nicholson;* 1 AD 14.8.35; attached to 1 Sqn/ North Australian Survey Flight after fitting equipment for air/ground photography; left Laverton 18.9.35 on 10,800-mile (17,380-km) tour of inspection of northern Australia; loaned 16.12.35 to Holyman's Airways Pty Ltd, Launceston, Tas, to cover aircraft shortage due to the loss of two DH.86 Express aircraft; used on Melbourne to Sydney route; regd **VH-UFF** (CoR 563) 30.12.35 to Holyman's Airways Pty Ltd, named *Memma*; operations commenced 27.1.36; regd 25.11.36 to Australian National Airways Pty Ltd, Melbourne; regd 28.6.38 to Airlines of Australia Ltd, Sydney (Mascot); regn cld 18.7.40; impressed into RAAF 12.7.40 as **A33-3**; 3 EFTS, Essendon; 1 AOS, Cootamundra 25.9.40; 3 CF, Mascot, 24.8.42; 36 Sqn, Essendon, 10.9.42; carried radio call sign **VHCRP**; 34 Sqn, Parafield, 2.1.43; to Department of Civil Aviation 15.11.43; restored to register as **VH-UFF** 21.11.43 to DCA for operation by Guinea Airways, Adelaide, SA; sold 17.2.45 and regd 30.6.45 to Airlines (WA) Ltd, Perth, and used for experimental sowing of clover seeds; sold 1.10.48 and regd 15.10.48 to Brown & Dureau Ltd, Geelong (Belmont Common), Vic, for photo survey work; regd 12.4.55 to W E James, t/a James Air Charter, Wollongong, NSW; regn cld 11.4.56 as sold in New Caledonia; regd **F-OAVG** 10.8.56 to Sté Calédonienne de Transports Aériens, Noumea for use by Transpac; last flight 11.6.57 and immediately broken up for spares for F-OATC; CoA suspended at Noumea (Magenta) 3.3.59.

6271   RAF serial **K4772**; the first DH.89M, ordered in response to Air Ministry specification G.18/35; TOC by A&AEE, Martlesham Heath, 13.4.35 for performance trials as GR aircraft;

Coast Defence Development Unit, Gosport, 13.5.35; A&AEE 3.6.35; RAE, Farnborough, 19.6.35; Instrument and Photographic Flight; Wireless & Telegraphic Flt 9.35; Instrument and Photographic Flt 5.36 for automatic control tests; 8 MU, Little Rissington, 13.11.39; RAE, Farnborough, 2.12.39; A&AEE, Boscombe Down, 4.4.40, used by 'B' Flt, Armament Testing Section, as communications aircraft; 9 MU, Cosford, 23.11.40; 38 MU, Llandow, 14.2.41; 32 MU, St Athan, 18.5.41; HQ SFS, Kemble, 18.7.41; DGRD at Lockheed Aircraft, Speke, 24.7.41; CRD at A&AEE 30.8.41; DH RU, Witney, 15.6.42; SOC 15.7.42; reduced to spares.

6272   Regd **G-ADAE** (CoR 5477) 20.2.35 to Northern & Scottish Airways Ltd, Newcastle and Renfrew; CoA (4699) issued 17.4.35; del with United Airways titles 19.4.35; regd 5.35 to United Airways Ltd, Blackpool; transferred to British Airways Ltd 1.10.35 and regd to them (CoR 6852) 24.3.36; based at Eastleigh; regd (CoR 8092) 28.8.37 to Airwork Ltd, Heston; regn cld 5.38; regd in Denmark as **OY-DIN** (CoR 101, CoA 79) 28.5.38 to Provins Luftfartsselskabet A/S and operated by DDL, Copenhagen (Kastrup); operated by 721 Sqn RDAF .40; regn cld as sold to UK 8.5.46; regd **G-ADAE** 12.6.46 to Stewart Smith and Co Ltd for operation by Southampton Air Services Ltd, Eastleigh; CoA renewed 29.7.46; regd 12.9.46 to Airborne Taxi Services Ltd, Elstree; regd 11.6.47 to Air Charter Experts Ltd, Ronaldsway; CoA lapsed 28.7.47; scrapped at Ronaldsway 8.48.

6273   CoA issued 13.3.35; originally regd **OO-APO** but NTU; regd **OO-JFN** to J Mahieu, Mons (CoR 325); regn cld 24.5.37, listed as sold to France but not regd there; possibly used in Spanish Civil War; NFT.

OY-DIN, c/n 6272, was operated by DDL of Copenhagen and later by the Royal Danish Air Force   *[G M Simons collection]*

Operated by the Nationalist side in the Spanish Civil War was DH.89 40-2, c/n 6277   *[P H T Green collection]*

6274   Regd **G-ACZU** (CoR 5450) 20.3.35 to the Rt Hon Viscount Furness, Burrough Court, Melton Mowbray; CoA (4748) issued 25.3.35; del to Cairo 28.3.35 by owner's personal pilot, Capt D P Cameron; regd (CoR 7616) 22.1.37 to Cinema Press Ltd, operated by Croydon Airways, Croydon; regn cld 7.37 as sold abroad; believed one of three aircraft purchased by Juan de la Cierva and Louis Bolín for use in Spanish Civil War; NFT.

6275   Regd **G-ADAO** (CoR 5499) 16.2.35 to T R A Bevan as nominee for Ethyl Export Corp, Brooklands; CoA (4697) issued 5.4.35; flown throughout Europe, Africa and the Middle East by D W Lucke; regn cld 9.36 as sold; purchased by Juan de la Cierva and Louis Bolín for use by Nationalists in Spanish Civil War; left Heston for Spain 13.8.36; converted to bomb-carrying Rapide with machine gun in side of nose; to Air Transportation Group 40, possibly as **40-1** (but 40-5 also quoted, see 6312); regd to Iberia Airlines 1.43 believed as **EC-CAQ**, to **EC-ABG** by 7.51; w/o Guinea 30.7.53. (Also suggested as EC-AAV 1.43, see 6425)

6276   Regd **G-ADAJ** (CoR 5485) .35 to unknown operator; regd (CoR 5869) 1.5.35 to Hillman's Airways Ltd, Stapleford Tawney; CoA (4829) issued 5.6.35; transferred to British Airways Ltd 11.12.35 and regd to them (CoR 6629) 10.1.36; regd (CoR 7364) 22.9.36 to Highland Airways Ltd, Kintore; del 26.12.36; named *Inverness* 7.37; merged into Scottish Airways Ltd, Inverness, 12.8.37 and regd (CoR 8565) to them 18.6.38; operated by AAJC during WW2; regd 1.2.47 to BEA; regn cld 21.11.47 as sold abroad; regd in France as **F-BEDY** 22.4.48 to Air France, Ivato, Madagascar; regd **F-OADY** 31.5.49 to same owner; retd to Le Bourget late .49; regd **F-BAHY** 21.10.50 to Air France and operated by Ecole de l'Aviation Civile; sold 10.7.52 to Sté Autrex Lopez & Cie, Hanoi, Indo-China; crashed

into trees on take-off from Séno, Savannakhet, Laos, 20.8.54; regn cld 22.12.56.

6277   Regd **G-ADCL** (CoR 5602) 16.4.35 to Anglo-American Oil Co Ltd, Redhill as replacement for G-ACTT; CoA (4784) issued 4.5.35; overturned on landing at Redhill 26.6.35, killing Brendan (Jimmy) Hanstock, Gen Mgr of Anglo-American; rebuilt by DH; regd (CoR 6607) 19.12.35 to Airwork Ltd, Heston; bought by Juan de la Cierva for Spanish Nationalists; left Heston for Spain 1.8.36, piloted by Lord Malcolm Douglas-Hamilton; converted by Capt A Salas as fighter-bomber fitted with forward-firing Vickers gun, almost certainly as serial **40-2** *Capitan Vela*; retained as personal aircraft of Maj J-A Ansaldo; later used as trainer by Spanish Air Force; regd **EC-AAY** to Iberia Airlines 1.40 (see also 6427); crashed in Spanish Guinea 22.6.46.

6278   Regd **G-ADAH** (CoR 5483) 30.1.35 to Hillman's Airways Ltd, Stapleford Tawney; CoA (4690) issued 19.2.35; transferred to British Airways Ltd 11.12.35; regd to them (CoR 6782) 27.2.36; regd (CoR 7275) 19.8.36 to Northern & Scottish Airways Ltd, Renfrew, and operated in joint livery; regd (CoR 8097) 31.8.37 to Airwork Ltd, Heston; sold 26.5.38 to E L Gandar Dower t/a Allied Airways (Gandar Dower) Ltd, Dyce, and regd to them (CoR 8843) 26.10.38, named *Thurso Venturer* (*Thurso Wanderer* ??) later *Pioneer*; operated by AAJC during WW2; regd 2.12.42 to Sec of State for Air, Dyce; regd 31.10.44 to Allied Airways (Gandar Dower) Ltd, Dyce; regd 25.7.46 to E L Gandar Dower t/a Allied Airways; CoA lapsed 9.6.47 and stored at Dyce; regn cld 18.2.59; moved by road to Personal Plane Services Ltd, Booker, 8.66 for rebuild; to Northern Aircraft Preservation Society, Peel Green, 10.70; loaned to Royal Scottish Museum, East Fortune, .74; to Manchester Museum of Science & Industry 7.4.89; refurbished .91-.95; extant.

Rapide G-ADAH, c/n 6278, in RAF camouflage on communications duty at Redhill in May 1940   *[C Nepean Bishop via P H T Green]*

CF-AEO, c/n 6279, was the prototype float conversion of the DH.89, but lasted only three weeks in the service of Quebec Airways before being written off

[Denis Fox collection]

6279   Del to Canada without UK CoA and issued with type approval 18.6.35 by RCAF at Rockcliffe; prototype floatplane conversion, fitted with Fairchild floats and longer dorsal fin; regd **CF-AEO** 28.6.35 to Quebec Airways Ltd, Montreal; crashed and DBF on take-off from Moncton, New Brunswick, 18.7.35; regn cld same day.

6280   Regd **G-ADBU** (CoR 5570) 27.4.35 to United Airways Ltd, Heston and Blackpool (Stanley Park); CoA issued 29.4.35; merged into British Airways Ltd 1.10.35 and regd to them (CoR 6697) 31.1.36; transferred to Northern & Scottish Airways Ltd, Renfrew, 11.6.36 and regd to them (CoR 7276) 19.8.36; DBR 11.36 and regn cld.

6281   Regd **G-ADAK** (CoR 5486) to Hillman's Airways Ltd but not delivered; regd (CoR 5869) 10.5.35 to British Continental Airways Ltd, Croydon, named *St Patrick*; CoA (4827) issued 14.5.35; transferred to British Airways Ltd 1.8.36 but not used; sold to Airwork Ltd, Heston, 8.36; sold to C Stave 8.36 on behalf of Spanish Republicans, financed through Union Founders Trust Ltd; sold to Le Fédération Populaire des Sports Aéronautiques 28.8.36; regd (CoR 7317) 3.9.36 to C H Stave, Croydon; a group of Frenchmen attempted to steal this aircraft from Air Dispatch's hangar on 5.9.36, but were foiled; sale to Spain for use by Republicans in Spanish Civil War banned by British Government; regd (CoR 7553) 15.12.36 to Union Founders Trust Ltd, Croydon; sold 1.37 to Air Dispatch Ltd, Croydon; regd (CoR 7737) 5.3.37 to Mutual Finance Ltd, Croydon; regd (CoR 8408) to J Wormald, Croydon, probably as nominee for Air Dispatch Ltd; regd 2.12.39 to Hon Mrs Victor Bruce and operated by Air Dispatch Ltd, Pengam Moors; regd 1.2.40 to Anglo-European Airways Ltd, Pengam

Moors; regd 14.5.40 to Air Dispatch Ltd, Pengam Moors; impressed into RAF 7.7.40 as **AW155**; 8 AACU, Filton, 7.7.40 (later Weston Zoyland, Old Sarum and Cardiff); DH 31.12.40; 18 MU, Dumfries, 28.6.41;1 OAPU, Kemble, 4.4.42; 6 AOS, Staverton, 9.8.42; unit redes 6 (O) AFU 11.6.43; DH RU, Witney, 17.6.43 as Cat B; SF Halton 21.9.43; DH RU, Witney, 11.9.44; SOC 26.9.44.

6282   Regd **G-ADDE** (CoR 5634) 7.5.35 to Aberdeen Airways Ltd, named *The Aberdonian;* CoA (4815) issued 31.5.35; del 9.7.35; regd 2.37 to Allied Airways (Gandar Dower) Ltd, Dyce; regd (CoR 8158) 21.10.37 to North Eastern Airways Ltd, Croydon; impressed into RAF 27.3.40; 110 Wg, Ringway, 27.3.40; allocated serial **X9386** 31.3.40; 6 AACU, Ringway, 25.5.40; regn cld 27.5.40; 24 Sqn, Hendon, 28.5.40 and detached to France; DH RU, Witney, 3.12.40; ATA, White Waltham, 3.6.41; 39 MU CF, Colerne, 1.10.41; stored at 39 MU 24.6.42; 24 Sqn, Gatwick, 11.9.42; SF Gatwick 8.2.43; DH RU, Witney, as Cat B 23.3.44; RAE, Farnborough, 10.6.44; DH RU, Witney, 18.8.45; 5 MU, Kemble, 8.11.45 for disposal; sold to Allied Airways (Gandar Dower) Ltd 24.3.47, presumably for spares as not restored to register.

6283   Regd **G-ADDD** (CoR 5632) 4.3.35 to Flt Lt Edward Fielden AFC on behalf of Edward, Prince of Wales; CoA (4802) issued 8.6.35; first aircraft to carry a reigning British monarch when King Edward VIII flew from Bircham Newton to Hendon on 21.1.36, the day after King George V died; King's Flight, Hendon, 21.7.36; sold to Norman Edgar (Western Airways) Ltd, Weston-super-Mare, 8.5.37; regd (CoR 7892) 25.5.37 to The Channel Trust Ltd (as nominee); regd (CoR 8444) 9.4.38 to Weston Airport Ltd and operated by Western Airways Ltd, Weston-super-Mare; regd (CoR

G-ADDD, c/n 6283, originally used by Prince Edward, in service later with Western Airways. The rudder stripes were red and white and the fuselage colour was dark blue, the colours of the Brigade of Guards

[via R C Sturtivant]

G-ADBV, c/n 6286, in the livery of Western Airways, was later impressed into the RAF as X8511   *[Denis Fox collection]*

G-ADAI, c/n 6287, its owner not recorded, with G-ADAK, c/n 6281 in the background. Their early careers were very similar   *[via A. Chivers]*

Rapide G-ADBW, c/n 6288, at Staverton in May or June 1940 when in use by 6 AONS, operated at the time by Airwork Ltd. This aircraft later became Z7262, although it never carried the serial   *[Denis Fox collection]*

8855) 1.11.38 to Western Airways Ltd, Weston-super-Mare; made first ever scheduled night service within the UK; impressed into RAF 1.6.40; 8 AACU, Pengam Moors; allocated serial **AW116** 25.7.40; DH RU, Witney, for inspection 7.4.41, but SOC 22.5.41 as BER.

6284 Regd **G-ADDF** (CoR 5635) .35 to Aberdeen Airways Ltd, Dyce, but probably not delivered; CoA (4994) issued 8.8.35; regd (CoR 6243) 27.8.35 to Hillman's Airways Ltd, Stapleford Tawney; transferred to British Airways Ltd 11.12.35 and regd to them (CoR 6628) 10.21.36; transferred to Northern & Scottish Airways Ltd, Renfrew, 29.6.36 and regd (CoR 7277) to them 19.8.36; regd (CoR 8098) 31.8.37 to Airwork Ltd, Heston; sold to Lejeune Aviation before 7.9.37; regn cld 9.37 as sold abroad; probably used by Republicans in Spanish Civil War; NFT.

6285 CoA (4966) issued 20.7.35; left Croydon 1.8.35, arr Salisbury, Southern Rhodesia, 11.8.35; regd **VP-YAU** 8.35 to Rhodesia and Nyasaland Airways Ltd, Salisbury; taken over by Southern Rhodesia Air Services 9.39 as **301**; restored to **VP-YAU** 4.42; SOC 8.44.

6286 Regd **G-ADBV** (CoR 5571) 4.35 to United Airways Ltd but not delivered; regd (CoR 5915) 28.5.35 to Jersey Airways Ltd, Heston, named *St Ouen's Bay II*; CoA (4795) issued 6.6.35; regd (CoR 7900) 31.5.37 to J Dade as nominee for Norman Edgar (Western Airways) Ltd, Weston-super-Mare; regd (CoR 8855) 1.11.38 to Western Airways Ltd, Weston-super-Mare; impressed into the RAF; 24 Sqn, Hendon, 3.10.39; regn cld 12.1.40; allocated serial **X8511** 2.3.40; DH RU, Witney, 22.10.41; SOC 2.11.41.

6287 Regd **G-ADAI** (CoR 5484) .35 to Hillman's Airways Ltd but not delivered; regd (CoR 5868) 10.5.35 to British Continental Airways Ltd, Croydon, named *St Andrew*; CoA (4828) issued 20.6.35; transferred to British Airways Ltd 1.8.36 and regd (CoR 7684) to them 17.2.37; regd (CoR 8091) to Airwork Ltd, Heston, 28.8.37 and operated by Martin's Navigation Ltd at 6 CANS, Shoreham (later Staverton); unit redes 6 AONS 1.11.39; allocated serial **Z7262** 7.40 but civil markings retained; SF Ringway 1.7.40; regn cld 15.7.40; 7 AACU, Castle Bromwich, 26.7.40; DBR in crash at Shawbury 31.7.40; SOC 2.12.40.

6288 Regd **G-ADBW** (CoR 5572) .35 to United Airways Ltd but not delivered; regd (CoR 5916) 28.5.35 to Jersey Airways Ltd, Heston; CoA (4796) issued 27.6.35; sold 21.7.38, possibly to Airwork Ltd, Heston, to whom regd 30.1.39; operated by 6 CANS, Shoreham (later Staverton); unit redes 6 AONS 1.11.39; impressed into RAF as **Z7265** 15.7.40; 6 AONS, Staverton; Ringway 17.7.40; 7 AACU, Castle Bromwich, 29.7.40; 8 AACU, Old Sarum, (later Pengam Moors) 9.10.40; SOC 17.11.41.

6289 Regd **G-ADBX** (CoR 5573) to United Airways Ltd, Blackpool (Stanley Park); CoA (4797) issued 4.7.35; transferred to

British Airways Ltd 1.10.35 and regd to them (CoR 6789) 2.3.36; crashed on landing at Newtownards 3.3.36; regn cld 5.36.

6290 Regd **G-ADFX** (CoR 5764) 17.6.35 to British-American Air Services Ltd, Heston; CoA (4903) issued 22.7.35; receiver appointed 6.1.37 and nominal change of ownership (CoR 7708) 23.2.37 to LHG Ltd, Heston (Lillian H Gibbs, wife of MD); regd 27.6.39 to (new) British-American Air Services Ltd, Heston; at DH RU, Witney, 22.4.40; regn cld 27.4.40; impressed into RAF 28.4.40 as **X9457**; 6 AACU, Ringway, 1.5.40; 24 Sqn, Hendon, 28.5.40; 1 ADF, Hendon, 11.4.41; 24 Sqn, Hendon, 31.7.41; DH RU, Witney, 17.9.41; 79 (Sigs) Wg Cal Flt, Long Kesh, 2.5.42; 77 (Sigs) Wg Cal Flt Speke, 7.11.42; 79 (Sigs) Wg Cal Flt, Speke, 4.1.43; force-landed in field near Sywell 17.5.43 and badly damaged when it hit ridge and tipped on nose; DH RU, Witney, for repair, but SOC 5.6.43.

6291 Regd **G-ADFY** (CoR 5769) 28.6.35 to W H Rhodes-Moorhouse, Heston; CoA (4928) issued 26.7.35; regd (CoR 6599) 14.12.35 to C E Gardner, Hamsey Green; regn cld 8.36 as sold abroad; purchased by Juan de la Cierva and Louis Bolín for use with Nationalist side in Spanish Civil War; flown to Spain 4.8.36 by A Rowley and probably allocated serial **40-3**; operated by El Conde de Cimera, Madrid; either shot down 27.8.36 or destroyed by fire at Aragón 13.9.36.

6292 CoA (5047) issued 30.8.35 to Asiatic Petroleum Co; regd **PH-AKV** 4.9.35 to KNILM for survey work in Dutch New Guinea on behalf of Asiatic Petroleum Co (Royal Dutch Shell), named *Vera*; regd in Dutch East Indies as **PK-AKV** 24.1.36 to KNILM; destroyed at Andir on request of the Army during invasion of Singapore by Japanese in 2.42.

6293 Regd **G-ADIM** (CoR 5933) 25.7.35 to British Continental Airways Ltd, Croydon, named *St David*; CoA (4972) issued 31.7.35; transferred to British Airways Ltd 1.8.36 and regd to them (CoR 7685) 18.2.37; regd (CoR 8093) 28.8.37 to Airwork Ltd, Heston; operated by Martin's Navigation Ltd/6 CANS, Shoreham (later Staverton); unit redes 6 AONS 1.11.39; impressed into RAF 15.7.40 as **Z7263**; 110 (AAC) Wg, Ringway 17.7.40; 8 AACU, Pengam Moors, 27.11.40; Old Sarum 24.9.41; 4 Sqn, Clifton, 14.3.42; on take-off from Doncaster 11.4.42 (still marked G-ADIM) made a half circuit of the airfield, dived, flattened out but struck a tree and burst into flames before crashing onto a road; SOC 9.5.42.

6294 CoA (5048) issued 30.8.35 to Asiatic Petroleum Co; regd **PH-AKW** 4.9.35 to KNILM for survey work in Dutch New Guinea on behalf of Asiatic Petroleum Co (Royal Dutch Shell); regd in Dutch East Indies as **PK-AKW** 24.1.36 to KNILM; DBR on overturning on landing at Babo, Dutch New Guinea, 7.3.36.

CF-AVJ, c/n 6295, which was used by Canadian Airways from September 1935 until it was burnt out in May 1939   *[G M Simons collection]*

6295 Regd **CF-AVJ** (CoR 1677) 24.9.35 to Canadian Airways Ltd, Winnipeg; fitted with additional door on starboard side; regd (CoR 2201/A168) 30.3.38 to (subsidiary) Quebec Airways Ltd, Montreal; DBF at St John, NB, 17.5.39 when port exhaust started a fire during engine start-up.

6296 CoA (5050) issued 2.9.35 to Asiatic Petroleum Co; regd **PH-AKU** (CoR 174) 4.9.35 to KNILM for survey work in Dutch New Guinea on behalf of Asiatic Petroleum Co (Royal Dutch Shell); regd in Dutch East Indies as **PK-AKU** 24.1.36 to KNILM; DBR in crash at Ketapang, Madura, West Borneo, 16.8.38.

6297 Regd **G-ADNG** (CoR 6157) 15.8.35 to Iraq Petroleum Transport Co Ltd, Haifa; CoA (5156) issued 5.10.35; del via Malta 14.10.35; crashed 30 mls E of Rutbah Wells 10.3.36; regn cld 8.36.

6298 CoA (5029) issued 27.8.35; regd **SU-ABP** 8.35 to Misr Airwork Ltd, named *Al Kahira*; crashed nr Maryut 6.2.45, killing pilot and six passengers.

6299 CoA (5074) issued 11.9.35; regd **SU-ABQ** 9.35 Misr Airwork Ltd, named *Thebes*; crashed on landing 18 mls N of Port Sudan 9.10.41.

6300 Regd **G-ADNH** (CoR 6158) 15.8.35 to Iraq Petroleum Transport Co Ltd, Haifa; CoA (5164) issued 11.10.35; regd (CoR 8571) 22.6.38 to Mutual Finance Ltd and operated by Air Dispatch Ltd, Croydon; regd 5.2.40 to Hon Mrs Victor Bruce and operated by Air Dispatch Ltd, Pengam Moors; impressed into RAF 11.1.40; 24 Sqn, Hendon 11.1.40; allocated serial **W6423** 1.3.40; regn cld 1.3.40; damaged by enemy action at Coulommiers, France, 16.5.40 (engines and equipment were salvaged, but remains were abandoned); SOC 3.6.40.

6301 Regd **G-ADNI** (CoR 6159) 15.8.35 to Iraq Petroleum Transport Co Ltd, Haifa; CoA (5166) issued 17.10.35; del 21.10.35; regd (CoR 8572) 22.6.38 to Mutual Finance Ltd and operated by Air Dispatch Ltd, Croydon; regd 27.2.40 to Anglo-European Airways Ltd, Pengam Moors; regn cld as sold 11.2.40 (sic); impressed into RAF 12.4.40 as **W9365**; 24 Sqn, Hendon, 12.4.40; damaged in France 5.40 and collected by 21 AD, Bouguenais, 7.6.40; SOC 22.6.40 upon inspection.

6302 CoA (5092) issued 20.9.35; regd **SU-ABR** 9.35 to Misr Airwork Ltd, named *Memphis*; believed sold 5.48 to Jordan or Yemen; regn cld; NFT.

The wreckage of Rapide PK-AKU, c/n 6296, of KNILM after its accident on 16th August 1938 at Ketapang, Borneo   *[Denis Fox collection]*

6303 CoA (5129) issued 25.9.35; regd **SU-ABS** 9.35 to Misr Airwork Ltd, named *Helwan*; believed sold 5.48 to Jordan or Yemen; regn cld; NFT.

6304 Regd **CF-AYE** (CoR 1689) 11.4.36 to de Havilland Aircraft of Canada Ltd, Toronto; to British North American Airways, Toronto, 13.5.37?; regd (CoR 2022) 5.9.38 to Quebec Airways Ltd, Montreal; merged 1.42 into Canadian Pacific Airlines; sometime named *Zeballos Empress* (but see 6679!); regd 31.7.47 to Central Northern Airways Ltd, Winnipeg; to Queen Charlotte Airlines Ltd, Vancouver, .49; WFU and to Vancouver Fire Dept; regn cld 24.8.51.

6305 CoA (5169) issued 18.10.35; regd **ZK-AED** (CoR 41) 9.12.35 to Cook Strait Airways Ltd, Wellington; assembled at Auckland by DH agent, Air Survey & Transport Co; arr Nelson 26.12.35 and based there, named *Venus*; inaugurated Wellington to Hokitika service 10.37; impressed into RNZAF 1.11.39 as **NZ556**; AG&AOS, Ohakea [6] 14.11.39; Fiji Det Flt, Nandi, 1.11.40 (fitted with bomb racks); wrecked during hurricane at Nausori 20.2.41.

6306 CoA (5174) issued 22.10.35; regd **ZK-AEE** (CoR 42) 9.12.35 to Cook Strait Airways Ltd, Wellington; assembled at Auckland by DH agent, Air Survey & Transport Co; arr Nelson 26.12.35 and based there, named *Jupiter*; badly damaged in hangar fire at Nelson 22.11.37 but repaired; impressed into RNZAF 10.11.39 as **NZ559**; AG&AOS, Ohakea 14.11.39; Fiji Det Flt 1.11.40; wrecked during hurricane at Nausori 20.2.41.

SU-ABQ, c/n 6299, "Thebes" was one of the five DH.89s aquired by Misr Airlines   *[G M Simons collection]*

CF-AYE, c/n 6304, as a landplane operated by Quebec Airways in 1942 on air survey tasks. Note the non-standard undercarriage fairings – no spats fitted to allow ease of float attachment when required

[G M Simons collection]

6307 Regd **CF-BBC** (CoR 1840) 2.11.36 to Canadian Airways Ltd, Winnipeg; regd (CoR 1852) 4.12.36 to same owner; regd (CoR 2198/A165) 28.3.38 to (subsidiary) Quebec Airways Ltd, Montreal, 28.3.38; taken over by Canadian Pacific Airways 1942; out of fuel, force-landed on floating ice on St Lawrence river nr Mont Joli, Quebec, 23.12.46; subsequently sank, but six of seven on board rescued after several days on ice floe.

6308 Regd **VT-AHB** (CoR 270) 6.12.35 to The Maharaja of Jammu and Kashmir, Srinagar; CoA (5256) issued 11.12.35; fitted with a luxury interior; regd (CoR 270/2) 6.5.37 to Air Services of India Ltd, Bombay; crashed at Kampur 30.12.45; regn cld 2.2.46.

6309 Used for design modifications and airworthiness tests at A&AEE, Martlesham Heath, 4.35, possibly under Class B markings; regd **G-ADWZ** (CoR 6466) 8.11.35 to de Havilland Aircraft Co Ltd, Hatfield as DH.89A; CoA (5206) issued 9.11.35; first aircraft to be fitted with cabin heat; regd (CoR 6866) 27.3.36 to Personal Airways Ltd, Croydon; Republican agents attempted to purchase aircraft for use in Spanish Civil War, but sale was blocked by British Government; flown to Paris and

regd **F-APES** (CoR 4888) 16.10.36, but was forced to return; regn cld 1.37 as 'sale cancelled'; re-regd (CoR 7618) 221.37 to Personal Airways Ltd, Croydon; regd (CoR 8893) 21.11.38 to North Eastern Airways Ltd, Doncaster (later Croydon); regn cld as sold 12.4.40; impressed into RAF 10.5.40 as **X9449**; 6 AACU, Ringway; 7 AACU, Castle Bromwich, 26.7.40; still marked as G-ADWZ, crash-landed at Llanrhaeadr-ym-Mochnant, Denbighshire, 2.8.40 due to fuel shortage while carrying out Army Co-operation duties at night; to Air Taxis Ltd, Manchester, for repair 7.8.40 but SOC as BER 7.9.40.

6310 DH.89M; regd **G-ADYK** (CoR 6540) 2.12.35 to de Havilland Aircraft Co Ltd, Hatfield; CoA (5252) issued 10.12.35; to Aviación Militar (Spanish Air Force); arrived at Cuatro Vientos airfield, Madrid, 1.36; regn cld 2.36 as sold abroad; based at Escuela de Vuelo y Combate, Alcalá de Henares, allocated serial **22-1**; taken over by Spanish Republicans 8.36, and named *Capitan Pouvo*; fuselage, nacelles and inner lower wings painted black, remainder in pale ochre; transferred to Basque front and destroyed by Nationalist bombing of Albericia airfield, Santander, 6.4.37.

G-ADWZ, c/n 6309, was the first DH.89A, and in this picture was with Personal Airways. A heater muff is visible on the starboard undercarriage leg

[via C N Dodds]

6311   DH.89M; regd **G-ADYL** (CoR 6541) 2.12.35 to de Havilland Aircraft Co Ltd, Hatfield; CoA (5153) issued 10.12.35; to Aviación Militar (Spanish Air Force); arr Cuatro Vientos airfield, Madrid, 1.36; regn cld 2.36 as sold abroad; based at Escuela de Vuelo y Combate, Alcalá de Henares; allocated serial **22-2**; taken over by Spanish Republicans 8.36; fuselage, nacelles and inner lower wings painted black, remainder in pale ochre; used by Alas Rojas Sqn at Sarinena from 5.8.36; shot down over Almudevar 19.10.36 when its pilot, Luis Aguilera Cullell, attacked a patrol of Nationalist He51s to draw them away from aircraft he was escorting.
[Note: the registration **G-ADYL** was reissued in 1955 to c/n 6895 which had not previously carried UK marks.]

6312   DH.89M; regd **G-ADYM** (CoR 6542) 2.12.35 to de Havilland Aircraft Co Ltd, Hatfield; CoA (5254) issued 10.12.35; to Aviación Militar (Spanish Air Force); arr Cuatro Vientos airfield, Madrid, 1.36; regn cld 2.36 as sold abroad; based at Escuela de Vuelo y Combate, Alcalá de Henares; allocated serial **22-3**; captured by Spanish Nationalists at Zaragoza 18.7.36 when flown there in an effort to persuade the military Governor, Gen Cabanellas, to remain loyal to the Republicans; the three on board, including Gen Nuñez de Prado, were charged with treason and shot; allocated Nationalist serial **40-5**; fuselage, nacelles and inner lower wings painted black, remainder in pale ochre; attached to the Fokker/Dragon Group at Olmedo; inadvertently shot down by He.51s near Segovia 26.8.36, killing Capts Pouzo and Vela, whose names were inscribed on 40-1 and 40-2 'in memoriam'.

6313   CoA (5217) issued 16.11.35; regd **SU-ABU** 11.35 to Misr Airwork Ltd, named *Heliopolis*; believed scrapped 1948.

6314   CoA (5304) issued 17.1.36 to de Havilland Aircraft (Pty) Ltd.; regn **VH-UVG** allocated but NTU; shipped to Sydney and handed over to RAAF 4.36 as **A3-2**; used for photographic survey duties; while flying from Camooweal to Wave Hill on 13.4.36, pilot (Flt Lt W L Hely) became lost and aircraft force-landed in scrub 90 mls west of Newcastle Waters, suffering a badly damaged undercarriage, but crew unhurt; aircraft (still carrying civil registration) and survivors located 22.4.36, but not rescued for two days; fuselage salvaged and shipped from Darwin to Sydney 13.5.36 on *Merkur,* but engines and mainplanes were abandoned as too badly damaged; reconditioning by DH completed 24.2.37, during which radio equipment was fitted, making this machine probably the first aircraft in Australia to carry radio; while flying from Tennant Creek to Tanami on 21.5.37, ran short of fuel and force-landed on shore of dry Lake Mackay (500 mls W of Alice Springs); flown out 31.5.37; crashed at Laverton 3.2.38 when wing-tip touched ground on approach, causing the

aircraft to cartwheel; Flg Off D McLean and two crew uninjured; remains sold to ANA for £912.

6315   Regd **G-ADUM** (CoR 6361) 16.3.36 to de Havilland Aircraft Co Ltd, Hatfield; CoA (5474) issued 30.4.36; regn cld 5.36 as sold abroad; regd in Turkey 5.36 as **TC-ARI** to Devlet Hava Yollari (fleet no 3); regd **TC-ALI** 4.7.47 to Hurkus Airlines, Ankara; WFU .59 but still regd 6.60.

6316   Regd **G-ADUN** (CoR 6362) 16.3.36 to de Havilland Aircraft Co Ltd, Hatfield; CoA (5475) issued 30.4.36; regn cld 5.36 as sold abroad 5.36; regd in Turkey 5.36 as **TC-BAY** to Devlet Hava Yollari (fleet no 4); to Hurkus Airlines, Ankara, pre-5.60; NFT

6317   Regd **G-ADUO** (CoR 6363) 16.3.36 to de Havilland Aircraft Co Ltd, Hatfield; CoA (5476) issued 30.4.36; regn cld 5.36 as sold abroad; regd in Turkey 5.36 as **TC-CAN** to Devlet Hava Yollari, Turkey (fleet no 5); to Hurkus Airlines, Ankara, pre-5.60; NFT

6318   CoA (5323) issued 7.2.36; regd **VH-UVI** (CoR 577) 15.4.36 to Adelaide Airways Ltd, Parafield, SA; used on routes to Melbourne via Mt. Gambier and to Broken Hill; taken over 1.11.36 and regd 25.11.36 to Australian National Airways Pty Ltd, Essendon, named *Moogana*; regd 8.8.39 to Guinea Airways Ltd, Adelaide, SA, named *Bulolo;* impressed into RAAF 12.7.40 as **A33-2**; 1 EFTS, Parafield, 12.7.40; 1 AOS, Cootamundra 18.10.40; crashed in heavily-wooded paddock 1 ml NW of Cootamundra 20.6.41 following engine failure on take-off, killing Flg Off W W Adrian and injuring four crew; SOC 30.7.41.

6319   Regd **G-ADUP** (CoR 6364), but NTU; CoA (5324) issued 11.2.36; arrived Australia 3.36; regd **VH-UVT** 15.4.36 to Adelaide Airways Ltd., Parafield, SA; used on routes to Melbourne via Mt Gambier and to Broken Hill; taken over 1.11.36 and regd 25.11.36 to Australian National Airways Pty Ltd, Melbourne, named *Monana*; crashed at Mount Gambier 30.6.37 when aircraft struck a windmill as pilot attempted to avoid birds on landing ground; pilot badly hurt but five passengers escaped; badly damaged aircraft trucked to Essendon for protracted rebuild; regd 17.4.41 to Airlines of Australia Ltd, Sydney, named *Memma;* regd 15.6.43 to Australian National Airways Pty Ltd, Melbourne; regd 7.2.50 to Butler Air Transport Pty Ltd, Sydney (Mascot); regd 14.2.53 to Connellan Airways Ltd, Alice Springs, NT; CoR lapsed 28.1.54; regn cld 5.11.54; WFU at Alice Springs.

6320   Regd **G-AEAJ** (CoR 6639) 22.2.36 to Railway Air Services Ltd, Barton, named *Star of Lancashire*; CoA (5349) issued 14.3.36; regd (CoR 8148) 19.10.37 to Isle of Man Air Services Ltd, Ronaldsway, named *RMA Castletown;* impressed

One of the Rapides, c/ns 6321-3, for the Imperial Iranian Air Force at Hatfield before delivery, its paintwork not yet completed. A fixed screened loop aerial by Marconi can be seen
[via C N Dodds]

into RAF; 24 Sqn, Hendon, 10.39; regn cld as sold 4.1.40; allocated serial **W6425** 1.3.40; 9 MU, Cosford, 17.9.40; Andover 25.10.40; 7 FPP, Sherburn-in-Elmet, 15.2.41; ATA, White Waltham, 23.2.41; 271 Sqn, Doncaster, 22.2.42; 9 MU, Cosford, 23.2.42; Exeter 6.8.42; collided with stationary Tiger Moth DE481 while taxying, 20.8.42; DH RU, Witney, for repair 2.10.42; 18 MU, Dumfries, 28.2.43; 55 OTU, Annan, 12.4.43; unit redes as 4 TEU 26.1.44 and 3 TEU 21.3.44; 53 OTU, Kirton-in-Lindsey, 22.4.44; 3 TEU, Aston Down, 8.8.44; DH RU, Witney, 7.9.44 for inspection but SOC 26.9.44.

6321   CoA (5503) issued 13.5.36 to Imperial Iranian War Ministry; del 7.36 and assembled by Peter de Havilland at Arvaz; used on internal services by Imperial Iranian AF in co-operation with Min of Posts Telegraphs & Telephones; regd **EP-AAA** 3.38 to Iranian State Airlines; seized by RAF .41 and impressed 1.43 as **HK917**; restored as **EP-AAA** .45 to Director General of Civil Aviation; NFT

6322   CoA (5449) issued 18.4.36 to Imperial Iranian War Ministry; del 7.36 and assembled by Peter de Havilland at Arvaz; used on internal services by Imperial Iranian AF in co-operation with Min of Posts Telegraphs & Telephones; regd **EP-AAB** 3.38 to Iranian State Airlines; seized by RAF .41 and impressed 1.43 as **HK916**; SOC by .45 (possibly crashed 4.43).

6323   CoA (5450) issued 18.4.36 to Imperial Iranian War Ministry; del 7.36 and assembled by Peter de Havilland at Arvaz; used on internal services by Imperial Iranian AF in co-operation with Min of Posts Telegraphs & Telephones; regd **EP-AAC** 3.38 to Iranian State Airlines; seized by RAF .41 and impressed 1.43 as **HK915**; SOC by .45 (possibly crashed 4.43).

6324   Regd **G-AEAK** (CoR 6640) 22.2.36 to Railway Air Services Ltd, Barton, named *Star of Mona*; CoA (5350) issued 4.4.36; regd (CoR 8149) 19.10.37 to Isle of Man Air Services Ltd, Ronaldsway; hit trees and crashed on landing at Speke, 25.4.39; Capt J Hesketh badly injured; regn cld 18.5.39.

6325   Regd **G-AEAL** (CoR 6641) 22.2.36 to Railway Air Services Ltd, Barton, named *Star of Yorkshire*; CoA (5351) issued 25.4.36; regd (CoR 8150) 19.10.37 to Isle of Man Air Services Ltd, Ronaldsway; impressed into RAF; 24 Sqn, Hendon, 30.9.39; no serial allocated; reverted to Isle of Man Air Services Ltd/AAJC 12.39 and operated during WW2 from Speke; regd 29.5.45 to Field Consolidated Aircraft Services Ltd, Croydon; regd 1.4.46 to Hunting Aerosurveys Ltd, Luton; regd 22.3.53 to Wolverhampton Aviation Ltd, Wolverhampton; merged with sister company Derby Aviation Ltd, Burnaston .54; sold 22.11.55 and regd 13.3.56 to R K Dundas Ltd; regn cld 10.4.56 as sold abroad; regd in France as **F-OAUE** 26.4.56

to Cie des Transports Aériens Intercontinentaux (TAI); operated by Air Ivoire, Abidjan; regd .60 to Sté Générale d'Affrètements Aériens (Air Fret), Algiers; CoA lapsed 9.1.62; regn cld 2.64.

6326   Regd **G-AEAM** (CoR 6642) 22.2.36 to Railway Air Services Ltd, Barton, named *Star of Ulster*; CoA (5352) issued 5.5.36; regd (CoR 8151) 19.10.37 to Isle of Man Air Services Ltd, Ronaldsway; impressed into RAF; 24 Sqn, Hendon, 4.9.39; regn cld 10.1.40; serial **W6424** allocated 1.3.40 but possibly not carried; force-landed at St Philbert, near Clisson, France, 23.2.40 due to fuel starvation, overran and hit ditch; dismantled and transported to 21 AD, Bouguenais, 27.2.40, where it was abandoned 16.5.40.

6327   Regd **G-AEBW** (CoR 6709) 22.2.36 to Railway Air Services Ltd, Barton, named *Star of Renfrew*; CoA (5353) issued 13.5.36; regd (CoR 8152) 19.10.37 to Isle of Man Air Services Ltd, Ronaldsway; impressed into RAF; 24 Sqn, Hendon, 4.9.39 and Le Bourget from 8.11.39; retd to Isle of Man Air Services 21.12.39 and operated by NAC; abandoned at Bordeaux 18.6.40, out of fuel.

6328   Regd **G-AEBX** (CoR 6710) 22.2.36 to Railway Air Services Ltd, Barton, named *Star of Scotia*; CoA (5354) issued 20.5.36; spun in and crashed near Belfast (Sydenham) airfield on take-off 3.7.38, killing Capt A C Larmuth and engineer R H Vaughan; regn cld 7.38.

6329   CoA (5539) issued 12.6.36 to Direction de l'Aviation Civile (Rumania); regd **YR-DRA** and operated by Liniile Aeriene Române Exploatate de Stat (LARES); destroyed in crash 29.4.37; regn cld same day.

6330   CoA (5546) issued 19.6.36 to Direction de l'Aviation Civile (Rumania) regd **YR-DRI** and operated by Liniile Aeriene Române Exploatate de Stat (LARES), renamed Liniile Aeriene Române Exploatate cu Statul 21.7.37; regd 31.3.42 to LARES; WFU .42.

6331   CoA (5568) issued 3.7.36 to Direction de l'Aviation Civile (Rumania); regd **YR-DRO** and operated by Liniile Aeriene Române Exploatate de Stat (LARES) from 21.9.36, renamed Liniile Aeriene Române Exploatate cu Statul 21.7.37; last CoA inspection 12.6.39; to Popesti-Leordeni 8.40; operated by Rumanian AF during WW2; NFT.

6332   Regd **G-AEKF** (CoR 7062) 15.6.36 to T G Mapplebeck, Belgrade as agent for Aeroput; CoA (5538) issued 15.6.36; regn cld 6.36 as sold abroad; regd in Yugoslavia 7.36 as **YU-SAS** to Aeroput; fate obscure – either captured by Germans intact or destroyed in a German air raid on Belgrade Airport 4.41.

6333   CoA (5581) issued 8.7.36; regd **CX-ABL** .36 to Ministerio de Salud Publica, Montevideo; used as air ambulance by Uruguayan Air Force; regn cld .47, but also on register .50?

Named "Star of Yorkshire", G-AEAL, c/n 6325, was used by Railway Air Services, and is seen here at Stoke-on-Trent (Meir)   [R. Lycett-Smith]

6334 CoA (5597) issued 22.7.36; regd **ZK-AEC** (CoR 65) 16.9.36 to Cook Strait Airways Ltd, Wellington; entered service 8.10.36, based at Nelson, named *Mercury;* inaugurated West Coast service 2.37; impressed into RNZAF 17.9.39 as **NZ555**; regn cld same day; AG&AOS, Ohakea [4] 14.11.39; shipped from Auckland to Nausori for Fiji Det Flt, Nandi, 1.11.40; Comms Flt Fiji 8.1.41; SOC 19.9.45 due to deterioration.

6335 Regd **G-AEGS** (CoR 6936) 13.5.36 to Iraq Petroleum Transport Co Ltd, Haifa; CoA (5497) issued 7.8.36; del via Malta 17.8.36; crashed at Affule, Palestine, 30 or 31.12.36; regn cld 12.36.

6336 Regd **G-AEMH** (CoR 7249) 8.36 to unknown operator; regd (CoR 7294) 25.8.36 to Personal Airways Ltd, Croydon; CoA (5639) issued 5.9.36; Republican agents attempted to purchase aircraft direct from DH for use in Spanish Civil War, but sale was blocked by British Government; regd (CoR 8892) 21.11.38 to North Eastern Airways Ltd, Doncaster (later Croydon); impressed into the RAF 28.3.40 as **X9387**; 6 AACU, Ringway, 28.3.40; 7 AACU, Castle Bromwich, 18.7.40; 110 (AAC) Wg, Ringway 26.7.40; 6 AACU, Ringway; force-landed near Warrington 14.8.41 due to engine failure in flight from Newtownards, overshot field and hit hedge; DH RU, Witney, for repair 18.8.41; 20 MU, Aston Down, 8.4.42; 22 MU, Silloth, 10.4.42; 41 OTU, Old Sarum, 27.6.42; damaged Cat B, to DH 12.4.43; SF Old Sarum 31.12.43; Doncaster 4.2.44; Staverton 22.10.44; 5 MU, Kemble, for disposal 25.7.45; sold to L E Hanson Air Charters 9.1.47; restored as **G-AEMH** 11.3.47 to A Hamson & Sons Ltd, Northampton; regd 11.7.47 to Air Charter Experts Ltd, Ronaldsway; re-regd 19.8.47 on take-over and change of name to Manx Air Charters Ltd; for sale by L E H Airways Ltd, Horsey Toll, 8.48; regd 9.3.49 to G Clifton, Spalding (but based at Horsey Toll); regd 4.6.52 to East Anglian Flying Services Ltd, Southend, t/a Channel Airways from .56; WFU at Ipswich 15.4.60; to Ipswich 7.60 for storage; re-regd 5.11.62 on change of name to Channel Airways Ltd; roaded to Southend 10.64 and fuselage seen there 21.7.68; roaded to Ian Jones, Burnham-on-Crouch, 19.8.72 for restoration; regn cld as 'destroyed' 14.2.73; parts to Chirk .81; reported as still owned by Ian Jones at Babbacombe, Devon, .85; remains probably at Chirk .03.

6337 Regd **G-AEML** (CoR 7260) 1.9.36 to Wrightways Ltd, Croydon; CoA (5643) issued 26.9.36; impressed into RAF 14.4.40 as **X9450**; 6 AACU, Ringway 14.4.40; damaged by AA fire 23.12.40; to DH RU, Witney, for repair; AFEE, Ringway, 27.10.41; Sir W G Armstrong Whitworth Aircraft Ltd, Baginton, 7.4.43 for communications duties; restored to civil register as **G-AEML** 13.3.46 to Sir W G Armstrong Whitworth Aircraft Ltd, Baginton; CoA renewed 17.5.46; regd 16.10.61 to Whitworth Gloster Aircraft Co Ltd, Baginton; regd 29.8.62 to Neil Tool Co Ltd, Panshanger; regd 10.11.65 to S J Lyons (Lines ?), Booker; del 16.12.67 and regd 26.1.68 to Liverpool Aero Engineering Co Ltd, Speke; operated by Liverpool Aero Club; regd 19.12.69 to J P Filhol Ltd, Baginton, named *The Cloth Bomber;* WFU 2.2.71; CoA lapsed 2.4.71; sold to V H Bellamy .78 and roaded to Land's End (St Just) for rebuild as Mk.4; regn cld 3.9.81; sold to Ian Jones, Babbacombe, 14.4.83 at Christie's auction; sold 4.86 to H A N Orde-Powlett; del to Barrow (Walney Island) for rebuild by Air

A fine picture of Rapide ZK-AEC, c/n 6334, of Cook Strait Airways over the city of Wellington in the late 1930s [*L L White via C N Dodds*]

Furness Ltd; sold to M V Gauntlet, Goodwood, 19.11.87 for restoration to flying condition and regd to him 11.1.88; to Rush Green 9.88 for completion of rebuild by Bowker Air Services Ltd; regd 6.1.89 to Proteus Petroleum Aviation Ltd (M V Gauntlett); regd 1.4.92 to Proteus Holdings Ltd; rebuild completed and reflown by Colin Dodds 16.4.93; CoA renewed 13.5.93; based Rendcomb, named *Proteus;* regd 14.6.95 to Amanda Investments Ltd, Rendcomb (K Whitehead); extant.

6338 CoA (5630) issued 25.8.36 to Direction de l'Aviation Civile (of Rumania) for use by N Caranfil, Under-Secretary of State for Air; regd **YR-DNC** 27.7.38 to Liniile Aeriene Române Exploatate cu Statul (LARES); to Popesti-Leordeni 8.40; written off in accident 17.7.42; regn cld 28.7.42.

G-AEMH, c/n 6336, being refuelled from a three-wheeled bowser [*via A. Chivers*]

Rapide G-AEMM of Anglo-Iranian Oil Co parked on the desert sand at Masjid-i-Sulaiman airstrip in 1938   *[via C N Dodds]*

6339   Regd **G-AEMM** (CoR 7262) 31.8.36 to Anglo-Iranian Oil Co Ltd, Abadan; CoA (5640) issued 10.10.36; retd to Heston 11.38 and regn cld 1.1.39; regd 17.3.39 to Airwork Ltd, Heston; regn cld as sold 1.4.39; regd 21.10.39 to Airwork Ltd; operated by 6 CANS, Staverton; unit redes 6 AONS 1.11.39; destroyed in mid-air collision 3.5.40; regn cld at census 30.3.46.

6340   Regd **G-AENN** (CoR 7344) 22.9.36 to Blackpool & West Coast Air Services Ltd but not del; CoA (5677) issued 25.11.36; sold by DH and regd (CoR 7489) 26.11.36 to C W F Wood (an Olley Air Service pilot) and officially based at Dar-es-Salaam but probably operated in Spain; if so, Wood probably returned to UK by 6.37; regd (CoR 8262) 13.12.37 to Olley Air Service Ltd, Croydon; impressed into RAF 23.1.40; 24 Sqn, Hendon, 23.1.40; serial **W6455** allocated 1.3.40; Skaebrae 27.5.42; 8 (C) OTU, Fraserburgh; engine failed over Rosehearty, Aberdeenshire, 13.12.42, causing the aircraft to crash-land near Fraserburgh; DH RU, Witney, as Cat B but SOC 18.1.43.

6341   Regd **G-AENO** (CoR 7345) 22.9.36 to Blackpool & West Coast Air Services Ltd, Blackpool; CoA (5667) issued 10.11.36; regd to Aer Lingus as **EI-ABP** 5.37; may have reverted to **G-AENO**; regn cld 2.38 as sold abroad; regd to Aer Lingus as **EI-ABP** 24.2.38, named *Iolar II* (since it replaced DH.84 EI-ABI); regn cld 10.2.40 as sold to Australia; erected and test flown 19.6.40; regd **VH-ADE** 27.6.40 to Guinea Airways Ltd, Adelaide, SA, named *Morobe*; impressed into RAAF 25.8.40 as **A33-7**;1 EFTS, Parafield, 25.8.40; regn cld 10.9.40; 3 EFTS, Essendon, 24.12.40;1 AOS, Cootamundra, 13.1.41; to Department of Civil Aviation 15.4.42; restored to civil register as **VH-ADE** 20.4.42 to Commonwealth of Australia Dept of Aviation; operated by Australian National Airways Pty Ltd, Melbourne; damaged 30.6.42 when struck by a DC-2 of USAAF in the ANA hangar at Essendon; repaired by 6.7.42; to Allied Works Council, Qld, 1943; struck an RAAF truck on landing at Iron Range 25.12.43 while on regular Cairns to Horne Island service; repaired by 1.1.44; damaged 26.1.44 in forced landing on a beach 13 mls S of Cape Sigmouth at Charlotte Bay, Qld; after being stripped for spares, remains were taken to Cairns and abandoned.

6342   Regd **G-AEOV** (CoR 7423) 9.12.36 to Rt Hon Viscount Forbes, Croydon (probably on behalf of Personal Airways Ltd); first flew 2.37 as **E.4**; prototype DH.89A, fitted with flaps and tested at A&AEE, Martlesham Heath; CoA (5806) issued 3.3.37; regd (CoR 8297) 14.1.38 to Mrs H Wood, Fittleworth, Sussex and operated by Personal Airways Ltd, Croydon; del 1.5.39 and regd 27.7.39 to W D T Gairdner, director/ nominee for Scottish Airways Ltd, Renfrew; impressed into RAF 1.40 as **W6456**; 24 Sqn, Hendon, 10.1.40; damaged 11.4.42 when port tyre burst while taxying at Hendon; DH RU, Witney, for repair 16.4.42, but SOC for spares.

Devoid of any other markings, c/n 6342 regd G-AEOV, was the prototype DH.89A   *[R C Sturtivant]*

EC-AKO, c/n 6345, of Aeromar at Barcelona/Sabadell on 1st August 1964   *[P H Butler]*

6343   CoA (5723) issued on 30.11.36; regd **ZK-AEW** (CoR
75) 24.2.37 to Cook Strait Airways Ltd, Wellington; based at
Nelson, named *Mars;* inaugurated Nelson – Greymouth – Hokitika
service 2.37; impressed into RNZAF 15.10.39 as **NZ557**;
AG&AOS, Ohakea [5] 14.11.39; Fiji Detd Flt 5.11.40; 4 Sqn; CF
Nausori; SOC 2.43 due to deterioration.

6344   Regd **G-AEPE** (CoR 7447) 27.11.36 to Personal
Airways Ltd, Croydon, named *Windermere*; CoA (5718) issued
24.2.37; regd (CoR 8001) 17.7.37 to Olley Air Service Ltd,
Croydon, named *The Luxembourg Listener*, used on charter to
Radio Luxembourg; impressed into RAF 4.10.39; 24 Sqn, Hendon,
11.10.39; retd to Olley Air Service Ltd/ NAC 10.2.40; retd to 24
Sqn, Hendon, 27.2.40; regd 12.7.40 to Scottish Airways Ltd,
Speke; regn cld as sold 24.7.40; impressed into RAF as **BD143**
28.7.40; 24 Sqn, Hendon; badly damaged in forced landing with
engine failure at Breston Farm, near Glengall Hospital,
Dalmellington, Ayrshire, 20.4.42; SOC 30.4.42.

6345   Regd **G-AERN** (CoR 7536) 13.1.37 to Blackpool &
West Coast Air Services Ltd, Blackpool (Squires Gate); CoA
(5820) issued 24.3.37; to West Coast Air Services Ltd, Croydon,
12.37; to AAJC for Scottish Airways Ltd, Inverness, 1.7.40; to
AAJC, Speke, 4.1.44 and operated by Railway Air Services Ltd;
regd 1.2.47 to British European Airways Corpn; regd 17.11.47 to
Gibraltar Airways Ltd; regd 29.6.53 to R A Peacock, Croydon; regn
cld 18.1.54 as sold in Spain; regd **EC-AKO** 1.12.54 to Soler de la
Riva, op by Aero Club de Barcelona-Sabadell; to Aeromar,
Barcelona; WFU .71 and stored at Barcelona/Sabadell to at least
.86; moved to Museo del Aire, Cuatro Vientos; at present undergoing major rebuild.

6346   CoA (5862) issued 2.4.37; shipped to Melbourne on
Moreton Bay; regd **VH-UXT** (CoR 641) 25.5.37 to Australian
National Airways Pty Ltd, Essendon, named *Mundoora;* test-flown
at Essendon 25.5.37; struck by strong wind gust when landing at
Kingscote strip, Kangaroo Island, SA, 5.2.38 and ran off airstrip,
causing substantial damage; shipped to Adelaide for rebuild and
test-flown 20.9.38; regn cld 19.7.40; impressed into RAAF 19.7.40
as **A33-4**; 3 EFTS, Essendon 19.7.40; 1 AOS, Cootamundra,
28.10.40; to Department of Civil Aviation 15.4.42; restored to
register as **VH-UXT** 21.4.42 for Airlines of Australia Ltd, Sydney; to
Allied Works Council, Qld, early .43; to Australian National Airways
Pty Ltd 26.6.43; over-ran landing strip into a ditch at Wynard, Tas,
18.8.43; Capt F H Dawson and three passengers uninjured; regn
cld 31.10.43; broken up for spares.

6347   CoA (5816) issued 5.3.37; regd **OH-BLA** (CoR 32)
9.3.37 to Aero O/Y, Helsinki, named *Salama;* del via Malmo and
Bromma 13.4.37; impressed into Ilmavoimat (Finnish Air Force)
14.10.39 to 19.3.40; regd 27.6.41 to Veljekset Karhumäki O/Y,
Kuorevesi; operated on behalf of Finnish Government on

ambulance flights; re-regd **OH-VKH** 20.6.46 to same owner; regd
27.11.50 to Savon Lentolinjat O/Y, Mikkeli; re-regd **OH-DHA**
31.5.54 to Lentohuolto O/Y, Helsinki; regd 4.55 to Pasenen &
Pasenen, Turku; regn cld 21.5.55 as sold in Denmark (del
14.4.55); regd **OY-DAS** 8.12.55 to Viggo Sylvest Jensen, Hillerod;
sold in West Germany 27.3.56; regd **D-IGEL** .56 to
Vermessungsburo Nico Rüpke, Hamburg and used for photographic survey work; damaged on landing at Mannheim 26.3.61;
regd 5.5.65 to Uwe Reszka, Flensburg; regd .67 to G Sueffert,
Bremen, 12.66; CoA expired 29.4.68; DBF at Weser-Wumme
27.4.72; regn cld 10.8.73.

6348   DH 89M; CoA issued 17.4.37 for Lithuanian Air Force,
serialled either **701** or **702** (see 6349); delivered via Schiphol
airport, Amsterdam; used by 3rd Sqn of Light Bombers at Shaulaj;
known to have been present with Karo Aviaijos 15.6.40 when
Russians invaded Lithuania; taken over by Luftwaffe 6.41; served
with Luftflotte 2 in communications role; NFT.

6349   DH 89M; CoA issued 17.4.37 for Lithuanian Air Force;
serialled either **701** or **702** (see 6348); delivered via Schiphol
airport, Amsterdam; used by 3rd Sqn of Light Bombers at Shaulaj;
known to have been present with Karo Aviaijos 15.6.40 when
Russians invaded Lithuania; taken over by Luftwaffe 6.41; served
with Luftflotte 2 in communications role; NFT.

6350   Regd **G-AEPW** (CoR 7475) 1.12.36 to Olley Air Service
Ltd, Croydon; used for trials leading to Type (MoD) CoA; CoA
(5819) issued 15.3.37; impressed into RAF 4.3.40; 24 Sqn,
Hendon, 4.3.40; allocated serial **X8510** 31.3.40; to Air Taxis Ltd,
Ringway, for inspection 5.7.40; 27 MU, Shawbury, 10.11.40;
Andover 25.11.40; DH RU, Witney, 7.11.41; SOC 11.12.41.

*The two DH.89s acquired by the Latvian Air Force, 701 and 702 (c/ns 6348,
6349), at Amsterdam during their ferry flight*   *[MAP via P H T Green]*

Operated by the Toronto Globe & Mail newspaper, CF-BBG, c/n 6354, rests on the water before another delivery flight. After only two months service it caught fire when being started and was destroyed

[G M Simons collection]

6351   DH.89M; CoA (5893) issued 30.4.37; regd **YL-ABC** to Post & Telecommunications Dept, Ministry of Commerce, Latvia; operated by Valsts Gaisa Satiksme (Latvian Post Office), which flew services from Riga to Liepaja between April and October only; first used 15.6.37; after 'voluntary take-over' of Latvia by the USSR, transferred to Pribaltijskoje Upravlenije Grazhdanskogo Vozdushnogo Flota (Baltic Board of the Civil Air Fleet) at Riga, where it was stored in a factory building; sometime regd **CCCP-L20**; captured by Germans 6.41; taken over by the Luftwaffe and probably used by an Estonian unit.

6352   DH.89M; CoA (6352) issued 30.4.37; regd **YL-ABD** to Post & Telecommunications Dept, Ministry of Commerce, Latvia; operated by Valsts Gaisa Satiksme (Latvian Post Office), which flew services from Riga to Liepaja between April and October only; first used 15.6.37; after 'voluntary take-over' of Latvia by the USSR, transferred to Pribaltijskoje Upravlenije Grazhdanskogo Vozdushnogo Flota (Baltic Board of the Civil Air Fleet) at Riga, where it was stored in a factory building; sometime regd **CCCP-L21**; captured by Germans 6.41; taken over by the Luftwaffe and probably used by an Estonian unit.
[Note: one was later operated by JG54, the other was damaged and abandoned at Riga; it was eventually repaired and operated by Sonderstaffel Buschmann from 4.42 to 8.42 as **SB+AH**.]

6353   Regd **G-AEPF** (CoR 7448) 10.3.37 to Air Commerce Ltd, Heston; CoA (5822) issued 17.4.37; company sold 6.38 to

Olley Air Service / British & Foreign Aviation Ltd; operated 6.38 by Isle of Man Air Services Ltd; operated 4.39 by Railway Air Services Ltd, Speke; impressed into RAF but no serial issued; 24 Sqn, Hendon; abandoned at Bordeaux 18.6.40.

6354   Regd (CoR 1985) **CF-BBG** 10.6.37 to The Toronto Globe & Mail Ltd; fitted with floats; DBF at Toronto Air Harbour during refuelling, 21.8.37; regn cld same day.

6355   Regd **G-AERE** (CoR 7491) 18.3.37 to L H G Ltd as nominee for British-American Air Services Ltd, Heston; CoA (5903) issued 11.5.37; regd (CoR 8586) 25.6.38 to director/ nominee Mrs L H Falk, Heston; re-regd 12.1.39 to LHG Ltd, Heston, still as nominee for BAAS; crashed at Ettersgill Fell End, nr Forest-in-Teesdale, Co Durham, 20.6.39 during flight to Gosforth Park racecourse; pilot F S Appi, engineer J E Elmslie and jockey J Crouch killed; regn cld 27.6.39.

6356   Regd **G-AERZ** (CoR 7577) 10.3.37 to Air Commerce Ltd, Heston (later Croydon); CoA (5823) issued 7.5.37; operated by AAJC during WW2; at DH RU, Witney, 18.9.40; to Scottish Airways Ltd, Renfrew, 15.11.40; cr Port Ellen 16.6.41; retd to Speke for repair 26.6.41; to Scottish Airways Ltd, Renfrew, 17.9.42; retd to Speke 26.8.43; operated by Railway Air Services Ltd.; crashed in fog on Royal Belfast golf course, Craigarad,1.4.46, killing six, inc pilot Capt E Tyrer; regn cld 4.5.46.

Rapide G-AERZ, c/n 6356, looking the worse for wear at Islay (Port Ellen) on 16th June 1941   [Denis Fox collection]

A posed photograph of c/n 6358 VP-YBJ "Bulawayo" of Rhodesia & Nyasaland Airways   *[via C N Dodds]*

A real African scene: VP-YBK, c/n 6359 of Rhodesia & Nyasaland Airways about to be loaded with sacks on 1st July 1939   [P Pennant via C N Dodds]

6357   CoA (5902) issued 7.5.37; regd **VP-KCG** 5.37 to Wilson Airways Ltd, Nairobi; impressed into Kenya Auxiliary Air Unit (KAAU) 9.39 as **K10**, **K11** or **K16** (probably the last); believed WFU .45.

6358   CoA (5921) issued 21.5.37; left Hatfield 27.5.37, arr Salisbury, Southern Rhodesia, 6.6.37; regd **VP-YBJ** 8.37 to Rhodesia & Nyasaland Airways Ltd, Salisbury, named *Bulawayo;* taken over by Southern Rhodesia Air Services 2.40 as **303**; restored to **VP-YBJ** 4.42; crashed and SOC 8.44; possibly used for spares by Central African Airways 6.46.

6359   CoA (5922) issued 24.5.37; left Hatfield 27.5.37, arr Salisbury, Southern Rhodesia, 6.6.37; regd **VP-YBK** 8.37 to Rhodesia & Nyasaland Airways Ltd, Salisbury, named *City of Salisbury*; taken over by Southern Rhodesia Air Services 9.39 as **304**; restored to register as **VP-YBK** 4.42; to Central African Airways Corpn 6.46; crashed at Balovale, Northern Rhodesia, 3.12.47; used for spares .48.

6360   CoA (5930) issued 28.5.37; regd **VR-SAV** (CoR 21) 6.7.37 to Wearne Bros Ltd. t/a Wearne's Air Service, Kallang, Singapore, named *Governor Raffles*; regd (CoR 28) 7.1.38 to Wearne's Air Service Ltd, Singapore; impressed into 'B' Flight, 1 Sqn, Malayan Volunteer Air Force (MVAF) 7.12.41; took off from Ipoh 18.12.41 to defend the airfield from the attacking Japanese; fragmentation bombs exploded across the airfield, hitting the aircraft and killing both crew, Sgt Trevethen and Sgt Cleaverley.

6361   CoA (5941) issued 9.6.37 as **CR-AAD** for Dept of Railways, Portuguese

East Africa, for operation by Direcçao de Exploraçao dos Transportes Aéreos (DETA), Lourenco Marques; current .41; NFT.

6362   CoA (5942) issued 9.6.37 as **CR-AAE** for Dept of Railways, Portuguese East Africa, for operation by Direcçao de Exploraçao dos Transportes Aéreos (DETA), Lourenco Marques; current .54; NFT.

6363   Regd **G-AESR** (CoR 7604) 18.3.37 to Iraq Petroleum Transport Co Ltd, Haifa; CoA (5954) issued 25.6.37; regd 18.10.47 to Airwork Ltd, Perth; operated by Channel Islands Air Services Ltd, Guernsey, .50; based at Blackbushe by Airwork Ltd .51; CoA lapsed 13.3.51 and stored/overhauled at Langley; CoA renewed 7.11.52; regd 18.3.53 to Air Kruise (Kent) Ltd, Lympne (also t/a Trans Channel Airways); leased to Oilfields Supply & Trading Co, Benghazi, Libya, .56; crashed on take-off from Gerdes el Abid, 30 mls E of El Marj, 22.7.56; regn cld 26.9.56.

C/n 6361, CR-AAD of DETA the airline of Portuguese East Africa   *[via K Smy]*

Apparently about to be swallowed by a Bristol freighter, Rapide c/n 6363 G-AESR in Trans Channel Airways titles taxies forward   *[MAP via P H T Green]*

CF-BFM and a DH.84 in a bleak Canadian wintry setting before the DH.89, c/n 6371, was exported to Uruguay to become CX-ABI   *[via C N Dodds]*

6364   CoA (5970) issued 7.7.37; regd **VR-SAW** (CoR 22) 30.8.37 to Wearne Bros Ltd, t/a Wearne's Air Service, Kallang, Singapore, named *Governor Fullerton;* regd (CoR 29) 7.1.38 to Wearne's Air Service Ltd, Singapore; impressed into 'B' Flight, 1 Sqn, Malayan Volunteer Air Force (MVAF); DBR at Palembang, Sumatra, 10.2.42 when struck by taxying Hurricane.

6365   CoA (5964) issued 1.7.37; test-flown at Essendon, Vic, 11.9.37; regd **VH-UXZ** (CoR 662) 15.9.37 to Australian National Airways Pty Ltd, Essendon, Vic, named *Marika;* crashed in forced landing at Tanners Bay, Flinders Island, Tas, 29.5.42, when attempting to return to island after an engine failed; four killed; regn cld 30.6.42.

6366   CoA (5965) issued 2.7.37; regd **VP-KCJ** (CoR 61) 20.7.37 to Wilson Airways Ltd, Nairobi; impressed into Kenyan Auxiliary Air Unit 9.39 as **K4**; restored to register 13.12.46 as **VP-KCJ** to East African Airways Corporation; regd 26.7.48 to Stirling Astaldi (EA) Ltd; regd 6.5.52 to Caspair Air Charters & Agencies Ltd, t/a Caspair, Nairobi; regn cld 7.5.52; regd 20.11.52 to J E F Wilkins, t/a Caspair, Nairobi; regd 22.11.55 to Caspair Air Charters & Agencies Ltd; regd 23.11.55 to East African Airways Corporation, Nairobi (unconfirmed); regd 15.8.60 to Caspair Ltd, Nairobi; crashed on landing at Entebbe 7.10.62; killing one.

6367   Regd **G-AEWL** (CoR 7772) 20.5.37 to Highland Airways Ltd, Inverness, named *Zetland;* CoA (5926) issued 18.6.37; del 25.6.37; merged into Scottish Airways Ltd 8.37; regd (CoR 8217) 15.11.37 to British Airways Ltd, Inverness; regd (CoR 8566) 8.6.38 to Scottish Airways Ltd, Inverness; damaged on landing at Kirkwall (Wideford) 8.7.38; DH, Hatfield, for rebuild, retd 26.10.38; regd 1.2.47 to British European Airways Corpn; regd 25.5.48 to C Allen, Croydon; regd 27.9.48 to M G H Fletcher, Croydon; regd 13.4.50 to Wg Cdr H C Kennard and operated by Air Kruise (Kent) Ltd, Lympne, named *Nicole;* regd 13.4.55 to Air Kruise (Kent) Ltd, Lympne; regd 14.12.55 to Aviation Supplies Co Ltd, Portsmouth; regn cld 24.1.56 as sold to French Ivory Coast; regd **F-OATT** 26.4.56 to Sté Navale Delmas & Vieljeux, Abidjan; regd 25.7.61 to Air Ivoire, Abidjan; sold 8.61 to SFATAT; regd **F-BJUY** 2.11.61 (or 27.7.61) to SFATAT, based Biscarosse, later Gaillac; crashed at Gaillac 29.7.62; regn cld 20.11.63.

6368   Regd **G-AEXO** (CoR 7839) 19.5.37 to North Eastern Airways Ltd, Croydon (later Doncaster); CoA (5915) issued 19.7.37; regn cld as sold 26.3.40; impressed into RAF; 24 Sqn, Hendon, 27.3.40; allocated serial **X8507** 31.3.40; SOC 13.6.41.

6369   Regd **G-AEXP** (CoR 7840) 19.5.37 to North Eastern Airways Ltd, Croydon (later Doncaster); CoA (5916) issued 19.7.37; operated by NAC 9.39; damaged in ground collision with Magister L5935 at Northolt 25.11.39; regn cld as sold 25.3.40; impressed into RAF 31.3.40 as **X8505**; 24 Sqn, Hendon, 9.4.40; still in civil markings when damaged by enemy action at St Omer, France, 21.5.40 and abandoned; SOC 28.5.40.

6370   Regd **CF-BBH** (CoR 2067) to de Havilland Aircraft of Canada Ltd, Toronto; floatplane; regd (CoR 2148/A71) 7.1.38 to Consolidated Mining & Smelting Co of Canada Ltd, Trail, BC; regd (CoR 2437/A71) 23.5.39 to Canadian Airways Ltd, Vancouver; merged 1.42 into Canadian Pacific Air Lines; wrecked at Pentecost, Quebec, 19.3.47 after stalling in sticky snow on third attempt to take off.

6371   Regd **CF-BFM** (CoR 2130) 26.11.37 to de Havilland Aircraft of Canada Ltd; fitted with floats; sold to Uruguay 13.1.38; regd **CX-ABI** 1.38 to B Scaglione, t/a Cia Expreso del Plata, Montevideo, named *Nuestra Senora del Carmen;* regn cld before .50.

6372   Regd **G-AFAO** (CoR 8016) 21.7.37 to de Havilland Aircraft Co Ltd, Hatfield; CoA (6007) issued 4.8.37; regn cld 9.37 as sold abroad; regd in Turkey as **TC-DAG** to Devlet Hava Yollari (fleet no 6); current 7.50.

6373   Regd **CF-BFL** (CoR 2110) 22.10.37 to Canadian Airways Ltd, Winnipeg; sold 17.2.38 to (subsidiary) Quebec Airways Ltd, Montreal; stalled in turn after take-off from Matane, Quebec, 23.2.38; to DH Canada for rebuild but never completed; believed scrapped for spares; regn cld 23.4.38.

6374   Regd **CF-BFP** (CoR 2297/A236) 23.8.38 to Quebec Airways Ltd, Montreal; merged into Canadian Pacific Air Lines .42; DBF at Walter Lake, Quebec, 5.7.45, when port engine caught fire during start-up.

Rapide floatplane CF-BND, c/n 6375, crashed on Digby Island, BC, in 1949 and the remains were not removed   *[Denis Fox collection]*

6375 Regd **CF-BND** 8.9.39 to Quebec Airways Ltd, Montreal; regd 2.6.47 to Central Northern Airways Ltd, Winnipeg; floatplane; leased to Queen Charlotte Airlines Ltd, Sea Island Airport, BC, named *Tsimpsean Queen;* ran out of fuel 29.7.49 and crashed into trees at Digby Island, BC; remains still on site 10.4.84 when acquired by Western Canada Aviation Museum, who intended to remove remains from cover built on site to its base at Winnipeg for rebuild when funds permit; possibly extant.

6376 Regd **CF-BNE** 4.11.39 to Quebec Airways Ltd, Montreal; lost when it broke through ice on Lake George, Man, 3.12.43 and sank.

6377 Regd **G-AFAH** (CoR 8007) 24.8.37 to Personal Airways Ltd, Croydon; CoA (6025) issued 26.8.37; regd (CoR 8539) 7.6.38 to Capt G S L Whitelaw and operated by Personal Airways Ltd, Croydon; regd 2.5.40 to Capt W Ledlie, MD of Personal Airways Ltd and continued to be operated by them; impressed into RAF 13.3.40; 24 Sqn, Hendon 13.3.40; allocated serial **X8508** 31.3.40; set alight and abandoned following damage at Merville, France, 21.5.40 while still in civilian markings; SOC 28.5.40.

6378 Regd **VT-AIZ** (CoR 319) 15.7.37 to Tata & Sons Ltd, Juhu, Bombay; CoA (6039) issued 8.9.37; regn cld 15.12.41; impressed into RAF 21.4.42 as **AX806**; 2 Coastal Def Flt, Juhu; stalled and crashed on landing at Juhu 22.10.42; SOC 1.7.43.

6379 Regd **VT-AJH** (CoR 320) 15.7.37 to Tata & Sons Ltd, Juhu, Bombay; CoA (6040) issued 8.9.37; crashed at Juhu 20.11.38; regn cld 9.12.38.

6380 CoA (6047) issued 13.9.37 to de Havilland Aircraft (South Africa) Ltd; regd **ZS-AKT** 11.10.37; impressed into SAAF 3.40 as **1560**; restored to register as **ZS-AKT** 13.3.46 to African Flying Services Ltd, Grand Central; regd 7.54 to Trans Oranje Air Services, Zastron; regd .55 to Drakensburg Air Services, Ladysmith; badly damaged on landing at Mokhotlong, Basutoland, 29.11.55 but repaired; regn cld 5.8.57 as sold in Belgian Congo; regd **OO-CJU** 7.12.57 to Air Brousse SPRL, Léopoldville; re-regd **9O-CJU** 17.3.61; re-regd **9Q-CJU** to AMAZ; NFT.

6381 Regd **VT-AJB** (CoR 321) 15.7.37 to Tata & Sons Ltd, Juhu, Bombay; CoA (6041) issued 8.9.37; impressed into RAF as **HX790** 21.1.42; 2 Coastal Def Flt, Juhu; to Director of Civil Aviation India 1.9.43; possibly restored as **VT-AJB**; SOC by RAF 31.5.45.

6382 CoA (6145) issued 2.12.37; regd **F-AQIL** (CoR 5513) 13.12.37 to Paul Legastelois, Paris; regd 12.37 to A Rodier, Coulommiers; to Spanish Republicans 18.1.38 (unconfirmed) for use in Spanish Civil War; regd 5.38 to Sté Française des Transports Aériens (SFTA), Paris; NFT

6383 CoA (6143) issued 1.12.37; regd **F-AQIM** (CoR 5497) 8.12.37 to Paul Legastelois, Paris; regd 12.37 to A Rodier, Coulommiers; to Spanish Republicans 10.12.37 (unconfirmed) for use in Spanish Civil War; regd 5.38 to Sté Française des Transports Aériens (SFTA), Paris; NFT

6384 CoA (6125) issued 12.11.37; test-flown at Sydney (Mascot) 17.1.38; regd **VH-UZY** (CoR 683) 25.1.38 to W R Carpenter and Co Ltd, Sydney, NSW; operated by North Queensland Airways Ltd, Cairns, Qld, 10.38; sold 25.10.38 and regd 1.12.38 to Airlines of Australia Ltd, Cairns; force-landed on beach near Townsville 8.1.40 and partly submerged by tide, but salvaged and returned to service; regn cld 9.8.40; impressed into RAAF 12.8.40 as **A33-6**; 3 EFTS, Essendon 12.8.40; 1 AOS, Cootamundra 23.9.40; 1 AD, Laverton, 2.6.42; 32 Sqn, Port Moresby (Horne Island ?), 15.6.42; 33 Sqn, Townsville 3.8.42 for use as air ambulance to evacuate troops from front line areas; 1 RCF, Port Moresby, New Guinea, 14.9.42; badly damaged 9.42; DH, Mascot, 3.12.42; 2 AAU, Port Moresby (Archerfield ?), 9.3.43; 1 RCS, Port Moresby, 4.4.43; damaged by fire 30. 6.43; crated and shipped to DH, Mascot, for repairs 24.9.43; to Department of Civil Aviation 19.1.44; crashed at Cape Sidmouth, Qld, 27.1.44; shipped to Perth, WA, on *Madura* 17.3.44 for rebuild by Airlines (WA) Ltd; restored to register as **VH-UZY** 19.11.43 to Airlines (Western Australia) Ltd, Perth, named *RMA Perth,* and del 19.1.44; regd 20.10.48 to Connellan Airways Ltd, Alice Springs, NT; crashed and DBF on take-off from Coolibah, NT, 21.10.49, killing pilot; regn cld 16.1.51.

6385 CoA (6127) issued 15.11.37 to Military Council of National Government of China; del via Far East Flying Training School Ltd, Hong Kong, 1.38; assembled and flown into China 2.38; understood to have been intended as ambulance aircraft with Red Cross markings but no identification.

6386 Regd **G-AFFF** (CoR 8354) 24.2.38 to de Havilland Aircraft Co Ltd, Hatfield; CoA (6222) issued 16.3.38; regd (CoR 8660) 27.7.38 to Railway Air Services Ltd, Croydon, named *Juno*; transferred to Scottish Airways Ltd, Renfrew, 26.5.39, but not regd to them; in bad weather, flew into Craigton Hill, nr Milngavie, 7 mls N of Renfrew, 27.9.46, killing seven, inc pilot, Capt F Stephens; regn cld 31.12.46.

The old and the new: VT-AJB, c/n 6381, and its load of freight at Juhu, Bombay, in 1937, when operated by Tata Airlines pre-war   *[BAE via G M Simons]*

Owners of this smart Rapide, ZS-AME, c/n 6387, were Allied American Corporation of South Africa Ltd. Note the cockpit sunblind, trailing aerial and position of the generator   *[via C N Dodds]*

6387   CoA (6129) issued 24.11.37; regd **ZS-AME** 22.12.37 to Anglo-American Trading Corporation of South Africa, Johannesburg; impressed into SAAF .39 as **1402**; restored to register as **ZS-AME** .46; regn cld 29.10.49 as sold in Kenya; regd **VP-KHJ** 29.10.49 to Tonk Aircraft; regd in South Africa 15.8.51 as **ZS-DFL** to Tonk Aircraft; regn cld 12.2.52; regd in Mozambique 19.2.52 as **CR-ADH** to Banco Nacional Ultrasino; broken up for spares 17.7.56.

6388   CoA (6130) issued 19.11.37 to Military Council of National Government of China; del via Far East Flying Training School Ltd, Hong Kong, assembled and flown into China 2.38; understood to have been intended as ambulance aircraft with Red Cross markings but no identification.

6389   CoA (6134) issued 24.11.37 to Military Council of National Government of China; del via Far East Flying Training School Ltd, Hong Kong, assembled and flown into China 2.38; understood to have been intended as ambulance aircraft with Red Cross markings but no identification.
[Note: the first three DH.89s purchased by China, 6385, 6388 and 6389, were delivered 2.38 from Kai Tak by Chinese pilots, during which two crashed on landing (one of them being written off) and the third was shot down by Chinese AA fire]

6390   CoA (6154) issued 11.12.37 to Military Council of National Government of China; del via Far East Flying Training School Ltd, Hong Kong, assembled and flown into China 7.38; NFT

6391   CoA (6155) issued 13.12.37 to Military Council of National Government of China; del via Far East Flying Training School Ltd, Hong Kong, assembled and flown into China 7.38; NFT

Rapide HK684 was the former G-AFEN, c/n 6399, and is seen here in service with 173 Squadron at Heliopolis in September 1942
[T L Edwards via A S Thomas and P H T Green]

6392   CoA (6163) issued 16.12.37 to Military Council of National Government of China; del via Far East Flying Training School Ltd, Hong Kong, assembled and flown into China 7.38; NFT

6393   CoA (6176) issued 4.1.38; regd **F-AQIN** 10.1.38 to Paul Legastelois, Paris; regd 1.38 to A Rodier, Coulommiers; to Spanish Republicans 5.1.38 for use in Spanish Civil War; regd 5.38 to Sté Française des Transports Aériens (SFTA), Paris; NFT.

6394   CoA (6188) issued 8.1.38; left Hatfield 18.1.38 on delivery, flown by Capt Geoffrey de Havilland and Frank Hearle and arrived Nairobi 27.1.38; regd **VP-KCL** (CoR 63) 5.2.38 to Wilson Airways Ltd, Nairobi; impressed into Kenyan Auxiliary Air Unit 3.9.39 as **K10**; broken up for spares for EAAC at Nairobi .46.

6395   CoA (6193) issued 21.1.38 to Paul Legastelois, Paris; regd **F-AQJH** 21.2.38 to Dr René Arbeltier, Coulommiers; to Spanish Republicans 22.2.38 (unconfirmed) for use in Spanish Civil War; regd 5.38 to Sté Française des Transports Aériens (SFTA), Paris; NFT.

6396   CoA issued 16.3.38; regd **F-AQJI** 4.4.38 to A Rodier, Coulommiers; regd 5.38 to Sté Française des Transports Aériens (SFTA); to Spanish Republicans 5.38 for Spanish Civil War; NFT.

6397   CoA (6239) issued 12.4.38 as **CR-AAM** for Dept of Railways, Portuguese East Africa, for operation by Direcçao de Exploraçao dos Transportes Aéreos (DETA), Lourenco Marques; current .54; NFT.

6398   CoA (6240) issued 12.4.38 as **CR-AAN** for Dept of Railways, Portuguese East Africa, for operation by Direcçao de Exploraçao dos Transportes Aéreos (DETA), Lourenco Marques; current .41; NFT.

6399   Regd **G-AFEN** (CoR 8312) 13.4.38 to Sir William Firth, Heston; CoA(6256) issued 25.4.38; regn cld as sold abroad 12.38; regd **VQ-PAC** 21.9.39 to Palestine Airways, Jerusalem; impressed into RAF as **Z7188** 1.7.40; Lydda CF; regd **G-AFEN** 25.7.40 to Sec of State for Air for operation by BOAC from Heliopolis for Gen Gifford; regn cld 1.8.40; CoA renewed 9.8.40; flown Cairo to Lagos 12-15.8.40 and still at Lagos 8.41; retd to Heliopolis and impressed again 17.2.42 as **HK864**; 173 Sqn, Heliopolis, 6.9.42; Iraq & Persia CF, Habbaniya, 24.10.42; allocated registration **TJ-AAI** 22.10.46 for Arab Airways Assoc Ltd but NTU; restored to British register as **G-AFEN** 21.4.47 to W A Rollason Ltd, Croydon; CoA renewed 18.11.48; regn cld 30.12.48 as sold in S America; regd in Argentina as **LV-AGV** 23.3.49 to ZONDA; to Aerolineas Argentinas 7.12.50; to Taxis Aéreos Argentinos SA, Buenos Aires 7.5.57; to F Doral & A Sayanes, Buenos Aires; CoA lapsed 29.4.60; moved to Don Torcuato, Buenos Aires, 9.61; still regd 5.67.

Albeit a partial one, this is one of the few photographs known to exist of the DH.92 Dolphin; it is the aircraft at the rear of this Hatfield scene
[via G M Simons and P H T Green]

6400   DH.92 DOLPHIN, the only example built; registration **G-AEMX** allocated 27.8.36 to de Havilland Aircraft Co Ltd, Hatfield, but not carried. Built in the experimental shop at Hatfield in an attempt to modernise the DH.89, with unequal-span swept wings as in the Dragonfly, a wing area 15.5% greater and an increase in all-up weight of 9%, a retractable undercarriage and side-by-side seating for two pilots. First flown 9.9.36 as **E.3** and continued to be flown for a short time with modifications during the summer of 1936 in Class B marks but the project was abandoned as structurally overweight; unused regn G-AEMX cld as pwfu 10.36, aircraft believed scrapped 12.36.
[Note: Entered by DH during 8.36 in Schlesinger African Air Race from Portsmouth to Johannesburg on 29.9.36, to be flown by Hugh Buckingham (Race No.9), but withdrawn early in 9.36.]

6401   Regd **OH-BLB** (CoR 41) 12.4.38 to Aero O/Y, Helsinki, named *Lappi;* CoA (6262) issued 2.5.38; del via Hamburg, Copenhagen and Stockholm 8.5.38; impressed into Ilmavoimat (Finnish Air Force) 14.10.39 to 3.5.40; used as air ambulance during the summer of 1941, named *Silver Star* after a DH.86B; forced down 8.11.41 by Luftwaffe Bf109 attacking in error between Kuusamo and Kiestinki and damaged, but repaired on site and flown out; re-regd **OH-VKI** 17.4.47 to Veljekset Karhumäki O/Y, Kuorevesi; regd 27.11.50 to Savon Lentolinjat O/Y, Mikkeli; re-regd **OH-DHB** 31.5.54 to Lentohuolto O/Y, Helsinki; regd 4.55 to Pasenen & Pasenen, Turku; regn cld 21.5.55 as sold in Denmark; del to Sylvest Jensen 14.4.55, but not regd in Denmark; sold in

The only DH.92 Dolphin, c/n 6400, E.3 (the registration G-AEMX was never applied to the single example) showing the retractable undercarriage, short nose, unique interplane strutting and fixed pitch propellers used for testing
[DH / AJJ via J Meaden]

OH-BLB, c/n 6401, "Lappi" at Hatfield just before delivery to Finland in May 1938   *[G M Simons collection]*

G-AGDP, c/n 6403, had seen service in Syria before coming onto the UK register (in Palestine) in November 1941   *[via A. Chivers]*

Norway and del from Copenhagen 4.6.55; regd **LN-BFB** (CoR 343) 20.7.55 to A/S Skogbruksfly, Sokna; regd 21.4.59 to Norsk Flyveselskap A/S, Honefoss, on take-over; CoA lapsed 30.12.60; WFU at Honefoss (Eggemoen); in open storage .64 carrying former Finnish name *Lappi*; remains burnt and regn cld 27.5.68.

6402   Regd **G-AFEY** (CoR 8342) 7.3.38 to Scottish Airways Ltd, Renfrew; CoA (6225) issued 11.4.38; opened Renfrew – Perth – Inverness– Northern Isles service 2.5.38; crashed at Kirkwall (Wideford) 18.3.40 and regn cld same day.

6403   CoA (6267) issued 5.5.38; regd **F-AQOH** 12.5.38 to Sté de Transport du Proche-Orient, Tripoli, Syria; probably taken over by associate company, Iraq Petroleum Transport Co Ltd, on invasion of Syria 5.41; regd **G-AGDP** 26.11.41 to Iraq Petroleum Transport Co Ltd, Haifa; CoA renewed 1.12.41; regd 12.1.49 to Short Bros & Harland Ltd, Rochester; regd 7.4.49 to Modern Transport (Wolverhampton) Ltd; regd 29.1.52 to Don Everall (Aviation) Ltd, Wolverhampton; CoA lapsed 24.7.58 and stored at Wolverhampton; DBF at Wolverhampton 8.69, perhaps burned deliberately; regn cld 7.60.

6404   CoA (6258) issued 28.4.38 as **VP-YBT**; left Croydon 10.5.38; damaged on landing at Khartoum 16.5.38 and repaired by Misr Airwork; arr Salisbury, Southern Rhodesia, 11.1.39; regd **VP-YBT** 1.39 to Rhodesia and Nyasaland Airways Ltd, Salisbury; taken over by Southern Rhodesia Air Services 9.39 as **305**; restored to **VP-YBT** 4.42; broken up for spares 12.44.

6405   Regd **G-AFEO** (CoR 8319) 11.4.38 to North Eastern Airways Ltd, Doncaster; CoA (6251) issued 9.5.38; regn cld as sold 26.3.40; impressed into RAF; 24 Sqn, Hendon 27.3.40; serial **X8506** allocated 31.3.40 but probably not carried; last recorded flight Hendon – Amiens – Hendon 18.5.40; abandoned in France during evacuation; SOC 22.6.40.

6406   Regd **G-AFEP** (CoR 8320) 11.4.38 to North Eastern Airways Ltd, Doncaster; CoA (6252) issued 13.5.38; regn cld as sold 23.3.40; impressed into RAF 25.3.40 as **X9388** at Benson; 6 AACU, Ringway, 17.4.40; transferred to FAA 4.40; SF Donibristle 5.5.40; 782 Sqn, Donibristle, 7.40; retd to RAF 8.40; restored to civil register as **G-AFEP** 13.11.40 to Air Commerce Ltd, Speke; regd 30.12.46 to parent company Olley Air Service Ltd, Croydon; regd 19.5.47 to Sir Brograve Beauchamp Bt; regd 2.9.47 to F A White & H C D Haytor, Croydon; regn cld 15.4.48 as sold abroad; regd in Kenya as **VP-KFV** 6.48 to Mrs E M Noon; DBF at Masindi 29.11.49.

6407   CoA (6283) issued 19.5.38; regd **F-AQOI** 8.6.38 to Sté de Transports du Proche-Orient, Tripoli, Syria; probably used as air ambulance during early days of WW2 but reported as destroyed in Allied invasion of Syria 5.41.

6408   Regd **G-AFEZ** (CoR 8343) 31.5.38 to Wrightways Ltd, Croydon; CoA (6296) issued 26.6.38; regn cld as sold 14.4.40; impressed into FAA 14.4.40 as **X9451**; restored to civil register as **G-AFEZ** 7.9.40 to Isle of Man Air Services Ltd, Speke; regd 1.2.47 to BEA; named *RMA Lord Shaftesbury* .52; regd 7.6.56 to Hants &

A classic view of G-AFEZ, c/n 6408, "RMA Lord Shaftesbury" of BEA   *[C N Dodds]*

Rapide SR8, c/n 6412, of the SRAF at Umtali, being inspected by a group of dignitaries [P H T Green collection]

Sussex Aviation Ltd, Portsmouth and converted to Mk.4 standard; regn cld 2.11.56 as sold to Laos; despatched from Portsmouth 15.11.56 and inspected at Toussus-le-Noble 15.12.56; regd **F-LAAL** 21.1.57 to Laos Air Service, Vientiane but not delivered and sent to Algeria in 1957 instead; regd **F-OBHI** 9.7.58 to Sté Générale d'Affrétements Aériens (Air Fret), Algiers; crashed on landing at Fort Flatters in Sahara 24.8.60.

6409   Regd **G-AFFB** (CoR 8345) 12.4.38 to Iraq Petroleum Transport Co Ltd, Haifa; CoA (6293) issued 27.5.38; CoA lapsed 14.5.46; sold 29.7.46; regd 30.6.47 to Air Transport Charter (CI) Ltd, Jersey, named *St Peter*; CoA renewed 5.7.47; nominal regn change 27.10.50 to Lambert's Trust Ltd (following take-over); CoA lapsed 12.6.51; regd 21.1.52 to Aerocontacts Ltd, Gatwick; CoA renewed 8.8.52; regd 4.11.52 to H J Rose, Christchurch; regd 17.7.53 to H C G Heathcote Stisted, Eastleigh; regd 12.4.54 to IAS (London) Ltd t/a Island Air Services, Heathrow (Ramsgate from .57); CoA lapsed 3.7.58; regd 19.3.59 to Air Couriers (Transport) Ltd, Croydon; CoA renewed 22.5.59; regd 29.5.59 to Trans European Aviation Ltd, Swansea (Fairwood Common) later to Baginton; damaged while taxying at Staverton 25.6.60; CoA lapsed 23.6.62; sold but not regd 15.5.63; regn cld 11.11.64; remains burnt at Baginton 12.8.67.

6410   Regd **G-AFFC** (CoR 8346) 12.4.38 to Iraq Petroleum Transport Co Ltd, Haifa; CoA (6297) issued 2.6.38; regn cld as sold 28.5.41 ("taken over by British Field Hospital, Jerusalem"); impressed into RAF 15.2.42 as **HK862**; 206 Gp CF, Heliopolis; Iraq & Persia CF, Habbaniya, 9.42; SOC 31.8.44.

6411   CoA (6338) issued 1.7.38; regd **ZS-AOM** 30.8.38 to Stewarts and Lloyds of South Africa Ltd; impressed into SAAF as **1401**; restored to register 24.7.45 as **ZS-CAB** to Department of Civil Aviation; re-regd **ZS-DDX** 13.5.50 to Pretoria Aircraft Co; to Drakensburg Air Services Pty Ltd, Ladysmith; badly damaged by tornado at Ladysmith 10.1.55 but repaired; crashed on landing at Mokhotlong, Basutoland, 24.6.55; regn cld 28.3.57.

6412   CoA (6343) issued 4.7.38 to Govt of Southern Rhodesia as **SR8**; named *Southern Rhodesia* at Hatfield 21.7.38; used by Maj D Cloete, DCA; regd **VP-YBU** .38 to Govt of Southern Rhodesia, probably for ferry flight by Maj Cloete; reverted to **SR8**; taken over by Southern Rhodesia Air Services 9.39 as **300**; restored to register as **VP-YBU** 4.42; to Central African Airways 6.46; to SRAF 9.46 as **SR23** and possibly to RRAF .53 as **RRAF23**; regd **VP-YNJ** 10.55 to Fishair (Pvt) Ltd, Marandellas; regn cld 6.59 as sold in France; inspected at Libreville 30.6.59; regd **F-OBOD** 22.7.59 to Cie Jean-Claude Brouillet, Libreville and operated by Transgabon; CoA suspended 26.11.60 but renewed 23.10.62; regd 25.5.64 to Transgabon, Libreville; crashed Libreville and CoA suspended 27.4.65; regn cld .65.

6413   CoA (6358) issued 23.7.38; regd **VP-KCR** to Wilson Airways Ltd, Nairobi; impressed into Kenyan Auxiliary Air Unit 9.39 as **K8**; 1 (Comm) Flt, Dar-es-Salaam; to RAF 1.11.40; AHQ East Africa CS, Nairobi (Eastleigh) 1.11.40; crashed into earth mound on landing at Tanga 16.5.43; SOC 30.6.43.

A rare photograph of c/n 6413 as K8, of the Kenya Auxiliary Air Unit. The GOC, Gen Alan Cunningham, and other senior officers, are about to greet an Italian envoy at Scenele airstrip. Note the SM.79 Sparviero transport in which the Italians had arrived. The reason for the meeting and its date are unknown [via K Smy]

Flying above the English countryside in 1938 before delivery to Iraq were Rapides YI-FYA, YI-HDA and YI-ZWA   *[via C N Dodds]*

6414   CoA (6359) issued 25.7.38; regd **YI-ZWA** (CoR 14) 25.7.38 to Iraqi Aeroplane Society, Baghdad; arr Baghdad 1.10.38 flown by Flt Lt Reed, Air Advisor to Iraqi AF; to Iraqi State Airlines 5.39; incorporated into IrAF but retained civil markings; used by 2 Sqn, Baghdad; possibly DBF on refuelling 30.9.43.

6415   CoA (6360) issued 25.7.38; regd **YI-HDA** (CoR 13) 25.7.38 to Iraqi Aeroplane Society, Baghdad; arr Baghdad 1.10.38; to Iraqi State Airlines 5.39; incorporated into IrAF but retained civil markings; used by 2 Sqn, Baghdad; possibly DBF on refuelling 30.9.43.

6416   CoA (6366) issued 4.8.38; regd **YI-FYA** (CoR 12) 25.7.38 to Iraqi Aeroplane Society, Baghdad; arr Baghdad 1.10.38; to Iraqi State Airlines 5.39; incorporated into IrAF but retained civil markings; used by 2 Sqn, Baghdad; badly damaged 31.8.40 at Mosul when flown by CO of IrAF; probably BER.

6417   Regd **G-AFHY** (CoR 8546) 1.7.38 to Anglo-Iranian Oil Co Ltd, Abadan; CoA (6387) issued 1.9.38; left UK 10.10.38 for Abadan, arrived 19.10.38; regd 23.9.46 to Aircraft & Engineering Services Ltd, Croydon; regd 23.8.47 to Air Charter Ltd, Croydon; crashed at Rotterdam 10.10.47; CoA renewed 23.2.49; regn cld 9.6.50 as sold abroad, reportedly to Belgium; NFT.

6418   Regd **G-AFHZ** (CoR 8547) 1.7.38 to Anglo-Iranian Oil Co Ltd, Abadan; CoA (6393) issued 15.9.38; left UK 10.10.38 for Abadan, arrived 19.10.38; CoA lapsed 30.5.46; sold 2.7.46; regd 21.6.47 to W A Rollason Ltd, Croydon; CoA renewed 3.7.47; regn cld 30.4.47 (sic) as sold abroad ; regd in Uganda 9.47 as **VP-UAX** to Uganda Co Ltd; sold to Kenya 4.48 as **VP-KFH**; broken up at Nairobi 10.52.

6419   Regd **G-AFIA** (CoR 8548) 1.7.38 to Anglo-Iranian Oil Co Ltd, Abadan; CoA (6398) issued 22.9.38; left UK 10.10.38 for Abadan, arrived 19.10.38; crashed near Abadan 20.8.42 and DBF; regn cld 30.10.42.

6420   Retained by DH and fitted with experimental Dowty levered suspension undercarriage; flew as **E.9** 9.38; CoA (6420) issued 11.11.38; regd **F-ARII** (CoR 6226) 2.12.38 to Paul Legastelois, Paris; regd 12.38 to Sté Française des Transports Aériens (SFTA); acquired for Spanish Republicans but presumed taken by Nationalists 12.38 as **40-6**; to Spanish Air Force .39; regd **EC-BAC** 2.6.42 to Iberia Airlines, possibly named *Marchenko*; re-regd **EC-AAR** .48; scrapped .60.

6421   RAF serial **P1764**; TOC by 24 Sqn, Hendon, 29.11.38; DBR in air raid on Coulommiers, France 16.5.40; SOC 3.6.40.

DH.89 P1764, c/n 6421, was one of a pair delivered to the RAF in 1938 and was lost in the fall of France   *[P H T Green collection]*

CS-AEB, c/n 6430, spent a short time in Portugal before going to Angola as CR-LCO   *[G M Simons collection]*

6422   RAF serial **P1765**; TOC by 24 Sqn, Hendon, 10.12.38; 1 ASR (??) 13.12.40; crashed and SOC 4.4.41 .

6423   CoA (6395) issued 19.9.38; shipped to New Zealand on *Rangitata*, arr 16.11.38; regd **ZK-AGT** (CoR 146) 24.11.38 to Cook Strait Airways Ltd, Wellington, named *Neptune;* impressed into RNZAF 15.10.39 as **NZ558**; CF Ohakea; CF Rongotai, 2.41; 42 Sqn, Rongotai, 24.12.43; regd **ZK-AHS** 2.12.44 to Air Travel (NZ) Ltd., Hokitika; taken over by New Zealand National Airways Corporation, Wellington, 1.4.47 and regd to them 4.11.48, named *Mokai;* to West Coast Airways Ltd, Hokitika, 1.57; regd 19.6.74 to Mount Cook & Southern Lakes Tourist Co, Christchurch; WFU .74; to Museum of Transport and Technology, Western Springs, Auckland, by .79 for static display (named *Huia / Mokai*); regn cld 21.6.91; extant.

6424   CoA (6446) issued 22.11.38; regd **F-ARIJ** (CoR 6223) 15.12.38 to Paul Legastelois, Paris; regd 12.38 to Sté Française des Transports Aériens (SFTA); to Spanish Republicans 12.38 for use in Spanish Civil War; to Spanish Air Force .39; regd **EC-AAS** 18.3.41 to Iberia Airlines, later based in Spanish Guinea; sold to Congo 2.57; inspected at Libreville 2.5.57; regd in France as **F-OBAQ** 27.5.57 to Cie Aéronautique Jean-Claude Brouillet, Libreville, Gabon; CoA suspended 5.11.57; regn cld 9.58 (or 28.7.62 ?).

6425   CoA (6448) issued 25.11.38; regd **F-ARIK** (CoR 6243) 20.12.38 to Paul Legastelois, Paris; regd 12.38 to Sté Française des Transports Aériens (SFTA); to Spanish Republicans 12.38 for use in Spanish Civil War, coded 7; to Spanish Air Force .39; regd **EC-AAV** 11.1.43 to Iberia Airlines; later based in Spanish Guinea; WFU .55 or .57 (alternatively believed to be EC-CAQ, see 6275).

6426   Regd **G-AFLY** (CoR 8878) 21.11.38 to Airwork Ltd, Heston; CoA (6443) issued 30.11.38; operated by C W Martin's School of Air Navigation, Shoreham, later 6 CANS; 7 AONS, Perth; 6 AONS, Staverton, 23.5.40; regn cld 15.7.40; impressed into RAF 15.7.40 as **Z7253**; 6 AACU, Ringway, 15.7.40; 9 MU, Cosford, 8.11.40; DH RU, Witney, 21.12.40; 10 B&GS, Dumfries, 24.8.41; unit redes 10 AOS 13.9.41 and 10 (O) AFU 1.5.42; 9 (O) AFU, Penrhos, 6.8.42; 18 MU, Dumfries, 11.9.42; to FAA; SF Stretton [ST9A] .43; 18 MU, Dumfries, 14.11.45; SOC 22.12.45.

6427   CoA (6449) issued 28.11.38; regd **F-ARIL** (CoR 6254) 3.1.39 to Paul Legastelois, Paris; regd 1.39 to Sté Française des Transports Aériens (SFTA); to Spanish Republicans 1.39 for use in Spanish Civil War; to Spanish Air Force .39; reported as regd **EC-AAY** .45 to Iberian Airlines; crashed in Spanish Guinea 6.46 (but see 6277).

6428   CoA (6457) issued 7.12.38; regd **F-ARIM** (CoR 6258) 3.1.39 to Paul Legastelois, Paris; regd 1.39 to Sté Française des Transports Aériens (SFTA); to Spanish Republicans 1.39 for use in Spanish Civil War; NFT.

6429   Regd **G-AFLZ** (CoR 8879) 21.11.38 to Airwork Ltd, Heston; CoA (6444) issued 14.12.38; operated by C W Martin's School of Air Navigation, Shoreham, later 6 CANS; 7 AONS, Perth;

6 AONS, Staverton, 23.5.40; impressed into RAF 15.7.40 as **Z7254** and retained by 6 AONS; DH RU, Witney, 2.7.42; DH for seating modifications 11.11.42; 1 SoTT Trg Flt, Halton, 17.12.42; damaged, Cat AC/FA 15.2.43, but ROS; DH as Cat B 27.8.43; 5 MU, Kemble, 23.11.43; 10 Gp CF, Colerne, 13.1.44; ROS by 50 MU 30.11.44; DH RU, Witney, 28.5.45; 5 MU, Kemble, 28.12.45; sold to Field Consolidated Aircraft Services Ltd .46; regd **G-AHPX** 22.5.46 to Field Consolidated Aircraft Services Ltd, Croydon; regn cld 12.8.46 as sold abroad; CoA (7913) issued 17.9.46; regd in S Africa 19.10.46 as **ZS-AYF** to Aircraft Operating Co of South Africa Pty, Rand; regn cld as sold to Belgian Congo 28.8.56; regd **OO-CJS** 31.7.56 to Air Brousse, Léopoldville; re-regd **9O-CJS** and **9Q-CJS**; badly damaged on landing nr Dakar 26.2.60; regn cld 23.5.60.

6430   Regd **G-AFMA** (CoR 8880) 21.11.38 to Airwork Ltd, Heston; CoA (6445) issued 3.1.39; operated by C W Martin's School of Air Navigation, Shoreham, later 6 CANS; 7 AONS, Perth, 30.1.39; force-landed 7.12.39 at Aboyne, Aberdeenshire, when aircraft ran down slope, collided with wall and overturned; 4 MU 14.12.39; 6 AONS, Staverton, 23.5.40; impressed into RAF 15.7.40 as **Z7255**; 7 FPP, Sherburn-in-Elmet, 17.1.41; 38 MU, Llandow, 19.2.41; ATA, White Waltham, 23.2.41; 38 MU, Llandow, 15.4.41; ATA, White Waltham, 28.6.41; DH RU, Witney, as Cat B 9.4.43; SF Halton [B, later THA:B] 9.8.43; 18 MU, Dumfries, 26.8.46; sold to Ciro's Aviation Ltd, Gatwick, 19.3.47 and regd **G-AFMA** to them 30.6.47; sold 14.10.48 and regd 24.1.49 to William Dempster Ltd, Blackbushe; regn cld 13.4.50 as sold abroad; regd in Portugal as **CS-AEB** .50 to Durval Ferreira da Costa Mergulhao; regd in Angola .51 as **CR-LCO** but del 28.3.53; to Direcçao de Exploraçao dos Transportes Aéreos (DETA), Luanda, .58; regn cld .61; to Museu do Ar, Alverca do Riba; 1968-99; NFT.

6431   Regd **G-AFME** (CoR 8902) 9.12.38 to Airwork Ltd, Heston; CoA (6459) issued 13.1.39; operated by C W Martin's School of Air Navigation, Shoreham, later 6 CANS; 7 AONS, Perth; 6 AONS, Staverton, 23.5.40; impressed into RAF 15.7.40 as **Z7257**; 8 AACU, Filton, 15.7.40; force-landed   at Newport, Shropshire, 17.12.40; Pengam Moors 31.12.41; DH RU, Witney, 29.6.42; 24 Sqn, Hendon, 14.10.42; 510 Sqn, Hendon; 5 MU, Kemble, 3.11.42; loaned to Allied Airways (Gandar Dower) Ltd, Dyce 23.12.42; DH RU, Witney, 23.4.43; SF Halton 12.7.43; DH RU 31.7.43; 5 MU, Kemble, 25.9.43; Heston 23.4.44; SF Skaebrae 3.9.44; DH RU, Witney, 20.2.45; SOC 3.3.45.

6432   Regd **G-AFMF** (CoR 8903) 9.12.38 to Airwork Ltd, Heston; CoA (6460) issued 20.1.39; operated by C W Martin's School of Air Navigation, Shoreham, later 6 CANS; 7 AONS, Perth; 6 AONS, Staverton, 23.5.40; impressed into RAF 15.7.40 as **Z7256** and retained by 6 AONS; DH RU, Witney, as Cat B 8.3.42; 5 MU, Kemble, 27.5.42; to Gloster Aircraft Ltd 13.10.42 for communications work; 5 MU, Kemble, 8.10.45; sold to Air Schools Ltd 11.2.46; regd **G-AFMF** 26.1.46 to N R Harben of Air Schools, Burnaston; CoA renewed 20.8.46; regd 24.8.46 to Kennings Ltd, Burnaston;

regd 17.1.47 to D L Steiner t/a Steiner's Air Services, Speke; regd 9.9.47 to R Jones t/a Belle Vue Flying Service, Barton; regd 4.3.48 to British Cellulose Industries (Manchester) Ltd t/a BCI Airways, Barton; damaged on landing at Barton 30.5.48 and sold 30.8.48; regd 19.1.49 to R C Jarvis, Leicester; regd 23.3.49 to Adie Aviation Ltd, Croydon; rebuilt early .50 using parts from G-AHXY; regd 18.4.50 to J W Adamson, trading as Oldstead Aircraft, Newcastle (Woolsington); CoA renewed 18.5.50; crashed on Stooprigg Fell, 2 mls W of Simonburn, nr Hexham, Northumberland due to icing, 19.2.54 and DBF, but no casualties; regn cld 17.9.54.

EI-AEA, c/n 6433 after its accident at Hutton Cranswick on 4th October 1949
[G M Simons collection]

6433   Regd **G-AFMG** (CoR 8904) 9.12.38 to Airwork Ltd, Heston; CoA (6461) issued 1.2.39; operated by C W Martin's School of Air Navigation, Shoreham, later 6 CANS; 7 AONS, Perth, 30.9.39; 6 AONS, Staverton, 23.5.40; impressed into RAF 15.7.40 as **Z7259** and retained by 6 AONS; DH RU, Witney, 27.6.42; 18 MU, Dumfries, 4.9.42; ATA, White Waltham, 21.2.43; DH RU, Witney, 1.8.44; 5 MU, Kemble, 2.12.44; sold to Portsmouth Aviation Ltd 5.12.46; regd **G-AFMG** 11.12.46 to Portsmouth Aviation Ltd, Portsmouth; CoA renewed 10.1.47; regn cld 21.5.48 as sold abroad; regd in Eire as **EI-AEA** 26.7.48 to Weston Air Services Ltd; crashed landing (without customs clearance) at Highfield Farm, nr Hutton Cranswick, Yorks, 4.10.49; wreck to Manchester 11.49 and later to Croydon for spares.

6434   Regd **G-AFMH** (CoR 8905) 9.12.38 to Airwork Ltd, Heston; CoA (6462) issued 6.2.39; operated by C W Martin's School of Air Navigation, Shoreham, later 6 CANS; 7 AONS, Perth, 30.9.39; 6 AONS, Staverton, 23.5.40; impressed into RAF 15.7.40 as **Z7258**; 6 AACU, Ringway; DH RU, Witney, for conversion to ambulance aircraft 10.40; 24 Sqn, Hendon, 15.5.41; nominally presented to the RAF by the Silver Thimble Fund and named *Women of the Empire* by Lady Maud Carnegie 21.5.41; 1680 Flt, Abbotsinch, 10.10.41; involved in air ambulance flight from Scatsta (Shetland) to Turnhouse with six wounded Catalina aircrew, 6.6.42; DH 20.10.42; SF Abbotsinch 23.1.43; 1680 Flt, Abbotsinch, 15.6.43; SOC 25.7.45.

6435   Regd **G-AFMI** (CoR 8906) 9.12.38 to Airwork Ltd, Heston; CoA (6463) issued 20.2.39; operated by C W Martin's School of Air Navigation, Shoreham, later 6 CANS; 7 AONS, Perth; 6 AONS, Staverton, 30.9.39; impressed into RAF 15.7.40 as **Z7260**; DH RU, Witney,19.8.42; DH for seating modifications 11.11.42; Halton 29.12.42; DH RU, Witney, 20.8.43; 5 MU, Kemble, 10.11.43; 13 OTU, Harwell, 6.11.44; 18 MU, Dumfries, 22.3.46; 63 MU, Carluke; SOC 23.4.46.

Two ambulance-fitted Dominies of 24 Squadron, Z7258, c/n 6434, "Women of the Empire" and Z7261, c/n 6436, "Women of Britain"   [MAP via P H T Green]

A post-war view of c/n 6436 as G-AFMJ of Air Enterprises Ltd standing in front of the Croydon terminal building   *[Denis Fox collection]*

6436 Regd **G-AFMJ** (CoR 8907) 9.12.38 to Airwork Ltd, Heston; CoA(6464) issued 27.2.39; operated by C W Martin's School of Air Navigation, Shoreham, later 6 CANS; 7 AONS, Perth, 30.9.39; impressed into RAF 15.7.40 as **Z7261**; 6 AONS, Staverton; DH RU, Witney, for conversion to ambulance 22.8.40; 24 Sqn, Hendon, 17.5.41; nominally presented to RAF 21.5.41 by the Silver Thimble Fund and named *Women of Britain* by Lady Maud Carnegie 21.5.41; Wick CF 22.8.41; DH RU, Witney; retd to Wick 3.4.42; involved in air ambulance flight from Scatsta (Shetland) to Turnhouse with six wounded Catalina aircrew 6.6.42; Wick 10.7.45; SF Kinloss 8.5.46; 18 MU, Dumfries, 25.5.47; sold to Air Enterprises Ltd; regd **G-AFMJ** 11.12.47, to Air Enterprises Ltd, Croydon; CoA renewed 27.7.48; to Palestine for use with UN forces 28.8.48 as **3**; returned to Air Enterprises Ltd 8.10.48 as **G-AFMJ** and operated on services to Sandown, IoW, from 5.49, named *Shanklin Flyer;* regd 13.4.53 to Airwork Ltd and operated by Airwork Training Services Ltd, Perth; regn cld 17.9.56 as sold to Paraguay; regd **ZP-TDH** 10.56 to Roland Degli Ubertti / Aero-Carga SRL, Asunción; DBR in hangar collapse at Stroessner Airport, Asunción, 10.62.

6437 CoA (6524) issued 22.3.39; regd **HB-AME** (CoR 505) 28.3.39 to Alpar Schweizerisch Luftverkehr AG, Berne (Belpmoos); regd 12.47 to Swissair AG, Dubendorf; re-regd **HB-APE** 19.4.48 to Swissair AG; overhauled c.8.54 by Farner-Werke AG, Grenchen; proposed sale to Spain abandoned; regd .55 to Motorfluggruppe Zurich, Aero Club de Suisse, Kloten; for sale 4.65; regn cld 16.4.69; regn **D-IGUN** reserved 15.4.69 for G Nitzsche; permit 28.5.69 for ferry Zurich-Egelsbach; overhauled by Röder Prasizion, Egelsbach; regd and CoA issued 1.12.69; sold to G Kurfiss (Air Classik GmbH), Stuttgart 3.74; last flown 9.74 to Frankfurt and placed on display on airport terrace 14.9.74; moved to Air Classik exhibition, Düsseldorf 8.76; to store (Malmsheim ?) by 7.85; sold to Ikarus Flugverkehrsmuseum GmbH, Marl .86; museum closed .88, aircraft sold to J Koch, Augsburg, who intended to restore it to flying condition; regn **D-ILIT** reserved 16.12.92 with c/n incorrectly quoted as 6347; parts used instead to rebuild c/n 6879 which became G-AMAI, D-ILIT.

6438 Regd **HB-AMU** (CoR 506) 28.3.39 to Alpar Schweizerische Luftverkehr AG, Berne (Belpmoos); CoA (6532) issued 29.4.39; regd 12.47 to Swissair AG, Dubendorf; re-regd **HB-APU** 14.5.48; regd .55 to Farner Werke AG, Grenchen; regd .55 to Motorfluggruppe Zurich, Aero Club de Suisse, Kloten; for sale 4.65; reduced to spares for HB-APE and regn cld 17.1.68.

6439 CoA (6561) issued 25.4.39 as **CR-AAT** for Dept of Railways, Portuguese East Africa, for operation by Direcçao de Exploraçao dos Transportes Aéreos (DETA), Lourenco Marques; current .54; NFT.

D-IGUN, c/n 6437, was purchased from Switzerland in 1970 and spent some time on display in Germany   *[G M Simons collection]*

6440 CoA (6571) issued 4.5.39 as **CR-AAU** for Dept of Railways, Portuguese East Africa, for operation by Direcçao de Exploraçao dos Transportes Aéreos (DETA), Lourenco Marques; current .54; NFT.

6441 Regd **G-AFRK** 9.3.39 to Isle of Man Air Services Ltd, Ronaldsway; CoA (6517) issued 8.5.39; regd 12.5.39 to Scottish Airways Ltd, Renfrew; believed used for AAJC services throughout the war; regd 1.2.47 to BEA, Northolt; named *RMA Rudyard Kipling* .52; regd 16.5.56 to Airviews Ltd, Ringway; regd 25.2.59 to T H Marshall, Christchurch; CoA lapsed 10.3.59; used for spares for G-AGJG and G-AKIF; remains extant at Christchurch 12.60; regn cld 12.2.62; parts to Durney Aeronautical Collection, Andover.

6442 Regd **G-AFNC** 1.2.39 to Aircraft Operating Co Ltd, Hatfield; CoA (6654) issued 21.6.39; impressed into RAF 8.9.39; 24 Sqn, Hendon; regn cld as sold 16.10.39; 1 Camouflage Unit, Baginton, 21.11.39; allocated serial **V4724** 6.2.40; 24 Sqn 23.2.40; 22 MU, Silloth, 7.10.40; 1 AONS, Prestwick, 10.10.40; 1 Camouflage Unit, Hendon, 4.1.41; USAAC Comm Flt 28.12.42; 8th Air Force Ferry & Transport Service, later 27th ATG; retd to RAF at Halton 20.10.43; DH RU, Witney, 17.3.45; 18 MU, Dumfries, 15.7.45; 5 MU, Kemble, 2.4.46; sold to Field Consolidated Aircraft Services Ltd 27.5.46; regd **G-AFNC** 26.6.46 to Field Consolidated Aircraft Services Ltd, Croydon; regn cld 14.8.46 as sold abroad; CoA renewed 23.10.46; regd in Belgian Congo as **OO-CCD** 10.2.47 to A Camelbeek, Elizabethville; WFU 5.7.47; regn cld 8.7.47.

6443 Regd **G-AFND** 1.2.39 to Aircraft Operating Co Ltd, Hatfield; CoA (6658) issued 29.6.39; impressed into RAF 9.9.39; 24 Sqn, Hendon; regn cld as sold 16.10.39; 1 Camouflage Unit, Baginton 27.11.39; allocated RAF serial **V4725** 6.2.40; 24 Sqn,

HB-AMU, c/n 6438, at Berne in 1939, when it was owned by Alpar Schweizerische Luftverkher AG   *[via C N Dodds]*

Airviews Ltd owned former BEA Rapide G-AFRK, c/n 6441, for about three years and based it at Ringway *[Denis Fox collection]*

Hendon, 25.2.40; 1 Camouflage Unit, Hendon, 14.3.40; Stapleford Tawney 11.6.42; damaged Cat B 15.6.42; DH RU, Witney, for repair 1.7.42; 19 Gp CF, Roborough, 16.10.42; 18 Gp CF, Leuchars, 25.10.43; DH RU, Witney, 7.5.45; 12 FU, Melton Mowbray, 12.10.45; 18 MU, Dumfries, 11.2.46; sold to W A Rollason Ltd 12.4.47; restored to civil register as **G-AFND** 4.12.47; CoA renewed 7.6.48; regn cld 1.7.48 as sold abroad; regd in Jordan 13.7.48 as **TJ-AAP** to Arab Airways Association Ltd; to Arab Legion Air Force .49 as **R301**; 3 Flt/Sqn .49; NFT.

6444   CoA (6583) issued 11.5.39 to China National Aviation Corporation; possibly CNAC fleet no 38; destroyed in hangar fire, Sanhupa, Chungking 27.1.40.

6445   Regd **G-AFSO** 21.4.39 to Western Airways Ltd, Weston-super-Mare; CoA (6554) issued 22.5.39; impressed into RAF 10.10.39; 24 Sqn, Hendon; regn cld as sold 4.1.40; allocated RAF serial **W6457** 1.3.40; force-landed and DBF near Aneuil, France, 31.5.40 when the aircraft came under fire from enemy ground troops; SOC 3.6.40.

6446   RAF serial **R2485**; TOC 2 E&WS, Yatesbury, 28.7.39; 8 MU, Little Rissington, 1.8.39; 2 E&WS (later 2 SS), Yatesbury, 11.10.39; DH RU, Witney, 12.9.42; SOC 21.9.42.

6447   RAF serial **R2486**; TOC 8 MU, Little Rissington, 28.7.39; RAE, Farnborough, 5.9.39; 2 E&WS (later 2 SS), Yatesbury, 3.10.39; to Wrightways Ltd 5.1.42; 2 SS, Yatesbury, 20.8.42; ROS by DH 20.8.42; 2 SS, Yatesbury, 22.1.43; ATA, White Waltham, 12.3.43; damaged Cat B; DH RU, Witney, 29.10.44; CC CF, Northolt, 19.1.45 and Leavesden 12.4.45; RAF NI CF, Sydenham; 5 MU, Kemble, 4.11.46; sold to Brooklands

Aviation Ltd 25.8.47; regd **G-AKJY** 22.12.47 to Brooklands Aviation Ltd, Shoreham; CoA (9937) issued 13.5.48; regd 18.2.54 to W S Shackleton Ltd; regn cld 7.4.54 as sold in Algeria; regd **F-OAPT** 11.6.54 to Sté Aérotechnique, Algiers; regd late .57 to Sté Générale d'Affrétements Aériens (Air Fret), Algiers; CoA suspended at Géryville 2.3.60; remains sold mid-.60 to Cie Gen de Transports en Algérie (CGTA) for spares.

6448   RAF serial **R2487**; TOC 8 MU, Little Rissington, 28.7.39; RAE, Farnborough, 30.9.39; 8 MU, Little Rissington, 14.10.39; 2 E&WS (later 2 SS), Yatesbury, 25.5.40; DH RU, Witney, 4.11.42; 18 MU, Dumfries, 4.2.43; ATC Flt, Halton, 20.3.43; DH RU, Witney, 27.7.43; 18 MU, Dumfries, 11.9.43; 59 OTU, Milfield, 17.9.43; unit redes FLS 27.1.44; DH RU, Witney, 12.4.45; A&AEE CF, Boscombe Down, 17.9.45; loaned to Vickers-Supermarine, High Post, 18.4.46 to 15.5.46; 5 MU, Kemble, 9.1.50; regd **G-ALZH** 24.3.50 to Le Bryan Group Products (GB) Ltd but officially sold to Hants & Sussex Aero Club 30.3.50; CoA (10874) issued 24.5.50; regd 24.5.50 to W J E Lee, Broxbourne; gained some notoriety 5.50 when it was looped at Bembridge air display; regd 6.4.51 to Aerocontacts Ltd, Gatwick; regn cld 2.4.52 as sold in Madagascar; inspected at Ivato 30.8.52; regd **F-OAKF** 25.10.52 to Sté Air Madagascar, Ivato; CoA suspended 21.4.62; regn cld .63.

6449   CoA (6751) issued 23.8.39; regd **PP-LAA** 30.3.40 to Cia Fabril de Juta; named *Maristella* 5.5.40; sold to VARIG 22.7.42; re-regd **PP-VAN** 19.8.42 to VARIG, named *Chui*; inaugurated Porto Alegre to Montevideo service 8.42; damaged in accident at Jaguarao, Rio Grande do Sul, 17.6.43, but repaired; sold to Organizacio Mineira de Transportes Aéreos (OMTA), Belo Horizonte, 5.11.45; re-regd **PP-OMA** 11.2.46; regn cld 24.10.62 as "deteriorated many years ago".

Dominie R2487, c/n 6448, sporting a wind-operated generator on the cabin roof *[via A J Jackson and P H T Green]*

Without fin and rudder, G-AFOI, c/n 6450, stands forlorn in the snow at Nottingham (Tollerton) on 3rd November 1957. In the background is Lincoln Freighter ZP-CBR-97!
[P H Butler]

6450 Regd **G-AFOI** 28.7.39 to Scottish Airways Ltd, Renfrew; CoA (6720) issued 28.8.39; believed used on AAJC services throughout WW2; regd 1.2.47 to BEA, Northolt; sold 7.6.48 and regd 20.1.49 to Gibraltar Airways Ltd; regd 18.5.50 to J H Hoggart-Hill t/a Airmotive, Taunton (based Speke); regd 28.6.50 to Airmotive Ltd, Speke; regd 5.6.52 to Handley-Page Ltd, Radlett; CoA lapsed 20.9.57 and in 'distressed' condition at Tollerton on 3.11.57; sold for spares .58 to Luton Airways Ltd; regn cld 20.3.59; remains extant at Luton 3.60.

6451 CoA (6752) issued 24.8.39; regd **CR-LAV** 24.8.39 to Portuguese Air Services; regd 10.5.40 to Direcçao de Exploraçao dos Transportes Aéreos de Angola (DTA), Luanda; current .59.

6452 CoA (6755) issued 29.8.39; regd **CR-LAU** 29.8.39 to Portuguese Air Services; regd .39 to Direcçao de Exploraçao dos Transportes Aéreos de Angola (DTA), Luanda; WFU at Luanda .56.

6453 CoA (6760) issued 29.8.39; regd **CR-LAT** 10.5.40 to Direcçao de Exploraçao dos Transportes Aéreos de Angola (DTA), Luanda; regn cld as sold in France; regd **F-OAVZ** 7.56 to Transports Aériens du Gabon, Libreville; crashed into tree 20 mls from Douala while flying from Kribi to Douala 18.9.56, killing pilot; wreck not found until 10.57.

6454 Regd **VT-ALO** (CoR 386) 6.39 to Air Services of India Ltd, Bombay (replacement for DH.90 VT-AKC); CoA (6715) issued 26.7.39; flown to India 25.8.39; probably to Tata and Sons Ltd, Juhu, Bombay; impressed into RAF 20.1.42 as **HX791**; 2 Coastal Def Flt, Juhu; to Director of Civil Aviation, India, 1.9.43; possibly restored as **VT-ALO**; SOC by RAF 29.3.45; regn cld 31.3.45.

6455 RAF serial **P9588**; TOC 10 MU, Hullavington, 21.9.39; 2 E&WS (later 2 SS), Yatesbury, 13.12.39; damaged and to Air Taxis Ltd 1.9.42; 18 MU, Dumfries, 21.11.42; loaned to Allied Airways (Gandar Dower) Ltd, Dyce, 15.1.43; sold to them 30.4.43 for £4300; regd **G-AGHI** 2.12.43 to Allied Airways (Gandar Dower) Ltd, named *The Shetlander;* CoA (7047) issued 18.3.44; taken over by BEA 12.4.47 and regd to them 13.11.47; regd 15.6.48 to Charles Allen, Croydon; regd 1.7.48 to C L Burton, t/a International Airways, Croydon; CoA lapsed 31.8.50; sold to Hants & Sussex Aviation Ltd, Portsmouth, for spares .52; regn cld 31.8.59.

6456 RAF serial **P9589**; TOC 10 MU, Hullavington, 21.9.39; 2 E&WS (later 2 SS), Yatesbury, 13.12.39; 1 SS, Cranwell, 2.10.41; damaged 3.8.42; DH RU, Witney, 27.9.42, awaiting collection 2.1.43; 18 MU, Dumfries, 21.1.43; 15 Gp CF, Speke, 10.4.43; DH RU, Witney, 26.9.44; 5 MU, Kemble, 6.12.44; sold to Wg Cdr Presland for RAF Flying Club 25.11.46; regd **G-AIYP** 9.12.46 to Wg Cdr W H Wetton, t/a Garden Corner, London; CoA (8806) issued 17.1.47; used by St Christopher Travel-Ways Ltd (associate company); regd 8.9.47 to R W Marsh and operated by Island Air Services at Heathrow; regd 11.3.49 to Autowork (Winchester) Ltd, Eastleigh; regd 29.3.50 to V H Bellamy t/a Flightways, Eastleigh; regd 28.3.52 to Murray Chown Aviation Ltd, Staverton; operated by Dragon Airways Ltd, Pwllheli, 6.53; crashed in fog 50 yds S of Four Crosses / Nevin Rd, Pentre Uchaf, 5 mls from Pwllheli, 5.7.53, and DBF; regn cld 27.8.53.

6457 RAF serial **R5921**; TOC 1 E&WS, Cranwell, 26.9.39; 2 E&WS (later 2 SS), Yatesbury, 13.10.39; damaged Cat B 11.8.42; DH RU, Witney, 25.8.42; 34 Wg 22.12.42; 2 Sqn, Sawbridgeworth, 3.1.43 (later Bottisham and Fowlmere); to Wrightways Ltd 11.7.43; SF Hartford Bridge 22.7.43; SF Old Sarum 5.4.44; overshot into ditch on landing at Andover 12.5.44; DH RU, Witney, 21.6.44; 12(P) AFU, Spitalgate, 25.10.44; 18 MU, Dumfries, 27.12.45; 16 FU, Dunkeswell, 1.2.46; Valley 12.4.46; 18 MU, Dumfries, 15.5.46; sold 10.3.47 to Lancashire Aircraft Corporation Ltd, Squires Gate and regd **G-AJKX** 22.3.47 to them; CoA (9438) issued 18.7.47; regn cld as to long term storage 9.11.50; regd 9.4.51 to same owner; regn cld 7.1.53 as sold in Pakistan; regd **AP-AGI** .53 to Crescent Air Transport, Karachi; shipped to UK in crates 19.7.56 for Morton Air Services Ltd, Croydon; restored to register as **G-AJKX** but WFU at Croydon; stored at Biggin Hill .62; presumed reduced to spares.

OO-AFG, c/n 6458, of Air Affairs owners of this Rapide from 1962 to 1964
[G M Simons collection]

C/n 6458 at Wevelgem about 1965, when operated by Centre National de Parachutisme and appropriately registered OO-CNP. It had been fitted with moulded top cockpit glazing, lowered cabin windows and navigation equipment located behind the pilot's bulkhead   *[via C N Dodds]*

6458   RAF serial **R5922**; TOC 2 E&WS (later 2 SS), Yatesbury, 13.10.39; Air Taxis Ltd for major inspection 3.8.42; 2 SS, Yatesbury, 20.9.42; Air Taxis Ltd 30.10.42; 18 MU, Dumfries, 24.2.43; ATC Flt, Halton, 20.3.43; DH RU, Witney, 25.8.43; 18 MU, Dumfries, 15.12.43; 2 DF, Cranfield, 2.4.44; 1 DF, North Weald, 5.7.44; Redhill 6.11.44; DH RU, Witney, 14.12.44; 18 MU, Dumfries, 27.4.45; 12 FU, Melton Mowbray, 7.10.45; 18 MU, Dumfries, 8.2.46; regd **G-AKNV** 2.12.47 to Lancashire Aircraft Corporation Ltd, Squires Gate and sold to them 9.12.47; CoA (9979) issued 24.3.48; regn cld as sold in Eire 11.12.53; regd **EI-AGK** 16.2.53 to J J Crowley, t/a Republic Air Charters; regn cld 12.6.55 as sold in UK; restored to register as **G-AKNV** 20.6.55 to Derby Aviation Ltd, Derby (Burnaston); CoA renewed 6.5.55 (sic); regd 12.7.55 to Fairey Aviation Co Ltd, White Waltham; regn cld 27.9.55 as sold in Belgium; regd **OO-AFG** 27.2.58 to Avions Fairey SA, Gosselies; stripped and rebuilt 1958, fitted with electric flaps, radio compass, moulded canopy and enlarged cabin windows, with an extra large folding door to allow carriage of bulky cargo; regd 10.4.62 to Air Affaires SPRL, Gosselies; re-regd **OO-CNP** 10.4.64 to L Huybrechts, Wevelgem; regd .66 to Abelag, Grimbergen; CoA lapsed 3.9.66; regn cld 10.8.70; stored at Korkrijk-Wevelgem until roaded to Musée Royal de l'Armée et de la Militaire, Brussels, 4.10.73; undergoing restoration from mid-.80s; extant.

6459   RAF serial **R5923**; TOC 2 E&WS (later 2 SS), Yatesbury, 13.10.39; swung on take-off from Yatesbury and hit fence 22.4.41; SOC 29.4.41.

6460   RAF serial **R5924**; TOC 2 E&WS (later 2 SS), Yatesbury, 13.10.39; undershot when landing at Yatesbury 23.3.42; DH RU, Witney, 28.3.42; 5 MU, Kemble, 22.7.42; 7 AGS, Stormy Down, 17.8.42 but probably to SF Croydon instead; 18 MU, Dumfries, 16.10.42; 2 (later 2 RS), Yatesbury, 19.11.42; 1 SoTT, Halton, 31.12.42; DH RU, Witney, 15.3.46; 5 MU, Kemble, 21.2.47; sold 29.5.47 to Southern Aircraft (Gatwick) Ltd and regd **G-AKFO** to them 3.9.47; sold 3.2.49 to unknown buyer; CoA 9780 allocated but aircraft not converted to civil standard; broken up for spares; regn cld 4.8.49.

6461   RAF serial **R5925**; TOC 10 MU, Hullavington, 6.10.39; 2 E&WS (later 2 SS), Yatesbury, 13.10.39; DH RU, Witney, 7.10.42 as damaged Cat B; 18 MU, Dumfries, 13.2.43; 24 Sqn, Hendon, 14.5.43; damaged 26.3.44; MCS, Hendon, 8.9.44; damaged 9.9.45; SOC 31.12.45.

6462   Experimental airframe for static use.

6463   RAF serial **R5926**; TOC 2 E&WS (later 2 SS), Yatesbury, 16.10.39; DH RU, Witney, 16.6.42; 18 MU, Dumfries, 26.9.42; sold 21.10.42 to Airwork General Trading Ltd, Gatwick, for packing for overseas shipment; regd **G-AGFU** 26.11.42 to Anglo-Iranian Oil Co Ltd, Abadan; CoA (6951) issued 1.2.43; shipped to Basra 24.3.43 on *Salawati* / LS405; sold 1.2.47 to Aircraft & Engineering Services Ltd, Croydon and regd to them 20.8.47; regd 29.8.47 to Air Charter Ltd, Croydon; CoA lapsed 24.5.50; regn cld 9.6.50 as sold abroad; to Belgium but not regd; derelict at Brussels .52.

6464   RAF serial **R5927**; TOC 2 E&WS (later 2 SS), Yatesbury, 18.10.39; struck balloon cable at Wiggins Field, Horton, Bucks, 14.2.42, crashed and DBF; 2 killed; SOC 14.3.42.

6465   RAF serial **R5928**; TOC 2 E&WS (later 2 SS), Yatesbury, 24.10.39; 1 SS, Cranwell, 2.10.41; DH RU, Witney, as damaged Cat B 7.7.42; SF Abbotsinch 11.10.42; 1 SS, Cranwell, 22.10.42; 1680 Flt, Abbotsinch, 15.6.43; crashed on Carricknowe golf course, Corstorphine, Edinburgh, 1.3.44 while force-landing in blizzard; SOC 2.3.44.

6466   RAF serial **R5929**; TOC 2 E&WS (later 2 SS), Yatesbury, 27.10.39; stalled and crashed while low flying at Bishops Cannings, Devizes, 27.5.41, killing seven; SOC 3.6.41.

6467   RAF serial **R5930**; TOC 2 E&WS (later 2 SS), Yatesbury, 6.11.39; 1 SS, Cranwell, 2.10.41; damaged on landing at Cranwell 23.3.42; DH RU, Witney, 1.4.42; 18 MU, Dumfries, 11.6.42; 2 SS, Yatesbury, 19.7.42; damaged in gale at Yatesbury 31.1.43; DH RU, Witney, 15.2.43; 57 OTU, Hawarden, 14.6.43; 56 OTU, Tealing, 4.7.43; 58 OTU, Grangemouth, 7.9.43; unit redes 3 TEU 5.10.43; 60 OTU, High Ercall, 2.7.44; 13 OTU, Harwell (later Middleton St. George) 22.3.45; 18 MU, Dumfries, 27.5.46; regd **G-AIUO** 20.11.46 to Air Schools Ltd, Derby (Burnaston); CoA (9011) issued 20.6.47; regd 26.6.47 to Hornton Airways Ltd, Gatwick; company ceased trading 5.50; regn cld 19.7.51 as sold in Sweden; regd **SE-BTT** 31.7.51 to Junex Konfektions AB, Huskvarna; regn cld 31.3.53 as sold in Denmark; regd **OY-ACV** 13.4.53 to Viggo Sylvest Jensen, Hillerod; sold in West Germany 10.4.56; regd **D-IDAK** .56 to Hamburger Aero Lloyd; regd .62 to Hanseatische Flugdienst GmbH, Hamburg; regn cld .63.

Hornton Airways Ltd used this Rapide, G-AIUO, c/n 6467, seen here at Croydon

[Denis Fox collection]

G-AKNW, c/n 6469, in the markings of Air Navigation & Trading Co Ltd, although this operator does not appear in the register   [G M Simons collection]

C/n 6470, 6V-AAC, originally R5933, when operated by Cie Sénégalaise de Transports Aériens   [G M Simons collection]

6468   RAF serial **R5931**; TOC 2 E&WS (later 2 SS), Yatesbury, 14.11.39; DH RU, Witney, as damaged 17.11.42; 24 Sqn, Hendon, 5.3.43; MCS, Hendon, 8.9.44; DH RU, Witney,1.6.45; 18 MU, Dumfries, 3.1.46; SF Halton 12.4.46; 18 MU, Dumfries, 3.6.47; regd **G-AKOO** 8.12.47 to Southern Aircraft (Gatwick) Ltd and sold to them 15.12.47; CoA (10056) issued 2.12.48; to Chile 4.12.48; regn cld 13.12.48 as sold abroad; this may be Rapide **CC-CIC-0034** regd to Club Aéreo de Linares which was damaged on take-off from El Maizal airstrip, Linares, 23.3.53.

6469   RAF serial **R5932**; TOC 2 E&WS (later 2 SS), Yatesbury, 20.11.39; DH RU, Witney, as damaged Cat B 6.8.42, after aircraft broke picketing ropes in strong gale; 18 MU, Dumfries, 30.11.42; 83 Gp CF, Redhill, 18.4.43; 3 Del Flt, High Ercall, 19.5.43; damaged on landing at Witney 18.10.43; 13 Gp CF, Speke, 11.10.43; 50 MU, Cowley, 2.11.43; 3 Del Flt, Acklington, 12.11.43; 13 Gp CF, Inverness, 7.12.43; 15 Gp CF, Speke, 11.10.44; repaired at 34 MU, Shrewsbury, 8.3.46; 18 MU, Dumfries, 3.10.46; regd **G-AKNW** 2.12.47 to Lancashire Aircraft Corporation Ltd, Squires Gate, and sold to them 9.12.47; CoA (9980) issued 7.4.48; regd 25.4.49 to R L Whyham, Squires Gate; regd 5.5.50 to Skyways Ltd, Dunsfold; regn cld 23.6.50 as sold in Lebanon; regd **LR-ABH** 23.6.50 to Arab Contracting & Trading, t/a Saad Transport, Beirut; re-regd **OD-ABH** 5.51; DBF on start-up at H3 airstrip, Syria, 30.7.54.

6470   RAF serial **R5933**; TOC 2 E&WS (later 2 SS), Yatesbury, 6.12.39; DH RU, Witney, 1.7.42; 18 MU, Dumfries, 15.10.42; BWF, Yatesbury, 28.10.42; 54 OTU, Charterhall, 1.1.44; DH RU, Witney, 1.6.45; 18 MU, Dumfries, 28.1.46; sold 9.12.47 to Air Enterprises Ltd; regd **G-AKNY** 11.12.47 to Air Enterprises Ltd,

CF-BNG, c/n 6472, on floats with beaching gear attached
[G M Simons collection]

Croydon; CoA (10014) issued 25.3.48; regd 22.1.49 to Patrick Motors Ltd, Elmdon; CoA lapsed 20.12.51; regd 25.3.52 to North Devon Flying Club Ltd, Chivenor; regd 29.7.53 to Air Couriers (Transport) Ltd, Croydon (Biggin Hill from 9.59); converted to Mk.6 3.4.59; regn cld 3.10.60 as sold in France; regd **F-OBRX** 13.10.60 to SA Ardic, Dakar, Senegal; regd in Senegal as **6V-AAC** 9.63 to Cie Sénégalaise de Transports Aériens, Dakar; regd mid-.65 to Centre de Parachutisme Sportif, Dakar; quoted as c/n 5933/W.1002 after rebuild at Dakar .66/.67 (implying that parts of G-AKJS were incorporated); CoA expired 4.70, regn cld .70.

6471   RAF serial **R5934**; TOC 2 E&WS (later 2 SS), Yatesbury, 6.12.39; BWF, Yatesbury, Cat B 3.3.43; DH RU, Witney, 26.3.43; 526 Sqn [MD:X], Inverness (Longman) 19.8.43; 527 Sqn, Digby, 3.5.45; RWE, Watton, 18.4.46; 5 MU, Kemble, 17.12.46; sold to Brooklands Aviation Ltd 25.8.47; regd **G-AKSH** 31.1.48 to Brooklands Aviation Ltd, Shoreham; CoA (9962) issued 14.5.48; regd 15.11.51 to W S Shackleton Ltd; regn cld 22.11.51 as sold in Fiji; despatched to H Gatty, Suva, 30.11.51, arr 2.52; regd **VQ-FAM** 11.2.52 to Katafanga Estates Ltd, t/a Fiji Airways; damaged by fire on start-up at Lambasa, Vanua Levu Island, 25.8.52 but repaired; CoA lapsed 17.3.55; broken up as spares for VQ-FAN (c/n 6577).

6472   Regd **CF-BNG** 12.9.40 to de Havilland Aircraft of Canada Ltd, Toronto; regd 6.1.41 to Ginger Coote Airways Ltd, Vancouver; became Canadian Pacific Air Lines 1.42; following forced landing on St Lawrence River ice, force-landed again with engine on fire at Great Lake, Quebec, 9.3.46, and DBF.

6473   RAF serial **R9545**; TOC 2 E&WS (later 2 SS), Yatesbury, 3.1.40; at DH RU, Witney, 5.40; DH RU, Witney, as damaged 5.11.42; 18 MU, Dumfries,18.2.43; ATA 23.3.43; DH RU, Witney, 30.11.44; A&AEE CF, Boscombe Down, 1.10.45; struck by fuel bowser 12.12.47; SOC 30.1.48 and to scrap dump at Boscombe Down 20.4.48.

6474   RAF serial **R9546**; TOC 2 E&WS (later 2 SS), Yatesbury, 12.1.40; DH RU, Witney, as damaged 11.12.42; 18 MU, Dumfries, 29.3.43; Old Sarum 11.4.43; ATA 26.5.43; DH RU Witney, as damaged 13.6.44; Vickers-Armstrongs Aircraft Ltd, Castle Bromwich, 11.10.44; 18 MU, Dumfries, 9.4.46; regd **G-AKOK** 18.6.48 to Mannin Airways Ltd, Ronaldsway; to North-West Airlines (IoM) Ltd 21.5.51 but not regd; regn cld 20.3.52 as sold abroad; regd in France as **F-BGPK** 30.4.52 to Sté Aigle Azur Indochine, Hanoi; CoA suspended at Phnom Penh 2.5.53; restored for single flight to Saigon 15.9.53; sold 3.54 to Cie Laotienne de Commerce et Transport, Hanoi, but probably used for spares.

F-BGPK, c/n 6474, the former G-AKOK, at Croydon in 1952 before leaving for French Indo-China
[via A. Chivers]

Rapide ZS-BCD, c/n 6477, of Owenair at Youngsfield, Cape Town, on 27th December 1950   *[P H T Green collection]*

6475 RAF serial **R9547**; TOC 2 E&WS (later 2 SS), Yatesbury, 12.1.40; damaged 29.6.42; DH RU, Witney, 8.7.42; 18 MU, Dumfries, 11.10.42; BWF, Yatesbury, 28.11.42; 18 MU, Dumfries, 18.2.44; 1680 Flt, Prestwick, 19.3.44; SOC 1.12.45.

6476 RAF serial **R9548**; TOC 2 E&WS (later 2 SS), Yatesbury, 12.1.40; damaged on landing at Yatesbury 9.12.42; DH RU, Witney, 9.12.42; 18 MU, Dumfries, 10.3.43; ATC Flt, Halton, 18.3.43; damaged Cat AC/FA 1.11.44; 1 SoTT, Halton [THA:A], 21.3.46; 5 MU, Kemble, 15.4.47; regd **G-AKVU** 10.3.48 to Surrey Financial Trust Ltd, Croydon; regd 19.3.48 to Aircraft & Engineering Services Ltd, Croydon; CoA (10397) issued 25.3.49; regd 30.9.49 to Patrick Motors Ltd, Elmdon; regd 30.5.50 to W S Shackleton Ltd; regd 26.10.50 to Goodhew Aviation Co Ltd, Kidlington; CoA lapsed 25.5.51; regd 17.3.52 to Transair Ltd, Croydon; regn cld 1.4.52 as sold in France; regd **F-BGPM** 25.6.52 to Aigle Azur Indochine, Hanoi; port engine caught fire on start-up at Siem Reap, Cambodia, 13.2.53 and aircraft DBF.

6477 RAF serial **R9549**; TOC 20 MU, Aston Down, 15.2.40; 44 MU, Edzell, 14.10.41; to Air Taxis Ltd as damaged Cat B 22.11.41; 44 MU 31.1.42; 24 Sqn, Hendon, 9.8.42; to Air Taxis Ltd 23.8.42; 18 MU, Dumfries, 21.11.42; 47 MU, Sealand, 2.1.43; shipped to South Africa on *Clan McNair*, arr 20.3.43; to SAAF as **1363**; 9 AD; 62 AS 28.5.43; 61 Sqn 14.11.44; Congella, Durban, 9.6.45; sold via 15 AD to Owenair Pty Ltd, Cape Town, 2.7.46 for £1950; regd **ZS-BCD** 21.10.46; regn cld 22.5.53 as sold in Southern Rhodesia; regd **VP-YKJ** 23.5.53 to Fishair (Pvt) Ltd, Marandellas; regn cld 10.58 as sold in France; regd **F-OBKH** 30.10.58 to Sté Franco-Africaine d'Exploitation, t/a Air Gabon, Libreville; regd mid-.59 to Groupement Aéronautique et Automobile, Libreville, but operated by Air Gabon; destroyed in Gabon 8.61.

6478 RAF serial **R9550**; TOC 20 MU, Aston Down, 6.3.40; damaged Cat B 12.10.41; HQ ATA, White Waltham, 31.12.41; 8 FPP, Hullavington, 4.43; DH RU, Witney, as damaged 8.8.43; RAE T Flt, Farnborough, 27.4.44; Hendon; 5 MU, Kemble, 31.4.46; regd **G-AHPT** 22.5.46 to Field Consolidated Aircraft Services Ltd, Croydon; regd 24.8.46 to Island Air Charters Ltd, Jersey; CoA (7912) issued 6.10.46; CoA lapsed 21.3.51; regd 11.5.51 to Aerocontacts Ltd, Gatwick; CoA renewed 18.3.52; regd 25.3.52 to Wright Aviation Ltd, Speke; regd 16.2.54 to Dragon Airways Ltd, Speke, named *Peter Tare;* regd 10.2.56 to Don Everall (Aviation) Ltd, Elmdon; while being operated for Tarmac Ltd, struck lorry on landing on St Albans bypass under construction nr Leverstock Green 7.7.59; pilot, E Ashton, and passenger T J Livesey (County Surveyor for Holland Division of Lincs) killed; regn cld 18.8.59.

6479 RAF serial **R9551**; TOC 12 MU, Kirkbride, 5.4.40; 18 MU, Dumfries, 12.8.40; 1 Cam Flt, Hendon, 24.12.40; badly damaged 25.3.41 in forced landing at Yoxall, Staffs, in bad weather; 51 MU, Lichfield, 29.3.41; SOC 14.4.41.

6480 RAF serial **R9552**; TOC 12 MU, Kirkbride, 5.4.40; 18 MU, Dumfries, 12.8.40; 1 Cam. Flt, Hendon, 22.12.40; unit redes 1 Cam Unit 13.3.41; SF Halton 5.8.42; 1 Cam. Unit, Stapleford Tawney, 6.8.42; 58 OTU, Grangemouth, 14.8.42; 57 OTU, Hawarden, 15.6.43; DH RU, Witney, as damaged 14.9.43; 18 MU, Dumfries, 15.12.43; 13 Gp CF, Inverness, 12.7.45 (later Dalcross); 1 FU, Pershore, 28.1.46; 18 MU, Dumfries, 10.4.46; sold to Air Navigation & Trading Ltd 15.12.47; regd **G-AKRO** 17.1.48 to East Anglian Flying Services Ltd, Southend; CoA (9994) issued 11.5.48; regd 4.4.49 to Inter-City Air Services Ltd, Hereford; CoA lapsed 8.4.50; regd 21.11.51 to Lancashire Aircraft Corporation Ltd, Squires Gate; CoA renewed 14.5.52; regn cld 16.1.54 as sold in France; regd **F-OAOY** 16.3.54 to Aéro Club de Colomb-Béchar, Algeria; DBF on starting up at Colomb-Béchar 22.10.54.

6481 RAF serial **R9553**; TOC 12 MU, Kirkbride, 3.5.40; 18 MU, Dumfries, 12.8.40; HQ FPP, Kemble, 27.3.41; 27 MU, Shawbury, 9.4.41; 10 FPP, Lossiemouth, 17.4.41; 9 MU, Cosford, 23.12.41; FTU, Honeybourne, 31.12.41; 24 Sqn, Hendon, 17.5.42; crashed on take-off from Rednal 27.4.43; SOC 13.5.43.

6482 RAF serial **R9554**; TOC 5 MU, Kemble, 2.5.40; 7 FPP, Sherburn-in-Elmet, 16.11.40; 10 FPP, Lossiemouth, 4.4.41; HQ FPP 16.5.41; SF Northolt 20.6.42; DH RU, Witney, as damaged 14.8.42; 18 MU, Dumfries, 8.12.42; 2 Del Flt, Colerne (later Cranfield), 29.3.43; DH RU, Witney, as damaged 2.5.44; 5 MU, Kemble, 23.8.44; SF Gatwick; SF Redhill 19.10.44; regd **G-AKTZ** 3.3.48 to D J Hayles, Portsmouth; sold to Denham Air Services 11.3.48; CoA (10057) issued 5.5.48; regd 9.6.48 to Airwork Ltd, Blackbushe; used

G-AHPT, c/n 6478, of Wright Aviation at Liverpool on 13th April 1952
[P H Butler]

Seen at Croydon on 18th June 1953 Rapide G-AKTZ, c/n 6482, in Olley Air Service titles although never registered to them!   *[Denis Fox collection]*

at Taif, Saudi Arabia, by British Civil Air Training Mission, operated by Airwork, 9.49 to 9.50; regd 25.10.50 to Birkett Air Service Ltd, Croydon; regd 14.5.53 to Morton Air Services Ltd, Croydon; converted to Mk.4 and CoA renewed 27.8.54; regd 25.8.54 to Iraq Petroleum Transport Co Ltd, Tripoli; regd 4.9.56 to Gordon, Woodroffe & Co Ltd, El Adem, Libya; regd 12.4.57 to Bahamas Helicopters (UK) Ltd, Libya; badly damaged when undercarriage collapsed on landing in desert nr Benghazi 27.5.57 but repaired; re-regd on name change 16.10.61 to Worldwide Helicopters (UK) Ltd; regn cld as 'destroyed' 23.4.63; rumoured that this aircraft survived in derelict condition on a military airfield in Libya.

6483 RAF serial **R9555**; TOC 5 MU, Kemble,11.4.40; 7 FPP, Sherburn-in-Elmet, 28.11.40; 2 FPP, Filton, 3.2.41; DH RU, Witney, as damaged 5.2.42; 37 MU, Burtonwood, 13.4.42; 2 Sqn, Sawbridgeworth, 9.7.42; DH RU, Witney, 9.1.43; 2 Sqn 31.1.43; 18 MU, Dumfries, 8.3.43; 4 DF, Turnhouse, 20.3.43; damaged 30.3.43, ROS by 50 MU 5.4.45; 4 DF, Hutton Cranswick, 13.7.45; SOC 13.3.46.

6484 RAF serial **R9556**; TOC 5 MU, Kemble,1.5.40; 7 FPP, Sherburn-in-Elmet, 22.11.40; HQ ATA, White Waltham, 8.9.41; 27 MU, Shawbury, 17.3.42; 24 Sqn, Hendon, 27.6.42; DH RU,

Dominie R9555, c/n 6483, on collection from Witney by ATA pilots   *[via P. Davis]*

Lancashire Aircraft Corporation's Rapide G-ALEJ, c/n 6484, crashed at Eccleshall on 14th September 1956   *[Denis Fox collection]*

G-AHJA, c/n 6486, and another Dragon Rapide advertising the Evening News *[via A. Chivers]*

Witney, as damaged 23.8.43; 4 RS, Madley, [A]11.11.43; 18 MU, Dumfries, 4.1.46; DH RU, Witney, as damaged 20.3.46; 18 MU, Dumfries, 12.12.46; sold to Tyne Taxis Ltd 27.5.48; originally allocated **G-ALAS** in error; regd **G-ALEJ** 1.6.48 to Tyne Taxis Ltd; on overhaul at Brough 8.48; CoA (10173) issued 1.4.49; regd 24.6.49 to Lancashire Aircraft Corporation Ltd, Squires Gate; crashed at Eccleshall, 10 mls S of Newcastle-under-Lyme, Staffs, 14.9.56, when smoke filled the cockpit; regn cld 22.11.56.

6485 RAF serial **R9557**; TOC 9 MU, Cosford, 3.5.40; 3 FPP, White Waltham, 1.11.40; damaged 1.11.41; 3 FPP, Hawarden, 29.11.41; blown into gun-pit while taxying at Edzell 14.4.43; DH RU, Witney, 1.45; SOC 11.1.45.

6486 RAF serial **R9558**; TOC 9 MU, Cosford, 13.5.40; 3 FPP, White Waltham, 1.11.40; DH RU, Witney, as damaged 25.1.44; 18 MU, Dumfries, 10.4.44; CRD at Vickers-Armstrongs (Aircraft) Ltd, High Post, 1.5.44; regd **G-AHJA** 8.4.46 to Vickers-Armstrongs (Aircraft) Ltd; CoA (7624) issued 8.5.47; regd 10.6.59 to Conway Hunt Ltd, Fairoaks; operated by Swansea Airways Ltd 11.60 to 7.61; regd 22.11.61 to Mexfield Aviation Co (Ireland) Ltd, Dublin; impounded by HM Customs at Luton 6.12.61 (13.12.61 ?) after illegal landing at Blackbushe; CoA lapsed 12.10.62; regd 18.6.63 to Air Navigation & Trading Co Ltd, Squires Gate; CoA renewed 24.11.66; regd 6.6.67 to D J Moores, East Midlands Airport; regd 28.3.68 to Trent Valley Aviation Ltd, East Midlands Airport; damaged in night landing at East Midlands Airport 20.5.69; sold 25.3.70; regn cld 9.4.70; believed moved to Abingdon before being shipped to Australia .78; probably stored at Berwick .78 but believed nothing now remains.

6487 RAF serial **R9559**; TOC 9 MU, Cosford, 3.5.40; 3 FPP, White Waltham, 3.11.40; DH RU, Witney, as damaged 11.4.43; SF Halton 30.8.43; hit obstruction on landing at Southend 30.11.44; DH RU, Witney, 12.12.44; 18 MU, Dumfries, 24.3.45; TTCCF,

White Waltham, (later Wyton) 16.8.45; Staff College CF, White Waltham, 21.3.46; RCCS, White Waltham, 28.11.46; 18 MU, Dumfries, 23.1.47; sold to D J Adey 31.5.47; regd **G-AKED** 25.8.47 to A Hamson & Son Ltd, Northampton; CoA (9702) issued 30.1.48; regd 3.2.48 to L E H Airways Ltd, London; regd 16.12.49 to W M Andrews, Nottingham (Tollerton); regd 21.11.50 to Patrick Motors Ltd, Elmdon; regd 9.4.51 to Airlines (Jersey) Ltd, t/a Jersey Airlines; converted to Mk.4 24.2.54; regd 10.3.55 to Eric Bemrose Ltd, Speke; regn cld 26.11.55 as sold in France; regd **F-DABY** 14.3.56 to Sté Norafor, Casablanca; regd **F-OBHH** 31.3.58 to Sté Générale d'Affrétements Aériens (Air Fret), Algiers; sold .60 to Cie Générale de Transports en Algérie (CGTA), Algiers; regd 1.61 to Air Fret; CoA suspended at Algiers 30.8.62; regn cld .64.

6488 RAF serial **R9560**; TOC 12 MU, Kirkbride, 12.5.40; 18 MU, Dumfries, 5.8.40; 8 MU, Little Rissington, 17.2.41; HQ SFPP, Kemble, 28.6.41; hit fence after ground-loop at Halton 28.11.41; DH RU, Witney, for repair 5.12.41; 9 MU, Cosford, 13.6.42; damaged 3.1.43 when part of blister hangar became detached during gale; SF Sealand 1.43; 30 MU, Sealand, 1.4.43; DH RU, Witney, as damaged 7.4.44; 5 MU, Kemble, 25.7.44; regd **G-AKUB** 3.3.48 to S K Davis, t/a Cambrian Air Services, Cardiff, and sold to them 11.3.48; CoA (10038) issued 2.4.48; regd 19.4.49 to J H Watts, S K Davies, E Keith-Davies & Care Lines Ltd, t/a Cambrian Air Services, named *Glamorgan;* regd 25.1.52 to Cambrian Air Services Ltd, Cardiff; regd 25.1.55 to Airwork Ltd, Blackbushe; regn cld 11.6.55 as sold in Iran; regd **EP-ADN** 7.55 to Iranian Oil Exploration & Production Co; regn cld before .59.

6489 RAF serial **R9561**; TOC 12 MU, Kirkbride, 12.5.40; 18 MU, Dumfries, 16.7.40; 7 FPP, Sherburn-in-Elmet, 28.11.40; HQ SFPP, Kemble, 2.41; swung on take-off from Prestwick and DBR 22.2.41; SOC 3.3.41.

Rapide G-AKSF, c/n 6490, of Scottish Aviation Ltd after it had caught fire at Prestwick on 23rd July 1949 *[P H T Green collection]*

6490   RAF serial **R9562**; 12 MU, Kirkbride, 28.5.40; 18 MU, Dumfries, 16.7.40; 15 MU, Wroughton, 23.2.41; 48 MU, Hawarden, 8.10.41; 4 Sqn, Clifton,1.8.42; damaged 24.3.43; DH RU, Witney, for repair 30.3.43; 18 MU, Dumfries, 15.7.43; SF Northolt 29.10.43; DH RU, Witney, 5.12.44; 18 MU, Dumfries, 11.3.45; MCS, Hendon, 11.10.45; damaged 13.5.46, ROS 22.5.46; SF Halton [THA:P] 8.9.46; 18 MU, Dumfries, 3.6.47; sold to Air Navigation & Trading Co Ltd 15.12.47; regd **G-AKSF** 14.2.48 to Scottish Aviation Ltd, Prestwick; CoA (10032) issued 23.6.48; DBF at Prestwick 23.7.49 after cabin fire; regn cld 25.7.49.

6491   RAF serial **R9563**; TOC 9 MU, Cosford, 26.5.40; 782 Sqn, Donibristle, 29.8.40; flew into high ground at Kempstone Hill, nr Cowie, Kincardineshire, (3 mls N of Stonehaven) 7.7.41 in bad weather while carrying personnel from Hatston to Donibristle, killing PO W C Jones, 1st Off M E J Dobson WRNS, Lt F P Tennyson, 2nd Ltd J L Day, C W Young of Vickers-Armstrongs and civilian W/T operator T McCabe.

6492   RAF serial **R9564**; TOC 9 MU, Cosford, 26.5.40; to 3 FPP, White Waltham, 20.11.40; DH RU, Witney, 4.9.43; 18 MU, Dumfries, 6.12.43; SF Kenley 16.2.44; SF Gatwick 11.8.44; DH RU, Witney, 24.7.45; 18 MU, Dumfries, 1.4.46; sold to Air Enterprises Ltd 9.12.47; regd **G-AKOB** 11.12.47 to Air Enterprises Ltd, Croydon; CoA (9964) issued 19.3.48; to Palestine 28.8.48 for use with UN forces as **4**; retd to UK 8.10.48; retd to Air Enterprises as **G-AKOB** by 5.49, named *The Sandown Flyer*; regd 2.10.52 to Eagle Aviation Ltd, Luton (later Blackbushe); del 10.9.53 and regd 20.3.54 to Dragon Airways Ltd, Speke, named *Oboe Baker*; regn cld 30.11.55 as sold in Kenya; regd **VP-KNS** 2.12.55 to East African Airways Corporation; regd 6.7.60 to Seychelles-Kilimanjaro Air Transport Ltd (SKAT), Nairobi; re-regd in Tanzania as **5H-AAM**; DBF at Dar-es-Salaam 13.9.66; regn cld .67.

6493   RAF serial **X7320**; TOC by DGRD at DH 3.8.40 as communications aircraft; allocated Class B marks **E-0228**; 18 MU, Dumfries, 13.2.42; 4 SS, Madley, 10.4.42 (later 4 RS); DH RU, Witney, 8.8.45; SOC 30.10.45.

6494   RAF serial **X7321**; TOC 9 MU, Cosford, 22.8.40; CRD at Westland Aircraft Co Ltd, Yeovil, 21.10.40, as communications aircraft; SOC 30.4.46; regd **G-AHLF** 26.4.46 to Westland Aircraft Co Ltd; CoA; (7706) issued 20.6.46; used until 8.2.58; regd 27.5.58 to Hants & Sussex Aviation Ltd, Portsmouth; regd 1.1.59 to Agricultural Aviation Co Ltd, Panshanger and operated by Luton Airways Ltd; repossessed by Hants & Sussex Aviation Ltd 2.11.59 and regd to them 4.12.59; regd 15.2.60 to R A Short, t/a Skycraft Services, Biggin Hill; CoA lapsed 22.2.60; regd 18.7.60 to F A Frampton Ltd, Biggin Hill; roaded to Portsmouth 9.60; remains extant 4.62; regn cld 1.11.62.

6495   RAF serial **X7322**; TOC 9 MU, Cosford, 21.8.40; 6 FPP, Ratcliffe, 22.11.40; 19 MU, St. Athan, 15.2.41; DBR in air raid on St Athan 29.4.41; DH RU, Witney, for repair 8.5.41 but SOC 12.6.41.

6496   RAF serial **X7323**; TOC 9 MU, Cosford, 25.8.40; A&AEE, Boscombe Down, 30.12.40; 9 MU, Cosford, 22.3.41; DH RU, Witney, 4.4.41; 1 Cam. Unit, Hendon 10.5.41; DH RU, Witney, 29.6.42; 1 SS, Cranwell, 16.9.42; DH as damaged 10.6.44; 44 Gp CF, Staverton, 28.9.44; 18 MU, Dumfries, 25.6.46; regd **G-AJFM** 29.1.47 to Field Aircraft Services Ltd, Croydon and sold to them 18.2.47; regn cld 15.4.47 as sold in Kenya; CoA (8981) issued 6.9.47; regd **VP-KEE** 5.47 to East African Airways Corporation, Nairobi; to IDFAF .48 as **1310**; regd in Israel as **4X-AEH** 27.11.53 to Arkia-Israel Inland Airlines, Eilat; crashed on take-off from Lydda airport, Tel Aviv, 2.7.54, following engine failure due to contaminated fuel; used as spares for 4X-AEI.

6497   RAF serial **X7324**; TOC 9 MU, Cosford, 29.8.40; 3 FPP, White Waltham, 2.11.40; damaged at Barton 2.1.43 when pilot taxied into stationary Anson DJ381; DH RU, Witney, 5.1.43; 18 MU, Dumfries, 13.5.43; SF Skaebrae 9.8.43; DH RU, Witney, 11.9.44; MCS, Hendon, 30.11.44; 5 MU, Kemble, 3.1.45; sold to North Sea Air Transport Ltd 8.11.46; regd **G-AIWG** 20.11.46 to North Sea Air Transport Ltd, Brough; CoA (8812) issued 6.1.47; regn cld 25.1.50 as sold in Australia but UK CoA renewed next day; regd **VH-AIK** 13.2.50 to E J Connellan, t/a Connellan Airways, Alice Springs, NT; arr Alice Springs 2.50; regd 14.3.51 to Connellan Airways Ltd, Alice Springs; DBF at Turkey Creek, WA, 29.9.51 when engine caused fabric fire during start-up; regn cld same day.

6498   RAF serial **X7325**; TOC 9 MU, Cosford, 4.9.40; 7 FPP, Sherburn-in-Elmet, 17.1.41; 18 MU, Dumfries, 5.3.41; HQ FPP, White Waltham, 15.4.41; 10 MU, Hullavington, 30.6.41; 8 MU, Little Rissington, 29.8.41; 10 MU, Hullavington, 3.10.41; 2 SS, Yatesbury, 3.8.42; 18 MU, Dumfries, 18.2.44; 1680 Flt, Prestwick, 19.3.44; to AAJC, Prestwick, 14.6.46; regd **G-AIHN** 5.9.46 to Railway Air Services Ltd, Speke; CoA (8512) issued 25.10.46; to Scottish Airways Ltd, Renfrew, 13.11.46; regd 1.2.47 to BEA; regd 26.11.47 to Gibraltar Airways Ltd; CoA lapsed 7.3.53; sold 24.6.53 and regd 7.1.54 to A J Whittemore (Aeradio) Ltd, Croydon; CoA renewed 3.3.54; regd 24.3.54 to General Mining & Finance Corpn. Ltd, Johannesburg; regn cld 23.7.54 as sold in South Africa; regd **ZS-DJT** 23.7.54 to General Mining & Finance Corpn, Rand; regd 1.59 to African Air Photo (Pty) Ltd, Germiston; to Drakensberg Air Services (unconfirmed); to Ladysmith Air Charter; ground-looped and badly damaged at Ladysmith 11.10.63; used as spares, some small parts going to SAAF Museum .78 after being found at Maritzburg (Oribi).

5H-AAM, c/n 6492, of SKAT was destroyed by fire at Dar-es-Salaam in September 1966   *[G M Simons collection]*

G-AIHN, c/n 6498, of Gibraltar Airways eventually found its way to South Africa   *[via A. Chivers]*

6499   RAF serial **X7326**; TOC 18 MU, Dumfries, 14.9.40; 6 MU, Brize Norton, 15.2.41; ATA, White Waltham, 31.12.41; DH RU, Witney, 3.5.43; 18 MU, Dumfries, 24.8.43; to AAJC 13.10.43; regd **G-AGJF** 25.10.43 to Scottish Airways Ltd; CoA (7029) issued 29.10.43; regd 1.2.47 to BEA; crashed at Barra, Hebrides, 6.8.47; regn cld 4.9.47.

6500   RAF serial **X7327**; TOC 18 MU, Dumfries, 23.9.40; 7 FPP, Sherburn-in-Elmet, 22.11.40; HQ FPP, White Waltham, 14.5.41; 9 MU, Cosford 14.10.41; Macmerry 22.11.42; 18 MU, Dumfries, 14.1.43; 1680 Flt, Abbotsinch, 2.8.43; 510 Sqn, Hendon, 8.9.43; DH RU, Witney, 27.9.43; 18 MU, Dumfries, 25.12.43; 526 Sqn, Inverness, 16.2.44; 527 Sqn, Digby 3.5.45; RWE (later CSE), Watton, 15.4.46; 5 MU, Kemble, 13.1.47; regd **G-AJSK** 8.5.47 to Field Aircraft Services Ltd, Croydon, and sold to them 29.5.47; regn cld as sold abroad 16.6.47, but sale abandoned; regd 17.1.48 to same owner; CoA (9373) issued 27.4.48; regd 17.5.49 to BEA, Renfrew, later named *RMA Lord Lister;* regd 1.1.53 to Gibraltar Airways Ltd; regd 13.1.54 to A J Whittemore (Aeradio) Ltd, Croydon; converted to Mk.4; regn cld 14.2.54 as sold in East Africa; regd in Kenya 15.2.54 as **VP-KMD** to J E F Wilkins, t/a

Caspair Air Charters, Nairobi; UK CoA renewed 16.4.54; regd 1.7.55 to Caspair Air Charters & Agencies Ltd, Nairobi; regd 16.1.56 to Airspray (East Africa) Ltd, Nairobi; to Southern Rhodesia 4.56; regd **VP-YOE** 4.56 to Richard Costain Ltd, Salisbury; CoA lapsed 27.3.57; regn cld 2.2.59.

6501   RAF serial **X7328**; TOC 18 MU, Dumfries, 27.9.40; SFPP 13.1.41; 11 FPP, Dumfries; overturned on landing at Abbotsinch 8.6.41; SOC 15.6.41.

6502   RAF serial X7329; TOC 18 MU, Dumfries, 10.10.40; 7 FPP, Sherburn-in-Elmet, 27.11.40; HQ ATA, White Waltham, 27.7.41; DH RU, Witney, as damaged 29.42; 18 MU, Dumfries, 13.1.44; CRD at DH 25.2.44; SOC 20.5.46.

6503   RAF serial **X7330**; TOC by DGRD at DH 18.1.41; 18 MU, Dumfries, 6.8.41; 47 MU, Sealand, 27.2.42 for packing; shipped on *City of Hong Kong* from Birkenhead 18.3.42; 1 (I) SFTS, Ambala; regd **VT-ARR** 29.12.43; sold to Indian National Airways 9.5.46; regd 4.6.46 to Indian Air Survey & Transport Co Ltd, Dum Dum, Calcutta; WFU at Calcutta .48/.49 and regn cld.

G-AGJF, c/n 6499, of Scottish Airways on the beach airstrip at Barra   *[J Stroud via GMS]*

After RAF service, G-AKOY, c/n 6504, was operated by Air Navigation & Trading Co Ltd and Lancashire Aircraft Corpn before being sold in Pakistan

[G M Simons collection]

6504   RAF serial **X7331**; TOC 2 ADF, Colerne, 15.3.41; SF Colerne 13.10.41; 418 Sqn, Debden, 6.2.42; damaged by electrical fire on landing at Bradwell Bay 22.7.42; DH RU, Witney, for repair 3.8.42; 3 Del Flt, High Ercall, 6.11.42; DH RU, Witney, 23.4.43; 18 MU, Dumfries, 13.8.43; 4 RS, Madley [4-92] 20.5.44; sold to Air Navigation & Trading Co Ltd 15.12.47; regd **G-AKOY** 31.12.47 to R L Whyham and operated by Air Navigation & Trading Co Ltd, Squires Gate; CoA (10016) issued 21.5.48; regd 8.5.49 to Lancashire Aircraft Corporation Ltd, Yeadon; regn cld 11.4.53 as sold in Pakistan; regd **AP-AGM** .53 to Crescent Air Transport, Karachi; possibly not used; sold in France 9.56; regd **F-OAYN** 27.6.57 to Sté Tunisienne de Réparation Aéronautique et de Construction (STRAC), Tunis, op as Aéro Sahara; destroyed in hangar fire at Tunis (El Aouina), 12.12.57.

6505   RAF serial **X7332**; TOC 3 Del Flt, Hawarden, 6.3.41; DH RU, Witney, 27.12.41; 4 SS, Madley, 8.4.42; unit redes 4 RS 1.1.43; DH RU, Witney, 1.7.44; 18 MU, Dumfries, 6.11.44; transferred to FAA 17.10.45; Evanton 31.10.45; AHS Arbroath 22.3.46; Crail 24.10.46; Culham 20.2.47; SF Lossiemouth 15.4.48; SF Eglinton [900:JR] 29.11.48; force-landed at Warmwell disused airfield 31.1.50 with engine fire; Culham 4.2.50; DH Leavesden for repair 29.4.50; AHS Arbroath 27.5.53; SF Lossiemouth 7.7.55; 1844 Sqn/ SF Bramcote [903:BR, later 890:BR] 24.8.55; port wing struck gatepost while taxying 21.1.56; over-ran parking area in strong wind, stbd lower wing damaged 1.7.56; port propeller spinner detached in flight, struck fuselage, 21.11.56; AHU Lossiemouth 15.1.58; SOC 13.1.59; scrapped by Hants & Sussex Aviation at Lossiemouth 8.60.

6506   RAF serial **X7333**; TOC 4 Del Flt, Grangemouth, 10.3.41; engine failed on take-off from Acklington 8.6.41, hit hedge and DBF; SOC 14.6.41.

6507   RAF serial **X7334**; TOC 18 MU, Dumfries, 17.3.41; 47 MU, Sealand, 14.4.41 for packing; shipped to South Africa on *Mandalay* 25.5.41; to SAAF as **1353** at 9 AD 5.41; 5 AS 27.8.41; 62 AS 5.9.41; 61 Sqn 13.3.45; sold to Maj J W O Billingham, Cape Town, 31.10.46 for £1485; regd **ZS-BEF** 18.12.46; to Aviation Industry Associated Services ?; regd .54 to South West Air Transport (Pty) Ltd, Windhoek; regn cld 2.8.58 as sold in Madagascar; inspected at Ivato 10.12.58; regd in France as **F-OBIO** 27.4.59 to Sté Air Madagascar; re-regd **5R-MAO** 3.63 to same owner; regn cld 7.67 on CoA expiry.

6508   RAF serial **X7335**; TOC 18 MU, Dumfries, 17.3.41; 47 MU, Sealand, 5.4.41 for packing; shipped to South Africa on *Mandalay* 25.5.41; to SAAF as **1354** at 9 AD 5.41; 5 AS 27.8.41; 62 AS 5.9.41; 61 Sqn 14.11.44; sold to African Flying Services 5.7.46; regd **ZS-BCS** 8.10.46; damaged in flying accident and listed as scrap, but rebuilt; regn cld 26.9.50 as sold in Southern Rhodesia; regd **VP-YNU** 5.56 to Victoria Falls Airways (Pvt) Ltd; to Air Brousse SPRL, Léopoldville; regd **9O-CJW** 17.3.61; re-regd **9Q-CJW** c.63 to Agence de Messageries Aériennes Zairoises (AMAZ); WFU .68.

6509   RAF serial **X7336**; TOC 18 MU, Dumfries, 20.3.41; 614 Sqn, Macmerry, 8.4.41; 225 Sqn, Macmerry, 15.9.42; Macmerry 30.10.42; DH RU, Witney, 13.2.43; 18 MU, Dumfries, 6.6.43; to AAJC 7.7.43; regd **G-AGIF** 15.7.43 to Great Western & Southern

X7332, c/n 6505, of the Fleet Air Arm at Blackbushe on 7th September 1955, with the terminal building in the background

[R A Walker]

G-AKRN, c/n 6513, in East Anglian Flying Services livery [*G M Simons collection*]

Airlines Ltd, Inverness; to Scottish Airways Ltd, Renfrew 19.7.43 and regd to them 6.3.44; CoA (7012) issued 20.7.43; regd 1.2.47 to BEA; regd 23.4.48 to Ulster Aviation Ltd, Newtownards; taken over by North-West Airlines (IoM) Ltd; CoA lapsed 24.1.50; regn cld 13.10.50; used for spares at Newtownards.

6510   RAF serial **X7337**; TOC 18 MU, Dumfries, 24.3.41; 47 MU, Sealand, 3.5.41 for packing; shipped to South Africa on *Lycason* 7.6.41; to SAAF as **1356** at 9 AD 5.41; 5 AS 28.8.41; 62 AS 5.9.41; 24 Gp CF 15.9.44; 61 Sqn 12.44; sold via 15 AD 5.7.46 to Coppen & Kotze, Windhoek, SWA, for £1350; regd **ZS-BCI** 2.9.46; to South West Air Transport 11.46; to President Motors; regd .52 to Anglo-Transvaal Consolidated Investments Co Ltd, Germiston, operated by Africair Ltd; leased to Commercial Air Services, Johannesburg; DBF during engine start-up at Welkom, OFS, 6.9.52.

6511   RAF serial **X7338**; TOC 9 MU, Cosford, 29.3.41; HQ FPP, White Waltham, 22.5.41; 10 FPP, Hullavington, 2.6.41; 12 MU, Kirkbride, 26.6.41; 19 MU, St. Athan, 3.10.41; 2 SS, Yatesbury, 22.10.42; DH RU, Witney, 30.10.42; 18 MU, Dumfries, 21.1.43; HQ ATA, White Waltham, 20.4.44; DH RU, Witney, 2.7.44; 19 Gp CF, Roborough, [G2:A] 29.7.44; DH RU, Witney, 16.4.46; 5 MU, Kemble, 21.2.47; sold to Aircraft & Engineering Services Ltd 29.5.47 and regd **G-AJMY** 13.6.47 to them; CoA (9901) issued 17.2.48; regd 30.3.48 to Sivewright Airways Ltd, Ringway; regd 6.6.51 to Melba Airways Ltd, Ringway; regd 17.7.51 to Wolverhampton Aviation Ltd, Wolverhampton; regn cld 21.8.52 as

sold in Portuguese Guinea; erroneously regd in UK 9.9.52 to Govt of Portuguese Guinea, Bissau; regd **CR-GAK** 10.52 to Transportes Aéreos da Guiné Portuguesa (TAGP); WFU and broken up as spares for CR-GAI and CR-GAJ before .63.

6512   RAF serial **X7339**; TOC 8 MU, Little Rissington, 28.3.41; 47 MU, Sealand, 18.4.41 for packing; shipped to South Africa on *Lycason* 7.6.41; to SAAF as **1355** at 9 AD 7.6.41; 5 AS 28.8.41; 62 AS 15.9.41; crashed at Bloemfontein 23.10.41; SOC 25.10.43.

6513   RAF serial **X7340**; TOC 9 MU, Cosford, 4.4.41; 6 MU, Brize Norton, 16.5.41; HQ ATA, White Waltham, 28.6.41; DH RU, Witney, 3.5.43; 2 RS, Yatesbury, [217] 31.8.43; 4 RS, Madley, 2.3.45; DH RU, Witney, 22.12.45; 18 MU, Dumfries, 27.8.46; sold to Air Navigation & Trading Co Ltd 15.12.47; regd **G-AKRN** 17.1.48 to East Anglian Flying Services Ltd, Southend; CoA (9913) issued 24.3.48; operated by Channel Airways; CoA lapsed 27.6.60 and stored at Southend and then Ipswich; retd to Southend 10.64 and fuselage seen there 21.7.68; to Ian Jones, Burnham-on-Crouch, 19.8.72; regn cld 14.2.73; parts to Chirk .80 for use in rebuild of G-AIUL; stored, with plans for restoration by Ian Jones at Babbacombe, Devon, .85 but little currently remains.

6514   RAF serial **X7341**; TOC 9 MU, Cosford, 8.4.41; 53 OTU, Heston, 30.5.41; DH RU, Witney, 3.2.42; 9 MU, Cosford, 19.3.42; 53 OTU, Heston, 28.3.42; 58 OTU, Grangemouth, 4.4.43; DH RU, Witney, 14.9.43; 18 MU, Dumfries, 22.12.43; transferred to

X7341, c/n 6514, served with the Fleet Air Arm from April 1945 to June 1963 [*via A. Chivers*]

FAA 3.4.45; Lee-on-Solent 3.5.45; Christchurch 4.6.45; 736B Sqn, Woodvale, 14.7.45; SF Hatston 8.8.45; 736B Sqn, Woodvale,18.8.45; SF Donibristle; SF Crail 25.6.46; 781 Sqn, Lee-on-Solent, 7.11.46; AHU, Stretton 8.7.47; SF Evanton 3.9.47; AHU, Stretton 14.10.47; Eglinton 14.1.48; Stretton (for 2 FF ?) 19.2.48; DH Witney 25.10.48; AHU, Stretton 18.5.49; AHU, Arbroath, 16.5.50; 782 Sqn, Donibristle [803:DO, later 801:DO] 14.7.51; nosed over after landing 24.8.51; DH Leavesden for repair 4.9.51; RDU, Arbroath, 30.1.52; AHU, Lossiemouth 17.3.53; Shorts Ferry Flight, Rochester, 24.11.54; SF Lossiemouth 15.9.55; AHS, Lossiemouth 3.10.55; SF Brawdy [910:BY] 30.11.55 (also attd to 7 FTS, Valley); groundcrew member SAC Cromarty walked into propeller and was killed while removing chocks, Brawdy, 11.3.57; Shorts Ferry Flight, Rochester, 3.3.58; AHU, Lossiemouth 18.7.58; SOC 22.6.63; sold to Anglo-Diesel Co., London, and left Lossiemouth 5.7.63.

6515 RAF serial **X7342**; TOC 9 MU, Cosford, 10.4.41; 56 OTU, Sutton Bridge, 3.6.41; 1 TEU, Tealing, 1.1.44; 54 OTU, Charterhall, 3.8.44; damaged 7.8.44; ROS by 63 MU 12.8.44; 53 OTU, Kirton-in-Lindsey, 6.9.44; DH RU, Witney, 31.5.45; 18 MU, Dumfries, 4.2.46; sold to Oxford Aero Club 11.12.47; regd **G-AKND** 29.11.47 to B T Aikman, t/a Aikman Airways, Croydon; CoA (9978) issued 1.4.48; regd 13.4.48 to W & H C V Hext, t/a Aikman Airways; regn cld 12.8.48 as sold in Kenya; regd **VP-KGE** to unknown owner; broken up for spares .50.

6516 RAF serial **X7343**; TOC 9 MU, Cosford 9.4.41; 52 OTU, Debden (later Aston Down), 3.6.41; Inverness 30.9.41; DH RU, Witney, as damaged 10.10.43; SF St Mawgan 31.5.44; 5 MU, Kemble, 25.11.46; regd **G-AJNA** 8.5.47 to Field Aircraft Services Ltd, Croydon, and sold to them 30.5.47; regd 15.7.47 to Franco-British Commercial & Industrial Co Ltd, London; CoA (9372) issued 23.7.47; regn cld 10.12.47 as sold abroad; regd in France 3.1.48 as **F-BEDI** to Sté Air Madagascar, named *Antalaha;* crashed at Tamatave 30.5.48.

6517 RAF serial **X7344**; TOC 9 MU, Cosford, 16.4.41; 1 Cam Flt, Hendon, 10.5.41; damaged 15.6.42; ROS 2.7.42; 18 MU, Dumfries, 10.10.42; to AAJC, Renfrew, 13.10.43; regd **G-AGJG** 25.10.43 to Scottish Airways Ltd, Inverness; CoA (7030) issued 15.2.44; regd 1.2.47 to BEA; regd 14.10.48 to Adie Aviation Ltd, Croydon; regd 10.1.49 to Mediterranean Air Services Ltd, Croydon, named *Isles of Scilly;* CoA lapsed 11.1.50; regd 4.8.50 to Adie Aviation Ltd, Croydon and stored until CoA renewed 23.8.52; regd 9.6.53 to E A Taylor, operated by Island Air Services, Heathrow; regd 2.4.54 to IAS (London) Ltd t/a Island Air Services, Heathrow (later Ramsgate); regd 13.3.59 to T H Marshall, operated by Christchurch Aero Club; regd 26.9.60 to E P Jones, t/a Swansea Airways, Fairwood Common; CoA lapsed 1.6.61; regd 18.12.61 to T H. Marshall, Christchurch; CoA renewed 27.4.62; regd 11.5.62 to G A Dommett, Thruxton (later Booker); damaged at Christchurch 20.5.62 whilst practising landings during gusty conditions; regd 8.6.67 to J A Galt, Booker; regd 25.3.68 to Aerial Enterprises Ltd, Booker; in open storage at Halfpenny Green when company ceased trading; CoA renewed 20.6.69, lapsed 15.11.74; sold by early .75 to Emanuel Wein & Duxford Aviation Society and ferried to Duxford 17.8.75; regd 20.3.86 to M J and J T Miller, Duxford; currently under restoration, with estimated first flight 2006.

6518 RAF serial **X7345**; TOC 18 MU, Dumfries, 20.4.41; 4 Del Flt, Grangemouth, 15.6.41; DH RU, Witney, 21.3.43; 1 RS, Cranwell, 24.7.43; DH RU, Witney, 3.1.46; 18 MU, Dumfries, 19.9.46; sold to Island Air Charter Ltd 9.12.47; regd **G-AKNF** 29.11.47 to R J Martin, Jersey; CoA (10019) issued 2.5.49; regd 11.5.49 to Airlines (Jersey) Ltd, t/a Jersey Airlines; converted to Mk.4 12.4.54; regd 25.1.55 to Airwork Ltd, Perth (Scone); regn cld 18.7.55 as sold in Iran; regd **EP-ADP** 7.55 to Iranian Oil Exploration & Production Co; regn cld before .60.

6519 RAF serial **X7346**; TOC 9 MU, Cosford, 24.4.41; 57 OTU, Hawarden, 27.6.41; DH RU, Witney, 5.4.42; 58 OTU, Grangemouth, 23.4.42; damaged, to Air Taxis Ltd 22.7.42; 18 MU, Dumfries, 19.8.42; 41 OTU, Old Sarum, 15.10.42; SF Old Sarum 31.12.42; DH RU, Witney, 17.3.44; 482nd BG, USAAF Alconbury, 9.5.44; damaged, ROS 4.7.44; returned to unit 26.7.44; 5 MU, Kemble, 28.8.44; regd **G-AIUM** 20.11.46 to Air Schools Ltd, Derby (Burnaston); regd 27.11.46 to Southern Aircraft (Gatwick) Ltd,

Gatwick; CoA (8778) issued 19.2.47; regd 7.5.47 to Hunting Flying Clubs Ltd, Luton; CoA lapsed 18.3.49; regd 30.6.50 to F C Gold, Southall; CoA renewed 3.7.50; regn cld 25.7.50 as sold abroad; regd in Sweden as **SE-BTA** 25.8.50 to Duells Aero AB, Göteborg, and operated occasionally on floats; to Ostermans Aero, Stockholm; regd 27.3.53 to Bolidens Gruv AB, Boliden; regd 13.5.60 to H Duell, Göteborg; regn cld 12.7.63.

6520 RAF serial **X7347**; TOC 18 MU, Dumfries, 25.4.41; 59 OTU, Crosby-on-Eden, 15.6.41; 4 SS, Madley, 12.12.41; 59 OTU, Crosby-on-Eden, 31.12.41; DH RU, Witney, as damaged 10.10.43; 18 MU, Dumfries, 12.2.44; 44 Gp CF, Staverton, 22.2.44; 1 FU, Pershore, 1.8.46; 18 MU, Dumfries, 21.8.46; regd **G-AJFN** 29.1.47 to Field Aircraft Services Ltd, Croydon, and sold to them 18.2.47; regn cld as sold in Belgium as **OO-CDE** 29.4.47 for John Mahieu Aviation but NTU; regd **G-AJFN** 15.7.47 to Franco-British Commercial & Industrial Co Ltd, London; CoA (8982) issued 23.7.47; sold to Air Madagascar, named *Majunga*, but was DBF 3.11.47 in a grass fire at Kosti, Sudan, while on delivery flight; regn cld 3.12.47.

6521 RAF serial **X7348**; TOC 9 MU, Cosford, 30.4.41; 4 SS, Madley, [J] 12.12.41; unit redes 4 RS 1.1.43; 18 MU, Dumfries, 17.3.45; transferred to FAA 17.10.45; Evanton 26.10.45; Crail 23.9.46; 782 Sqn, Donibristle, 10.10.46; DH Witney 29.9.47 (for CoA); AHU, Stretton 2.2.48; SOC 12.6.58.

6522 RAF serial **X7349**; TOC HQ SFPP 5.5.41; 10 FPP, Hullavington, 16.5.41; DH RU, Witney, 3.2.43; 18 MU, Dumfries, 23.4.43; to AAJC 7.43; regd **G-AGIC** 6.7.43 to Scottish Airways Ltd, Inverness; CoA (7011) 20.8.43 to Great Southern & Western Airlines Ltd; regd 1.2.47 to BEA; regn cld 20.11.47 as sold abroad (but CoA renewed 16.3.48); regd in France 22.4.48 as **F-BEDZ** to Air France, Ivato, Madagascar; regd **F-OADZ** 1.6.49 to Air France; transferred to Algeria late .49; retd to Le Bourget late .50; regd **F-BAHZ** 10.10.50 to Air France for operation by Ecole de l'Aviation Civile, Dreux; crashed at La Madeleine par Nonencourt, Eure, 24.2.51.

6523 RAF serial **X7350**; TOC 18 MU, Dumfries, 11.5.41; 57 OTU, Hawarden, 5.6.41; DH RU, Witney, 12.7.41; 9 MU, Cosford, 12.10.41; transferred to FAA 17.2.42; 781 Sqn, Lee-on-Solent 2.42; DH RU, Witney, 24.12.42; retd to 781 Sqn 6.2.43; DH RU, Witney, 25.10.43; 781 Sqn [L9C] 28.1.44; DH RU, Witney, 23.4.45; 782 Sqn, Donibristle, 27.8.45; nosed over in strong wind 17.9.48; AHU, Stretton 9.48 to 1.50; 782 Sqn, Donibristle [802:DO] 6.50 to 9.50 (as ambulance); DH Leavesden 1.51; retd to 782 Sqn; SOC 18.6.51.

6524 RAF serial **X7351**; TOC 18 MU, Dumfries, 12.5.41; 55 OTU, Usworth, 10.6.41; hit fence on take-off from Usworth 11.7.41; DH RU, Witney, for repair 16.7.41; 24 Sqn, Hendon, 5.11.41; 9 MU, Cosford, 15.1.42; 271 Sqn, Doncaster, [YS:A] 8.3.42; damaged on landing at Brockworth 13.9.43; to Gloster Aircraft for repair 21.9.43; 1680 Flt, Abbotsinch, 7.1.44; to AAJC, Prestwick, 16.4.46, but not civil regd; believed broken up for spares.

6525 RAF serial **X7352**; TOC 18 MU, Dumfries, 21.5.41; 58 OTU, Grangemouth, 11.6.41; DH RU, Witney, 4.4.42; 2 SS, Yatesbury, [219 and 224] 21.8.42; unit redes 2 RS 1.1.43; DH RU, Witney, 5.4.45; MCS, Hendon, 12.10.45; 18 MU, Dumfries, 7.8.46; sold to Scottish Aviation Ltd 24.5.48; regd **G-ALBI** 7.6.48 to Scottish Aviation Ltd, Prestwick; regn cld 1.6.49 as sold in Luxembourg; regd **LX-LAD** to Luxembourg Airlines; UK CoA (10213) issued 17.7.49; UK CoA lapsed 16.7.50; regn cld 8.50 and restored as **G-ALBI** 14.9.50 to Scottish Aviation Ltd, Prestwick; CoA renewed 14.4.53; regd 19.5.53 to Airwork Ltd, Perth (Scone); regd 25.6.55 to Air Couriers (Transport) Ltd, Croydon and operated in Evening News livery in .56; converted to Mk.6 3.4.59; based at Biggin Hill from 9.59; regn cld 16.8.60 as sold in Senegal; regd **F-OBRV** 29.8.60 to SA Ardic, Dakar, op by Air Sénégal; crashed at Boghé, Mauritania, 4.8.61.

6526 RAF serial **X7353**; TOC 9 MU, Cosford, 22.5.41; 52 OTU, Aston Down, 31.8.41; damaged 10.5.42, ROS 27.5.42; 52 OTU, Aston Down, 26.5.42; 63 OTU, Honiley, 28.8.43; 54 OTU, Charterhall, 1.4.44; 2 Del Flt, Cranfield, 3.4.44; DH RU, Witney, 18.8.44; 5 MU, Kemble, 10.11.44; A&AEE, Boscombe Down, 19.1.48, as replacement for R9545; DBR in taxying accident at

Dominie X7372, c/n 6532, of 1680 Flight with which it served for the second half of its career　　　*[MAP via P H T Green]*

Hatfield 18.1.49; SOC 21.2.49; sold 9.11.49 to Air Navigation & Trading Co Ltd; regd **G-ALVU** 27.10.49 to G C S Whyham, Squires Gate; not converted, although CoA (10744) allocated; used as spares before being burnt at Squires Gate early .62; regn cld 13.5.64.

6527　　RAF serial **X7354**; TOC 9 MU, Cosford, 28.5.41; 3 DF, Hawarden, 28.6.41; struck by lightning, abandoned, crashed at Hordley, Salop, 7.12.41 and DBF.

6528　　RAF serial **X7368**; TOC 18 MU, Dumfries, 4.6.41; 10 AGS, Castle Kennedy (later Barrow) 25.9.41; 2 (O) AFU, Millom, 12.8.42; 18 MU, Dumfries, 11.9.42; 51 OTU, Cranfield, 31.12.42; collided with Beaufighter R2252 on approach to Cranfield, 11.11.43, killing five.

6529　　RAF serial **X7369**; TOC 18 MU, Dumfries, 27.5.41; 1 Del Flt, Hendon (later Croydon, North Weald, Gatwick, Redhill and Odiham) 9.6.41 (named *Galloping Gertie*); DH RU, Witney, 4.6.45; 18 MU, Dumfries, 12.2.46; 21 Gp CF, Cranwell, 11.10.46; 23 Gp CF, Halton, 12.4.47; 21 Gp CF 15.4.47; 18 MU, Dumfries, 21.8.47; regd **G-AKZH** 19.5.48 to Herts & Essex Aero Club (1946) Ltd, Broxbourne, and sold to them 24.5.48; CoA (10053) issued 10.8.48; regd 8.9.49 to Kenning Aviation Ltd, Sherburn-in-Elmet; regn cld 7.5.52 as sold in Portuguese Guinea (erroneously regd in UK 24.5.52 to Govt of Portuguese Guinea and then deleted); regd **CR-GAJ** to Transportes Aéreos da Guiné Portuguesa (TAGP) 5.52 (del 19.6.52); regn cld after .63.

6530　　RAF serial **X7370**; TOC 18 MU, Dumfries, 16.6.41; 60 OTU, East Fortune, 2.7.41; 52 OTU, Aston Down, 1.9.42; 2 Del Flt, Colerne, 22.9.42; DH RU, Witney, 23.4.43; 18 MU, Dumfries, 14.8.43; 1 RS, Cranwell, 4.9.43; SF Halton [THA:D] 26.3.45; 5 MU, Kemble, 12.12.46; sold to Field Aircraft Services Ltd 29.5.47; regd **G-AJXB** 14.6.47 to Field Aircraft Services Ltd, Croydon; CoA (9479) issued 15.12.48; regd 21.12.48 to BEA, later named *RMA William Gilbert Grace;* regd 29.4.55 to Eagle Aviation Ltd, Blackbushe; regd 20.2.56 to Independent Air Travel Ltd, Hurn; regn cld 4.3.56 as sold in Sweden; regd **SE-CBU** 2.8.56 to Dragon Aviation AB, Stockholm (Bromma); regd 5.8.60 to Petur W A Ahrens (of Dragon Aviation), Ekero and flown by him with his family on emigration from Sweden to Australia, arriving Darwin, NT, 26.9.60; regd **VH-CBU** 12.5.61 to Ahrens and based at Burleigh Heads, Qld; re-regd **VH-ECW** 7.6.62 to Ahrens' new company, East Coast Airways Pty Ltd, Coolangatta, Qld; regd 11.1.63 to R H Healey, RAAF Darwin; to Parafield 12.63 for major overhaul which took three years; regd 29.1.55 to M Ward, t/a Pastoral Aviation (Queensland) Pty Ltd, Brisbane, Qld; DBF at Blackall, Qld, 30.3.68 during engine start-up.

6531　　RAF serial **X7371**; TOC 2 Del Flt, Colerne, 16.6.41; force-landed at Old Sodbury, Glos, 20.10.41 when lost at dusk and DBR; SOC 12.11.41.

6532　　RAF serial **X7372**; TOC 18 MU, Dumfries, 18.6.41; SF Abbotsinch 17.7.41; 1680 Flt, Abbotsinch 15.6.43 (later Prestwick); damaged 8.11.45; SOC 5.4.46.

6533　　RAF serial **X7373**; TOC 33 MU, Lyneham, 19.6.41; 51 OTU, Debden (later Cranfield) 1.8.41; 1 ADF, Croydon, 23.8.42 (later North Weald, Gatwick, Redhill and Odiham) named *Leaping Lena II;* damaged 31.7.45; SOC 3.10.45.

6534　　RAF serial **X7374**; TOC 18 MU, Dumfries, 23.6.41; 24 Sqn, Hendon, 17.7.41; DBF in hangar at Hendon 21.4.42; SOC 6.5.42.

6535　　RAF serial **X7375**; TOC 9 MU, Cosford, 25.6.41; 61 OTU, Heston (later Rednal) 8.7.41; damaged 5.6.42; returned to 61 OTU, Rednal, 27.6.43; damaged 16.8.43; DH RU, Witney, 30.10.43; 18 MU, Dumfries, 21.2.44; RAE, Farnborough, 30.7.45; SOC 28.8.48 and RTP.

6536　　RAF serial **X7376**; TOC 33 MU, Lyneham, 28.6.41; 57 OTU, Hawarden, 25.7.41; damaged 6.5.42; returned to 57 OTU 12.10.44; DH RU, Witney, 26.3.45; 18 MU, Dumfries, 22.7.45; 16 FU, Dunkeswell, 1.2.46; Valley 7.5.46; 18 MU, Dumfries, 17.6.46; regd **G-AKZI** 19.5.48 to Adie Aviation Ltd, Croydon, and sold to them 31.5.48; regd 11.8.48 to Mayfair Air Services Ltd, London; ferried to Palestine, arr 14.9.48; to Israeli AF as **S-76**; 1 and 4 Sqns, Sde Dov; hit by AA fire and force-landed behind enemy lines nr Wadi Rabin, S of Tel Aviv, 21.10.48; captured and set on fire by Egyptians; regn cld 16.5.50 as 'destroyed in Palestine'. (Also reported as being the Rapide recaptured at Al Arish LG 29.12.48 and returned to Israel for repair).

6537　　RAF serial **X7377**; TOC 9 MU, Cosford, 30.6.41; HQ SFPP, Kemble, 7.7.41; DH RU, Witney, 8.3.42; 55 OTU, Usworth, 25.4.42; DH RU, Witney, 8.4.43; 18 MU, Dumfries, 7.7.43; 3 Gp CF, Newmarket (later Wyton) 29.10.44; 18 MU, Dumfries, 16.9.46 and SOC same day.

6538　　RAF serial **X7378**; TOC 9 MU, Cosford, 5.7.41; 55 OTU, Usworth, 1.8.41; damaged on take-off from Usworth 2.4.42; DH RU, Witney, 8.4.42; 18 MU, Dumfries, 23.7.42; 271 Sqn, Doncaster, 6.8.42; damaged in forced landing in field near Doncaster 3.2.44; Staverton 6.2.44; repaired by 60 MU 19.2.44; 4 Gp CF, Staverton, 20.5.44; DH RU, Witney, 15.9.44; SF Old

The remains of F-BGON, c/n 6541, at La Ferté-Alais in the late 1970s prior to restoration   [G M Simons collection]

Sarum 6.1.45; FCCS, Northolt, 18.1.45; 10 Gp CF, Colerne; FCCS, Northolt, 10.5.45; 1 ADF, Andrewsfield, [N] 16.8.45 (later Hawkinge); 18 MU, Dumfries, 19.10.45; regd **G-AKOF** 4.12.47 to W A Rollason Ltd, Croydon, and sold to them 19.12.47; CoA (9954) issued 18.6.48; regd 18.6.48 to Mannin Airways Ltd, Ronaldsway; crashed, out of fuel, into River Mersey at Garston Channel, nr Liverpool, 11.11.48, while flying from Dublin to Ronaldsway but diverted due to fog; Capt J C Higgins (MD of Mannin), co-pilot and five of six passengers drowned; Rapide sank in 25 minutes; regn cld same day; remains salvaged to Hooton Park and eventually dumped in Manchester Ship Canal.

6539   RAF serial **X7379**; TOC 9 MU, Cosford, 9.7.41; HQ ATA, White Waltham, 13.10.41; 3 FPP, White Waltham, 31.12.41; HQ ATA; DH RU, Witney, 29.3.43; 1 RS, Cranwell, 26.7.43; 27 Gp CF, Aston Down, (later Southrop) 26.7.44; 1 RS, Cranwell, 19.2.45; 18 MU, Dumfries, 13.5.46; sold to Lancashire Aircraft Corporation 10.3.47 and regd **G-AJKW** 22.3.47 to them; CoA (9437) issued 30.7.48; CoA lapsed 9.11.50; regn cld as to long term storage 28.12.50; regd 9.6.52 to same owner; CoA renewed 17.7.52; to Silver City Airways Ltd 12.56; regd 17.6.57 to W Westoby, t/a Westair, Squires Gate; sold 22.2.63; CoA lapsed 15.5.63; regd 21.5.63 to Air Navigation & Trading Co Ltd, Squires Gate; CoA renewed 6.7.65; regd 12.5.66 to P J Amor and D J A Smith, t/a Skydivers Flying Club, 22 (Air) SAS, Shobdon (or Halfpenny Green); overturned on take-off from Halfpenny Green 7.5.67 and DBR; regn cld 26.7.67.

6540   RAF serial **X7380**; TOC 9 MU, Cosford, 8.7.41; 1 Del Flt, Hendon (later Croydon), 10.9.41 (named *Leaping Lena*); damaged on landing at North Weald 4.1.42; DH RU, Witney, for repair 12.1.42; 1 DF, Croydon, 3.3.42; 1 Cam. Unit, Stapleford Tawney, 1.7.42; 18 MU, Dumfries, 12.10.42; 2 SS, Yatesbury, [211] 4.11.42 (later 2 RS); 18 MU 11.4.45; SOC 29.3.46.

6541   RAF serial **X7381**; TOC 9 MU, Cosford, 14.7.41; HQ ATA, White Waltham, 13.10.41; 9 MU, Cosford, 17.3.42; 18 MU, Dumfries, 9.8.42; 2 SS, Yatesbury, [201] 7.9.42; damaged 22.12.42, ROS by 50 MU; unit redes 2 RS 1.1.43; DH RU, Witney, 23.5.45; A&AEE, Boscombe Down, 29.11.45; 5 MU, Kemble, 5.1.50; regd **G-ALZF** 24.3.50 to Herts & Essex Aero Club (1946) Ltd, Broxbourne, and sold to them 30.3.50; CoA (10919) issued 5.7.50; regd 2.8.50 to East Riding Flying Club (Speeton) Ltd, Bridlington (Speeton); regd 2.8.51 to F J R Elliott, Neasham (Croft); sold 5.9.51 to unknown buyer; regn cld 8.52 as sold in France; regd **F-BGON** 24.9.52 to Direction de l'Aviation Légère et Sportive, Buc; regd .62 to CIC Parachutisme, Gisy-les-Nobles (later La Ferté-Gaucher); regd .65 to CIC Parachutisme de l'Ouest, Nantes (Chateau Bougon); CoA exp 9.69, sold to Dan Hollander and used as prop in film 'Stavisky' .73; damaged in forced landing in mid .70s; regn cld .75; to J Salis, La Ferté-Alais, by .77 in semi-derelict condition; rebuilt .80/.81 and regd **F-AZCA** 4.81 to the Jean Salis Collection; participated in Paris (Le Bourget) to New York Air Race, departing 6.6.81; repainted and named *Blue Way* to launch new cigarette; repainted in RAF camouflage with code ZC:A; extant at La Ferté-Alais.

6542   RAF serial **X7382**; TOC 9 MU, Cosford, 14.7.41; HQ ATA, White Waltham, 13.10.41; DH RU, Witney, 20.4.44; to 5 MU, Kemble, 31.7.44; RAE, Farnborough ('C' Flt) 15.1.48; SOC 4.5.50 and RTP; remains to 49 MU, Colerne, 10.7.50.

6543   RAF serial **X7383**; TOC 18 MU, Dumfries, 20.7.41; 18 Gp CF, Leuchars 24.8.41; 5 MU, Kemble, 18.12.44; regd **VH-BKM** 10.2.48 to E J Connellan, t/a Connellan Airways, Alice Springs, NT; CoA (10039) issued 25.3.48; left Croydon on delivery flight 13.4.48; crashed on take-off from Daly Waters, NT, 6.5.48 when both engines failed and aircraft impacted heavily with ground; all aboard (pilot, engineer and two women) injured but escaped before aircraft burst into flames.

Misrair's SU-ACS, c/n 6544, the second allocation of these marks was written off in July 1948   [P H T Green collection]

6544 RAF serial **X7384**; TOC 18 MU, Dumfries, 20.7.41; 55 OTU, Usworth, 23.7.41; 54 OTU, Church Fenton, (later Charterhall)13.3.42; SF Northolt 19.8.42; DH RU, Witney, 10.10.42; 18 MU, Dumfries, 18.2.43; sold to Misr Airwork Ltd, Egypt, 25.3.43 as replacement aircraft for c/n 6641, which was lost at sea during delivery; regd **SU-ACS** (second), named *Jerusalem* (*Al Quds* in Arabic); DBR at Zaafarane 27.7.48.

6545 RAF serial **X7385**; TOC 18 MU, Dumfries, 21.7.41; CFS, Upavon, 17.8.41; 4 AOS, West Freugh, 15.5.42; 18 MU 17.9.42; 4 RS, Madley, 19.4.43; damaged 13.6.43; DH RU, Witney, 5.1.45; Flight Refuelling Ltd 11.5.45; sold to Flight Refuelling Ltd, Ford, .3.46; regd **G-AHFJ** 25.3.46 to Skyways Ltd, named *Sky Trail*; CoA (7592) issued 28.5.46 (applied for by W A Rollason Ltd); sold 26.6.48; regd **VP-KFW** 6.48; crashed on landing at Mauritius 8.8.48 while on delivery flight from the UK (still as G-AHFJ).

6546 RAF serial **X7386**; TOC 18 MU, Dumfries, 27.7.41; CFS, Upavon, 17.8.41; 4 AOS, West Freugh, 4.6.42; 18 MU, Dumfries, 17.9.42; 2 SS, Yatesbury, 21.10.42 [205]; unit redes 2 RS 1.1.43; DH RU, Witney, 20.6.45; 5 MU, Kemble, 8.11.45; DH RU, Witney, 28.11.45; 18 MU 8.5.46; regd **G-AKOI** 4.12.47 to W A Rollason Ltd, Croydon, and sold to them 19.12.47; CoA (10098) issued 7.5.48; regn cld 7.7.48 as sold abroad but later amended to 'destroyed 23.9.48'; actually shipped to South Africa and painted in Pan African Air Charter colours; purchased by Boris Senior for Israeli AF but impounded in Egypt 5.48 while being ferried by A Lindsay; del to Jordan and regd **TJ-AAQ** 7.48 to Arab Airways Assoc Ltd; shot down by G Lichtmann in Israeli AF Bf109 at Irbid, Jordan, 23.9.48 while flying from Beirut to Amman; three killed, inc BBC correspondent John Nixon and Daily Telegraph journalist David Woodford.

6547 RAF serial **X7387**; TOC 18 MU, Dumfries, 28.7.41; to DGA for AAJC 7.9.41; regd **G-AGDG** 11.9.41 to Scottish Airways Ltd, Inverness and Renfrew; CoA (6910) issued 21.10.41; to BEA 1.2.47; regn cld 21.11.47 as sold abroad; CoA renewed 16.3.48; regd in France 22.4.48 as **F-BEDX** (CoR 20382) to Air France, Ivato, Madagascar; re-regd **F-OADX** 31.5.49; retd to Le Bourget late .49; regd **F-BAHX** 10.10.50 to Air France for operation by Ecole de l'Aviation Civile, Dreux; sold to Société Autrex Lopez & Cie, Hanoi, Indo-China, 10.7.52; damaged on landing at Nam-Dinh, Vietnam, 15.3.53; believed not repaired and destroyed 29.6.53 on French evacuation from Hanoi; regn cld 5.7.53.

6548 RAF serial **X7388**; TOC 18 MU, Dumfries, 20.7.41; to DGA for AAJC 7.9.41; regd **G-AGDH** 11.9.41 to Scottish Airways Ltd, Inverness and Renfrew; CoA (6909) issued 10.10.41; DBR in gale at Stornoway 25.11.41 and regn cld same day.

6549 RAF serial **X7389**; TOC 9 MU, Cosford, 5.8.41; 3 FPP, Hawarden, 13.10.41; DH RU, Witney, 20.2.43; 18 MU 8.4.43; 2 RS, Yatesbury, 29.4.43; 18 MU 4.5.45; DH RU, Witney, 12.3.46; 18 MU, Dumfries, 3.12.46; regd **G-AKZJ** 19.5.48 to Adie Aviation Ltd, Croydon, and sold to them 31.5.48; CoA (10175) issued

29.6.48; regd 5.7.48 to Mayfair Aviation Services Ltd, London; export to Israel blocked in Cyprus 12.48; regd 17.12.48 to Mediterranean Air Services Ltd, Nicosia, Cyprus; regn cld 6.5.49; regd **4X-ACU** 13.11.49 to Arkia - Israel Inland Airlines; regd by 1.53 to M Lang (unconfirmed); regd 9.3.53 to Arkia - Israel Inland Airlines; broken up for spares at Lydda .54; remains extant 8.57; regn cld 18.12.57.

6550 RAF serial **X7390**; TOC 9 MU, Cosford, 6.8.41; HQ ATA, White Waltham, 13.10.41; 27 MU, Shawbury, 22.10.41; 3 FPP, Hawarden, 31.12.41; DH RU, Witney, 19.5.43; 18 MU, Dumfries, 26.8.43; 1 DF, Redhill, (later Odiham, Andrewsfield and Hawkinge) 31.12.44; 18 MU, Dumfries, 14.5.46; sold to Air Enterprises 9.12.47; regd **G-AKNZ** 11.12.47 to Air Enterprises Ltd, Croydon; CoA (9940) issued 9.3.48; regd 29.11.48 to W A Rollason Ltd, Croydon; regn cld 30.12.48 as sold in South America; regd in Argentina as **LV-AGY** 23.3.49 to Zonas Oeste y Norte de Aerolineas Argentinas (ZONDA), via Sfreddo y Paolini Ltda, aircraft brokers; re-regd **LV-FEP** 25.9.51; to Ricardo Alvarez, San Justo, Buenos Aires, 25.9.51; crashed 3.11.52 while engaged in smuggling, but still shown as regd 5.67.

6551 RAF serial **X7391**; TOC 18 MU, Dumfries, 7.8.41; 10 AOS, Dumfries, 13.9.41; damaged 10.9.42; Air Taxis Ltd for repair; 18 MU 24.2.43; sold to Misr Airwork Ltd, Egypt, 25.3.43; regd **SU-ACT** (second) 28.9.43 to Misr Airlines Ltd, named *Al Alamein;* DBF at Almaza 25.2.51. (This was a replacement aircraft for c/n 6642, which was lost at sea during delivery).

6552 RAF serial **X7392**; TOC 18 MU, Dumfries, 14.8.41; 10 AOS, Dumfries, 13.9.41; 3 (O) AFU, Bobbington (later renamed *Halfpenny Green*), 14.8.42; 18 MU 9.9.42; 54 OTU, Charterhall, 3.2.43; DH RU, Witney, 28.12.43; retd to 54 OTU 10.1.44; 18 MU 21.3.44; 7 Gp CF, Bottesford, (later Spitalgate) 23.11.44; 18 MU 16.1.46; SF Halton [THA:I] 25.3.46; 18 MU 11.8.46; regd **G-AJFK** 29.1.47 to Field Aircraft Services Ltd, Croydon, and sold to them 14.2.47; regd 19.2.47 to Island Air Charters Ltd, Jersey; CoA (8979) issued 29.4.47; regd 21.5.51 to Aerocontacts Ltd, Gatwick; regn cld 21.2.52 as sold in Pakistan; regd **AP-AFN** 3.52 to Crescent Air Transport Ltd, Karachi; DBF at Karachi 28.9.52.

6553 RAF serial **X7393**; TOC 18 MU, Dumfries, 13.9.41; 10 AOS, Dumfries; 1 (O) AFU, Wigtown, 4.8.42; DH RU, Witney, 9.4.42; 18 MU, Dumfries, 29.11.42; 1 SS, Cranwell, 15.1.43; DH RU, Witney, 28.6.44; 6 (O) AFU, Staverton, 28.10.44; 44 Gp CF, Staverton, 6.11.44; SoAT, Netheravon, 9.1.46; 18 MU, Dumfries, 23.5.46; sold to Lancashire Aircraft Corporation Ltd, Squires Gate, 10.3.47 and regd **G-AJKY** 22.3.47 to them; CoA (9303) issued 22.3.47; regn cld as to long term storage 9.11.50; regd 9.4.51 to same owner; CoA renewed 25.5.51; regd 14.4.54 to Aeroservices Ltd, Croydon; regn cld 23.6.54 as sold in Indo-China; inspected at Hanoi 14.7.54; regd **F-OAQZ** 7.10.54 to Cie Autrex, Saigon; CoA suspended at Sam Neua 17.4.55, probably after accident.

G-AJKY, c/n 6553, of Lancashire Aircraft Corporation, apparently operating pleasure flights at an air show [via A. Chivers]

G-APSD, c/n 6556, when in the ownership of Air Navigation & Trading Co Ltd   [G M Simons collection]

6554   RAF serial **X7394**; TOC 9 MU, Cosford, 18.8.41; 782 Sqn, Donibristle [Merlin V], 25.9.41 as ambulance; det. to Inverness 1.42–4.42; DH RU, Witney, 6.8.42; retd. to 782 Sqn 19.9.42; damaged when tipped up while taxiing at Eglinton 22.10.42; DH RU, Witney, 7.11.42 for repair; retd to 782 Sqn 18.1.43; det to Inverness 27.1.43; DH RU, Witney, 31.7.43; retd to 782 Sqn 23.9.43; nosed over while taxiing at Hatston 20.3.44; DH RU, Witney presumed; retd to 782 Sqn 21.7.44; DH RU, Witney, 11.9.45; flew into Broadcrag, Scafell Pike, Lake District, 30.8.46 while on ambulance flight from Abbotsinch to Stretton; pilot Sub Lt S K Kilsby, CPO H J Clark, SBA   L H Watkinson, Comm Wardmaster C R Allwright, Surg Cdr W M T Gwynne-Jones and one patient killed.

6555   RAF serial **X7395**; TOC 9 MU, Cosford, 18.8.41; SF Northolt 21.9.41; DH RU, Witney, 15.12.41; 18 MU, Dumfries, 9.4.45; SF Halton [THA:D and THA:E] 25.10.45; 5 MU, Kemble, 10.10.46; sold to C W Potter 10.3.47; regd **G-AJKE** 12.3.47 to Private Air Hire Service Ltd, London; CoA (9646) issued 28.8.47; regd 29.11.48 to W A Rollason Ltd, Croydon; regn cld 20.5.52 as sold in France; regd **F-BEFU** 23.5.52 to Sté Violet Frères, Perpignan; regd 1.56 to Sté Aéro-Sud, Bône (later Algiers); crashed and written off at M'laca 30.4.60.

6556   RAF serial **X7396**; TOC 9 MU, Cosford, 22.8.41; 24 Sqn, Hendon, 5.10.41; 4 Del Flt, Grangemouth, (later Turnhouse) 6.11.41; 3 DF, High Ercall, 9.8.42; DH RU, Witney, 25.11.42; 18 MU, Dumfries, 27.1.43; HQ ATA, White Waltham, 21.3.43; DH RU, Witney, 30.11.44; 18 MU 22.4.45; 12 FU, Melton Mowbray, 7.10.45; 18 MU 8.2.46; RAE, Farnborough, ('A' Flt) 23.9.46; DH, Leavesden, 10.9.52; ATDU, Gosport, 13.9.53; ATDU det, St Mawgan, by 11.9.58; sold 22.1.59 to Air Navigation & Trading Co Ltd, Squires Gate and regd **G-APSD** to them 4.2.59; CoA issued 19.7.60; regd 24.5.63 to Stramsway Ltd, Shoreham, named *Cookie;* CoA lapsed 10.7.64; airframe burnt at Shoreham 4.5.66; regn cld 22.5.69.

6557   RAF serial **X7397**; TOC 9 MU, Cosford, 25.8.41; HQ ATA, White Waltham, 18.11.41; DH RU, Witney, 25.8.43; 18 MU, Dumfries, 1.12.43; transferred to FAA 13.4.45; 782 Sqn, Donibristle, 2.5.45; AHU, Stretton 4.46 to 7.46; DH Witney 25.9.46; AHU, Stretton 14.3.47; SF/2 FF Stretton [901:JA] 20.1.48; nosed over after landing 6.7.49; DH Leavesden by road 19.7.49; RDU Arbroath 12.5.50; AHU, Lossiemouth 24.3.53; RN Unit, SLAW, Old Sarum, 6.11.53; Yeovilton [921:VL] 14.4.56; nosed over when brakes failed while taxiing at Yeovilton 3.8.56 and DBR; SOC 13.9.56.

Fleet Air Arm Dominie X7397, c/n 6557, carried the code 921:VL when used by the RN Section of SLAW, Old Sarum, a unit parented by RNAS Yeovilton

[Denis Fox collection]

A well-known photograph of two Dominies of 2 Signals School at Yatesbury, with X7398 [209] in the foreground and X7386 [205] behind

[G M Simons collection]

6558 RAF serial **X7398**; TOC 18 MU, Dumfries; 10 AOS, Dumfries, 27.8.41; 9 (O) AFU, Penrhos, 6.8.42; Air Taxis Ltd 14.9.42; 18 MU, Dumfries, 12.10.42; 2 RS, Yatesbury [209], 22.10.42; DH RU, Witney, 21.3.45; 18 MU 12.7.45; 1 RS, Cranwell, 16.1.46; Staff College Comm Flt, White Waltham [TBR:R], 24.5.46; 18 MU 9.1.47; regd **G-AJTU** 21.5.47 to Southern Aircraft (Gatwick) Ltd and sold to them 31.5.47; regd 11.6.47 to J E Coxon of Southern Aircraft, Gatwick; CoA (9530) issued 7.10.47; regd 19.5.48 to Southern Aircraft (Gatwick) Ltd; sold 21.6.48 and regn cld 31.12.48; regd in Kenya 12.48 as **VP-KGS**; broken up for spares at Mombasa 10.52.

6559 RAF serial **X7399**; TOC 18 MU, Dumfries; 10 AOS, Dumfries, 29.8.41; 1 (O) AFU, Wigtown, 3.8.42; DH RU, Witney, 9.9.42; 18 MU, Dumfries, 17.11.42; 2 RS, Yatesbury, 31.12.42; DH RU, Witney, 21.3.45; 18 MU 10.7.45; 4 Gp CF, Full Sutton, (later Rufforth and Abingdon) 16.11.45; 18 MU 16.10.47; sold to R A Short 2.2.49; regd **G-ALGM** 17.2.49 to Sqn Ldr K J Nalson,

Croydon; CoA (10437) prepared, date unknown; regn cld 21.7.52 as sold in France; regd **F-BGOL** 26.8.52 to Transportes Aériens Waldberg, Nice; regd 2.54 to Aéro Club Paul Tissandier, St Cyr; sold in Belgian Congo 8.55; regd **OO-CRS** to Air Brousse SPRL, Léopoldville; badly damaged on landing at Maimanimba 5.7.56; regn cld 16.2.59; intended to become **OO-CJW** but ntu 16.2.59; reported as returned to France instead as **F-BEOL** but believed crashed in Atlantic .60 en route.

6560 RAF serial **X7400**; TOC 18 MU, Dumfries; 10 AOS, Dumfries, 29.8.41; 18 MU, Dumfries, 7.10.42; 2 SS, Yatesbury, 21.10.42; unit redes 2 RS [204] 1.1.43; overshot landing at Yatesbury 7.12.44; DH RU, Witney, for repair 15.12.44; 18 MU 13.4.45; transferred to FAA 17.10.45; Evanton 12.45; 782 Sqn, Donibristle, by 10.48; unable to maintain height, flew into hill at Dun Rig, Peebleshire, 28.2.49 when port engine failed at 6500 feet above cloud.

G-ALGM, c/n 6559, owned by Sqn Ldr K J Nalson at Croydon prior to sale to France in 1952 [via A. Chivers]

Named "Monmouth", G-AKUC, c/n 6565, of Cambrian Air Services is seen being refuelled

6561 RAF serial **X7401**; TOC 18 MU, Dumfries; 10 AOS, Dumfries, 1.9.41; 6 AOS, Staverton, 31.7.42; DH RU, Witney, 23.9.42; 18 MU, Dumfries, 8.12.42; 32 Wg 16.2.43; Macmerry 22.6.43; 32 Wg, Turnhouse, 1.3.44; DH RU, Witney, 18.9.44; 56 OTU, Milfield, 6.1.45; 18 MU 28.3.46; regd **G-AHPY** 22.5.46 to Field Consolidated Aircraft Services Ltd, Croydon; regn cld 12.8.46 as sold abroad; UK CoA (8014) issued 18.10.46; regd in South Africa as **ZS-BCP** 14.8.46 to Owenair (Pty) Ltd; regd to O G Davies t/a Owenair, Youngsfield; regd .55 to Owenair (Pty) Ltd; converted to Mk.4; to Drakensberg Air Services; to D Steyn, Ladysmith; scrapped at Virginia Airport, Durban c.1967 and parts used for **ZS-DLS**; regn cld 31.3.71.

6562 RAF serial **X7402**; TOC 18 MU, Dumfries, 4.9.41; 10 AOS, Dumfries, 13.9.41; hit water when flying low over Derwentwater, Cumberland, 28.11.41, killing six; SOC 10.12.41.

6563 RAF serial **X7403**; TOC 18 MU, Dumfries, 7.9.41; 24 Sqn, Hendon, 20.8.42; to USAAF 1.12.42; 8th Air Force Ferry and Transport Service, later 27th ATG; DH RU, Witney,19.5.44; 5 MU, Kemble, 11.9.44; regd **G-AKTY** 3.3.48 to L E Gisborne & D J Hayles, t/a Ocean Airways, Portsmouth; regd 15.4.48 to Herts & Essex Aero Club (1946) Ltd, Broxbourne; CoA (10081) issued 5.5.48; regn cld 11.5.51 as sold in France; regd **F-BFVR** 11.8.51 to SCA, Toussus-le-Noble; regd 2.54 to Air Madagascar, Ivato; re-regd as **5R-MAM** to same owner 3.63; sold 1.64 and regd **F-OCBX** 13.3.64 to Air Djibouti; restored as **5R-MAM** 31.5.65 to Air Madagascar, Ivato; regn cld 11.66 on CoA enquiry.

6564 RAF serial **X7404**; TOC 18 MU, Dumfries, 12.9.41; 10 AOS, Dumfries, 18.9.41; 3 (O) AFU, Bobbington, 14.8.42; 18 MU 9.9.42; 47 MU, Sealand, 25.10.42 for packing; to Liverpool 20.11.42, dispatched to Cape Town on *Priam* 2.12.42, arrived 3.2.43; to SAAF as **1362**; 9 AD; 62 AS 3.8.43; Congella 28.12.44; sold to N Shand, Cape Town, 5.7.46 for £1921; regd **ZS-BCR** 22.8.46; regn cld 17.6.53 as sold in Mozambique; regd **CR-ADT** to DETA 6.53; reduced to spares 1.58.

6565 RAF serial **X7405**; TOC HQ FPP, White Waltham, 12.9.41; DH RU, Witney, 6.3.43; retd to HQ FPP 21.5.43; damaged while taxying at Charterhall 15.3.44; 5 MU, Kemble, 9.7.44; regd **G-AKUC** 3.3.48 to S K Davies, t/a Cambrian Air Services, Cardiff, and sold to them 11.3.48; CoA (10036) issued 14.5.48; regd 13.4.49 to J H Watts, S K Davies, E Keith-Davies & Care Lines Ltd, t/a Cambrian Air Services; named *Monmouth*; regd 25.1.52 to Cambrian Air Services Ltd, Cardiff; regd 26.2.55 to Airwork Ltd, Blackbushe; regn cld 13.6.55 as sold in Iran; regd **EP-ADM** 7.55 to Iranian Oil Exploration & Production Co; regn cld before .60.

6566 RAF serial **X7406**; TOC 18 MU, Dumfries, 17.9.41; 10 AOS, Dumfries, 22.9.41; 2 (O) AFU, Millom, 12.8.42; 18 MU 11.9.42; 1 SS, Cranwell, 24.9.42; unit redes 1 RS 1.1.43; 1 APS, Fairwood Common 26.10.44; 84 Gp CF, Gilze-Rijen, 22.3.45; 1 APC, Fairwood Common, 19.7.45; 18 MU 31.10.45; 1 FU, Pershore, 17.1.46; 18 MU 10.4.46; regd **G-AKOD** 3.12.47 to Darlington and District Aero Club Ltd, Neasham (Croft) and sold to them 9.12.47; CoA (10152) issued 30.9.48; regd 26.5.49 to

G-AKOD, c/n 6566, probably photographed when in the hands of Lancashire Aircraft Corpn Ltd

Lancashire Aircraft Corporation Ltd, Bovingdon (later Yeadon); regn cld as to long-term store 24.11.50; regn restored 4.7.51; CoA renewed 16.1.52, lapsed 15.1.53; regd 12.4.54 to Aeroservices Ltd, Croydon; CoA renewed 14.4.54; regn cld 23.6.54 as sold in Indo-China; regd **F-OAQY** 31.8.54 to Cie Autrex, Saigon; regd mid-.55 to Sté Laos Air-Service, Vientiane; crashed in downwind landing at Sam Neua, Laos 9.4.57, with one fatality.

6567   RAF serial **X7407**; TOC 18 MU, Dumfries, 19.9.41; 3 Del Flt, Hawarden, 21.10.41; DH RU, Witney,15.7.42; 18 MU 24.8.42; SF Abbotsinch 16.9.42; 1680 Flt, Abbotsinch, (later Prestwick) 15.6.43; reputed to have been the last aircraft to use Dundonald airfield, 23.7.45; damaged 1.10.45; SOC 29.11.46.

6568   RAF serial **X7408**; TOC 18 MU, Dumfries, 29.9.41; 47 MU, Sealand, 30.1.42 for packing; shipped from Birkenhead to Karachi on *Streelkerk* 10.3.42; GR School, Bombay; Bengal Comm Unit, Dum Dum, Calcutta; Comm Sqn, Willingdon; SOC 16.12.44.

6569   RAF serial **X7409**; TOC 18 MU 2.10.41; 47 MU, Sealand, 1.3.42 for packing; shipped from Birkenhead to India on *City of Hong Kong* 18.3.42; GR School, Bombay; 2 Coastal Def Flt, Juhu; regd **VT-ARF** 11.6.43 to Air Service Co of India; to Director of Civil Aviation 1.9.43; regd 26.6.46 to Indian National Airways; regd 5.6.47 to Indian Air Survey & Transport Co Ltd, Dum Dum, Calcutta; name changed .48 to Air Survey Co of India Ltd; crashed .50 (or broken up for spares at Dum Dum .49?).

6570   RAF serial **X7410**; TOC 18 MU, Dumfries, 3.10.41; 41 OTU, Old Sarum, 17.10.41; DH RU, Witney, 21.10.41; 18 MU 2.1.43; 53 OTU, Llandow, (later Kirton-in-Lindsey) 27.2.43; 18 MU, Dumfries, 5.7.45; SOC 18.10.45.

6571   RAF serial **X7411**; TOC 9 MU, Cosford, 2.10.41; HQ ATA, White Waltham, 13.10.41; 271 Sqn, Doncaster, 17.3.42; 24 Sqn, Hendon, 6.1.44; MCS, Hendon, 8.9.44; DH RU, Witney, 14.5.45; A&AEE, Boscombe Down, 27.11.45; DH, Witney, 9.2.49; damaged in taxying accident there 10.2.49 but repaired; retd to A&AEE 13.4.49; 5 MU, Kemble, 11.1.50; sold to Adie Aviation 31.3.50; regd **G-AMAM** 11.4.50 to Adie Aviation Ltd, Croydon; regd 21.3.51 to Martin-Baker Aircraft Co Ltd, Denham; CoA issued 29.3.51; regd 24.11.59 to Fieldair Ltd, Croydon (based at Wymeswold); CoA lapsed 20.11.60; regd cld 13.2.62 as 'destroyed'; remains extant at Wymeswold 6.62.

6572   RAF serial **X7412**; TOC 9 MU, Cosford, 12.10.41; 2 Del Flt, Colerne, 24.10.41; DH RU, Witney, 17.3.42; retd to 2 Del Flt 15.4.42 (named *Thermo Excreta*); DH RU, Witney, 24.5.43; 18

MU, Dumfries, 29.8.43; 27 Gp CF, Aston Down [TSO:A], 28.10.44; DH RU, Witney, 29.3.46; 18 MU, Dumfries, 15.1.47; sold to Aeroways 21.5.48; regd **G-ALBC** 27.5.48 to A W Coombs, t/a Aeroways, Croydon; CoA (10188) issued 15.6.48; regd 24.7.48 to Sir Robert McAlpine & Sons Ltd, t/a Luton Airways, Luton; regd 24.3.55 to K McAlpine, Croydon; converted to Mk.6 2.8.61; operated by Solair Flying Services Ltd, Baginton, from 5.62 and regd to them 26.6.63; struck rising ground on Wove Hill, 1,900 ft asl on Kinder Scout, Edale Moor, Derbyshire, while flying from Middleton St. George to Birmingham on 30.12.63, injuring two; cause was severe turbulence; remains burnt on site due to difficulty of salvage; regn cld 9.1.64.

6573   RAF serial **X7413**; TOC 24 Sqn, Hendon, 7.10.41; damaged 3.8.44, ROS by 71 MU 11.8.44; retd to 24 Sqn 19.10.44; Yatesbury 31.10.44; DH RU, Witney, 27.7.45; 18 MU, Dumfries, 29.9.45; Gloster Aircraft 6.11.45; Power Jets Ltd, Bitteswell, 26.6.46; loaned to Martin-Baker Aircraft, Chalgrove, 3.9.48 to 11.9.48; retd to Bitteswell; loaned to Martin-Baker Aircraft 26.7.49 to 30.7.49; Bitteswell to 5 MU, Kemble, 4.1.50; regd **G-ALZJ** 27.3.50 to Cambrian Air Services Ltd, Cardiff, and sold to them 31.3.50, named *Caernarvon*; CoA (10855) issued 21.4.50; regd 7.7.50 to J H Watts, E Keith-Davies, S K Davies & Care Lines Ltd, t/a Cambrian Air Services; regd 25.1.52 to Cambrian Air Services Ltd; regd 12.3.56 to Cambrian Airways Ltd; regd 24.4.56 to Independent Air Travel Ltd, Hurn; regn cld 30.4.56 as sold in French Morocco; inspected at Tunis 2.6.56; regd **F-OAME** 6.56 to Sté Tunisienne de Réparations Aériennes et de Construction (STRAC), Tunis; CoA suspended at Tunis (El Aouina) 19.1.60; re-regd **TS-BME** 3.60 to same owner; remained unairworthy, regn cld .64.

6574   RAF serial **X7414**; TOC 9 MU, Cosford, 12.10.41; HQ ATA, White Waltham, 28.10.41; DH RU, Witney, 2.6.43; 18 MU, Dumfries, 8.9.43; transferred to FAA 11.10.44; 782 Sqn, Donibristle, 10.44; overshot downwind landing and went through fence, 18.1.45.

6575   RAF serial **X7415**; TOC 9 MU, Cosford, 15.10.41; 4 SS, Madley, 2.1.42; unit redes 4 RS [4-85] 1.1.43; 18 MU, Dumfries, 4.1.46; DH RU, Witney, 19.3.46; 18 MU 10.12.46; regd **G-AKZO** 20.5.48 to J Nesbit Evans & Co Ltd, Wednesbury, and sold to them next day; CoA (10205) issued 24.7.48; regd 11.4.53 to Don Everall (Aviation) Ltd, Elmdon; regn cld 9.8.60 as sold in France; regd **F-BHFM** 12.4.61 to Aéro Club d'Alsace, Strasbourg; regd .63 to CIC de Parachutisme d'Alsace, Strasbourg, transferred to La Ferté-Gaucher; CoA suspended 11.66; regn cld .67.

X7413, c/n 6573, in service as a 'hack' with Gloster Aircraft in 1948, with a Hastings and a Sturgeon in the background, probably at an SBAC show

[MAP via P H T Green]

Dominie X7413, c/n 6573, eventually became Rapide G-ALZJ, seen here in the hands of Cambrian Air Services and named "Caernarvon" [Denis Fox collection]

6576   RAF serial **X7416**; TOC 20 MU, Aston Down, 17.10.41; 24 Sqn, Hendon 7.1.42; 1 ADF, Croydon, (later North Weald and Gatwick) 23.1.42; Redhill 6.11.44; DH RU, Witney, 19.3.45; 18 MU, Dumfries, 20.6.45; 1680 Flt, Prestwick, 14.12.45; to AAJC, Prestwick, 16.4.46; regd **G-AHLL** 8.5.46 to Scottish Airways Ltd, Renfrew; CoA (7779) issued 28.6.46; regd 1.2.47 to BEA, later named *RMA Sir Henry Lawrence* (name later transferred to G-AJCL); overshot on landing at Land's End (St Just) 21.5.59; regn cld 30.7.59; broken up by 2.60, but remains still at Exeter 10.68.

6577   RAF serial **X7417**; TOC 9 MU, Cosford, 22.10.41; HQ ATA, White Waltham, 18.11.41; DH RU, Witney, 11.1.45; 18 Gp CF, Leuchars [2V:D] 25.5.45; DH RU, Witney, 4.2.46; 18 MU, Dumfries, 17.10.46; sold to W A Webb 19.12.47; regd **G-AKOR** 31.12.47 to W A Webb, Croydon; CoA (9918) issued 1.3.48; regd 9.3.48 to Morton Air Services Ltd, Croydon; regd 5.5.48 to John Mowlem & Co Ltd, London; regd 11.7.49 to Morton Air Services Ltd, Croydon; regd 25.5.50 to Skyways Ltd, Dunsfold; regd 5.5.52 to W S Shackleton Ltd, Croydon; regn cld 4.12.52 as sold in Fiji; regd **VQ-FAN** 20.2.53 to Katafanga Estates Ltd, t/a Fiji Airways; damaged on landing at Matei, Taveuni Island, 10.8.56; regn cld as sold in French Noumea 9.10.56; regd **F-OAZT** 12.7.57 to Sté Calédonienne de Transports Aériens (Transpac), Nouméa, New Caledonia; CoA suspended at Nouméa (Magenta) 11.3.58 (but also reported as written off 13.12.58).

6578   RAF serial **X7437**; TOC 9 MU, Cosford, 24.10.41; 4 SS, Madley, 12.12.41; unit redes 4 RS 1.1.43; overshot landing at Perdiswell 31.8.43; DH RU, Witney, 13.9.43 for repair; 18 MU, Dumfries, 15.12.43; transferred to FAA 13.4.45; 782 Sqn, Donibristle, 27.4.45 (det to Lee-on-Solent 10.45–3.46); AHU,

Stretton, 9.46; SOC 21.2.55; sold 6.55 to Federated Fruits, Speke (disposal subject of court martial); used for spares and painted as 'G-AZZZ'; to Continental Aircraft Services Ltd, Croydon, 3.56 and rebuilt; regd **G-APJW** 2.1.58 to S J, K and H J Stevens, t/a Missionary Aviation Fellowship; sold 13.2.58 and regd 16.4.58 to Tarmac Ltd, Wolverhampton; CoA issued 20.5.58; regd 29.4.59 to (associate company) Plascom (1909) Ltd, Wolverhampton; damaged in heavy landing nr Gleneagles Hotel, Perthshire, 3.6.59 but repaired; converted to Mk.4; regd 13.9.60 to Direct Air Ltd, Elstree; sold 17.7.62 to unknown buyer; regn cld 9.8.62 as sold in France; inspected at Dinard 23.8.62 by Rousseau Aviation; regd **F-BHOB** 3.10.62 to Aéro Club Centre Alsace, Colmar; regd to Aéro Club de Normandie, Rouen; regd 2.68 to M Rouchaud, t/a Transaero, Bordeaux (Merignac) (later Belle Ile); CoA suspended 17.2.70 at St Nazaire (Montoir); regn cld.

6579   RAF serial **X7438**; TOC 9 MU, Cosford, 30.10.41; HQ ATA, White Waltham, 18.11.41; DH RU, Witney, 24.1.43; 18 MU, Dumfries, 18.3.43; 33 Wg CF, Clifton, 26.3.43; SF Church Fenton 29.10.43; SF Grimsetter 6.12.45; SOC 18.2.46.

6580   RAF serial **X7439**; TOC 9 MU, Cosford, 1.11.41; 4 SS, Madley, [K]15.12.41 (later 4 RS); DH RU, Witney, 11.7.45; 18 MU, Dumfries, 19.3.46; regd **G-AKOJ** 4.12.47 to W A Rollason Ltd, Croydon, and sold to them 19.12.47; CoA (9955) issued 20.4.48; regn cld 14.5.48 as sold abroad; regd in Jordan as **TJ-AAJ** 5.48 to Arab Airways Assoc Ltd; damaged at Amman 8.5.48 and repaired; re-regd **JY-AAJ** .54, possibly NTU; regd in France as **F-OARH** 29.12.54 to Sté Air Madagascar, Ivato; CoA suspended at Majunga 14.11.62; regn cld as destroyed.

G-APJW, c/n 6578, in the snow at an unrecorded location

Formerly X7440 of the RAF, civil registration G-AKYW has been crudely applied to this Dominie, c/n 6581 [*A J Jackson via P H T Green*]

6581 RAF serial **X7440**; TOC 9 MU, Cosford, 12.11.41; 4 SS, Madley, 12.12.41 (later 4 RS); DH RU, Witney, 5.7.45; 18 MU, Dumfries, 14.3.46; regd **G-AKYW** 18.5.48 to D J Hayles, Croydon, and sold to him 27.5.48; regd 24.6.48 to W A Rollason Ltd, Croydon; CoA (10199) issued 2.11.48; regn cld 23.11.48 as sold abroad; regd in Argentina as **LV-AGR** 26.2.49 to Zonas Oeste y Norte de Aerolineas Argentinas (ZONDA) via Sfreddo y Paolini Ltd (aircraft brokers); to Aerolineas Argentinas .50; to Centro Universitario de Aviación, Matanza, Buenos Aires 30.5.57; CoA lapsed 28.9.65 but still regd 5.67.

6582 RAF serial **X7441**; TOC 9 MU, Cosford, 12.11.41; 4 SS, Madley, 12.12.41 (later 4 RS); DH RU, Witney, 7.4.45; 18 MU 2.10.145; 1 FU, Pershore, 16.1.46; 18 MU, Dumfries, 10.4.46; regd **G-AKOH** 4.12.47 to W A Rollason Ltd, Croydon, and sold to them 19.12.47; CoA (9992) issued 21.5.48; regd 21.5.48 to Mannin Airways Ltd, Ronaldsway; CoA lapsed 10.8.50; regd 21.5.51 to North-West Airlines (IoM) Ltd, Ronaldsway; CoA renewed 5.3.53; regn cld 12.5.53 as sold in France; regd **F-BGXH** 18.6.53 to Aéro Club du Dauphiné, Grenoble; regd .62 to Aero Club du Rhône et du Sud-Est, Lyon (Bron); CoA suspended 3.11.64; destroyed in hangar, Lyon (Corbas) 23.1.65; regn cld .65.

6583 RAF serial **X7442**; TOC 9 MU, Cosford, 12.11.41; 4 SS, Madley, 15.12.41 (later 4 RS); damaged 4.11.42; damaged 21.11.43; 18 MU, Dumfries, 22.4.44; 16 Wg CF, Hendon, 23.12.44; 23 MU, Aldergrove, 8.1.45; 18 MU, Dumfries, 5.2.45; sold to Hawker Aircraft Ltd 4.12.45; regd **G-AHGC** 28.3.46 to Hawker Aircraft Ltd, Langley (later Dunsfold); CoA (7591) issued 25.6.46; regd 18.7.63 to Hawker Siddeley Aviation Ltd; regd 20.7.65 to Hawker Siddeley Aviation (Leasing) Ltd; CoA lapsed 21.6.65 and WFU at Dunsfold; roaded to Blackbushe 1.2.66 and to Booker 1.5.66 for rebuild; regd 5.4 66 to K B Neely t/a Scillonia Airways, Land's End (St. Just), named *Tresco;* sold, but not regd, to Trent Valley Aviation .68 and del to Halfpenny Green; CoA lapsed 4.7.68; to Army Parachute Association, Netheravon, for spares by 7.70; regn cld 16.5.72; parts to Durney Aeronautical Collection, Andover.

6584 Regd **G-AGDM** 1.11.41 to Allied Airways (Gandar Dower) Ltd, Dyce, named *Eldorado;* CoA (6913) issued 8.11.41; CoA lapsed 7.8.46; taken over by BEA 4.47 and regd to them 15.11.47; regd 25.5.48 to Charles Allen, Croydon; regd 29.12.48 to R A Short, M Marodeen and D J Hayles, Croydon; CoA renewed 1.1.49; regd 18.1.49 to R A Short, Croydon; regd 24.1.49 to Sqn Ldr K J Nalson, Croydon; regd 23.6.49 to Sivewright Airways Ltd, Barton; CoA lapsed 23.2.51; regd 11.9.51 to Airviews Ltd, Ringway; regd 1.11.56 to Hants & Sussex Aviation Ltd, Portsmouth; converted to Mk.4; regn cld 30.3.57 as sold in France; regd **F-OAXK** 6.6.57 to Sté Aérienne de Transport Guyane-Antilles (SATGA), Cayenne; CoA suspended 17.12.65; regn cld .66.

F-BGXH, c/n 6582, was used by Aero Clubs in the south east of France [*G M Simons collection*]

Manx Air Charters Ltd was the owner of this smart Rapide G-AJGV c/n 6589, named "Glen Helen"   *[Denis Fox collection]*

6585 RAF serial **X7443**; TOC 33 MU, Lyneham, 18.11.41; BW Flt, Yatesbury, 6.9.42; 22 Gp CF, Ternhill, 19.7.45; damaged 2.10.46; DH RU, Witney, 31.10.46; 5 MU, Kemble, 21.2.47; sold to Field Aircraft Services Ltd, Croydon, 29.5.47 and regd **G-AKBW** to them 18.7.47; CoA 9611 allocated but regn cld 5.5.48; broken up for spares.

6586 RAF serial **X7444**; TOC 9 MU, Cosford, 25.11.41; 4 SS, Madley, 12.12.41 (later 4 RS); collided with Proctor DX223 and crashed at Langwardine, Hereford, 12.4.43; SOC 25.4.43.

6587 RAF serial **X7445**; TOC 9 MU, Cosford, 27.11.41; HQ ATA, White Waltham, 5.12.41; ACCCF (later 2nd TAF CF), White Waltham, 21.4.43; TTCCF, Wyton, 5.12.45; SF Northolt 30.11.45; MCS, Hendon, 16.7.46; damaged 29.8.46; Kirkbride 30.10.46; MCS, Hendon; 18 MU, Dumfries, 11.10.46; regd **G-AJFJ** 29.1.47 to Field Aircraft Services Ltd, Croydon, and sold to them 17.2.47; regd 17.3.47 to T L E B Guiness, London; CoA (8978) issued 27.6.47; regd 29.10.47 to Airwork Ltd and operated by Kuwait Oil Co Ltd from 8.47; CoA lapsed 26.6.48; regd 20.12.49 to C W J Allen, Croydon; regd 4.5.50 to Allen Aircraft Services Ltd, Croydon; WFU 20.4.51 and broken up for spares 6.51; regn cld 20.4.59.
[Note: this aircraft was to be deleted from contract B1045495/40 when that contract was reduced, but as it had already been delivered, X7526 was substituted.]

6588 RAF serial **X7446**; TOC 18 MU, Dumfries, 27.11.41; 47 MU, Sealand, 16.2.42 for packing; shipped from Liverpool to Karachi on *Steelkerk* 11.3.42; AHQ India CU; regd **VT-ASA** 1.9.44; regd 4.6.46 (CoR 550/2) to Indian Air Survey & Transport Co Ltd, Dum Dum, Calcutta; name changed .48 to Air Survey Co of India Ltd; badly damaged on running into ditch on take-off from Ondal 24.3.59 but repaired; regn cld 7.78; shipped to Portland, OR, USA .78 and regd in USA as **N2290B** to E J Gothard, Chevalis, WA; regd .79 to M G Kimbrell, Oakville, WA, named *Mary Linda*; aircraft fitted with non-standard nose glazing; regd 11.92 to J J Schell, Puyallup, WA, based at Thun, nr Seattle; aircraft current and flown under experimental certificate.

6589 RAF serial **X7447**; TOC 9 MU, Cosford, 1.12.41; 4 SS, Madley, 12.12.41; 1 SS, Cranwell, 12.7.42; 4 RS, Madley, 1.1.43; struck by Proctor LX793 on Madley runway 28.8.44; DH RU, Witney, 14.9.44 for repair; 5 MU, Kemble, 6.12.44; sold to Air Charter Experts Ltd 6.1.47; regd **G-AJGV** 11.2.47 to A Hamson & Son Ltd, Northampton; operated by Air Charter Experts Ltd, Ronaldsway; CoA (9149) issued 30.4.47; regd 26.8.47 (on name change) to Manx Air Charter Ltd, named *Glen Helen;* regd 20.8.53 (on name change) to Manx Airlines Ltd (actually 2.53); regn cld 5.5.55 as sold in Paraguay but NFT.

The postwar Jersey Airlines operated this Rapide, G-AKNE c/n 6591, which became F-OBDV in Madagascar   *[C N Dodds]*

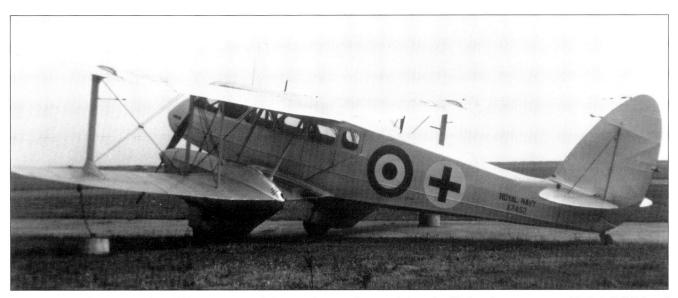

Dominie X7542, c/n 6594, seen about 1951 carrying air ambulance markings; at the time it belonged to 782 Squadron   *[MAP via P H T Green]*

6590   RAF serial **X7448**; TOC 9 MU, Cosford, 2.1.42; transferred to FAA; 781 Sqn, Lee-on-Solent, 17.2.42; DH RU, Witney, 27.2.43; retd to 781 Sqn 26.3.43; DH RU, Witney, 21.1.44; retd to 781 Sqn 30.3.44; 782 Sqn, Donibristle, 2.45, named *Merlin XIII;* tipped onto nose on landing 27.3.45; Crail 5.7.46; 781 Sqn, Lee-on-Solent [854:LP] 2.8.46 to 6.48; AHU, Stretton, 1.49; SOC 27.8.49.

6591   RAF serial **X7449**; TOC 18 MU, Dumfries, 8.12.41; damaged on landing at Dumfries on delivery flight that day; ROS and TOC again 27.12.41; 4 SS, Madley, 27.3.42 (later 4 RS [4-92]); DH RU, Witney, 23.12.45; 18 MU 6.9.46; sold to Island Air Charters Ltd 9.12.47; regd **G-AKNE** 29.11.47 to R J Martin, Jersey; CoA (10018) issued 30.5.49; regd 23.6.49 to V H Bellamy, t/a Flightways, Eastleigh; regd 25.1.50 to M L Thomas, t/a Jersey Airlines; regd 30.5.57 to Hants & Sussex Aviation Ltd, Portsmouth; left Portsmouth 1.9.57 on ferry flight to Madagascar; regn cld 23.9.57 as sold in Madagascar; inspected at Ivato 25.11.57; regd **F-OBDV** 21.1.58 to Sté Air Madagascar, Ivato; re-regd **5R-MAN** to Sté Air Madagascar 3.63; CoA suspended 18.5.68, destroyed.

6592   RAF serial X7450; TOC 18 MU, Dumfries, 8.12.41; 47 MU, Sealand, 16.2.42 for packing; shipped to Karachi from Birkenhead on *Steelkerk* 10.3.42; AHQ India CF, Lahore; damaged when taxied into Hurricane HW468 5.9.43 and repaired; DBF during refuelling at Vizagapatam 24.12.43; SOC 31.8.44.

6593   RAF serial **X7451**; TOC 18 MU, Dumfries, 12.12.41; 47 MU, Sealand, 16.2.42 for packing; shipped to Karachi from Birkenhead on *City of Hong Kong* 18.3.42; 2 Coastal Rec Flt, Juhu; damaged on hitting fence on take-off from Ahmadabad 7.8.42 and repaired; SF Chaklala; damaged when taxied into Hudson V9199 at Chaklala 3.2.43 and repaired; 152 OTU, Peshawar; damaged when struck by Vengeance on ground at Peshawar 22.1.43 and repaired; 223 Gp CF, Chaklala (or AHQ India CF, Willingdon (later Palam)); damaged on landing at Razmak 17.7.44; PSOC 1.1.47.

6594   RAF serial **X7452**; TOC 18 MU, Dumfries, 17.12.41; transferred to FAA; 781 Sqn, Lee-on-Solent, 13.3.42; DH RU, Witney, 28.3.43; retd to 781 Sqn 23.6.43; DH RU, Witney, 19.4.44; retd to 781 Sqn 21.6.44; DH RU, Witney, 23.5.45; 799 Sqn, Lee-on-Solent [L9B], 10.10.45 to 3.46; 782 Sqn, Donibristle, to Crail 31.7.46; 782 Sqn, Donibristle [802:DO] 1.49 as ambulance; nosed over in soft ground on landing 16.1.50; DH Leavesden 7.50; AHU, Stretton, 2.51; 782 Sqn, Donibristle [809:DO, later 804:DO] 6.51; DH Leavesden 23.7.53; Northern Comms Sqn, Donibristle [802:DO] 31.3.54; brakes seized on landing due to icing, tipped on nose, damaging propellers and nose, 20.1.55; SOC 27.4.55.

6595   RAF serial **X7453**; TOC 782 Sqn, Donibristle, 22.12.41 (det to Inverness 2.42 to 8.42); DH RU, Witney, 7.11.42; retd to 782 Sqn 18.11.42; DH RU, Witney, 22.9.43; retd to 782 Sqn 24.12.43; DH RU, Witney, 6.12.44; retd to 782 Sqn 29.3.45; collided with Seafire SW822 from Stretton over Wimboldsley, between Middlewich and Medwich, Cheshire, 11.2.46, killing Lt (E) A W Watson MBE, Lt A H Lavington, PO(A) G G Reynolds DSM and Cdr (E) L B Sharman; SOC 12.2.46.

X7454, c/n 6596, at Witney on 28th October 1943, when it was in for repair after being damaged at Prestwick on 8th June   *[via P. Davis]*

G-AHKB, c/n 6596, in use by Hampshire Aeroplane Club was the former RAF and USAAF X7454   *[via A. Chivers]*

C/n 6596 in its final guise in France as F-BEKB   *[G M Simons collection]*

6596   RAF serial **X7454**; TOC HQ ATA, White Waltham, 2.1.42; 4 FPP, Prestwick; damaged while taxiing at Prestwick 8.6.43; DH RU, Witney, 23.8.43 for repair; 18 MU, Dumfries, 17.11.43; USAAF, Alconbury, for 27th ATG 5.4.44, named *Wee Wullie;* retd to RAF; 57 OTU, Hawarden, 17.8.44; 10 Gp CF, Colerne, 3.9.44; DH RU, Witney, 20.2.45; CRD at Vickers-Armstrongs Ltd, South Marston, 1.6.45; converted to civilian standard 30.5.45; Castle Bromwich 30.8.45; regd **G-AHKB** 16.4.46 to Vickers-Armstrongs Ltd, South Marston; CoA (7640) issued 11.5.46; re-regd by .51 to Vickers-Armstrong (Aircraft) Ltd; regd 2.4.59 to V H Bellamy, t/a Hampshire Aeroplane Club, Eastleigh; regn cld 16.10.61 as sold in France; regd **F-BEKB** 29.11.61 to Ateliers Aéronautiques de la Côte d'Emeraude, Dinard (Rousseau Aviation); operated by RF Para Club, Bergerac; regd .62 to Etat SFATAT, Bergerac; regd 28.12.64 to CIC Parachutisme du Sud-Ouest, Bergerac; WFU on expiry of CoA 12.65; regn cld .67.

6597   RAF serial **X7455**; TOC HQ ATA, White Waltham, 24.12.41; DH RU, Witney, 28.9.43; 18 MU, Dumfries, 9.2.44; 1 DF, Andrewsfield, (later Hawkinge) 6.7.45; Hawarden 27.9.45; 5 MU, Kemble, 22.1.47; SOC 30.5.47.

6598   RAF serial **X7456**; TOC 9 MU, Cosford, 4.1.42; 4 SS, Madley, 28.3.42; unit redes 4 RS 1.1.43; DH RU, Witney, 22.12.45; 18 MU, Dumfries, 26.8.46; sold to West Cumberland Air Services 11.12.47; regd **G-AKNN** 8.12.47 to W A Herbert & E C Wilson t/a West Cumberland Air Services Ltd, Workington; CoA (9981) issued 22.4.48; regd 26.5.48 to Astral Aviation Ltd, Newcastle

(Woolsington); regd 26.2.49 to Air Couriers (Transport) Ltd, Croydon; regd 16.4.51 to Air Couriers (Properties) Ltd, Croydon; regd 12.10.53 to Air Couriers (Transport) Ltd; regd 18.5.54 to Marshall's Flying Services Ltd, Cambridge; converted to Mk.6 21.6.60; regd 18.1.62 to William Tomkins Ltd, Apethorpe and used for parachuting duties at Podington as *The Brown Bomber;* deconverted from Mk.6 5.2.62; regd 4.4.67 to British Skydiving Ltd, Thruxton; regd 9.10.68 to G H Smale, t/a Trak Air, Dunkeswell; CoA lapsed 29.8.69; sold 28.10.70 to M de Cartier; in external storage at East Midlands Airport by 11.71; regn cld 10.9.73 and broken up for spares.

6599   RAF serial **X7482**; TOC 9 MU, Cosford, 4.1.42; 3 Del Flt, High Ercall, 16.4.42; DH RU, Witney, 27.7.42; retd to 3 Del Flt; DH RU, Witney, 21.8.42; 2 SS, Yatesbury, 9.9.42; damaged 22.9.42; unit redes 2 RS 1.1.43; DH RU, Witney, 5.4.45; 18 MU, Dumfries, 2.9.45; transferred to FAA 17.10.45; Evanton 12.45; RN Unit, SLAW, Old Sarum, 1.49; AHU, Stretton, 4.49 to 4.50; AHU, Arbroath, 7.50 to 1.51; 782 Sqn, Donibristle, 7.51; attd to RN Unit, SLAW, Old Sarum, 12.52 to 3.53; overshot landing at Lee-on-Solent 3.3.53, ran onto soft ground and tipped on nose; SOC 25.3.53.

6600   RAF serial **X7483**; TOC 9 MU, Cosford, 2.1.42; 4 SS, [P] Madley, 9.3.42; unit redes 4 RS [4-91] 1.1.43; TTCCF, Wyton, 26.3.46; 27 Gp CF, Southrop, 4.46; damaged, ROS by 49 MU, 3.7.46; SF Halton 20.8.46; 5 MU, Kemble, 18.12.46; regd **G-AJVA** 29.5.47 to Airwork Ltd, Heston; regd 30.6.47 to Iraq Petroleum

Transport Co Ltd, Tripoli; CoA (9596) issued 1.3.48; CoA lapsed 26.4.51; regn cld 13.12.51 as sold abroad; regd in Jordan as **TJ-ABM** 10.52 to Arab Airways Association Ltd, Amman; destroyed in hangar fire at Amman 9.5.53; regn cld 5.6.53.

6601 RAF serial **X7484**; TOC PTS, Ringway, 25.1.42; damaged 2.12.43; DH RU, Witney, 3.2.46; 18 MU, Dumfries, 29.10.46; regd **G-AKOE** 3.12.47 to Darlington & District Aero Club Ltd, Neasham (Croft) and sold to them 9.12.47; CoA (10023) issued 26.5.48; regd 26.5.49 to Lancashire Aircraft Corporation Ltd, Bovingdon (later Squires Gate); regn cld as to long-term storage 9.11.50; regn restored 3.2.51; CoA renewed 20.4.51; regd 28.10.57 to Silver City Airways Ltd; CoA lapsed 26.5.58; regd 16.10.58 to Hants & Sussex Aviation Ltd, Portsmouth; converted to Mk.4 and reflown 10.12.58; CoA renewed 27.10.59; regd 6.11.59 to Air Rectification Ltd, Hurn, named *The Water's Edge;* sold 9.10.61 and regd 8.1.62 to E M Brain and S M Harley, Baginton; regd 31.5.62 to Rapide Flying Group Ltd, Baginton; regd 31.10.62 to J E Pierce, Baginton; CoA lapsed 9.7.65, stored at Baginton; to Ley Farm, Chirk, for rebuild by Pierce / North Western Aero Engineering Ltd; reflown 17.10.78; leased to British Airways 18.10.78 and operated by them in 'modern' BA colours after CoA renewal 26.7.79, named *Sir Henry Morgan* and used in Islander Class 25 celebrations; CoA lapsed 25.7.82 and stored at Chirk; regn cld 16.5.89; regd 12.12.89 to same owner; stored (9.99).

6602 RAF serial **X7485**; TOC 4 SS, Madley, [O] 24.11.42 (later 4 RS [4-90]); DH RU, Witney, as damaged 11.7.45; loaned to BOAC Training Flight, Hurn, 15.3.46; 18 MU, Dumfries, 10.4.46; regd **G-AIUN** 20.11.46 to Air Schools Ltd, Derby (Burnaston) and sold to them 10.3.47; regd 30.7.47 to D L Steiner, t/a Steiner's Air & Travel Services Ltd, Speke; CoA (9614) issued 7.8.47; regd 25.5.48 to Mayfair Air Services Ltd, London; to Israel 6.48 but allegedly written off at Sodom 6.6.48 (still carrying UK regn) when bomb exploded; rebuilt and to Israeli AF as **S-75**; operated by 1 and 4 Sqns, Sde Dov, 7.48; became IDFAF **1305** c12.48; WFU .49; UK regn cld 16.5.50 as 'disappeared in Palestine'.

6603 RAF serial **X7486**; TOC 18 MU, Dumfries, 14.2.42; transferred to FAA; 782 Sqn, Donibristle, 1.4.42; DH RU, Witney, 2.3.43; retd to 782 Sqn 7.4.43; DH RU, Witney, 29.3.44; retd to 782 Sqn 27.5.44; braked to avoid lorry at Belfast 8.6.44 and nosed up; DH RU, Witney, 18.5.45; retd to 782 Sqn 27.11.45; Crail 22.5.46; RNARY Donibristle 25.11.46; 782 Sqn, Donibristle [802:DO] 4.5.48 as ambulance; DH Leavesden 13.6.49; AHS, Arbroath 1.5.50; 782 Sqn, Donibristle [802:DO] 17.11.50; RNARY Donibristle 19.11.51; DH Leavesden 17.6.52; retd to 782 Sqn [804:DO] 16.2.53; Northern Comms Sqn, Donibristle [805:DO] 10.10.53; AHU, Donibristle 9.12.54; deteriorated by 6.55; SOC and sold 19.12.56; regd

G-AOZG 23.1.57 to Hants & Sussex Aviation Ltd, Portsmouth; regd 11.3.57 to R E Webb; regd 22.7.57 to A V Boella & W Bogatto, Eastleigh; converted to Mk.4 and CoA issued 18.10.57; regd 11.11.57 to West African Airways Corpn, Lagos, Nigeria; regn cld 10.12.57 as sold in Sierra Leone; regd **VR-LAC** 1.58 to Sierra Leone Airways, Freetown, named *Mount Mamba;* damaged at Hastings, Sierra Leone, 30.5.58 and presumably WFU.

6604 RAF serial **X7487**; TOC 18 MU, Dumfries, 13.2.42; transferred to FAA; 782 Sqn, Donibristle, 13.3.42, named *Merlin VII;* 781 Sqn, Lee-on-Solent, by 3.43; DH RU, Witney, 22.5.43; 782 Sqn, Donibristle, 30.7.43; DH RU, Witney, 15.8.44; retd to 782 Sqn; SOC 12.8.48; wings on Balado Bridge dump 3.52.

6605 RAF serial **X7488**; TOC 18 MU, Dumfries, 12.2.42; transferred to FAA; 782 Sqn, Donibristle, 13.3.42, named *Merlin XIII;* DH RU, Witney; retd to 782 Sqn 30.10.42; DH RU, Witney, 15.2.43; retd to 782 Sqn 24.12.43; RNARY, Donibristle, 7.2.45; 782 Sqn, Donibristle, 25.6.45; SF Donibristle 13.9.45; Donibristle SS; 782 Sqn, Donibristle, 28.2.46; 767 Sqn, Yeovilton [VL] 11.11.49; 767 Sqn to Henstridge 4.1.52; AHS Arbroath 5.2.52; AHU Lossiemouth 26.8.53 as spares source; SOC 13.1.59; remains still extant 7.60.

6606 RAF serial **X7489**; TOC 18 MU, Dumfries, 13.2.42; 4 SS, Madley, 29.3.42; unit redes 4 RS 1.1.43; DH RU, Witney, 15.3.45; 18 MU 22.7.45; CRD at Power Jets Ltd, Bitteswell, 9.11.45; sold to D J Adie, Croydon, 25.4.47; regd **G-AKRE** 21.1.48 to L E H Airways Ltd, London; CoA (9945) issued 16.2.48; regn cld 7.1.49 as sold in French Indo-China; inspected at Saigon 21.4.49; regd **F-OABH** 12.5.49 to Cie de Transports Aériens Autrex, Hanoi; destroyed in hangar fire at Gia-Lam, Hanoi, 4.6.52.

6607 RAF serial **X7490**; TOC SFC, Watchfield, 17.3.42; damaged on landing at Watchfield 31.8.42; DH RU, Witney, 31.8.42 for repair; 18 MU, Dumfries, 22.12.42; SF Old Sarum 5.3.43; DH RU, Witney, 14.5.45; 18 MU, Dumfries, 31.10.45; MCS, Hendon, 27.12.45; 18 MU, Dumfries, 7.8.46; sold to Scottish Aviation Ltd 24.5.48; regd **G-ALBH** 7.6.48 to Scottish Aviation Ltd, Prestwick; CoA (10212) issued 9.8.49; sold to Luxembourg Airlines as **LX-LAC** .49 but NTU; CoA lapsed 7.6.53; regd 20.3.54 to Mitchell Engineering Ltd, Croydon; CoA renewed 18.6.54; regd 26.7.57 to Morton Air Services Ltd, Croydon (later Gatwick); regd 23.6.60 to Aerocontacts (Aircraft Distributors) Ltd, Gatwick; regn cld 28.9.60 as sold in Congo; regd **OO-CJD** 15.11.60 to Air Brousse SPRL, Léopoldville; to Cogeair, Kinshasa; to Agence de Messageries Aériennes Zairoises (AMAZ), Ndolo; re-regd **9O-CJD** .61; crashed on take-off from Boma 7.6.62; rebuilt and re-regd to AMAZ as **9Q-CJD** 6.63; current .69; NFT.

X7488, c/n 6605, "Merlin XIII" of 782 Squadron at Donibristle; note the unusual presentation of the letters RN on the fin and rudder [R C Sturtivant]

G-ALBH, c/n 6607, in Olley Air Service Ltd titles with a Dove in the background. It was actually registered to Morton Air Services, which bought Olley in 1953 [via A. Chivers]

6608 RAF serial **X7491**; TOC SFC, Watchfield, 27.3.42; damaged on landing at Watchfield 10.4.42; DH RU, Witney, 18.4.42 for repair; 1 BAS, Watchfield, 2.6.42; 41 OTU, Old Sarum, 6.11.42; damaged 1.8.43; 41 OTU, Hawarden, 20.8.43; damaged 20.9.43 and ROS; 3 TEU, Aston Down, 10.11.44; FCCS, Northolt, 2.8.45; 4 DF, Hutton Cranswick, 6.9.45; civilianised by General Aircraft 16.11.45; sold to General Aircraft Ltd, Hanworth, 28.3.46; regd **G-AHTY** 5.6.46 to Airtraining (Fairoaks) Ltd, Fairoaks; CoA (7865) issued 1.8.46; regd on change of name to Universal Flying Services Ltd 26.2.47; CoA lapsed 23.3.49; regd 31.10.49 to North Sea Air Transport Ltd, Hanworth and Brough; CoA renewed 28.5.52; regn cld 21.7.52 as sold; regd in France as **F-BGIS** 28.8.52 to Sté Turboméca, Pau (Idron); regn cld; regn restored 3.9.56; regd. 56 to Air Ouest, Nantes; CoA suspended 2.2.58; permit issued 14.6.58 for flight to Algiers; operated 9.58 to 60 by Sté Générale d'Affrétements Aériens (Air Fret), Algiers; regd late .60 to Sté Transport Air Saoura, Colomb-Béchar; CoA suspended at Benoud 1.11.60; regn cld .63.

6609 RAF serial **X7492**; TOC SFC, Watchfield, 5.4.42; 1 BAS, Watchfield, 7.42; 81 Gp CF, Perdiswell, 2.11.42; 9 Gp CF, Samlesbury, 29.4.43; 61 OTU, Rednal, (later Keevil) 10.2.44; DH RU, Witney, 21.3.46; 18 MU, Dumfries, 6.1.47; regd **G-ALAU** 26.5.48 to W A Webb, Croydon, and sold to him next day; CoA (10235) issued 21.9.48; sold 5.10.48 (but not regd) to W A Rollason Ltd, Croydon; regn cld 15.10.48 as sold abroad; regd in Argentina as **LV-AER** 31.12.48 to Zonas Oeste y Norte de Aerolineas Argentinas (ZONDA) through Sfreddo y Paolini Ltda (aircraft brokers); to Aerolineas Argentinas .50; to Aeroclub Argentino 3.62; to Tuvavion SRL, Buenos Aires, 15.9.65; CoA lapsed 30.9.66, but still regd 5.67; moved to Don Torcuato 7.67; noted WFU at Asuncion, Paraguay, 3.72, but essentially complete.

6610 RAF serial **X7493**; TOC SFC, Watchfield, 5.2.42; 18 MU, Dumfries, 7.11.42; 24 Sqn, Hendon, 4.9.43; MCS, Hendon, 8.9.44; damaged 3.9.45; SOC 20.11.45.

LV-AER, c/n 6609, parked on grass in 1968,with what appears to be a Ryan Navion behind it. By that time the DH.89s CoA had expired [M Magnusson]

Used in Iran by Iranian Oil Exploration & Production Co Ltd, EP-ADO, c/n 6618, was the former G-AKOA   *[Denis Fox collection]*

6611   RAF serial **X7494**; TOC by FAA at Lee-on-Solent 16.2.42; 782 Sqn, Donibristle, 25.2.42; damaged on landing 8.42; DH RU, Witney, for repair 25.8.42 but SOC.

6612   RAF serial **X7495**; TOC 32 MU, St. Athan, 16.2.42; 18 MU, Dumfries, 29.5.47; 32 MU, St Athan, 12.6.47; sold to Air Navigation & Trading Ltd 15.12.47; regd **G-AKOV** 17.12.47 to East Anglian Flying Services Ltd, Southend; CoA (10112) issued 18.9.48; sold 28.1.49 and regd 4.4.49 to Inter-City Air Services Ltd, Hereford; regd 9.8.50 to Wolverhampton Aviation Ltd, Wolverhampton, and also used by Derby Aviation Ltd; regn cld 7.2.55 as sold in Kenya; regd **VP-KNC** 7.2.55 to J E F Wilkins, t/a Noon & Pearce Air Charters, Mazinde; sold to Madagascar 4.56 and inspected at Ivato 11.5.56; regd in France as **F-OAUH** 5.56 to Air Madagascar, Ivato; DBF 14.11.56.

6613   RAF serial **X7496**; TOC by FAA at Lee-on-Solent 19.2.42; 782 Sqn, Donibristle, 26.5.42 as VIP aircraft, known as the 'Admiral's Barge'; stalled on landing 11.1.43; DH RU, Witney, 8.3.43 for repair; retd to 782 Sqn 16.6.43; DH RU, Witney, 7.5.44; retd to 782 Sqn 16.8.44; flew into hill in mist, 13.9.44 (no casualties).

6614   RAF serial **X7497**; TOC by FAA at Donibristle 23.2.42; 782 Sqn, Donibristle 23.2.42 (det to Inverness 3.42 to 8.42); DH RU, Witney, 6.1.43; retd to 782 Sqn 12.2.43; DH RU, Witney, 15.2.44; retd to 782 Sqn 21.4.44; DH RU, Witney, 10.4.45; retd to 782 Sqn 13.9.45 (detd to Eglinton 11.45 and to Lee-on-Solent 12.45); 2 FP, Stretton, 5.1.46 to 4.46; AHU, Stretton 7.7.46; DH Witney; AHU, Stretton 25.6.47; 781 Sqn, Lee-on-Solent [860:LP] 12.10.49; AHU, Arbroath 14.11.51; AHU, Stretton 24.8.53; SOC 12.6.58.

6615   RAF serial **X7498**; TOC by FAA at Donibristle 9.3.42; 782 Sqn, Donibristle, 13.3.42; accident 28.3.42; DH RU, Witney, 24.4.42; 781 Sqn, Lee-on-Solent, 4.7.42; DH RU, Witney, 31.7.43; retd to 781 Sqn 17.9.43; DH RU, Witney, 21.7.44; 782 Sqn, Donibristle, 9.11.44; DH RU, Witney, 6.45; 18 MU, Dumfries, 19.7.45; retd to 782 Sqn 9.45; DH RU, Witney, 31.10.45; retd to 782 Sqn 8.7.46 to 1.47; DH Witney 5.48; AHU, Stretton 3.7.48; SOC 21.2.55; sold to Federated Fruit Ltd, Speke, 3.55 (disposal subject of court martial); to Vendair Ltd, Croydon, for spares .55.

6616   RAF serial **X7499**; TOC by FAA at Donibristle 10.3.42; 782 Sqn, Donibristle, 13.3.42, named *Merlin XII*, as ambulance; DH RU, Witney, 18.11.42; retd to 782 Sqn 12.1.43; swung while taxiing 12.8.44; DH RU, Witney, 22.2.45; retd to 782 Sqn 8.6.45; Donibristle 11.10.45; 790 Sqn, Dale, 30.12.45; 782 Sqn, Donibristle, 25.7.46; DH Witney 9.2.47 for CoA; AHU Stretton 9.10.47; SOC 12.6.58.

6617   RAF serial **X7500**; TOC 4 SS, Madley, 14.3.42 (later 4 RS); damaged on landing at Yeovil 7.5.44; DH RU, Witney, 19.5.44; 5 MU, Kemble, 30.8.44; sold to Goodhew Aviation Co Ltd 11.3.48; regd **G-AKMF** 23.2.48 to C F Cockburn, Oxford; CoA (10074) issued 11.5.48; regd 26.5.48 to Mayfair Air Services Ltd, London; to Israel 6.48; to Israeli AF as **S-74**, operated by 1 and 4 Sqns, Sde Dov, by 7.48; became IDFAF **1304** c12.48; CoA lapsed 10.5.49; UK regn cld as 'disappeared' 17.5.50; NFT.

6618   RAF serial **X7501**; TOC 4 SS, Madley, 17.3.42; unit redes 4 RS 1.1.43; damaged 13.8.43; retd to 4 RS 3.9.43; 18 MU, Dumfries, 12.7.45; DH RU, Witney, 4.10.45; 18 MU 23.5.46; sold to Air Enterprises Ltd 9.12.47; regd **G-AKOA** 11.12.47 to Air Enterprises Ltd, Croydon; CoA (10024) issued 18.3.48; regd 22.1.49 to Patrick Motors Ltd, Elmdon; regd 8.12.50 to M L Thomas, t/a Jersey Airlines; regd 25.2.55 to Airwork Ltd, Blackbushe; regn cld 15.6.55 as sold in Iran; regd **EP-ADO** 7.55 to Iranian Oil Exploration & Production Co; damaged when tipped on nose at Masjid-i-Sulaiman, Iran, 3.1.56 and presumed repaired; regn cld before .59.

6619   RAF serial **X7502**; TOC 9 MU, Cosford, 18.3.42; 47 MU, Sealand, 24.5.42 for packing; shipped from Glasgow 18.8.42 to Cape Town on *Empire Might*, arriving 16.9.42; to SAAF as **1357** at 9 AD 9.42; 62 AS 21.10.42; 24 Gp CF 15.9.44; sold to Aircraft Operating Co via 15 AD 31.10.46; regd **ZS-BMV** 13.1.47; regn cld 20.4.49 as sold in Uganda; regd **VP-UBB** 4.49; regd in Kenya as **VP-KFI** 1.1.48 [sic] to Jivraj's Air Services; to Air Travel (Charters) Ltd .51; reduced to spares at Nairobi 10.52.

6620   RAF serial **X7503**; TOC 9 MU, Cosford, 27.3.42; BW Flt, Yatesbury, 30.4.42; DH RU, Witney, 20.6.45; 18 MU, Dumfries, 12.2.46; regd **G-AKON** 8.12.47 to Southern Aircraft (Gatwick) Ltd and sold to them 15.12.47; CoA (9910) issued 29.1.48; regd 29.1.48 to J E Coxon, Gatwick; regn cld 8.7.48 as sold abroad; regd in Kenya as **VP-KFX** 7.48; regd 7.12.51 to Noon & Pearce Air Charters Ltd, Nairobi; sold in Madagascar 11.53; regd in France as **F-OAOS** 11.1.54 to Soc Air Madagascar, Ivato; re-regd **5R-MAP** 3.63 to same owner; CoA expired 3.64, cld.

6621   RAF serial **X7504**; to AAJC, Speke, 29.3.42; regd **G-AGED** 21.4.42 to Scottish Airways Ltd, Renfrew; CoA (6932) issued 25.4.42; crashed into fence on take-off from Renfrew 2.2.43; regn cld same day.

6622   RAF serial **X7505**; to AAJC, Speke, 3.4.42; regd **G-AGEE** 16.4.42 to Great Western & Southern Airlines Ltd; CoA (6924) issued 15.5.42; to Scottish Airways Ltd 5.2.43; retd to AAJC 7.7.43; regd 1.2.47 to BEA; regd 26.11.47 to Gibraltar Airways Ltd; regn cld 1.7.53 as sold to Iceland; del from Croydon 4.7.53; regd **TF-KAA** (CoR 074) 7.53 to Flugskolinn Thytur HF, Reykjavik; regd 3.7.61 to Daniel Petursson; CoA lapsed 18.5.63; broken up and burnt .66.

Before becoming TF-KAA, c/n 6622, G-AGEE spent time with Gibraltar Airways, whose interesting badge was sported on its fin   *[via C N Dodds]*

The same aircraft as TF-KAA in Iceland soon after delivery in 1953   *[via C N Dodds]*

6623   RAF serial **X7506**; TOC 9 MU, Cosford, 8.4.42; 1 SS, Cranwell, 29.4.42 (later 1 RS); DH RU, Witney, 29.4.43; 18 MU, Dumfries, 31.12.43; transferred to FAA 13.4.45; 782 Sqn, Donibristle, 29.4.45; 781 Sqn, Lee-on-Solent, 28.7.45; 782 Sqn det, Lee-on-Solent, 1.8.45 (det to Belfast 11.45 to 3.46); Stretton [902:JA] 6.46; made precautionary landing on beach at Tenby in bad weather 2.7.46 but later reached Dale; retd to Stretton 4.7.46; DH Witney 5.47; Stretton 16.5.47; Donibristle 28.5.47; 703 Sqn, Thorney Island [A] 24.6.47; 703 Sqn. Lee-on-Solent, 25.5.48; AHU, Stretton 14.9.48; SOC 21.2.55; sold to Federated Fruit Ltd for civil conversion but sale became subject of court martial and was abandoned.

6624   RAF serial **X7507**; TOC 9 MU, Cosford, 12.4.42; transferred to FAA 6.5.42; 787 Sqn, Duxford, 29.4.42; 787Y Flt, Arbroath and Burscough, 6.44 to 10.44; DH RU, Witney, 1.1.45; Lee-on-Solent 4.5.45; SF Woodvale 25.6.45; SF Arbroath 19.8.45; SF/2 FS, Stretton [905:JA], 6.11.45; Crail 31.5.46; Donibristle 18.3.47; RAD Donibristle 12.5.47; Evanton 29.5.47; DH Witney 29.8.47; Stretton 31.12.47; SF/2 FS, Stretton [905:JA, later 902:JA] 21.1.48; DH Leavesden 11.10.49; AHS Arbroath 26.6.50; 782 Sqn, Donibristle [803:DO] 31.8.51; AHU Lossiemouth 30.4.53; SOC 13.1.59; cut up and burnt by Hants & Sussex Aviation 8.60.

6625   RAF serial **X7508**; TOC 9 MU, Cosford, 18.4.42; TOC by FAA at Yeovilton 2.5.42; 776 Sqn, Speke, 17.6.42; 781 Sqn, Lee-on-Solent, 29.9.42; 2 MU, Worthy Down, 8.10.42; retd to 776 Sqn 17.6.42; 2 MU, Worthy Down, 6.11.42; 776 Sqn, Speke, 1.12.42; 781 Sqn, Lee-on-Solent, 8.3.43; 776 Sqn, Speke, 12.3.43; accident at Speke 16.6.43; DH RU, Witney, 11.11.43; retd to 776 Sqn 15.2.44 for C-in-C's Flt; DH RU, Witney 8.6.45; Evanton 26.2.46; Crail 19.10.46; RDU Culham 24.1.47; AHU Stretton 18.2.49; AHS Arbroath 22.9.50; SF Machrihanish [901:MA] 18.10.51; caught by gust while taxying in high wind 26.10.51 and wingtip hit hangar wall; DH Leavesden 11.3.52; RDU Arbroath 8.11.52; AHU Lossiemouth 11.2.53; 787 Sqn, West Raynham, 22.9.54; swung off perimeter track while taxying in strong wind at West Raynham 2.5.55 and hit notice board; AHU Lossiemouth 4.2.56; SF Lossiemouth 9.3.56; AHU Lossiemouth 23.3.56; overshot runway on landing at Tain 2.8.56 and fell into ditch; roaded to RNARY Donibristle 31.8.56; SOC 8.11.56.

6626   RAF serial **X7509**; TOC 9 MU, Cosford, 30.4.42; 47 MU, Sealand, 24.5.42 for packing; to Glasgow docks 1.8.42; shipped to Cape Town 18.8.42 on *Empire Might*, arriving 16.9.42; to SAAF as **1358** at 9 AD 9.42; 62 AS 15.10.42; 11 OTU 15.9.44; 61 Sqn 12.44; sold via 15 AD 5.7.46 to Aircraft Operating Co, Germiston, for £2250; regd **ZS-BEA** 10.8.46; regd .53 to OFS Air Services Pty Ltd,

Bloemfontein; regd 7.54 to Trans Oranje Air Services (Pty) Ltd, Zastron, OFS; operated by Maputi Air Services, Johannesburg; to South West Air Transport; crashed at Leribe, Basutoland, 24.7.54 while on flight from Ficksburg to Tlokoenga but rebuilt; DBF during engine start-up at Otjiwarongo, SWA, 22.2.55.

6627 RAF serial **X7510**; TOC 9 MU, Cosford, 30.4.42; 47 MU, Sealand, 24.5.42 for packing; to Glasgow docks 1.8.42; shipped to Cape Town 18.8.42 on *Empire Might*, arriving 16.9.42; to SAAF as **1359** at 9 AD 9.42; 62 AS 15.10.42; 61 Sqn 2.3.45; sold to African Flying Services 5.7.46 for £2040; regd **ZS-BCT** 29.1.47; regn cld 23.5.49 as sold in Kenya; regd **VP-KHF** 5.49 to ??; regd 20.9.52 to Caspair Air Charters & Agencies Ltd, Nairobi; operated by E E (Ted) Fresson as anti-locust sprayer 12.53 to 2.54; crashed on take-off and DBF 1 ml N of Garissa 23.1.55, killing one.

6628 RAF serial **X7511**; TOC 18 MU, Dumfries, 15.5.42; 47 MU, Sealand, 24.5.42 for packing; to Glasgow docks 1.8.42; shipped to Cape Town 18.8.42 on *Empire Might*, arriving 16.9.42; to SAAF as **1361** at 9 AD 9.42; 62 AS 15.10.42; crashed Bloemfontein 22.10.42; SOC by RAF 6.1.43; SOC by SAAF 31.8.43.

6629 RAF serial **X7512**; TOC SF Abbotsinch 26.5.42; damaged when struck wall in forced landing at Hawes, Yorks, 23.8.42; DH RU, Witney, for repair; 18 MU, Dumfries, 22.1.43;

2 SS, Yatesbury, 25.1.43; unit redes 2 RS [212] 1.1.43; 4 RS, Madley, 2.3.45; DH RU, Witney, 29.10.45; 18 MU 24.6.46; regd **G-AKNX** 4.12.47 to Air Enterprises Ltd, Croydon, and sold to them 9.12.47; CoA (9911) issued 13.2.48; to Palestine 28.8.48 for use with UN forces as **5**; returned to UK 8.10.48; sold 1.12.48 and regd as **G-AKNX** 14.2.49 to Patrick Motors Ltd, Elmdon; regd 24.4.52 to Airlines (Jersey) Ltd, t/a Jersey Airlines; regn cld 13.9.55 as sold in France; regd **F-OATD** 20.9.55 to Transports Aériens du Gabon (Air Gabon), Libreville; regd .58 to M Boulame-Lafond, Port-Gentil, Central African Republic; regd .58 to Groupement Aéronautique et Automobile, Port-Gentil and operated by Air Gabon; destroyed at Tchibanga 8.11.60; regn cld 1.61.

6630 RAF serial **X7513**; TOC SF Abbotsinch 31.5.42; 1680 Flt, Abbotsinch, 15.6.43; iced up and flew into ground at Braehead, 2 mls SW of Barrhead, Renfrewshire, 1.3.44, injuring six.

6631 RAF serial **X7514**; TOC 9 MU, Cosford, 11.6.42; 1 SS, Cranwell, 19.6.43 (later 1 RS); DH RU, Witney, 18.7.44; 18 MU, Dumfries, 29.10.44; TTCCF, White Waltham, (later Wyton) [TWY:C] 2.6.45; 18 MU 20.6.46; regd **G-AJFL** 29.1.47 to Field Aircraft Services Ltd, Croydon, and sold to them 19.2.47; regn cld 28.3.47 as sold in Uganda; erroneously 'restored' to the Uganda Co Ltd 10.4.47; CoA (8980) issued 30.4.47; regd **VP-UAW** 4.47 to Uganda Co Ltd; written off at Zanzibar 21.9.47.

Rapide G-AKNX, c/n 6629, was operated by Jersey Airlines from 1952 to 1955   *[Denis Fox collection]*

After use by Jersey Airlines, G-AKNX was sold in Gabon as F-OATD   *[Denis Fox collection]*

6632   RAF serial **X7515**; TOC 9 MU, Cosford, 11.6.42; 47 MU, Sealand, 20.6.42 for packing; to Liverpool docks; shipped to West Africa 2.9.42 on *Nigerian*, arriving 3.10.42; SF Ikeja [1]; SOC 22.11.44.

6633   RAF serial **X7516**; TOC 18 MU, Dumfries, 17.6.42; 2 SS, Yatesbury, 26.6.42 (later 2 RS [206]); DH RU, Witney, 21.3.45; 18 MU 19.7.45; transferred to FAA 17.10.45; 18 MU 24.10.45; to CRD at Blackburn Aircraft Ltd, Brough, 14.11.45; sold to Blackburn Aircraft Ltd 31.7.46; regd **G-AHLU** 2.5.46 to Flying Training Ltd, Hanworth; regd 22.5.46 to North Sea Air Transport Ltd, Hanworth; CoA (7792) issued 20.7.46; regd 21.11.49 to E J Connellan t/a Connellan Airways, Alice Springs, NT, Australia; flown from UK, arr Alice Springs 8.12.49; regd **VH-AHI** 14.12.49 to E J Connellan t/a Connellan Airways and operated for Flying Doctor Service; regd 14.3.51 to Connellan Airways Ltd, Alice Springs; badly damaged in take-off crash in bush at Hookers Creek, NT, 5.1.53; roaded 1000 mls to Alice Springs and rebuilt over 12 months; WFU at Alice Springs and regn cld 13.5.58.

6634   RAF serial **X7517**; TOC 18 MU, Dumfries, 19.6.42; 2 SS, Yatesbury, 27.6.42 (later 2 RS [207]); 18 MU 5.4.45; SOC 3.9.45.

6635   RAF serial **X7518**; TOC 18 MU, Dumfries, 24.6.42; 1 SS, Cranwell, 20.7.42 (later 1 RS); DH RU, Witney, 26.5.44;. 5 MU, Kemble, 24.9.44; regd **G-AKMG** 24.2.48 to Aircraft & Engineering Services Ltd, Croydon, and sold to them 25.3.48; regd 9.4.48 to

After war service, X7523, c/n 6640, was civilianised as G-AIUK and is seen here in the hands of Derby Aviation Ltd   *[Denis Fox collection]*

Now registered VP-KND, the former G-AIUK was photographed at Croydon just before its departure to Caspair Air Services at Nairobi. It seems that seats have yet to be reinstalled   *[Denis Fox collection]*

Sivewright Airways Ltd, Manchester (Barton); CoA (10061) issued 13.5.48; CoA lapsed 18.6.51; regd 3.3.52 to Transair Ltd, Croydon; regn cld 23.4.52 as sold in France; regd **F-BGPI** 25.6.52 to Aigle Azur Indochine, Hanoi; regd 10.53 to Cie Autrex, Hanoi; CoA suspended at Sam Neau 22.5.58, probably as result of an accident.

6636   RAF serial **X7519**; TOC 18 MU, Dumfries 30.6.42; 271 Sqn, Doncaster, 11.7.42; 24 Sqn, Hendon, 6.1.44; MCS, Hendon, 8.9.44; DH RU, Witney, 17.9.45; 18 MU 3.4.46; regd **G-AKOP** 9.12.47 to T H Morton, Croydon; regd 11.12.47 to W A Webb, Croydon, and sold to him by RAF 19.12.47; CoA (9909) issued 14.1.48; regd 9.2.48 to Denham Air Services Ltd, Denham; regn cld 3.5.48 as sold abroad; to Israeli AF ?.

6637   RAF serial **X7520**; TOC 18 MU, Dumfries, 7.7.42; 27 MU, Sealand, 15.7.42 for packing; to Glasgow docks 1.8.42; shipped to South Africa 18.8.42 on *Empire Might*, arriving 16.9.42; to SAAF as **1360** at 9 AD; 62 AS 15.10.42; 11 OTU 15.9.44; 61 Sqn 6.45; sold 31.10.46; regd **ZS-BMW** .47 but NTU; regn cld 9.8.47.

6638   RAF serial **X7521**; TOC 18 MU, Dumfries, 17.7.42; DH RU, Witney, 20.9.42; 18 MU 17.10.42; 2 SS, Yatesbury, 30.12.42 (later 2 RS); 5 MU, Kemble, 20.9.44; Church Fenton 20.4.47 for GOC Northern Command; 18 MU 24.1.49; sold to Short Bros 28.4.49; regd **G-ALOV** 29.9.49 to Short Bros & Harland Ltd, Rochester; CoA (10583) issued 30.5.49; sold 14.1.54 to unknown buyer, probably W A Rollason Ltd, Croydon; regn cld 1.3.54 as sold in French Equatorial Africa; regd **F-OAPS** 1.4.54 to Sté Transports Aériens du Gabon; Libreville; DBF on start-up at Ekouata, French Equatorial Africa, 16.3.55.

6639   RAF serial **X7522**; TOC 18 MU, Dumfries 2.8.42; 24 Sqn, Hendon, 17.8.42; to USAAF 1.12.42; 8th Air Force Ferry and Transport Service, later 27th ATG; damaged 12.3.43; retd to USAAF 12.12.43; DH RU, Witney, 17.5.44; 5 MU, Kemble, 14.9.44; regd **G-AKTX** 1.3.48 to L E Gisborne, t/a Denham Air Services, Denham, and sold to them 11.3.48; CoA (10054) issued 8.4.48; regd 22.4.48 to Mayfair Air Services Ltd, London; ferried from Croydon to Palestine via Nicosia, arr Tel Aviv 5.5.48; to Israeli AF as **S-72**; Galil Sqn, Yavne (redes 3 Sqn 6.48); became IDFAF **1302** c12.48; still with 3 Sqn, Yavne (redes 100 Sqn 5.49); UK regn cld 17.5.50 as 'disappeared'; NFT

6640   RAF serial **X7523**; TOC 18 MU, Dumfries, 18.8.42; 24 Sqn, Hendon, 25.8.42; to USAAF 1.12.42; 8th Air Force Ferry and Transport Service, later 27th ATG; damaged, but ROS 21.3.43; DH RU, Witney, 13.4.44; SF Old Sarum 20.6.44; 18 MU 4.4.46; regd **G-AIUK** 8.11.46 to Kenning Aviation Ltd, Derby (Burnaston) and sold to them 17.1.47; CoA (9012) issued 26.9.47; regd 18.6.48 to Air Schools Ltd, t/a Derby Flying Club, Burnaston; operated by Wolverhampton Aviation / Derby Aviation; converted to Mk.4; regn cld 14.2.55 as sold in Kenya; regd **VP-KND** 14.2.55 to J E F Wilkins t/a Caspair Air Charters, Nairobi; badly damaged by fire on start-up at Kisumu 18.3.55 but repaired; regd 16.4.56 to Caspair Air Charters & Agencies Ltd, Nairobi; regd .58 to Caspair Ltd, Nairobi; regn cld .64.

In USAAF markings and RAF serial, X7523, c/n 6640 was used by the 8th Air Force for communication purposes   *[G M Simons collection]*

C/n 6641, built as X7524, was one of the Dominies lost at sea on the way to Egypt for service with Misr Airlines   [G M Simons collection]

ZK-AKS, c/n 6647 of Southern Scenic Air Services at Queenstown crashed in the mountains of New Zealand's South Island in 1965 but was salvaged and earmarked for rebuilding   [G M Simons collection]

6641   RAF serial **X7524**; CoA (6948) issued 4.11.42; shipped direct to Misr Airways, Egypt, as **SU-ACS** but ship sunk on voyage; replaced by X7384.

6642   RAF serial **X7525**; CoA (6949) issued 4.11.42; shipped direct to Misr Airways, Egypt, as **SU-ACT** but ship sunk on voyage; replaced by X7391.

6643   RAF serial **HG644**; to R & J Park Ltd, Chiswick, for packing 3.5.43; despatched on LS320 5.7.43; arr in Turkey 21.8.43; regd **TC-LAV** 4.44 to Devlet Hava Yollari; fleet no 5; current 7.50; NFT.

6644   RAF serial **HG645**; to R & J Park Ltd, Chiswick, for packing 18.5.43; despatched on LS322 18.5.43; arr Turkey 21.8.43; regd **TC-MUT** 4.44 to Devlet Hava Yollari; current 7.50; NFT.

6645   RAF serial **HG646**; to R & J Park Ltd, Chiswick, for packing 31.5.43; despatched on LS1053 23.8.43; arr Turkey 20.9.43; regd **TC-NUR** 4.44 to Devlet Hava Yollari; current 7.50; NFT.

6646   RAF serial **HG647**; to R & J Park Ltd, Chiswick, for packing; despatched on LS1063 11.9.43; arr Turkey 10.10.43; regd **TC-ZOR** 8.44 to Devlet Hava Yollari; current 7.50; NFT.

6647   RAF serial **HG648**; TOC 76 MU, Wroughton, 13.5.43; shipped to New Zealand 4.8.43 on *Sussex*, arr 5.9.43; to RNZAF as **NZ523**; TOC at Hobsonville 8.9.43; CF Nausori 10.43; 42 Sqn, Rongotai, 12.11.45; regd **ZK-AKS** 25.7.46 to NZNAC, named *Tara* (later *Teoteo*); regd 11.9.56 to Southern Scenic Air Services Ltd, Queenstown; caught in downdraught and crashed at Mount Soho, nr Arrowtown, 15.6.65 while on sheep-spotting charter; three occupants survived; regn cld 29.11.65; salvaged and to MoTaT Auckland for rebuild; being rebuilt .98 by Croydon Aircraft Co at Old Mandeville; current status uncertain.

6648   RAF serial **HG649**; TOC 76 MU, Wroughton, 19.5.43; shipped to New Zealand 4.8.43 on *Sussex*, arriving 5.9.43; to RNZAF as **NZ524**: TOC at Hobsonville 8.9.43; CF Rongotai 9.43; 42 Sqn, Rongotai, 20.12.43; CF Nausori 15.10.45; GP Flt Rongotai 22.8.47; GP Flt Rongotai 10.47; 42 Sqn, Ohakea, 3.50; for sale 1.12.52; regd **ZK-BCP** 17.12.53 to Airwork (NZ) Ltd, Christchurch; CoA issued 1.2.54; to Trans Island Airways, Oamaru, 5.56; to Coastal Airways, Auckland, 9.58; regd 16.9.59 to B G Chadwick, South Brighton, t/a Air Charter (NZ) Ltd, Christchurch; badly damaged on striking fence when landing at Queenstown 7.2.62 but repaired; regd 7.7.64 to Southern Scenic Air Services Ltd, Queenstown; taken over by New Zealand Tourist Air Travel Ltd

1.5.65; taken over by Mount Cook Airlines Ltd 1.1.68; regd 18.7.73 to Mount Cook & Southern Lakes Tourist Co Ltd, Christchurch; WFU and stored at Lake Te Anau; sold to W Waterton and ferried to Manapouri 1.11.73 and thence to Queenstown; overhauled by Southair Aviation Services, Taieri, Dunedin; left Christchurch 14.1.75 for Melbourne via Auckland, Kaitaia, Norfolk Island and Brisbane, arr 21.1.75; regd **VH-BGP** 31.1.75 to C Tracey & Co Pty Ltd, Melbourne, Vic; regd 20.5.75 to J Drage, Woodonga, Vic and preserved in museum; regd 3.4.84 to Drage's Air World & City of Wangaratta, Vic; regd 3.4.85 to City of Wangaratta; extant.

6649   RAF serial **HG650**; TOC 76 MU, Wroughton, 3.6.43; shipped to India on *Fort Camouson* 16.8.43; arr 23.9.43; regd **VT-ARL** 13.10.43 to Govt of India for operation by Air India; impressed into RAF 3.12.43 as **MA964**; regn cld 30.5.45; SOC 31.2.46.

6650   RAF serial **HG651**; TOC 76 MU, Wroughton, 3.6.43; shipped to India on *Fort Camouson* 16.8.43; arr 23.9.43; regd **VT-ARM** 13.10.43 to Govt of India for operation by Air India; impressed into RAF 3.12.43 as **MA965**; restored to register 4.46 as **VT-ARM** to Govt of India; regd 9.4.47 to Air Services of India Ltd, Bombay; regd 19.10.49 to Varadaraja Airways Ltd, Madras; regd 27.8.57 (CoR 535/5) to Madras Presidency Airways Ltd, Madras; regn current 30.6.68 and it is possible that this aircraft existed until at least .78.

6651   RAF serial **HG652**; TOC 76 MU, Wroughton, 12.6.43; shipped to India on *Fort Camouson* 16.8.43; arr 23.9.43; regd **VT-ARN** 13.10.43 to Govt of India for operation by Air India; impressed into RAF 1.12.43 as **MA966**; restored to register as **VT-ARN** to Govt of India 1.1.47; NFT.

6652   RAF serial **HG653**; TOC 76 MU, Wroughton, 11.6.43; shipped to India on *Fort Camouson* 16.8.43; arr 23.9.43; regd **VT-ARK** 13.10.43 to Govt of India for operation by Air India; impressed into RAF 31.12.43 as **MA963**; SOC 1.1.47; restored to register as **VT-ARK** to Govt of Bengal, Calcutta, 29.3.47; regn cld 24.2.48.

[Note: there remains some uncertainty of the serial/registration tie-ups for the above four aircraft. Information shown above is from the RAF Record Cards (Form 78) and from Indian records.]

6653   RAF serial **HG654**; TOC 76 MU, Wroughton, 3.7.43; shipped to New Zealand on LS732 26.8.43, arr Auckland 6.10.43; to RNZAF as **NZ525**; TOC at Hobsonville 13.10.43; Northern Group CF, Mangere, 10.43; 42 Sqn, Rongotai, 1.10.44; regd **ZK-AKY** 12.8.46 to New Zealand National Airways Corporation, Wellington, named *Tui*; regd 19.5.64 to Ritchie Air Services Ltd, Te Anau; regd to Tourist Air Travel Ltd, Queenstown; regd 18.7.73 to Mount Cook Airlines Ltd, Christchurch; WFU at Queenstown; regd 28.3.78 to T C Williams, Masterton, for rebuild; rebuilt .83/.86, restored in NZNAC colours, named *Tui* and flew Palmerston North

C/n 6648 as ZK-BCP of Trans Island Airways who operated it from 1956 to 1958   [BAe Systems]

VH-BGP was the former ZK-BCP and is preserved at Wangaratta in Victoria, Australia   [G M Simons collection]

ZK-AKY, c/n 6653, of NZNAC had seen service in the RNZAF as NZ525 and is still in existence [via C N Dodds]

to Dunedin 1.86 to commemorate fifty years since New Zealand's first main trunk flight; operated .86 on pleasure flights by White Island Airways, Rotorua; also carried spurious RNZAF colours as 'AKY/NZ525' in .80s; regd 1.2.93 to Croydon Aircraft Co Ltd, Mandeville; took part in celebrations 12.94 to mark sixty years since New Zealand's first scheduled air service; regd 2.10.95 to Biplane Adventures Ltd (Sir T Wallis), Wanaka; regd 18.12.97 Croydon Air Services, Mandeville; then to Croydon Aircraft Co Ltd, Mandeville 14.2.01; extant.

6654   RAF serial **HG655**; TOC 76 MU, Wroughton, 22.7.43; shipped to New Zealand on LS732 26.8.43, arr Auckland 6.10.43; to RNZAF as **NZ526**; TOC at Hobsonville 13.10.43; Central Group CF, Rongotai, 10.43; 42 Sqn, Rongotai, 20.12.43; GP Flt, Rongotai, 1.9.46; GP Flt, Ohakea, 10.47; 42 Sqn, Ohakea, 3.50; for sale at 1 Stores Depot 18.2.52; regd **ZK-BAU** 28.4.52 to Auckland Aero Club, Mangere, named *City of Auckland*; CoA issued 14.5.52; regd 1.3.56 to Southern Scenic Air Services Ltd, Queenstown; crashed on take-off from Milford Sound 22.4.64; engines salvaged, airframe burnt; regn cld 5.5.64.

6655   RAF serial **HG656**; TOC 76 MU, Wroughton, 23.7.43; shipped to New Zealand on LS732 26.8.43, arr Auckland 6.10.43; to RNZAF as **NZ527**; TOC at Hobsonville 13.10.43; Southern Gp CF, Wigram, 10.43; 42 Sqn, Rongotai, 1.10.44; regd **ZK-ALB** 30.8.46 to New Zealand National Airways Corporation, Wellington, named *Tikaka;* badly damaged while taxying at Whenuapai 24.5.56 but repaired; regd 22.7.57 to Trans Coastal Airways Ltd, Oamaru; regd 31.7.58 to Coastal Airways Ltd, Auckland; regd 2.6.59 to Marlborough Aero Club; regd 2.7.61 to Ritchie Air Services Ltd, Te Anau; regd to Tourist Travel Ltd, Queenstown; regd to Mount Cook Airlines Ltd, Christchurch; WFU 4.11.71; sold 11.73 to Bill Waterton, Australia and ferried from Auckland to Australia 15.6.74; regn cld 10.7.74; regd **VH-IAN** 2.8.74 to C Tracey & Co Pty Ltd, Melbourne, Vic; regd 10.74 to K E Orrman, Shepparton, Vic; CoA lapsed .94; sold late .98 to Sydney syndicate; regd **VH-UTV** 4.6.99 to K E Orrman, Bankstown; reflown early .99 and ferried from Bankstown to Sydney 5.99 for R Fox, Kellyville, NSW; extant.

Seen in splendid New Zealand mountain scenery in 1965 is ZK-ALB, c/n 6655, of Ritchie Air Services Ltd, Te Anau [MAP via P H T Green]

VH-IAN, c/n 6655, originally NZ527 of the RNZAF and ZK-ALB, is still extant as VH-UTV   *[G M Simons collection]*

6656   RAF serial **HG657**; TOC 76 MU, Wroughton 23.8.43; shipped to India on *Chyebassa* 3.12.43, arr Karachi 12.1.44; regd **VT-ART** 15.3.44 to Indian Air Survey & Transport Co Ltd, Dum Dum, Calcutta; loaned to Tata Airlines 12.45; operated by Indian National Airways; crashed at Pratapgarth, 35 mls N of Allahabad, 8.4.46, killing Capt B Ramchandra and Capt H O'Neill; regn cld same day.

6657   RAF serial **HG658**; TOC 76 MU, Wroughton, 23.8.43; shipped to India on *Chyebassa* 3.12.43, arr Karachi 12.1.44; to Indian Air Survey & Transport Co Ltd; regd **VT-ARV** .44; regd 1.7.46 to Indian National Airways, New Delhi; regd 5.6.47 Indian to Air Survey & Transport Co Ltd, Dum Dum, Calcutta; name changed .48 to Air Survey Co of India Ltd; regn cld 26.4.51 as sold in UK; regd **G-AMJK** 17.5.51 to Fairey Aviation Co Ltd, White Waltham; CoA issued 24.9.51; regd 24.9.59 to Fairey Aviation Ltd; regd 17.8.60 to Hants & Sussex Aviation Ltd, Portsmouth; converted to Mk.6 .60; CoA lapsed 31.3.61; regn cld 9.10.61 as sold in France; inspected at Toussus-le-Noble 28.10.61; regd **F-OBVL** 15.12.61 to Dept de la Guyane and operated by Sté Aérienne de Transport Guyane-Antilles (SATGA), Cayenne; CoA suspended 16.12.65; regn cld .66.

6658   RAF serial **HG659**; DH for storage 18.8.43; CoA (7035) issued 9.11.43; to R & J Park Ltd, Chiswick, for packing 15.11.43; shipped to Southern Rhodesia on *Fort Jackson* 12.12.43, arr Cape Town 8.1.44; regd **VP-YCI** 1.44 to Southern Rhodesia Air Services; regd 6.46 to Central African Airways; regn cld 12.49 as sold in South Africa; regd **ZS-DDI** 19.10.49 to Associated Manganese

Mines of South Africa Ltd, Postmasburg; regn cld 30.11.59 as sold in Belgian Congo; regd **OO-CJX** 10.11.59 to Air Brousse SPRL, Léopoldville; re-regd **9O-CJX** 17.3.61; re-regd **9Q-CJX** .62 to Agence de Messageries Aériennes Zairoises (AMAZ); NFT.

6659   RAF serial **HG660**; DH for storage 18.8.43; CoA (7034) issued 6.11.43; to R & J Park Ltd, Chiswick, for packing 10.11.43; shipped to Southern Rhodesia on *Roslin Castle* 20.11.43, arr Cape Town 11.12.43; regd **VP-YCJ** 1.44 to Southern Rhodesia Air Services; regd 6.46 to Central African Airways; regn cld 1.50 as sold in Nyasaland; regd **VP-NAK** 1.50 to Govt of Nyasaland, Zomba; regd **VP-RCP** 1.52 to DCA, Govt of Northern Rhodesia, Lusaka; crashed at Rhodesia/Nyasaland border, 100 mls from Landazi, 30.8.53, injuring four.

6660   RAF serial **HG661**; DH for storage 1.9.43; CoA (7036) issued 15.11.43; to R & J Park Ltd, Chiswick, for packing 9.10.43; shipped to Southern Rhodesia on *Sandown Castle* 13.12.43, arr Cape Town 24.1.44; regd **VP-YCK** 29.1.44 to Southern Rhodesia Air Services; regd 6.46 to Central African Airways; regd early .50 to H Tevis, c/o Victoria Falls Airways, Victoria Falls; regn cld .51 as sold in Northern Rhodesia; regd **VP-RCI** .51 to Zambesi Airways Ltd, Livingstone; regd in Southern Rhodesia as **VP-YLV** .54 to same owner; DBR in hangar collapse in storm at Victoria Falls 6.1.55.

6661   RAF serial **HG662**; TOC 76 MU, Wroughton, 14.9.43; shipped to India on *Chyebassa* 3.12.43, arr Karachi 12.1.44; regd **VT-ARW** 6.5.44; regd 20.5.46 to Indian National Airways, New Delhi; regn cld 16.5.47.

G-AMJK, c/n 6657, had been used exclusively in India before returning to the UK in 1951 for operation by Fairey Aviation   *[G M Simons collection]*

ZK-AKU, c/n 6662, of Nelson Aero Club, named "Tawaka", had carried that name earlier when with NZNAC   *[via A. Chivers]*

6662   RAF serial **HG663**; TOC 76 MU, Wroughton, 14.9.43; shipped to New Zealand on *Glenbeg* 28.9.43, arr Auckland 21.11.43; to RNZAF as **NZ528**; TOC at Hobsonville 22.11.43; Northern Gp CF, Mangere, 11.43; 42 Sqn, Rongotai, 1.10.44; regd **ZK-AKU** 30.8.46 to New Zealand National Airways Corporation, Wellington, named *Tawaka;* del to Nelson Aero Club 19.5.63 and regd to them 24.5.63; regd 2.11.65 to Patchett Tours Ltd, Christchurch; regd 15.9.66 to Rotorua Aero Club; regd 22.7.68 to D W Gray, Auckland (Ardmore); took part in London to Sydney Air Race, arriving at Parafield, Vic, 28.12.69, crewed by D Gray, R Cooney and J Moon; WFU .71; rebuilt by Gray and reflown at Ardmore 23.1.77, named *Tawaka* again; damaged .80, rebuilt by .84 in Rothmans Sports Foundation colours; painted as "AKU" in Monteith's Brown Beer colours .88; later painted as NZ528; WFU and stored by Gray at Dairy Flat, Auckland; regn cld 1.4.92; re-regd 12.10.94 to same owner; extant and airworthy at Ardmore.

6663   RAF serial **HG664**; TOC 76 MU, Wroughton, 5.10.43; shipped to Madagascar on *Clan McBrayne* 7.12.43, arr Diego Suarez 5.3.44; to Free French Air Force; PSOC 1.1.47.

6664   RAF serial **HG665**; TOC 76 MU, Wroughton, 11.10.43; shipped to New Zealand on *Port Alma* 17.10.43, arr Auckland 26.11.43; to RNZAF as **NZ529**: TOC at Hobsonville 29.11.43; Southern Group CF 1.44; 42 Sqn, Rongotai, 1.10.44; flew military scheduled services from Rongotai to New Plymouth, Rukuhia, Ardmore and Whenuapai; regd **ZK-ALC** 30.8.46 to New Zealand National Airways Corporation, Wellington, named *Tiora;* DBF on ground at Rotorua 14.1.50 when exhaust flames set grass alight; no casualties; regn cld 3.3.50.

6665   RAF serial **HG666**; DH for storage 11.10.43; to R & J Park Ltd, Chiswick, for packing 29.11.43; CoA (7043) issued 5.12.43; shipped to Southern Rhodesia on *Umtali* 22.12.43, arr Cape Town 30.1.44; regd **VP-YCL** 3.44 to Southern Rhodesia Air Services; regd 6.46 to Central African Airways; regn cld 10.49 as sold in Northern Rhodesia; regd **VP-RBT** 10.49 to Northern Rhodesia Aviation Services Ltd; reverted to **VP-YCL** 5.50; crashed nr Fort Manning, Nyasaland, 28.9.50.

6666   RAF serial **HG667**; DH for storage 19.10.43; to R & J Park Ltd, Chiswick, for packing 4.12.43; CoA (7044) issued 5.12.43; shipped to Southern Rhodesia on *Empire Grove* 11.1.44, arr Cape Town 5.2.44; regd **VP-YCM** 3.44 to Southern Rhodesia Air Services; regd 6.46 to Central African Airways; to SRAF 7.49 as **SR57**, possibly later to RRAF as **RRAF-57**; regd **VP-YOL** 5.56 to Victoria Falls Airways (Pvt) Ltd, Victoria Falls; regn cld .62 as sold in Congo; regd **9Q-CJD**, rebuilt using parts of c/n 6607 for Agence de Messageries Aériennes Zairoises (AMAZ); regn cld.

6667   RAF serial **HG668**; TOC 76 MU, Wroughton, 5.1.44; to R & J Park Ltd, Chiswick, for packing 18.1.44; CoA (7053) issued 28.1.44; shipped to Southern Rhodesia on *Neleus* 29.1.44, arr Cape Town 21.2.44; regd **VP-YCN** 4.44 to Southern Rhodesia Air Services; regd 6.46 to Central African Airways; regd 4.50 to Trevor

Construction Co Ltd; regd .50 to Air Carriers Ltd, Bulawayo; regn cld 4.6.51 as sold in South Africa; regd **ZS-DFG** 4.6.51 to Bechuanaland Air Services; regd .53 to Anglo-Transvaal Consolidated Investment Co Ltd, Rand; restored to Southern Rhodesian register as **VP-YMW** 24.2.55 to Victoria Falls Airways (Pvt) Ltd, Victoria Falls; regd .57 to Zambesi Airways Ltd, Victoria Falls; regd .60 to Victoria Falls Airways (Pvt) Ltd; regn cld 24.8.62 as sold in Belgian Congo; regd **9Q-CJK** 24.8.62 to Agence de Messageries Aériennes Zairoises (AMAZ); NFT

6668   RAF serial **HG669**; TOC 76 MU, Wroughton, 5.11.43 ; shipped to New Zealand 1.12.43 on *Port Huon*, arr Auckland 18.1.44; to RNZAF as **NZ531**; TOC at Hobsonville 25.1.44; 42 Sqn, Rongotai, 1.44; GP Flt, Rongotai, 1.9.46; GP Flt, Ohakea, 10.47; 42 Sqn, Ohakea, 3.50; for sale 28.7.52; sold 8.52 to Airwork (NZ) Ltd, Christchurch and regd **ZK-BBP** to them 4.9.52; CoA issued 12.12.52; inaugurated services from Christchurch to Ashburton, Oamaru, Timaru and Nelson; regd to South Island Airways Ltd, Christchurch; regn cld 24.1.57; regd **VH-AAG** 19.8.58 to Alpine Airways (Pty) Ltd, Cooma, NSW, and shipped to Sydney; entered service 11.58; regd 16.8.60 to R G Carswell, t/a Carsair Air Service Pty Ltd, Archerfield to carry buffalo meat from hunters' camps to Darwin; badly damaged 12.12.60 by fire during start-up at Banyan Station airstrip, NT, but ROS and flown to Darwin 16.2.61; leased to Darwin Air Taxis 10.61; collided with a kangaroo at Wolner Station .63, breaking the lower centre section spar; engines removed and aircraft scrapped at Darwin 21.12.64; remains to RAAF and used as target for Sabres on Leanyea Range near Darwin; regn cld 12.12.64.

Dominie NZ531, c/n 6668, of the Royal New Zealand Air Force, carrying an unusual fin flash   *[Denis Fox collection]*

C/n 6668 later as VH-AAG of Alpine Airways Pty Ltd   *[via A. Chivers]*

At an RAF airfield in Iceland, TF-ISM, c/n 6670, is made ready for service with Flugfelag Islands HF   *[G M Simons collection]*

6669   RAF serial **HG670**; TOC 76 MU, Wroughton, 15.11.43; shipped to Madagascar on *Clan McBrayne* 7.12.43, arriving Diego Suarez 5.3.44; to Free French Air Force; PSOC 1.1.47; taken to France; stored at Villacoublay .58; NFT.

6670   RAF serial **HG671**; DH for storage 28.12.43; to R & J Park Ltd, Chiswick, for packing; shipped to Iceland on *Horsa* 9.4.44, arr Reykjavik 15.4.44; CoA (7065) issued 12.4.44; regd **TF-ISM** (CoR 009) 5.4.45 to Flugfelag Islands HF, Reykjavik, named *Sviffaxi;* WFU .49/50 and burnt .52; regn cld .61.

6671   RAF serial **HG672**; TOC 76 MU, Wroughton, 23.11.43; shipped to Madagascar on *Clan McBrayne* 7.12.43, arriving Diego Suarez 5.3.44; to Free French Air Force; PSOC 1.1.47; inspected at Ivato 30.5.53; regd **F-OANU** 9.9.53 to Soc Air Madagascar, Ivato; CoA suspended at Tananarive 19.1.54, probably following earlier damage at Tamatave.

6672   RAF serial **HG673**; TOC 18 MU, Dumfries, 2.12.43; 4 RS, Madley, [TML:A] 12.2.44; 5 MU, Kemble, 2.12.46; sold to Airwork Ltd 27.8.47 and regd **G-AKEU** 5.9.47 to them; regd 29.9.47 to Iraq Petroleum Transport Co Ltd, Haifa; CoA (9781) issued 3.6.48; CoA lapsed 8.11.50; regn cld 21.6.51 as sold in Lebanon; regd **OD-ABL** 9.7.51 to Arab Contracting and Trading Co. t/a Saad Transport, Beirut; DBF while refuelling at Baghdad 26.7.55.

6673   RAF serial **HG674**; TOC 76 MU, Wroughton, 10.11.43; shipped to New Zealand on *Port Huon* 1.12.43, arr Auckland 18.1.44; to RNZAF as **NZ530**; TOC at Hobsonville 25.1.44; 42 Sqn, Rongotai, 1.44; regd **ZK-AKT** 30.8.46 to NZNAC, Wellington, named *Tareke;* regd 17.1.56 to West Coast Airways Ltd, Hokitika; regd 4.12.56 to (parent company) Southern Scenic Air Services Ltd, Queenstown; both engines failed while overshooting Queenstown, 15.4.67, and fell into Shotover River in an attempted forced landing; regn cld 12.5.67; wreckage burned and remains buried in riverbed.

6674   RAF serial **HG689**; TOC 76 MU, Wroughton, 26.11.43; shipped to Madagascar on *Atlantean* 5.3.44, arr Diego Suarez 20.5.44; to Free French Air Force 5.44; NFT.

6675   RAF serial **HG690**; TOC 18 MU, Wroughton, 11.12.43; 2 RS, Yatesbury, [208] 28.12.43; 5 MU, Kemble, 16.8.45; regd **G-AIUI** 8.11.46 to Kenning Aviation Ltd, Derby (Burnaston) and sold to them 20.12.46; CoA (8974) issued 29.5.47; regd 26.6.47 to Wings & Wheels Ltd, t/a Hargreaves Airways Ltd, Elmdon; crashed on west face of Cronk ny Laa, nr Dalby, Isle of Man, 30.6.48 while being flown by Capt C S M Herbert, whose first flight to the Isle of Man it was; two of the seven passengers were found alive in the wreckage; regn cld same day.

6676   RAF serial **HG691**; TOC 18 MU, Dumfries, 11.12.43; 2 RS, Yatesbury [219], 28.12.43; 5 MU, Kemble, 16.8.45; sold to Reid & Sigrist Ltd 22.11.46; regd **G-AIYR** 11.12.46 to Reid & Sigrist Ltd, Desford; CoA (8830) issued 26.2.48; CoA lapsed 15.3.50; regd 31.3.52 to R R Carne, Elstree; regd 23.1.53 to Hunting Aerosurveys Ltd, Elstree; CoA renewed 13.2.53; regd 31.5.60 to Hunting Surveys Ltd, Elstree (later Leavesden); regd 4.5.67 to Hunting Surveys & Consultants Ltd; sold 22.4.71 and regd 22.7.71 to V H Bellamy, Land's End (St Just); operated by Westward Airways (Land's End) Ltd and Land's End Flying Club; regd 10.1.79 to C D Cyster, C A Cyster and D I Rendall, RAF Valley (later Shipdham and RAF Coningsby); flown by Flt Lt C D Cyster and C A Cyster from Hatfield (4.7.80) to Cape Town (31.7.80) to commemorate Alan Cobham's 1925 flight; to British Aerospace Ltd, Chester; restored following undercarriage collapse on 16.5.82; regd 2.10.85 to C D and C A Cyster; later based at Edinburgh (Turnhouse); CoA lapsed 17.9.88 and renewed 11.4.90; regd 17.4.91 to Clacton Aero Club (1988) Ltd, Clacton and Duxford, named *Classic Lady* and operated by Classic Wings; regd 24.8.99 to Fairmont Investments Ltd; 19.9.02 to Spectrum Leisure Ltd, remaining in use by Clacton Aero Club; extant.

G-AIYR, c/n 6676, visiting Liverpool on 25.10.58 from its Elstree base when in service with Hunting Aerosurveys Ltd   *[P H Butler]*

Seen at Kumalo in 1948 is Dominie SR24 of the SRAF, c/n 6678 [R C Sturtivant]

6677 RAF serial **HG692**; TOC 18 MU, Dumfries, 12.12.43; 1 RS, Cranwell, [TCR:Q] 7.6.44; 18 MU 9.7.46; sold to A Hamson & Son Ltd, Brixworth, Northants, 27.1.48; believed used for spares.

6678 RAF serial **HG693**; TOC 18 MU, Dumfries, 4.1.44; 87 Gp CF, Buc, 30.5.45; 428 R&SU, Buc, 21.6.45; Croydon 30.1.46; 18 MU 4.4.46; regd **G-AHPW** 22.5.46 to Field Consolidated Aircraft Services Ltd, Croydon; regn cld 12.8.46 as sold abroad; regd in South Africa as **ZS-BCO** 7.9.46 to Field Aircraft Services Ltd; UK CoA (8160) issued 9.10.46; to SRAF as **SR24** 22.8.47; regd **VP-YOY** .56 to Gibb, Coyne & Sager (Kariba) (Pvt) Ltd, Salisbury; regd .57 to Sir Alexander Gibb & Ptnrs (Africa) Ltd, Salisbury; DBF on start-up at Kariba 25.11.57.

6679 RAF serial **HG694**; TOC 18 MU, Dumfries, 28.12.43; transferred to FAA 3.3.45; 781 Sqn, Lee-on-Solent, 7.3.45; 782 Sqn, Donibristle, 1.8.45 to 1.46; AHU Stretton; 782 Sqn, Donibristle, 7.47 to 2.48; SF Culham [900:CH]; Stretton 1.49 to 8.49; Lee-on-Solent 1.50; Donibristle 22.3.50; SF Eglinton [900:GN] 5.50 to 1.53; heavy landing 27.7.52; taxying over bridge, Eglinton 5.12.52, swung to port, wheel and propeller hit parapet; DH, Leavesden; Lossiemouth 28.9.53; 782 Sqn, Donibristle [803:DO], 13.10.53; Northern CF, Donibristle [803:DO] 1.54; AHU Lossiemouth 8.12.55; 700Z Flight (Buccaneer S.1 IFTU), Lossiemouth 10.62;

sold to F B Sowery & Ptnrs 5.2.63; regd **G-ASFC** 25.2.63 to F B Sowery, M M C Stamford & B W Rigold, t/a RAF Abingdon Sport Parachuting Club; CoA issued 5.7.63; sometime named *Zaballos Empress;* CoA lapsed 27.8.65 and stored at Weston-on-the-Green; regn cld 10.1.66; fuselage converted into ground trainer 1.67 but wings burnt; remains burnt at Weston-on-the-Green 11.79.

6680 RAF serial **HG695**; TOC 76 MU, Wroughton, 10.1.44; shipped to South Africa on *Ville d'Amiens* 12.2.44, arr Cape Town 26.3.44; to SAAF as **1364**; 62 AS 12.7.44; Signal School 8.44; 61 Sqn 10.12.44; 28 Sqn 4.46; sold to Southern Rhodesia Air Services for £3913; regd **VP-YEZ** 6.46 to Central African Airways; SOC by RAF 26.9.46 as sold locally; regd 4.50 to C A Pritchard, Victoria Falls; regd .51 to Victoria Falls Airways Ltd, Victoria Falls; DBR in hangar collapse at Victoria Falls 6.1.55.

6681 RAF serial **HG696**; TOC 76 MU, Wroughton, 10.1.44; shipped to India on *Custodian* 28.3.44, arr Bombay 11.5.44; ACSEA 26.10.44; regd **VT-ARY** 1.7.44; regd 12.9.46 to Indian National Airways, New Delhi; regd 5.6.47 Indian Survey & Transport Co Ltd, Dum Dum, Calcutta; name changed .48 to Air Survey Co of India Ltd; regd 7.3.53 to Jokai (Assam) Tea Co Ltd, Mohanbari, Assam; crashed and DBF nr Mohanbari 9.2.59, killing two; regn cld 7.4.59.

C/n 6679, HG694 at Abingdon early in 1963, just after disposal by the Fleet Air Arm [R A Walker]

6682   RAF serial **HG697**; TOC 18 MU, Dumfries, 21.1.44; transferred to FAA 1.3.45; 782 Sqn, Donibristle, 1.3.45 to 2.46 (det to Lee-on-Solent 8.45 to 10.45, Belfast 11.45, Lee-on-Solent 12.45); tipped onto nose while taxying at Belfast 4.2.46; Stretton [900:JA] by 5.46 to 7.49; used by Test Flight .46/7; 50 TrAG, Yeovilton, 9.49; 767 Sqn, Yeovilton, 10.49; AHS Arbroath 7.52 to 1.53; AHU Stretton 7.53; regd **G-ANZP** 24.2.55 to R J Gates, t/a Federated Fruit Co, Speke (disposal subject of court martial) and del 2.3.55; SOC by FAA 21.8.55; CoA issued 15.9.56; name of operator altered to Federated Air Transport before 3.61; converted to Mk.6 8.61; CoA lapsed 30.7.62; stored at Speke; sold 3.11.64 to H Best-Devereux, Panshanger; regn cld 21.6.55 as sold in France, but not regd there; ferried to Rousseau Aviation, Dinard, and engines and other components used to build replica Fokker D VII for film 'The Blue Max'.

6683   RAF serial **HG698**; TOC 18 MU, Dumfries, 21.1.44; transferred to FAA 1.2.45; 781 Sqn, Lee-on-Solent, 1.2.45; Stretton 1.49; FP Anthorn 3.46; Crail SS; SF Anthorn 24.1.47 to 2.47; AHU Stretton 1.49 to 10.49; SF Anthorn 11.49 to 1.51; RDU Anthorn 10.3.51; Gosport (NARIU ?) 7.51 to 7.52; 782 Sqn, Donibristle, [805] 9.52 to 11.52; Arbroath 1.53; AHU, Lossiemouth, for mods; roaded to DH, Leavesden 22.11.53; AHU Lossiemouth 18.1.54; Shorts Ferry Flight, Rochester, 1.2.54; Shorts Ferry Flight, Belfast, 20.2.54; retd to Rochester 15.5.55; AHU Lossiemouth, 24.7.57; SF Lossiemouth 6.2.58; bowser reversed into nose of aircraft 4.6.58; AHU, Lossiemouth, 9.12.58; SOC 22.6.63; sold to Anglo-Diesel Co, London, for scrap and del 5.7.63.

6684   RAF serial **HG699**; TOC 18 MU, Dumfries, 21.1.44; 80 (French) OTU, Morpeth, (later Ouston) 26.5.45; to l'Armée de l'Air 11.11.46 for Ecole de Chasse, Meknes; NFT.

6685   RAF serial **HG700**; TOC 18 MU, Dumfries, 21.1.44; transferred to FAA 24.3.45; 782 Sqn, Donibristle, 27.3.45 (det to Eglinton 10.45, Belfast 2.46 and Lee-on-Solent 2.46 to 3.46); AHU, Stretton, .47; 782 Sqn, Donibristle, 11.47; struck by lightning at Machrihanish 6.2.48; RNARY, Donibristle, 23.8.48; SOC 25.8.48 and RTP.

6686   RAF serial **HG701**; DH for storage 24.1.44; to R & J Park Ltd, Chiswick, for packing 3.3.44; CoA (7066) issued 26.4.44; shipped to Turkey 4.44; regd **TC-AGA** 8.44 to Devlet Hava Yollari; current 7.50; NFT.

6687   RAF serial **HG702**; DH for storage 31.1.44; to R & J Park Ltd, Chiswick, for packing 10.3.44; CoA (7067) issued 26.4.44; shipped to Turkey 4.44; regd **TC-HAD** 8.44 to Devlet Hava Yollari; regd 26.9.57 to Hurkus Airlines, Ankara; WFU .59; still regd 6.60; NFT.

6688   RAF serial **HG703**; DH for storage 1.2.44; to R & J Park Ltd, Chiswick, for packing 19.3.44; CoA (7068) issued 26.4.44; shipped to Turkey 4.44; regd **TC-PER** 8.44 to Devlet Hava Yollari; regd 19.6.57 to Hurkus Airlines, Ankara; WFU .59; still regd 6.60; NFT.

6689   RAF serial **HG704**; DH for storage 1.2.44; to R & J Park Ltd, Chiswick, for packing 30.3.44; CoA (7069) issued 26.4.44; shipped to Turkey 4.44; regd **TC-VUR** 8.44 to Devlet Hava Yollari; current 7.50; NFT.

6690   RAF serial **HG705**; TOC 18 MU, Dumfries, 28.1.44; MCS, Hendon [CB:U], 22.8.45; 18 MU, Dumfries, 9.11.46; 5 MU, Kemble,11.1.49; sold to Air Navigation & Trading Co Ltd 16.1.50; regd **G-ALXI** 31.1.50 to Mrs D L Whyham for Air Navigation & Trading Co Ltd, Squires Gate (ferried as **G-ALXJ**, repainted as **G-ALXI**); CoA (10869) issued 25.5.50; regd 3.2.51 to W Stevens, Exeter; CoA lapsed 24.5.51, returned to Air Navigation & Trading Co Ltd and regd 21.1.52 to them; CoA renewed 21.8.52; regd 13.5.55 to T W Williams, White Waltham; regn cld 15.10.55 as sold in Austria; regd **OE-FAA** to Österreichische Rettungsflugwacht (Austrian Rescue Service) 28.11.55; used as air ambulance, including support for refugees during Hungarian uprising of 1956; regn cld 10.5.63; listed as preserved in Techniches Museum fur Industrie und Gewerbe, Vienna, but according to curator of museum it was scrapped many years ago.

6691   RAF serial **HG706**; TOC 18 MU, Dumfries, 8.2.44; transferred to FAA 24.3.45; 782 Sqn, Donibristle, 6.45 to 2.46, named *Merlin XXI* (det to Eglinton 10.45 to 11.45, Lee-on-Solent 1.46 to 2.46); 782 Sqn 3.47 to 8.47; AHU Stretton 2.48; 782 Sqn, Donibristle, [806:DO] 3.49; RNARY, Donibristle, 16.12.49; DH, Leavesden, 8.5.50; AHS Arbroath 12.2.51; SF Machrihanish [901:MA] 15.3.52; AHS Arbroath 14.10.52; AHU Stretton 10.2.53; SOC 17.7.54 and RTP.

6692   RAF serial **HG707**; DH 8.2.44; to R & J Park Ltd, Chiswick, for packing 20.6.44; shipped to Middle East on *Salawata* 30.6.44, arr Alexandria 22.7.44; UK CoA (7086) issued 22.8.44; regd **EP-AAD** 22.8.44 to Iranian State Airlines, Teheran; to Aero Club Dosahn Teppah; regn cld before .59.

6693   RAF serial **HG708**; 18 MU, Dumfries, 8.2.44; transferred to FAA 24.3.45; Lee-on-Solent 25.4.45; 701 Sqn, Heston [L0X] 31.5.45; DH RU, Witney, 9.8.46; RDU, Culham, 18.2.47; 1 FF, Culham [601:CH], 12.12.47; DH, Leavesden, 24.11.50; AHS, Arbroath, 10.9.51; SF Anthorn [901:AH] 2.7.52; AHS, Arbroath, 2.2.53; SF Arbroath [AO] 22.9.53; used by FORA Command Flt .56; AHU, Lossiemouth, 28.3.57; SOC 13.1.59; cut up and burnt by Hants & Sussex Aviation at Lossiemouth 8.60.

Dominie HG708, c/n 6693, when with Station Flight Anthorn, coded AH; note the Sturgeon behind it   *[MAP via P H T Green]*

HG709, c/n 6694, carrying the code 801:VL when in service with the RN Unit at the School of Land/Air Warfare at Old Sarum   *[G J Cruikshank]*

6694   RAF serial **HG709**; 18 MU, Dumfries, 15.2.44; transferred to FAA 24.3.45; 782 Sqn, Donibristle, 10.4.45; (det Lee-on-Solent by 1.46); DH RU, Witney, 28.10.46; Stretton 28.4.47; 703 Sqn, Thorney Island, [A] 10.6.47; RNARY, Donibristle, 24.6.47; AHS Arbroath 19.8.47; 4 FF, Arbroath, 5.1.48; AHU Stretton 8.9.48; RN Unit, SLAW, Old Sarum, [801:VL] 18.2.49; DH, Leavesden, 27.8.51; AHS Arbroath 3.3.52; RDU Anthorn 13.5.53; SF Abbotsinch [901:AC] 7.10.53; AHU Lossiemouth, 3.12.57; SF Culdrose [999:CU]14.7.60; used during Operation 'Tiger' at Dartmouth 15.8.61; det to RNEC Manadon, Roborough; nosed over on landing at Roborough 31.8.61; RNAY Fleetlands; SOC 18.9.61; sold to Hants & Sussex Aviation Ltd, Portsmouth,10.61; remains burnt on Portsmouth Corpn rubbish tip 12.62.

6695   RAF serial **HG710**; DH 8.2.44; to R & J Park Ltd, Chiswick, for packing 16.8.44; CoA (7087) issued 22.8.44; shipped to Middle East on *Glenogle* from Glasgow 26.8.44, arr Alexandria 14.9.44; regd **EP-AAE** 30.11.44 to Iranian State Airlines, Teheran; regn cld before .59.

6696   RAF serial **HG711**; DH 12.2.44; to R & J Park Ltd, Chiswick, for packing 16.8.44; CoA (7088) issued 22.8.44; shipped to Middle East on *Glenogle* from Glasgow 26.8.44, arr Alexandria 14.9.44; regd **EP-AAT** 30.11.44 to Iranian State Airlines, Teheran; to Aero Club Doshan Teppah; NFT.

6697   RAF serial **HG712**; 18 MU, Dumfries 19.2.44; MCS, Hendon, 10.1.45; force-landed near Eindhoven when engine fell out after take-off, 17.5.45 (pilot Capt Lutz, RNethAF); seven slightly injured; SOC 17.5.45.

This is what happened when brakes were applied too harshly! HG713, c/n 6698, on its nose at Lee-on-Solent on 11th October 1950   *[G M Simons collection]*

6698   RAF serial **HG713**; 18 MU, Dumfries, 12.2.44; transferred to FAA 24.3.45; 782 Sqn, Donibristle, [B], named *Merlin XXII* 6.4.45 (detached to Belfast 11.45); collided with motor-cycle whose engine had stalled at Donibristle 28.7.45; DH RU, Witney, 17.4.46; Culham 18.2.47; AHU Stretton 23.10.47; 781 Sqn, Lee-on-Solent, 13.2.48; DH, Leavesden, 5.50; AHS Arbroath 26.6.50; 781 Sqn, Lee-on-Solent, [858:LP, later 854:LP] 30.6.50; brakes bound on touching down 11.10.50, nosed over at end of runway; blown onto

Dominie c/n 6699, HG714 [902:ST] of Station Flight, Stretton   *[Denis Fox collection]*

nose when visiting B-25 Mitchell of RNethAF revved engines on ground 18.9.51; damaged on landing 14.5.52; DH Leavesden, by road 30.5.52; AHU Lossiemouth 25.2.53; NARIU, Gosport, 29.9.53; 781 Sqn, Lee-on-Solent [854] 17.2.54; landed at Bramcote 23.7.54 when port engine ran rough during flight from Lee-on-Solent to Lossiemouth; AHU Lossiemouth 25.2.57; RDU Anthorn 20.6.57 (also used by SF); AHU Lossiemouth 3.12.57; SOC 22.6.63 and despatched to Anglo-Diesel Ltd, London, for scrap 5.7.63.

6699 RAF serial **HG714**; 18 MU, Dumfries, 25.2.44; transferred to FAA 24.3.45; 701 Sqn, Heston [L0R] 6.45 to 9.46; 4 FP, Anthorn, 5.48; 781 Sqn, Lee-on-Solent [LP] 6.48; DH, Leavesden, 17.10.49; SF Arbroath [900:AO, later 903:AO, 902:AO and 906:AO] 6.50 to 5.53; DH, Leavesden, 8.10.53; AHU, Lossiemouth, 11.5.54; Short Bros & Harland Ltd, Rochester, 17.8.54; SF Stretton [903:ST unconfirmed, later 902:ST and 963:ST] 18.5.55; AHU, Lossiemouth, 22.10.57; SOC 22.6.63 and sold to Anglo-Diesel Co Ltd, London, for scrap.

6700 RAF serial **HG715**; 18 MU, Dumfries, 3.3.44; A&AEE, Boscombe Down, 29.8.45; ETPS, Cranfield, 24.10.45 (later Farnborough) [5]; regd **G-ANET** 5.10.53 to Hants & Sussex Aviation Ltd, Portsmouth and sold to them 13.10.53; CoA issued 18.11.53; regd 8.3.54 to Silver City Airways Ltd, Blackbushe; regd 17.3.55 to BOAC; regn cld 29.5.55 as sold in Aden; modified to Mk.4 6.55 and flown 31.8.5; regd **VR-AAL** .55 to Aden Airways, named *Dhala;* leased to Amerada Petroleum Corpn; regn cld 5.9.58; regd in Ethiopia as **ET-P-22** 9.58 to L Mascheroni & C Tonna, Asmara, c/o Italian Consulate; reported as crashed at Gondra, but more likely CoA lapsed 26.6.0 at Old Airport, Addis Ababa, after death of Tonna in motoring accident; later scrapped.

6701 RAF serial **HG716**; 18 MU, Dumfries, 11.3.44; transferred to FAA 3.3.45; 782 Sqn, Donibristle, 9.3.45 to 4.46; (det to Lee-on-Solent 8.45 and Belfast 11.45 to 1.46); AHU Stretton 3.47 to 5.49; AHU/SF Anthorn [903:AO] 7.49 to 10.51, also used by 2 FF 2.50; Shorts Ferry Flight, Rochester, 28.11.51; AHU Lossiemouth 30.8.54; SOC 12.7.56.

6702 RAF serial **HG717**; 18 MU, Dumfries, 29.2.44; transferred to FAA 2.2.45; 781 Sqn, Lee-on-Solent, 15.2.45; 782 Sqn, Donibristle, 26.7.45; DH RU, Witney, 23.9.45; Crail 6.6.46; RDU Culham 14.1.47; 1 FF, Culham, 12.12.47; DH, Leavesden, 3.11.49; AHS Arbroath 5.7.50; Short Bros & Harland Ltd, Belfast, 31.10.51; AHU Lossiemouth, 1.4.54; SOC 29.4.54 and RTP.

6703 RAF serial **HG718**; 18 MU, Dumfries, 3.3.44; 4 RS, Madley, 7.8.45 [TML:B and TML:D] (later Swanton Morley [TSM:T]); 5 MU, Kemble, 3.4.49; sold to Short Bros 11.1.50; regd **G-ALWI** 21.1.50 to Short Bros & Harland Ltd, Rochester; ferried as **G-ALWJ**, repainted as **G-ALWI**; CoA (10801) issued 28.3.50; used by Shorts Air Charter Services; regd 20.2.52 to Transair Ltd, Croydon; regn cld 19.3.52 as sold in France; regd **F-BGPJ** 30.4.52 to Sté Aigle Azur Indochine, Hanoi; regd 11.53 to Cie Autrex, Hanoi; regd .55 to Soc Laos Air-Service, Vientiane; damaged 31.5.57; CoA suspended at Vientiane 22.5.59; regn cld .63; to Veha Akat, Laos and seen awaiting rebuild at Vientiane 7.63; NFT.

6704 RAF serial **HG719**; 18 MU, Dumfries, 1.3.44; SF Halton [THA:B], 6.9.45; Staff College Flt, White Waltham, [TBR:D] 21.3.46; 18 MU 24.11.47; regd **G-AKMH** 28.2.48 to W Westoby, Squires Gate, t/a Westair Flying Services, and sold to him 11.3.48; CoA (10055) issued 16.6.48; sold 24.2.49 and regd 24.5.49 to Isle of

Originally HG715 and then G-ANET, c/n 6700 became VR-AAL in the service of Aden Airways in 1955 [Denis Fox collection]

Photographed at an unrecorded location, Dominie HG716 of the Fleet Air Arm is parked beside an Oxford, with a Varsity and a Proctor in the background and a Navion next to the control tower. C/n 6701's last unit was Short's Ferry Flight at Rochester [Denis Fox collection]

G-AKMH, c/n 6704, of The Contracting & Trading Co. being refuelled from a 40-gallon drum somewhere in the Middle East [via A. Chivers]

Wight Flying Club Ltd, Sandown; operated by associate company to Bees Flight; regd 11.2.53 to Bees Flight Ltd, Sandown; regd 30.3.55 to S G Newport, t/a The Contracting & Trading Co Ltd, Beirut, Lebanon, possibly for crop-spraying; CoA lapsed 16.7.63; regd 3.4.64 to Aerocontacts (Aircraft Distributors) Ltd, Gatwick; regn cld 22.10.64 as sold in Congo; regd 10.64 to Agence de Messageries Aériennes Zairoises (AMAZ), but regn unknown; NFT.

6705   RAF serial **HG720**; 18 MU, Dumfries, 11.3.44; damaged 10.4.45, ROS by 63 MU; 18 MU 20.6.45; 5 MU, Kemble, 9.10.45; despatched to l'Armée de l'Air 15.11.45, arr Bordeaux 16.11.45; Ecole de Radio-Navigants; NFT.

6706   RAF serial **HG721**; 18 MU, Dumfries, 11.3.44; 527 Sqn, Digby, 16.4.45; damaged 7.7.45, ROS by 63 MU 3.8.45; RWE, Watton, 18.4.46; 18 MU 22.11.46; 61 Gp CF, Kenley, 29.4.48; 5 MU, Kemble, 7.9.48; sold to Air Navigation & Trading Co. Ltd 10.12.48; regd **G-ALGB** 17.12.48 to G C S Whyham, Squires Gate; regd 1.4.49 to R H Braime & A G Wilson, t/a Yorkshire Aeroplane Club, Sherburn-in-Elmet; CoA (10443) issued 5.11.49; regd 7.5.54 to R A Peacock (Aviation) Ltd, Croydon; regn cld 26.10.54 as sold in France; regd **F-BHCD** 10.12.54 to SALS, St Cyr; regd .62 to Centre National de Parachutisme de Bourgogne Franche-Comté, Chalons-sur Saône; CoA expired 10.66; regn cld .67; to Musée de l'Air et de l'Espace, Paris (Le Bourget) by 9.68 and initially stored at St Cyr, then at Villacoublay; on display at Le Bourget since .81.

Rapide G-AKMH when being operated by Westair Flying Services at Blackpool c.1948 [Denis Fox collection]

6707   RAF serial **HG722**; 18 MU, Dumfries, 10.3.44; MCS, Hendon [CB:E], 24.9.45; 18 MU 6.8.46; 5 MU, Kemble, 11.1.49; regd **G-ALWP** 23.1.50 to Allen Aircraft Services Ltd, Croydon, and sold to them 13.2.50; regd 4.5.50 to C W J Allen, Croydon; CoA (10892) issued 26.7.50; regd 23.8.50 to Airwork Ltd, Gatwick; regd 4.6.51 to W S Shackleton Ltd; regn cld 28.6.51 as sold in Fiji; del to H Gatty, Suva, 27.7.51; regd **VQ-FAL** 21.8.51 to Gatty's company, Katafanga Estates Ltd, t/a Fiji Airways; crashed and DBF on take-off from Labasa, Vanua Levu Is, 24.4.54, due to engine failure; no casualties.

F-BHCD, c/n 6706, at Chalons-sur-Saône in the early 1960s. It is now a museum resident at Le Bourget [via C N Dodds]

G-AHLM, c/n 6708, of Marshall's Flying Services Ltd, Cambridge, had been owned, but probably not used, by BEA and ended its days by crashing in the Scilly Isles in July 1963   *[via A. Chivers]*

EI-AML, c/n 6709, of Aer Turas, which flew it from 1962 to 1964, when it went to France   *[G M Simons collection]*

As F-BLHZ, c/n 6709, was used by the Para Club at Nancy prior to sale to the USA in 1972   *[A D Pearce]*

Dominie HG729, c/n 6714, carrying the code letters of 64 Group Communications Flight in 1948   *[G M Simons collection]*

6708   RAF serial **HG723**; 18 MU, Dumfries, 18.3.44; 1680 Flt, Prestwick [MJ:XN], 17.10.45; to AAJC, Prestwick, 16.4.46; regd **G-AHLM** 8.5.46 to Scottish Airways Ltd, Renfrew; CoA (7780) issued 13.7.46; del 23.10.46; regd 1.2.47 to BEA; regd 6.3.48 to Marshall's Flying School Ltd, Cambridge; regd 9.4.52 to Marshall's Flying Services Ltd, Cambridge; converted to Mk.6 27.9.60; regd 13.6.61 to K P H Cleife t/a Mayflower Air Services, Plymouth (Roborough); written off at Scilly Isles (St. Mary's) 20.7.63 while on scheduled service; during take-off in calm conditions the aircraft bounced a number of times, swung left and right, became airborne, then banked to the right; the starboard wing cut through gorse bushes, hit a rock, the aircraft cartwheeled and caught fire before coming to rest with the rear fuselage overhanging a cliff; all seven passengers escaped through the emergency hatches, the seriously injured pilot being removed from cockpit wreckage by fire service; regn cld 26.10.63.

6709   RAF serial **HG724**; 18 MU, Dumfries, 18.3.44; CRD at DH 4.2.45; 5 MU, Kemble, 21.2.47; sold to Newman Aircraft 25.8.47; regd **G-AKPA** 12.1.48 to Newman Aircraft Co Ltd, t/a Newman Airways, Croydon; CoA (9919) issued 25.6.48; regd 16.3.51 to Midland Metal Spinning Co Ltd, Wolverhampton; sold 17.5.62 and regn cld 8.6.62 as sold in Eire; regd **EI-AML** 25.6.62 to F J Connolly, t/a Aer Turas; regd 11.9.62 to Aer Turas Teoranta, Dublin; regn cld 19.6.64 as sold in France; regd **F-BLHZ** 2.2.65 to Aéro Club de Lorraine, Luneville; regd .68 to Centre Ecole Régional de Para Sportif de Nancy-Lorraine, Nancy; sold in USA 11.72; regd **N89DH** to D W Cotton and W F Watson, Tulsa, OK and painted in RAF colour scheme; regd 1.90 to R C Hood, Carthage, MO; extant.

6710   RAF serial **HG725**; TOC 782 Sqn, Donibristle, 21.3.44; port engine failed on approach, force-landed in field, 5.3.45; SOC 6.3.45.

6711   RAF serial **HG726**; TOC 782 Sqn, Donibristle 21.3.44 to 10.45; RNARY, Donibristle; retd to 782 Sqn; port engine failed, made precautionary landing at St Merryn 15.8.46; SOC.

6712   RAF serial **HG727**; TOC 782 Sqn, Donibristle, 22.3.44; DH RU, Witney, 29.3.45; retd to 782 Sqn, Lee-on-Solent, 13.8.45; 2 FP, Stretton, 8.5.46; DBF on ground during engine test 4.47.

6713   RAF serial HG728; 18 MU, Dumfries, 31.3.44; 527 Sqn, Digby, 20.4.45; 57 OTU, Hawarden, 26.4.45; 53 OTU, Kirton-in-Lindsey, 14.6.45; 18 MU 1.7.46; 66 Gp CF, Turnhouse [RCI:K], 29.4.48; 18 MU 12.1.49; regd **G-ALNT** 21.4.49 to R A Short & J H Tattersall, Croydon and sold to R A Short 25.4.49; CoA (10604) issued 8.7.49; regd 15.9.49 to W Hutchinson, Eastleigh; regd 2.12.50 to Hampshire School of Flying Ltd, Eastleigh; regn cld 26.2.52 as sold in Australia; regd **VH-CFA** (second) 21.11.52 to Queensland Ambulance Transport Brigade, Cairns, named *Clive Jones;* pilot, Capt Brampton, became lost on approach to Townsville, Qld, 26.10.53 and crashed into sea near Hinchinbrook Island, 20 mls N of Ingham; aircraft broke up and sank; ambulance officer Andrew Courser pulled pilot out of wreck with a broken leg, but the boy patient was drowned; pilot later drowned, but Courser was picked up six hours later; regn cld same day.

In later life HG729 became G-AMCT of Short Bros & Harland Ltd and then F-BHTH at Aero-Sud, Algiers   *[C N Dodds]*

6714   RAF serial **HG729**; TOC 1 RS, Cranwell [TCR:P], 30.3.44; DH RU, Witney, 1.4.46; 18 MU, Dumfries, 24.1.47; 64 Gp CF, Linton-on-Ouse [RCH:H], 21.4.48; 5 MU, Kemble, 27.2.50; regd **G-AMCT** 13.7.50 to Short Bros & Harland Ltd, Rochester, and sold to them next day; CoA (10982) issued 9.10.50; CoA lapsed 2.4.55; CoA renewed 29.3.56; regn cld 13.8.56 as sold in France; regd **F-BHTH** 3.9.56 to Groupement d'Etudes et de Consultations Aéronautiques (GECA), Toussus-le-Noble; regd mid-.57 to Sté Gen d'Affrétements Aériens (Air Fret), Algiers; regd .59 to Sté Aéro-Sud, Algiers (later Dar-el-Beida); CoA expired 4.66; regn cld 9.67.

6715   RAF serial **HG730**; TOC 18 MU, Dumfries, 6.4.44; MCS, Hendon, 24.9.45; 18 MU 7.8.46; 63 Gp CF, Hawarden, 23.4.48; 5 MU, Kemble, 20.5.49; sold to R A Short 2.1.50; regd **G-ALXS** 24.1.50 to R A Short, Croydon; regd 16.4.50 to W A Rollason Ltd, Croydon; converted at Eastleigh and CoA 10871 allocated but replaced by A2812 (date unknown); sale to Arab Airways Assoc Ltd, Transjordan, as **TJ-AAU** 5.50 not concluded and regn NTU; regn cld 22.5.51 as sold in France; inspected at Toussus-le-Noble 30.6.51; regd **F-OAIH** 21.8.51 to Jean-Marc Dulas, Port-Gentil; regd by .54 to Sté Transports Aériens du Gabon, Libreville; regd .57 to Cie Aéronautique Jean-Claude Brouillet (Transgabon), Libreville; re-regd **F-OBGU**; regd .64 to Cie Transgabon, Libreville; regd in Gabon as **TR-LKQ** 12.65 to same owner; WFU and stored at Libreville on CoA expiry 14.11.66; regn cld .67.

6716   RAF serial **HG731**; TOC CRD at DH 15.4.44; SF Halton [THA:E] 29.6.44; damaged 30.3.45; ROS by 49 MU 11.4.45; damaged when taxying at Dishforth 24.2.46; DH RU, Witney, 25.4.46; 5 MU, Kemble, 21.2.47; SOC 6.3.47 and sold to D J Adie as spares.

6717   RAF serial **HG732**; TOC 76 MU, Wroughton, 12.4.44; shipped on *Fort Louisburg* from Middlesbrough to India 31.5.44, arr Bombay 18.6.44; regd **VT-ARZ** 14.9.44; regd 22.5.46 to Govt of Bihar; regd 25.7.46 to Tata (Civil Airlines); crashed 17.2.51 and regn cld same day.

A particularly fine view of c/n 6718, NF847, coded 903:AO as a member of Station Flight, Arbroath in 1960   *[P H T Green collection]*

6718   RAF serial **NF847**; TOC 18 MU, Dumfries, 7.4.44; transferred to FAA 6.11.44; 781 Sqn, Lee-on-Solent, 23.11.44; used by 781X Flight, Toussus-le-Noble, France and Wunsdorf, Germany, 5.45 to 6.45; AHU Stretton (tested 22.3.47); 782 Sqn, Donibristle [803] 5.47; DH, Witney, 16.1.48; DH, Leavesden, 27.10.48; AHU Stretton 7.10.49; 781 Sqn [851:LP] 10.50 to 1.54; tyre burst whilst taxiing, nosed up, 1.6.51; DH, Leavesden, 7.54; AHU, Lossiemouth, 11.3.55; Yeovilton for FOFT 3.55; AHU Anthorn; 782 Sqn, Donibristle, 8.6.55; AHU Lossiemouth 8.7.55; SF Lossiemouth [931:LM] 27.7.55; AHU, Lossiemouth, 31.1.58; SF Lossiemouth 2.59; SF Arbroath [903:AO]11.5.59 to 1.62; AHU, Lossiemouth, 1.63; sold to F B Sowery & Ptnrs 5.2.63; regd **G-ASIA** 6.5.53 to F B Sowery, M M C Stamford & B W Rigold, t/a RAF Abingdon Sport Parachuting Club but not converted or registration taken up; fully complete in FAA markings at Abingdon in .63; regn cld 11.65.

Another RNAS Stretton-based Dominie, c/n 6719, NF848 [902:ST]
[MAP via P H T Green]

NF850 after being cocooned at Stretton; the marking of the nacelle indicates
that the engine was inhibited on 15th September 1955 [MAP via P H T Green]

6719   RAF serial **NF848**; TOC 18 MU, Dumfries, 7.4.44; transferred to FAA 20.8.45; 782 Sqn, Donibristle [B], named *Merlin XI*, 30.8.45 (det. to Belfast 11.45, Lee-on-Solent 12.45 to 3.46); Crail 19.9.46; RNARY, Donibristle, 28.11.46; RAD Donibristle 11.9.47; RARA Command Flt, Donibristle, 29.9.47; 782 Sqn [803:DO] 7.11.47; SF Arbroath [901:AO] 19.12.47; DH, Leavesden, 16.6.50; AHS Arbroath 11.5.51; SF Stretton [902:JA, later 902:ST] 26.6.53; tyre burst on landing at Valley 7.7.54; AHU, Lossiemouth, 4.2.55; SOC 13.1.59; remains still at Lossiemouth 7.60.

6720   RAF serial **NF849**; TOC 18 MU, Dumfries, 7.4.44; transferred to FAA 6.11.44; 781 Sqn, Lee-on-Solent, 12.44 to 7.45; SF/FP Stretton [ST9A] 10.45 to 1.46; DH, Witney; 782 Sqn, Donibristle [B], 5.10.46; 1 FF, Culham, [602:CH] 8.49 to 11.50; nosed over at Yeovilton 5.5.50; Shorts Ferry Flt, Rochester .52; AHU Lossiemouth, 18.6.54; SOC 7.54 and RTP.

6721   RAF serial **NF850**; TOC 18 MU, Dumfries, 24.4.44; transferred to FAA at Lee-on-Solent 17.11.44; 787Y Sqn, Speke, 23.11.44; 782 Sqn, Donibristle, 16.3.45 (det to Lee-on-Solent 11.45, Eglinton 1.46 and Belfast 2.46 to 3.46); AHU Stretton 20.5.46; DH, Witney, 19.10.46; AHU Stretton 25.4.47; 2 FF, Stretton, 1.10.47; AHU Stretton 21.1.48; 2 FF, Stretton, 8.7.49; AHU Stretton 1.11.49; cocooned 22.6.54; SOC 12.6.58.

6722   RAF serial **NF851**; TOC 18 MU, Dumfries, 22.4.44; 13 OTU, Harwell, 26.4.45 (later Middleton St. George); 85 Gp CF, Leuchars, 18.10.45; 61 OTU, Keevil, 27.12.45; 18 MU 3.12.46; regd **G-AJCL** 7.9.48 to Butlins Ltd, London and sold to them 14.9.48; CoA (10364) issued 29.5.49; regd 2.7.49 to Allgood Mfg Co Ltd and operated by Cambrian Air Services, Cardiff, named *Flint*; regd 18.1.54 to Cambrian Air Services Ltd; regd 19.6.59 to BEA, Land's End (St Just), named *RMA Sir Henry Lawrence;* used to replace G-AHLL following accident 21.5.59; converted to Mk.6 7.60; regd 16.7.65 to F H Mann, t/a British Westpoint Airlines; sold 9.6.66 and regd 12.10.66 to K B Neely, t/a Scillonia Airways, Land's End (St. Just), named *Samson;* sold 2.4.70 and regd 24.9.70 to Maj J P Epplestone t/a Rhine Army Parachute Association; CoA lapsed 11.1.71; to Fairoaks; regn cld as 'destroyed' 24.5.71; fuselage and other components to J Pierce, Lay Farm, Chirk for store.

G-AKGY, c/n 6723, of Manx Airlines Ltd which ended its days in Algeria as F-BFEH   [G M Simons collection]

6723   RAF serial **NF852**; TOC 18 MU, Dumfries, 24.4.44; MCS, Hendon, [CB] 24.9.45; 5 MU, Kemble, 25.3.47; sold to A Hamson & Son Ltd 25.8.47; regd **G-AKGY** 29.9.47 to A Hamson & Son Ltd, Northampton; regd 22.10.47 to Manx Air Charters Ltd, Ronaldsway, named *Glen Maye;* CoA (9797) issued 20.5.48; re-regd on change of name 20.8.53 to Manx Airlines (actually 2.53); regn cld 5.12.56 as sold in France; regd **F-BFEH** 25.1.57 to Sté Vignafibre France, Algiers; regd .57 to Sté Générale d'Affrétements Aériens (Air Fret), Algiers; CoA suspended 5.6.63; regn cld .65.

6724   RAF serial **NF853**; TOC 18 MU, Dumfries, 22.4.44; 41 OTU, Hawarden, 3.10.44 (later Chilbolton); SF Northolt 28.6.45; 5 MU, Kemble, 1.8.45; regd **G-AIUJ** 8.11.46 to Kenning Aviation Ltd, Derby (Burnaston) and sold to them 2.12.46; CoA (8779) issued 23.7.47; regd in India as **VT-CHZ** 16.4.47 to Air Services of India Ltd, Bombay; sold in French Indo-China 11.50; regd **F-OAIL** 15.2.51 to Cie Laotienne de Commerce et du Transport, Hanoi; damaged by fire at Gia-Lam airport, Hanoi, 5.6.52 and repaired; overturned on landing at Gia-Lam 25.10.53 and repaired; regd in Laos as **F-LAAB** 13.10.55 to Cie Veha Akat, Vientiane; CoA suspended 27.3.61; believed scrapped.

6725   RAF serial **NF854**; TOC 18 MU, Dumfries, 26.4.44; transferred to FAA 20.8.45; Evanton SS 2.9.45; 799B Sqn, Lee-on-Solent 9.45; became 781 Sqn, Lee-on-Solent, 27.6.46 to 9.46; Stretton 1.48 to 1.49; Abbotsinch .49; 782 Sqn [809:DO] 4.49 to 7.50; DH, Leavesden, 1.51; 781 Sqn, Lee-on-Solent, [854:LP] 6.51 to 7.54; SOC 15.12.54; on Lee-on-Solent dump 7.55.

6726   RAF serial **NF855**; TOC 18 MU, Dumfries, 27.4.44; transferred to FAA 17.10.45; Evanton SS 27.10.45; AHU Stretton 17.1.47; DH, Leavesden, 21.1.48; AHU Stretton 5.48; 782 Sqn, Donibristle 8.48 to 7.49; AHS Arbroath 7.50 to 1.51; Anthorn 6.51; AHU Stretton 7.51 to 7.53; DH, Leavesden, .53; AHU Lossiemouth 28.1.54; SF Anthorn [AH] 27.5.54; AHU Lossiemouth 25.6.57; sold to Anglo-Diesel Co Ltd, London, 5.7.63 for scrap.

6727   RAF serial **NF856**; TOC 18 MU, Dumfries, 28.4.44; SHAEF CF, Gatwick, 7.6.45 (later Detmold); RAF Mission Denmark CF, Kastrup, 15.11.45; 18 MU 20.2.46; 4 RS, Swanton Morley, 19.4.48; 5 MU, Kemble, 8.6.48; sold to Darlington and District Aero Club 11.1.50; regd **G-ALXA** 16.1.50 to Darlington & District Aero Club Ltd, Neasham (Croft); CoA (10852) issued 8.6.50; regd 14.12.51 to W S Shackleton Ltd; regn cld 25.2.52 as sold in Vietnam [sic]; sold to Cie de Transports Aériens Autrex, Hanoi, but not regd locally; destroyed in hangar fire at Gia-Lam, Hanoi, 5.6.52.

6728   RAF serial **NF857**; TOC 18 MU, Dumfries, 30.4.44; transferred to FAA 17.10.45; damaged 2.11.45; ROS by 63 MU 5.11.45; retd to RAF; 62 Gp CF, Colerne, 22.4.48; flew into high ground 1 ml N of Chipping Sodbury 18.1.49; SOC 19.1.49.

6729   RAF serial **NF858**; TOC 18 MU, Dumfries, 30.4.44; SHAEF CF, Gatwick, 7.6.45; 85 Gp CF, Northolt, 16.8.45; 18 MU 4.4.46; 5 MU, Kemble, 11.1.49; sold to Wilks & Chandler 11.1.50; regd **G-ALWN** 30.1.50 to V H Bellamy, t/a Flightways, Eastleigh;

A lack of code letters means that the unit to which Dominie NF854, c/n 6725, was attached when the photo was taken cannot be determined
[Denis Fox collection]

CoA (10889) issued 24.7.50; regd 24.10.50 to Southern Aerowork Ltd, Eastleigh; regd 28.2.52 to Transair Ltd, Croydon; regn cld 5.3.52 as sold in France; regd **F-BGPG** 7.4.52 to Sté Aigle Azur Indochine, Hanoi; sold 12.53 and regd .54 to Cie Laotienne de Commerce et du Transport, Hanoi; regd in Laos as **F-LAAC** 13.10.55 to Cie Veha Akat, Vientiane; CoA suspended at Luang Prabang 15.10.58; destroyed.

6730   RAF serial **NF859**; DH 8.5.44; to R & J Park Ltd, Chiswick, for packing 1.7.44; shipped to Iceland on *Nadin* 24.7.44, arr Reykjavik 28.7.44; CoA (7089) issued 22.8.44; regd **TF-ISO** (CoR 010) 5.4.45 to Flugfelag Islands HF, Reykjavik; ditched in sea off NE coast of Iceland 27.8.45 (also reported as having crashed at Grimseyjarsundi).

6731   RAF serial **NF860**; TOC 18 MU, Dumfries, 5.5.44; transferred to FAA 6.11.44; retd to RAF at 18 MU 5.11.45; St. Mawgan 17.5.46; despatched to Pau, France, 22.5.46 for l'Armée de l'Air; NFT

6732   RAF serial **NF861**; TOC 18 MU, Dumfries, 8.5.44; transferred to FAA 6.11.44; 781 Sqn, Lee-on-Solent, 21.11.44; taxying accident 13.4.45; Western Aircraft for repairs 5.7.45; 782 Sqn, Donibristle, 7.3.46; AHU Stretton, tested 11.2.47; 703 Sqn, Lee-on-Solent [002:LP] 7.48 to 10.48; AHU Stretton 16.11.48 to 1.51; 782 Sqn, Donibristle, [804:DO] 2.51; DH, Leavesden, 7.51; AHS Arbroath 1.52 to 1.53; 744 Sqn/SF Eglinton [900:GN] 3.53; crashed in Glendone Mountains, 6 mls W of Cushenden, Co. Antrim, 15.9.53, while flying from Stretton to Eglinton, killing Teleg H L Charlesworth, inj pilot Lt A G Cronin; SOC 25.9.53.

6733   RAF serial **NF862**; TOC 18 MU, Dumfries, 11.5.44; SHAEF Mission to Denmark, Kastrup, 7.6.45; 18 MU 24.1.46; 62 Gp CF, Colerne, 22.4.48; 5 MU, Kemble, 17.6.49; sold to Short Bros & Harland Ltd, Rochester, 11.1.50 for Shorts Air Charter Service, but never regd; used as spares for G-ALPK .56.

6734   RAF serial **NF863**; TOC 18 MU. Dumfries, 11.5.44; 4 RS, Madley [TML:B], 28.10.44; damaged and SOC 13.4.48.

This Dominie, c/n 6732, NF861 of Station Flight Eglinton, was wrecked in Northern Ireland on 15th September 1953   *[MAP via P H T Green]*

NF864, c/n 6735, was another of the many Dominies used by the Fleet Air Arm   *[G M Simons collection]*

The former NF864, now registered G-ASKO after a long period of service in the Fleet Air Arm, in the hands of Hants & Sussex Aviation Ltd at Portsmouth on 20th August 1963 with military markings crudely erased   *[Denis Fox collection]*

This photo was taken at Woodley in March 1947, at which time Dominie NF868, c/n 6739, was serving with the Metropolitan Communications Squadron at Hendon. It then went to the Belgian Air Force as D-3
[Denis Fox collection]

6735 RAF serial **NF864**; TOC 18 MU, Dumfries, 9.5.44; transferred to FAA 6.11.44; Lee-on-Solent 17.11.44; 781 Sqn, Lee-on-Solent, 26.11.44; 781X Flt, Toussus-le-Noble, 5.45; taxiing in strong wind, swung into Barracuda LS961 12.6.45; Hatston 24.6.45; RNAY, Donibristle, 7.8.45; DH RU, Witney, 14.8.45; 782 Sqn, Donibristle, 18.4.46; AHU Stretton 20.4.46; 782 Sqn 19.9.46; RNARY, Donibristle, 4.12.46; 781 Sqn, Lee-on-Solent, [857:LP] 1.6.48; AHU Abbotsinch 12.12.49; DH, Leavesden, 13.5.50; AHU Arbroath 6.4.51; AHU Lossiemouth 19.5.53; RNARY, Donibristle, 29.10.54; Northern CS/Airwork Ltd, Donibristle, [804:DO] 9.12.54; RNARY, Donibristle, 11.1.56; retd to Northern CS [049:DO] 2.5.56; RNAY, Donibristle, 29.6.56; retd to Northern CS [804:DO] 5.57; AHU, Lossiemouth, 13.6.57; 781 Sqn, Lee-on-Solent, 4.3.60; sold to Hants & Sussex Aviation 8.7.63; regd **G-ASKO** 22.7.63 to Hants & Sussex Aviation Ltd, Portsmouth; converted to Mk.6 and CoA issued 13.3.64; regd 25.5.64 to Mayflower Air Services Ltd; regd 8.10.64 to British Westpoint Airlines Ltd, Exeter; regd 15.6.65 to Hantsair Ltd, Eastleigh; regd 1.9.65 to 20th Century Fox Productions Ltd, Dublin (Baldonnel) for use as camera platform in making of film 'The Blue Max'; regn cld 17.1.66 as sold in France; inspected at Cayenne 11.7.67; regd **F-OCHF** 29.8.67 to Soc Eurafair; operated by Sté Aérienne de Transport Guyane-Antilles (SATGA), Cayenne; CoA suspended at Cayenne (Rochambeau) 22.3.68; regn cld .68.

6736 RAF serial **NF865**; TOC 18 MU, Dumfries, 12.5.44; MCS, Hendon [CB:P], 6.7.45; 18 MU 7.8.46; 5 MU CF, Kemble [3D] 25.1.49; sold to R A Short 2.1.50; regd **G-ALXT** 24.1.50 to R A Short, Croydon; regd 24.2.50 to A R Frogley, Broxbourne, probably for Herts & Essex Aero Club; CoA (10824) issued 2.5.50; regn cld 5.7.51 as sold abroad; regd in Ceylon as **CY-AAI** 3.7.51

to DCA and operated by Ceylon Air Academy, Colombo; re-regd **4R-AAI** 1.12.54; to Rapid Air Transport Ltd, Ratmalana; left Ratmalana (now in Sri Lanka) 14.2.74 piloted by Gary Studd and arrived at Biggin Hill 10.3.74; to Dismore Aviation Ltd, Staverton for storage pending sale; sold to Strathallan Collection and del 4.8.75; repainted as **G-ALXT** .79 in Railway Air Services colours, named *Star of Scotia;* sold by auction 14.7.81 to Science Museum at Wroughton for display; extant.

6737 RAF serial **NF866**; TOC 18 MU, Dumfries, 15.5.44; transferred to FAA 6.11.44; 781 Sqn, Lee-on-Solent, 12.44; 799 Sqn, Lee-on-Solent, 30.7.45; force-landed in field due to engine failure, 15.11.45; SOC.

6738 RAF serial **NF867**; TOC 18 MU, Dumfries, 15.5.44; transferred to FAA 23.2.45; 782 Sqn, Donibristle, 24.2.45 (det. to Inverness 7.45); DH RU, Witney, 13.8.45; 782 Sqn [B8V] 10.4.46 (det to Lee-on-Solent 5.46); RNARY, Donibristle, 27.3.47; RAD Donibristle 15.12.47; 3 FF, Anthorn, 8.1.48; AHU Abbotsinch 10.3.50; DH, Leavesden, 13.3.50; AHS Arbroath 7.3.51; RDU, Culham, 26.4.51; Southern Air Division, Culham/Benson [905:CH] 7.7.53; Yeovilton 6.10.54; AHU Lossiemouth 22.11.55; 781 Sqn, Lee-on-Solent, 4.3.57; SF Lossiemouth 6.58; 781 Sqn, Lee-on-Solent, 7.58; AHU Lossiemouth 21.3.60; SOC 22.6.63; despatched to Anglo-Diesel Co Ltd, London, 5.7.63 for scrap.

6739 RAF serial **NF868**; TOC 18 MU, Dumfries, 18.5.44; MCS, Hendon, 19.9.44; DH RU, Witney, 15.1.45; 18 MU 26.4.45; 16 FU, Dunkeswell, 11.2.46; 1316 Flt, Hendon, 25.5.46; to Belgian AF as **D-3** 4.9.46; 367e Escadrille [ZC:K], Evere; 21e Escadrille 1.2.48; damaged 5 21.8.52 and SOC.

C/n 6740, PH-VNC in UN markings at Schiphol in 1948 although it never saw service in Palestine

PH-TGC was the third Dutch registration of c/n 6740, the aircraft which had started life as NF869 of the RAF [KLM]

6740 RAF serial **NF869**; TOC 18 MU, Dumfries, 22.5.44; 1316 Flt, Hendon, 14.9.44; to RNethAF 17.11.45 as **V-3**, named *Gelderland;* 334 Sqn; at DH, Witney, 13.1.46; regd **PH-RAE** 16.3.46 (CoR 423) to RLD; retd to RNethAF 15.5.46 as **V-3**; regd **PH-VNC** 30.8.48 (CoR 640) to Staat der Nederlanden for operation by UN in Palestine as **7**, with c/n as NF877 but amended to NF869 with the comment 'ex PH-RAE'; did not, after all, go to Palestine; regn cld 8.10.48 and returned to RNethAF as **V-3**; SOC 23.1.52; regd **PH-TGC** 19.11.52 (CoR 312) to KLM, Amsterdam (Schiphol); re-regd **PH-OTA** 3.5.54 to same owner; regd 30.8.54 to KLM Aerocarto and Aero Camera, Schiphol; regd 6.7.62 to Aero Ypenburg NV, Rotterdam; regd 5.8.66 to NV General Aviation, Rotterdam; regn cld 9.11.66; was on display for many years in the Aviafauna Playground at Alphen; removed from playground .68, restored as **V-3** and placed on display in KLM Museum before being moved to the RNethAF Museum at Soesterberg; extant.

6741 RAF serial **NF870**; TOC 18 MU, Dumfries, 22.5.44; 1316 Flt, Hendon, 15.9.44; damaged on hitting bowser at Hendon 7.12.44; DH RU, Witney, 2.1.45, for repair; 18 MU 17.4.45; 63 Gp CF, Hawarden, 16.4.48; 5 MU, Kemble, 8.6.49; sold to Air Enterprises Ltd 13.1.50; regd **G-ALWY** 18.1.50 to Air Enterprises Ltd, Croydon; CoA (10804) issued 24.3.50; operated on services to Sandown, IoW, named *The Ventnor Flyer*; undercarriage collapsed when aircraft undershot landing at Islay (Port Ellen), 19.4.52; regn cld 19.5.52.

6742 RAF serial **NF871**; TOC 18 MU, Dumfries, 23.5.44; transferred to FAA 17.10.45; NARIU, Middle Wallop, 25.10.45; 781 Sqn, Lee-on-Solent, 15.7.46; 778 Sqn (Service Trials Unit), Ford, [002, later 057] 15.10.47; DH 22.3.48; AHU Stretton 1.7.48; 782 Sqn, Donibristle, [803:DO] 2.3.49; collided with lorry on perimeter track, damaging starboard lower wing, 25.3.49; DH, Leavesden, 3.11.50; AHS Arbroath 5.7.51; 781 Sqn, Lee-on-Solent, [859:LP, later 858:LP] 20.5.52; AHU, Lossiemouth, 1.11.55; Shorts Ferry Flt, Rochester, 5.6.57; AHU Lossiemouth 24.6.57; SOC 22.6.63; despatched to Anglo-Diesel Co Ltd, London, 5.7.63 for scrap.

6743 RAF serial **NF872**; TOC 18 MU, Dumfries, 20.5.44; transferred to FAA 17.10.45; Evanton 27.10.45; Crail 2.9.46; 782 Sqn, Donibristle, 15.10.46; 781 Sqn, Lee-on-Solent, [857:LP] 7.11.46; AHU Stretton 20.7.48; 782 Sqn [803:DO] 26.10.50; RNARY, Belfast, 13.2.51; RDU Arbroath 26.3.52; AHU Lossiemouth 25.3.53; 787 Sqn, West Raynham, 9.4.54; undershot landing at West Raynham 1.9.54 due to loss of aileron control on approach and landed in field; AHU Lossiemouth; SOC 10.9.54.

6744 RAF serial **NF873**; TOC 18 MU, Dumfries, 26.5.44; transferred to FAA 22.8.45; Evanton 7.9.45; 701 Sqn, Heston 9.8.46; DH, Witney, 23.9.47; AHU Stretton 13.11.47; RDU Anthorn 20.1.50; Shorts Ferry Flt, Rochester, [602] 3.11.50; DH, Leavesden, 16.2.54; AHU, Lossiemouth, 22.10.54; SF Lossiemouth 9.12.54; AHU Lossiemouth 12.2.55; RNAY Belfast 31.3.55 for conversion to ambulance; Northern CS/Airwork Ltd,

G-ALWY, c/n 6741, of Air Enterprises Ltd, at one time named "The Ventnor Flyer", often carried holiday makers to the Isle of Wight [Denis Fox collection]

Dominie c/n 6745 had become D-2 of the Belgian Air Force at Smalldeel in 1946 [C N Dodds]

Donibristle [802:DO, 048:DO] 29.6.55; AHU, Lossiemouth, 11.3.57; SOC 13.1.59 and RTP; parts sold to Hants & Sussex Aviation Ltd 8.60; fuselage at Portsmouth 3.63.

6745   RAF serial **NF874**; TOC 18 MU; Dumfries, 30.5.44; Berlin Air Command Flt, Gatow, 15.6.45; 18 MU 26.7.45; MCS, Hendon, [ZA:W] 15.1.46; to Belgian AF as **D-2** 4.9.46; 367e Escadrille [ZC:K], Evere (radio call-sign OTZCK); 21e Escadrille 1.2.48, named *Raymond Chartier*; damaged 2.6.55; NFT

6746   RAF serial **NF875**; TOC 18 MU, Dumfries, 26.5.44; issued to Airwork General Trading Ltd 5.9.45 for modifications; regd **G-AGTM** 19.9.45 to Iraq Petroleum Transport Co Ltd, Haifa; CoA (7229) issued 6.12.45; regn cld 24.4.53 as sold in Lebanon; regd **OD-ABP** 23.9.53 to Arab Contracting & Trading Co, t/a Saad Transport, Beirut; regd **JY-ACL** 4.62 to Contracting & Trading Co Ltd, Amman; converted to Mk.6; regd **G-AGTM** 25.3.64 to E A J Gardener t/a Army Parachute Training Association, Netheravon, named *Valkyrie;* CoA issued 12.5.64; regd 1.3.67 to R C J Brinton, t/a Parachute Regt Free Fall Club, Netheravon; badly damaged in landing accident at Netheravon 26.2.68 but repaired; sold 1.3.68 and regd 4.11.68 to D Hughes t/a Army Parachute Association, Netheravon; CoA renewed 6.3.69; sold 9.77 to Martin Barraclough & Partners, overhauled at Netheravon and painted in RN colours as NF875 [603:CH]; regd 8.3.78 to Sealion Shipping Ltd (M Barraclough), Duxford; regd 25.9.80 to Airborne Taxi Services Ltd,

Duxford; regd 1.3.83 to Russavia Ltd, t/a Russavia Collection, Duxford, for pleasure flying; damaged when it swung into parked cars on landing at Duxford 21.6.87; to Audley End 2.88 for rebuild; to Rush Green 10.93 for sale; sold 20.1.94 and regd 28.3.94 to Aviation Heritage Ltd (D Geddes); to Ben Borsberry, Kidmore End, Reading, 1.3.94, for restoration; to S Evans at Farnborough 1.8.95 for completion; flown 13.11.96, CoA renewed 15.11.96; based at Kemble in civil markings; sold 1.99 to Air Atlantique Ltd, Coventry (but still regd to Aviation Heritage Ltd); extant.

6747   RAF serial **NF876**; TOC DH, Witney, 30.5.44; 5 MU, Kemble, 5.8.44; DH 19.3.46; regd **G-AHXV** 11.7.46 to MoS; regd 14.8.46 to BEA; CoA (8059) issued 16.8.46; overshot landing at Ronaldsway 15.11.49 and ran into ditch; regn cld 1.1.50.

6748   RAF serial **NF877**; TOC 18 MU, Dumfries, 7.6.44; 1316 Flt, Hendon, 14.9.44; to RNethAF as **V-1** 15.5.46, named *Limburg;* regd as **PH-VNA** to Staat der Nederlanden (CoR 639) 30.8.48 for operation by UN in Israel as **6**; did not, after all, go to Palestine; regn cld 8.10.48 and returned to RNethAF as **V-1**; 334 Sqn 1.12.52; SOC 28.9.56; retd to UK and regd **G-APBM** 13.5.57 to Aerocontacts (Aircraft Distributors) Ltd, Croydon; regd 21.5.57 to Air Couriers (Transport) Ltd, Croydon (Biggin Hill from 9.59); CoA issued 3.9.57; converted to Mk.6 1.9.58; regn cld 21.7.60 as sold in France; regd **F-OBRU** 1.8.60 to SA Ardic, Dakar, Senegal; crashed and written off at Podor, Sénégal, 8.6.62.

C/n 6746, G-AGTM masquerading as NF875 (its original serial number) and carrying representative code 603:CH when owned by Martin Barraclough & Partners in the late seventies [via A. Chivers]

C/n 6748 became V-1 of the Royal Netherlands Air Force, probably photographed before delivery   *[via A. Chivers]*

The wreckage of Rapide TJ-ABJ, c/n 6749, of Air Jordan at Amman, where it crashed on take-off on 1st May 1953   *[Denis Fox collection]*

6749   RAF serial **NF878**; TOC 18 MU, Dumfries, 3.6.44; issued to Airwork General Trading Ltd 26.8.45 for modifications; regd **G-AGTN** 19.9.45 to Iraq Petroleum Transport Co Ltd, Haifa; CoA (7230) issued 17.12.45; regn cld as sold in Jordan 20.5.52; regd **TJ-ABJ** 2.52 to Air Jordan Co, Amman; crashed into electricity standard and destroyed on take-off from Amman 1.5.53.

6750   RAF serial **NF879**; TOC RNAS Donibristle 31.5.44; 787 Sqn, Wittering, 31.5.44 (later Tangmere 17.1.45 and Westhampnett 15.7.45); DH RU, Witney, 10.10.45; 5 FS, Crail, 8.5.46; Culham 13.1.47; AHU Stretton 1.2.48; 2 FF, Stretton, [903:JA] 16.2.48; AHU Stretton 18.10.48; 781 Sqn, Lee-on-Solent, [859] 16.9.49; DH, Leavesden, 13.11.50; AHS Arbroath 20.8.51; 782 Sqn, Donibristle, [802:DO] 6.6.52; Northern CS/ Airwork Ltd, Donibristle, [802:DO]10.10.53; AHU Lossiemouth 9.2.54; SOC 13.1.59 and RTP; remains burnt by Hants & Sussex Aviation Ltd 8.60.

6751   RAF serial **NF880**; TOC RNAS Donibristle 31.5.44; 782 Sqn, Donibristle 9.6.44; 781 Sqn, Lee-on-Solent, 17.9.44; 782 Sqn 5.12.44; DH RU, Witney, 5.6.45; retd to 782 Sqn 4.1.46 (detached to Lee-on-Solent 21.1.46 to 28.2.46, Eglinton 20.3.46 to 6.4.46 and Belfast 6.46); SoAS (RN Section), Old Sarum, 22.5.46; DH, Witney, 9.6.47; AHU Stretton 1.9.47; RDU Culham 3.11.47; 3 FF, Anthorn, 7.1.48; engine fire 28.3.49; RNARY, Donibristle,14.11.49; DH, Leavesden, by road 3.5.50; AHS Arbroath 7.3.51; RN Unit, SLAW, Old Sarum, 25.3.53; heavy landing 24.9.53; DH, Leavesden, 2.11.53; AHU Lossiemouth 11.5.54; RRE, Defford, 3.9.54; SF Ford 8.6.56; AHU Lossiemouth 19.2.57; Shorts Ferry Flight, Rochester, 18.6.57; AHU, Lossiemouth, 30.9.58; SOC 22.6.63; sold to Anglo-Diesel Co Ltd, London .63 for spares.

6752   RAF serial **NF881**; TOC RNAS Donibristle 31.5.44; 782 Sqn, Donibristle, 9.6.44; DH RU, Witney, 5.6.45; retd to 782 Sqn [B8H] 18.12.45 to 9.46 (det to Eglinton 1.46 and Lee-on-Solent 3.46 to 4.46); DH, Witney; AHU Stretton 12.5.47; 782 Sqn [804:DO] 31.8.49; force-landed in bad weather 31.1.50, damaging tail oleo; DH, Leavesden, 26.1.51; AHS Arbroath 25.9.51; SF Brawdy [901:BY] 1.9.52; propeller of main generator detached and cut into top starboard fuselage longeron 24.11.54, made precautionary landing at Yeovilton; AHU Lossiemouth 29.11.55; SF Brawdy [909] 17.6.57; Yeovilton 29.7.58; Brawdy 10.9.58; SF Culdrose [999:CU] 10.11.58; AHU Lossiemouth, 18.8.60; SOC 22.6.63; sold to Anglo-Diesel Co Ltd, London, 5.7.63 for scrap.

Seen at Llanbedr in about 1948 is Dominie NF880, c/n 6751, then in service with the Fleet Air Arm's 3 Ferry Flight at Anthorn   *[N D Welch via C N Dodds]*

NF881, c/n 6752, of Station Flight Brawdy, at Blackbushe on 6th September 1955, with Belgian Air Force Dakota K10 and a Beech 18 behind [R A Walker]

6753   RAF serial **NF882**; TOC Yatesbury 9.6.44; 4 RS, Madley [4-96, later TME:B], 2.3.45; 5 MU, Kemble, 2.12.46; regd **G-AJVB** 29.5.47 to Airwork Ltd, Heston; regd 30.6.47 to Iraq Petroleum Transport Co Ltd, Tripoli; CoA (9597) issued 10.5.48; CoA lapsed 7.9.51; regn cld 13.12.51 as sold abroad; regd in Jordan as **TJ-AAZ** 12.51 to Arab Airways Association Ltd; change of name to Arab Airways (Jerusalem) Ltd 23.8.53; re-regd **JY-AAZ** 4.54; sold to France and inspected at Toussus-le-Noble 26.4.55; regd **F-BHDY** 19.7.55 to Cie Bretonne Aéronautique (COBRA), Brest; CoA suspended at Ouessant 24.11.56; regd .62 to Aero Club du Limousin, Limoges; CoA suspended 16.8.63; regn cld .63; stored at Limoges 6.65; NFT.

6754   RAF serial **NF883**; TOC ATA, White Waltham, [M]13.6.44; 32 MU, St. Athan, 28.11.44; retd to ATA 5.45; 1680 Flt, Prestwick, 27.12.45; to AAJC, Prestwick, 16.4.46; regd **G-AHLN** 8.5.46 to Scottish Airways Ltd, Inverness; CoA (7781) issued 6.10.46; regd 1.2.47 to BEA; regd 23.4.48 to Ulster Aviation Ltd, Newtownards; regd 21.5.51 to North-West Airlines (IoM) Ltd, Ronaldsway; CoA lapsed 15.6.51, renewed 7.11.52; regn cld 1.12.52 as sold in France; regd **F-BGOQ** 7.4.53 to Ets Jules Richard, Toussus-le-Noble; believed to have crashed at Toussus-le-Noble 6.7.53; regn cld 10.12.53.

6755   RAF serial **NF884**; TOC 13 Gp CF, Inverness, 13.6.44; DH RU, Witney, 19.7.45; 18 MU, Dumfries, 28.3.46; 66 Gp CF, Turnhouse [RCI:J], 21.8.48; 5 MU, Kemble, 20.12.48; sold to Wilks & Chandler 11.1.50; regd **G-ALWM** 30.1.50 to V H Bellamy, t/a Flightways, Eastleigh; regn cld 20.6.50 as sold in France; CoA (10888) issued 24.6.50; inspected at Rabat 11.7.50; regd **F-OAGP** 23.8.50 to Maroc Air Service, Rabat; regd 7.5.53 to Cie de Transports Aériens Autrex, Hanoi; wrecked in forced landing at Mellila, Spanish Morocco, 17.5.53, before proposed delivery.

6756   RAF serial **NF885**; TOC 4 ADF, Clifton, 14.6.44 (later Hutton Cranswick); 18 MU, Dumfries, 11.10.45; MCS, Hendon [CB:Z], 20.12.45; 18 MU 1.9.46; regd **G-AJFO** 29.1.47 to Field Aircraft Services Ltd, Croydon, and sold to them 19.2.47; regn cld as sold in Belgium as **OO-CDF** 29.4.47 but NTU; regd **G-AJFO** 15.7.47 to Franco-British Commercial & Industrial Co Ltd, London; CoA (8983) issued 23.7.47; sold to Air Madagascar (named either *Tamatave* or *Antananarivo*); DBF 3.11.47 at Kosti, Sudan, while on delivery flight; regn cld 3.12.47.

6757   RAF serial **NF886**; TOC ATA, White Waltham, [L] 16.6.44; 32 MU, St. Athan, 3.12.44; retd to ATA 9.12.44; damaged 26.3.45, but ROS by 29.3.45; 1 PTS, Ringway, 27.12.45; damaged 18.5.46; 1 P&GTS, Upper Heyford, 3.12.47; 38 Gp CF, Upavon, 2.48; 5 MU, Kemble, 25.6.48; sold to Air Navigation & Trading Co Ltd 29.10.48; regd **G-ALPK** 3.5.49 to Lancashire Aircraft Corpn Ltd, Squires Gate (later Yeadon); CoA (10573) issued 17.8.49; reportedly rebuilt at Squires Gate using fuselage of NF862 (itself sold 11.1.50 to Short Bros & Harland); regd 22.10.57 to Air Taxis (Cumberland) Ltd, Crosby (later Prestwick); regd 18.4.61 to Tyne Tees Air Charter Ltd, Newcastle (Woolsington); regd 22.2.63 to Tyne Tees Airways Ltd on change of name; sold 20.7.64 and regd 31.3.65 to K G Dobson, Blackbushe; CoA lapsed 4.6.66 and to Netheravon late .66; regd 18.10.66 to Maj M R Heerey. t/a Parachute Regt. Free Fall Club, Netheravon; regn cld 1.2.67; broken up for spares at Netheravon 7.68.

6758   RAF serial **NF887**; Heston Aircraft Co 23.7.44 for 1422 Flt; retd to Brush Coachworks Ltd; DH RU, Witney, 22.10.44; 1422 Flt, Heston, 13.2.45 (but it became S Flt 3.6.44!); ATA, attached to Heston Aircraft Co for use by MoAP, 11.7.45; 5 MU, Kemble, 11.6.47; regd **G-AKOM** 8.12.47 to Southern Aircraft (Gatwick) Ltd and sold to them 17.12.47; CoA (9913) issued 12.7.50; regn cld 6.12.51 as sold in Belgium; regd **OO-DCB** 14.12.51 to C le Clerq, Het Zoute; regn cld 3.11.54 as sold in UK; restored to register as **G-AKOM** 12.11.54 to Avionics Ltd, Croydon; converted to Mk.4 9.3.55 and CoA renewed 12.4.55; regn cld as sold in France 12.4.55; inspected at Cayenne 1.12.55; regd **F-OGAU** 7.5.56 to Dept de la Guyane and operated by Sté Aérienne de Transport Guyane-Antilles (SATGA), Cayenne; written off at Inini 5.8.60.

6759   RAF serial **NF888**; TOC ATA, White Waltham, 19.6.44; 32 MU, St. Athan, 25.1.45; retd to ATA 19.2.45; 18 MU, Dumfries, 27.12.45; regd **G-AHPV** 22.5.46 to Field Consolidated Aircraft Services Ltd, Croydon; regn cld 12.8.46 as sold abroad; CoA (8013) issued 19.9.46; regd in South Africa as **ZS-AYG** 30.10.46 to Field Aircraft Services Ltd for Aircraft Operating Co of South Africa, but crashed at El Adem, Libya, on delivery flight, 31.10.46.

6760   RAF serial **NF889**; TOC 1 RS, Cranwell, 19.6.44; collided with Spitfire AR395 of 1653 CU which was making practice attacks on Lancaster over Witham-on-the-Hill, Rutland, 20.3.45; six killed, inc pilot Flt Sgt C S Jones.

Three Rapides lined up at Newcastle (Woolsington): G-AKLA (c/n 6764), G-AKOY (c/n 6504) and G-AHLN (c/n 6754)   *[MAP via P H T Green]*

G-ALPK, c/n 6757, at Blackbushe on 10.9.64, by which time its owner was K G Dobson [P H Butler]

Still showing signs of its former registration G-AKOM, Rapide OO-DCB, c/n 6758, is seen parked at Croydon in December 1951, after sale to Belgium
[V Jacobs via C N Dodds]

6761 RAF serial **NF890**; TOC 76 MU, Wroughton, 21.6.44; to Glasgow docks 5.7.44; shipped to South Africa on *Clan Chattan* 12.7.44, arr Cape Town 11.8.44; to SAAF as **1365**; 9 AD; Signal School, presumed 66 AS, 4.45; sold to Southern Rhodesia Air Services 7.46 for £3522; regd **VP-YFA** 7.46 to Central African Airways; regn cld 14.7.49 as sold in South Africa; regd **ZS-BZU** 14.7.49 to Commercial Air Services Ltd, t/a Comair; to Drakensberg Air Services (Pty) Ltd, Ladysmith; overturned on landing in high winds at Mokhotlong, Basutoland, 10.9.54; regn cld 7.2.55.

6762 RAF serial **NF891**; TOC 76 MU, Wroughton, 24.6.44; shipped to India on *City of Canterbury* 20.8.44, arr Bombay 26.9.44; ACSEA 26.10.44; regd **VT-ASC** 1.11.44 to Govt of India, Bombay; sold 27.3.47 by Director-General of Disposals; regd 22.7.47 (CoR

552/2) to Indian Air Survey & Transport Co Ltd, Dum Dum, Calcutta; name changed .48 to Air Survey Co of India Ltd; crashed nr Somarampet 22.1.60, killing three, but regn still current on 30.6.68! [Note: the fuselage number quoted, BCL89403, would indicate c/n 6752, which was NF881 of the FAA.]

6763 RAF serial **NF892**; TOC ADGB CS, Northolt, 23.6.44; FCCS, Northolt, 16.10.44; TCCF, Northolt, 15.3.45; 18 MU, Dumfries, 4.7.45; MCS, Hendon, 15.1.46; 18 MU 14.5.46; regd **G-AJKH** 19.3.47 to Airwork Ltd, Heston and sold to them 3.10.47; regd 16.5.47 to Iraq Petroleum Transport Co Ltd; regd 3.11.47 to Anglo-Iranian Oil Co Ltd; CoA (9290) issued 8.1.48; seized in Iran 4.51 but UK CoA renewed 30.7.51; regd **EP-AAV** 10.51 to National Oil Co; UK regn cld 29.10.54 as sold in Iran; current 6.59; NFT.

G-AKLA, c/n 6764, had three civilian owners and was written off in India in 1954 while on a ferry flight to Indo-China   *[G M Simons collection]*

6764 RAF serial **NF893**; TOC 1 RS, Cranwell, 24.6.44; TTCCF, Wyton, 29.10.45; 18 MU, Dumfries, 11.4.47; sold to Darlington & District Aero Club 26.8.47; regd **G-AKLA** 23.10.47 to Darlington & District Aero Club Ltd, Neasham (Croft); regd 8.6.49 to Lancashire Aircraft Corporation Ltd, Squires Gate; CoA (9829) issued 18.1.50; regn cld as to long-term storage 9.11.50; restored 3.2.51 and CoA renewed 23.2.51; regd 6.4.54 to Aeroservices Ltd, Croydon; crashed 38 mls NW of Jodhpur, India, 15.6.54, when on delivery flight to Hanoi, Indo-China; regn cld same day.

6765 RAF serial NF894; TOC 1 RS, Cranwell, [J] 29.6.44; 18 MU, Dumfries, 26.4.46; regd **G-AJBJ** 20.1.47 to Birkett Air Service Ltd, Croydon; CoA (8928) issued 26.3.47; regd 1.5.53 to Airwork Ltd and operated by Airwork Services Training Ltd, Perth (Scone); CoA lapsed 24.1.55; regd 19.7.55 to Air Navigation & Trading Co Ltd, Squires Gate; CoA renewed 11.9.56 and lapsed 10.10.57; stored at Kirkham; CoA renewed 15.5.59 and lapsed 14.9.61; stored at Squires Gate; to S Westwell / Northern Aircraft Preservation Society, Peel Green, 9.69; to Midland Aircraft Preservation Society, Baginton, .70; regn cld 12.1.72; roaded to Ley Farm, Chirk, 16.6.78; regd 15.8.78 to John Pierce Aviation Ltd, Chirk; rebuild well advanced by 10.78 and unofficially referred to as Mk.7, with Gipsy Queen 30 engines; was intended to fly around the world, but still being rebuilt 9.00; regn cld 16.12.91.

6766 RAF serial **NF895**; TOC 4 RS, Madley, [4-97] 29.6.44; damaged 6.3.46; DH 9.4.46; 5 MU, Kemble, 21.2.47; sold to D J Adie 29.5.47, but no CoA issued; presumed scrapped.

6767 RAF serial **NF896**; TOC 16 Gp CF, Detling, (later Rochester) [9S:A] 30.6.44; DH 8.3.46; 18 MU, Dumfries, 25.10.46; regd **G-AKME** 1.3.48 to Tyne Taxis Ltd, Newcastle (Woolsington) and sold to them 11.3.48; CoA (10106) issued 7.5.48; regd 21.2.50 to Wolverhampton Aviation Ltd, Wolverhampton; DBF during refuelling and engine start-up at Lympne 30.6.50; regn cld same day.

6768 RAF serial **NR669**; TOC 18 MU, Dumfries, 4.7.44; transferred to FAA 20.8.45; Evanton 7.9.45; 2 FS, Stretton, 12.45; 781 Sqn, Lee-on-Solent, [855:LP] 7.47; 2 FF, Stretton, 15.3.48; Shorts, Belfast 30.11.50; Shorts Ferry Flt, Rochester, 2.12.50; DH, Leavesden, 6.12.51; AHS Arbroath 25.8.52; AHU Lossiemouth 16.7.53; Shorts Ferry Flt, Rochester, 5.3.54; AHU, Lossiemouth, 16.6.55; SF Lossiemouth 28.10.55; SF Brawdy [909:BY] 18.11.55; braked near end of landing run, handbrake fouled, tipped onto nose, damaging propellers, 18.4.56; AHU, Lossiemouth, 2.7.57; SOC 13.1.59 and RTP; remains burnt by Hants & Sussex Aviation 8.60.

6769 RAF serial **NR670**; TOC 18 MU, Dumfries, 7.7.44; St Mawgan 30.5.46; despatched to Pau, France, 25.6.46 for l'Armée de l'Air; regd **F-BDJX** 29.10.57 to Etat SFASA, St Yan (later Strasbourg); regd .63 to Etat SFATAT, Lille; regd 12.3.64 to CIC de Centre Parachutisme Alsace, Strasbourg; CoA lapsed 1.68; painted as 'F-BGXT' and sunk off Deauville for film 10.68; regn cld .69.

6770 RAF serial **NR671**; TOC DH, Witney, 7.12.44; SF Halton [THA:A, later THA:B], 10.6.45; damaged 27.6.45; ROS by 49 MU 18.7.45; 18 MU, Dumfries, 10.5.46; regd **G-AJHP** 14.2.47

The partial remains of G-AJBJ, c/n 6765, of Air Navigation & Trading Co Ltd; in more recent years this aircraft was intended to make a round-the-world flight after restoration
[MAP via P H T Green]

G-AKME, c/n 6767, of Wolverhampton Aviation being destroyed by fire at Lympne on 30th June 1950   *[G M Simons collection]*

to Brooklands Aviation Ltd, Shoreham, and sold to them 27.2.47; CoA (9155) issued 16.5.47; converted to Mk.6; regd 25.7.51 to GQ Parachute Co Ltd, Brooklands; sold to Hants & Sussex Aviation Ltd, Portsmouth; regn cld 12.3.60 as sold in Algeria; regd **F-OBOI** 6.5.60 to Cie Générale de Transports en Algérie (CGTA), Algiers; regd .61 to Sté Générale d'Affrétements Aériens (Air Fret), Algiers; CoA suspended 18.4.62 at Algiers; regn cld .64.

6771   RAF serial **NR672**; TOC 18 MU, Dumfries, 1.7.44; transferred to FAA 30.10.45; Evanton SS 12.11.45; Crail 19.9.46; SF Arbroath 31.10.46; 781 Sqn, Lee-on-Solent, [859:LP] 25.11.46; precautionary landing 14.1.47 after engine failure; retd to 781 Sqn 14.5.48; DH, Witney, 7.6.48; AHU Stretton 27.10.48; SOC 29.11.54 and RTP; remains extant 5.55.

6772   RAF serial **NR673**; TOC 18 MU, Dumfries, 6.7.44; DH 23.7.44; Brush Coachworks 21.8.44; CoA (7093) issued 11.9.44 to Sec of State for Air; shipped to Uruguay on LS1696 29.9.44, arr Montevideo 20.10.44 for use of Air Attaché to Uruguay; SOC 25.6.47 as sold locally; NFT.

6773   RAF serial **NR674**; TOC 18 MU, Dumfries, 11.7.44; MoAP at DH 27.10.45; MoAP at Hanworth 3.12.45; regd **G-AGZU** 22.1.46 to Hunting Air Travel Ltd, Luton; CoA (7359) issued 19.2.46; regd 25.10.46 to Cecil Kay Aircraft (1945) Ltd, Elmdon; re-regd 18.11.47 to Cecil Kay Ltd; regd 1.4.48 to Herts & Essex Aviation Ltd, Broxbourne (later Stapleford Tawney); regd 22.4.48

to Herts & Essex Aero Club (1946) Ltd; regd 24.3.55 to A C Williams, Durban, South Africa; regn cld 28.4.55 as sold in South Africa; regd **ZS-DLS** 24.4.55 to Enterprise Clothing Manufacturers (SA) Ltd, Durban; regd 7.57 to J L Palframan, Durban; regd 3.60 to General Aircraft (Pty) Ltd, Durban; regd c.8.68 to D Steyn t/a Ladysmith Air, Ladysmith; to A Mechin, Baragwanath; WFU at Baragwanath and regn cld 19.4.71 and later vandalised; remains to Oribi airport, Maritzburg; centre section, wings and tail transferred to SAAF Museum at Lanseria 6.76 for possible restoration; current status unknown.

6774   RAF serial **NR675**; TOC 5 MU, Kemble, 12.7.44; sold to DH 15.4.46; CoA (8819) issued 6.12.46; sold to Organizacio Mineira de Transportes Aereos, Belo Horizonte; regn **PP-OMD** reserved but formal registration did not take place; last temporary CoA issued 26.10.47; NFT

6775   RAF serial **NR676**; TOC 5 MU, Kemble, 12.7.44; sold to DH 15.4.46; regd **G-AIWY** 22.11.46 to de Havilland Aircraft Co Ltd, Witney; CoA (8740) issued 26.11.46; regn cld 7.1.47 as sold abroad; regd in Denmark as **OY-AAO** 6.10.47 to Falcks Redningskorps, Copenhagen; regd 23.6.61 to Peer Perch, Esbjerg; regd 26.2.63 to Danfly, Kalundborg; CoA lapsed 29.11.63 and aircraft donated to children's playground; regn cld 4.4.66; rescued .66 by Historical Branch of Royal Danish Aero Club and taken to Technical Museum, Elsinore; preserved in store at Veteranmuseum, Kvaerdrup.

OY-AAO, c/n 6775, in a sorry state at Kalundborg on 26th March 1966   *[Denis Fox collection]*

6776   RAF serial **NR677**; TOC 18 MU, Dumfries, 15.7.44; transferred to FAA 20.6.45; 782 Sqn, Donibristle, 30.8.45 (det to Lee-on-Solent 10.45 to 11.45); Crail 24.9.46; DH, Witney, 30.10.46; AHU Stretton 25.4.47; 1 FF, Culham [601:CH] 17.1.50; Shorts Ferry Flt, Rochester, 16.12.50; DH, Leavesden, 9.11.51; AHS Arbroath 6.6.52; RNARY, Belfast, 30.6.53; Eglinton 9.10.53; Shorts Ferry Flt, Rochester, 4.6.54; force-landed due to fire in port engine 18.11.54; MARU, Lee-on-Solent, 25.11.54; SF Lee-on-Solent 15.12.54; AHS, Lossiemouth, 3.10.55; RTP 13.1.59; remains extant 7.60.

6777   RAF serial **NR678**; TOC 1 RS, Cranwell [TCR:C, later TCR:U], 17.7.44; 18 MU, Dumfries, 1.10.47; 5 MU, Kemble, 26.10.48; sold to Short Brothers 11.11.50; regd **G-ALWJ** 21.1.50 to Short Bros & Harland Ltd, Rochester; ferried as **G-ALWI**, repainted as **G-ALWJ**; CoA (10802) issued 21.4.50; used by Shorts Charter Service; regn cld 12.10.53 as sold in Kenya; regd **VP-KLL** 20.10.53 to Noon & Pierce Air Charters Ltd, Nairobi; regd 1.7.55 to J E F Wilkins, t/a Caspair Air Charters, Nairobi; damaged on landing at Kisimu 9.10.55 but repaired; regd 16.4.56 to Caspair Air Charters & Agencies Ltd, Nairobi; regd .58 to Caspair Ltd, Nairobi; badly damaged 20.1.58 in forced landing at Magadi Road, 40 mls from Nairobi, when out of fuel; regn cld but regd .60 to same owner; converted to Mk.4; re-regd **5Y-KLL** 1.65; CoA lapsed 31.7.65; regn cld .66.

6778   RAF serial **NR679**; TOC 18 MU, Dumfries, 17.7.44; damaged 5.11.45; DH 17.12.45 for repair; 18 MU 15.7.46; 25 Gp CF, Spitalgate, 12.9.47; 18 MU 17.2.48; 61 Gp CF, Kenley, 20.4.48;

damaged 5.12.48; 5 MU, Kemble, 25.2.49; regd **G-ALNS** 21.4.49 to R A Short & J H Tattersall, Croydon; regd 15.9.49 to W Hutchinson, Eastleigh; CoA (10603) issued 16.6.49; regd 2.12.50 to Hampshire School of Flying Ltd, Eastleigh; regd 11.12.51 to S G Newport, t/a The Arab Contracting & Trading Co, Beirut, Lebanon, reportedly for crop-spraying; converted to Mk.4 12.1.55; CoA lapsed 22.2.56, renewed 5.4.57, lapsed 4.4.58, renewed 26.5.59; regd 3.4.64 to Aerocontacts (Aircraft Distributors) Ltd, Gatwick; deconverted from Mk.4 22.4.64; regn cld 22.10.64 as sold in Congo; regd **9Q-CJK** to Agence de Messageries Aériennes Zairoises (AMAZ); NFT.

6779   RAF serial **NR680**; TOC DH, Witney, 11.8.44; 6 MU, Brize Norton, 9.9.44; DH for conversion to Dominie II; CRD at RAE, Farnborough, 12.2.45; CRD at DH 30.8.45; 18 MU, Dumfries, 20.8.46; regn **G-AGLO** may have been allocated to Sec of State for Air 27.10.44 for use by Allied Airways (Gandar Dower) Ltd but was NTU; retd to RAF **NR680** 23.11.44; regd **G-AKSC** 27.1.48 to Olley Air Service Ltd, Croydon; regd 28.2.48 to Sir Brograve Beauchamp, Croydon; CoA (9970) issued 16.3.48; regd 8.7.49 to The Demolition & Construction Co Ltd, Croydon (Beauchamp's company); regd 4.5.53 to East Anglian Flying Services Ltd, Southend; regd 27.9.54 to Aeroservices Ltd, Croydon; regn cld 3.8.55 as sold in French New Caledonia; ferried to New Caledonia 27.6.55 to 9.8.55 by P Palmer of Independent Air Transport, Hurn; regd **F-OATC** 22.9.55 to Sté Calédonienne de Transports Aériens (Transpac), Nouméa (Magenta); converted to Mk.6 by .63; regd 25.11.65 to Aero Club Calédonien, Nouméa (Magenta); CoA lapsed 8.66; regn cld .67.

G-ALNS, c/n 6778, of The Arab Contracting & Trading Co of Beirut, Lebanon, was formerly NR679   *[G M Simons collection]*

NR680, c/n 6779, which became G-AKSC and ended its days in New Caledonia in 1967   *[G M Simons collection]*

Rapide G-AHXW, c/n 6782, in original BEA livery at St Mary's on the Scilly Isles   *[Denis Fox collection]*

6780 RAF serial **NR681**; TOC DH, Witney, 11.8.44; regd **G-AGLP** 28.10.44 to Railway Air Services Ltd, Speke; CoA (7111) issued 2.2.45 and del to AAJC, Speke, 8.2.45; to Scottish Airways Ltd, Renfrew, 27.2.45; on 26. 5 45, chartered to Jersey Airways, was first civilian aircraft to land in Channel Islands after liberation; to Scottish Airways Ltd 17.4.46; regd 1.2.47 to BEA; regd 15.6.48 to C Allen, Croydon; regd 1.7.48 to C L Burton, t/a International Airways, Croydon; leased to Jersey Airlines 3.49 to 4.49; CoA lapsed 17.10.50; regn cld 31.8.59.

6781 RAF serial **NR682**; TOC DH, Witney, 11.8.44; regd **G-AGLR** 28.10.44 to Railway Air Services Ltd, Speke; CoA (7112) issued 13.1.45 and issued to AAJC, Speke, 20.1.45; to Scottish Airways Ltd, Renfrew, 2.5.45; regd 1.2.47 to BEA; regd 24.6.48 to Lees-Hill Aviation (Birmingham) Ltd, Elmdon; name changed 9.51 to Don Everall (Aviation) Ltd and re-regd as such 29.1.52; force-landed, out of fuel, at Four Oaks cross-roads, Berkswell, nr Coventry, 7.10.56 while flying from Le Touquet to Elmdon and DBF; regn cld 30.5.57.

6782 RAF serial **NR683**; TOC 5 MU, Kemble, 28.7.44; DH for civil conversion 19.3.46; regd **G-AHXW** 11.7.46 to MoS; regd 14.8.46 to BEA, later named *Sir John Nicholson*; CoA (8060) issued 16.8.46; CoA lapsed 10.1.53; regd 14.4.53 to A J Whittemore (Aeradio) Ltd, Croydon; modified to Mk.4 and CoA renewed 20.10.54; regd 2.11.54 to Fairey Aviation Co Ltd, White Waltham; regd 25.6.59 to Fairey Aviation Ltd, White Waltham; regd 30.8.60 to Fairey Air Surveys Ltd, White Waltham; retitled Fairey Surveys Ltd 30.12.63; regd 27.2.68 to GRM Airwork Ltd, Staverton; regd 14.8.69 to GRM Developments Ltd; re-regd on name change 20.7.70 to PSL Developments Ltd, Worcester; claimed to be the last DH.89 on

air survey work; regn cld 16.3.71 as sold in USA; regd **N683DH** 3.71 to J R O'Brien and R M Puryear, Portola Valley, San Jose, CA; flown from Booker to Rotterdam 6.71 and shipped to Newark, NJ on *Atlantic Champagne;* reassembled by Butler Aviation at Newark and flown 18.7.71; flown to San Jose 12.8.71; donated to EAA Museum Foundation Inc, Oshkosh, WI, 4.75 and restored in quasi BEA colours and markings, named *Sir Robert Puryear;* regd 12.2.98 to W B Field and J M Reed, Portland, OR, for rebuild at Calaveras Co Airport, San Andreas, CA; extant.

6783 RAF serial **NR684**; sold to DH 3.5.46; CoA (8834) issued 16.12.46 to Peruvian Govt; transfer date 19.3.47; regd **OB-RAH-197**; used by Estado, 41 Escuadron de Transporte, Transportes Aereos Militares, the airline branch of the Peruvian AF, Iquitos, Pucalipa or Puerto Maldonado; NFT.

6784 RAF serial **NR685**; TOC 5 MU, Kemble, 28.7.44; regd **G-AGLE** 14.12.44 to Railway Air Services Ltd, Speke; at DH RU, Witney, 3.2.45; del to AAJC, Speke, and CoA (7152) issued 12.2.45; to Scottish Airways Ltd, Renfrew, 14.3.45; regd 1.2.47 to BEA; regd 15.6.48 to C Allen, Croydon; regd 1.7.48 to C L Burton t/a International Airways, Croydon; damaged in forced landing at Morden, Surrey, 17.3.49; stored at Croydon until sold to Hants & Sussex Aviation Ltd, Portsmouth, for spares .52; regn cld 31.8.59.

6785 RAF serial **NR686**; TOC 1316 Flt, Hendon, 15.8.44; to Belgian AF as **D-4** 3.9.46; 367e Escadrille [ZC:M], Evere (radio call-sign OTZCM); 21e Escadrille 1.2.48; EVS, Koksijde; damaged while taxying 22.9.55 but repaired; regd **OO-ARN** (CoR 1145) 25.7.57 to COGEA Nouvelle SA, Keerbergen for anti-aircraft co-operation duties; regd .59 to Air Brousse SPRL, Léopoldville; crashed at Louzi, Congo, 20.6.60; regn cld 5.9.60.

C/n 6785, OO-ARN of COGEA is seen here at Dakar in West Africa   *[Denis Fox collection]*

The significance of number 14 on the fuselage of Rapide CX-API, c/n 6786, formerly G-ANAH, is not known [Denis Fox collection]

6786 RAF serial **NR687**; TOC 15 Gp CF, Speke, 9.9.44; CCCF, Leavesden, [QX:F] 18.8.45; DH, Witney, 14.3.46; Leavesden 27.3.46; 18 MU, Dumfries, 19.11.46; Staff College CF, Andover, [KE:B] 4.10.47; 32 MU, St Athan, 12.10.50; BLEU, Andover, 14.11.50; sold to Vickers-Armstrongs Ltd 22.5.52; regd **G-ANAH** 24.6.53 to Hants & Sussex Aviation Ltd, Portsmouth; CoA issued 3.3.54; regd 19.3.54 to Vickers-Armstrongs Ltd, Weybridge; regn cld 26.8.54 as sold in Uruguay; regd **CX-API** 9.54 to Delfin Dias Gibils, Montevideo; to F Deismann (or Oetzmann), Montevideo; current on 8.72 register; NFT.

6787 RAF serial **NR688**; TOC 24 Sqn, Hendon, 18.8.44; MCS, Hendon, 8.9.44; to Belgian AF 4.9.46 as **D-5**; 367e Escadrille [ZC:N], Evere (radio call-sign OTZCN); 21e Escadrille 1.2.48; SOC 1.9.55; regd **OO-ARI** (CoR 1085) 11.7.56 to COGEA Nouvelle SA, Keerbergen, for anti-aircraft co-operation duties; ferried to Croydon 24.4.57; regn cld as sold in UK 7.5.57; regd **G-APBN** 16.5.57 to Crewdson Aviation Ltd, Croydon; regn cld 29.9.57 as sold in Belgium; restored as **OO-ARI** 10.12.57; del from Croydon 4.58; sold in France 25.4.58; inspected at Tunis 15.10.58; regd in France as **F-OBIA** 2.12.58 to SA Aéro Sahara, Tunis (El Aouina); damaged when ground-looped on landing at Mohging 26.10.60 and possibly not repaired; CoA suspended 28.11.62; regn cld .64 but in store .66.

6788 RAF serial **NR689**; TOC 76 MU, Wroughton, 23.8.44; to Birkenhead docks 19.9.44; shipped to South Africa on *City of*

Calcutta 22.9.44, arr 12.10.44; to SAAF as **1366** at 9 AD; 61 Sqn 1.45; sold via 15 AD for £3340 to Civil Aviation Council, Dept of Transport, 9.8.46; SOC by RAF 26.9.46 as sold locally; regd **ZS-CAC** 10.9.46 to Dept of Transport; re-regd **ZS-BZC** 11.5.48; impounded in Cairo 29.4.48 [sic] when in transit to Israeli AF but later released; NFT.

6789 RAF serial **NR690**; TOC ATA, White Waltham, [AB] 16.9.44; 32 MU, St. Athan, 25.10.44; retd to ATA 23.11.44; DH 22.10.45; 18 MU, Dumfries, 21.6.46; regd **G-AKYZ** 18.5.48 to D J Hayles, Croydon; regd 24.6.48 to W A Rollason Ltd, Croydon; CoA (10209) issued 6.9.48; regn cld 15.9.48 as sold abroad; regd in Argentina as **LV-AEO** 30.11.48 to Zonas Oeste y Norte de Aerolineas Argentinas (ZONDA) through Sfreddo y Paolini Ltda (aircraft brokers); crashed 22.11.48, and again 24.1.49 at Gral Pacheco airport, Buenos Aires; regn cld 6.1.54.

6790 RAF serial **NR691**; TOC ATA, White Waltham, [C] 23.9.44; 32 MU, St. Athan, 25.10.44; 5 MU, Kemble, 1.11.44; retd to ATA 13.11.44; DH 11.12.45; 18 MU, Dumfries, 20.8.46; regd **G-AKZB** 18.5.48 to D J Hayles, Croydon; CoA (10187) issued 13.7.48; regd 15.7.48 to L D Trappitt, Croydon; regd 25.10.48 to C W J Allen, Croydon; regd 11.2.49 to BEA, named *RMA Lord Baden Powell* 1.9.50; converted to Mk.6 29.8.60; crashed at Land's End (St Just) 12.12.61 when port undercarriage struck concrete post and port lower wing fouled top wire of fence; regn cld 27.12.61; parts in store at Exeter .68.

G-AKZB, c/n 6790, at Croydon soon after civilianisation, traces of RAF roundels and serial number still apparent [G M Simons collection]

6791 RAF serial **NR692**; TOC ATA, White Waltham, 23.9.44; 32 MU, St. Athan, 23.11.44; retd to ATA 23.11.44; DH for inspection 22.11.45; 18 MU, Dumfries, 18.7.46; regd **G-AKTD** 19.2.48 to Butlins Ltd, London and sold to them 16.3.48; CoA (10025) issued 14.4.48; regd 17.2.49 to Air Couriers Ltd, Croydon; regn cld 4.5.51 as sold in France; regd **F-BFVM** 8.5.51 to Aéro Club du Touquet, Le Touquet; regd 8.54 to Transports Autonomes du Tréport-Eu-Mers (TATEM), Eu; CoA suspended 23.4.55; ferried to Toussus-le-Noble 3.7.56; regd .57 to Aéro Club de Colomb-Béchar; regd 1.60 to Cie Générale de Transports en Algérie (CGTA), Algiers; regd 1.61 to Sté Générale d'Affrétements Aériens (Air Fret), Algiers; crashed at Amenas 9.10.61.

6792 RAF serial **NR693**; TOC 5 MU, Kemble, 1.12.44; DH 14.3.46; to AAJC, Speke, 26.7.46; regd **G-AHKV** 23.4.46 to MoS;

CoA (7673) issued 25.7.46; regd 25.7.46 to BOAC (BEA Divn) and operated by Isle of Man Air Services Ltd; regd 6.5.47 to BEA, later named *RMA Sir James Outram* but name not painted on aircraft; CoA lapsed 27.12.52; regd 14.4.53 to A J Whittemore (Aeradio) Ltd, Croydon; CoA renewed 25.1.54; regd 4.2.54 to Sky Neon Aviation Co Ltd, Croydon; thought to have been only DH.89 used for aerial advertising, with neon tubes fitted to framework under lower mainplanes; CoA lapsed 24.2.55; regd 3.1.56 to Ind Coope & Allsopp Ltd, Wolverhampton; regd 29.11.57 to Automobile Association, Fairoaks (later Panshanger) and used for aerial patrols; converted to Mk.6 3.61; regd 20.6.63 to Solair Flying Services Ltd, Elmdon; regd 5.1.65 to Mid-Fly Ltd, Elmdon; regd 23.8.66 to Cartographical Services (Southampton) Ltd, Eastleigh; CoA lapsed 3.12.68; sold 2.2.69 and regn cld 9.9.69; burnt by Birmingham Airport Fire Section.

G-AHKV of brewers Ind, Coope & Allsopp Ltd, who used it for a time in 1956/57 [via A. Chivers]

Visiting Liverpool (Speke) on 23rd March 1961 was G-AHKV, c/n 6792, of the Automobile Association [P H Butler]

C/n 6793 as NR694 during its very short service with the RAF in India [*G M Simons collection*]

6793   RAF serial **NR694**; TOC 76 MU, Wroughton, 29.9.44; to Middlesbrough docks 20.10.44; shipped to India on *Martaban* 30.10.44, arr Bombay 8.12.44; regd **VT-ASJ** 15.1.45 to Govt of India, Bombay; regn cld 29.4.47, possibly after a crash.

6794   RAF serial **NR695**; TOC 76 MU, Wroughton, 29.9.44; to Middlesbrough docks 20.10.44; shipped to India on *Martaban* 30.10.44, arr Bombay 8.12.44; regd **VT-ASQ** 27.3.45; regd 21.5.46 (CoR 566/2) to Indian Air Survey & Transport Co Ltd, Dum Dum, Calcutta; name changed .48 to Air Survey Co of India Ltd; regn current on 30.6.68; shipped to Portland, OR, USA, 7.78; regd **N2290F** .78 to E J Gothard, Chevalis, WA; regd .79 to J Schell, Graham, WA and based at Oakville, WA; regn cld 31.1.90; to USAF Museum, Wright-Patterson AFB, Dayton, OH, where it is currently on display as X7454 *Wee Wullie*.

6795   RAF serial **NR696**; TOC by Airwork Ltd 27.9.44; regd **G-AGLN** 2.10.44 to Anglo-Iranian Oil Co Ltd, Abadan; CoA (7106) issued 1.12.44; to Birkenhead docks 27.12.44; shipped to Middle East, arr Basra 20.1.45; written off in crash near Abadan 15.12.46; regn cld 2.1.47.

The colour scheme for c/n 6794 when N2290F epitomises the Dragon name. Note the extra glazed panels below the normal cockpit windows [*G M Simons collection*]

Suspended from the roof of the USAF Museum at Dayton, Ohio, is Dominie NR695, c/n 6794, masquerading as X7454, which was used by the USAAF in the UK during the Second World War [*via author*]

C/n 6796, F-BFPU of Sté Air Caen is still extant in Canada as C-FAYE

[via A. Chivers]

6796   RAF serial **NR697**; TOC 12 (P) AFU, Spitalgate, 1.10.44 for 21 Gp CF [FKO:A]; damaged and ROS by 58 MU 10.9.45; 17 SFTS, Cranwell, 29.9.45; damaged on landing at Brize Norton 28.9.46; Bircham Newton; sold to Cirrus Club, t/a Ciro's Aviation, 9.3.47; regd **G-AKGV** 9.10.47 to Ciro's Aviation Ltd, Gatwick; CoA (9796) issued 17.10.47; regd 11.11.48 to William Dempster Ltd, Blackbushe; regd 20.7.50 to J A Longmoor, t/a Vendair, Croydon; regn cld as sold abroad 25.7.50; regd in France as **F-BFPU** 11.8.50 to SA Air Caen, Carpiquet; CoA lapsed 1.71; sold to S J Filhol and del to Baginton for storage 26.9.73; restored as **G-AKGV** 7.11.75 to S J Filhol, Baginton, but UK regn not applied; to Booker mid.75 ?; regn cld as sold in Canada 21.6.76; regd **C-GXFJ** to G M LeMay, Acme, nr Calgary; regn lapsed; rebuilt and regd **C-FAYE** 9.82 to same owner, named *Lady Faye;* fitted with extended fin; owner died .96 and aircraft for sale .98; regd to B J LeMay; regd 6.12.99 to Ontario Bushplane Heritage & Forest Fire Educational Centre, Sault Ste Marie, Ont; extant.

6797   RAF serial **NR698**; TOC 5 MU, Kemble, 6.10.44; TFU, Defford 27.9.45; loaned to NGTE, Bitteswell, 2.9.47; retd to Defford 13.10.47; 5 MU 22.3.48; sold to R A Short 2.1.50; regd **G-ALXU** 24.1.50 to R A Short, Croydon; regd 16.4.50 to W A Rollason Ltd, Croydon; CoA (10872) issued 24.1.50; converted at Eastleigh; regn cld 20.5.50 as sold in Transjordan; regd **TJ-AAV** 29.9.50 (or

29.8.50) sold to Arab Airways Association Ltd; nominal change 23.8.53 to Arab Airways (Jerusalem) Ltd; re-regd **JY-AAV** 4.54; regn cld; inspected at Ivato, Madagascar, 2.3.55; regd in France as **F-OASC** 22.4.55 to Sté Air Madagascar, Ivato; DBF at Fort Dauphin, Madagascar, 20.5.57.

6798   RAF serial **NR699**; sold to DH 3.5.46; CoA (8820) issued 6.12.46 to Peruvian Govt; transfer date 13.3.47; regd **OB-RAG-196**; used by Estado, 41 Escuadron de Transporte, Transportes Aéreos Militare, the airline branch of the Peruvian Air Force, Iquitos, Pucalipa or Puerto Maldonado; NFT

6799   RAF serial **NR700**; TOC 76 MU, Wroughton, 19.10.44; to Liverpool docks 23.11.44; shipped to West Africa on *Silver Walnut,* 2.12.44; arr Takoradi 20.2.45; West Africa CS, Accra; SOC 1.1.47.

6800   RAF serial **NR701**; TOC 5 MU, Kemble, 17.10.44; DH 19.3.46; regd **G-AHXX** 11.7.46 to MoS; regd 9.8.46 to BEA; CoA (8061) issued 9.8.46; prototype of BEA Islander Class, named *RMA Islander;* used by Channel Islands Airways; regn cld 1.8.52 as sold in Malaya; regd in Borneo as **VR-OAB** 1.53 to Malayan Airways Ltd; to Borneo Airways Ltd 4.58; damaged at Lahad Dutu 27.3.59 and probably not repaired; regn cld 10.3.61.

The former BEA "Islander", G-AHXX, c/n 6800, seen in Channel Islands Airways livery at Croydon

[Denis Fox collection]

6801 RAF serial **NR713**; TOC 18 MU, Dumfries, 1.11.44; TTCCF, White Waltham, 8.9.45 (later Wyton [TWY:G]); SF Halton 24.8.46; 5 MU, Kemble, 16.1.47; regd **G-AJSL** 8.5.47 to Field Aircraft Services Ltd, Croydon, and sold to them 29.5.47; regn cld as sold abroad 16.6.47, but sale abandoned; regd 29.9.49 to Trent Valley Aviation Ltd, Nottingham (Tollerton), named *Friar Tuck;* CoA (9373) issued 26.10.49; regd 8.9.50 to Eagle Aviation Ltd, Luton; CoA lapsed 25.10.50; regd 24.12.51 to Air Charter Ltd, Croydon; CoA renewed 21.3.52; regd 9.4.52 to Eagle Aviation Ltd, Blackbushe; regd 10.4.52 to Surrey Flying Services Ltd, Southend; regd 26.3.56 to Southern Flying Services Ltd, t/a Portsmouth Aero Club, Portsmouth; regd 10.1.61 to Portsmouth Aero Club Ltd; regd 9.5.62 to T H Marshall, Christchurch (del 3.62); regd 28.8.62 to P E Palmer Holdings Ltd, Hurn; regd 2.5.63 to Shackleton Aviation Ltd; CoA lapsed 19.6.63; regd 5.10.64 to Airgeneers Ltd, Staverton; CoA renewed 28.7.65; regd 18.10.66 to Maj M R Heerey, t/a Parachute Regt. Free Fall Club, Netheravon, named *Pegasus;* nominal re-regn 1.3.67 to Lt R C J Brinton; sold 31.1.68 and regd 30.5.68 to Trent Valley Aviation Ltd, East Midlands Airport; damaged at Usworth 16.5.69 when aircraft tipped onto nose; CoA lapsed 16.5.69; sold to unidentified buyer 25.3.70; stored at Usworth until at least 8.76; reported to Biggin Hill .78; exported to Australia .78/.79; to M Rolfe, stored nr Melbourne .83; to Moorabbin by .85; regd **VH-UXZ** (second) 31.1.95 to M Rolfe, Moorabbin; rebuild almost complete 4.01; extant.

6802 RAF serial **NR714**; TOC 18 MU, Dumfries, 3.11.44; FCCF, Northolt, 18.12.44; CCCF, Leavesden, 12.4.45; damaged 30.5.45, ROS by 5 MU 4.6.45; retd to CCCF 12.7.45; 18 MU 1.4.46; sold to Air Navigation & Trading Co Ltd 11.3.48; regd **G-AKMD** 2.3.48 to R L Whyham, Squires Gate; regd 18.5.48 to Butlin's Ltd, London; CoA (10143) issued 10.9.48; sold 1.6.49 and regd 9.8.49 to Aviation Traders Ltd, Gatwick; regd 19.2.51 to Aerocontacts Ltd, Gatwick; regn cld as sold abroad 17.12.51; inspected at Ivato, Madagascar, 28.12.51; regd in France as **F-OAKD** 5.2.52 to Sté Air Madagascar, Ivato; DBF during engine start at Béalanana, Madagascar, 15.3.52.

6803 RAF serial **NR715**; TOC 18 MU, Dumfries, 4.11.44; regd **G-AGNH** 9.1.45 to BOAC; CoA (7158) issued 16.5.45; allocated serial **VG764** 17.5.45 for ferry flight from Witney to Hurn and onward flight to Nairobi 19.5.45 to 25.5.45 in order to overcome ban on non-US civil aircraft flying through west and south of France, a ploy intended to keep non-US civil aircraft out of Middle East and Africa pending the establishment by Pan American Airways of a post-war network; reverted to **G-AGNH** on arrival and regd **VP-KCT** 9.8.45 to BOAC for operation by East African Airways Corpn; restored to register as **G-AGNH** 13.8.49 to MoCA, Stansted; CoA renewed 20.8.49 and lapsed 19.4.52; regd 19.1.54 to MoT&CA (by then based at Baghdad West for use of British Air Attache, possibly since .49); regn cld as sold in Aden 6.7.56; regd **VR-AAP** to Aden Airways 3.56; broken up Salalah 11.59.

6804 RAF serial **NR716**; sold to DH 2.5.46; CoA (8811) issued 25.11.46 to Peruvian Govt; transfer date 12.3.47; regd **OB-RAF-195**; used by Estado, 41 Escuadron de Transporte,

Transportes Aéreos Militare, the airline branch of the Peruvian Air Force, based at Iquitos, Pucalipa or Puerto Maldonado; NFT

6805 RAF serial **NR717**; TOC 5 MU, Kemble, 9.11.44; MCS, Hendon, 17.10.45; SF Halton [THA:I] 31.7.46; 18 MU, Dumfries, 3.6.47; regd **G-AKUS** 11.3.48 to T W Morton, t/a Morton Air Services, Croydon; regd 26.4.48 to A W Weyman, London; CoA (10072) issued 19.8.48; regd 20.8.48 to Mayfair Air Services Ltd, London; ferried to Palestine 15.9.48; to Israeli AF as **S-77**; became IDFAF **1306**; regn cld 16.5.50 as 'disappeared in Palestine'; NFT

6806 RAF serial **NR718**; TOC 5 MU, Kemble, 6.11.44; 18 MU, Dumfries; 4 RS, Madley, 9.8.45; 5 MU 21.3.46; sold to DH 9.5.46; CoA (9014) issued 18.2.47; regd **VQ-PAR** 12.47 to Aviron (also operated by Shirut Avir); to Israeli AF 11.47, probably as **S-71**; fitted to carry four 250lb bombs; regd **4X-ACU** 13.11.49; reported damaged in Egyptian air attack on Sde Dov 15.5.48; converted to air ambulance by 14.10.48; became IDFAF **1301** c12.48; broken up 1957.

6807 RAF serial **NR719**; TOC 5 MU, Kemble, 6.11.44; sold to DH 14.5.46; CoA (8945) issued 15.1.47; regd **PP-DPH** 8.4.49 to Distribuidora de Automovies Studebaker Ltda, Sao Paulo; sold to Joaquim Lemos 6.10.49; sold to Adhemar de Barros Filho 25.10.51; sold to Servicios Aereos Estrela Matutina, Sao Luiz, State of Maranhao, 24.12.53; sold to Jose Ribamar Campos da Silva 5.11.54; sold to Jose Laureano Couto Mello 8.9.56; CoA expired 9.9.57; regn cld 2.12.71 due to "lack of inspection for more than ten years".

6808 RAF serial **NR720**; TOC 5 MU, Kemble, 10.11.44; DH for civil conversion 15.4.46; regd **G-AHXY** 11.7.46 to MoS; regd 11.9.46 to BEA; CoA (8062) issued 13.9.46; crashed in fog on Renfrew golf course 27.12.48 while on approach to Renfrew airport from Benbecula (an ambulance flight); regn cld 17.2.49; parts used in rebuild of G-AFMF (c/n 6432); remains extant 1.50.

6809 RAF serial **NR721**; TOC 5 MU, Kemble, 15.11.44; BOAC, Whitchurch, 9.3.46; RAE, Farnborough, 14.1.48; used by Transport Flt from 27.4.48; ATDU, Gosport, as spares source 14.4.53; SOC 19.5.53.

6810 RAF serial **NR722**; TOC 5 MU, Kemble, 13.11.44; DH for civil conversion 11.3.46; regd **G-AHKU** 23.4.46 to MoS; CoA (7672) issued 14.6.46; regd 14.6.46 to BOAC (BEA Divn) and operated by Isle of Man Air Services Ltd; to AAJC, Speke, 24.6.46; regd 6.5.47 to BEA, later named *RMA Cecil John Rhodes;* converted to Mk.6 7.60; regd 20.5.64 to British Westpoint Airlines Ltd, Exeter; regd 16.7.65 to F H Mann, but still operated by British Westpoint Airlines until company ceased trading early .66; regd 26.7.66 to Treffield Aviation, and operated by Dominie Airways, East Midlands Airport; regd 30.12.66 to Treffield International Airways Ltd, later named *Sir Richard Hawkins;* sold 24.7.67 and regd 8.11.67 to Pamela M Scholfield, Exeter; sold 30.5.68 and regd 6.1.69 to K B Neely, t/a Scillonia Airways, Land's End (St Just), named *Bishop;* CoA lapsed 12.8.70; regn cld 16.5.72; some parts at Biggin Hill .80 as spares for G-AGTM and G-AIDL.

Although allocated to BOAC post-war, NR721, c/n 6809, remained in service use [MAP via R C Sturtivant]

C/n 6810 saw extensive post-war service with BEA as G-AHKU "RMA Cecil John Rhodes" of BEA [via A. Chivers]

G-AHKU after sale to British Westpoint Airlines with the colour scheme little changed from its BEA days [via A. Chivers]

6811 RAF serial **NR723**; TOC 5 MU, Kemble, 15.11.44; DH for civil conversion 11.3.46; to AAJC, Speke, 27.6.46; regd **G-AHKT** 23.4.46 to MoS; CoA (7671) issued 24.4.46; regd 20.6.46 to BOAC (BEA Divn) and operated by Isle of Man Air Services Ltd; regd 6.5.47 to BEA, later named *RMA Lord Tennyson;* CoA lapsed 6.12.52; regd 14.4.53 to A J Whittemore (Aeradio) Ltd, Croydon; converted to Mk.4 and CoA renewed 1.6.54; regd 22.6.54 to Whiteley (Rishworth) Ltd and operated by Yeadon Aero Club; regd 10.10.57 to Hants & Sussex Aviation Ltd, Portsmouth; regn cld as sold in South America 17.2.58; shipped from London Docks 11.2.58;

regd in French Guiana 10.9.58 as **F-OAUG** to Sté Aérienne de Transport Guyanne-Antilles (SATGA), Cayenne; damaged at Rochambeau 20.11.61 and CoA suspended; regn cld .64.

6812 RAF serial **NR724**; 5 MU, Kemble, 15.11.44; DH for civil conversion 19.3.46; regd **G-AHKS** 23.4.46 to MoS; regd 23.8.46 to BEA, later named *Robert Louis Stevenson;* CoA (7670) issued 26.8.46; converted to Mk.4 6.55 by Hants & Sussex Aviation Ltd; regd 2.6.55 to Eagle Aviation Ltd, Singapore, and regn cld same day; regd **VR-OAC** 6.55 to Malayan Airways Ltd; operated by Borneo Airways Ltd from 4.58; crashed and written off at Jesselton 21.12.60; regn cld 10.3.61.

6813 RAF serial **NR725**; TOC 5 MU, Kemble, 24.11.44; DH for civil conversion 11.3.46; 2 FP, Aston Down; damaged while taxying at Kemble 6.5.46 and ROS; sold to BOAC 1.7.46; regd **G-AIBB** 25.9.46 to BOAC, Aldermaston; regd 20.10.47 to Airways Training Ltd, Aldermaston; CoA (8470) issued 6.5.48; sold 28.9.48 and regd 6.12.48 to Patrick Motors Ltd, Elmdon; operated by Jersey Airlines 5.50; regd 27.4.51 to F H Wilson t/a Starways, Speke; used by Wright Aviation .53; regd 2.12.53 to R J Gates. t/a Federated Fruit Co, Speke and operated by Federated Air Transport; CoA lapsed 10.10.56; CoA renewed 10.4.58; regd 1.5.58 to Luton Airways Ltd, Luton; converted to Mk.6 10.58; regd 23.3.60 to Hants & Sussex Aviation Ltd. Portsmouth; regn cld as sold in France 21.8.61; regd in Senegal as **F-OBVJ** 6.9.61 to SA Ardic, Dakar, op Air Sénégal; CoA suspended 8.62; regn cld .64.

G-AHKT, c/n 6811, with Yeadon Aero Club in the mid-1950s [via A. Chivers]

G-AIYE, c/n 6815, of Olley Air Service Ltd at Croydon   *[via A. Chivers]*

6814   RAF serial **NR726**; TOC 5 MU, Kemble, 28.11.44; 428 R&SU, Buc, 4.10.45; 87 Gp CF, Buc, (later Le Bourget) 6.10.45; damaged 24.6.46; 18 MU, Dumfries, 13.12.46; sold to West Cumberland Air Services 11.3.48; regd **G-AKOC** (second) 18.3.48 to W A Herbert, t/a West Cumberland Air Services, Workington; CoA (10171) issued 2.7.48; sold 10.6.49 to unknown buyer; regn cld as sold abroad 21.7.49; shipped to Cairns, Qld, by sea; regd **VH-CFA** (1) 11.11.49 to Queensland Ambulance Transport Brigade, Cairns, named *Gron Owens;* crashed into sea 6 mls off coast near Double Island, Qld, 26.11.51 when returning from Vanrook Station with seriously injured patient; Capt. Hook searched for lights of Cairns until he ran out of fuel and ditched; he and ambulance officer were unable to drag the patient out of the aircraft before it sank; they were rescued by police search party six and a half hours later.

6815   RAF serial **NR727**; TOC 5 MU, Kemble, 1.12.44; sold to de Havilland Aircraft Co Ltd 17.5.46; regd **G-AIYE** 12.12.46 to Olley Air Service Ltd, Croydon; CoA (8823) issued 23.12.46; regd 16.2.53 to British Transport Commission; regd 19.2.53 to Cambrian Air Services Ltd, Cardiff; CoA lapsed 20.9.53; regd 3.5.54 to R A Peacock (Aviation) Ltd, Croydon; converted to Mk.4 and CoA renewed 21.9.54; regd 22.9.54 to L S Dawson, Sherburn-in-Elmet; regn cld 20.3.57 as sold in France; regd **F-OAYS** 5.4.57 to Sté Nord-Africaine de Travaux Aériens, Bône, Algeria; CoA suspended 18.5.62; regn cld .64

6816   RAF serial **NR728**; TOC 5 MU, Kemble, 2.12.44; RAE, Farnborough, 15.1.48; RPE, Westcott, 17.11.49; sold 2.12.53 and regd **G-ANJR** 12.12.53 to A J Whittemore (Aeradio) Ltd, Croydon; del 26.1.54; CoA issued 15.4.54; force-landed in bush nr Gulu,

Uganda, 27.4.54, on ferry flight to Sté Air Madagascar; regn cld 8.7.54 as sold in Madagascar; inspected at Ivato 23.9.54; regd **F-OAKX** 25.11.54 to Sté Air Madagascar, Ivato; regn cld as 'destroyed' 8.56.

6817   RAF serial **NR729**; TOC 4 RS, Madley, 9.1.45; damaged 18.7.46; DH for repair 30.7.46; 5 MU, Kemble, 21.2.47; Cat E 16.3.47; remains sold to D J Adie for spares 29.5.47.

6818   RAF serial **NR730**; TOC 5 MU, Kemble, 8.12.44; 64 Gp CF, Linton-on-Ouse [RCH:K], 26.4.48; 5 MU 27.2.50; sold to International Air Exports 16.8.50; regd **G-AMDG** 17.8.50 to International Air Exports Ltd, London; regd 26.10.50 to Autowork (Winchester) Ltd, Eastleigh; CoA issued 26.2.51; regn cld 8.3.51 as sold in France; regd **F-OAIR** 3.4.51 to COTECI, Casablanca; regd mid.52 to Maroc Air Service, Rabat; regd mid.53 to Cie de Transports Aériens Autrex, Hanoi; crashed and DBF, nr Nam-Dinh, S of Phu-Nhac 2.4.54, killing nine.

6819   RAF serial **NR731**; TOC 1316 Flt, Hendon, 31.12.44; transferred to RNethAF 17.4.45; sold to RNethAF 17.11.45 as **V-4**; 334 Sqn; regd **PH-RAF** 31.1.46 (CoR 393) to Ministerie van Verkeer en Energie/RLD and operated by KLM; retd to RNethAF 15.5.46 as **V-4** 15.5.46; regd **PH-VND** 4.9.48 (CoR 643) to Staat der Nederlanden for use with UN in Palestine as **9**; retd to Holland 7.10.48; regn cld 22.9.48 and returned to RNethAF as **V-4**; SOC 23.1.52; broken up .57.

6820   RAF serial **NR732**; TOC DH, Witney, 14.1.45; to R & J Park Ltd, Chiswick, for packing 26.4.45; shipped to Peru on *Laguna*, arriving Callao 4.7.45 for British Air Attaché; sold to Lineas Aéreas del Pacifico 1.48; NFT.

NR732, c/n 6820, the aircraft used by the British Air Attache in Peru, at an up-country airstrip. The inscription on the fuselage reads: Agregado Aereo Embajada Britanica, Lima, Peru   *[BAe Systems]*

G-ALBA, c/n 6821, of Trans-European Aviation who owned it in 1959-60, with another Rapide in the background   *[G M Simons collection]*

6821   RAF serial **NR733**; TOC School of Air Support, Old Sarum, 10.1.45; damaged in taxying accident at Weston Zoyland 2.1.46; DH 24.2.46; 18 MU, Dumfries, 26.9.46; sold to Aeroways 21.5.48; regd **G-ALBA** 27.5.48 to A W Coombs, t/a Aeroways, Croydon; regd 17.7.48 to Autowork (Winchester) Ltd, Eastleigh; CoA (10201) issued 24.7.48; regd 8.6.49 to R A Gunton, Cowes; sold 23.8.50 and regd 6.1.51 to Somerton Airways (Cowes) Ltd, Cowes; regd 8.8.51 to R A Short, Croydon; regd 3.10.51 to Skegness Airport Ltd, Ingoldmells; to Stanley Spencer's Tours Ltd .52; sold 12.12.52 and regd 19.3.53 to Skegness Air Taxi Service Ltd, Ingoldmells; to Ringway Air Charter Services .54; regd 11.7.55 to Airviews Ltd, Ringway; regd 19.1.59 to E D Kayton & A Ross, t/a Trans European Aviation, Swansea (Fairwood Common); regd 29.1.60 to Trans European Aviation Ltd, Swansea (later Baginton); leased to Skycraft Services 2.60 to 3.60; CoA lapsed 29.9.61; WFU at Baginton 9.61; sold 15.5.63 to unknown buyer; regn cld 23.8.64; remains scrapped at Baginton 11.64.

6822   RAF serial **NR734**; TOC CCCF, Northolt, 5.2.45; 41 OTU, Hawarden, 15.2.45; 58 OTU, Poulton, (later Hawarden) 22.3.45; SF Hawarden 21.8.45; DH 11.10.45; 18 MU, Dumfries, 14.5.46; regd **G-AKYY** 18.5.48 to D J Hayles, Croydon; regd 24.6.48 to W A Rollason Ltd, Croydon; CoA (10208) issued 8.11.48; regn cld 23.11.48 as sold abroad; regd in Argentina as **LV-AES** 26.2.4 to Zonas Oeste y Norte de Aerolineas Argentinas (ZONDA) through Sfreddo y Paolini Ltda (aircraft brokers); to Aerolineas Argentinas .50; to Taxis Aéreos Argentinas SA (TAASA), Buenos Aires; to Aero Expreso Barcella, named *Marmolin I;* to Aria Vilalta y Pizarro, Villa Maria, 12.62; CoA lapsed .64 but still regd 5.67.

6823   RAF serial **NR735**; TOC 5 MU, Kemble, 23.11.44; CRD at Gloster Aircraft Ltd 3.10.45; damaged, ROS by 67 MU 12.12.45; retd to Gloster Aircraft 28.2.46; sold to Gloster Aircraft Ltd 30.7.46; regd **G-AHRH** 22.5.46; CoA (7793) issued 18.10.46; CoA lapsed 5.9.58; regd 2.2.59 to Hants & Sussex Aviation Ltd, Portsmouth; converted to Mk.6 and CoA renewed 12.2.60; regn cld 12.2.60 as sold in Algeria; regd **F-OBOH** 25.2.60 to Sté Air Oasis, Laghouat, Algeria; CoA suspended 20.5.60, and regn cld.

6824   RAF serial **NR736**; TOC 5 MU, Kemble, 15.11.44; DH for civil conversion 11.3.46; regd **G-AHKR** 23.4.46 to MoS; to AAJC, Speke, 12.7.46; regd 6.6.46 to BOAC (BEA Div) and operated by Isle of Man Air Services Ltd; CoA (7669) issued 9.7.46; in bad weather, crashed onto hill between Greeba and Mt Slieu Ruy, Isle of Man 15.4.47, injuring seven; regn cld 19.9.47.

5H-AAN, c/n 6831, at a small airstrip in Tanzania   [G M Simons collection]

6825   RAF serial **NR737**; TOC 5 MU, Kemble, 20.11.44; DH for civil conversion 25.3.46; regd **G-AHXZ** 11.7.46 to MoS; CoA (8063) issued 5.9.46; regd 5.9.46 to BEA; operated by Channel Islands Airways Ltd 9.46 to 3.47; later named *RMA Charles Dickens;* DBF at Renfrew 28.8.51 while undergoing maintenance; regn cld same day.

6826   RAF serial **NR738**; TOC DH, Witney, 7.12.44; SF Halton [THA:C] 6.6.45; 5 MU, Kemble, 21.1.47; regd **G-AJSJ** 8.5.47 to Field Aircraft Services Ltd, Croydon, and sold to them 29.5.47; regd 15.7.47 to Franco-British Commercial & Industrial Co Ltd, London; CoA (9375) issued 25.7.47; crashed in Tunisia 18.9.47 on delivery flight to Sté Air Madagascar; regn cld 3.12.47.

6827   RAF serial **NR739**; TOC DH, Witney, 7.12.44; SF Halton [THA:H] 6.6.45; 4 RS, Swanton Morley, 22.3.48; 5 MU, Kemble, 8.4.49; ATDU, Gosport, 6.2.51; DH, Leavesden, 1.4.55; retd to ATDU 19.9.55; damaged in taxying accident 16.1.56; SOC 26.3.56; sold 21.6.57 to Hants & Sussex Aviation and del 27.6.57 from Weston-super-Mare; regd **G-APKA** 7.1.58 to Hants & Sussex Aviation Ltd, Portsmouth; converted to Mk.4 and CoA issued 6.5.58; regn cld 8.2.58 (?) as sold in Sierra Leone; del 1.7.58; regd **VR-LAE** .58 to Sierra Leone Airways, Freetown, named *Kassewe;* DBF at Hastings.

6828   RAF serial **NR740**; TOC 5 MU, Kemble, 17.1.45; transferred to FAA 17.10.45; Evanton SS 27.10.45; 781 Sqn, Lee-on-Solent [860], 23.8.46; AHU Stretton 9.7.47; SOC 19.9.49 and RTP; remains noted 26.3.50.

6829   RAF serial **NR741**; TOC 18 MU, Dumfries, 12.1.45; sold to Aeroways 21.5.48; regd **G-ALBB** 27.5.48 to A W Coombs, t/a Aeroways, Croydon; regd 24.8.48 to C W J Allen, Croydon; regd 9.9.48 to E A Taylor and operated by IAS (London) Ltd (Island Air Services), Heathrow, named *Pickles III;* CoA (10271) issued 10.9.48; entered into 1952 King's Cup Air Race with Monique Agazarian as pilot but failed to finish due to engine problems; crashed at London (Heathrow) Airport 1.8.52 during pleasure flight, when it was caught in the wake from a Stratocruiser; pilot (Wg Cdr Brian McGinn) and five of eight passengers injured; regn cld 19.12.52.

6830   RAF serial **NR742**; TOC SF Skaebrae 10.1.45; SF Grimsetter 27.8.45; SF Turnhouse 7.2.46; 66 Gp CF, Turnhouse [RCI:H] 17.10.46; damaged 9.6.47, ROS 16.6.47; 18 MU, Dumfries, 7.10.48; sold to R A Short 2.2.49; regd **G-ALGO** 17.2.49 to Sqn Ldr K J Nalson, Croydon; regd 14.9.49 to Airwork Ltd, Langley; regd 25.10.49 to Anglo-Iranian Oil Co Ltd, Abadan; CoA (10710) issued 2.12.49; hit refinery mast and crashed at Abadan, Iran, 10.7.51 and subsequently DBF; regn cld 11.7.51.

6831   RAF serial **NR743**; TOC 4 RS, Madley, [4-89] 10.1.45; 5 MU, Kemble, 2.12.46; sold to BOAC 1.7.47; CoA (9851) issued 14.11.47; regd **VP-KEF** .47 to East African Airways Corpn, Nairobi; regd 6.7.60 to Seychelles-Kilimanjaro Air Transport, Nairobi; re-regd in Tanzania as **5H-AAN** .64 to same owner; regd .69 to A-D Aviation Co Ltd, Nairobi; regd .71 to W J Baker, named *African Queen;* ferried from Dar-es-Salaam to Mahé 2.73 for Air Mahé; regd **VQ-SAD** or **VQ-SAG** 3.76, but NTU; to South Africa 12.74; regd **ZS-JGV** 20.1.75 to J English, Plettenburg Bay, Durban; regd 18.9.81 to J English, Greenbushes; still current.

G-ALET, c/n 6832, in the livery of North West Airlines, a company to which it was not registered!   *[Denis Fox collection]*

6832   RAF serial **NR744**; TOC DH, Witney, 14.1.45; 18 MU, Dumfries, 20.6.45; GOC Eastern Command, Langley; 61 Gp CF, Kenley, [RCE:A] 29.5.47; 18 MU 12.3.48; sold to Mannin Airways 20.9.48; regd **G-ALET** 15.10.48 to Capt J C Higgins, Ronaldsway; sold 1.12.48 and regd 14.2.49 to Mannin Airways Ltd, Ronaldsway; CoA (10403) issued 21.11.49; regn cld 10.9.51 as sold abroad; regd in France as **F-OALD** 4.6.52 to Sté des Caoutchoucs d'Extrême Orient (Far East Rubber Co), Saigon, Indochina; regd in Laos as **XW-TAB** 4.60 but believed NTU; NFT.

6833   RAF serial **NR745**; TOC DH, Witney, 18.12.44; CoA (7166) issued 24.3.45; 2 Aircraft Preparation Unit, Filton, 27.3.45; left UK 9.4.45, arr Cairo 13.4.45 and Salisbury, Southern Rhodesia, 21.4.45; regd **VP-YCO** 9.45 to Southern Rhodesia Air Services; regd 6.46 to Central African Airways; regn cld 23.8.49 as sold in South Africa; regd **ZS-DDH** 23.8.49 to Africair Ltd, Germiston; CoA lapsed 28.3.57; regn cld 26.1.60; believed scrapped and sold to Rhodesia as spares.

6834   RAF serial **NR746**; TOC DH, Witney, 18.12.44; CoA (7165) issued 24.3.45; 2 Aircraft Preparation Unit, Filton, 27.3.45; left UK 9.4.45, arr Cairo 13.4.45 and Salisbury, Southern Rhodesia, 21.4.45; regd **VP-YCP** 21.9.45 to Southern Rhodesia Air Services; regd 6.46 to Central African Airways; regn cld 4.48 as sold in South Africa; regd **ZS-BYT** 9.4.48, but NTU; to Israeli AF 29.6.48, possibly as **S-73**; NFT.

6835   RAF serial **NR747**; TOC DH, Witney, 12.12.44; SF Halton 10.6.45; 18 MU, Dumfries, 10.5.46; regd **G-AJHO** 14.2.47 to Brooklands Aviation Ltd, Shoreham (later Sywell) and sold to

them 10.3.47; CoA (9380) issued 27.6.47; CoA lapsed 13.4.62 and renewed 13.6.63; regd 27.6.63 to J S Weeks. t/a Army Free Fall Parachute Association; painted in colours of Rothmans Sports Foundation and nicknamed *Groanin Granny;* operated by Rhine Army Parachute Association, named *Siegfried;* converted to Mk.4 2.68; damaged in landing accident at Netheravon 27.7.75; sold 7.10.75 and regd 9.6.76 to East Anglian Aviation Society Ltd, Bassingbourn, for rebuild; collected from Netheravon 2.7.76; rebuilt at Tadlow, nr Bassingbourn, 1976-87 and flown 20.5.87 in colours of first aircraft used by King's Flight, G-ADDD; CoA renewed 14.3.88; regd 19.4.88 to M V Gauntlett and repainted in Brooklands Aviation colours as G-AJHO 10.88; regd 6.1.89 to Proteus Petroleum Aviation Ltd (Gauntlett's company); following winter overhaul, aircraft took off from Kidlington for Shoreham on 5.2.89 piloted by Charles Shea-Simmonds, who reported engine trouble and turned back to airfield; engine caught fire, prompting forced landing near Sescut Farm, Woodeaton; aircraft turned over on landing and was DBF, but pilot escaped; regn cld 31.3.89.

6836   RAF serial **NR748**; TOC DH, Witney, 12.12.44; 18 MU, Dumfries, 13.6.45; 1680 Flt, Prestwick, 9.8.45; damaged on landing at Hawarden 22.10.45; DH RU, Witney, 12.11.45 for repair; 18 MU 10.7.46; FCCS, Bovingdon, 8.9.47; 5 MU, Kemble, 22.2.49; ATDU, Gosport, 6.2.51; sold to C E Harper Aircraft 1.10.53; regd **G-ANEU** 5.10.53 to C E Harper Aircraft Co Ltd, Exeter; CoA issued 27.11.53; regn cld 26.8.54 as sold in France; regd **F-OAQU** 10.9.54 to Sté Transports Aériens du Gabon, Libreville; crashed on landing at Ekouata, French Equatorial Africa, 18.1.55.

C/n 6836 as NR748 at Croydon; this was one of the few late-built Dominies that saw lengthy RAF service   *[P H Dobbs via R C Sturtivant]*

Derby Aviation Ltd and its sister company Wolverhampton Aviation Ltd flew G-AIUL, c/n 6837, for several years in the mid-1950s [Denis Fox collection]

6837 RAF serial **NR749**; TOC 2 RS, Yatesbury, 14.1.45; 5 MU, Kemble, 16.8.45; regd **G-AIUL** 8.11.46 to Kenning Aviation Ltd, Derby (Burnaston) and sold to them 4.12.46; CoA (8814) issued 8.5.47; regd 9.6.47 to Air Transport Charter (CI) Ltd, Jersey (later Blackbushe), named *Saint Clement;* CoA lapsed 22.2.51; regd 21.1.52 to Aerocontacts Ltd, Gatwick; CoA renewed 20.6.52; regd 18.7.52 to C G Bowers, Newcastle-under-Lyme; regd 7.8.52 to Keele Street Pottery Co Ltd, Stoke-on-Trent (based at Wolverhampton); regd 9.6.54 to Wolverhampton Aviation Ltd and also used by Derby Aviation Ltd, Derby (Burnaston); these companies merged .54; regd 22.3.57 to A S Hubbard and operated by Olley Air Service Ltd, Croydon; CoA lapsed 8.3.58; modified to Mk.6 and CoA renewed 9.5.59; regd 1.5.59 to R K Dundas Ltd; regd 21.5.59 to Cumberland Aviation Services Ltd, t/a Casair, Silloth (later Crosby); regd 2.4.63 to Mayflower Air Services Ltd, Plymouth (Roborough); CoA lapsed 28.3.64; taken over 5.64 by British Westpoint Airlines Ltd, Exeter; regd 15.10.64 to A J Collins, t/a Flower Air Services, Jersey; CoA renewed 21.6.65; sold 18.3.67 and regd 30.5.67 to A F Ward, Booker; CoA lapsed 29.9.67 and aircraft stored at Booker; said to have been acquired by Historic Aircraft Museum, Southend, .72; regn cld 6.4.73; sold to I Jones and roaded to Southend by 3.75; roaded to J Pierce, Ley Farm, Chirk, 7.9.78; rebuild began 10.79 and still under way 9.95, but later abandoned; fuselage stored 2.00; extant.

6838 RAF serial **NR750**; TOC SF Halton [THA:F] 9.1.45; 5 MU, Kemble, 3.3.47; sold to A Hamson & Son Ltd 25.8.47; regd **G-AKIF** 24.9.47 to A Hamson & Son Ltd, Northampton; regd 22.10.47 to Manx Air Charters Ltd, Ronaldsway, named *Glen Wyllin;* CoA (9807) issued 22.12.47; for sale by L E H Airways Ltd, Horsey Toll (L E H was L E Hamson); regd 20.8.53 on name change to Manx Airlines Ltd (actually 2.53); leased to Skyflights 6.58 to 8.58; regd 16.10.58 to Hants & Sussex Aviation Ltd, Portsmouth; regd 5.2.59 to T H Marshall, Christchurch; regd 2.3.62 to Southern Counties Aerial Contracts Ltd, Staverton; CoA lapsed 28.6.62; re-regd on change of name 5.3.63 to Bardock Aviation Services Ltd; CoA renewed 5.3.64; company ceased trading late .64; CoA lapsed 4.3.65; sold 25.4.66 to Kentair Charters (Biggin Hill) Ltd, Biggin Hill, and regd to them 15.7.66; regd 2.5.68 to B S Schofield, t/a Parachute Regt Free Fall Club, Netheravon; rebuilt by Arrow Air Services, Shipdham, for Rothmans sales promotion in Norway, operated in the colours and markings of Rothmans Sports Foundation and named *The Rothmans Skydiver;* regn cld as sold in Norway 2.8.71; regd **LN-BEZ** 6.8.71 (CoR 1227) to Paralift Petter Ringvold, Asker; regn cld as sold to UK 30.4.73; restored to register as **G-AKIF** 15.6.73 to Sir Adrian C Swire, Booker; CoA renewed 17.8.73; regd 12.9.73 to Airborne Taxi Services Ltd, Booker; (temporarily painted as G-ADAE 5.74 for filming); operated by Classic Air Wings, Duxford; extant.

In its early life, c/n 6838 was Dominie NR750, which is seen here carrying the early postwar code THA denoting Station Flight Halton, but without an individual aircraft letter [M W Payne via R C Ashworth and P H T Green]

6839 RAF serial **NR751**; TOC 18 MU, Dumfries, 14.1.45; DH for civil conversion 27.3.46; regd **G-AHKA** 16.4.46 to de Havilland Aircraft Co Ltd and sold to them 31.8.46; CoA (7726) issued 20.5.46; used as company hack; equipped with manual variable pitch propellers by DH .49 to become first DH.89A Mk.5; regn cld as sold 7.12.53; regd **F-OAQL** 12.7.55 to Dept de la Guyane and operated by Sté Aérienne de Transport Guyane-Antilles (SATGA), Cayenne; DBR in ground accident at Sophie Inini airfield, Cayenne, 30.10.57.

6840 RAF serial **NR752**; TOC 18 MU, Dumfries, 14.1.45; MCS, Hendon, [CB:D] 24.9.45; 18 MU 1.11.46; 5 MU, Kemble, 9.12.48; regd **G-ALWO** 23.1.50 to Allen Aircraft Services Ltd, Croydon, and sold to them 13.2.50; regd 14.4.50 to Wesley & Nash Ltd, Croydon; CoA (10879) issued 10.5.50; regn cld 1.6.51 as sold abroad; regd in S Rhodesia as **VP-YHE** 7.51 to Rhodesian Investments Trust Ltd, Umtali; regd in Mozambique as **CR-ADM** .52 (to whom ?); crashed at Praia, Zululand, 15.3.55.

6841 RAF serial **NR753**; TOC 18 MU, Dumfries, 14.1.45; transferred to FAA 20.8.45; 782 Sqn, Donibristle, 30.8.45 to 9.47; 783 Sqn, (unconfirmed) Lee-on-Solent [601:LP]; RN Section, SLAW, Old Sarum, 3.48; collided with Anson NL248 in Old Sarum circuit 31.5.48, cutting off tailplane; crashed nr Bulford, Wilts, killing RAF pilot, AM(O)1 P J Bartlett and AM(A)1 P C Damon.

6842 RAF serial **NR754**; TOC 18 MU 17.1.45; transferred to FAA 20.8.45; 799B Sqn, Lee-on-Solent .45; collided with Anson NK738 in Lee-on-Solent circuit 25.1.46, crashed and DBF, killing CPO C J Holden and Sub Lt E T Alwood.

6843 RAF serial **NR755**; TOC 18 MU, Dumfries, 17.1.45; sold to BOAC 27.10.45; regd **LR-AAD**; CoA (7237) issued 16.10.45; del to Beirut 26.10.45; regd 27.11.45 to Middle East Air Line Co, Beirut, named *Sun'Neen;* sold in UK 19.12.47 and stored at Manchester; regd **G-AKZV** 24.5.48 to W A Rollason Ltd, Croydon; CoA renewed 12.11.48; regn cld 30.12.48 as sold in South America; regd in Argentina as **LV-AGW** 23.3.49 to ZONDA; to Aerolineas Argentinas .50; to Aerotransportes Rosario SRL 1.64; CoA lapsed 11.4.65; still regd 5.67.

G-AKIF, c/n 6838, in use for dropping parachutists of the Red Devils team at the Newcastle Town Show [G M Simons collection]

Rapide G-AHKA, c/n 6839, the Mk.5 prototype, at Hatfield in 1948. It had Gipsy Queen III engines with manually-operated variable-pitch propellers [via C N Dodds]

Post-war, c/n 6843 went to the Lebanon as LR-AAD of Middle East Air Line Co, Beirut   *[G M Simons collection]*

C/n 6843 was finally registered in Argentina, seen here as LV-AGW at Rosario on 11th April 1964   *[M Magnusson]*

The all-white c/n 6844, F-BHGR, with Nr.756 marked on the rudder, had originated as NR756 of the Fleet Air Arm   *[G M Simons collection]*

6844 RAF serial **NR756**; TOC 18 MU, Dumfries, 19.1.45; transferred to FAA 24.10.45; Evanton 24.10.45; 781 Sqn, Lee-on-Solent, 3.48 to 9.48; AHU Stretton 1.49; SOC 21.2.55; sold to Federated Fruit Co, Speke, 2.55; sale became subject of court martial; regd **G-AOAO** 22.3.55 to R J Gates, t/a Federated Fruit Co, Speke, and del 3.55; regd 2.8.55 to Hants & Sussex Aviation Ltd, Portsmouth; regn cld 4.1.56 as sold in France but CoA issued 5.1.56; regd **F-BHGR** 28.1.56 to SFASA, Toussus-le-Noble; transferred to Biscarosse .57, La Ferté-Gaucher 3.59, Biscarosse .59; regd to CN de Parachutisme de Biscarosse .63; to Chalon 10.69; regd .70 to Interclubs de Para de Bourgogne-Franche-Comté, Dijon; regd 7.71 to Jacques Noari, Toussus; CoA expired 26.10.71; regn cld 5.74; to Jean Salis, stored at Etampes and then La Ferté-Alais; NFT.

6845 RAF serial **NR769**; TOC 18 MU, Dumfries, 20.1.45; 4 RS, Madley, 17.7.46 [TML:C] (later Swanton Morley [TSM:S]); 5 MU, Kemble, 8.4.49; sold to Wilks & Chandler 11.1.50; regd **G-ALWL** 30.1.50 to V H Bellamy, t/a Flightways, Eastleigh; regd 24.10.50 to Southern Aerowork Ltd, Eastleigh; CoA issued 25.1.51; regd 3.3.52 to Transair Ltd, Croydon; regn cld 5.3.52 as sold in France; regd **F-BGPH** 7.4.52 to Sté Aigle Azur Indochine, Hanoi; regd **F-BEPE** 4.1.54 to Cie Laotienne de Commerce et Transport, Hanoi (reported as carrying serial no F-90); regd in Laos as **F-LAAE** 20.10.55 to Veha-Akat, Vientiane; crashed at Ban-Ban 23.12.60.

6846 RAF serial **NR770**; TOC DH, Witney, 14.2.45; CoA (7167) issued 19.6.45; shipped from Liverpool to Portugal on *Pandorian* 1.8.45, arr Lisbon 4.8.45; regd **CR-LBH** 26.1.46 to Direcçao de Exploraçao dos Transportes Aéreos (DTA), Luanda; DBF on start-up at Ambriz 10.5.57.

6847 RAF serial **NR771**; TOC DH, Witney, 14.2.45; CoA (7168) issued 19.6.45; shipped from Liverpool to Portugal on *Pandorian* 1.8.45, arr Lisbon 4.8.45; regd **CR-LBG** 19.1.46 to Direcçao de Exploraçao dos Transportes Aéreos (DTA), Luanda; sold to Transportes Aéreos Sao Tome 10.5.57; regd either **CR-SAB** or **CR-SAC**; flown to Angola 1970; derelict Angola 1976; NFT.

6848 RAF serial **NR772**; TOC DH, Witney, 20.2.45; regd **G-AGOX** 31.5.45 to BOAC, Nairobi; CoA (7184) issued 4.7.45; left UK 12.7.45, arr Nairobi 19.7.45; regd **VP-KCU** 10.8.45 to East African Airways Corp, Nairobi; force-landed in bush nr Garsen, 130 mls N of Mombassa, 28.6.46 and abandoned; regn cld .49.

6849 RAF serial **NR773**; TOC DH, Witney, 20.2.45; regd **G-AGOW** 31.5.45 to BOAC, Nairobi; CoA (7183) issued 6.7.45; left UK 11.7.45, arr Nairobi 19.7.45; regd **VP-KCV** 10.8.45 to East African Airways Corpn, Nairobi; retd to MoCA 11.8.49 and stored locally; regd .51 to Airwork (East Africa) Ltd; sold 10.51 and regd 16.4.52 to J E F Wilkins t/a Caspair, Mazinde; regd 26.7.54 to Sudan Interior Mission, Khartoum/Malakal (later renamed Missionary Aviation Fellowship); retd to UK 9.56; restored as **G-AGOW**

13.11.56 to S J Stevens, K Stevens and H J Adams, Croydon; used as spares at Croydon for **G-APJW**; regn cld 10.12.57.

6850 RAF serial **NR774**; TOC DH, Witney 20.2.45; sold to Scottish Airways Ltd; regd **G-AGOJ** 27.4.45 to Isle of Man Air Services Ltd, Ronaldsway; regd 10.9.45 to Scottish Airways Ltd, Renfrew; CoA (7177) issued 27.9.45; regd 1.2.47 to BEA; regd 8.7.48 to Lancashire Aircraft Corporation Ltd, Squires Gate; regd 28.2.55 to Skyways Ltd, Squires Gate, as company hack; operated by Deutsche Luftwerbung, Dusseldorf, .55; regd 27.5.59 to Skyways Coach Air Ltd, Lympne; modified to Mk.4; crashed on landing at Lympne 1.5.61; regn cld 13.6.61.

6851 RAF serial **NR775**; TOC 18 MU, Dumfries, 30.1.45; MCS, Hendon, 24.9.45; 18 MU 16.10.46; sold to W A Webb 24.5.48; regd **G-ALAT** 26.5.48 to W A Webb, Croydon; CoA (10211) issued 31.7.48; regd 9.8.48 to Elliot Trades Ltd, Cardiff; regd 13.4.49 to J H Watts, S K Davies, E Keith-Davies & Care Lines Ltd, t/a Cambrian Air Services Ltd, Cardiff, named *Anglesey*; regd 25.1.52 to Cambrian Air Services Ltd; CoA lapsed 16.11.53; regd 3.5.54 to R A Peacock (Aviation) Ltd, Croydon; regd 18.11.54 to A J Whittemore (Aeradio) Ltd, Croydon; CoA renewed 6.1.55; regn cld 24.1.55 as sold in France; regd **F-BHCE** to SALS, Avignon; regd .62 to Etat CR 10e Subdivision, Avignon; regd .63 to CIC de Parachutisme de Bourgogne Franche-Comté, Dijon; regd .66 to Centre Nationale de Parachutisme d'Aquitaine, Bergerac; regd .68 to CIC de Parachutisme Alsace, Strasbourg; CoA expired 3.69; WFU at Strasbourg; regn cld .70.

6852 RAF serial **NR776**; TOC RAF (Belgian) TS, Snailwell and Bottisham, 22.2.45; to Belgian AF 7.46 as **D-6**; 367e Escadrille [ZC:J], Evere (radio call-sign OTZCJ); 21e Escadrille; WFU 27.2.54; SOC 8.7.55.

6853 RAF serial **NR777**; TOC RAF (Belgian) TS, Snailwell and Bottisham, 22.2.45; to Belgian AF 7.46 as **D-7**; 367e Escadrille, Evere; 21e Escadrille; SOC 8.7.55 and stored; to L Vlieghe .62 and stored nr Antwerp (Duerne); shipped to R Souch in UK .94; shipped .97 from Southampton to New Zealand for rebuild by C Smith/Croydon Aircraft Co, Mandeville for The Rapide Group (Benno Tissi, Chris Hart, Steve Turner and Gerald Grocott, all Swissair pilots); on rebuild .01 for proposed flight from New Zealand to Switzerland and then to be painted in Swissair colours for use by Fliegersmuseum Altenrhein; regn **ZK-SWR** reserved; to Southair Ltd, Taieri, nr Dunedin, by 4.02 for completion of rebuild; extant.

6854 RAF serial **NR778**; TOC 18 MU, Dumfries, 15.2.45; 1 FU, Pershore, 11.10.45; MU 12.6.46; sold to Reid & Sigrist Ltd 5.12.46; regd **G-AIYY** 19.12.46 to Reid & Sigrist Ltd, Desford; CoA (8848) issued 23.1.47; regd 22.5.53 to Seear & Morford Ltd, Rochester; name changed to J K Seear & Co Ltd 29.5.54; CoA lapsed 30.4.64; stored at Rochester; regn cld 16.6.65.

G-ALAT, c/n 6851, of Cambrian Air Services, named "Anglesey" [via A. Chivers]

G-AGUF, c/n 6855, of Island Air Services, Heathrow, ended its life by crashing at Ramsgate in 1957 [via A. Chivers]

6855 RAF serial **NR779**; TOC 18 MU, Dumfries, 20.5.45; issued to MoCA 17.10.45; regd **G-AGUF** 18.10.45 to MoCA; operated by Railway Air Services Ltd, Speke; CoA (7235) issued 29.10.45; to Channel Islands Airways Ltd 14.1.46; regd 1.1.47 to BEA; regd 2.6.48 to J A R Helps, t/a Island Air Services, Heathrow; regd 7.10.48 to J A R Helps, Monique M Agazarian (later Mrs Rendall) and R C Rendall; regd 4.2.54 to Mrs M Rendall and R C Rendall t/a Island Air Services; based at Ramsgate from .57; crashed on take-off from Ramsgate 29.6.57; regn cld 9.8.57.

6856 RAF serial **NR780**; TOC CRD at DH, Hatfield, 27.2.45; 18 MU, Dumfries, 26.6.47; 5 MU, Kemble, 12.7.48; sold to Bendix Home Appliances Ltd 11.1.50; regd **G-ALWK** 26.1.50 to R C Cox, Fairoaks; CoA (10816) issued 12.4.50; regd 21.8.51 to Wg Cdr H C Kennard, t/a Air Kruise (Kent), Lympne; regd 25.2.55 to Air Kruise (Kent) Ltd; regd 8.8.55 to H C Kennard, initially t/a Air Kruise (Kent) and later as Trans Channel Airways, Ramsgate; regn cld 15.4.57 as sold in Algeria; regd **F-OBAL** 31.7.57 to Sté Gen d'Affrétements Aériens (Air Fret). Algiers; CoA suspended 28.7.62; regn cld .64.

6857 RAF serial **NR781**; TOC 18 MU, Dumfries, 23.2.45; transferred to FAA 24.10.45; Evanton SS 24.10.45; 782 Sqn, Donibristle, 2.46; 799B Sqn, Lee-on-Solent, 2.46; became 781 Sqn [858:LP, later 859:LP] 27.6.46; SF Lossiemouth 23.2.48; AHU Stretton 26.7.48; 782 Sqn, Donibristle, 27.7.48; DH, Witney, 5.11.48; AHU Stretton 18.5.49; AHU Arbroath 26.7.50; AHU Stretton (cocooned) 28.3.53; SOC 12.6.58 and RTP.

6858 RAF serial **NR782**; TOC 18 MU, Dumfries, 1.3.45; Berlin Air Cmd CF, Gatow, 30.5.45; 18 MU 26.7.45; transferred to FAA 26.7.45; Evanton 24.10.45; AHS Arbroath 8.10.46; Culham 1.5.47; 739 Sqn, Culham, 26.2.48; RDU Culham 1.8.50; AHS Arbroath 21.2.51; DH, Leavesden, 31.3.51; RDU Arbroath 23.10.51; Lossiemouth 12.2.53; 782 Sqn, Donibristle, [801:DO] 16.7.53; Northern CS/Airwork Ltd, Donibristle [901:DO] 10.10.53; AHU Lossiemouth 31.11.55; SF Culrose 16.12.61; SF Yeovilton 2.7.62; SF Culrose [999:CU] 25.9.62; sold to J H J Maxwell-Jones, Devonport, 25.6.63; regd **G-ASKI** 12.7.63 to W H W Lucas, Plymouth (Roborough); regd 14.10.64 to Hants & Sussex Aviation Ltd, Portsmouth; CoA issued 28.1.65; regn cld 16.2.65 as sold in Italy; regd **I-BOBJ** 8.4.65 to Aero Club Torino, Turin; damaged at Venaria Reale, Turin, .67; CoA lapsed 28.4.67; regn cld .71.

Air Kruise (Kent) Ltd owned G-ALWK, c/n 6856, from August 1951 to April 1957, when it was sold in Algeria [Denis Fox collection]

Dominie NR782, c/n 6858, carrying Station Flight Culdrose codes

Later as I-BOBJ of Aero Club Torino, c/n 6858 was damaged beyond repair in 1967

6859 RAF serial **NR783**; TOC 18 MU, Dumfries, 1.3.45; issued to MoCA 11.45; regd **G-AGUG** 18.10.45 to MoCA, operated by Railway Air Services Ltd, Speke; CoA (7236) issued 8.11.45; to Channel Islands Airways Ltd 15.1.46; regd 1.1.47 to BEA; regd 8.7.48 to Lancashire Aircraft Corporation Ltd, Squires Gate; leased to Standard Vacuum Oil Co Ltd for survey work in India and Pakistan; regn cld 11.4.53 as sold in Pakistan; regd **AP-AGL** .53 to Crescent Air Transport, Karachi; returned to Croydon in crates 19.7.56; restored as **G-AGUG** 4.9.56 to Morton Air Services Ltd, Croydon (later Gatwick); CoA renewed 11.3.57; badly damaged on take-off from Paksey, East Pakistan, 31.5.59 but repaired; converted to Mk.6; regn cld 10.1.63 as sold in France; regd **F-OCAG** 22.12.62 to Sté Eurafair; operated by Air Sénégal, Dakar, Senegal; CoA suspended at Ziguinchor, Senegal 27.3.63; regn cld .65.

6860 RAF serial **NR784**; TOC 57 OTU, Hawarden, 7.3.45; SF Skaebrae 5.7.45; SF Grimsetter 27.8.45; 13 Gp CF, Dalcross,

(later Turnhouse) 28.3.46; 18 MU, Dumfries, 26.6.46; sold to Birkett Air Service Ltd, Croydon, 20.1.47 and regd **G-AJDN** to them 27.1.47; CoA (8967) issued 30.4.47; regd 20.4.53 to Airwork Ltd, Blackbushe (later operated by AST, Perth); CoA lapsed 10.6.55; regd 28.4.58 to Hants & Sussex Aviation Ltd, Portsmouth; converted to Mk.4 and CoA renewed 29.8.58; regn cld as sold in Algeria 29.8.58; regd **F-OBIV** 8.9.58 to Sté Nord-Africaine de Travaux Aériens, Bône; CoA suspended 18.5.62; regn cld .65.

6861 RAF serial **NR785**; TOC 18 MU, Dumfries, 5.3.45; Berlin Air Cmd CF, Gatow, 30.5.45; 18 MU 29.7.45; 1 FU, Pershore, 8.11.45; 18 MU 12.6.46; sold to Reid & Sigrist Ltd, Desford, 5.12.46 and regd **G-AIZI** to them 30.12.46; CoA (8863) issued 25.3.47; regd 31.3.52 to R R Carne, Elstree; CoA renewed 2.5.52; after taking off from Croydon, crashed at Wallington 14.9.52 and DBF; R R Carne killed; regn cld same day.

Although never a BEA aircraft G-AHGD, c/n 6862, was painted specially in the then current colour scheme with a barely-readable legend commemmorating 25 years of the airline, 1947-1972 [via A. Chivers]

6862 RAF serial **NR786**; TOC 18 MU, Dumfries, 29.3.45; CRD at Lancashire Aircraft Corporation 8.7.45; sold to Lancashire Aircraft Corporation Ltd 28.3.46; regd **G-AHGD** 1.4.46 to them; CoA (7646) issued 17.5.46; regd 17.10.46 to Universal Flying Services Ltd, Kidlington (later Fairoaks); regd 31.10.49 to North Sea Air Transport Ltd, Hanworth (later Brough); regd 6.4.51 to L H Riddell, Sherburn-in-Elmet (later Yeadon and Tees-side); regd 22.2.70 to Lowe & Oliver Ltd, Booker; regd 1.5.75 to M R L Astor, Booker; painted as Z7258 *Women of the Empire* .80; repainted as G-AHGD; to Old Warden .87; sold 15.4.91 at Robert Brooks auction at Duxford and regd 28.5.91 to P and A Wood; loaned to Shuttleworth Collection, Old Warden; stalled and spun in from 500 feet at Wings & Wheels airshow at Audley End airfield 30.6.91 (pilot Peter Treadaway killed); regn cld 9.10.91; regd 27.11.91 to R Jones, Membury, for rebuild or spares; current status uncertain.

6863 RAF serial **NR787**; TOC 18 MU, Dumfries, 8.3.45; 87 Gp CF, Buc, (later Le Bourget) 30.5.45; 428 R&SU, Buc, 21.6.45; 87 Gp CF, Croydon, 30.1.46; DH 13.3.46; 18 MU 8.11.46; 4 RS, Swanton Morley, 12.2.48; 5 MU, Kemble, 8.4.49; sold to Air Navigation & Trading Co. Ltd 18.1.50; regd **G-ALXJ** 31.1.50 to Mrs D L Whyham for Air Navigation & Trading Co Ltd, Squires Gate; CoA(10831) issued 6.4.50; struck cliffs and crashed in sea off Skeirrid, nr Laxey Head, Isle of Man, 10.7.51 while flying from Blackpool (Squires Gate) to Ronaldsway; Capt Walker killed; regn cld 11.7.51.

6864 RAF serial **NR788**; TOC HQ ATA, White Waltham, 15.3.45; 32 MU, St. Athan, 20.4.45; retd to ATA; 18 MU, Dumfries, 10.11.45; regd **G-AKYX** 18.5.48 to D J Hayles, Croydon; CoA (10231) issued 29.7.48; sold 14.9.48 (but not regd) to W A Rollason Ltd, Croydon; regn cld 15.9.48 as sold abroad; regd in Argentina as **LV-AEN** 30.11.48 to Zonas Oeste y Norte de Aerolineas Argentinas (ZONDA) through Sfreddo y Paolini Ltda (aircraft brokers); re-regd **LV-FFO** 19.1.53 to O Arizaga & F Escales, Victoria, Entre Rios; CoA lapsed .60; re-regd **LV-AEN** to P Socca Gallegos, Rosario; derelict at Don Torcauto, Buenos Aires, .66

6865 RAF serial **NR789**; TOC 13 Gp CF, Inverness (later Dalcross), 16.3.45; SF Grimsetter 17.1.46; 13 Gp CF, Dalcross, (later Turnhouse) 28.3.46; FCCS, Northolt, (later Bovingdon) 6.2.47; 18 MU, Dumfries, 27.10.47; sold to Goodhew Aviation Co Ltd 27.1.48; regd **G-AKSL** 4.2.48 to Goodhew Aviation Co Ltd, Kidlington; CoA (10075) issued 28.5.48; CoA lapsed 18.5.51; regd 17.3.52 to Transair Ltd, Croydon; regn cld 28.4.52 as sold in France; regd **F-BGPL** 30.4.52 to Sté Aigle Azur Indochine,

Hanoi; CoA suspended at Saigon 14.6.52, probably as the result of an accident; regn cld 9.52.

6866 RAF serial **NR790**; TOC 18 MU, Dumfries, 16.3.45; CCCF, Leavesden, 7.6.45; starboard engine failed after take-off from Manorbier 14.1.46, force-landed but struck bank; SOC 14.2.46.

6867 RAF serial **NR791**; TOC 18 MU, Dumfries, 16.3.45; 1 FU, Pershore, 11.10.45; 18 MU 12.6.46; sold to Blackburn Aircraft Ltd 12.11.46; regd **G-AIWZ** 21.11.46 to North Sea Air Transport Ltd, Brough; CoA (8773) issued 13.1.47; crashed on landing at Brough 30.7.49; regn cld same day.

6868 RAF serial **NR792**; TOC 18 MU, Dumfries, 20.3.45; 87 Gp CF, Buc, 6.6.45; 428 R&SU, Buc, 21.6.45; 87 Gp CF, Croydon, 21.3.46; 18 MU 22.6.46; regd **G-AJKI** 19.3.47 to Airwork Ltd, Heston and sold to them 3.10.47; regd 16.5.47 to Anglo-Iranian Oil Co Ltd; CoA (9291) issued 31.10.47; seized in Iran 4.51 but UK CoA renewed 12.5.51; regd **EP-AAY** 10.51 to National Oil Co; UK regn cld 29.10.54 as 'sold in Iran'; current 6.59; NFT.

6869 RAF serial **NR793**; TOC 76 MU, Wroughton, 20.3.45; to South Shields docks 19.4.45; shipped to India on *City of Florence* 23.4.45, arr Bombay 1.6.45; sold to Nizam of Hyderabad 25.4.46; regd **VT-CBY** 8.5.47 to Air Services of India Ltd, Bombay, named *Gaganrekh;* regd 19.10.49 to Vardaraja Airways, Madras; regd 21.3.55 (CoR 777/5) to Madras Presidency Airways Ltd, Madras; damaged in gales at Calcutta 14.6.60 but possibly repaired; regn still current 30.6.68; NFT.

6870 RAF serial **NR794**; TOC SF Peterhead 23.3.45; damaged 18.5.45; ROS by 56 MU; SF Church Fenton 6.9.45; 18 MU, Dumfries, 10.6.47; sold to A Hamson and Son Ltd 11.12.47; regd **G-AKSE** 27.1.48 to L E H Airways Ltd, London; regd 16.2.48 to Manx Air Charters Ltd, Ronaldsway, named *Glen Mona;* CoA (9963) issued 10.3.48; regd on change of name to Manx Airlines Ltd 2.53; regd 10.10.58 to V H Bellamy, Eastleigh; regn cld 10.4.59 as sold in Eire; regd **EI-AKH** 14.5.59 to Skycraft Services Ltd; regn cld 22.12.60 as sold in UK; restored to register as **G-AKSE** 3.1.61 to Air Couriers (Transport) Ltd, Biggin Hill; converted to Mk.6 and CoA renewed 8.6.61; regn cld 7.4.63 as sold in France; regd **F-BLHE** 11.4.63 to Ets Rousseau, Dinard; crashed at Ouessant 28.9.66; regn cld .67.

6871 RAF serial **NR795**; TOC SF Skaebrae 26.3.45; crashed 1.6.45 when making a low pass over Millfield Camp, Orkney, during which undercarriage hit a Nissen hut; pilot, Flg. Off. J G R Lowe, and three others on board were killed; SOC 14.6.45.

G-AKSE, c/n 6870, of Manx Air Charters Ltd (later Manx Airlines Ltd)   *[G M Simons collection]*

C/n 6872 as V-2 of the Royal Netherlands Air Force was originally NR796 and was named "Zeeland" by the Dutch   *[Denis Fox collection]*

V-2 was registered PH-VNB for a time before returning to the UK as G-APBJ, seen here at Croydon in 1957 with a tiny registration on the fin and an Austin Ruby car and Bonanza EI-AJG for company   *[Denis Fox collection]*

6872   RAF serial **NR796**; TOC 18 MU, Dumfries, 29.3.45; 1316 Flt, Hendon, [CB:L] 31.5.45 for use by Dutch Naval Air Service; damaged 18.12.45; retd to 1316 Flt 8.3.46; to RNethAF 15.5.46 as **V-2**, named *Zeeland;* 334 Sqn; regd **PH-VNB** 3.9.48 to Staat der Nederlanden (CoR 642) for use by UN in Palestine as **8**; regn cld 22.9.48 and retd to Holland 7.10.48; retd to RNethAF as **V-2**; SOC 28.9.56; regd **G-APBJ** 14.5.57 to Aerocontacts (Aircraft Distributors) Ltd, Croydon; regn cld 6.9.57 as sold in Tunisia; inspected at Tunis 31.1.58; regd **F-OBGE** 20.3.58 to Sté Tunisienne de Réparations Aéronautiques et de Constructions (STRAC), Tunis; regd .62 to parent company SA Aéro Sahara, Tunis; CoA suspended 19.8.63; regn cld .64; broken up at Tunis.

G-AGOR, c/n 6877, never saw service as a Dominie before being registered to the Iraq Petroleum Transport Co Ltd at Haifa in 1945 [Denis Fox collection]

G-AGOR went to the Sudan in new hands in 1953 as VP-KLB and ended its days in Kenya as 5Y-KLB   *[Denis Fox collection]*

6873   RAF serial **NR797**; TOC DH, Witney, 10.4.45; issued to Airwork Ltd 30.4.45; regd **G-AGOP** 25.5.45 to Iraq Petroleum Transport Co Ltd, Haifa; CoA (7178) 3.8.45; left UK 11.8.45, arr Haifa 18.8.45; crashed nr Milepost 100, Syria, 25.6.48; regn cld same day.

6874   RAF serial **NR798**; TOC DH, Witney, 10.4.45; retd to Brush Coachworks 31.4.45; regd **G-AGOV** 31.5.45 to BOAC, Nairobi; CoA (7182) issued 29.8.45; left Hurn 31.8.45, arr Nairobi 7.9.45; re-regd **VP-KCY** 10.8.45 to East African Airways Corpn, Nairobi; regd 8.51 to Noon & Pierce Air Charters Ltd; regd 28.11.51 to Caspair Air Charter & Agencies Ltd, Nairobi; regd 6.6.53 to East African Airways Corpn, Nairobi; regd 15.8.60 to Caspair Ltd, Nairobi; crashed on take-off from Kaabong 23.12.61.

6875   RAF serial **NR799**; TOC DH, Witney, 12.4.45; regd **G-AGOU** 31.5.45 to BOAC, Nairobi; CoA (7181) 21.7.45; left UK 25.7.45, arr Nairobi 31.7.45; re-regd **VP-KCW** 10.8.45 to East African Airways Corpn, Nairobi; regd 2.9.49 to Sir Alexander Gibb & Ptnrs, Nairobi; regd in Southern Rhodesia as **VP-YNN** 11.55 to Sir Alexander Gibb & Ptnrs (Africa) Ltd, Salisbury; CoA lapsed 24.11.56; regn cld 27.12.57 and broken up for spares.

6876   RAF serial **NR800**; TOC DH, Witney, 12.4.45; regd **G-AGOT** 31.5.45 to BOAC, Nairobi; CoA (7180) 21.7.45; left UK 25.7.45, arr Nairobi 1.8.45; re-regd **VP-KCX** 10.8.45 to East African Airways Corpn, Nairobi; regn cld as sold 2.8.46; regd 18.10.48 to Jivrajs Air Services Ltd; WFU at Mombasa and regn cld 31.10.50.

6877   RAF serial **NR801**; TOC DH, Witney, 18.4.45; issued to Airwork Ltd 30.4.45; regd **G-AGOR** 25.5.45 to Iraq Petroleum Transport Co Ltd, Haifa; CoA (7179) 3.8.45; left UK 17.8.45, arr Haifa 21.8.45; converted to Mk.4; regd 10.4.53 to W H Knights, t/a The Missionary Aviation Fellowship; regn cld as transferred to Kenya 29.4.53; regd **VP-KLB** 11.8.53 to The Missionary Aviation Fellowship, Khartoum, Sudan; regd 14.9.54 to Caspair Air Charters & Agencies Ltd, Nairobi; re-regd **5Y-KLB** 8.65 to same owner; written off at Bukoba 7.8.68.

6878   RAF serial **NR802**; TOC 18 MU, Dumfries, 20.4.45; 87 Gp CF, Buc, 30.5.45; 428 R&SU, Buc, 29.6.45; 18 MU 4.4.46; regd **G-AKOG** (second)19.5.48 to Butlins Ltd, London, and sold to them 24.5.48; CoA (10154) issued 12.7.48; sold 1.6.49 and regd 9.8.49 to Aviation Traders Ltd, Gatwick; regd 7.11.50 to Bond Air Services Ltd, Gatwick; regd cld as sold in N Rhodesia 8.10.51; del from Croydon as **'VP-YCH'** 17.10.51; regd **VP-RCH** 10.51 to A Mechin, Lusaka; regd .52 to Lusaka Air Charter Ltd, Lusaka; regd .53 to Windsor Aviation Ltd, Lusaka; regd early .54 to Fishair (Pvt) Ltd, Marandellas; regd in S Rhodesia as **VP-YLF** 6.54 to Fishair (Pvt) Ltd, Marandellas; regd in France as **F-OBMQ** 5.5.9 to Sté l'Okoumé de Libreville and operated by Transgabon; regd mid-.59 to Cie Aéronautique Jean-Claude Brouillet, Libreville, but still operated by Transgabon; CoA suspended 30.5.63; regn cld .65.

6879   RAF serial **NR803**; TOC SF Talbenny 24.4.45; Dunkeswell 1.2.46; Valley 10.4.46; TCCF, Hendon, (later Upavon)

25.4.46; 18 MU, Dumfries, 7.10.46; to Airwork Ltd 1.7.47 for operation by Sperry Gyroscope Ltd, Langley until 15.7.49; 5 MU, Kemble, 5.1.50; sold to Fielding Aircraft 31.3.50; regd **G-AMAI** 4.4.50 to W J Nobbs, Fairoaks; CoA (10895) issued 7.7.50; regd 12.12.51 to A G Sheppard, Fairoaks; regn cld 10.7.52 as sold in Spain; regd **EC-AGP** 6.5.52 to F B Guell; regd .65 to Comercial Exportadora de Articules Perecederos SA (CEAPSA), Madrid; regn cld .82; sold to G Kurfiss (Air Classik GmbH) .85; to Frankfurt Airport authority and displayed in terminal as **"G-RYCR"**; sold to J Koch, Augsburg c.92 (later Lahr); rebuilt using parts of c/n 6437 D-ILIT and Permit issued 26.6.95 as **D-ILIT** with incorrect c/n "6347"; reflown 21.7.95 by C N Dodds; del to Sandown, IoW 15.10.95; regd **G-AMAI** 13.11.95 to J Koch t/a Island Aeroplane Co, Sandown (quoting correct c/n 6879); CoA issued 8.11.96; regn cld 19.4.99 and re-regd **D-ILIT**, Permit issued 23.12.99, CoR and CoA 22.5.00; extant at Grossenhain.

6880   RAF serial **NR804**; TOC 4 Del Flt, Clifton, 20.4.45; damaged 28.4.45; ROS by 50 MU 7.5.45; 4 ADF, Hutton Cranswick, 11.10.45; 18 MU, Dumfries, 15.11.45; SF Halton [THA:J] 10.5.46; 18 MU 4.6.47; sold to Air Navigation & Trading Co. Ltd 15.12.47; regd **G-AKJZ** 17.12.47 to East Anglian Flying Services Ltd, Southend; CoA (10262) issued 3.6.49; sold 28.2.57; CoA lapsed 27.3.57 and renewed 14.7.58; regd 14.8.58 to A S Hubbard, Biggin Hill; CoA lapsed 13.7.59; regn cld same day (notified 22.10.63!).

6881   RAF serial **NR805**; TOC 18 MU, Dumfries, 25.4.45; Berlin Air Cmd CF, Gatow, 30.5.45; damaged Cat AC/FA 6.6.45; 108 R&SU, Miramas, 19.7.45; 151 RU, Courtrai, 27.9.45; 18 MU 3.10.45; MCS, Hendon, 29.10.45; to Belgian Air Force 2.9.46 as **D-1**; 367e Escadrille [ZC:H], Evere (radio call-sign OTZCH); 21e Esc 1.2.48; SOC 24.2.53 after accident.

6882   RAF serial **NR806**; TOC 18 MU, Dumfries, 27.4.45; Berlin Air Cmd CF, Gatow, 30.5.45; 151 RU, Courtrai, 2.8.45; 18 MU 17.1.46; regd **G-AKZP** 20.5.48 to G C H Last, Croydon, and sold to him 24.5.48; CoA (10179) issued 2.6.49; regd 2.6.49 to E Holden, Speke; regd 14.1.53 to F Swift, Handforth; regd 1.4.54 to Ringway Air Charter Services Ltd, t/a Manchester Air Charter, Ringway; regd 14.3.56 to Gordon, Woodroffe & Co Ltd, El Adem, Libya, and operated by Oilfields Supply & Trading Co; regd 12.4.57 to Bahamas Helicopters (UK) Ltd, Libya; DBF after forced landing on Nabuel beach, nr Hammamet, 25 miles SE of Tunis, when flying to UK for overhaul 16.3.57; regn cld 20.5.57.

6883   RAF serial **NR807**; TOC 18 MU, Dumfries, 27.4.45; 87 Gp CF, Buc, 15.5.45; 428 R&SU, Buc, 29.6.45; 87 Gp CF; 18 MU 15.4.46; sold to Airwork Ltd 20.12.46; regd **G-AJGZ** 12.2.47 to Anglo-Iranian Oil Co Ltd; CoA (9030) issued 13.5.47; DBF at Agha Jari 16.7.49; regn cld 30.7.49.

6884   RAF serial **NR808**; TOC DH, Witney, 25.5.45; regd **G-AGSH** 25.7.45 to Channel Islands Airways Ltd, Croydon, t/a Jersey Airways; del to AAJC, Speke, 24.8.45 and CoA (7205) issued 25.8.45; regd 22.11.46 to MoCA, Jersey, for same operator; regd 1.5.47 to BEA, later named *RMA James Keir Hardie;* regd 4.5.56 to Airviews Ltd, Ringway; regn cld 17.4.57 as sold to Eire; regd **EI-AJO** 26.4.57 to Air Kruise (Ireland) Ltd; regn cld 1.7.57; restored as **G-AGSH** 18.7.57 to W S Shackleton Ltd, Kidlington; regd 7.2.58 to M L Thomas, t/a Jersey Airlines; regd 12.2.59 to Airlines (Jersey) Ltd; wore Alderney Airlines titles c.60; converted to Mk.6 8.60; regd 9.8.61 to Alares Development Co Ltd, Jersey, t/a Jersey Airlines; sold 12.1.62 and regd 25.1.62 to BEA, Land's End (St Just), named *RMA Lord Baden Powell;* sold 2.5.64 (the last Rapide in BEA service, and also the last biplane) and regd

As EI-AJO, c/n 6884 was used by Air Kruise (Ireland) Ltd for a very short time in 1957   *[G M Simons collection]*

As G-AGSH of Specialist Flying Training Ltd, c/n 6884 is seen on a visit to Cranwell on 5th July 1987; it was painted in the red & white colours of Alderney Airlines, who had operated it in 1960   *[P Ponting via P H T Green]*

Seen here with registration G-AGSI painted faintly on the fin and rudder, c/n 6886 was converted to Mk.4 with an ambulance configuration, and left Croydon in December 1954 to become VH-BFS   *[Denis Fox collection]*

TJ-ABP, c/n 6887, of Air Jordan was re-registered JY-ABP in 1954   *[via C N Dodds]*

Claiming to be the only Rapide to fly below sea level was JY-ABP, formerly G-AGSK of BEA   *[Denis Fox collection]*

20.5.64 to British Westpoint Airlines Ltd, Exeter; sold 30.5.65 to Gp Capt L C P Marton & Sqn Ldr J Grant, as nominees for RAF (Abingdon) Sport Parachute Association, Abingdon; del 28.5.65; named *Paranymph* in .74; nominees altered later; regd 8.4.75 to A V Heath t/a Pioneer Aviation Trust, Jersey; CoA lapsed 11.7.75 and rebuilt .75/.76; first flight 4.10.76 sold 19.10.76; CoA renewed 26.10.76; regd 16.3.77 to B Haddican, R W Archdale, C Edis, A Somers and P Harrison, t/a Pioneer Aviation Trust, Jersey; regd 10.4.81 to Pioneer Aviation Ltd, Jersey; CoA lapsed 7.6.82; regd 21.3.83 to Exair Travel Ltd, Exeter; CoA renewed 15.8.83; repossessed by Air & General Finance Ltd and ferried to Biggin Hill .84; rebuilt by Cobbaircraft and del to Carlisle (Crosby) 2.3.85; regd 8.3.85 to Specialist Flying Training Ltd, Crosby, and painted in Alderney Airlines colours; regd 15.6.89 to Venom Jet Promotions Ltd (Phillip Meeson), Hurn, named *Jemma Meeson;* CoA lapsed 10.5.92; to C Lovell, Bishops Waltham, for overhaul 6.93 and to Lower Upham .94; CoA renewed 20.6.95; repainted in BEA colours; regd 29.3.00 to Techair (London) Ltd (Phillip Meeson), Hurn; extant

6885 RAF serial **NR809**; TOC DH, Witney, 5.45; sold to Jersey Airways Ltd 30.6.45; regd **G-AGPI** 13.6.45 to Channel Islands Airways Ltd, Croydon, t/a Jersey & Guernsey Airways; CoA (7187) issued 30.6.45; regd 22.11.46 to MoCA, Jersey for same operator; regd 1.2.47 to BEA; regd 19.4.48 to F A Hill, t/a Lees-Hill Aviation, Elmdon; regd 17.5.49 to Somerton Airways Ltd, Cowes; overshot on landing and crashed at Cowes (Somerton) 16.6.49; regn cld same day; remains still at Somerton 3.52.

6886 RAF serial **NR810**; TOC DH, Witney, 15.5.45; regd **G-AGSI** 25.7.45 to Olley Air Service Ltd, Speke; CoA (7206) issued 15.8.45 and del to AAJC, Speke, 17.8.45; regd 16.2.53 to British Transport Commission, London; regd 19.2.53 to Cambrian Air Services Ltd, Cardiff; CoA lapsed 23.6.53; regd 21.4.54 to W. A. Shackleton Ltd on behalf of Queensland Ambulance Transport Brigade, Cairns, Qld, and converted to Mk.4; regd 28.10.54 to Queensland Ambulance Transport Brigade, Cairns; ferried to Cairns by Bush Pilots Airways 12.54 to 1.55; regn cld as sold to Australia 16.2.55; regd **VH-BFS** 16.2.55 to QATB (the first Rapide Mk.4 in Australia); regn cld as sold in New Hebrides 4.5.60 but operated in Australian markings by New Hebrides Airways Ltd, Port Vila, from 2.4.60, named *Miti Vaku;* regd **VQ-FAZ** 27.10.60 to

New Hebrides Airways Ltd; written off 17.5.62 due to deterioration and regn cld.

6887 RAF serial **NR811**; TOC DH, Witney, 18.5.45; issued to AAJC, Jersey, 23.10.45; regd **G-AGSK** 25.7.45 to Channel Islands Airways Ltd, Croydon and operated by Jersey Airways; CoA (7208) issued 27.8.45; regd 22.11.46 to MoCA, Jersey, for same operator; regd 1.1.47 to BEA, later named *RMA Lord Kitchener;* regd 15.12.52 to Gibraltar Airways Ltd; regn cld 2.10.53 as sold in Jordan (via Aerocontacts Ltd); regd **TJ-ABP** 10.53 to Air Jordan Co; re-regd **JY-ABP** 4.54; operated by Below Sea Level Flying Club; WFU at Amman 2.56.

6888 RAF serial **NR812**; TOC DH, Witney, 17.5.45; regd **G-AGSJ** 25.7.45 to Isle of Man Air Services Ltd, Speke; CoA (7207) issued 15.8.45 and del to AAJC, Speke, 20.8.45; regd 1.2.47 to BEA; regd 13.5.48 to W Hills-Grove-Hills, t/a Island Air Services, Scilly Isles (St Mary's), named *Isles of Scilly;* regn cld by Sec of State 18.9.48; to Trent Valley Aviation 9.48; regd 7.10.48 to The British Wagon Co Ltd, Rotherham; overhauled at Copenhagen (Kastrup) 11.49; regn cld 2.12.49 as sold abroad; regd **OY-ACZ** 12.5.50 to Zone-Redningskorpset, Copenhagen; force-landed, out of fuel, nr Lynge, Frederikssund, 3.3.54; regn cld 4.8.54.

6889 RAF serial **NR813**; TOC DH, Witney, 29.5.45; regd **G-AGPH** 13.6.45 to Channel Islands Airways Ltd, Croydon, t/a Jersey & Guernsey Airways; CoA (7186) issued 30.6.45; del 12.7.45; regd 22.11.46 to MoCA, Jersey, (but same operator); regd 1.2.47 to BEA, later named *RMA Sir Henry Havelock;* overturned on landing at Barra 6.12.51; regn cld same day.

6890 RAF serial **NR814**; TOC DH, Witney, 31.5.45; CoA (7223) issued 1.9.45; sold to KLM 7.9.45; regd **PH-RAA** 19.9.45 (CoR 369) to Ministerie van Verkeer en Energie/RLD and operated by KLM; regd **VP-KEA** 8.5.47 to East African Airways Corpn, Nairobi; CoA renewed 16.7.47; crashed on take-off from Butaiba, Lake Albert, 24.1.54 and DBF.

6891 RAF serial NR815; TOC DH, Witney, 31.5.45; CoA (7224) issued 6.9.45; sold to KLM 7.9.45; regd **PH-RAB** 19.9.45 (CoR 370) to Ministerie van Verkeer en Energie/RLD and operated by KLM; regd **VP-KEB** 5.47 to East African Airways Corpn, Nairobi; CoA renewed 30.7.47; written off in landing accident at Kasese 15.10.51.

PH-RAA, c/n 6890, is believed to have operated KLM's first post-war service from Amsterdam (Schiphol) on 6th September 1945   *[G M Simons collection]*

6892 RAF serial **NR828**; TOC 18 MU, Dumfries, 28.5.45; MCS, Hendon, 21.3.46; 18 MU 7.8.46; regd **G-AKZA** 18.5.48 to D J Hayles, Croydon; CoA (10198) issued 2.7.48; sold 5.10.48 (but not regd) to W A Rollason Ltd, Croydon; regn cld 15.10.48 as sold abroad; regd in Argentina as **LV-AEP** 31.12.48 to Zonas Oeste y Norte de Aerolineas Argentinas (ZONDA) through Sfreddo y Paolini Ltda (aircraft brokers); to Aerolineas Argentinas .50; to L Garrido, Villa Maria, Cordoba; to Aero Expreso Barcella, named *El Santo;* to Aria Vilalta y Pizarro 30.3.62; moved to Comodoro Rivadavia 2.63; CoA lapsed 3.63 but at Villa Maria 7.65 and still regd 5.67.

6893 RAF serial **NR829**; TOC DH, Witney, 30.5.45; CoA (7225) issued 19.9.45; sold to KLM 22.9.45; regd **PH-RAC** 1.10.45 (CoR 371) to Ministerie van Verkeer en Energie/RLD and operated by KLM; regd **VP-KEC** 5.47 to East African Airways Corpn, Nairobi; CoA renewed 3.9.47; written off in landing accident at Mafia Island, Tanganyika, 12.5.50.

6894 RAF serial **NR830**; TOC DH, Witney, 18.6.45; CoA (7233) issued 1.10.45; sold to BOAC 1.11.45; del to Beirut 2.10.45; regd **LR-AAE** 27.11.45 to Middle East Air Line Co, Beirut, named

A'Shahbah; sold in UK 19.12.47 and stored at Manchester; regd **G-AKZT** 28.5.48 to R L Whyham; operated by Air Navigation & Trading Co Ltd, Squires Gate; CoA renewed 30.3.49 (initially new CoA 10287 allocated); regd 28.3.52 to R K Dundas Ltd; regn cld 9.4.52 as sold in Ceylon; regd **CY-AAK** 9.4.52 to DoCA and operated by Ceylon Air Academy; re-regd **4R-AAK** .54; regn cld before .70.

6895 RAF serial **NR831**; TOC DH, Witney, 15.6.45; CoA (7226) issued 19.9.45; sold to KLM 24.9.45; regd **PH-RAD** 8.10.45 (CoR 372) to Ministerie van Verkeer en Energie/RLD and operated by KLM; regd **VP-KED** 5.47 to East African Airways Corpn, Nairobi; CoA renewed 3.9.47; sold to IDFAF 5.5.51, possibly as **1306**; regd **4X-AEI** 27.11.53 to Arkia-Israel Inland Airlines, Eilat, named *The Rover;* del to UK 11.8.55; regn cld as sold in UK 19.8.55; regd **G-ADYL (2)** 22.8.55 to Aeroservices Ltd, Croydon, taking registration of c/n 6311; CoA issued 28.11.55; regd 6.2.56 to Mitchell Aircraft Ltd, Portsmouth; regd 17.2.56 to F G Fox, Fairoaks; CoA lapsed 16.12.58; stored at Fairoaks; to Luton 31.1.62 for possible overhaul but reduced to spares; regn cld 28.3.63; airframe burned at Luton 7.64.

The result of a poor landing by Rapide VP-KEC, c/n 6893, at Mafia Island, Tanganyika, on 12th May 1950 [Denis Fox collection]

After restoration work as G-ADYL was abandoned at Luton, c/n 6895 was dumped outside revealing its former identity 4X-AEI on the rudder. It was finally burned in July 1964 [G M Simons collection]

Used in Portuguese East Africa as CR-GAI, this Rapide, c/n 6896, was formerly G-AKZW [via C N Dodds]

6896 RAF serial **NR832**; TOC DH, Witney, 18.6.45; CoA (7234) issued 5.10.45; sold to BOAC 1.11.45; del to Beirut 17.10.45; regd **LR-AAF** 27.11.45 to Middle East Air Line Co, Beirut, named *Al Carmel;* sold in UK 19.12.47 and stored at Manchester; regd **G-AKZW** 24.5.48 to W A Rollason Ltd, Croydon; CoA renewed 16.8.48; regd 19.8.48 to Mayfair Air Services Ltd, London; sold in Israel and flown to Cyprus but sale blocked; regd 3.5.49 to H A E Towle (prop of Mayfair Air Services Ltd), Denham; regd 21.6.49 to Adie Aviation Ltd, Croydon; regd 16.5.50 to Morton Air Services Ltd, Croydon; regn cld 26.4.52 as sold in Portuguese Guinea; erroneously regd in UK 24.5.52 to Govt of Portuguese Guinea and entry deleted; regd **CR-GAI** 5.52 to Transportes Aéreos da Guiné Portuguesa (TAGP); del 19.6.52; current .63; NFT

6897 RAF serial **NR833**; TOC DH, Witney, 18.6.45; CoA (7254) issued 23.10.45 to MoAP; sold to BOAC 6.12.45 for Iraqi Airways; regd **YI-ABD** 1.46 to Iraqi Airways, Baghdad and del 2.2.46; ferried to Almaza 7.47; regn cld 11.8.47; retd to UK; regd **G-AKDW** 25.8.47 to BEA and operated by Gibraltar Airways; inaugurated (with G-AKDX) Gibraltar to Tangier route; CoA renewed 24.8.47; stored at Manchester 4.48; regd 30.5.49 to Short Bros & Harland Ltd, Rochester; regd 27.5.58 to Avionics Ltd, Croydon; regn cld 23.6.58 as sold in Belgium; del via Ostend but not regd; del to Sté Aéro Sud 6.58; inspected at Toussus-le-Noble 6.8.58; regd **F-BCDB** 1.11.58 to Sté Aéro Sud, Maison Blanche, Algeria; regd mid-.59 to Sté Générale d'Affretements Aériens (Air Fret), Algiers; regd 1.61 to Sté Aéro Sud, Algiers; to Avignon 5.63; CoA suspended at Nîmes 7.6.63; still there 5.77 but removed by 8.78; to the Jean Salis Collection 8.7.83; to the Aviodome Museum, Schiphol-Centrum, Amsterdam, 18.4.84 for restoration as G-AKDW *City of Winchester*; on display .91; to Guy Black, Paddock Wood, early .93; to Mosquito Aircraft Museum, Salisbury Hall, London Colney, 12.93; regd **G-AKDW** 3.5.94 to de Havilland Aircraft Museum Trust Ltd, Salisbury Hall, where it is on display; museum renamed de Havilland Heritage Museum; extant.

6898 RAF serial **NR834**; TOC DH, Witney, 18.6.45; sold to BOAC 17.11.45; CoA (7255) issued 24.10.45 to MoAP; del to Iraq 5.1.46 to 13.1.46; regd **YI-ABE** 1.4.46 to Iraqi Airways, Baghdad; ferried to Almaza 7.47; regn cld 11.8.47; regd **G-AKDX** 25.8.47 to BEA and operated by Gibraltar Airways; inaugurated (with G-AKDW) Gibraltar to Tangier route; CoA renewed 24.8.47; regd 25.7.49 to Adie Aviation Ltd, Croydon; regd 11.2.50 to World Evangelisation Trust Ltd, London and operated by Missionary Aviation Fellowship in Sudan, named *Asfur Allah (God's Bird)*; regn cld 5.2.51 as transferred to Kenya; regd **VP-KIO** 6.2.51 to same owner; overhaul at Khartoum abandoned 10.52 and scrapped; regn cld 23.6.53.

6899 RAF serial **NR835**; TOC DH, Witney, 20.6.45; CoA (7245) issued 1.11.45; ferried from Witney 8.11.45; regd **CS-ADI** 11.45 to Companhia de Transportes Aéreos, Lisbon; to Portuguese AF 1.3.50 as **2307**; operated on communications duties until WFU .68 and stored at Sintra AFB; to Museo do Ar, Alverca for display; in store at Sintra 3.95/3.01; extant.

An engineless F-BCDB, c/n 6897, now restored as G-AKDW and displayed at Salisbury Hall [G M Simons collection]

On their way to Portugal the three Rapides, c/ns 6899-6901, were accompanied by a new Percival Proctor, CS-ADN   *[via P. Davis]*

6900   RAF serial **NR836**; TOC DH, Witney, 21.6.45; CoA (7246) issued 3.11.45; ferried from Witney 8.11.45; regd **CS-ADJ** 11.45 to Companhia de Transportes Aéreos, Lisbon; regd **CR-SAD** 27.2.50 to Linhas Aéreas São Tomé e Príncipe; regd .70 to Aeroclube de Angola; wfu .74 and acquired by VARIG for their museum at Porto Alegre; shipped to Brazil as **CR-LKR** and painted as 'PP-VAN' .80 to represent VARIG's first aircraft; stored for several years at Porto Alegre before being rebuilt in VARIG's workshops .86/,87; official presentation 7.5.87; lent to Museu Aerospacial, Rio de Janeiro, .96 and extant there 11.01.

6901   RAF serial **NR837**; TOC DH, Witney, 21.6.45; CoA (7247) issued 6.11.45; ferried from Witney 8.11.45; regd **CS-ADK**

11.45 to Companhia de Transportes Aéreos, Lisbon; to Linhas Aéreas São Tomé e Príncipe 27.2.50 as **CR-SAE**; to Angola for Aeroclube de Angola as **CR-LKS**; derelict in Angola after civil war in .74; to Germany, and stored at Wilhelmshaven docks to be restored; shipped to Museum of Flight & Transportation, Richmond, BC, Canada by .79; present status uncertain.

6902   RAF serial **NR838**; TOC DH, Witney, 23.6.45; CoA (7277) issued 26.11.45 for MoAP pre-civil regn, possibly for aborted export; to AAJC 11.4.46; regd **G-AHGG** 2.5.46 to Railway Air Services Ltd, Speke; regd 19.8.46 to Air Commerce Ltd, Croydon; taken over by Olley Air Service Ltd and regd to them 27.12.46; CoA lapsed 1.4.49; CoA renewed 9.4.52; regn cld as sold to Liberia

CR-LKS, c/n 6901, was found in semi-derelict condition at Luanda, Angola in 1975   *[MAP via P H T Green]*

G-AHGG, c/n 6902, of Olley Air Service Ltd in a hangar at Croydon [via A. Chivers]

VH-BIF, c/n 6903, of Airflite at Archerfield, Queensland, was used for grass-seeding [G M Simons collection]

10.4.52; del to Liberia 26.4.52; regd **EL-AAA** to Liberian National Airways; sold to Belgian Congo 4.11.55; regd **OO-CMS** 13.3.56 to Air Brousse, Léopoldville; DBR in forced landing nr Kikwit while flying from Léopoldville to Port Francqui 8.7.56; regn cld 11.10.56.

6903 RAF serial **NR839**; TOC DH, Witney, 29.6.45; CoA (7268) issued 19.11.45 to MoAP pre-civil regn, as possibly earmarked for Portugal; to AAJC 13.4.46; regd **G-AHGF** 2.5.46 to Railway Air Services Ltd, Speke; regd 1.2.47 to BEA; CoA lapsed 16.1.48; regd 5.7.48 to Lees-Hill Aviation (Birmingham) Ltd, Elmdon; intended for operation by Solent Airways .48/.49; regd 28.4.49 to F A Hill t/a Lees-Hill Aviation; CoA renewed 8.9.49; regd 30.6.52 to W A Shackleton Ltd; sold 25.11.52; regd 23.2.53 to V H

Bellamy, t/a Flightways, Eastleigh; converted to Mk.4 at Eastleigh 1953; regd 26.9.53 to K G R Bloomfield, Gisborne, New Zealand; regn **ZK-BCP** possibly allocated 11.53 but NTU; left UK 4.3.54, arr Gisborne 17.4.54; regd **ZK-BFK** 30.4.54 to K G R Bloomfield, Waitangi sheep station, Karaka, nr Gisborne; regn cld as sold in Australia 4.11.57; regd **VH-AWG** 4.11.57 to Airwork Co Pty Ltd, Archerfield, Qld; regd **VH-BIF** 15.6.59 to R G Carswell t/a Carsair Air Service Pty Ltd, Archerfield, Qld; regd 9.11.60 to M Ward, Archerfield, t/a Airflite, for grass-seeding and dingo bait dropping; to Northern School of Parachuting, Archerfield, .63, but sale not completed and retained by Airflite for charter work; WFU at Archerfield 10.65; regn cld 6.5.66 and burnt by fire service 3.6.68.

The first civil operator of c/n 6906 was Iraqi Airways, for whom the aircraft was purchased by BOAC as YI-ABF [Denis Fox collection]

G-ALGC, c/n 6906, in the colours of the short-lived Luton Airways about 1959   [Denis Fox collection]

6904   RAF serial **NR840**; TOC DH, Witney, 25.7.45; CoA (7269) issued to MoAP 16.11.45; regd **CR-LBN** 17.6.46 to Direcçao de Exploraçao dos Transportes Aéreos (DTA), Luanda; current .59; NFT.

6905   RAF serial **NR841**; TOC DH, Witney 30.7.45; retd to Brush Coachworks for civil conversion; CoA (7271) issued to MoAP 20.11.45; regd **CR-LBO** 24.5.46 to DTA, Luanda; sold to Transportes Aéreos de Cabo Verde as **CR-CAA**; probably the Rapide operated by Aeroclube de Cabo Verde, Santiago, which was used from 7.55 on local services in the Cape Verde Islands; NFT.

6906   RAF serial **NR842**; DH, Witney, 27.7.45; retd to Brush Coachworks for civil conversion 10.8.45; CoA (7299) issued

The remains of N8053 at St. Maarten, Netherlands Antilles, on 4th December 1986   [G M Simons collection]

17.12.45 to MoAP; sold to BOAC 1.1.46; regd **YI-ABF** 46 to Iraqi Airways, Baghdad; del 13.1.46; retd to UK 2.48 (or 12.48 ?); regd **G-ALGC** 3.1.49 to A R Pilgrim, London; CoA renewed 5.3.49; regd 22.6.49 to W H Cornish, Denton, Lancs; regd 8.9.49 to Melba Airways Ltd, Ringway; regd 17.7.52 to Wolverhampton Aviation Ltd, Wolverhampton; regd 11.2.53 to Heliwells Ltd, Walsall; regd 4.9.58 to TI (Group Services) Ltd, Birmingham (Elmdon); regd 10.10.58 to Luton Airways Ltd, Luton; conv to Mk.6 24.3.59; regd 9.2.60 to Keens (Watford) Ltd, Elstree; CoA lapsed 16.3.62; sold 12.11.62 and regd 21.5.63 to D C Cole and K B Kneely; CoA renewed 30.5.63; deconverted from Mk.6 14.5.63; sold 23.12.63; shortly after taking off from Biggin Hill for Coventry 9.3.64 with three passengers, pilot decide to return as ammeter failed to indicate a charge; overran taxiway and nosed over into piles of earth; regd 23.10.64 to Booilushag Ltd, Isle of Man; operated by Scillonia Airways, Shobdon, named *The Bishop*; CoA lapsed 21.7.66; used for spares at Shobdon, still extant 7.68; regn cld 28.2.73.

6907   RAF serial **NR843**; TOC DH, Witney, 23.7.45; retd to Brush Coachworks for civil conversion 10.8.45; CoA (7300) issued 17.12.45 to MoAP; sold to BOAC 1.1.46; regd **YI-ABG** .46 to Iraqi Airways, Baghdad; del 29.1.46; retd to UK 2.48 and stored at Manchester; regd **G-ALGE** 5.1.49 to W A Rollason Ltd, Croydon; CoA renewed 26.8.49; regd 8.9.49 to Melba Airways Ltd, Ringway; regd 6.5.52 to Wolverhampton Aviation Ltd, Wolverhampton; regd 3.6.54 to Kenning Aviation Ltd, Derby (Burnaston); regd 1.6.56 to L S Dawson, Yeadon; operated by Yorkshire Aeroplane Club; regd 8.12.59 to MacSmith Ltd, Newcastle (Woolsington); regd 7.3.60 to MacSmith Air Charter Ltd & Cumberland Aviation Services Ltd, t/a Casair, Carlisle (Crosby); CoA renewed 6.4.62; regn cld 5.7.62 as sold in Irish Republic; regd **EI-AMN** 31.7.62 to A C O'Hara & Ptnr; regd .62

VR-OAA, c/n 6908, had seen service with Railway Air Services, BEA and Gibraltar Airways before being modified to Mk.4 standard and exported to Malayan Airways in 1953   [via C N Dodds]

C/n 6911 as F-OBGY of Air Ivoire, Abidjan, with whom it served for three years   *[via A. Chivers]*

to J Farrell, Co Roscommon; regn cld 25.8.64 as sold in France; regd **F-BLXX** 15.9.64 to Aéro Club Centre Alsace Marin-la-Meslée, Colmar, named *Desirée II;* regd to CIC de Para-Alsace, Strasbourg 2.70; regd 8.70 to Aéro Club de Moselle-Parachutisme, Doncourt-les-Conflans; ferried to Meaux 31.10.72, for sale to USA; crated at Rotterdam 9.73; first deld to UK for restoration by Doug Bianchi, then shipped to USA; regd in USA as **N8053** to G E Frank; regd to D S Foley & N Peckham, Bloomfield Hills, MN; painted in BEA 1950 colour scheme and named *RMA Lord Shaftesbury;* to W Crorely (Leach ?); impounded at Phillipsburg, St Maarten, Dutch Antilles, .75 for drug smuggling; hit by hurricane 'David' 9.79, suffering much damage, including broken back; left derelict and scrapped by .90.

6908   RAF serial **NR844**; TOC DH, Witney, 28.7.45; regd **G-AGUU** 30.10.45 to Railway Air Services Ltd, Speke; CoA (7262) issued 10.1.46 and del to AAJC, Speke, 12.1.46; regd 1.2.47 to BEA, later named *RMA Sir Colin Campbell;* leased to Gibraltar Airways .47; regn cld 1.8.52 as sold in Malaya; regd **VR-OAA** 9.52 to Malayan Airways; converted to Mk.4 and del 1.53; sold 1.3.58 to Borneo Airways Ltd; regn cld 10.3.61.

6909   RAF serial **NR845**; TOC DH, Witney, 30.7.45; retd to Brush Coachworks for civil conversion 10.8.45; CoA (7309) issued 18.12.45 to MoAP; sold to BOAC 1.1.46; regd **YI-ABH** 1.46 to Iraqi Airways, Baghdad; del 20.1.46; retd to UK 2.48 and stored at Manchester; regd **G-ALGI** 13.1.49 to W Westoby, Squires Gate t/a Westair Flying Services; CoA renewed 7.7.49; regd 13.3.52 to W S Shackleton Ltd; regd 7.4.52 to C E Harper Aircraft Co Ltd, Exeter; regn cld 21.9.53 as sold in France; regd **F-OAND** 25.9.53 to Sté Transports Aériens du Gabon, Libreville; crashed 6.54; regn cld 23.9.54.

6910   RAF serial **NR846**; TOC DH, Witney, 30.7.45; retd to Brush Coachworks for civil conversion 10.8.45; regd **G-AGUR** 9.11.45 to Scottish Airways Ltd, Renfrew; CoA (7257) issued 20.12.45; del 12.1.46; regd 1.2.47 to BEA, later named *RMA Lord Roberts;* CoA lapsed 2.11.53; regd 30.11.53 to C E Harper Aircraft Co Ltd, Exeter; regd 15.7.54 to R Myhill and operated by his company Autair Ltd at Frankfurt; CoA renewed 16.7.54; DBR when overshot on landing at Frankfurt (Rhein Main) 2.8.54; regn cld 28.9.54.

6911   RAF serial **NR847**; TOC DH, Witney, 3.8.45; sold to Isle of Man Air Services Ltd 21.12.45; regd **G-AGUP** 24.10.45 to Isle of Man Air Services Ltd, Ronaldsway; CoA (7256) issued 20.12.45; regd 1.2.47 to BEA, later named *RMA Robert Peel;* damaged on landing at Alderney 21.7.52 but repaired; regd 18.8.52 to Airlines (Jersey) Ltd t/a Jersey Airlines; regd 30.5.57 to Hants & Sussex Aviation Ltd, Portsmouth; regn cld 26.2.58 as sold to French Ivory Coast; del 19.2.58; regd **F-OBGY** 6.5.58 to Air Ivoire, Abidjan; sold 25.7.61 to ETAT/SFATAT; regd **F-BJUZ** 22.3.62 to Centre Nationale de Parachutisme de Biscarosse; regd .63 to CIC de Parachutisme de l'Ile de France, La Ferté-Gaucher; regn cld .65.

6912   RAF serial **NR848**; TOC DH, Witney, 8.8.45; retd to Brush Coachworks for civil conversion 19.8.45; regd **G-AGUV** 30.10.45 to Great Southern & Western Airlines Ltd, Speke; CoA (7263) issued 9.1.46 and del to AAJC, Speke, same day; regd 1.2.47 to BEA, later named *RMA General Gordon;* regd 13.1.53 to Gibraltar Airways Ltd; regd 18.2.54 to A J Whittemore (Aeradio) Ltd, Croydon; modified to Srs.4; regd 5.4.54 to Iraq Petroleum Transport Co Ltd, Tripoli, Lebanon; crashed and DBF at Tarif, nr Bahrain, 26.4.54; regn cld 25.5.54.

G-AGZO, c/n 6913, of Marshalls of Cambridge was later sold to Belgium via France, only to be destroyed in the civil war in the Belgian Congo [via A. Chivers]

Named "Saint Lawrence", G-AGWC, c/n 6916, was used by Air Transport Charter (CI) Ltd from 1947 to 1952   *[Denis Fox collection]*

6913   RAF serial **NR849**; TOC DH, Witney, 10.8.45; retd to Brush Coachworks for civil conversion 16.8.45; regd **G-AGZO** 26.1.46 to Air Taxis (Croydon) Ltd and sold to them 16.2.46; CoA (7405) issued 11.2.46; Air Taxis (Croydon) Ltd ceased trading early .48; regd 13.1.48 to F T Bingham (of Air Taxis); regd 31.7.48 to Marshall's Flying School Ltd, Cambridge; regd 9.4.52 to Marshall's Flying Services Ltd, Cambridge; regn cld as sold in France 24.5.62; regd **F-BGZT** 3.7.62 to Ets Rousseau Aviation, Dinard; sold to Belgium 11.62; regd **OO-ITI** 5.10.62 to R Van Risseghem Lint, Antwerp; destroyed by SAAB J29 fighters of UN at Kolwezi, Belgian Congo, 29.12.62; regn cld 28.7.64.

6914   RAF serial **NR850**; TOC DH, Witney, 14.8.45; retd to Brush Coachworks for conversion to Mk.3 Rapide 29.8.45; CoA (7540) issued 18.3.46; sold to Aircraft Operating Co Ltd 23.3.46; regd **ZS-ATV** to Aircraft Operating Co of South Africa Pty Ltd 12.4.46; DBF on take-off from Thysville, Congo 5.6.51.

6915   RAF serial **NR851**; TOC DH, Witney, 14.8.45; retd to Brush Coachworks for conversion to Mk.3 Rapide 29.8.45; CoA (7539) issued 22.3.46; sold to Aircraft Operating Co Ltd 23.3.46; regd **ZS-ATW** 12.4.46 to Aircraft Operating Co of South Africa Pty Ltd; DBF during engine start-up (or crashed and DBF ?) at Beit Bridge 11.12.46 .

6916   RAF serial **NR852**; TOC DH, Witney, 23.8.45; regd **G-AGWC** 13.12.45 to British-American Air Services Ltd, White Waltham, and sold to them 21.1.46; CoA (7316) issued 21.1.46; del 28.1.46; regd 9.4.47 to Air Transport Charter (CI) Ltd, Jersey (later Blackbushe), named *Saint Lawrence;* nominal regn change on take-over by Lambert's Trust Ltd 27.10.50; regd 21.1.52 to Aerocontacts Ltd, Gatwick; regn cld as sold in Pakistan 9.7.52; regd **AP-ADM** 8.52 to Crescent Air Transport Ltd, Karachi; DBR when tyre burst on landing at Nawabshah, Sind, 17.3.53; regn cld .54.

6917   RAF serial **NR853**; TOC DH, Witney, 31.8.45; regd **G-AGWR** 8.12.45 to Morton Air Services Ltd, Croydon and sold to them 27.1.46; at DH, Witney, 13.1.46; CoA (7302) issued 25.1.46; to Palestine 28.8.48 for use with UN forces as **1**; returned to UK 8.10.48; regn cld as sold to Denmark 30.4.54; regd **OY-DYA** 15.6.54 to Zone-Redningskorpset, Copenhagen (Kastrup); regn cld 21.4.56 as sold to Sweden; regd **SE-CDI** 20.4.56 to AB Europa-Flyg, Bromma; crashed into trees at Jusdala, nr Vimmerby, 23.12.56, during forced landing in snowstorm; was returning from Denmark after overhaul and fitting with under-wing lighting system; regn cld 31.12.56.

6918   RAF serial **RL936**; TOC DH, Witney, 31.8.45; regd **G-AGWP** 8.12.45 to Morton Air Services Ltd, Croydon and sold to them 19.1.46; CoA (7301) issued 18.1.46; to Palestine 28.8.48 for use with UN forces as **2**; returned to UK 6.10.48, re-regd

G-AGWP; operated by Pakistan Petroleum 12.57; regd 22.6.60 to Aerocontacts (Aircraft Distributors) Ltd, Gatwick; regn cld as sold in Congo 28.9.60; regd **OO-CJE** to Air Brousse, Léopoldville, 15.11.60; to Cogeair, Kinshasa; to AMAZ, Ndola; re-regd **9O-CJE** .61; re-regd **9Q-CJE**; WFU after accident at Mweka 1962.

6919   RAF serial **RL937**; TOC DH, Witney, 5.9.45; CoA (7358) issued 16.1.46; sold to Sweden 26.1.46 and del from Hatfield 7.2.46; regd **SE-APH** 15.3.46 to Svensk Flygtjänst AB, Stockholm (Bromma); destroyed by fire in hangar at Bromma 9.4.47; regn cld 19.11.47.

6920   RAF serial **RL938**; TOC DH, Witney, 12.9.45; CoA (7396) issued 18.1.46; sold to Rootes, Blades, Wharf & Smith for Brazil 27.1.46; shipped to Brazil on *Potaro*, arr Rio de Janeiro 16.3.46; regd **PP-AIA** 11.9.46 to Arco-Iris Viacao Aerea SA, São Paulo; auctioned 20.10.49 at Caxias do Sul and bought by Vicente Sangiacomo; sold to Armando Azevedo Andrade 30.3.50; sold to Adhemar de Barros Filho 25.10.51; donated to Erlono Salzano 14.1.54; crashed at Coroata, Maranhao, 10.5.56.

6921   RAF serial **RL939**; TOC DH, Witney, 17.9.45; CoA (7410) issued 25.1.46; sold to Rootes, Blades, Wharf & Smith for Brazil 17.2.46; regd **PP-AID** 11.9.46 to Arco-Iris Viacao Aerea SA, São Paulo; crashed on take-off from Congonhas airport .46; regn cld 18.12.46.

6922   RAF serial **RL940**; TOC DH, Witney, 9.10.45; CoA (7409) issued 25.1.46; sold to Rootes, Blades, Wharf & Smith for Brazil 9.2.46; shipped to Brazil on *Potaro,* arr Rio de Janeiro 16.3.46; regd **PP-AIB** 11.9.46 to Arco-Iris Viacao Aerea SA, São Paulo; crashed at Fartura, State of São Paulo, 24.12.46; regn cld 21.1.47.

6923   RAF serial **RL941**; TOC DH, Witney, 9.10.45; CoA (7411) issued 28.1.46; sold to Rootes, Blades, Wharf & Smith for Brazil 9.2.46; shipped to Brazil on *Potaro,* arr Rio de Janeiro 3.5.46; regd **PP-AIC** 11.9.46 to Arco-Iris Viacao Aerea SA, São Paulo; auctioned 20.10.49 at Caxios do Sul and bought by Vicente Sangiacomo; sold 30.3.50 to Armando Azevedo Andrade; sold 25.10.51 to Adhemar de Barros Filho; regn cld 11.5.53.

6924   RAF serial **RL942**; TOC DH, Witney, 30.10.45; CoA (7462) issued 14.2.46 to de Havilland Aircraft of South Africa; sold in Southern Rhodesia 17.3.46; regd **VP-YDF** 4.46 to Southern Rhodesia Air Services; regd 6.46 to Central African Airways; regn cld 10.49 as sold in Northern Rhodesia; regd **VP-RBU** 10.49 to Northern Rhodesia Aviation Services Ltd; to Zambesi Airways Ltd .50; re-regd VP-YDF 10.50 to Field Aircraft Services of Rhodesia Ltd, Salisbury; regd .52 to Fishair Ltd, Marandellas; regd .54 to Fishair (Pvt) Ltd; CoA lapsed 10.8.54; regn cld late .56.

VP-YDF, c/n 6924, at Belvedere, Salisbury, Southern Rhodesia, on 9th July 1951   *[L T Chamberlain via P H T Green]*

G-AHAG, c/n 6926, was based at Brough and used by Blackburn Aircraft and later by Hawker Siddeley Aviation as the company 'hack' until 1965
[via C N Dodds]

G-AHAG, later with Thames Valley Airsport displaying the repairs made after being involved in a strange accident in July 1972   *[via C N Dodds]*

CF-DIM, c/n 6928, showing the extended fin incorporated when Rapides were fitted with floats, which in this case have been replaced by a conventional wheeled undercarriage   *[via C N Dodds]*

6925   RAF serial **RL943**; TOC DH, Witney, 30.10.45; CoA (7513) issued 20.2.46 to de Havilland Aircraft of South Africa; sold in Southern Rhodesia 17.3.46; regd **VP-YDE** 4.46 to Southern Rhodesia Air Services; regd 6.46 to Central African Airways; regn cld 8.49 as sold in South Africa; regd **ZS-BZV** 15.8.49 to Commercial Air Services Ltd, t/a Comair; regd 8.53 to Drakensberg Air Services (Pty) Ltd, Ladysmith; badly damaged in tornado at Ladysmith 10.1.55 but repaired; regn cld 26.10.56 as sold in Belgian Congo; regd **OO-CJT** 27.10.56 to Air Brousse SPRL, Léopoldville; re-regd **9O-CJT**; crashed at Malegbe 6.10.60 due to fuel starvation; regn cld 30.11.60.

6926   RAF serial **RL944**; TOC DH, Witney, 31.10.45; regd **G-AHAG** 31.1.46 to Lancashire Aircraft Corpn Ltd, Squires Gate; CoA (7437) issued 18.2.46; regd 17.10.46 to Universal Flying Services Ltd, Kidlington and Fairoaks; regd 31.10.49 to North Sea Air Transport Ltd, Hanworth and Brough (operated by Blackburn Aircraft Ltd); regd 6.12.63 to Hawker Siddeley Aviation Ltd, Brough; transferred to Dunsfold 5.7.65 but WFU same month; regd 20.7.65 to Hawker Siddeley Aviation (Leasing) Ltd; regn cld 20.10.65 as 'destroyed'; roaded to Blackbushe 1.2.66 and to Booker 1.5.66 for rebuild; CoA renewed 8.6.66; regd 5.4.66 to K B Neely, t/a Scillonia Airways, Land's End (St Just), named *Bryher;* to Scenic Air Flights ?; to M de Cartier t/a Thames Valley Airsport, Compton Abbas (later Halfpenny Green), used for parachuting; on 17.7.72 this aircraft was the subject of one of the strangest accidents involving a DH.89, when at 10,500ft in formation with an Islander of Thruxton Aviation. At the time of exit the DH.89 slid

under the Islander from which Mike Taylor exited and hit the rear fuselage of 'HAG, breaking his wrist. Mike Bolton crashed through the roof of the Rapide, ending up in the main cabin with both wrists smashed; all involved landed safely; sold 1.10.72 and regd 1.2.73 to M E R Coughlan t/a MM Aviation, Lympne (later Ford); CoA lapsed 17.7.73 and stored at Blandford Forum; regd 14.3.80 to R Jones t/a Southern Sailplanes, Membury; under restoration; regd 2.3.00 to Pelham Ltd, Membury; extant.

6927   RAF serial **RL945**; TOC DH, Witney, 13.11.45; sold to Canada 11.1.46 but sale cancelled; sold to DH 23.3.46 for Organizacio Mineira de Transportes Aéreos, Belo Horizonte; regn **PP-OMB** reserved but formal registration did not take place; crashed at São Joao del Rei, Minas Gerais, 20.9.46.

6928   RAF serial **RL946**; TOC DH, Witney, 31.10.45; sold to DH Canada 11.1.46; regd **CF-DIM** 9.8.46 to de Havilland Aircraft of Canada Ltd, Toronto; regd 4.51 to G H Wheeler, Toronto; to Matane Air Transport, Quebec, 14.12.51; DBF at Matane 19.6.53.

6929   RAF serial **RL947**; TOC 18 MU, Dumfries, 1.1.46; TTCCF, Wyton, 20.6.46; 18 MU 23.7.47; initially allocated regn **G-AKMD** but NTU; sold to R N W Miller of Connellan Airways 11.3.48; regd **VH-BKR** 4.3.48 to E J Connellan, t/a Connellan Airways, Alice Springs, NT; CoA (10059) issued 9.4.48; flown to Australia; regd 14.3.51 to Connellan Airways Ltd; re-regd **VH-CLH** 5.11.58 to same owner; WFU at Alice Springs 31.7.62 and scrapped after failing major inspection.

G-AKSG , c/n 6631, of Air Navigaton & Trading Co Ltd who later sold it to Silver City   *[G M Simons collection]*

6930 RAF serial **RL948**; TOC 18 MU, Dumfries, 1.1.46; 27 Gp CF, Southrop, [TSO:C] 26.6.46 (later Fairford and Debden); ERS, Debden, 29.9.47; 18 MU 26.2.48; sold to Aeroways Ltd 21.5.48; regd **G-ALAX** 27.5.48 to A W Coombs, t/a Aeroways Ltd, Croydon; CoA (10282) issued 4.9.48; regd 7.9.48 to Autowork (Winchester) Ltd, Eastleigh, and operated by Flightways Ltd; regd 10.6.49 to Saunders-Roe Ltd, Bembridge (later Sandown); badly damaged on take-off from Bembridge 26.10.53 but repaired; regd 21.7.60 to G K Tulloch, Leuchars, and operated by Scottish Parachute Club, Perth; sold 8.11.66 to unknown buyer, possibly at Luton; used in 20th Century Fox film 'Fathom' starring Raquel Welch, .66; CoA lapsed 8.3.67 and WFU at Luton; regn cld 7.12.67; roaded to Old Warden; to D D Johnson, t/a Durney Aeronautical Collection, Andover, .71 for eventual rebuild (a composite airframe consisting of components from G-AFRK, G-AHGC, G-AHJS and G-ASRJ); still stored in garden at Andover .94; current staus uncertain.

6931 RAF serial **RL949**; TOC 18 MU, Dumfries, 3.1.46; TTCCF, Wyton [TWY:D], 29.6.46; 18 MU 18.9.47; sold to Air Navigation & Trading Co Ltd 27.1.48; regd **G-AKSG** 28.1.48 to R L Whyham and operated by Air Navigation & Trading Co Ltd, Squires Gate; CoA (10146) issued 25.8.49; regd 10.2.54 to Silver City Airways Ltd, Blackbushe; regd 27.5.55 to V H Bellamy, Eastleigh; converted to Mk.4 4.56; regn cld 10.5.56 as sold in France; regd **F-BHAF** 10.7.56 to Air Ouest, Nantes; sold late .58 to Sté Générale d'Affrétements Aériens (Air Fret), Algiers; regd late .60 to Sté Air Oasis, Laghouat, Algeria; CoA suspended at Bastia 7.3.62; regn cld .63.

6932 RAF serial **RL950**; TOC 18 MU, Dumfries, 2.1.46; EFS Handling Sqn, Hullavington, 31.7.46; 18 MU 23.9.46; Staff College CF, Booker, 19.2.47; 21 EFTS, Booker; 18 MU 14.1.48; sold to Aeroways Ltd 21.5.48; regd **G-ALAZ** 27.5.48 to A W Coombs, t/a Aeroways Ltd, Croydon; regd 17.7.48 to Autowork (Winchester) Ltd, Eastleigh; regn cld 27.7.48 as sold abroad; CoA (10200) issued 7.8.48; regd in Belgian Congo as **OO-CFI** 5.8.48 to Air Congo, Léopoldville; regd 18.5.50 to SABENA, Léopoldville; regd cld 19.11.50 (or 19.12.50) as sold in Angola; regd **CR-LCK** 20.12.50 to Direcçao de Exploraçao dos Transportes Aéreos (DTA), Luanda; to Aeroclube de Angola, Luanda; WFU .75, derelict in Angola, complete with instruments.

6933 RAF serial **RL951**; TOC 18 MU, Dumfries, 4.2.46; King's Flight, Benson, 16.7.46; crashed in field 1 ml NW of Mount Farm airfield on night of 1.11.46 when engine failed over Oxford due to fuel starvation; SOC 10.2.47.

6934 RAF serial **RL952**; TOC DH, Witney, 20.2.46; CoA (7525) issued 6.3.46 to MoAP pre-civil regn; to AAJC 2.4.46; regd **G-AHGH** 2.5.46 to Railway Air Services Ltd, Speke; regd 1.2.47 to BEA; regd 8.6.48 to Patrick-Duval Aviation Ltd, Elmdon; regd 9.8.48 to Patrick Motors Ltd; operated by Flightways Ltd, Eastleigh, .52-.53; regn cld as sold to Sweden 10.6.53; regd **SE-BXZ** 31.7.53 to Svenska Aero Westlund, Orebro; regd 16.8.55 to Svenska Aero Westlund, Rosen & Gustavsson AB, Orebro; damaged in crash at Bromma 29.7.57; regd 2.12.58 to Svenska Aero, K O Gustavsson AB, Orebro; CoA lapsed 23.4.59; to A Fredriksson, Goteborg; regn cld 31.12.65; wings to Luftfartsmuseet, Arlanda.

SE-BXZ was the former G-AHGH, c/n 6934, and was owned by Svenska Aero whose titles it wears [Denis Fox collection]

A rare picture of Venezulan Rapide YV-P-BPE, a former floatplane minus spats, at Toronto in June 1949; this was c/n 6938, the only member of the DH Dragon family to be registered in Venezuela [Denis Fox collection]

6935   RAF serial **RL953**; TOC DH, Witney, 1.1.46; CoA (7562) issued 18.3.46 to MoAP pre-civil regn; to AAJC 5.4.46; regd **G-AHGI** 2.5.46 to Railway Air Services Ltd, Speke; regd 1.2.47 to BEA; to Scottish Airways Ltd 9.9.46; regd 3.6.48 to Patrick-Duval Aviation Ltd, Elmdon; regd 9.8.48 to Patrick Motors Ltd; CoA lapsed 12.7.49; renewed 19.8.52; regn cld as sold to French Indochina 13.11.52; regd **F-OANF** 30.5.53 to Sté Indochinoise des Plantations Réunies, Mimot, Saigon; regd in Laos .56 as **F-LAAF** to Veha Akat, Vientiane; crashed at Phong Savanh 2.5.58.

6936   RAF serial **RL954**; TOC DH, Witney, 1.1.46; regd **G-AGZJ** 12.1.46 to British-American Air Services Ltd, White Waltham and sold to them 6.4.46; CoA (7463) issued 1.4.46; regd 23.6.47 to S K Davies t/a Cambrian Air Services, Cardiff; nominal change of regn 13.4.49 to J H Watts, S K Davies, E Keith-Davies and Care-Lines Ltd t/a Cambrian Air Services, named *Carmarthen;* CoA lapsed 30.6.50; regn cld as sold 3.9.50 but not re-regd; WFU at Cardiff 1.52 and used for spares.

6937   RAF serial **RL955**; TOC DH, Witney, 2.1.46; regd **G-AGZK** 12.1.46 to British-American Air Services Ltd, White Waltham; CoA (7464) issued 21.3.46; regd 30.10.47 to Iraq Petroleum Transport Co Ltd, Tripoli, Lebanon; CoA lapsed 13.1.51; regn cld as sold 13.12.51; sold to Arab Airways Assoc Ltd, Amman, Jordan, for spares or rebuild; DBF in hangar at Amman 9.5.53.

6938   RAF serial **RL956**; TOC DH, Witney, 2.1.46; sold to DH Canada 16.3.46; regd **CF-DIN**, but NTU; regd **YV-P-BPE** .46 (? .49) to Riego Oil Co; regn cld before .51

6939   RAF serial **RL957**; TOC 18 MU, Dumfries, 10.1.46; TTCCF, Wyton, 21.6.46; crashed into hedge when engine failed on take-of from Staverton, 24.1.47; SOC 10.3.47.

6940   RAF serial **RL958**; TOC 18 MU, Dumfries, 4.2.46; regd **G-AKRP** 26.1.48 to Short Bros & Harland Ltd and sold to them next day; operated by Short's Air Charter Service, Rochester; CoA (9952) issued 14.2.48; converted to Mk.4 3.12.54; regd 20.6.57 to Avionics Ltd, Croydon; CoA lapsed 12.6.58; regn cld 2.10.58 as sold in France; regn **F-DAFS** reserved for Sté Agricolavia, but NTU; regd **CN-TTO** 13.2.59 to SA Agricolavia, Rabat; regd .65 to H Carton, Casablanca (Tit-Mellil); regd .67 to Parachute Club de Maroc, Casablanca (Tit-Mellil); WFU .72; sold to French collector .74 but remained at Casablanca in deteriorating condition; sold .79 to US syndicate and shipped to Bremerhaven docks, Germany, but owing to dispute over harbour dues was detained in open storage; sold .80 to Bob Wirth and stored in barn in north Germany; sold 8.8.94 to R H Ford, t/a Fordaire Aviation, and moved to Little Gransden for rebuild; to Sywell .95; taxying trials 1.10.98; regd **G-AKRP** 15.10.99 to R H Ford of Fordaire Ltd, Sywell, named *Northamptonshire Rose;* reflown 6.4.00 and CoA renewed 27.6.00; extant.

6941   RAF serial **RL959**; TOC 18 MU, Dumfries, 4.2.46; Staff College CF, White Waltham, [KE:B] (later Andover) 3.7.46; MCCS, Andover, 16.10.46; Staff College CF, Andover, 11.3.48; 5 MU, Kemble, 15.10.48; sold to Cambrian Air Services Ltd 13.5.49; regd **G-ALRW** 16.5.49 to Cambrian Air Services Ltd, Cardiff, named *Meirionydd;* CoA (10624) issued 29.7.49; regd 7.7.50 to J H Watts, E Keith-Davies, S K Davies & Care Lines Ltd, t/a Cambrian Air Enterprises, Cardiff; CoA lapsed 28.7.50; regd 25.1.52 to Cambrian Air Services Ltd; regd 30.10.52 to Patrick Motors Ltd, Elmdon; CoA renewed 11.5.53; regn cld 25.9.53 as sold in France via W A Shackleton Ltd; regd **F-BGXT** 7.10.53 to Sté Française Radio Electrique, Angers; regd 3.9.56 to Air Ouest, Nantes; operated 12.57 by Sté Générale d'Affrétements Aériens (Air Fret), Algiers; regd 2.61 to Sté Air Saoura, Colomb-Bechar; CoA lapsed 3.63; ferried from Nimes to Rousseau Aviation, Dinard, 9.7.65 and regd to them .66; regd 1.67 to Sté Aéronautique de l'Est Marie et Cie, Strasbourg; regd .68 to Aéro Club de l'Aube, Troyes; regd .69 to Aéro Club Moselle Parachutisme, Doncourt-les-Conflans; CoA expired 10.70; for sale 8.71; NFT.

F-BGXT, c/n 6941, seen in the colours of Air Saoura at Nîmes-Garons on 3rd August 1964   *[P H Butler]*

Parked at Rosario in Argentina in the 1950s is LV-AES, c/n 6942, in the titles of Aero Expreso Barcella   *[via C N Dodds]*

The first operator of G-AHED, c/n 6944, was Marshall's of Cambridge, as seen here at Liverpool (Speke)on 25th March 1954 [P H Butler]

6942 RAF serial **RL960**; TOC 18 MU, Dumfries, 4.2.46; Staff College CF, White Waltham, (later Andover) 6.8.46; 18 MU 13.2.48; sold to Aeroways 21.5.48, regd **G-ALAY** 27.5.48 to A W Coombs. t/a Aeroways, Croydon; CoA (10270) issued 29.7.48 to Autowork (Winchester) Ltd; regd 23.11.48 to W A Rollason Ltd, Croydon; regn cld 30.12.48 as sold in South America; regd in Argentina 23.3.49 as **LV-AGX** to Zonas Oeste y Norte de Aerolineas Argentinas (ZONDA) through Sfreddo y Paolini Ltda (aircraft brokers); to Aerolineas Argentinas .50; re-regd **LV-FET** 5.10.51; to Taxis Aéreos Argentinios (TAASA) as **LV-AES** (second); fitted with steel plate undersides to protect from stones on primitive airstrips; to Aero Expresso Barcella; to D Errecaborde. t/a Aero Services Errecaborde, Mar del Plata, Buenos Aires, 1.59; crashed 29.2.60; regn cld 20.2.61 (but still on 5.67 register).

6943 RAF serial **RL961**; TOC 18 MU, Dumfries, 28.2.46; TTCCF, Wyton [TWY:G], 28.3.47; 18 MU 16.10.47; sold to R A Short 2.2.49; regd **G-ALGN** 17.2.49 to Sqn Ldr K J Nalson, Croydon; CoA (10438) issued 11.10.51; regd 14.12.51 to Aerocontacts Ltd, Gatwick; regn cld 28.1.52 as sold in Madagascar; inspected at Ivato 5.2.52; regd **F-OAKE** 28.2.52 to Sté Air Madagascar, Ivato; crashed on landing at Port-Bergé, Madagascar, 17.2.53.

6944 RAF serial **RL962**; TOC DH, Witney, 18.2.46; sold to DH 16.3.46; regd **G-AHED** 27.2.46 to Marshall's Flying School Ltd, Cambridge; CoA (7537) issued 25.4.46; regd 9.4.52 to Marshall's Flying Services Ltd, Cambridge; modified to Srs.6 21.7.60; regd 20.4.61 to Hunting Aerosurveys Ltd, Leavesden; CoA lapsed 17.4.68; sold 28.2.69 and regn cld 3.3.69; to RAF Museum store at Henlow .69; to Cardington .82; to Wyton 1.00; extant.

In the RAF Museum store at Cardington on 12th November 1999 was the hull of G-AHED, looking more like a boat than an aircraft

[W J Taylor via P H T Green]

A pristine G-AHEB, c/n 6945, of Jersey Airlines; to whom it was registered from 11.55 to 2.57 [Denis Fox collection]

Many French-registered Dragon Rapides were used by parachute clubs, as was F-BHVQ, c/n 6945

[G M Simons collection]

RL964, c/n 6946 was quickly sold to Lancashire Aircraft Corporation as G-AHEA

[R C Sturtivant]

6945   RAF serial **RL963**; TOC DH, Witney, 18.2.46; regd **G-AHEB** 27.2.46 to Portsmouth Aviation Ltd and sold to them 20.4.46; CoA (7535) issued 17.4.46; regn cld as sold abroad 2.8.47; regd **EI-ADP** to Weston Ltd; retd to UK 30.3.55; restored as **G-AHEB** 2.4.55 to J B Peak and J Chapman, Cambridge; regd 25.11.55 to Airlines (Jersey) Ltd t/a Jersey Airlines; regn cld 8.2.57 as sold in France; regd **F-BHVQ** 25.3.57 to SFASA, Toussus-le-Noble, based Biscarosse (later Avignon); regd .63 to Centre Régional de Parachutisme Provence-Mediterranée, Avignon; ferried to Castelnaudry 30.6.65 and reduced to spares; regn cld .66.

6946   RAF serial **RL964**; TOC DH, Witney, 18.2.46; regd **G-AHEA** 27.2.46 to Lancashire Aircraft Corpn Ltd, Squires Gate and sold to them 13.4.46; CoA (7536) issued 12.4.46; regn cld (long term storage) 9.11.50; regd 3.2.51 to same owner; CoA lapsed 6.8.53; regd 31.3.54 to R A Peacock (Aviation) Ltd, Croydon; regd 18.11.54 to A J Whittemore (Aeradio) Ltd, Croydon; regn cld 22.1.55 as sold in France; regd **F-BHCF** 9.3.55; regn cld, restored 12.6.57 to SFASA, Chalon; regd .62 to Etat, CR No.2, Chalon-sur-Saône; regd .63 to CIC de Parachutisme de Bourgogne Franche-Comté, Chalon-sur-Saône; CoA suspended at Castelnaudry 19.10.64; regn cld .65.

6947   RAF serial **RL965**; TOC DH, Witney, 4.2.46; CoA (7625) issued 12.4.46; regd **VT-AVW** 9.3.46 to Air Services of India Ltd, Bombay, named *Gagenratna*, and sold to them 4.5.46; regn cld .47.

G-AHIA, c/n 6948, of Morton Air Services Ltd outside a Croydon hangar

[Denis Fox collection]

6948 RAF serial **RL966**; TOC DH, Witney, 4.2.46; sold to Morton Air Services Ltd 6.4.46 and regd **G-AHIA** 8.4.46 to them; CoA (7606) issued 8.4.46; regd 27.2.50 to Skyways Ltd, Dunsfold; DBR when it fell into an excavation while taxying at Maritse, Rhodes, 5.3.51; regn cld 11.6.51.

6949 RAF serial **RL967**; TOC 18 MU, Dumfries, 11.3.46; 25 Gp CF, Ternhill, 17.3.47; 18 MU 31.7.47; regd **G-AKSD** 27.1.48 to Olley Air Service Ltd, Croydon; regd 24.11.48 to Windmill Theatre Transport Co Ltd, White Waltham (later Portsmouth), named *Windmill Girl II;* CoA (9971) issued 26.11.48; badly damaged in forced landing nr Villefranche-de-Rouergue, France, 22.12.52 but repaired; regd 7.3.60 to Hants & Sussex Aviation Ltd, Portsmouth; operated by Hunting Surveys Ltd .61; regn cld 24.8.61 as sold in France; regd **F-OBVI** 19.9.61 and del 7.11.61 to SA Ardic, Dakar, Senegal; CoA suspended at Podor 18.9.62; regn cld .64.

6950 RAF serial **RL968**; TOC 18 MU, Dumfries, 11.3.46; DH, Witney, 9.4.47 for mods before intended loan to Sperry Gyroscope Co Ltd, Hanworth; 18 MU 24.7.47; regd **G-AKRR** 26.1.48 to Short Bros & Harland Ltd, Rochester, and sold to them next day; CoA (9953) issued 25.2.48; regd 9.4.52 to G C Heighington, Gatwick; regn cld 14.5.52 as sold in Sudan; sold to V Vanian and regn **SN-ABB** reserved 8.52 but NTU and cld 9.52; restored to UK register as **G-AKRR** 16.9.52 to G C Heighington, Gatwick; regn cld 8.11.52 as sold in Sudan; regd **SN-ABB** 13.11.52 to V Vanian; regd in Ethiopia 18.11.52 as **ET-P-16** to K Marru, t/a Meat Export and Supply Co, Dire Dawa; DBF while refuelling at Dire Dawa 3.9.53.

6951 RAF serial **RL980**; TOC 18 MU, Dumfries, 11.3.46; sold to Olley Air Service Ltd 27.1.48 and regd **G-AKSB** to them same day; CoA (9969) issued 14.2.48; sold 14.10.49 to R T Briscoe Ltd, Gold Coast; regn cld 17.2.50 as sold in Gold Coast; regd **VP-AAA** 17.2.50 to R T Briscoe Ltd, Sekondi; fate uncertain but believed scrapped before 1.59.

6952 RAF serial **RL981**; TOC 18 MU, Dumfries, 5.3.46; regd **G-AKRS** 21.1.48 to J Dade, Croydon and sold to him 27.1.48; CoA (9972) issued 9.4.48; operated by Air Enterprises Ltd, of which Capt Dade was MD; regd 1.2.49 to Air Enterprises Ltd, Croydon; regd 13.4.53 to Airwork Ltd, Blackbushe, and later operated by Air Service Training at Perth (Scone); CoA lapsed 3.12.54 and renewed 28.6.56; regd 13.5.60 to W Westoby, t/a Westair Flying Services, Squires Gate; regd 23.5.62 to Bournemouth Air Taxi Ltd, t/a Bournair, Hurn; regd 16.1.64 to Piper Products (Poole) Ltd, Hurn; sold 20.7.64 and regd 5.10.64 to Tippers Air Transport Ltd, Baginton; CoA lapsed 24.2.65; regd 2.9.65 to Shackleton Aviation Ltd; CoA renewed 6.5.66; regd 23.5.66 to B W Holman, Middleton St. George; sold 2.6.68 and regd 15.10.68 to Trent Valley Aviation Ltd, East Midlands Airport; CoA lapsed 7.11.69; sold 25.3.70 to Arrow Air Services Ltd, Shipdham and del 5.70; regd 24.11.70 to R V Snook and N C L Wright, t/a Toftwood Aviation, Shipdham; CoA lapsed 30.12.71 and stored at Shipdham; rebuilt for Israeli Air Force Museum; flew again 28.4.78 before departing for Tel Aviv 20.5.78 as **4X-970**; to IDFAF Museum, Ben Gurion Airport, carrying museum serial **002**; UK regn cld 29.2.84 as sold in Israel; repainted as 'VQ-PAR' in Aviron colour scheme at IDFAF Museum, Hatzerim; extant.

SN-ABB, c/n 6950, was briefly owned by V Vanian in the Sudan before moving to Ethiopia as ET-P-16   *[Denis Fox collection]*

G-AKRS, c/n 6952, at Liverpool (Speke) on 14.7.59 when in use by Air Service Training Ltd at Perth (Scone)   *[P H Butler]*

VT-AVX, c/n 6953, "Gagenraj" of Air Services of India Ltd was destroyed at Juhu in November 1948   *[G M Simons collection]*

6953 RAF serial **RL982**; TOC DH, Witney, 21.2.46; regd **VT-AVX** 9.3.46 to Air Services of India Ltd, Bombay, named *Gagenraj,* and sold to them 4.5.46; CoA (7724) issued 1.5.46; destroyed in hangar collapse in cyclone at Juhu 11.48; regn cld .50; possibly spares to SE Asia.

6954 RAF serial **RL983**; TOC DH, Witney, 28.2.46; CoA (7723) issued 1.5.46; sold to Arab Airways, Transjordan, 29.5.46; at DH, Witney, 4.7.47 and from there flown to Little Horwood; regd **TJ-AAA** to Arab Airways Association Ltd, Amman, named *Yarmouk;* DBF in hangar at Amman 4.5.53.

TJ-AAB, c/n 6955, of Arab Airways Association Ltd, apparently on its way through Egypt to Transjordan   *[P H T Green collection]*

6955 RAF serial **RL984**; TOC DH, Witney, 28.2.46; CoA (7775) issued 8.5.46; sold to Arab Airways, Transjordan, 30.5.46; at DH, Witney, 7.47 and from there flown to Little Horwood; regd **TJ-AAB** to Arab Airways Association Ltd, Amman, named *El Ordan;* strayed into Israel 13.6.50 while flying from Amman to Almaza and forced to land at Be'er Sheva (Beersheba) by IDFAF Spitfires; taken over by IDFAF, possibly as one of three serialled **1311** to **1313**; crashed into sea off Ashkelon, Gaza, 18.12.50 (pilot Hoffshi); seven passengers killed.

6956 RAF serial **RL985**; TOC DH, Witney, 14.3.46; sold to Dansk Rode Kors & Zone-Redningskorpset, Copenhagen, (Danish Red Cross) 24.4.46; CoA (7799) issued 23.5.46; regd **OY-DZY** 28.6.46; at DH, Witney, 2.6.47; crashed 40 metres off-shore in The Sound after engine failure on take-off from Kastrup 16.7.60; eight amateur footballers killed, pilot S Windelow injured.

6957 RAF serial **RL986**; TOC DH, Witney, 14.3.46; regd **VT-AXG** 9.3.46 to Air Services of India Ltd, Bombay, named *Gagenrup,* and sold to them 18.5.46; CoA (7769) issued 8.5.46; regn cld .50 as sold in French Indo-China; inspected at Hanoi 17.10.50; regd **F-OAHL** 19.1.51 to Autrex, Lopez & Cie, Hanoi; crashed at Quang Tri, Indo-China, 26.4.54.

6958 RAF serial **TX300**; TOC DH, Witney, 19.3.46; CoA (7835) issued 15.5.46; sold to Arab Airways 6.46; regd **TJ-AAC** 6.46 to Arab Airways Association Ltd, Amman, named *Balka;* at DH, Witney, 7.47 and from there flown to Little Horwood; to Arab Legion Air Force .49 as **R300**; 3 Flt/Sqn .49; crashed at Jerusalem .56.

OY-DZY, c/n 6956, which crashed into Danish waters off Kastrup in July 1960, killing eight passengers   *[Denis Fox collection]*

TJ-ACE, c/n 6959, owned by Arab Contracting & Trading Co of Amman with trademark black cat symbol on the fin [Denis Fox collection]

JY-AAE, c/n 6961, of the Arab Contracting & Trading Co at Amman, Jordan in the late 1950s. This aircraft eventually returned to the UK register as G-ASRM [via C N Dodds]

6959   RAF serial **TX301**; TOC DH, Witney, 19.3.46; CoA (7836) issued 23.5.46; sold to Arab Airways 6.46; regd **TJ-AAD** 6.46 to Arab Airways Association Ltd, Amman, named *Raghadan;* at DH, Witney, 7.47 and from there flown to Little Horwood; re-regd **TJ-ACE** 16.6.52 to Arab Contracting & Trading Co, Amman; re-regd **JY-ACE** 4.54 to same owner; sold in France 10.60 but NTU; regd **JY-ACG** 10.61 to Arab Contracting & Trading Co; retd to UK and regd **G-ASRJ** 25.3.64 to E A J Gardener, t/a Parachute Regt Free Fall Club; CoA issued 26.5.64; regd 19.11.64 to T Leask, t/a Army Parachute Association; regd 30.4.65 to T C Wilson, t/a Rhine Army Parachute Association, named *Rhinegold* but popularly known as *Ringo*; nominal re-regns 4.3.69 to D C Parker and 10.2.70 to J P Epplestone; WFU and regn cld 16.2.70 when extensive plywood rot discovered; stored dismantled at Netheravon before being scrapped; parts to Durney Collection, Andover.

6960   RAF serial **TX302**; TOC DH, Witney, 22.3.46; sold to Organizacio Mineira de Transportes Aereos, Belo Horizonte; regn **PP-OMC** reserved but formal registration did not take place; crashed at Araguari, Minas Gerais, 4.2.47.

6961   RAF serial **TX303**; TOC DH, Witney, 22.3.46; CoA (8016) issued 14.6.46; sold to Arab Airways 6.46; regd **TJ-AAE** to Arab Airways Association Ltd, Amman, named *Moab* (later

Yarmouk);   at DH, Witney, 7.47 and from there flown to Little Horwood; nominal change to Arab Airways (Jerusalem) Ltd 23.8.53; regd to Arab Contracting & Trading Co, Amman; re-regd **JY-AAE** 4.54; re-regd **JY-ACF**; to UK 5.64; regd **G-ASRM** 26.3.64 to Aerocontacts (Aircraft Distributors) Ltd, Gatwick; CoA issued 30.4.64; regn cld 27.7.64 as sold in Congo; regd **9Q-CPF** 8.64 to Dr Gorecki, Ndola; believed scrapped.

6962   RAF serial **TX304**; TOC DH, Witney, 28.3.46; regd **G-AHTS** 3.6.46 to Anglo-Iranian Oil Co Ltd, Abadan; CoA (7859) issued 22.6.46; crashed in Middle East 29.4.47; regn cld 29.1.48.

6963   RAF serial **TX305**; sold to DH 28.3.46; regd **G-AHPU** 25.6.46 to Hunting Air Travel Ltd, Luton, named *Avon;* CoA (7957) issued 29.6.46; regd 28.7.49 to J E Steel, t/a Steel and Co. Ltd, Newcastle (Woolsington); regd 3.4.57 to Luton Flying Club Ltd, Luton; regd 1.7.57 to V H Bellamy, Eastleigh; converted to Mk.4 1.58; regn cld as sold in Nigeria 5.3.58; regd in Sierra Leone to Sierra Leone Airways, Freetown, as **VR-LAD** 4.58, named *RMA Loma;* del 26.5.58; DBF at Hastings.

6964   RAF serial **TX306**; sold to DH 1.4.46; regd **G-AHTR** 3.6.46 to Anglo-Iranian Oil Co Ltd, Abadan; CoA (7858) issued 4.7.46; DBF at Abadan 21.4.50; regn cld 10.7.50.

Seen in 1948 at Naft-i-Shah, a major oilfield region near the Iraqi border, is Rapide G-AHTS, c/n 6962, of the Anglo-Iranian Oil Co Ltd   [via C N Dodds]

Another Rapide used by the Anglo-Iranian Oil Co Ltd was G-AHTT, c/n 6966, here about to leave Kermanshah, western Iran, in December 1948

[via C N Dodds]

G-AHPU, c/n 6963, was operated by the Hampshire Aeroplane Club when owned by V H Bellamy at Eastleigh 1957-8   *[via A. Chivers]*

C/n 6963 was later VR-LAD "RMA Loma" of Sierra Leone Airways but was only in use for a few weeks before being destroyed by fire   *[Denis Fox collection]*

6965   RAF serial **TX307**; sold to DH 1.4.46; regd **G-AHWF** 25.6.46 to Hunting Air Travel Ltd, Luton; CoA (7958) issued 4.7.46; regd 7.3.49 to Iraq Petroleum Transport Co Ltd; regd 10.11.50 to Anglo-Iranian Oil Co Ltd, Abadan; regd in Iran as **EP-AAW** 10.51 to National Oil Co; NFT.

6966   RAF serial **TX308**; sold to DH 4.4.46; regd **G-AHTT** 3.6.46 to Anglo-Iranian Oil Co Ltd, Abadan; CoA (7860) issued 18.7.46; seized by Iranian Govt 4.51; regn cld 29.10.54 as sold to Iran; regd **EP-AAX** 10.51 to National Oil Co; regn cld; NFT.

6967   RAF serial **TX309**; sold to DH 8.4.46; regd **G-AHJS** 16.4.46 to Fairey Aviation Co Ltd, White Waltham; CoA (7725) issued 18.7.46; crashed on take-off from Charleroi, Belgium, 4.5.56 and flown to Lydd (Ferryfield) in a Bristol Freighter for repair; regd 20.6.61 to Westland Aircraft Ltd, Fairey Aviation Divn; regd 11.1.65 to Hantsair Ltd, Eastleigh; regd 22.6.65 to Robin Air Ltd, t/a Three Counties Aero Club, Blackbushe; to Lasham 1.2.66; CoA lapsed 20.5.66; regn cld 13.7.73; to Army Parachute Training Association, Netheravon, for spares; parts to The Durney Collection, Andover.

In derelict condition at Lasham on 28th May 1966 was G-AHJS, c/n 6967, last operated by the Three Counties Aero Club at Blackbushe   *[Denis Fox collection]*

An early shot of Rapide G-AIDL, c/n 6968, in the hands of E L Gandar Dower and named "The Wanderer"   *[Denis Fox collection]*

6968   RAF serial **TX310**; sold to DH 7.5.46; regd **G-AIDL** 23.8.46 to E L Gandar Dower, t/a Allied Airways, Dyce; named *The Wanderer,* mainly used by Gandar Dower as personal aircraft and retained after nationalisation in 4.47; CoA (8252) issued 5.9.46; seized by High Sheriff of Oxfordshire and auctioned at Witney 19.4.50 with spare engine; regd 27.4.50 to Goodhew Aviation Co Ltd, Kidlington; regd 12.10.50 to W S Shackleton Ltd, Kidlington; regd 25.10.50 to Fox's Glacier Mints Ltd, Rearsby; converted to Mk.6 8.59; regd 11.12.61 to A J Flatley, Poynton, based at Wolverhampton; regd 11.4.62 to Midland Metal Spinning Co Ltd, Wolverhampton (later Halfpenny Green); regd 17.3.67 to Maj G C Stacey t/a Army Parachute Association, Netheravon; CoA lapsed 29.1.72, renewed 3.7.73; regd 17.5.73 to Army Parachute Association; regd 13.6.77 to Southern Joyrides Ltd, Biggin Hill and used by Mike Hood for pleasure flights; to Llandwrog (Caernarfon) 10.86 and regd 11.3.87 to R Mackenzie-Blyth, t/a Snowdon Mountain Aviation Ltd; operated by Air Caernarfon for pleasure flights; regd 26.5.95 to Atlantic Air Transport Ltd, Caernarfon; to Air Atlantique, Baginton; extant

6969   RAF serial **TX311**; sold to DH, 15.4.46; CoA (8641) issued 24.10.46; regd **ZS-AXS** 30.10.46 to South West Air Transport Pty Ltd; to Sud Air International Airways 12.49; to A Shabum 1.51; regd in Southern Rhodesia 30.3.51 as **VP-YIU** to Igusi (Rhodesia) Ltd, Bulawayo; regd .52 to H D Hooper, Kumalo; regn cld early .55; regd in Mozambique as **CR-AEQ** 15.2.55 to Taxi Aéro de Mocambique (TAM); NFT.

6970   RAF serial **TX312**; sold to DH 7.5.46; CoA (8588) issued 10.10.46; shipped to Brazil on *Potaro,* arr Rio de Janeiro 3.5.46; regd **PP-AIE** 11.3.47 to Arco-Iris Viacao Aerea SA, São Paulo; damaged at Ararangua 31.10.48; regn cld 11.2.49; remains auctioned at Caxios do Sul 20.10.49 and bought by Vicente Sangiacomo.

6971   RAF serial **TX313**; sold to DH 7.5.46; CoA (8589) issued 10.10.46; regd **PP-AIF** 7.3.47 to Arco-Iris Viacao Aerea SA, São Paulo; auctioned at Caxios do Sul 20.10.49 and bought by Vicente Sangiacomo; sold 30.3.50 to Armando Azevedo Andrade sold 25.10.51 to Adhemar de Barros Filho; crashed at Malhada de Pedra-Baia 26.4.52; regn cld 13.6.52.

6972   RAF serial **TX314**; sold to DH 20.5.46; CoA (8621) issued 15.10.46; regd **PP-AIG** 6.3.47 to Arco-Iris Viacao Aerea SA, São Paulo; CoA expired 20.3.49; auctioned at Caxios do Sul 20.10.49 and bought by Vicente Sangiacomo; remained on register for many years in the name of Arco-Iris; regn cld 23.11.71 due to "lack of inspection for more than ten years."

6973   RAF serial **TX315**; sold to DH 20.5.46; CoA (8590) issued 10.10.46 to Peruvian Govt; regd **OB-RAA-156**; used by Estado, 41 Escuadron de Transporte, Transportes Aéreos Militare, the airline branch of the Peruvian Air Force, Iquitos, Pucalipa or Puerto Maldonado; NFT.

6974   RAF serial **TX316**; sold to DH 28.5.46; CoA (8591) issued 10.10.46 to Peruvian Govt; regd **OB-RAB-157**; used by

After a period in South Africa, c/n 6969, the former TX311 was registered VP-YIU in Southern Rhodesia in 1951 before passing to Mozambique as CR-AEQ in 1955

[Denis Fox collection]

The final Brush-built Dominie, TX319, c/n 6977, seen at Loughborough in June1946. No roundels have been applied, as the aircraft went straight to DH at Witney for civil conversion [via N Franklin and P H T Green]

Estado, 41 Escuadron de Transporte, Transportes Aéreos Militare, the airline branch of the Peruvian Air Force, Iquitos, Pucalipa or Puerto Maldonado; NFT.

6975 RAF serial **TX317**; sold to DH 14.6.46; CoA (8656) issued 24.10.46 to Peruvian Govt; regd **OB-RAC-158**; used by Estado, 41 Escuadron de Transporte, Transportes Aéreos Militare, the airline branch of the Peruvian Air Force, Iquitos, Pucalipa or Puerto Maldonado; NFT.

6976 RAF serial **TX318**; sold to DH 19.6.46; CoA (8657) issued 29.10.46 to Peruvian Govt; regd **OB-RAD-159**; used by Estado, 41 Escuadron de Transporte, Transportes Aéreos Militare, the airline branch of the Peruvian Air Force, Iquitos, Pucalipa or Puerto Maldonado; NFT.

6977 RAF serial **TX319**; sold to DH 2.7.46; CoA (8716) issued 5.11.46 to Peruvian Govt; regd **OB-RAE-160**; used by Estado, 41 Escuadron de Transporte, Transportes Aéreos Militare, the airline branch of the Peruvian Air Force, Iquitos, Pucalipa or Puerto Maldonado; NFT.

89232 Built from spare fuselage number 89232 shipped to Downsview, Canada 11.41; regd **CF-BNJ** 2.6.42 to Maritime Central Airways Ltd, Charlotteville; regd 30.4.52 to Spartan Air Services Ltd, Ottawa; WFU .55 and sold to S Banville, Quebec; regn cld 20.8.55; believed used by children as plaything until DBF by irate mother!

W1001 Built at DH, Witney, from spares and remains of **G-ACZE** (c/n 6264); regd **G-AJGS** 24.10.47 to de Havilland Aircraft Co Ltd, Witney; regd 23.2.48 to Mrs M L Wilson t/a Allied Airways (Gandar Dower) Ltd, Dyce, named *The Vagabond;* CoA (10004) issued 12.3.48; WFU 18.2.49 and stored at Dyce; regd 19.12.49 to Caroline Brunning, Dyce (nominal change only); regn cld 18.2.59; sold 28.5.66 to A F Ward and del to Booker by road 26.8.66; regd 30.5.67 to A F Ward and rebuilt by Personal Plane Services (aircraft had flown only 47 hours from new); reflown 2.68 and regd 25.3.68 to Aerial Enterprises Ltd, Booker, for parachuting duties; sold .69 to Fritz Luddington, Delray Beach, FL, and flown across Atlantic by C D Downes and T Wein from Castle Donington via Glasgow, Kulusuk, Narssarssuaq, Goose Bay and Burlington to

This DH.89, c/n 89232, was built in Canada from components sent from de Havilland Aircraft in the UK. The lack of spats and the extended fin/rudder point to this being capable of use on floats [G M Simons collection]

The nose of c/n W1001, registered G-AJGS "The Vagabond" to Allied Airways (Gandar Dower) Ltd; photographed at Booker on 2nd October 1966, by which time it was owned by A F Ward [Denis Fox collection]

Miami between 28.8.70 and 13.9.70; regn cld 15.11.73; to R M Schultz of Hamburg Airdrome Inc, Lakeview, NY by .77 for overhaul and storage; no US regn allotted; sold to Brian Woodford and returned to UK by sea .84; to R Souch, Hamble, for rebuild; regd **G-ACZE** 23.1.85 to Wessex Aviation & Transport Ltd, Chalmington Manor, Dorchester; overhauled by R Souch at Hamble and Sarisbury Green and painted in Brigade of Guards / King's Flight colours; CoA renewed 12.8.86 and based at Henstridge; CoA lapsed 11.8.95 and stored; for sale 8.00 and stored at Haverfordwest (Withybush) 9.00; extant.

W1002   Built at DH, Witney, from spares and regd **G-AKJS** 3.11.47 to Fairey Aviation Co Ltd, White Waltham; CoA (9863) issued 2.12.47; CoA lapsed 23.4.58; converted to Mk.6 and CoA renewed 10.6.59; regd 21.9.59 to Airwork Services Ltd, Hurn and Perth (Scone); regd 26.7.62 to R J Gates, Speke; sold 3.11.64 and flown to Panshanger that day; CoA lapsed 4.3.65; regd 13.5.65 to H Best-Devereux, Panshanger; regn cld as sold in France 21.6.65 but not regd there, as it was used for components in construction of a Fokker D.VIII replica for the film "The Blue Max" by Rousseau Aviation, Dinard (see also c/n 6470).

One of two DH.89s built at Witney from spares, c/n W1001, was registered G-AJGS and is still current as G-ACZE   [C N Dodds]

The last Rapide, G-AKJS, c/n W1002, at Dinard in 1965, before components were used in the construction of a Fokker D.VIII replica [Denis Fox collection]

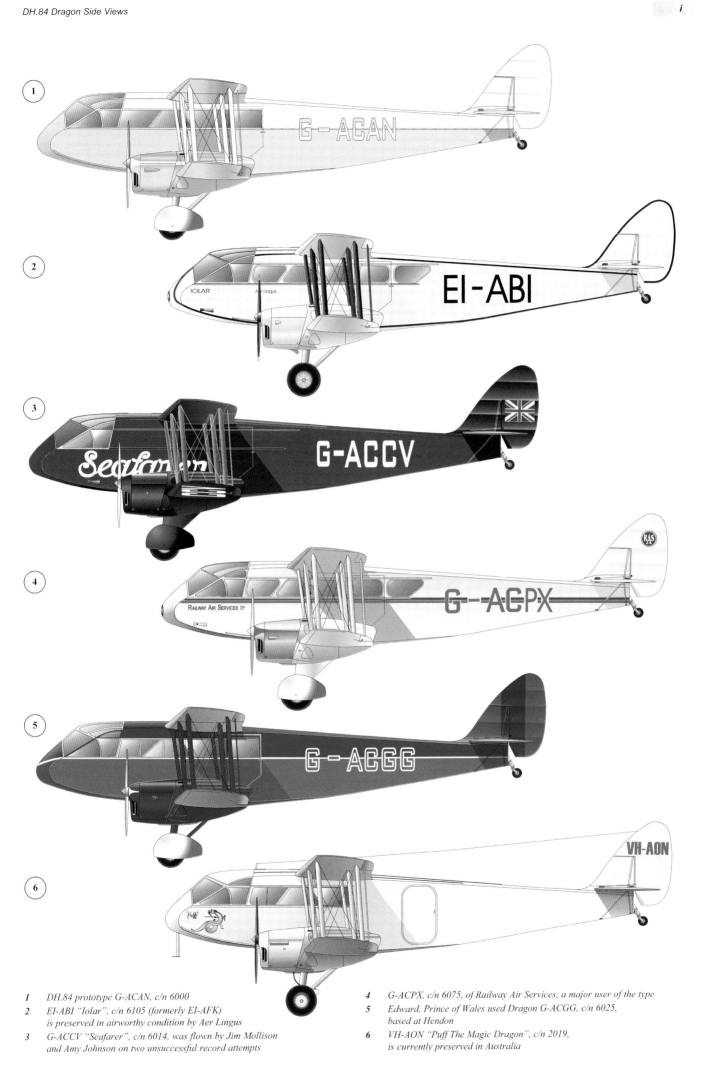

1   DH.84 prototype G-ACAN, c/n 6000

2   EI-ABI "Iolar", c/n 6105 (formerly EI-AFK)
     is preserved in airworthy condition by Aer Lingus

3   G-ACCV "Seafarer", c/n 6014, was flown by Jim Mollison
     and Amy Johnson on two unsuccessful record attempts

4   G-ACPX, c/n 6075, of Railway Air Services, a major user of the type

5   Edward, Prince of Wales used Dragon G-ACGG, c/n 6025,
     based at Hendon

6   VH-AON "Puff The Magic Dragon", c/n 2019,
     is currently preserved in Australia

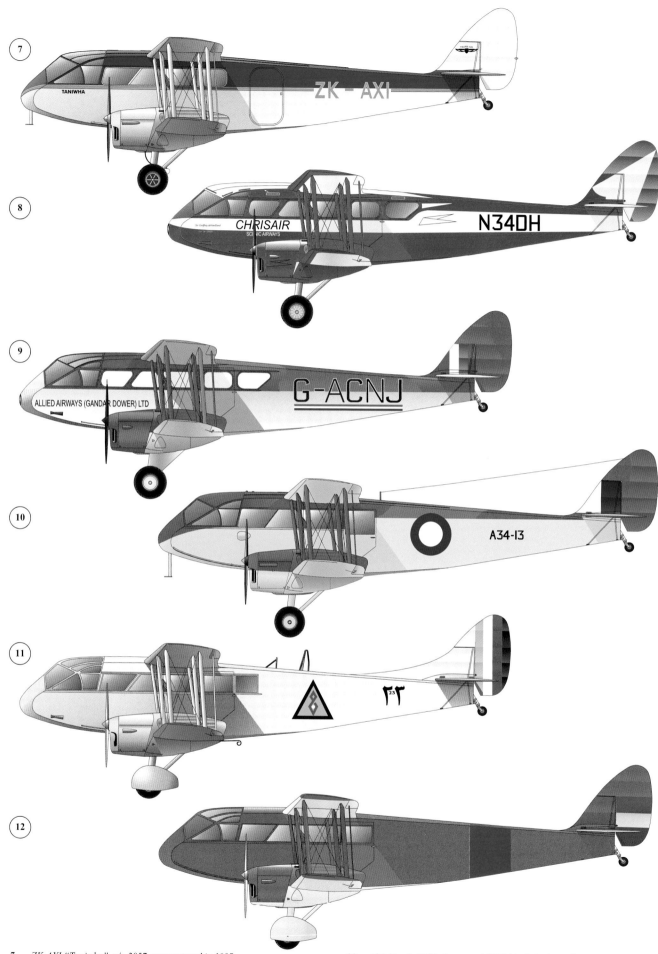

7   ZK-AXI "Taniwha", c/n 2057, was restored in 1997

8   C/n 6096, named "Sir Geoffrey de Havilland",
    N34DH began life as G-ADDI of Railway Air Services

9   G-ACNJ, c/n 6072, of Allied Airways (Gandar Dower) Ltd
    continued in use during the early part of the Second World War

10 A34-13, c/n 2002, the second DH.84 built in Australia,
    is currently at the Museum of Flight at East Fortune

11 23, c/n 6013, one of several DH.84Ms exported to the Iraqi Air Force

12 A Dragon typical of those in use by the Republicans
    in the Spanish Civil War

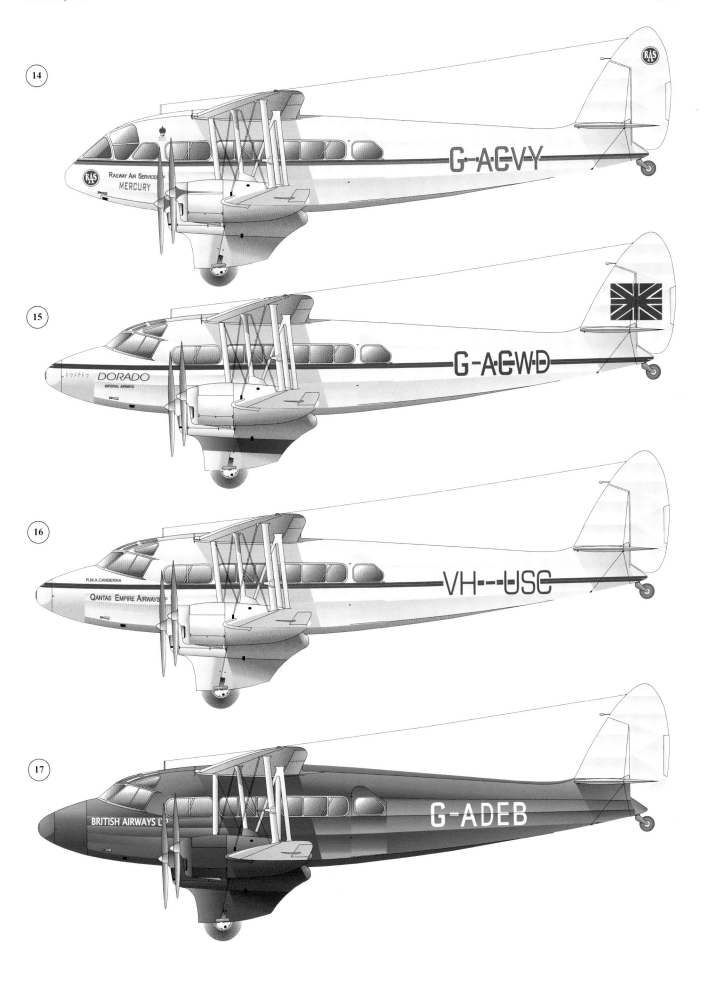

14 Railway Air Services' second DH.86 was G-ACVY "Mercury", c/n 2302, which was operated by AAJC throughout the Second World War

15 Imperial Airways used DH.86 G-ACWD, c/n 2305, which was eventually impressed into the RAF as HK829

16 VH-USC "RMA Canberra", c/n 2307, of Qantas became A31-5 in the RAAF before being returned to Qantas in 1942

17 G-ADEB, c/n 2324, of British Airways was the ill-fated DH.86 that crashed in Germany in 1936

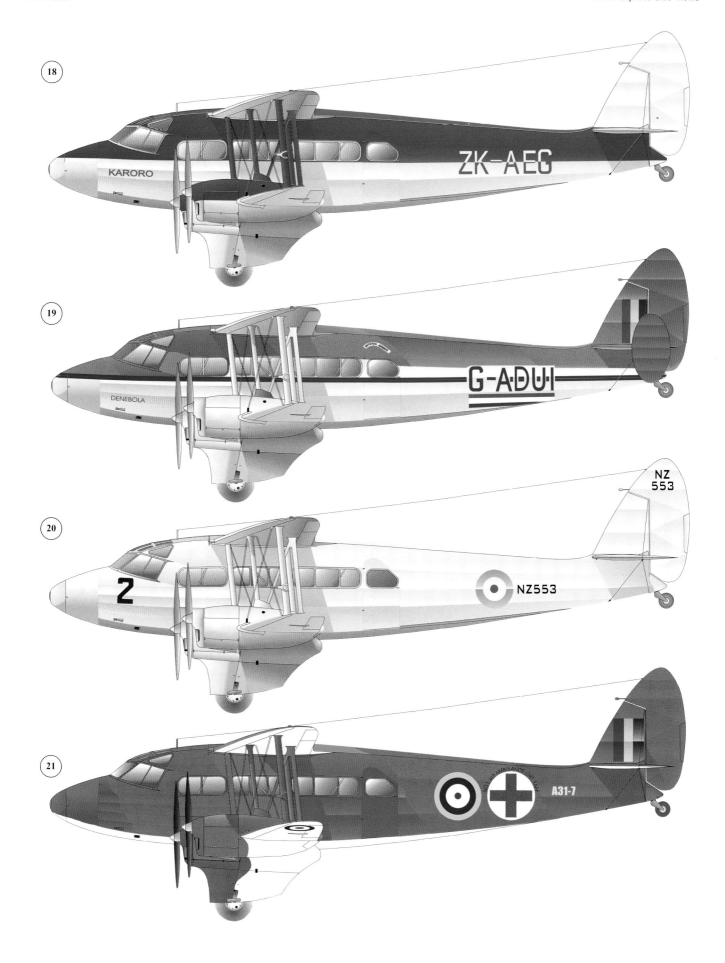

18   *ZK-AEG "Karoro", c/n 2331, of Union Airways in New Zealand saw war service with the RNZAF before being returned to civil use as ZK-AHW*

19   *G-ADUI "Denebola", c/n 2337, of Imperial Airways in early wartime garb was a DH.86B conversion*

20   *The former ZK-AEG, c/n 2331, as RNZAF NZ553 between 1939 and 1945*

21   *Originally G-ADEA, c/n 2323 of Hillman's Airways, A31-7 was used as an air ambulance in the Middle East*

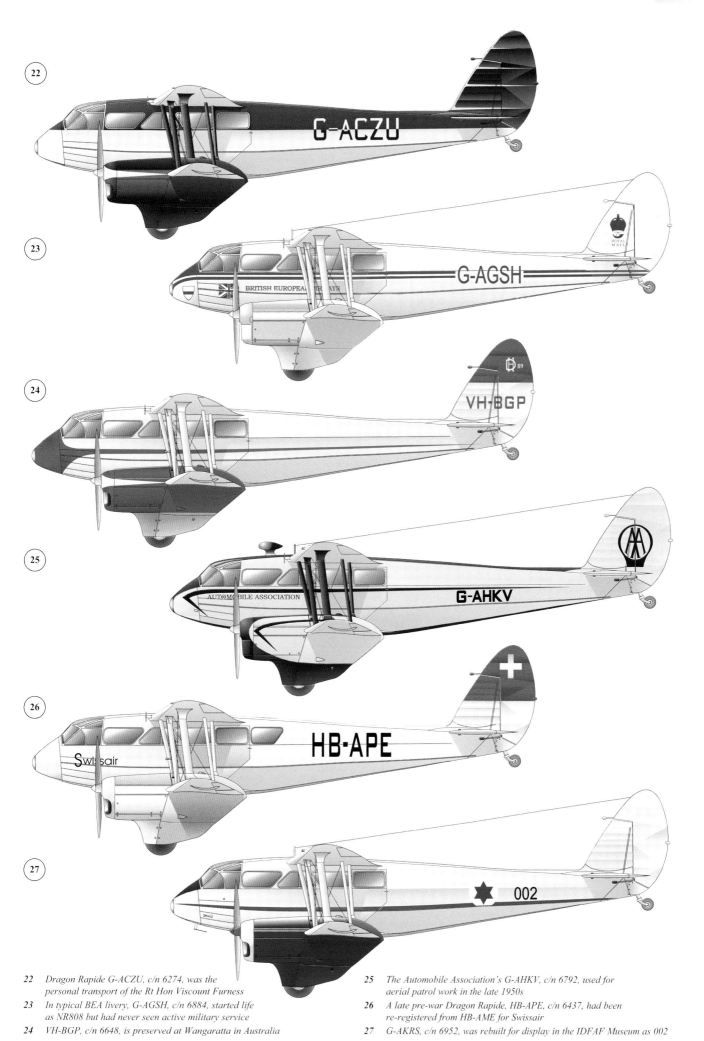

22   Dragon Rapide G-ACZU, c/n 6274, was the personal transport of the Rt Hon Viscount Furness

23   In typical BEA livery, G-AGSH, c/n 6884, started life as NR808 but had never seen active military service

24   VH-BGP, c/n 6648, is preserved at Wangaratta in Australia

25   The Automobile Association's G-AHKV, c/n 6792, used for aerial patrol work in the late 1950s

26   A late pre-war Dragon Rapide, HB-APE, c/n 6437, had been re-registered from HB-AME for Swissair

27   G-AKRS, c/n 6952, was rebuilt for display in the IDFAF Museum as 002

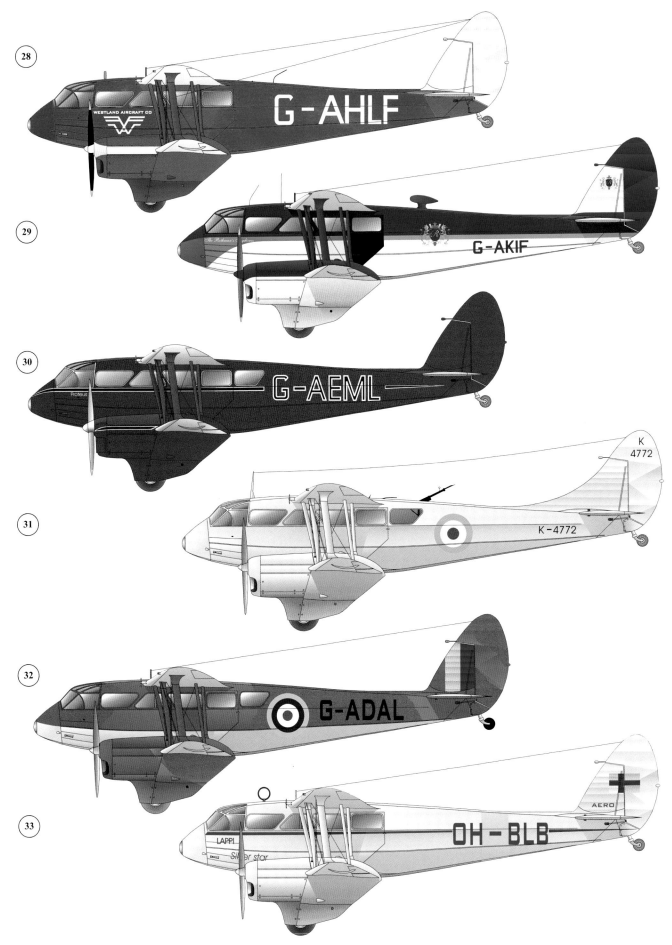

28 G-AHLF, c/n 6494, was Westland Aircraft Co's hack from 1940 to 1958

29 Rothmans Sports Foundation used G-AKIF, c/n 6838,
    the former NR750, as a parachuting platform

30 G-AEML "Proteus", c/n 6337, which was constructed
    in 1936 and is still active

31 K4772, c/n 6271, was the first DH.89M, built as a contender for the
    Air Ministry contract which was awarded to the Avro Anson

32 A typical early wartime camouflage scheme applied to G-ADAL,
    c/n 6263, of Wrightways Ltd before impressment

33 OH-BLB "Lappi", c/n 6401, spent its entire thirty-year
    working life in Scandinavia

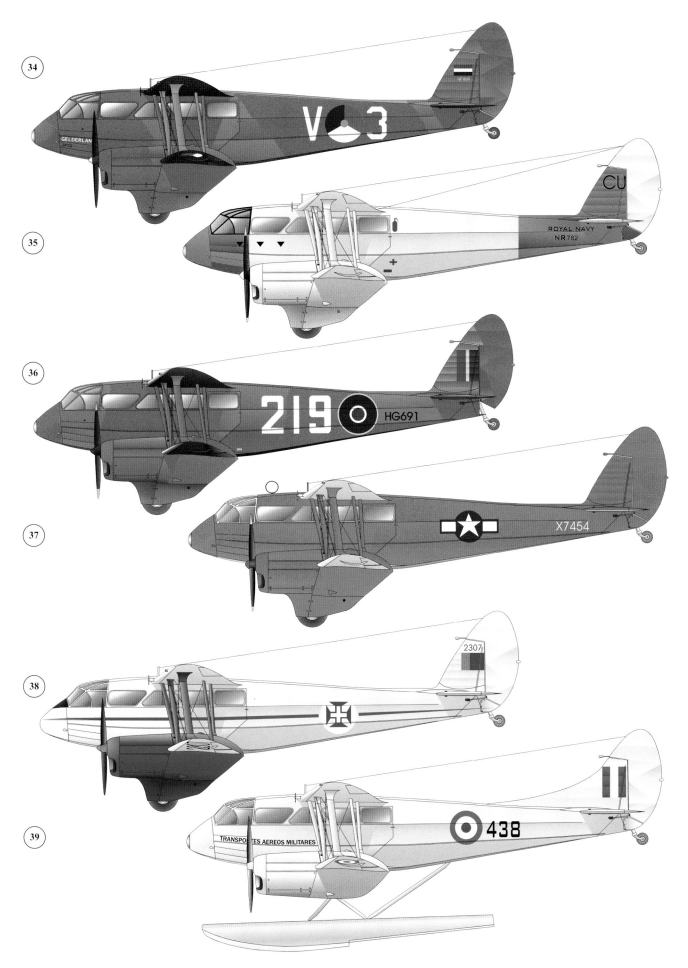

34 V-3, c/n 6740, of the Royal Netherlands Air Force is currently in the RNethAF Museum

35 NR782, c/n 6858, seen in the markings of Station Flight Culdrose

36 2 Radio School at Yatesbury used many Dominies, among them HG691, c/n 6676

37 X7454, c/n 6596, in the markings of the USAAF, which used it at Alconbury and named it "Wee Wullie"

38 This Dominie 2307, c/n 6899, of the Portuguese Air Force is extant at Sintra

39 438 of the Peruvian Air Force was one of six DH.89s supplied in 1946-7

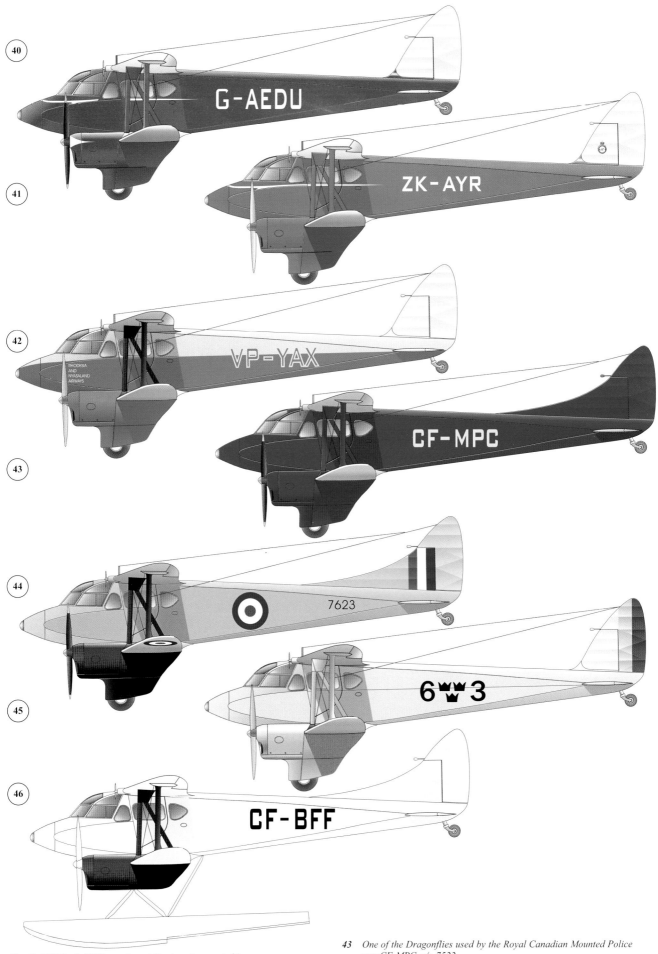

40 G-AEDU, c/n 7509, survives at Rendcomb, operated by
    the Norman Aeroplane Trust

41 Currently airworthy in New Zealand is ZK-AYR, c/n 7508, originally G-AEDT

42 VP-YAX, c/n 7512, of Rhodesia & Nyasaland Airways
    crashed within eighteen months

43 One of the Dragonflies used by the Royal Canadian Mounted Police
    was CF-MPC, c/n 7522

44 RCAF 7623, c/n 7543, was originally CF-BFF and as such was fitted with floats

45 Swedish Air Force Fv906, c/n 7550, coded 6:3, was a VIP transport

46 Fitted with floats for use by Consolidated Mining & Smelting Co
    of Canada was CF-BFF, c/n 7543

The power of advertising! VH-AQU, c/n 2048, carrying Coca-Cola artwork　　　　　　　　*[via T Hancock and P H T Green]*

Dragon VH-AML, c/n 2081, owned by Mrs M C Hoskin, at Jandakot on 8th June 1986　　　　　　　　*[N Appleby via P H T Green]*

Resplendent in Aer Lingus colours, EI-ABI, c/n 6105, originally EI-AFK, is seen here at a PFA rally at Cranfield　　　　　*[W J Taylor via P H T Green]*

Seen here at White Waltham in 1958 is G-ACZP, c/n 2321, of Hampshire Aero Club, the last DH.86 in airworthy condition [MAP via P H T Green]

Rapide HB-APE, c/n 6437, in 1960, when operated by Aero Club de Suisse [MAP via P H T Green]

Colourful Rapide G-AHLF, c/n 6494, at Biggin Hill in 1960, probably when owned by F A Frampton Ltd [MAP via P H T Green]

Rapide G-AGJG, c/n 6517, seen here in a smart livery, is currently under restoration at Duxford [MAP via P H T Green]

G-AHGC, c/n 6583, in a line of Devons and Princes at an unrecorded location [MAP via P H T Green]

ZK-AKY, c/n 6653, was painted as NZ525, its former serial in the 1980s [via C N Dodds]

ZK-AKU, c/n 6662, in Rothmans Sports Foundation colours in December 1986 [J N Geelen]

G-AGTM, c/n 6746, of Aviation Heritage Ltd at Kemble in 1997 [P Harrison via P H T Green]

Fairey Surveys Ltd operated Rapide G-AHXW, c/n 6782, from White Waltham for many years [MAP via P H T Green]

Perhaps one of the best-known Rapides was c/n 6792 when it was in use by the AA as G-AHKV [MAP via P H T Green]

In high-visibility colour scheme but without port engine, F-BHCE c/n 6851, had been wfu at Strasbourg / Neuhof when seen on 11th August 1969
[via D Partington]

Flying as it used to be! G-AGSH, c/n 6884, of BEA at Land's End (St Just) [MAP via P H T Green]

In beautiful condition, G-AKRP, c/n 6940, "The Northamptonshire Rose" of Fordaire Aviation at Sywell on 27th July 2002   *[via author]*

In Atlantic Air Transport colours and operated from Caernarfon, G-AIDL c/n 6968, was joy-riding at White Waltham on 16th May 1998

[via D Partington]

Built at Witney from c/n 6264 and spares becoming G-AJGS, c/n W.1001 was restored for Brian Woodford as G-ACZE, seen here at Woburn on 15th August 1987

[P Ponting via P H T Green]

PP-VAN represents VARIG's first aircraft but is in fact a rebuild of the ex-Portuguese c/n 6900   [G M Simons collection]

In Scillonian colours and named "Samson", G-AJCL, c/n 6722, was photographed at East Midlands Airport in April 1968   [P H Butler]

G-AKNN, c/n 6598, in a gold and blue colour scheme when used as a parachuting platform during the sixties   [G M Simons collection]

C/n 6736 as Rapid Air's 4R-AAI at Staverton in June 1975 just before it was acquired for the Strathallan Collection   [P H Butler]

VP-YOL, c/n 6666, of Victoria Falls Airways (Pvt) Ltd had seen service with the RRAF, among other users   [G M Simons collection]

D-ILIT, c/n 6879 at Lahr, Germany, in July 1995 after restoration and before its delivery to Joseph Koch at Sandown by Colin Dodds   [C N Dodds]

The colourful markings applied to c/n 6694 when in use by Station Flight, Culdrose as HG709   [R C Sturtivant]

C/n 6899 was the only DH.89 used by the Portuguese Air Force, as 2307, and was finally stored at Sintra for the Museu do Ar   [G M Simons collection]

G-AEDT, c/n 7508, at Woburn on 20th August 1988, when it was owned by Brian Woodford's Wessex Aviation & Transport Ltd   [P Ponting via P H T Green]

C/n 7526 was a late arrival on the UK register as G-AEDU, having seen much service in Portuguese East Africa and South Africa until 1979
[P H T Green collection]

G-ANYK, c/n 7529, in its attractive two-tone blue livery   *[MAP via P H T Green]*

The prototype DH.90 Dragonfly c/n 7500 with engines running and test identification E.2 as it first flew on 12.8.35. Red primer paint is still much in evidence and initial tests were flown in this form prior to finish painting and applying registration G-ADNA   *[Aeroplane via J Meaden]*

Part 4: The DH.90 Dragonfly

Background

Essentially a smaller, more streamlined, version of the DH.89, the DH.90 Dragonfly first took to the air at Hatfield on 12th August 1935. The prototype, G-ADNA, took part in the King's Cup Air Race at Hatfield on 10th July 1936 in the hands of Capt Geoffrey de Havilland and finished in eighth position. As a type which today would be classified as an 'executive' aircraft, the Dragonfly did not secure a large number of orders, particularly in Great Britain, where only twenty-one of the sixty-six aircraft built were delivered as new. At a price of about £2650 only wealthy organisations or individuals could afford one during the hard times of the 1930s, notable purchasers being Lord Beaverbrook, the Guinness family and Sir Philip Sassoon. Many went overseas, however, to such owners as King Faisal of Iraq and a number of wealthy Frenchmen. Others were delivered to airlines such as QANTAS in Australia, Wearne's Air Service in Singapore, Rhodesia & Nyasaland Airways, PLUNA in Uruguay and several in Europe, while some were acquired by charter operators. Perhaps surprisingly, the Swedish Air Force and Danish Army bought examples of the Dragonfly, using them mainly as VIP transports.

Dragonflies began drifting back to Great Britain by the time production ended in 1938, and a number were used as Army co-operation aircraft by Air Dispatch Ltd. During the Second World War several Dragonflies saw service with National Air Communications before most of them were impressed for RAF service at Anti-Aircraft Co-operation Units, and six were likewise used by the RCAF in Canada. By the end of the war all but one of the RAF aircraft had been struck off due to lack of spare parts. In other parts of the world, however, Dragonflies survived and continued in service for several years. In 2003, two Dragonflies exist in flying condition, and others may survive in the form of wrecked airframes.

Technical specification

A twin-engined two-bay biplane, the Dragonfly had a monocoque plywood shell fuselage with spruce stringers, similar to the construction of the DH.88 Comet Racer and the DH.91 Albatross. Strengthened spars in the wing centre sections allowed bracing wires at that point to be dispensed with, thus providing easier access to the luxury cabin for up to four passengers. The fuselage was sheathed in 1.5 mm plywood which in turn was covered with doped-on fabric. A tailplane of spruce spars and ribs was also plywood-covered. The fixed undercarriage was encased in streamlined fairings. Two 130 hp four-cylinder Gipsy Major engines powered the Dragonfly, and sufficient fuel could be carried in three tanks to allow a respectable range with a full load. Dual controls were provided for the crew.

The following information is from the maker's manuals:

Dimensions:

Span	43 ft 0 in (13.11 m)	upper mainplane
	38 ft 6 in (11.74 m)	lower mainplane
Length	31 ft 8 in (9.65 m)	
Height	9 ft 2 in (2.79 m)	
Wing area	288 sq ft (26.76 sq m)	

Weights:

Tare	2500 lbs (1136 kg)
All-up	4000 lbs (1818 kg)

Maximum speed:	147 mph (237 kph)
Cruising speed:	125 mph (201 kph)
Initial climb:	7.5 mins to 5000 ft (1524 m)
	19.5 mins to 10,000 ft (3049 m)
Range:	625 mls (1006 km) with 60 galls (107 ltrs) of fuel
	885 mls (1423 km) with the maximum
	85 galls (151 ltrs) of fuel
Service ceiling:	15,700 ft (4786 m)

Production

7500 – 7546	DH.90 Dragonfly
7547 – 7566	DH.90A Dragonfly

Individual Aircraft Histories

7500 First flown 12.8.35 at Hatfield as **E.2**; regd **G-ADNA** (CoR 6135) 15.8.35 to de Havilland Aircraft Co Ltd; first CoA (5305) issued 17.1.36; CoA lapsed 16.1.37, but visited Farnborough 9.37, so probably operated by DH under manufacturer's permit; regd (CoR 8313) 22.1.38 to Albert Batchelor, and probably operated by Thanet Aero Club Ltd, Ramsgate; CoA renewed 14.3.38; regd 27.1.39 to Southern Airways Ltd, Ramsgate and operated by (associate) Western Airways Ltd, Weston-super-Mare; regn cld as sold 17.4.40; impressed into RAF 17.4.40; 6 AACU, Ringway, same day; allocated serial **X9452** 10.5.40; 8 AACU, Pengam Moors, 24.8.41; to Air Service Training Ltd CRD 8.6.42; DH RU, Witney, 19.8.42; SOC 30.8.42.

7501 Regd **G-AEBU** (CoR 6705) 8.2.36 to de Havilland Aircraft Co Ltd, Hatfield; first CoA (5322) issued 15.2.36; regn cld as sold 5.38 (and CoA renewed 19.5.38); regd **F-AQEU** 31.3.38 to Auguste A Boyer, (via Paul Legastelois ?) Paris; to Sté Française de Transports Aériens 6.38; to Spanish Republicans and flown to Barcelona by A Boyer; probably recovered by Nationalists at end of war in 1939; reported as possibly to Ejercito del Aire as **40-3.**

7502 First CoA (5469) issued 28.4.36 to HM King Ghazi of Iraq; regd **YI-HMK** 27.5.36 to King Ghazi of Iraq, Akerkuf, named *The Golden Eagle*; impressed into Iraqi AF .41; NFT.

7503 Regd **G-AEDW** (CoR 6784) 10.3.36 to H B Legge & Sons Ltd, Hamsey Green; first CoA (5388) issued 9.5.36; regn cld as sold 2.38 (and CoA renewed 11.3.38); regd **VP-YBR** (CoR 51) 2.38 to Rhodesia & Nyasaland Airways Ltd, Salisbury; badly damaged in crash on take-off from Gwelo 5.10.38; crashed nr Kasama 1.1.39.

7504 Regd **G-AECW** (CoR 6747) 29.2.36 to The London Aeroplane Club Ltd, Hatfield; first CoA (5369) issued 28.7.36; regd (CoR 8393) 9.3.38 to de Havilland Aircraft Co Ltd, Hatfield; operated on MoAP permit during war until expiry 10.10.44; RTP and regn cld as PWFU at census 23.11.45.

7505 Regd **G-AECX** (CoR 6748) 28.4.36 to Arthur H Youngman as nominee for H Gordon Selfridge, Heston; first CoA (5462) issued 20.5.36; operated by Selfridge (pilot son-in-law Vicomte de Sibour) on clandestine flight to Spanish Nationalists late 7.36 on behalf of Socony-Vacuum Oil Co to arrange oil supplies; regn cld as sold abroad 3.38 (and CoA renewed 2.3.38); regd **VT-AKC** 4.38 to Air Services of India Ltd, Bombay; flown back to Britain 17.7.39-24.7.39; regd **G-AECX** 9.8.39 to International Air Freight Ltd; operated by Air Dispatch Ltd, Croydon; regd 23.1.40 to Hon Mrs Victor Bruce, Cardiff, still operated by Air Dispatch Ltd; regn cld as sold 22.6.40; impressed into RAF as **AX855** 2.6.40; ATA White Waltham; to Hawker Aircraft CRD 26.8.41; SF Northolt 16.12.41; to DH RU, Witney, 29.1.42; SOC 22.2.42.

G-AEBU, c/n 7501, was registered to its makers before being sold in France as F-AQEU after which it was used in the Spanish civil war [via A Chivers]

The DH.90 used by King Ghazi of Iraq, YI-HMK "The Golden Eagle", c/n 7502; the King was a very enthusiastic aviator [MAP via P H T Green]

G-AEDT, c/n 7508, was the private aircraft of the Rt Hon Sir Philip Sassoon before being sold in Australia   *[via A Chivers]*

7506 To DH Canada with CoA (5461) issued 28.5.36; erected and flown at Downsview 26.6.36; regd **CF-AYF** (CoR 1758) 16.7.36 to W M Archibald, Creston, BC; regd (CoR 1849) 3.11.36 to Consolidated Mining & Smelting Co of Canada Ltd, Trail, BC; badly damaged in heavy landing at Kimberley, BC, 12.10.46; wreck donated to Trail Flying Club.

7507 Regd **G-AEFN** (CoR 6876) 28.4.36 to Walter G Robson, Heston; first CoA (5460) issued 6.6.36; regd 18.2.39 to Air Commerce Ltd, Heston; regn cld as sold 28.3.40; impressed into RAF 28.3.40; 6 AACU, Ringway, same day; allocated serial **X9390** 31.3.40; 7 AACU, Castle Bromwich, 3.5.40; to DH RU, Witney, 20.9.40; 7 FPP, Sherburn-in-Elmet, 3.2.41; 9 MU, Cosford, for store 4.4.41; crashed nr Cosford waterworks after engine failure on take-off 10.9.41; SOC 18.9.41.

7508 Regd **G-AEDT** (CoR 6777) 9.5.36 to Sqn Ldr Rt Hon Sir Philip A G D Sassoon Bt, the Under-Secretary of State for Air (regn reserved 2.36); first CoA (5490) issued 19.6.36; based at Lympne; regn cld as sold 7.38; regd in Australia as **VH-AAD** (CoR 697) 25.3.38 to Adastra Airways Pty Ltd, Mascot for aerial survey work; slightly damaged during forced landing on Gerringong Beach, NSW, 20.1.39; regd 14.6.51 to Bush Pilots Pty Ltd, Cairns as ambulance aircraft; leased to Queensland Ambulance Transport Brigade, Cairns 11.51-11.52 to replace lost DH.89 VH-CFA and again 10.53-11.54 to replace second lost VH-CFA!; regd 25.11.54 to Kingsford-Smith Aviation Service Pty Ltd, Bankstown, NSW; regd 8.6.56 to Griffith Aero Club, Griffith, NSW; sold 8.63 to Charles Masefield & Lord Trefgarne; regn cld 2.9.63;

regd **G-AEDT** 3.10.63 to David, Lord Trefgarne, named *Endeavour;* flown back to UK by Masefield/Trefgarne, departing Bankstown 1.12.63 and arriving Gatwick 23.12.63; to Shoreham for overhaul and CoA renewed 30.7.64; flown to Tallmantz Museum, Santa Ana, CA, USA via Iceland departing 30.7.64; regn cld as sold in USA 2.5.66; regd **N2034** 1.67 to Rosen Novak Auto Co, Omaha, Nebraska (delivered 1.67); regd to Joe L Terteling, Boise, Idaho and del 4.69; US regn probably not used and to store; auctioned 20.9.86 and bought by Brian Woodford for $41,000; regn cld 23.4.87; retd to UK .87 for rebuild by Ron Souch of The Aeroplane Co, Sarisbury Green; regd **G-AEDT** 27.4.87 to Wessex Aviation & Transport Ltd (Brian Woodford), Henstridge; reflown at Lee-on-Solent 15.7.88 and CoA renewed 19.7.88; CoA lapsed 18 7.91 but renewed 25.5.93; sold 9.96 to Colin Smith, Mandeville, New Zealand: shipped out 8.97; regd 12.9.97 to Barry K Donovan, c/o Cathay Pacific Airways, Kai Tak, Hong Kong; regn cld as sold to New Zealand 23.3.98; regd **ZK-AYR** 1.4.98 to Croydon Aircraft Co Ltd (Colin Smith), Mandeville; assembled and reflown 7.4.98; extant at Gore.

7509 Regn **G-AEDU** reserved 3.36 but not taken up; regd **G-ADXM** (CoR 6480) 9.5.36 to William Lindsay Everard MP, Ratcliffe, named *The Leicestershire Vixen II* (regn originally reserved 11.35); CoA (5488) issued 20.6.36; del 27.6.36; regn cld as sold 4.40; impressed into RAF 3.40; 110 (AAC) Wg, Ringway, 3.40; allocated serial **X9327** 31.3.40; 6 AACU, Ringway, 21.5.40; 8 AACU, Cardiff, 24.8.41; ACCCF, White Waltham; 2nd TAF CF, White Waltham 21.6.43; SOC 22.7.44.

G-ADXM, c/n 7509, was owned and used as a business aircraft by Sir William Lindsay Everard MP, who based it on his private airfield at Ratcliffe (Leics) and named it "The Leicestershire Vixen II"   *[via A Chivers]*

7510 Regd **G-AEDH** (CoR 6766) .36 to Samuel Harris, Redhill and operated by Croydon Airways Ltd, Croydon (also t/a Croydon Flying Club); first CoA (5489) issued 2.7.36; receiver appointed to Croydon Airways Ltd 16.3.37 and aircraft sold; regd (CoR 8119) 25.9.37 to Plymouth Airport Ltd, Roborough; regd 15.2.39 to (associate) Western Airways Ltd, Weston-super-Mare; regn cld as sold 8.3.40; impressed into RAF as **AV987** 12.5.40; 110 (AAC) Wg, Ringway, 10.5.40 6 AACU, Ringway, 16.5.40 (16.8.40 ?); SF Ringway 5.12.40; SOC 1.1.41.

7511 Regd **G-AEDI** (CoR 6767) 14.5.36 (reserved 2.36) to British Continental Airways Ltd, Croydon but not delivered; first CoA (5513) issued 13.10.36; regn cld as sold abroad 10.36; flown to Singapore, departing Croydon 27.12.36 and arriving Penang 26.1.37; regd **VR-SAX** (CoR 17) 4.2.37 to Asiatic Petroleum Co (SS) Ltd, Singapore; damaged when swung on landing at Tourane, Indo-China, 20.11.37; rebuilt in situ over three months, departing 27.2.38 only to suffer undercarriage collapse on landing at Vientiane; rebuilt again and flown out 31.5.38 to Singapore; badly damaged again on landing at Alor Star 1.12.38 en route to UK; shipped to Penang and sold for rebuild; regd .39 to Wearne's Air Services Ltd, Singapore; impressed into 'B' Flight MVAF 1.12.41; destroyed in air raid on Kallang 20.1.42.

7512 CoA (5595) issued 21.7.36; regd **VP-YAX** 8.36 to Rhodesia & Nyasaland Airways Ltd, Salisbury; crashed near Gwelo 20.12.38; no casualties.

7513 CoA (5615) issued 6.8.36; regd **VH-UXB** (CoR 612) 26.10.36 to Qantas Empire Airways Ltd, Archerfield; damaged on take-off from Mount Isa, Qld, 25.12.38 but repaired; camouflaged and used during Second World War on USAAF charters; damaged in forced landing at Alexandra 19.6.41 when propeller failure caused engine damage, and repaired; damaged in forced landing at Daly Waters 8.5.43 after generator failure, and repaired; badly damaged when swung on take-off from Archerfield 13.7.43 and repaired; undercarriage collapsed on landing at Cloncurry 28.1.46 and again on take-off from Cloncurry 16.1.47; repaired; regd 25.2.47 to E J Connellan t/a Connellan Airways, Alice Springs; regd 14.3.51 to Connellan Airways Ltd; regn cld as PWFU 17.9.51.

7514 Regd **G-AEHC** (CoR 6919) 5.36 to Lord Beaverbrook, Croydon (possibly regd in name of A E Millar?); first CoA (5516) issued 14.7.36; regd (CoR 7586) 9.1.37 to The London Express Newspapers Ltd and operated by Personal Airways Ltd, Croydon on behalf of Daily Express on internal route survey following the Maybury Committee Report; crashed at Darnaw, Minnigaff Parish, Kircudbrightshire 2.2.37 while flying from Renfrew to Speke, killing L T Jackson of Personal Airways, Maj Harold Pemberton, aviation editor of Daily Express and two other Express staff members; regn cld 4.37.

7515 Regd **G-AEDJ** (CoR 6768) 6.36 to T Loel E B Guiness, Heston; first CoA (5514) issued 3.7.36; regd (CoR 8227) 17.11.37 to A J D Jameson, Heston; regd 11.10.39 to International Air Freight Ltd, Croydon and operated by Air Dispatch Ltd; regn cld as sold 22.6.40; impressed into RAF 2.6.40 as **AV992**; ATA (3 FPP), White Waltham; to Vickers-Armstrongs Ltd for communications by 6.41; SOC 12.2.45.

G-AEDJ, c/n 7515, was first registered to the Guinness brewing family but later saw war service with the RAF and Vickers-Armstrongs *[via A Chivers]*

G-AEDG, c/n 7576, was bought by James Fairbairn, the Australian Minister for Air, who flew it to his homeland in 1937 *[via A Chivers]*

The four Dragonflies operated by the RCMP posed outside the de Havilland factory at Toronto with a group of pilots and engineers in front of each aircraft
[via C N Dodds]

7516 Regd **G-AEDG** (CoR 6764) 29.7.36 (reserved 2.36) to James V Fairbairn, Hatfield, named *Spirit of Flinders;* first CoA (5606) issued 13.8.36; left Lympne 14.9.36 and arrived Darwin 3.10.36, flown by Fairbairn and Owen Thomas; regd cld as sold abroad 10.37; regd in Australia as **VH-ADG** (CoR 673) 12.10.37 to James V Fairbairn, Derrinallum, Vic; (Fairbairn was Australian Minister for Air but this was his private aircraft, based on his strip); requisitioned by Government and del 10.39 to Airlines (WA) Ltd to replace DH.84 VH-URY; regd 5.9.40 to Airlines (WA) Ltd, Maylands, named *Murchison*, later *RMA Port Hedland;* overturned on take-off Guilford, WA,1.12.47; regn cld 12.1.48.

7517 Regd **G-AEDK** (CoR 6769) 3.7.36 to C J Donada, Heston; first CoA (5569) issued 5.9.36; regd 30.1.39 to Mutual Finance Ltd, and operated by Air Dispatch Ltd, Croydon; regd 12.3.40 to (associate) Anglo-European Airways Ltd, Cardiff; regn cld as sold 7.7.40; impressed into RAF; SF Gosport 2.7.40; allocated serial **AW164** 7.7.40; 15 Gp CF, Hooton Park (later Speke), 21.3.41; SOC 16.12.42; BBOC 27.10.43; SOC by 2 MPRD Eaglescliffe as scrap 17.12.43.

7518 Regd **G-AEEK** (CoR 6817) 27.6.36 to Sir William J Firth, Heston/Brooklands; first CoA (5555) issued 11.9.36; struck power lines and crashed at Beeding, Sussex 17.8.37; Sir William and pilot unhurt; wreck to Hatfield 18.8.37; regn cld 12.37.

7519 CoA (5633) issued 27.8.36; regd **F-AOZC** (CoR 4870) 23.9.36 to Baron Sternberg de Armella, Paris; regd 5.38 to Marcel Bleustein, Paris; retd 1.39 to Air Dispatch Ltd, Croydon; regn cld 3.39 as sold abroad; regd **G-AFRF** 9.3.39 to Mutual Finance Ltd, and operated by Air Dispatch Ltd, Croydon; CoA renewed 7.3.39; regd 12.3.40 to (associate) Anglo-European Airways Ltd, Cardiff; regn cld as sold 22.6.40 impressed into RAF as **AV993** 2.6.40; ATA (3 FPP), White Waltham; to Vickers-Armstrongs Ltd, Brooklands,10.6.41; damaged at Brooklands 24.6.41, presumed repaired; to DH RU, Witney, 27.7.42; SOC 11.8.42.

7520 CoA (5575) issued 8.7.36; regd **VP-YBB** 7.36 to London & Rhodesian Mining & Land Co Ltd, Salisbury; crashed in fog at Donga, 13 mls from Selukwe, 20.10.38, while being operated by Flights Ltd; five killed, including pilot Danby Gray & A R Metlerkamp, Chairman of Southern Rhodesia Electricity Supply Commission.

7521 CoA (5655) issued 14.9.36; regd **F-AOYK** 23.9.36 to Baron Jules de Koenigswarter, Paris; to Roger Seligman 1.38; regd **G-AFVJ** 12.6.39 to Airwork Ltd, Heston; CoA renewed 11.7.39; sold 13.7.39, but not regd, to Allflights Ltd, Heston; impressed into RAF 31.3.40 as **X9337**; 110 (AAC) Wg, Ringway; 7 AACU, Castle Bromwich, 3.5.40; damaged 24.9.40 when struck by bullets whilst target towing; 8 AACU, Pengam Moors, 11.12.40; undercarriage collapsed on take off from Old Sarum 24.6.41; to DH RU, Witney; SOC 2.7.41.

7522 Regd **CF-BBD** (CoR 1836) 24.10.36 to DH Aircraft of Canada Ltd, Toronto; (no UK CoA); operated by Royal Canadian Mounted Police by 3.37; regd **CF-MPC** (CoR 2019/A31) 15.7.37 to Royal Canadian Mounted Police, Ottawa, named *Crocus;* impressed into RCAF as **7628**; TOC 23.7.40 at Rockcliffe; SOC 12.6.41 as returned to RCMP, presumably as **CF-MPC**; regd **CF-BXU** 30.5.45 to Johannesson Flying Service, Winnipeg; regd 30.10.45 to A J Danes & F B Wilson, Yellowknife, NWT; badly damaged in forced landing following engine failure at Thorhild, Alberta, 23.12.45.

7523 CoA (5653) issued 12.9.36 to Vacuum Oil Co Ltd, South Africa; flown out late 9.36 by Capt Walters; regd **ZS-AHV** 9.2.37 to Vacuum Oil Co of South Africa Ltd; impressed into SAAF 3.40 as **1403**; NFT.

7524 Regd **G-AEDV** .36 to Hon Charles J Winn, Croydon; first CoA (5580) issued 8.10.36; regd (CoR 7940) 16.6.37 to Birkett Air Service Ltd, Heston; regn cld as sold 27.3.40; impressed into RAF same day;110 (AAC) Wg, Ringway, same day; allocated serial **X9389** 31.3.40; 7 AACU, Castle Bromwich, 3.5.40; 8 AACU, Pengam Moors, 25.8.41; took off from Weston Zoyland 3.9.41 for night-flying exercise with 222 Searchlight Battery but due to fog crashed on the Polden Hills at Chedzoy, killing Flt Lt J R M Sales and Sgt H W Bellingham.

7525 CoA (5663) issued 17.9.36; regd **YI-OSD** to Director of Railways, Iraq; possibly to Iraqi AF; NFT.

ZS-CTR, the former CR-AAB, c/n 7526, at Johannesburg in the hands of A G Mechin
[A G Mechin via P H T Green]

7526 CoA (5689) issued 14.10.36; regd **CR-AAB** to Railway Administration of Portuguese East Africa and operated by DETA, Lourenco Marques; to South Africa and regd **ZS-CTR** 27.9.61 to A G Mechin, Johannesburg; WFU at Baragwanath 8.74; sold to Wayne Kerr c76/77 but remained stored; sold to UK 6.79 and regd **G-AEDU** 4.6.79 to Anthony Haig-Thomas & Martin C Barraclough; briefly stored at Hatfield until rebuilt by Cliff Lovell at Walkeridge Farm and reflown 1.7.81; CoA renewed 10.7.81 and based at Duxford, later Old Warden; sold at Christie's auction at Duxford 14.4.83 for £35,000; regn cld as sold 2.6.83; flown to USA, departing UK 13.6.83 and arriving Clark County Airport, Sellersburg, IN, 15.7.83; regd **N190DH** 6.83 to Charles A Osborne Jr, Louisville, KY; badly damaged on take-off from Clark County Airport, 22.9.87; US regn cld 8.4.88; wreck bought by Torquil Norman and returned to UK for rebuild by Cliff Lovell at Coombe Bissett (7.88), later Lower Upham; regd **G-AEDU** 28.4.92 to Torquil Norman, Rendcomb; rebuilt and reflown at Old Sarum 8.92; CoA renewed 2.12.92; flown to USA, departing UK 11.7.95, arr Portland, ME, 16.7.95 for visit to Oshkosh; returned to UK 12.8.96; regd 8.7.97 to Alexander J Norman, t/a Norman Aeroplane Trust, Rendcomb; to Langham .98 for refurbishing by H Labouchere; retd to Rendcomb; extant.

7527 Regd **VT-AHW** (CoR 290) 15.7.36 to R E Grant-Govan, Delhi; first CoA (5676) issued 29.9.36; del 9.11.36; regn cld 2.9.41; impressed into RAF as **AX797** .41; SF Ratmalana 7.43 until at least 26.11.43; SOC 31.12.43.

7528 CoA (5646) issued 1.9.36; regd **VP-KCA** 30.9.36 to Wilson Airways Ltd, Nairobi; impressed into KAAU 9.39 as either **K13** or **K14** (see c/n 7554); NFT.

7529 CoA (5674) issued 29.9.36; regd **F-APDE** (CoR 4880) 9.10.36 to Gustave Wolf, Constantine, Algeria; regd 3.38 to Georges Prieur, Algiers; regd 10.38 to Sté Française de Transports Aériens, Paris (Le Bourget); to Spanish Republicans 1.38; used at Totana as liaison trainer and allocated type code LY; fled to Argelia, Oran 24.3.39 but recovered by Nationalists 4.39 as **40-4**; to Spanish AF (Ejercito del Aire) as **756**; regd **EC-BAA** 3.41 to Iberia; re-regd **EC-AAQ** .47; sold to Rodolfo Bay Wright, Tangier 7.48; regn cld 12.3.49; regd **OO-PET** 13.9.49 to M Petermans, Brussels (acquired in exchange for Argus OO-PET, which became EC-AEN in 1953); regn cld as sold to France 24.2.53; regd **F-OAMS** 16.7.53 to I Daunes, Tangier; flown Toussus-le-Noble to Jersey 8.54 and regd **G-ANYK** 20.1.55 to BEA (initially intended as executive aircraft with regn G-ABEA?); air-freighted to Eastleigh in Bristol 170 G-AMWC 1.7.56 and regd 25.7.56 to Owen Hill; rebuilt and reflown 27.3.59; CoA renewed 27.5.59; regd 27.11.59 to John R T G Jarvie and Bryan H M Winslett; regd 20.12.60 to Metropolitan Air Movements Ltd, Biggin Hill; DBR when undercarriage collapsed on landing at La Baule 23.6.61; regn cld 2.10.61.

7530 To DH Canada without CoA; regd **CF-MPA** (CoR 1945) 1.5.37 to Royal Canadian Mounted Police, Ottawa, named *Anemone;* impressed into RCAF as **7626** 29.7.40; operated by unit(s) of 3 Training Command; SOC 28.1.43 and RTP.

7531 To DH Canada without CoA; regd **CF-MPB** (CoR 1974) 29.5.37 to Royal Canadian Mounted Police, Ottawa, named *Buttercup;* impressed into RCAF as **7627** 23.7.40; crashed at Oshawa 19.6.42 but repaired; SOC 19.6.44; regd **CF-BZA** 1.6.45 (or 11.6.45) to T P Fox, Verdun, PQ; regd 1.11.45 to Associated Airways Ltd, Edmonton; crashed at Indian Lake, NWT, 17.11.48; regn cld 8.10.49.

7532 CoA (5665) issued 18.9.36 to Alberto & Jorge Marquez Vaeza (founders of PLUNA), Uruguay; regd **CX-AAR** 10.36 to PLUNA, Montevideo, named *Churrinche;* believed WFU .49; to Uruguayan Air Force Museum (Museo Aeronáutica), Montevideo by .79; DBF at museum 4.12.97.

7533 CoA (5695) issued 21.10.36 to DH, Australia; regd **VH-UXA** (CoR 622) 24.1.37 to Fostars Shoes Air Transport Pty Ltd, Mascot; operated by Harry McEvoy of Fostars and flown on Australia-Hong Kong trip by Frank McEvoy and family; left Mascot 27.5.37, retd Darwin 7.7.37; flown on Donald Mackay's Central Australian Expedition 19.7.37-21.8.37; left Mascot 23.2.39 for UK via China, flown by Harry McEvoy; regn cld 17.4.39; regd **G-AFTF** 15.4.39 to Eric E Noddings (director) for Air Dispatch Ltd, Croydon; CoA renewed 29.4.39; regn cld as sold 11.8.40; impressed as **BD149** 11.8.40; 8 AACU, Weston Zoyland same day (later to Old Sarum 10.40 and Pengam Moors 11.40); damaged 16.5.42; SOC 21.5.42.

7534 CoA (5668) issued 22.9.36 to Alberto & Jorge Marquez Vaeza (founders of PLUNA, Uruguay); regd **CX-AAS** 10.36 to PLUNA, Montevideo, named *San Alberto;* regn cld as WFU .46 (but still apparently on register .50).

7535 CoA (5704) issued 4.11.36 to DH South Africa; regd **ZS-AIK** 18.12.36 to Witwatersrand Technical College; impressed into SAAF .40 as **1408**; restored as **ZS-AIK**; crashed at Rustenburg 31.5.51.

7536 CoA (5729) issued 7.12.36; regd **F-APAX** (CoR 4974) 31.12.36 to Jacques Dupuy, Paris; regd 7.37 to Edouard Daubree (Daulory?), Tangier; retd to UK 1.39 and with Air Dispatch Ltd, Croydon; regn cld 3.39 as sold abroad; regd **G-AFRI** 27.3.39 to Hon Mrs Victor Bruce, Croydon (operated by Air Dispatch Ltd); CoA renewed 4.4.39; regd 24.1.40 to Anglo-European Airways Ltd, Cardiff; regn cld as sold 2.6.40; impressed into RAF as **AV994** 2.6.40; ATA (3 FPP), White Waltham; struck by Tiger Moth BB687 while taxying at Peterborough (Westwood) 4.5.41; to DH RU, Witney, 8.5.41; SOC 24.5.41.

7537 CoA (5691) issued 16.10.36; regd **R326** 12.36 to Shell Mex Argentina Ltd, named *Gavilan de la Selva (Jungle Hawk)* (also reported as named *Gavilan de la Pampa (Pampas Hawk)* but see c/n 7563); erected and flown 6.1.37; re-regd **LV-RDA** 11.11.37; destroyed in hangar fire at San Fernando, Buenos Aires, 25.11.37, when still marked as R326!.

C/n 7538, CF-BPD began life as CF-MPD of the RCMP at Ottawa, and later was operated by four airlines or charter companies   *[MAP via P H T Green]*

The first launching of DH.90 floatplane CF-BFF, c/n 7543, at Longueuil, PQ on 21st July 1937   *[P H T Green collection]*

After time spent as a floatplane, CF-BFF was impressed into the RCAF as landplane 7623   *[P H T Green collection]*

7538 To DH Canada without CoA; regd **CF-MPD** (CoR 2017) 26.6.37 to Royal Canadian Mounted Police, Ottawa, named *Dandelion;* regd (CoR 2312/A29) 2.9.38 to Noorduyn Aviation Ltd, St Laurent; regd **CF-BPD** 8.12.38 to same owner; regd (CoR 2404/A295) 6.4.39 to Leavens Bros Air Services Ltd, Toronto; regd 1.9.41 to Ginger Coote Airways Ltd, Vancouver; became Canadian Pacific Air Lines 1.42; ground-looped on take-off and DBR at Edmonton 13.4.43.

7539 CoA (5705) issued 9.11.36; regd **PH-KOK** (CoR 236) 11.11.36 to J E F de Kok, Ypenburg (General Manager of Royal Dutch Shell); regd **PH-ATK** (CoR 325) 4.7.38 to same owner; impressed into Netherlands Army Air Corps 1.9.39 as **LVA962**; destroyed Ypenburg 10.5.40; regn cld 4.7.41.

7540 CoA (5715) issued 20.11.36; regd **VT-AHY** (CoR 292)15.1.37 to Maharaja of Myurbhati, Orissa (based at Dum Dum, Calcutta); impressed into RAF 15.5.40 as **V4734**; AHQ India CF, New Delhi; Bengal CF/CU, Barrackpore, .43; swung on take-off from Barrackpore in crosswind and crashed into ditch 28.5.43; SOC 1.2.44.

7541 CoA (5712) issued 17.11.36; regd **I-DRAG** (CoR 1977) 19.1.37 to Conte Franco Mazzotti Biancinelli, Milan; possibly operated by Ala Littoria; damaged 2.37 and returned by road to Rollasons at Croydon for repairs; regd 20.1.39 to Conte Carlo Felice Trossi, Caglianico; NFT.

7542 CoA (5735) issued 15.12.36; regd **F-APFK** 31.12.36 to Jean Raty, Neuilly-sur-Seine; regn cld after.39.

7543 To DH Canada without CoA; erected and first flown Downsview 19.7.37; regd **CF-BFF** (CoR 2040/A45) 20.7.37 to de Havilland Aircraft of Canada Ltd, Toronto and fitted with Fairchild floats 21.7.37; regd (CoR 2082) 6.8.37 to Consolidated Mining & Smelting Co of Canada Ltd, Trail, BC; sold back to DH 9.37 and leased to Canadian Airways Ltd, Montreal .37; impressed into RCAF as **7623** and TOC 30.7.40 at Trenton; crashed at Toronto Island Airport 23.9.41 but repaired; crashed at Toronto Island Airport 4.5.42 but repaired; to storage 3.8.42; sold 15.11.42 to Clark Ruse Aircraft but sale cancelled; sold 26.1.43 to de Havilland Aircraft of Canada Ltd; regd **CF-BFF** 5.12.42 to Quebec Airways Ltd, Montreal; regd 14.12.45 to de Havilland Aircraft of Canada Ltd, Toronto; regd 16.2.46 to L A Seguin, Rouyn, PQ; regd 16.7.48 to Gold Belt Air Service Ltd, Rouyn; hit soft spot on ice while landing on Ottawa River 20.12.49; partly submerged and DBR.

7544 Regd **G-AESW** (CoR 7617) 3.2.37 to W A Rollason, Croydon; first CoA (5815) issued 4.3.37; regd 12.7.39 to Nash Aircraft Sales & Hire Ltd, Croydon; regd 24.7.39 to Air Taxis Ltd, Croydon; operated by ATA, White Waltham, on outbreak of WWII; regn cld as sold 10.5.40; impressed into RAF as **AV976** 12.5.40; 110 (AAC) Wg, Ringway, 13.5.40; 7 AACU, Castle Bromwich, 16.5.40 but possibly not delivered; used for spares at Ringway and SOC 11.11.40.

The Maharaja of Indore owned c/n 7545, VT-AIE, which sported the final version of the cockpit and special cabin windows   *[Aeroplane (9905E)]*

7545   Regd **VT-AIE** (CoR 298) 3.10.36 to HH Maharaja of Indore, Indore; CoA (5804) issued 27.2.37; loaned to RAF .41 as **HX792**; SOC 4.9.43; possibly restored to **VT-AIE**; regn cld 4.1.46.

7546   CoA 5764 issued 19.1.37 to DH Australia; regd **VH-UXS** (CoR 655) 5.8.37 to Southern Airlines & Freighters Ltd, Mascot; sold 21.7.39 and regd 2.10.39 to T H McDonald, Cairns; regn cld 16.1.42; impressed into RAAF 16.1.42 as **A43-1**; converted to air ambulance by Guinea Airways; 2 CF, Mascot, 11.2.42; damaged on landing at Archerfield 10.8.42; 3 AD, Archerfield, 17.8.42; to Aircrafts Pty Ltd 21.8.42 for repair; 3 AD 23.4.43; PTU, Laverton 10.6.43; 3 AD, Amberley, 6.12.44; sold 9.3.45 to T H McDonald for £850; regd **VH-UXS** 8.8.45 to T H McDonald, Cairns; regd 12.11.45 to Brown & Dureau Pty Ltd, Melbourne; regn cld 28.9.49; regd 28.12.50 to same owner; regd 21.7.54 to R N Hunt, Conargo, NSW; regd 21.1.56 to Austral Motorcycles Pty Ltd, Newcastle, NSW; regd 9.4.56 to D L Hilder, Merewether, NSW; regd 20.5.65 to L G Randall, Shoal Bay, NSW; WFU at Darwin; regn cld 17.7.68; reportedly to Nowra, NSW, .90 as a derelict airframe for rebuild.

7547   CoA (6051) issued 20.9.37 to L'Aviation Civile Romaine; regd **YR-FLY** 1.10.37 to Liniile Aeriene Române Exploatate cu Statul (LARES); believed scrapped or destroyed by .43 but also listed as scrapped 10.45.

7548   CoA (6066) issued 27.9.37 to L'Aviation Civile Romaine; regd **YR-FLO** 1.10.37 to Liniile Aeriene Române Exploatate cu Statul (LARES); believed scrapped or destroyed by .43 but also listed as WFU 9.44

7549   CoA (6083) issued 14.10.37 to L'Aviation Civile Romaine; regd **YR-FLU** 23.10.37 to Liniile Aeriene Române Exploatate cu Statul (LARES); WFU .40.

7550   CoA (5940) issued 9.6.37 to Swedish Air Force; serial **Fv906** (in type Trp3; later Tp3, transport category); Staff Flt of F8 Wg, Stockholm for use as VIP transport by C-in-C of Swedish Air Force, Lt Gen Torsen Tris, and Chief of Staff Col Arthur Ornburg; coded 6-3 (6 indicating Staff Flt, 3 the individual aircraft); later coded 8-99, 8-67, 8-57 & 8-68; some time operated on skis; DBR in heavy landing 8.6.42; SOC 28.5.43.

VH-UXS, c/n 7546, minus its undercarriage spats   *[via A Chivers]*

Danish Army S-24, c/n 7552, was used as a training aircraft pre-war

[via author]

7551 CoA (5882) issued 24.4.37 to Haerens Flyvertropper (Danish Army AF); serial **S-23**; to Army Aviation workshops at Clover Field nr Copenhagen for installation of military equipment; used as blind-flying and navigation trainer; 3 Esk, Vaerlose; damaged by Luftwaffe attack on Vaerlose 9.4.40; stored after German occupation until removed to an unknown location and fate.

7552 CoA (5888) issued 27.4.37 to Haerens Flyvertropper (Danish Army AF); serial **S-24**; to Army Aviation workshops at Clover Field nr Copenhagen for installation of military equipment; used as blind-flying and navigation trainer; stored after German occupation until removed to an unknown location and fate.

7553 CoA (5981) issued 22.7.37; regd **SU-ABW** to Misr Airwork Ltd; flown back to UK by Geoffrey Allington, arriving Lympne 18.11.46; to Gatwick 21.11.46 for overhaul; regd **G-AIYJ** 5.12.46 to C G (Geoffrey) Allington, Birmingham; based at Gatwick and used as ferry aircraft on behalf of Air Transport SA, Brussels; regd 2.3.48 to Southern Aircraft (Gatwick) Ltd, Gatwick; sold 7.3.49 and regn cld 14.3.49.

7554 Regd **G-AEXI** (CoR 7825) 20.5.37 to Lt Col E T Peel DSO MC, Alexandria, Egypt; CoA (5929) issued 27.5.37; regn cld 11.38; regd in Kenya as **VP-KCS** 11.38 to Wilson Airways Ltd, Nairobi; impressed into KAAU 9.39 as either **K13** or **K14** (see c/n 7528); NFT.

7555 Regd **G-AEWZ** (CoR 7805) 10.4.37 to Air Service Training Ltd, Hamble; CoA (5971) issued 9.7.37; operated for 3 E&RFTS and (wef 11.39) 11 AONS, Hamble (later Watchfield); regn cld 10.1.41; impressed into RAF 10.1.41 as **DJ716** and remained operated by 11 AONS; 10 MU, Hullavington, 19.3.41; crashed 8.7.41; repaired and to 39 MU, Colerne, 29.8.41; to Short Bros Ltd for communications duties 30.11.41; sold 5.46 to Short Bros (Rochester and Bedford) Ltd, Rochester; regd **G-AEWZ** 30.5.46 to Short Bros (Rochester and Belfast) Ltd and operated by Rochester Air Charter Service, Rochester; CoA renewed 23.8.46; regd 12.1.48 to Short Bros & Harland Ltd, Rochester; regd 20.12.48 to F T Bingham; operated by Hampshire School of Flying, Eastleigh; regd 23.6.49 to V H Bellamy, t/a Flightways, Eastleigh; regd 19.7.50 to Silver City Airways Ltd, Eastleigh; regd 9.6.60 to V H Bellamy, Eastleigh; regd 7.10.60 to R M Wilson of Devonair Ltd, operated by Coventry Flying & Country Club, Baginton; ground-looped on take-off from Elmdon for Wolverhampton 3.3.61; wreck to Baginton but repairs abandoned; regn cld 30.7.64.

7556 Regd **G-AFAN** (CoR 8105) 21.7.37 to de Havilland Aircraft Co Ltd, Hatfield; CoA (6008) issued 5.8.37; regn cld as sold abroad 9.37; regd in Turkey as **TC-IDE** 8.37 to Devlet Hava Yollari; NFT but possibly acquired by Spanish Republicans.

7557 To DH Canada without CoA; stored until RCAF acceptance flight 27.7.40; to RCAF 1.8.40 as **7624**; operated by units of 4 Training Command; SOC 8.1.45; regd **CF-BXV** 22.2.45 to Johannesson Flying Service, Winnipeg; ground-looped and undercarriage collapsed on landing at Winnipeg 3.4.45.

VP-KCS, c/n 7554, was another of the Wilson Airways fleet to be taken over by the Kenya Auxiliary Air Unit

[via A Chivers]

G-AEWZ, c/n 7555, saw wartime service as a communications aircraft before reverting to civilian use   *[P Clifton via R C Sturtivant]*

7558   To DH Canada without CoA; stored until issued to RCAF as **7625** 1.8.40; operated by units of 4 Training Command; crashed at Claresholm 6.5.42; SOC 8.3.43.

7559   Regd **G-AEXN** (CoR 7838) 30.4.37 to de Havilland Aircraft Co Ltd, Hatfield; CoA (5892) issued 16.6.37; regd (CoR 8008) 19.7.37 to E D Spratt, Hatfield; regd (CoR 8392) 8.3.38 to Hon Max Aitken & Brian S Thynne, Hendon; regd 30.1.39 to Mutual Finance Ltd; operated by Air Dispatch Ltd, Croydon; crashed at Hampden, nr High Wycombe, 21.7.39; regn cld 29.3.40.

7560   CoA (5989) issued 22.7.37; regd **ZK-AFB** (CoR 98) 23.9.37 to Air Travel (NZ) Ltd, Hokitika; regd 3.52 to Canterbury Aero Club, Christchurch; to Aircraft Engineering of NZ Ltd and operated by Wairarapa & Ruahine Aero Club; to A J Bradshaw, named *Kiwi Rover;* regd 13.5.61 to Air Charter (NZ) Ltd, Christchurch; missing between Christchurch and Milford Sound 12.2.62; five killed included pilot B G Chadwick (owner of company).

7561   CoA (6011) issued 6.8.37; regd **OO-JFN** (CoR 416) 25.9.37 to Louis J Mahieu, Brussels; possibly operated by Banque Nationale de Belgique, where owner was director; to Estafette Escadrille, Aéronautique Militaire, 10.9.39; II Group, 2 Regt, 4.40; retreated to Fréjorgues, France 5.40; handed over to Vichy Government on Franco-German armistice 8.40; Belgian regn cld 4.3.46.

7562   CoA (6105) issued 28.10.37 to DH Australia; erected at Mascot and flown 28.1.38; regd **VH-UTJ** (CoR 691) 23.2.38 to North Western Airlines Ltd, Moree, NSW; camouflaged for use on USAAF charter flights; undercarriage collapsed on take-off from Narromine 16.1.40 and repaired; regd 3.10.40 to Qantas Empire Airways Ltd, Sydney; damaged on landing at Breddon, Qld, 6.5.43 when starboard brake seized, causing undercarriage damage and broken centre section spar; repaired; swung on landing at Breddon 21.10.43 due to jammed throttle, causing similar damage; repaired; swung on landing at Cloncurry 14.10.45, causing starboard undercarriage to collapse and damaging mainplanes and propellers; repaired; regd 18.10.46 to E J Connellan t/a Connellan Airways, Alice Springs; regd 14.3.51 to Connellan Airways Ltd, Alice Springs; damaged by fire at Ammaroo, NT, 8.1.48 (or 9.1.48) and repaired; DBF while refuelling at Tennant Creek, NT, 9.8.55; regn cld 28.9.55.

7563   CoA (6218) issued 4.3.38 to Eagle Oil, Argentina; regd **LV-KAB** to Shell Mex Argentina (Pty) Ltd, (or Eagle Oil); erected and test flown 21.5.38; named *Gavilan de la Selva (Jungle Hawk);* crashed into hill nr Rio de Janeiro 8.11.40 after collision with Ju52/3m PP-SPF over Presidential Palace while on anti-submarine patrol; Shell pilot C F Abbott killed.

7564   CoA (6261) issued 29.4.38; regd **ZS-ANM** 28.6.38 to Miss M Reynolds; impressed into SAAF .40 as **1404**; restored as **ZS-ANM** .46; crashed Pietersburg 18.8.49.

7565   CoA (6246) issued 7.4.38 to Shell Co of Nigeria; regd **VR-NAA** (CoR 1) 18.5.38 to Shell Co of East Africa Ltd, Lagos; left Croydon 16.6.38 on delivery via Cairo and Khartoum but hit six-foot high anthill on take-off from Abecher, Chad, 25.9.38 while still on delivery flight (pilot F/O J R Van).

7566   CoA (6390) issued 5.9.38; regd **ZK-AGP** (CoR 143) 1.11.38 to Air Travel (NZ) Ltd, Hokitika (fleet No 5); propeller came off in flight and aircraft crashed in sea off Westport 21.12.42, killing four passengers.

ZK-AFB, c/n 7560, operated by Air Charter NZ Ltd, the owners when it crashed fatally in February 1962   *[via C N Dodds]*

Appendix 1

UNITED KINGDOM AIRLINES AND CHARTER OPERATORS WHICH USED THE DH.84, DH.86, DH.89 OR DH.90

Note: some of the aircraft in the list below each operator's entry were registered not to the company itself but to nominees, while others were borrowed. Reference to the individual aircraft listings will give further information.

ABERDEEN AIRWAYS Ltd

With three other companies, Aberdeen Airways Ltd was registered on 2nd January 1934 by Eric Leslie Gandar Dower, with a capital of £8000 in £1 shares. Delivery of its first aircraft, DH.84 Dragon G-ACRH *Aberdonian,* was made to Dyce airfield, Aberdeen on 6th July, but this aircraft was written off a week later and was replaced by a Short Scion. The airline's share capital was increased to £20,000 on 20th July, and a week later Dyce Airport was opened officially.

Scheduled services began on 10th September 1934, when the Scion flew from Dyce to Glasgow (Renfrew), and Dragon G-ACAN joined in next day, but poor passenger figures forced the closure of the route on 24th October. The return fare had been £5-5-0 (£5.25). Aberdeen Airways' second route was from Dyce to Stromness (Howe), which G-ACAN opened on 27th May 1935. On 4th June another service, to Edinburgh (Turnhouse) began, but again a low number of passengers forced its closure on 3rd August, apart from a few 'on demand' trips during the following year or so. More effective was the Stromness route, into which a call at Thurso (Claredon) was inserted from 11th June. On 3rd December 1935 the aircraft on this service began to call at South Ronaldsay (St Margaret's Hope) on request, but ten days later the Dyce to Thurso sector closed down for the winter. During its first year of operation, Aberdeen Airways had carried 480 passengers but had suffered a loss of £8000. Two more aircraft had been added to the fleet in October: Dragon G-ADFI and Dragon Rapide G-ADDE.

The first air ambulance service flown by Aberdeen Airways carried a sick islander from St. Margaret's Hope to Stromness on 2nd February 1936. On 13th April the Dyce to Thurso sector reopened, and on 2nd June Aberdeen Airways inaugurated its Dyce to Shetland (Sumburgh) route, one day ahead of Highland Airways. This flight was made non-stop, but afterwards calls at Thurso and Stromness or Kirkwall (Quanterness) were made routinely. Again, the Dyce to Thurso sector was not flown that winter, leaving the services northward intact.

On 17th November 1936 a resolution was passed altering the name of the company to Allied Airways (Gandar Dower) Ltd, and this change came into effect on 13th February 1937.

Aircraft: DH.84 G-ACAN, G-ACRH, G-ADFI

ADIE AVIATION Ltd

Principally involved in aircraft maintenance, Adie Aviation of Croydon maintained Dragon Rapides for ad-hoc charter work between 1948 and 1954.

Aircraft: DH.89 G-AFMF, G-AGJG, G- AKDX, G-AKRE, G-AKZI, G-AKZJ, G-AKZW, G-AMAM

ADVANCE AIR LINES Ltd

Formed at Croydon on 1st December 1937 by J F Armitage and Mrs J E Grave, this very short-lived company may have had connections with the Hon Mrs Victor Bruce (see Air Dispatch Ltd). Four DH.84s were acquired in March 1938 but passed to Anglo-European Airways Ltd the following month.

Aircraft : DH.84 G-ACBW, G-ACEK, G-ACHV, G-ACKU

AERIAL ENTERPRISES Ltd

A small charter company based at Booker, Aerial Enterprises owned two DH.89s for about a year from March 1968, using them for parachute-dropping and photographic work.

Aircraft: DH.89 G-AGJG, G-AJGS

AERO ENTERPRISES (JHS) Ltd

This company owned a Dragon which was operated by Chrisair at Ramsgate and Sywell between November 1962 and May 1968.

Aircraft: DH.84 G-ADDI

AIKMAN AIRWAYS Ltd

One Rapide joined the recently-formed Aikman Airways at Croydon in April 1948 for pleasure flying and charter work, but the company, the brain-child of Wg Cdr B T Aikman, ceased flying at the end of 1950.

Aircraft: DH.89 G-AKND

AIR CHARTER Ltd

Air Charter Ltd was the first company formed by the redoubtable Freddie Laker, and began charter and freight-carrying operations from Croydon in March 1947 with Dragon G-ADDI and Dragon Rapide G-AFHY. Dragon Rapide G-AGFU entered service in August of that year, as did a pair of Miles Geminis and an Airspeed Consul. Between them, these aircraft continued the company's work until larger aircraft entered service in the early 1950s.

Aircraft: DH.84 G-ADDI
DH.89 G-AFHY, G-AGFU, G-AJSL

Air Charter Ltd had the use of Rapide G-AFHY for less than two months in 1947 before it crashed at Rotterdam [Denis Fox collection]

AIR CHARTER EXPERTS Ltd

Formed by Capt G H Drummond in March 1947, Air Charter Experts Ltd was based at Ronaldsway in the Isle of Man, from where two elderly DH.89s were flown on charter work. The company was very short-lived, however, as in August of the same year it was taken over by Manx Air Charters Ltd.

Aircraft: DH.89 G-ADAE, G-AEMH, G-AJGV

AIR COMMERCE Ltd

Three DH.84s were acquired by this company, founded by British & Foreign Aviation, in the summer of 1936. By the time scheduled services from Liverpool to the Isle of Man, Belfast and London began in 1938 a DH.89 had been added to the fleet. These services came to an end on the outbreak of war in September 1939, by which time another DH.89 and DH.90 Dragonfly G-AEFN had joined the company. These two were among the five aircraft taken over by National Air Communications in September 1939 and based at Ronaldsway.

Services were resumed in 1945, but the original Dragon was lost in April 1946, although replaced later in the year. Air Commerce was absorbed into Olley Air Service in December 1946, but the company name survived until 1950 as a charter operator using aircraft from the Olley fleet.

Aircraft: DH.84 G-ACEK, G-ACGG, G-AEKZ
DH.89 G-AEPF, G-AERZ, G-AFEP, G-AHGG
DH.90 G-AEFN

AIR COURIERS (TRANSPORT) Ltd
AIR COURIERS (PROPERTIES) Ltd

A development of a prewar aircraft maintenance company, Air Couriers (Transport) Ltd was formed at Croydon early in 1948 under the directorship of G G Glanville, F W Griffith and C P Godsal. The company's fleet was varied, and included a number of Dragon Rapides which were widely used for charter operations and pleasure flying until 1960, by which time the company had moved to Biggin Hill.

Aircraft: DH.89 G-ACPP, G-ACYR, G-AFFB, G-AKNN, G-AKNY, G-AKSE, G-AKTD, G-ALBI, G-APBM

AIR CRUISES Ltd

Set up by Amy Johnson and Francois Dupré at Hatfield in early 1936, this company used a DH.84. Its task seems to have been quality air touring, but the aircraft was sold early in 1937, apparently after the venture failed.

Aircraft: DH.84 G-AECZ

AIR DISPATCH Ltd

Wholly-owned by wealthy amateur racing driver and pilot the Hon Mrs Victor Bruce, this company was formed on 9th July 1934 and came about when that lady responded to an advertisement for aircraft to deliver London daily newspapers to Paris, a service which Air France had been providing but was not keen to continue. The other original directors were Flt Lt H Thomas (of Provincial Airways Ltd) and N M Poole. To operate its service, Air Dispatch acquired two DH.84s and began dawn flights from Croydon to Le Bourget. The operation was not without troubles, and on one occasion papers had to be dumped into the English Channel after an engine failed. Unfortunately, the newspaper service failed to make money, and a fatal crash did not improve matters. A mystery surrounds the identity of the aircraft reported lost in this incident, as records do not show the involvement of any of the company's aircraft. As an alternative operation an air ambulance service was started, for which two more DH.84s were purchased.

The two Dragons involved in the newspaper flights were, fortunately for the ailing company, sold for use in the Spanish civil war and in their place two DH.89s were bought. In 1938 the threat of war persuaded Mrs Bruce that she should give up all other activities to concentrate on Army co-operation flying, for which she soon received a contract. This involved flying for the benefit of gunners and searchlight operators, and before long the company had a fleet of nineteen DH.84s, DH.89s and DH.90s, plus four other types, all concentrating on this contract. Soon after the Munich crisis, the company signed a 'dormant contract', whereby in the event of war the entire fleet of 23 aircraft would be placed under orders from the Air Ministry. On 31st August 1939 this happened, and the aircraft were speedily flown away from Croydon, some to Cardiff (Pengam Moors) and others elsewhere. Between then and June 1940 Air Dispatch took part in the task of ferrying RAF officers and urgent supplies to and from France, after which all the aircraft were impressed. Air Dispatch spent the war years as an aircraft maintenance organisation and did not operate aircraft again before going out of business just after the war.

It should be noted that aircraft used by Air Dispatch Ltd were registered from time to time not only to the company but to the Hon Mrs Victor Bruce, Anglo European Airways Ltd, Commercial Air Hire Ltd, International Air Freight Ltd and E E Noddings.

Aircraft: DH.84 G-ACBW, G-ACCZ, G-ACEK, G-ACET, G-ACHV, G-ACKB, G-ACKU, G-ACVD, G-AEMK

DH.89 G-ADAK, G-ADNH, G-ADNI

DH.90 G-AECX, G-AEDJ, G-AEDK, G-AEXN, G-AFRF, G-AFRI, G-AFTF

AIR ENTERPRISES Ltd

Set up at Croydon in April 1947 by H, A and F Carr and T Hudson, Air Enterprises began passenger and freight charter operations. A Dragon Rapide was acquired in December 1947, and several more were added in the spring of

G-AKOB "The Sandown Flier" was used by Air Enterprises Ltd on holiday flights to the Isle of Wight [G M Simons collection]

1948. An out-station was set up at Glasgow (Renfrew) from where the charter work was continued, as well as some pleasure flying. The company was one of the first to operate passenger services under the BEA Associate scheme, and from July 1948 the Rapide fleet was used on summer services from Cowes to Southampton, Gatwick and Croydon, mainly at weekends. By 1951 scheduled services were being flown from Heathrow, Northolt and Gatwick to Sandown instead of Cowes and from Shoreham to Jersey and Sandown. The company's Rapides were also often seen at race meetings around the country and on ad-hoc charters, particularly in the winters. The Isle of Wight services continued until the end of the 1952 season, after which the Rapides were sold.

Aircraft: DH.89 G-AFMJ, G-AKNX, G-AKNY, G-AKNZ, G-AKOA, G-AKOB, G-AKRS, G-ALWY

AIR KRUISE (KENT) Ltd

The first DH.89 acquired by this company, whose chairman and managing director was Wg Cdr H C Kennard, arrived in April 1950. In July that year this Rapide began flying a route from Lympne to Le Touquet three times per day. To cope with demand, a second Rapide was soon added. From June 1953 the route was extended to run from Ramsgate to Ostend via Lympne and Le Touquet, the aircraft carrying Trans Channel Airways titles as well as those of Air Kruise.

Following its take-over by the British Aviation Services group in 1953, Air Kruise continued to operate, gradually replacing its older aircraft with larger and more modern types and moving to a better operating base at Lydd (Ferryfield).

Aircraft: DH.89 G-AESR, G-AEWL, G-ALWK

Registered to Wg Cdr H C Kennard of Air Kruise (Kent) Ltd, G-AEWL was operated under the title Trans Channel Air Services, and is seen at London Airport (Heathrow) on 23rd September 1950 [Denis Fox collection]

AIRLINES (JERSEY) Ltd (see Jersey Airlines Ltd)

AIRMOTIVE (LIVERPOOL) Ltd

One Dragon Rapide was the only aircraft owned by this company, which was set up at Liverpool (Speke) in January 1950 by Capt J H Hoggart-Hill. Pleasure flying and Army co-operation work formed the basis of the company's operations until June 1952, when the company was liquidated.

Aircraft: DH.89 G-AFOI

AIR NAVIGATION & TRADING Co Ltd

A significant user of Dragon Rapides, Air Navigation & Trading Co Ltd was formed at Blackpool (Squires Gate) in March 1947 by R L Whyham, who before the war had been chief engineer with Allied Airways (Gandar Dower) Ltd. A Rapide was acquired to carry out charter operations, and in 1948 AN&T was awarded the right to operate a scheduled service from Carlisle (Kingstown) to the Isle of Man (Ronaldsway), under the BEA Associate

G-AKZT of Air Navigation & Trading Co Ltd at Newcastle (Woolsington) [G M Simons collection]

scheme. A base was therefore established at Kingstown, and the route was opened, using Rapides.

In 1951 two DH.84s were bought, specifically for pleasure flying at Blackpool, always involving a circuit of the famous tower. These remained in service until 1961, after which they were replaced by Rapides, the last of which was disposed of in 1967.

Aircraft: DH.84 G-ACIT, G-ADDI

DH.89 G-ACPP, G-AHJA, G-AJBJ, G-AJKW, G-AKMD, G-AKOY, G-AKSG, G-AKZT, G-ALXI, G-ALXJ, G-APSD

AIR TAXIS Ltd

Formed in 1934 by C W Allen, J D Smith and F Bingham to operate air charters, Air Taxis Ltd used three DH.84s and added DH.90 Dragonfly G-AESW to the fleet in 1939. Surviving aircraft were taken over by National Air Communications in September 1939 and were impressed into the RAF in April 1940, but the company worked through the war by carrying out aircraft repairs and maintenance at Manchester (Barton).

Aircraft: DH.84 G-ACHV, G-ACNJ, G-ACPX

DH.90 G-AESW

AIR TAXIS (CROYDON) Ltd

Registered on 4th December 1946 by B Quinn and H Bryan, this company carried out charter work with two Proctors, a Dragon and a Dragon Rapide. Notable among the tasks handled was the repatriation of stranded Britons from Paris during a strike of French railwaymen in June 1947. The company also co-operated closely with Southampton Air Services, often pooling aircraft and work. In February 1948, however, Air Taxis (Croydon) Ltd went into liquidation and its aircraft were sold.

Aircraft: DH.84 G-AECZ

DH.89 G-AGZO

AIR TAXIS (CUMBERLAND) Ltd

Formed in 1957 to operate charter flights and pleasure flying in Scotland from a base at Carlisle (Crosby), this concern used one Rapide between October 1957 and April 1961, when the company ceased trading.

Aircraft: DH.89 G-ALPK

AIR TRANSPORT CHARTER (CHANNEL ISLANDS) Ltd

Established in July 1946 at Jersey, this company originally used Miles Aerovans to carry flowers and vegetables to the mainland. The Aerovans were replaced by Rapides a year later, but the Rapides were used mainly on charter flights between the three main islands. Considerable work was undertaken during the next few years by the Rapides and a number of Dakotas, but in 1952 the company was forced to cease flying after falling foul of the licensing authorities.

Aircraft: DH.89 G-AFFB, G-AGWC, G-AIUL

G-AIUL's second owner was Air Transport Charter (CI) Ltd, who named it "Saint Clement"   *[Denis Fox collection]*

AIRVIEWS Ltd

In September 1951, this company, based at Manchester (Barton and Ringway) acquired a Rapide to add to its small fleet of aircraft devoted to pleasure flying. This aircraft was also used on a scheduled service from Manchester to the Isle of Wight via Eastleigh, and three similar aircraft were added. Two of them had to be sold during temporary financial difficulties in 1957, but by 1958 the remaining aircraft were flying the scheduled service three times per week in the summer months. In addition, the company frequently carried members of the racing fraternity to meetings at many courses. However, in 1959 the company went into liquidation and its aircraft were sold.

Aircraft: DH.89 G-AFRK, G-AGDM, G-AGSH, G-ALBA

G-ALBA when in service with Airviews Ltd   *[P H T Green collection]*

AIRWORK Ltd
AIRWORK SERVICES Ltd

Originally formed at Heston in 1928, Airwork Ltd survived the Second World War and almost immediately afterwards built up a fleet of Consuls, Proctors and Rapides for passenger and freight charter operations. In addition, the company was involved in sales of second-hand aircraft. At least three of the Rapides were used at Perth (Scone) under the banner of Airwork Services Training until the last one was disposed of in July 1962.

Aircraft: DH.84 G-ACEU, G-ACEV, G-ACHV, G-ACIE, G-ACLE, G-ACMC, G-ACMJ, G-ACNI, G-AEKZ

DH.89 G-ACZE, G-ACZF, G-ADAE, G-ADAG, G-ADAH, G-ADAI, G-ADBW, G-ADCL, G-ADDF, G-ADIM, G-AEMM, G-AESR, G-AFLY, G-AFLZ, G-AFMA, G-AFME, G-AFMF, G-AFMG, G-AFMH, G-AFMI, G-AFMJ, G-AJBJ, G-AJDN, G-AJFJ, G-AJKH, G-AJKI, G-AJVA, G-AJVB, G-AKEU, G-AKJS, G-AKNF, G-AKOA, G-AKRS, G-AKTZ, G-AKUB, G-AKUC, G-ALBI, G-ALGO, G-ALWP

DH.90 G-AFVJ

Rapide G-AJBJ in its heyday at Newcastle when owned by Airwork Ltd
[Denis Fox collection]

ALLFLIGHTS Ltd

Flying from Heston, this company used, among other aircraft, a DH.90 that was acquired in July 1939 but had not been registered to the company by the time it was impressed for military service in March 1940.

Aircraft: DH.90 G-AFVJ

ALLIED AIRWAYS (GANDAR DOWER) Ltd

At the time of its change of name from Aberdeen Airways Ltd on 13th February 1937, this airline was flying a route between Thurso and Sumburgh, with intermediate stops. Its eponymous Managing Director had visions of setting up a route to Norway, and on 22nd May a proving flight was made from Dyce to Stavanger (Sola) in Dragon Rapide G-ADDE, with Mr Gandar Dower on board. To operate the service, a larger aircraft was required, and a DH.86B Express was ordered. This aircraft, G-AETM, was delivered to Dyce on 29th June and made a proving flight from Newcastle (Woolsington) to Stavanger on 5th July. On this service, to be flown five times per week, the return fare was set at £15-15-0 (£15.75). The first scheduled flight was made on 12th July, but due to a poor response closed down for the winter on 27th September.

G-ACNJ of Allied Airways (Gandar Dower) Ltd, flying low over the Scottish countryside [*via A Chivers*]

Another Dragon, G-ACLE, was acquired in September to replace G-ADFI, which had been written off in July, and G-ACNJ arrived on 21st November, ready to fly the official Royal Mail service from Dyce to Sumburgh via Stromness two days later. Competing with Highland Airways, Allied Airways opened a twice-weekly service from the municipal airfield at Inverness (Longman) to Thurso on 30th November, but it closed on 9th April 1938 due to lack of passengers. In 1938 the Newcastle to Stavanger route was reopened on 16th April, but after losing £16,000 in two seasons the service closed again on 19th September. The Inverness to Thurso route, however, was reopened on 4th November and flew for a short time during that winter.

In January 1939 the new Air Transport Licensing Authority met to decide the future of air routes in northern Scotland, and in February announced that Allied Airways would continue to operate between Aberdeen, Thurso and the Orkneys, while Scottish Airways would fly northward from Inverness. The two airlines would share services between the Orkneys and Shetlands. A non-stop service from Aberdeen to the Shetlands would be Allied Airways' prerogative, while Scottish Airways would have the use of Dyce airport for the first time to fly a service to Inverness and Stornoway.

Allied Airways' last route, the non-stop service to Sumburgh, opened on 10th July 1939, but on the outbreak of war on 3rd September all operations ceased. Apart from the new non-stop service and trans-Pentland services, flying recommenced two weeks later under the auspices of National Air Communications, and continued for the time being, although by now there was only one pilot, the others having been 'called up'. During the spring of 1940 Allied Airways aircraft were involved in the evacuation of troops from France, often crewed by pilots from other airlines. On 27th June all internal airlines except Allied Airways joined forces under the Associated Airways Joint Committee, pooling their aircraft for general use, but Gandar Dower believed he could weather the storm without such co-operation, and carried on by himself, flying his remaining routes for the benefit of mainly Service passengers for the duration of hostilities.

In 1942 and 1943 more aircraft were acquired to replace those written off in accidents. Twelve thousand passengers were carried in 1945, providing revenue of £45,000. Two more Dragon Rapides were taken on strength in 1946, but soon the company became one of those taken by British European Airways. Due to difficulties in the reorganisation, Allied Airways continued to fly under its own name, but operating on behalf of BEA, between 2nd August 1946 and 31st January 1947. During that time the services from Aberdeen to Sumburgh, some of them via Wick and Kirkwall, were maintained. When Allied Airways became unable to carry on due to shortage of aircraft, BEA took over fully on 11th April 1947. Ironically, the only profit ever made by Allied Airways and its predecessor was £5000 in 1946/47.

Aircraft: DH.84   G-ACAN, G-ACLE, G-ACNJ, G-ADFI
        DH.86   G-AETM
        DH.89   G-ACZE, G-ACZF, G-ADAH, G-ADDE,
                   G-AGDM, G-AGHI, G-AIDL

Undergoing start-up, probably at Dyce post-war, was G-ADAH of Allied Airways [*via C N Dodds*]

ALLIED BRITISH AIRWAYS Ltd

Owned by Whitehall Securities Ltd, this company was registered on 30th September 1935 to act as the holding company for United Airways Ltd and Spartan Airlines Ltd and to absorb Hillman's Airways. Before the latter move could take place, however, the word Allied was dropped and the company became British Airways Ltd on 29th October 1935.

ANGLO-EUROPEAN AIRWAYS Ltd

Established on 18th January 1937 at Croydon by T Nash (the MD of Nash Aircraft Sales) and C J Roberts, this company operated two DH.84s from April 1938 but sold them before the outbreak of war. Early in 1940 two DH.89s and two DH.90s were registered to the company but were soon impressed for RAF service.

Aircraft: DH.84   G-ACHV, G-ACKU
        DH.89   G-ADAK, G-ADNI
        DH.90   G-AFRF, G-AFRI

ARROW AIR SERVICES (CHARTER) Ltd

Established at Shipdham in 1969, this company took delivery of a Rapide in July 1970 but never made use of it, selling it four months later.

Aircraft: DH.89   G-AKRS

ASSOCIATED AIRWAYS JOINT COMMITTEE

In order to co-ordinate essential internal scheduled services, the Government established the Associated Airways Joint Committee (AAJC) on 5th May 1940. The seven airlines involved were Air Commerce Ltd, Great Western & Southern Airlines Ltd, Isle of Man Air Services Ltd, Olley Air Service Ltd, Railway Air Services Ltd, Scottish Airways Ltd and West Coast Air Services Ltd. For some reason Allied Airways (Gandar Dower) Ltd was treated separately. A headquarters for AAJC was set up at Liverpool (Speke), where excellent maintenance facilities were available, with Wg Cdr A H Measures as manager and Capt G P Olley as his deputy. To operate the scheme, AAJC had the use of four DH.86s, fourteen DH.89s and three DH.84s. Routes were re-established without delay, but on 17th May the Air Ministry, desperate for transport aircraft to help evacuate personnel from France, ordered all AAJC aircraft and crews to fly to RAF Stations in the south of England to await instructions. This order was countermanded soon afterwards, but reinstated on 22nd May and again cancelled on 31st May when it was accepted that sending unarmed aircraft to a war zone was not a good idea!

All services were again suspended on 15th June and the aircraft flown to Exeter and on to France, where they put in sterling service in the evacuation, adding to the effort being made by certain RAF squadrons. Two DH.86s and two DH.89s had to be abandoned, although their crews survived.

AAJC continued to control internal air services throughout the war and beyond, surviving until all its assets were taken over by British European Airways on 1st February 1947.

ASTRAL AVIATION Ltd

This company took over the route to the Isle of Man previously operated by West Cumberland Air Services Ltd and its surviving Rapide, but within a few months was taken over by Lancashire Aircraft Corporation Ltd.

Aircraft: DH.89   G-AKNN

BARDOCK AVIATION Ltd

Formerly Southern Counties Aerial Contracts Ltd, this Staverton-based company, one of whose directors was Sir Bernard Docker, used Rapide G-AKIF for charter work and as a parachuting vehicle. After an abortive attempt to obtain licences for scheduled services, the company lost interest and all flying ceased at the end of 1964.

Aircraft: DH.89   G-AKIF

BARNSTAPLE & NORTH DEVON AIR SERVICES

This company, owned by R T Boyd, operated his DH.84 on a service from Barnstaple to Lundy Island between October 1933 and June 1934, when the aircraft crashed on the island.

Aircraft: DH.84   G-ACCR

BCI AIRWAYS Ltd

The air charter department of British Cellulose Industries (Manchester) Ltd, BCI Airways began life in early 1948 with a Rapide, two Austers and a Gemini at Manchester (Barton). After a summer spent on pleasure flying and charters, the company ceased operations in January 1949.

Aircraft: DH.89 G-AFMF

BEES FLIGHT Ltd

One Rapide was among several aircraft used by this company, which had been established at Sandown, Isle of Wight, in February 1947 by J P Stephenson and M Williams. It was used for pleasure flying, ambulance flights and general charter work until 1955.

Aircraft: DH.89 G-AKMH

BIRKETT AIR SERVICE Ltd

George Birkett formed his company at Heston in 1935, initially using a number of DH.85 Leopard Moths for passenger and freight charter work. The only member of the Dragon family used by Birkett Air Service before hostilities began was DH.90 Dragonfly G-AEDV. Birkett Air Service was one of the many companies to lose its aircraft to National Air Communications in September 1939, and later the DH.90 was impressed for RAF service.

After the war, the company moved to Croydon and acquired three Dragon Rapides, which were used for many types of charter operations, including flying jockeys and trainers to race meetings. Maintenance of these aircraft was in the hands of Olley Air Service. The company provided some of the aircraft and crews when, under a BEA Associate arrangement, Island Air Services opened a route from Shoreham to Deauville on 1st July 1950. This service was not financially viable, however, and soon closed. Afterwards, Birkett's Rapides were seen at London Airport (Heathrow), providing pleasure flights, and this facility was extended to Northolt and Croydon. Although applications to operate a number of scheduled services with Rapides were filed, the company began to run down its operations, and all flying ended on 31st July 1953.

Aircraft: DH.89 G-AJBJ, G-AJDN, G-AKTZ

DH.90 G-AEDV

G-AJDN of Birkett Air Services Ltd, its first civilian owner [via A. Chivers]

Dragonfly G-AEDV in use with Birkett Air Service, based at Heston
[MAP via R C Sturtivant]

BLACKPOOL & WEST COAST AIR SERVICES Ltd

Formed on 25th March 1933 and based at Blackpool (Squires Gate), this company's managing director was the well-known G P Olley, and the other members of the Board were J C Higgins and J W Comber. On 3rd July the company opened its route from Liverpool (Speke) to Blackpool (Squires Gate) and the Isle of Man (Ronaldsway), using DH.84 aircraft, and by the summer of 1934 this service was flown twice daily. On 17th April 1935 three flights daily from Liverpool to the Isle of Man and from Blackpool to the Isle of Man

began; from Belfast and Carlisle to the Isle of Man there was one flight per day on each route, while between Liverpool and Blackpool a flight every two hours was operated. A jointly-operated service from Dublin (Baldonnel) to Bristol (Whitchurch), using DH.86 Express aircraft, was opened with Aer Lingus on 27th May 1936 and extended to Croydon on 14th September the same year. On 23rd September a new route from Carlisle (Kingstown) to Belfast (Newtownards) was opened, using DH.84s three times per week.

During the summer of 1937 the Isle of Man services continued from Blackpool's other airport, Stanley Park, and a route from Manchester (Barton) to Liverpool was opened. However, in September the company became part of the newly-reorganised Isle of Man Air Services Ltd.

Aircraft: DH.84 G-ACGU, G-ACPY, G-ADCP, G-ADCR

DH.86 G-ADVJ, G-ADVK, G-AENR

DH.89 G-EANO, G-AERN

G-AENR of Blackpool & West Coast Air Services, the first production DH.86B, probably seen at Blackpool (Squires Gate) soon after delivery in February 1937 [via C N Dodds]

BOND AIR SERVICES Ltd

Formed at Gatwick in 1946 by D E Bond, the company devoted its early months to pleasure flying. In July a DH.86B was acquired for passenger charter work, and the company was expanded later that year when R D Gillmore and R A Treen took over control. A second DH.86B was added to the growing fleet and carried on the company's operations while several larger aircraft were devoted to the Berlin airlift. From May 1950 these two workhorses formed the mainstay of Bond's operations, which in 1950 included pleasure flying at an air display at the tiny Skegness (Ingoldmells) airfield! Race meetings were often served by the two DH.86s and by a Rapide which was acquired in November 1950. By February 1951, however, the DH.86s proved too large for the company's needs, and they were sold. The Rapide, however, soldiered on until the company ceased trading at the end of the year.

Aircraft: DH.86 G-ADVH, G-ADVJ

DH.89 G-AKOG

In early postwar years, G-ADUH saw service with Bond Air Services Ltd among others [M W Manderfield via R C Sturtivant]

BRITISH AIRWAYS Ltd

Formerly (for a short time) Allied British Airways Ltd, this company underwent a name change on 29th October 1935 and on 11th December that year absorbed Hillman's Airways Ltd, Spartan Airlines Ltd, United Airways Ltd and British Continental Airways Ltd. Operations from Heston with DH.86s began on 1st January 1936, and in May the terminal of most routes was moved from Croydon to Gatwick. Another service, operated by DH.84s, was opened between Gatwick, Ryde and Cowes (Somerton) on 25th May 1936 and provided nine flights per day until 3rd October. Until January 1937 the constituent companies continued to operate under their own titles.

At least four of the DH.86s were equipped with the Lorenz beam approach system, Marconi radio and de-icing equipment. On 1st April 1940 the company and Imperial Airways merged to form BOAC.

Aircraft: DH.86 G-ACYF, G-ACZP, G-ADEA, G-ADEB,
G-ADEC, G-ADYC, G-ADYD, G-ADYE,
G-ADYF, G-ADYG, G-ADYH, G-ADYI,
G-ADYJ, G-ADMY

Before being modified to DH.86B standard, G-ADYJ of British Airways is seen at Gatwick early in 1937, with the Southern Railway station in the back-ground *[via C N Dodds]*

BRITISH-AMERICAN AIR SERVICES Ltd

Under the direction of D S Gibbs in the United States and Maj M Peto and H Falk in London, BAAS began operations from Heston in April 1935. DH.89 G-ADFX was acquired in July 1935 to expand the charter operations to race meetings which formed the mainstay of the company's work, and in 1938 DH.86 G-ADMY was added to the small fleet. All operations stopped on the outbreak of war, however, and the fleet became part of National Air Communications before being impressed in 1940.

Charter operations recommenced in January 1946, this time from White Waltham, using DH.89 G-AGWC, which was soon joined by G-AGZJ and G-AGZK. All three, however, were disposed of by the summer of 1947 to make way for larger aircraft and expanded operations.

Aircraft: DH.84 G-ACGU

DH.86 G-ADMY, G-ADUE

DH.89 G-ADFX, G-AGWC, G-AGZJ, G-AGZK

BRITISH CONTINENTAL AIRWAYS Ltd

This company was formed on 15th April 1935 by a number of influential people in the aviation world, headed by Sir Percy Mackinnon. Other original directors were F W Farley-Jones of F W Jones & Ptnrs (aviation insurers), Capt W Fry and J R Bryans. Operations began on 1st July 1935, using DH.86 Express Air Liners on scheduled services from Croydon to Ostend to Brussels via Knocke (Le Zoute). Other destinations included Lille and Brussels direct from October; and Antwerp and Amsterdam, which opened in November.

British Continental Airways Ltd was converted to a public company on 31st October 1935 and took over Rollason Aircraft Services Ltd in January 1936. The joint service to Amsterdam operated with KLM altered its intermediate point of call from Hull to Doncaster on 1st July 1936, but the company ended its days as an airline when it was taken over by British Airways on 11th December (12th October ?), although it continued to exist as a major shareholder.

Aircraft: DH.84 G-ACOR

DH.86 G-ADYC, G-ADYD, G-ADYE, G-ADYF, G-ADMY

DH.89 G-ADAK

G-ADAK of British Continental Airways, who operated it from May 1935 to August 1936 *[Denis Fox collection]*

BRITISH EAGLE
EAGLE AVIATION Ltd

Founded in 1948, Eagle Aviation Ltd based three Rapides at Blackbushe between September 1950 and February 1956, either for small charter operations or as support for the Eagle Group's larger aircraft, or both.

Aircraft: DH.89 G-AJSL, G-AJXB, G-AKOB

G-AJXB of Eagle Aviation Ltd, who owned it for a few months in 1955/56 *[via A. Chivers]*

BRITISH EUROPEAN AIRWAYS CORPORATION

In 1946 the Civil Aviation Act was passed, with the aim of nationalising all internal airlines in the UK. British European Airways was established on 1st August 1946 in accordance with the Act, to take over the services, aircraft and personnel of the erstwhile Associated Airways Joint Committee. Still operating at that time were Railway Air Services Ltd, Great Western & Southern Airlines Ltd, Isle of Man Aviation Ltd and Scottish Airways Ltd. Two companies outside AAJC, Allied Airways Ltd and Channel Islands Airways Ltd, were also swallowed up, and the names of four dormant companies, Highland Airways Ltd, North Eastern Airways Ltd, West Coast Airlines Ltd and Western Isles Airways Ltd, were absorbed. As the reorganisation involved was so large-scaled, the companies were permitted to continue flying under their own names but on behalf of BEA between 2nd August 1946 and 31st January 1947, when BEA came into its own. Details of the routes flown during that winter period will be found under the individual companies' names.

The four operating companies brought to BEA thirty-nine Rapides and one Dragon, G-ACIT, as well as other types. UK internal services were arranged in two operating areas, English Division with HQ at Liverpool (Speke) and Scottish Division with HQ at Glasgow (Renfrew). Many of the Rapides were, it seems, stored and not used by BEA before being sold. It is possible that only seventeen aircraft that were given names and three that were not named saw service, plus a further five that were acquired in later years, a total of twenty-five. Routes flown were in the Highlands and Islands of Scotland and the Land's End to the Scillies route, which Rapides, known as the 'Islander' Class, continued to fly until being replaced by helicopters in 1964. The final Rapide operation was an ambulance charter from St Mary's to St Just on 1st May 1964, flown by G-AJCL, soon after which that aircraft and G-AGSH were sold to British Westpoint Airlines, ending BEA's fourteen years' use of the Rapide.

Aircraft: DH.84 G-ACIT

DH.89 G-ADAJ, G-AFEZ, G-AFOI, G-AFRK,
G-AGDG, G-AGDM, G-AGEE, G-AGHI,
G-AGIC, G-AGIF, G-AGJF, G-AGJG, G-AGLE,
G-AGLP, G-AGLR, G-AGOJ, G-AGPH,
G-AGPI, G-AGSH, G-AGSJ, G-AGSK,
G-AGUF, G-AGUG, G-AGUP, G-AGUR,
G-AGUU, G-AGUV, G-AHGF, G-AHGH,
G-AHGI, G-AHKR, G-AHKS, G-AHKT,
G-AHKU, G-AHKV, G-AHLL, G-AHLM,
G-AHLN, G-AHXW, G-AHXX, G-AHXY,
G-AHXZ, G-AIHN, G-AJCL, G-AJSK, G-AJXB,
G-AKDW, G-AKDX, G-AKZB

G-AKZB of BEA ended its life at Land's End (St Just) in December 1961 *[via A. Chivers]*

BRITISH OVERSEAS AIRWAYS CORPORATION

Royal Assent was given in August 1939 for the merger of Imperial Airways and British Airways, and came into effect on 1st April 1940. Nine Express Air Liners were taken over from Imperial Airways and were in use in Africa and the Far East, and most of them were impressed into the RAF in 1941.

Aircraft: DH.86 G-ACPL, G-ACWC, G-ACWD, G-ADFF,
G-ADUE, G-ADUF, G-ADUG, G-ADUI, G-AEAP

In service with BOAC in the Western desert, G-ACWD carried a fin flash and registration underlining   *[MAP via P H T Green]*

BRITISH WESTPOINT AIRLINES Ltd

In May 1964 British Westpoint Airlines Ltd, based at Exeter since its formation in 1960 by F H and J F Mann, took control of Mayflower Air Services. This brought them two Rapides, and three more were soon acquired from BEA. Mayflower's scheduled services to the Scilly Isles were also taken over, after which Westpoint passengers could fly from Heathrow to Exeter or Newquay (St Mawgan) by Dakota and change to a Rapide for their onward journey to the Scillies. A few services were flown regularly from Cardiff and Bristol to the Scillies, sometimes direct and sometimes via Exeter or Plymouth.

In September 1965 Westpoint was acquired by Metropolitan Air Movements, but continued to operate under its own name. The company found itself in financial difficulties early in 1966, and in May was put into liquidation and its assets sold.

Aircraft: DH.89 G-AGSH, G-AHKU, G-AIUL, G-AJCL, G-ASKO

Used by British Westpoint between May 1965 and June 1966, Rapide G-AJCL was then sold to Scillonia   *[C N Dodds]*

BROOKLANDS AVIATION Ltd

Long-established Brooklands Aviation Ltd began air charter operations in 1947 with two Rapides and added two more a year later. These were used on a scheduled service between Shoreham and Southampton via Cowes from 6th August 1948, under an early BEA Associate agreement. Connecting at Southampton with services to the Channel Islands, this route was very well-patronised, and in April 1949 another BEA agreement was implemented, this time between Shoreham and Jersey via Southampton. However, at the end of the 1950 summer season the scheduled services closed down, and for a couple of years the Rapides carried out charter work before being sold.

Aircraft: DH.89 G-AJHO, G-AJHP, G-AKJY, G-AKSH

Brooklands Aviation Ltd operated Rapide G-AJHO from Shoreham and then Sywell for several years before it became a parachute platform in 1963
[Denis Fox collection]

CAMBRIAN AIR SERVICES Ltd
CAMBRIAN AIRWAYS Ltd

Formed in 1936 as Cambrian Air Services Ltd by S K Davies, this company did not begin flying until after the Second World War, when on 1st January 1946, the first day of civil flying, Auster Autocrat G-AFWN flew from Cardiff (Pengam Moors) to Filton. In June 1947 Rapide G-AGZJ arrived to boost the company's small fleet, and early in 1948 Cambrian Air Services entered into the first of the BEA Associate agreements, allowing the company to operate a route from Cardiff to Weston-super-Mare from May. For this, two more Rapides were acquired.

J H Watts & Ptnrs took control of Cambrian in 1949, and three more Rapides were added to the fleet to operate a lucrative route to the Channel Islands. A service between Cardiff and Haverfordwest (Withybush) was operated for a short time in 1952 but proved unsuccessful. In February 1953, when Olley Air Service Ltd and Morton Air Services Ltd merged, two former Olley Rapides joined Cambrian, which was in the process of enlarging its route structure through Gloucester/Cheltenham (Staverton) and Bristol. Murray Chown Aviation Ltd was absorbed in May 1953, but this did not include any aircraft. By the 1954 season, Cambrian's operation had moved from Pengam Moors to Rhoose, and services were being flown to Manchester, Liverpool, Southampton, Haverfordwest (Withybush) and to Paris, in addition to the routes already mentioned.

The Rapides were by now somewhat outdated, and more modern equipment such as Dakotas and Herons was being acquired. On 23rd May 1955 the company took up its new title, Cambrian Airways Ltd, which still used a couple of Rapides. In February 1958 BEA bought a one-third share in the company, which by that time had only one Rapide on its books, two Dakotas and four Herons carrying out most of the work. Bad passenger figures that year forced the company to offer most of its equipment for sale, apart from Rapide G-AJCL.

Aircraft: DH.89 G-AGSI, G-AGZJ, G-AIYE, G-AJCL, G-AKUB,
                          G-AKUC, G-ALAT, G-ALRW, G-ALZJ

Cambrian Air Services displayed their name prominently on G-AJCL, seen at Liverpool (Speke) on 21.3.59   *[P H Butler]*

CASAIR Ltd (see Cumberland Aviation Services Ltd)

CECIL KAY AIRCRAFT (1945) Ltd

One Rapide was used by this company between October 1946 and April 1948, flying on air taxi services from Birmingham (Elmdon).

Aircraft: DH.89 G-AGZU

CHANNEL AIR FERRIES Ltd

A subsidiary of Olley Air Service Ltd, Channel Air Ferries Ltd was registered on 8th May 1936 and began to operate routes in the south and south-west of England. The first, opened on 23rd May, was between Shoreham and Ryde, using DH.84s and Scions. The company did not at that stage purchase its own aircraft, but instead used those of other companies under Olley's control. On 1st July 1937 a route between Shoreham and Christchurch via Bembridge and Ryde started, and on 15th September the popular route from Land's End (St Just) to the Scillies (St Mary's) was inaugurated. A more important but very roundabout route, from Heston to Cardiff via Croydon, Shoreham, Bembridge, Christchurch and Bristol (Whitchurch), was opened.

From August 1938, when the company took over much of the Railway Air Services activities in the south of England, services were operated under the Channel Air Ferries title until Great Western & Southern Airlines Ltd was formed in December.

Aircraft: DH.84 G-ACPY, G-ADCR, G-ADDI, G-AEKZ

Channel Air Ferries' G-ACPY, probably at Land's End (St Just)
[via M J Ingham and P H T Green]

CHANNEL AIRWAYS Ltd

Originally East Anglian Flying Services Ltd, Channel Airways Ltd came into being in 1957, and used two Rapides spasmodically until 1960, the company's main equipment being Doves.

Aircraft: DH.89 G-AEMH, G-AKRN

CHANNEL ISLANDS AIR SERVICES Ltd

Formed at Guernsey early in 1950, this company leased a Rapide from Airwork Ltd for a few months and used it on charters between the islands and to France and the UK mainland.

Aircraft: DH.89 G-AESR

CHANNEL ISLANDS AIRWAYS Ltd

Registered on 1st December 1934, this was a holding company for Guernsey Airways Ltd and Jersey Airways Ltd, shares being held in equal proportion by the Great Western Railway Co Ltd, the Southern Railway Co Ltd and Whitehall Securities Ltd. On 2nd March 1943, however, these two railway companies acquired the shares of Whitehall Securities Ltd.

On 1st September 1945, after Jersey Airways and Guernsey Airways had established their new postwar schedules, they merged as Channel Islands Airways Ltd. Jersey Airways brought four Rapides to the new company. Ten days later, Channel Airways reopened its route from Jersey and Guernsey to Southampton, and the Croydon service soon followed. Two more Rapides were added to the fleet in January 1946, and inter-island flights became a regular feature. Significant use of the Rapides was made by flower-growers who wanted their products to reach the mainland markets quickly. Services of all types increased during the summer of 1946, but the prospect of being absorbed by BEA hung over the company, which hoped that its registration in the Channel Islands would help to avoid this fate. It was not possible, but from 2nd August 1946 the company flew its services under contract to BEA. The six routes flown during the winter of 1946/47 were between Guernsey and Alderney, Jersey, Southampton and Croydon and from Jersey to Southampton and Croydon. On 1st April 1947, however, Channel Islands Airways Ltd formally became part of the BEA empire, all its services and equipment being absorbed.

Aircraft: DH.89 G-AGPH, G-AGPI, G-AGSH, G-AGSK,
G-AGUF, G-AGUG

G-AGPI of Channel Islands Airways Ltd, trading as Jersey & Guernsey Airways, who used it before being taken over by BEA   [via A. Chivers]

CHRISAIR Ltd

This company was formed in 1961 by Mr and Mrs C Roberts at Luton, and in November 1962 DH.84 G-ADDI, owned by Aero Enterprises (JHS) Ltd, was operated on pleasure flights at Ramsgate and later from the company's second home at Northampton (Sywell). Freight charters to and from many locations were also flown by this elderly aircraft until its C of A expired in May 1968 and Chrisair ceased operating.

Aircraft: DH.84 G-ADDI

G-ADDI, operated by Chrisair, was owned by Aero Enterprises (JHS) Ltd
[via A Chivers]

CIRO'S AVIATION Ltd

This unusual organisation was registered in December 1946 by Ciro's Club in the West End of London. It began flying a Dakota on luxury passenger flights but was also involved in low-cost travel. A Rapide was bought in June 1947 for passenger and freight charter operations, and another one followed in October, but both were disposed of in 1948/49.

Aircraft: DH.89 G-AFMA, G-AKGV

G-AKGV, its owner not apparent in this view, was used by Ciro's Aviation Ltd,
1947-8   [G M Simons collection]

COMMERCIAL AIR HIRE Ltd

Located at Croydon, Commercial Air Hire Ltd had as its managing director J Pugh DFC, with the Hon Mrs Victor Bruce as co-director, and work was closely co-ordinated with that lady's Air Dispatch Ltd. Operations began in the summer of 1934 with an early-morning newspaper flight to Paris, using a Dragon. From 14th April 1935 the 'Inner Circle Air Line' between Croydon and Heston was operated four times daily by this company, again using Dragons, and the intention was to extend this service to other London-area airports, but this plan did not materialise.

Commercial Air Hire seems to have remained active until its remaining Dragons were impressed into the RAF in July 1940.

Aircraft: DH.84 G-ACAP, G-ACBW, G-ACCR. G-ACDL,
G-ACDN, G-ACDR,G-ACEK, G-ACKB,
G-ACKC, G-ACKU, G-AEMR

CRILLY AIRWAYS Ltd

Directors of Crilly Airways Ltd were F L Crilly (managing), H P Gowen JP and W H Parkin, and the company's office was at Leicester. DH.84 Dragons were used by Crilly Airways on two routes which opened in 1935, from Croydon to Doncaster (from 11th March) and twice daily from Norwich (Mousehold) to Leicester (Braunstone) and Bristol (Whitchurch), which opened on 2nd April. Crilly Airways was taken over by the new British Airways in March 1936.

Aircraft: DH.84 G-ACCZ, G-ACDN, G-ACLE

CROYDON AIRWAYS Ltd

A subsidiary of Cinema Press Ltd, Croydon Airways Ltd was formed on 22nd June 1936 by S Harris, S F Woods, J Armstrong and H H S Harris.

However, in February 1937 the company was advertised for sale by Harris & Gillow and a receiver was appointed on 16th March.

Aircraft: DH.89 G-ACZU

DH.90 G-AEDH

CUMBERLAND AVIATION SERVICES Ltd / CASAIR Ltd

Based originally at RAF Silloth, this company flew a Rapide and an Auster on charter work from May 1959. Its directors were M Kidd, L A Kidd and L P Marshall. Business grew rapidly, and within two months flying training, surveys and aerial photography were being undertaken as well as charter and pleasure flying. In the summer of 1960 the company moved to Carlisle (Crosby) and changed its name to Casair Ltd. A second Rapide was acquired in February 1961, and the two were occupied on charter work, largely in Scotland, but one was sold in July 1962 and the other in March 1963.

Aircraft: DH.89 G-AIUL, G-ALGE

Seen at Cranfield on 18th September 1959 was Rapide G-AIUL in the livery of its then owner, Cumberland Aviation Services Ltd [Denis Fox collection]

DENHAM AIR SERVICES Ltd

An established aircraft maintenance company, Denham Air Services acquired three Rapides early in 1948 and after refurbishing them, sold them on to other operators.

Aircraft: DH.89 G-AKOP, G-AKTX, G-AKTZ

DERBY AVIATION Ltd

Based at Burnaston airport, Derby Aviation Ltd was registered as an airline operator by Gp Capt C A Willcock MP and E W Phillips on 16th February 1949. Charter flights, pleasure flying and Army co-operation work occupied the company's fleet, which included a Rapide. The growth of holiday flights prompted Derby Aviation to begin one of their own, between Derby, Wolverhampton and Jersey, on 18th July 1953, using two Rapides. Another Rapide was acquired for the 1954 season, when weekend flights to Jersey from Birmingham and Nottingham (Tollerton) were added to the programme. There was a significant amount of aircraft-sharing between Derby Aviation and Wolverhampton Aviation Ltd at times. In 1955 a Dakota took over some flights, but for a time those from Wolverhampton and Nottingham continued to be flown by Rapides. The last Rapide used by the company was disposed of in March 1957.

Aircraft: DH.89 G-AEAL, G-AIUL, G-AKNV

At Newcastle (Woolsington) in 1960 was Rapide G-AIUL of Derby Aviation, with a Dakota of the same operator behind it [MAP via P H T Green]

DEVONAIR Ltd

Devonair Ltd came into being in December 1952, when it was registered as a charter company and took over the operation of the North Devon Flying Club. The service to Lundy Island continued under the new operator, which by 1960 had become the operator of the Coventry Flying Club at Baginton. In

September of that year Dragonfly G-AEWZ was acquired for charter operations from Coventry but was written off in March 1961.

Aircraft: DH.90 G-AEWZ

DOMINIE AIRWAYS Ltd

A subsidiary of Treffield Aviation Ltd, based at Northampton (Sywell), Dominie Airways flew a Rapide on charters from East Midlands airport between August 1966 and January 1967.

Aircraft: DH.89 G-AHKU

DON EVERALL (AVIATION) Ltd

The result of a take-over of Lees-Hill Aviation by Modern Transport (Wolverhampton) Ltd in September 1951, this company had two Rapides that were used intensively on summer holiday services to the Channel Islands and the Isle of Man from Birmingham and Wolverhampton. In the summer of 1953 a batch of licence applications was approved, and scheduled services from Birmingham to Jersey, Guernsey and Weston-super-Mare via Cardiff and from Wolverhampton to the Isle of Man began. During 1954 services from Coventry and Leicester to the Channel Islands and from Coventry to the Isle of Man were added. Yet another summer service was flown in the 1955 season – between Birmingham and Sandown, Isle of Wight. Passenger numbers grew steadily, and when it was realised that the Rapides were becoming inadequate for the services a Dakota was acquired and began to take over most of the services. The Rapides, now three in number, were then relegated to charter work, the last one remaining until the summer of 1960.

Aircraft: DH.89 G-AGDP, G-AGLR, G-AHPT, G-AKZO

G-AGLR of Don Everall (Aviation) Ltd was written off in a crash in October 1956 [via A. Chivers]

DRAGON AIRWAYS Ltd

This company was set up at Broomhall airfield, Pwllheli, early in 1953 specifically to provide pleasure flights for holiday-makers at the local Butlin's Holiday Camp. A Rapide was leased from Murray Chown Aviation in June but was written off in an accident within a few weeks. A replacement was purchased in September and flying resumed, including some passenger and freight charter flights. On 16th January 1954 Dragon Airways Ltd was registered by Capt M A Guinane, D H Todd and H R Bamberg as an airline company and moved to Liverpool (Speke). There, application for a number of scheduled services was made, and subsequently an irregular service was flown from Manchester and Liverpool to Pwllheli. Pleasure flights continued, and Army co-operation exercises were also undertaken. However, when longer-distance services were approved it became clear that the Rapides were no longer a suitable aircraft, and they were replaced by DH.114 Herons in 1955.

Aircraft: DH.89 G-AHPT, G-AIYP, G-AKOB

Named "Peter Tare", G-AHPT was owned by Dragon Airways Ltd at Liverpool (Speke) for two years before it was passed to Don Everall (Aviation) Ltd at Birmingham [Denis Fox collection]

EAGLE AVIATION Ltd (see BRITISH EAGLE)

EAST ANGLIAN FLYING SERVICES Ltd

One of the earliest of the post-war UK airlines, East Anglian Flying Services was registered in January 1946 by Sqn Ldr R J Jones. In January 1948 four Rapides were bought for charter work and pleasure flying from Southend, with a trip across the Channel to France or Belgium as a bonus. That summer, a BEA Associate agreement was signed, and the company began operating the short hop across the Thames from Southend to Rochester. A route from Southend to Ostend via Lympne opened in 1949, and extended to Birmingham in 1950. Another BEA Associate agreement in 1950 permitted East Anglian to begin weekend flights between Southend and Jersey. 1951, however, was a bad year for the company, which almost failed, but the following year saw the reintroduction of the Southend to Ostend and Jersey routes.

In January 1953 a route from Ipswich to Jersey via Southend, Rochester and Shoreham was among several licensed. Ipswich airport came into use on 1st April 1954 and flights then began to Southend to connect with services to the Channel Islands, Rochester, Shoreham, Le Touquet, Ostend and Paris. Sandown, Isle of Wight, was served from Portsmouth, and passenger numbers dictated that larger and faster aircraft than the faithful Rapide became necessary.

Still using two Rapides among a growing number of other types, the company changed its name in 1957 to Channel Airways Ltd.

Aircraft: DH.89 G-AEMH, G-AJHO, G-AKJZ, G-AKOV,
G-AKRN, G-AKRO, G-AKSC

G-AKJZ of East Anglian Flying Services Ltd at Southend [via A. Chivers]

FEDERATED AIR TRANSPORT Ltd

A fruit and vegetable wholesaler in Liverpool, Federated Fruit Co, had used the services of Wright Aviation to transport its produce until that company went into liquidation in 1953. Federated Fruit's owner, R J Gates, then decided to carry on the operation himself, and acquired two Ansons and a Rapide, which became busy flying produce from Ireland to Liverpool for onward distribution. Early in 1955, he bought five former Fleet Air Arm Dominies, but three never entered service, as they were the subject of court-martial proceedings within the Royal Navy. In the event, one Rapide and one Anson carried out most of the work, and the Rapide flew no more serviecs after the end of October 1960. It remained airworthy, however, and was subsequently flown by R J Gates as a personal aircraft.

Aircraft: DH.89 G-AIBB, G-ANZP, G-AOAO

G-ANZP of Federated Air Transport had been the subject of a court martial concerning its sale by the Fleet Air Arm [via A. Chivers]

FLIGHT CHARTER Ltd
FLIGHTWAYS Ltd

These two companies were registered on 8th March 1948 by V H Bellamy, who began passenger and freight charter operations from Southampton (Eastleigh) that autumn. Early in 1950 the companies entered into a BEA Associate agreement and began to fly between Portsmouth and Ryde, Isle of Wight, a route which was extended in 1951 to include Southampton. A service from Bournemouth to Jersey was also flown in the summer of 1950. Many other applications for permission to fly scheduled services were filed, but none came to fruition, and charter flights and pleasure flying formed most of the company's work until 1954, when all flying ceased.

Aircraft: DH.89 G-AHGF, G-AHGH, G-AIYP, G-AKNE,
G-ALAX, G-ALWL, G-ALWM, G-ALWN
DH.90 G-AEWZ

Rapide G-ALWL of Flightways Ltd, who owned it for a few months in 1950 [Denis Fox collection]

GOODHEW AVIATION Ltd

This company, which had owned Oxford (Kidlington) airfield since 1946, acquired a Rapide in January 1948 for charter operations, and during that summer it carried many holiday-makers to the Channel Islands, the Isle of Wight and the Isle of Man. In addition, it took racegoers to several meetings and flew many people on pleasure flights. A further Rapide was acquired in May 1950, and the two were used intensively until 1952, when the company devoted itself to the operation of the Oxford Aeroplane Club.

Aircraft: DH.89 G-AIDL, G-AKSL, G-AKVU

GREAT WESTERN & SOUTHERN AIRLINES Ltd

This company was incorporated on 5th December 1938 as the result of an agreement between the Great Western Railway, the Southern Railway and British & Foreign Aviation Ltd to amalgamate certain services which had been worked by Railway Air Services and Olley Air Services's subsidiary Channel Air Ferries. Its capital was £100,000, the participating companies providing 25%, 25% and 50% respectively. The directors representing the GWR and SR companies were J O H Elliot, K W C Grand and Wg Cdr A H Measures, while Gordon Olley, J W S Comber and J S Wells represented British & Foreign Aviation Ltd, the Olley group holding company. A management Committee was set up to combine the activities of the companies until 24th March 1939.

The new airline's specified area of operation was south-west of a line drawn between North Foreland, London, Manchester, Liverpool, Anglesey and the Scilly Isles, and excluded the Channel Islands but included Luxembourg. The fleet of aircraft contributed by the participating companies totalled three DH.89s, two DH.84s and other types. The company's headquarters was at Shoreham airport.

On 3rd April 1939 GW&SA began flying from Shoreham to Ryde and Bournemouth and on 1st May the former Railway Air Services route between Shoreham, Ryde, Southampton, Bristol, Birmingham (Elmdon), Manchester (Ringway) and Liverpool (Speke) was reopened on a daily basis. A service between Croydon and Luxembourg, mainly for the transportation of gramophone records to Radio Luxembourg, began on 16th May, followed ten days later by new routes from Heston to Ryde via Croydon and Croydon to Deauville and Le Touquet, sometimes with a call at Shoreham.

After a short break when war was declared, GW&SA recommenced flying on the former Railway Air Services Scilly Isles route, and in May 1940 became a member of AAJC, with whom it maintained the service throughout the war, losing a DH.84 to enemy action in the process.

Following the end of the war in Europe, the company continued the Scilly Isles service and opened new routes between Cardiff and Bristol and Cardiff and Weston-super-Mare on 31st July 1946, the later with fourteen daily return flights. The threat of nationalisation was now present, and the airline should have been taken over by BEA in April 1946, but problems intervened and several three-month delays were allowed. In the end, GW&SA was among those companies allowed to continue flying under their own names for a time. Routes flown during the winter of 1946/47 were from Bristol (Whitchurch) to Southampton and Cardiff, from Cardiff to Weston-super-Mare (still running eight times daily) and the Land's End to the Scillies service. However, on 1st February 1947 BEA finally took over the company and its assets.

Aircraft: DH.84 G-ACPY, G-ADDI

DH.89 G-ACPP, G-ACPR, G-ACYM, G-AGEE, G-AGIF

G-AGEE of Great Western & Southern Airlines in camouflage finish in 1942, possibly at Liverpool (Speke). The presentation of the red, white and blue stripes under the registration is unusual *[via C N Dodds]*

GUERNSEY AIRWAYS Ltd

Registered on 24th November 1934, Guernsey Airways Ltd flew amphibious aircraft until 1939, when the new airport on the island was opened on 5th May. From there, the airline used DH.86s until June 1940, when refugees were flown to England in advance of the German occupation of the Channel Islands.

Aircraft: DH.86 G-ADVK, G-AENR

G-ADVK wearing Guernsey & Jersey Airways titles on the nose *[S Flatt]*

HARGREAVES AIRWAYS Ltd
(see WINGS AND WHEELS Ltd)

HERTS & ESSEX AERO CLUB (1946) Ltd

Well-known in early postwar days as a major flying club based at Broxbourne, this company had already flown many charter flights when the first of several Rapides was acquired in May 1948. Of the five Rapides operated, three had been disposed of by 1952, when the company moved to Stapleford Tawney, and the last one was sold in 1955.

Aircraft: DH.89 G-AGZU, G-AKTY, G-AKZH, G-ALXT, G-ALZF

HIGHLAND AIRWAYS Ltd

Highland Airways first used Dragons in April 1933, when they replaced Monospars on the airline's route from Inverness to Wick and Kirkwall. For its Aberdeen to Kirkwall route via Wick a temporary airfield at Seaton, just outside Aberdeen, was used, but Highland Airways moved its operation on 23rd May 1935 to a new terminal at Kintore. Great Britain's first internal air mail service, between Inverness and Wick, was flown by Highland Airways on 29th May 1934. On 3rd June 1936 another route was added, from Aberdeen to Kirkwall and Sumburgh in the Shetlands. Highland Airways merged on 31st May 1935 with United Airways Ltd (part of Whitehall Securities) and on 12th August 1937 with Northern & Scottish Airways Ltd to become Scottish Airways Ltd.

Aircraft: DH.84 G-ACCE, G-ACET, G-ACGK, G-ACIT, G-ADCT

HILLMAN'S SALOON COACHES & AIRWAYS Ltd
HILLMAN'S AIRWAYS Ltd

Registered as Hillman's Saloon Coaches & Airways Ltd on 12th November 1931 by Edward Hillman, this pioneering company opened a

HILLMAN'S AIRWAYS
MAYLANDS AERODROME.
'Phone : ROMFORD 1700.

LONDON — PARIS SERVICE.

London	TWICE DAILY.	Paris
10. 0 a.m.		10. 0 a.m.
13.45 p.m.		13.45 p.m.
Single fare - £3 10 0		Period return fare - £5 10 0

Special week-end, Friday to Tuesday - £4 15 0

A Hillman's Airways advertisement proclaiming the Romford (Maylands) to Paris service *[via author]*

route from Romford (Maylands) to Clacton on 1st April 1932, using Fox Moths. Originally a farm worker, Hillman had been an NCO in the First World War, after which he had worked as a chauffeur, taxi driver, car hire operator and a large-scale coach operator. His airline venture was immediately successful, and Hillman soon asked de Havilland to produce an economical twin-engined aircraft to operate a route from Clacton to Ramsgate via Maylands. This resulted in the DH.84, and Hillman's Airways took delivery of the former prototype, G-ACAN, on 26th December 1932, and it was 'christened' by Amy Johnson. More Dragons had arrived by April 1933, enabling him to open his route to Paris from Maylands. It is said that Hillman remarked "I'm going to run to Paris like a bus service from my field at Maylands" and that is what he did – the service was an instant success.

In April 1934 Hillman's Airways began operating a through service to Belfast (Aldergrove) in conjunction with Midland & Scottish Air Ferries Ltd, and on 16th July took the route over completely. By this time the company had moved to a new airfield at Stapleford Tawney as Maylands was too small for safety. From August the Belfast route was flown by new DH.89 aircraft, which also replaced the DH.84s on the Paris service. On 29th September the Belfast service was closed for a time, but on 1st December it was recommenced, in competition with Railway Air Services. The shorter title for the company came into use on 12th December 1934, and a week later the company became a public one, but on 31st December Edward Hillman died of a heart attack. Most of the shares were bought by the Erlanger merchant bank, and although Hillman's son took over as Managing Director he resigned on 21st July 1935.

Three new DH.86s were delivered in June 1935 and were placed into service on a new route to Ostend and Brussels and also replaced DH.89s on the Paris service. Other routes operated by Hillman's Airways that year were to Ramsgate and Knocke (Le Zoute) and to Brussels via Knocke and Antwerp.

On 11th December 1935, however, Hillman's Airways became a constituent of the new British Airways, to whom its aircraft were handed over.

Aircraft: DH.84 G-ACAN, G-ACAO, G-ACAP, G-ACBW, G-ACEU, G-ACEV

DH.86 G-ADEA, G-ADEB, G-ADEC

DH.89 G-ACPM, G-ACPN, G-ACPO, G-ADAG, G-ADAH, G-ADAJ, G-ADAK, G-ADAL, G-ADDF

The naming ceremony of G-ADEA "Drake" of Hillman's Airways at Essex Airport (Stapleford Tawney) on 20th June 1935; from left to right: 1st Off Hill, Lady Cunliffe-Lister, ?, Capt Neville Stack, W Anderson (chief pilot), ? (chief engineer), H C Robinson (chief Radio Operator), and ? (traffic manager) *[P H T Green collection]*

HORNTON AIRWAYS Ltd

Formed at Gatwick in 1946, Hornton Airways used a small fleet of Consul aircraft to which a Rapide was added in 1947. This was used in 1949 on BEA Associate services to Land's End, Exeter and Plymouth and for race-meeting charters, but early in 1950 all flying was suspended.

Aircraft: DH.89 G-AIUO

HUMBER AIR FERRY

One of the UK's earliest domestic air services, the Humber Air Ferry opened on 1st July 1933 between Hull (Hedon) and Grimsby (Waltham), using a DH.84 and a Seagrave on a frequent cross-river route. The service was operated jointly by North Sea Aerial & General Transport Co and East Yorkshire Motor Services, and ended on 4th November 1933. However, it appears to have reopened in August 1936 under the auspices of North Eastern Airways.

HUNTING AIR TRAVEL Ltd

Formed in December 1945 by Wg Cdr G Hunting, Capt P L Hunting and C Hunting, this company was initially based at Luton. Among the aircraft acquired in the early days were three Rapides which were used on charter work in the UK and overseas. A subsidiary company was the Aircraft Operating Company of Africa, which also used Rapides. While Hunting Air Travel embarked on plans to acquire larger and more modern aircraft for a range of international services, the Rapides, with Avro 19s and Doves, continued in use for carrying holiday-makers to UK and close Continental airfields and racegoers to meetings. They were also used, in June 1947, to repatriate stranded people from France during a railway strike. The two remaining Rapides lasted until the mid 1950s.

Aircraft: DH.89 G-AGZU, G-AHPU, G-AHWF

The Halifax of LAMS in the background gives a clue that this picture of G-AEAL in use by Hunting Aerosurveys was taken at Elstree in 1946
[P H T Green collection]

IMPERIAL AIRWAYS Ltd

The British national carrier, Imperial Airways, placed an order in 1934, on behalf of QANTAS, for a number of DH.86s for use on the final section of the infant route from England to Australia. In August 1935 a subsidiary company was formed to handle routes in the Far East, and on 16th September a DH.86 left England for Penang to carry out survey flights. A route from Penang to Hong Kong opened on 23rd March 1936, and in the autumn of 1937 two more DH.86s were sent to cover increasing traffic. This route was flown throughout the remainder of Imperial Airways' life.

In February 1936 a DH.86 was despatched to Khartoum in the Sudan to survey a route across Africa to Lagos in Nigeria, but it was September of that year before landing grounds west of Kano were established. During October the new route was extended to Accra in the Gold Coast (now Ghana).

In Europe, pilots of DH.86s which were used on the Cologne service complained of severe icing condition in March 1937, and the manager of the European Division, Wolley Dod, flew on it to see for himself. Sadly, the aircraft crashed and he and others on board lost their lives.

Just before the outbreak of war, Imperial Airways' sole UK-based DH.86 was moved to Bristol (Whitchurch) and then to Exeter, where it took part in NAC operations before being impressed into the RAF. On 1st April 1940 Imperial Airways became a constituent of BOAC.

Aircraft: DH.86 G-ACPL, G-ACVZ, G-ACWC, G-ACWD, G-ACWE,
G-ACYG, G-ACZN, G-ACZR, G-ADCM, G-ADCN,
G-ADFF, G-ADMY, G-ADUE, G-ADUF,
G-ADUG, G-ADUH, G-ADUI, G-AEAP

INDEPENDENT AIR TRAVEL Ltd

This company, formed in 1953 as a travel agent, was bought a year later by a number of pilots and began charter flights with an Anson, which was soon replaced by two Doves. Two Rapides were added in 1956 but were disposed of the same year.

Aircraft: DH.89 G-AJXB, G-ALZJ

INTER-CITY AIR SERVICES Ltd

Originally known as Aircraft (Hereford) Ltd, this company changed its title in 1949 and purchased two Rapides for charter work. One of them was later disposed of, but the other continued until the company ceased trading when its Hereford airfield was bought for industrial development.

Aircraft: DH.89 G-AKOV, G-AKRO

Although marked 'Hereford Aviation Centre', G-AKRO was registered to Inter-City Air Services Ltd
[Denis Fox collection]

INTERNATIONAL AIRWAYS Ltd

Based at Croydon, this company had been formed in 1946 by T Barclay as Barclay's International Airways. Its fleet consisted of Consuls and other aircraft until, in July 1948, three Rapides were bought from BEA to be used on a route awarded under the BEA Associate scheme. This was between Croydon, Bournemouth (Hurn) and Cowes, and was flown at weekends during that summer, proving popular. In September another BEA Associate route, between Croydon and Birmingham (Elmdon) was opened, and continued during 1949, but the Isle of Wight service was taken over by Air Enterprises Ltd. The British Industries Fair at Birmingham in May 1949 spawned a number of temporary routes, among them a frequent service from Croydon via RAF Hendon to Castle Bromwich, which was flown jointly by International Airways, Air Enterprises and Patrick Aviation. For most of that summer the Rapides operated Jersey Airlines services from the Channel Islands to destinations in France and the UK as well as International's own route to Cowes and ad-hoc charters. After a slack winter in 1949, the company carried on until the end of the 1950 summer season, when it ceased trading and the aircraft were either sold or scrapped.

Aircraft: DH.89 G-AGHI, G-AGLE, G-AGLP

International Airways Ltd operated this Rapide, G-AGLE, seen here at Croydon in the company of Consuls of Morton Air Services and a Proctor
[Denis Fox collection]

ISLAND AIR CHARTERS Ltd

After being established at Jersey airport in 1946 by S R Lempriere and Capt W Gratrix, this company took delivery of several aircraft, including a Rapide. Charter flights to many destinations in the UK and France began, and in May 1947 a second Rapide was acquired so that a scheduled inter-island service could be operated. In addition, a good deal of produce was carried from the Channel Islands to airfields on the south coast of England for onward transport to Covent Garden. By the end of 1949 only the two Rapides were still in use, and the company's operations were being integrated with those of Air Transport Charter, so that by the early months of 1950 Island Air Charters Ltd no longer existed.

Aircraft: DH.89 G-AHPT, G-AJFK, G-AKNE

An evocative picture of Island Air Charters' Rapide G-AJFK at Jersey about 1950; in the background is a Dakota of Air Transport Charter Ltd, who gradually took over IAC services [Denis Fox collection]

ISLAND AIR SERVICES (LONDON) Ltd

Founded in June 1945 as Island Air Services by D Hills-Grove-Hills, this company originally operated two Proctor aircraft. One was based at Elstree for general charter work and the other in the Scillies to specialise in the flower trade. In 1947 a Dragon Rapide was acquired by the company, which had by then moved from Elstree to Croydon. This aircraft was quickly put into use on a frequent passenger service to Jersey, sometimes flown by the well-known former ATA pilot Monique Agazarian, who managed the Croydon part of the business.

In 1948 the company was awarded a concession to carry out pleasure flying at Northolt, soon followed by a similar arrangement at London Airport (Heathrow), for which two more Rapides were put to use. This enterprise soon became very profitable, and the Scilly Isles operation was ended so that the company could concentrate its efforts. On 31st December 1948 the company was reformed as Island Air Services (London) Ltd, with Monique Agazarian as chairman and chief pilot. The Croydon base was retained, and some charter flights were flown from there. During 1950 regular flights were made from Shoreham to Deauville carrying passengers eager to enjoy a weekend's gambling in the casinos! In addition, the company was awarded a BEA Associate agreement on 1st July 1948 for a service between Shoreham and Deauville, later extended to La Baule and Le Touquet, but this lasted only one season. Pleasure flying from Heathrow continued to provide a good income for the company, and no further operations from Croydon were carried out after 1952.

An accident to G-ALBB occurred on 1st August 1952, when the slipstream from a Stratocruiser caused the pilot of the Rapide to lose control. Luckily, there were no serious injuries to the passengers in the ensuing crash, although the pilot, Wg Cdr B J McGinn, was badly hurt. Pleasure flying continued, although it was becoming clear that Heathrow was now far too busy for such an operation, and a ban was placed on it. In total, 30,000 pasengers had been flown safely from Heathrow. The Rapides were then moved to Ramsgate, where pleasure flying carried on in 1957. It was not successful, however, and at the end of that season the company ceased trading.

Aircraft: DH.89 G-AFFB, G-AGJG, G-AGSJ, G-AGUF, G-AIYP, G-ALBB

G-AGSJ, c/n 6888, was used for a short time by Island Air Services, Land's End [via A. Chivers]

ISLE OF MAN AIR SERVICES Ltd

Registered on 21st January 1935 with a capital of £1000, all owned by Olley Air Service Ltd, Isle of Man Air Services Ltd was reorganised in September 1937 with a capital of £75,000. A third of the shares were now owned by Olley, a third by the London, Midland & Scottish Railway Co Ltd and a third by the Isle of Man Steam Packet Co Ltd. All services flown to and from the Isle of Man by Blackpool & West Coast Air Services and Railway Air Services were withdrawn, apart from the B&WCAS route to Dublin. On 26 September five DH.89s were transferred from RAS to Isle of Man Air Services Ltd, as were two DH.86s from B&WCAS and two DH.84s. The new airline began operations that day, flying routes from Manchester (Barton) to Liverpool (Speke), Blackpool (Squires Gate) and Isle of Man (Ronaldsway) and from Liverpool to Ronaldsway and on to Belfast.

The 1938 summer schedule opened on 1st June on the same routes and four new ones: Isle of Man – Blackpool – Liverpool – Leeds/Bradford (Yeadon); Isle of Man – Belfast; Isle of Man – Carlisle (Kingstown); and Isle of Man – Glasgow (Renfrew). These services closed down on 10th September and reopened on the following 1st July, in the final year of peace. Everything

came to a halt, however, on 3rd September 1939, when the four DH.89s and one DH.84 were taken over by National Air Communications. Later IoMAS came under the control of AAJC and restarted its Isle of Man service from Liverpool, which was continued throughout the war, using just one Rapide, the others having been impressed.

After the end of hostilities in Europe, Isle of Man Air Services acquired two more Rapides and opened routes from the island to Blackpool, Carlisle and Manchester. A route to Glasgow (Renfrew) followed in 1946, but by that time the prospect of nationalisation was evident. Before formal take-over by British European Airways, the company continued to fly under its own name from 2nd August 1946, and during the following winter operated daily services from the island to Liverpool, Carlisle, Blackpool and Manchester. On 1st February 1947, however, Isle of Man Air Services Ltd formally became part of British European Airways Corporation.

Aircraft: DH.84 G-ADCP, G-ADCR

DH.86 G-ADVK, G-AENR

DH.89 G-AEAJ, G-AEAK, G-AEAL, G-AEAM, G-AEBW, G-AEPF, G-AFRK, G-AGOJ, G-AGSJ, G-AGUP, G-AHKR, G-AHKT, G-AHKU, G-AHKV

G-ADCP of Isle of Man Air Services, displaying the island's three-legged symbol on its rudder [via A Chivers]

JERSEY AIRLINES
AIRLINES (JERSEY) Ltd

This company was established in 1948 by M L Thomas as a travel agency, using chartered aircraft to fly trips to France. Due to possible confusion with Jersey Airways Ltd, permission to register as a limited company was refused, and therefore a slight change of name to Airlines (Jersey) Ltd was settled in December 1948.

At first, leasing of aircraft continued, but on 3rd May 1949 Rapide G-AKNF was delivered as the nucleus of the company's own fleet. That summer this and two leased Rapides were intensively used on holiday flights to Dinard and St Brieuc in northern France and to bring French agricultural workers to Jersey to help lift potatoes. Regular charter flights were made from Jersey to Toussus-le-Noble later in 1949. By 1950, four Rapides were on the company's strength, and on 16th June 1951 scheduled services on summer Saturdays from Jersey and Guernsey to Southampton were introduced.

On 7th April 1952 Exeter became a second destination, while the service to Toussus-le-Noble was moved to Le Bourget. Further routes, to Bournemouth (Hurn), Gatwick, Coventry and Manchester were opened in the summer of 1952.

By now a larger aircraft was becoming essential, and the company therefore ordered two DH.114 Herons, which took over some of the services and allowed expansion of the route structure. In 1956 the company took over most of BEA's services to and from the Channel Islands, and the three remaining Rapides were relegated to inter-island services and charter work. The last example of the Rapide departed in October 1961, by which time Herons, Bristol Freighters and Dakotas had replaced the faithful biplane.

Aircraft: DH.89 G-AGLP, G-AGSH, G-AGUP, G-AHEB, G-AIBB, G-AKED, G-AKNE, G-AKNF, G-AKNX, G-AKOA

Rapide G-AKED of Jersey Airlines later spent several years in Algeria [Denis Fox collection]

Owned by Patrick Motors Ltd and based at Birmingham (Elmdon), G-AIBB was borrowed by Jersey Airlines for the 1950 summer season

[Denis Fox collection]

One of Jersey Airlines' Rapides on the apron at Jersey Airport

[G M Simons collection]

JERSEY AIRWAYS Ltd

Prominent among users of the DH Dragon series of aircraft was Jersey Airways. Registered by the Royal Court on 9th December 1933, the airline announced that scheduled services between Portsmouth and Jersey would begin at once. A major director was W L Thurgood, a bus and coach operator from Hertfordshire who was the promoter of the venture. At Stag Lane on 15th December, Jersey Airways took delivery of its first aircraft, six-seat DH.84 Dragon G-ACMJ, and W B Caldwell flew it at once to Portsmouth and on to Jersey, landing on the beach at St Aubin's Bay, the terminal for the new route. Two more Dragons were rented so that the new route could become established quickly, G-ACCE from Brian Lewis Ltd and the other from Scottish Motor Traction. The inaugural service took off from Portsmouth at 10.00 on 18th December with just one passenger, and arrived at St. Aubin's Bay about an hour and a quarter later. For the return flight, which left at 11.50, there were twelve passengers, almost a full complement for the two aircraft. Next day few passengers presented themselves at Portsmouth airport, and after that the weather became progressively worse, few flights being made until conditions improved on 31st December. On 9th January 1934 the airline's second Dragon, G-ACMC *St Brelade's Bay*, was delivered, releasing one of the rented aircraft, and passengers handled rapidly increased.

Although Jersey Airways had begun operating in the 'off' season, the winter service often had to be doubled to cope with demand. The Portsmouth route was followed by one from Heston which opened on 28th January 1934, with an initial frequency of one flight per day. By the summer of 1934 about a thousand passengers per week were making use of the services. Timings were arranged so that both services arrived at and left St. Aubin's at about the same time, minimising use of the beach, and the Heston-bound aircraft could make an extra landing if there were more passengers for Portsmouth than could be carried in one aircraft.

Jersey Airways' third Dragon, G-ACMO *St. Ouen's Bay*, was delivered on 1st February 1934, by which time traffic figures were beginning to justify the airline promoter's faith in his operation. At this time Jersey Airways' fares were higher than the rail / sea fares but much more acceptable given the very much shorter point-to-point time of three hours from central London to St. Helier via Heston airport.

Although the permissible all-up weight of the DH.84 had been set at 4200 lbs (1909 kg) by its makers, the Air Ministry was not happy where long over-water flights were concerned, and suggested that the limit should be reduced to 3850 lbs (1750 kg). As this was not a direct order, Jersey Airways did not comply, but every flight undertaken with an all-up weight of over 3850 lbs was reported to the Air Ministry by official inspectors and it was proposed that further tests on the Dragon type should be undertaken by the A&AEE at Martlesham Heath.

Use of St Aubin's beach by aircraft caused increasing concern, and clearly could not continue as a permanent feature, but at Easter 1934 no less than six Dragons were to be seen there at one time, and Jersey Airways

claimed that it could have filled six double-deck flying buses! The Portsmouth service was extended to Southampton on 18th March, providing yet more capacity for passengers keen to visit Jersey. Two more Dragons, G-ACNG and G-ACNH, were put into service that month. Expanding rapidly, the airline opened a twice-weekly service from Jersey to Paris (Le Bourget) on 4th June, and soon the last two Dragons, G-ACNI and G-ACNJ, were delivered.

By now, Jersey Airways' success was the envy of most of the other small British airlines. It had become the habit for several aircraft to make the sea crossing together in a 'flock', partly to avoid protracted use of the beach at St. Aubin's and partly for safety's sake. Nevertheless, the problem of holiday-makers and aircraft in close proximity was becoming serious, and reports of close encounters culminated in a tragic accident on 25th August 1934, when a Jersey Airways Dragon hit the sea wall at St. Aubin's on take-off, killing a ten-year-old boy who was watching the proceedings, and injuring another. An Air Ministry report blamed the pilot for errors of judgment stemming from lack of experience in piloting twin-engined aircraft.

During August hundreds of would-be passengers were disappointed when Jersey Airways could not accommodate them. After the holiday season, however, the service to the English mainland were reduced to one per day and the Paris route closed down. In its first twelve months of operation the airline carried almost 20,000 passengers, an excellent result.

The advantages of carrying modern radio equipment in their aircraft were seen by Jersey Airways by the end of 1934, when four of the eight Dragons were fitted with HF radio. With this, pilots could communicate with Portsmouth airport after take-off from Jersey, while pilots flying to Heston called the Croydon zone controller.

On 1st December 1934, Channel Islands Airways Ltd. was formed as a holding company for the shares of Jersey Airways and recently-formed Guernsey Airways. Mr Thurgood, Jersey Airways' founder, and Whitehall Securities Corpn Ltd each held one third of the share capital, the remaining third being divided between the Great Western Railway and the Southern Railway. Jersey Airways then became a subsidiary company, although continuing to operate in its own name.

Still growing quickly, Jersey Airways opened a route to Rennes in Brittany on 8th January 1935, connecting with flights from London to give a fast service into western France or by connecting train to Paris. However, this route had to be closed down after about two months, as the States of Jersey and local potato growers were concerned about the possible import of Colorado beetles.

To cope with ever-expanding passenger numbers and to provide a 90-minute service from Heston, Jersey Airways had placed an order on 10th November 1934 for six DH.86 Express aircraft.

The first new fourteen-passenger aircraft, G-ACYF, made a trial flight from Heston to St. Aubin's on 7th February 1935, with a number of airline executives and members of the aviation press on board. The outward trip took only 71 minutes and the return journey 95 minutes against a head wind. Timings for the Heston—Jersey route were reduced to 90 minutes when the DH.86s came into use in February. Deliveries continued until the sixth and last of Jersey Airlines' DH.86s came into service in May 1935.

As an intermediate call on the Heston—Jersey route, Portsmouth was dropped on 1st March 1935 in favour of Southampton (Eastleigh), a customs airport, with perceived better interchange facilities with the Southern Railway; this increased the Heston—Jersey timing to 105 minutes. In addition Southampton Docks was nearby, where transatlantic steamer services were available to Jersey Airways passengers.

A route from Jersey to Plymouth (Roborough) was opened on 3rd March 1936, flown twice a week by DH.84s and DH.89s. By this time the new States Airport was under construction, and a DH.86 made trial landings there in January 1937.

The 85-acre (34 hectare) new airport was opened officially on 10th March 1937, when at long last the use of St. Aubin's beach could be ended. A new route to Shoreham was opened on 31st May by a DH.86, and Exeter also became a DH.86 destination. On 28th February 1938 the Portsmouth service reopened, again using DH.86s, and on 9th August a service to Dinard operated jointly with Air France began. In the summer of 1939 scheduled services from Jersey operated to Guernsey, Heston, Southampton, Shoreham and Exeter, the last three via Guernsey, but any further development was inhibited by the outbreak of war on 3rd September. The airline's aircraft were then put at the disposal of the UK government, and in October 1939 the route to Shoreham was reopened under the auspices of National Air Communications. With invasion of the islands imminent, all operations were suspended on 15th June 1940, after which the airline evacuated thousands of residents from Jersey to England (mainly Exeter from 18th June). Subsequently, Jersey Airways aircraft were absorbed into the general fleet controlled by AAJC.

Immediately after the end of the war in Europe, Jersey Airways was back in business. On 26th May 1945 Rapide G-AGLP, chartered from Railway Air Services, touched down at Jersey airport, which at the time was an RAF

Evocative view of DH.86 G-ACYG "Gronville Bay" of Jersey Airways landing at Jersey (St Aubin's beach) in 1936

[via C N Dodds]

Staging Post. Flights to Guernsey and Croydon then began, and a formal schedule was established on 21st June. A merger between Jersey Airways and Guernsey Airways took place on 1st September 1945 under the title Channel Islands Airways, the name of the prewar holding company for the group. Four Rapides formed the equipment of Jersey Airways at the time.

Aircraft: DH.84   G-ACCE, G-ACET, G-ACMC, G-ACMJ, G-ACMO,
G-ACMP, G-ACNG, G-ACNH, G-ACNI, G-ACNJ

DH.86   G-ACYF, G-ACYG, G-ACZN, G-ACZO,
G-ACZP, G-ACZR, G-ADVK

DH.89   G-ADBV, G-ADBW, G-AGSH, G-AGPI, G-AGSK

Surely this picture captures the feeling of pre-war commercial flying? Before the construction of Jersey Airport the beach at St Aubin was used and here three DH.86s of Jersey Airways are lined up on the firm sand, with G-ACZR in the foreground. Coaches await the disembarking passengers
[P H T Green collection]

KENNING AVIATION Ltd

Based at Derby (Burnaston), this company was a subsidiary of a well-known motor dealership. In December 1946 four Rapides were purchased, but only one entered service, the others being sold. This single Rapide was employed on charter operations. However, by 1948 the operation was being curtailed, although a further Rapide was registered in 1949 and was based at Sherburn-in-Elmet for a time before the company ceased operations in 1950.

Aircraft: DH.89   G-AIUI, G-AIUJ, G-AIUK, G-AIUL,
G-AKZH, G-ALGE

KENTAIR (CHARTERS) Ltd

This company was formed early in 1966 and flew one Rapide on passenger and freight charters from Biggin Hill and also provided pleasure flights at the local air show. The Rapide was replaced by an Aztec in 1968.

Aircraft: DH.89   G-AKIF

G-AKIF of Kentair Charters, with whom it spent two years in the 1960s
[via A. Chivers]

LANCASHIRE AIRCRAFT CORPORATION Ltd

A major operator of the DH.89, Lancashire Aircraft Corpn began its life in February 1946 by flying them from Blackpool (Squires Gate) on charter and pleasure flights. Very quickly, the company expanded by acquiring other, larger, types of aircraft, but many more Rapides were also added to the fleet. Pleasure flying was also undertaken at Northolt. In July 1948 Rapides and Consuls opened a scheduled service from Leeds/Bradford (Yeadon) to the Isle of Man under a BEA Associate agreement. Other similar services followed in May 1949, when routes from Northolt to Blackpool and Leeds/Bradford were opened. Yet more scheduled services operated by Lancashire Aircraft Corpn at this time were Leeds – Blackpool – Isle of Man, Blackpool to Southport, Leeds/Bradford to Jersey and Blackpool to Jersey. Following the opening of a base at Newcastle (Woolsington) in the summer of 1949, the route from Northolt to Leeds/Bradford was extended to serve that city.

In 1950 another BEA Associate agreement was entered into, for a service from Northolt to Penzance [sic], flown, as all the company's routes were, by Rapides and Consuls. Other work was still undertaken, and included the inevitable charter flights and, in the winter of 1950, eight Rapides gathered at Newcastle to take part in Exercise 'Emperor' to act as bombers!

The BEA Associate scheme came to an end in 1951, after which Lancashire Aircraft Corpn flew many routes under its own auspices, still using the faithful Rapides and Consuls. By now headquartered at Samlesbury, the company bought the aircraft of Skytravel Ltd, which was in liquidation, in 1951, including DH.86 G-ACZP. The routes being flown now consisted on Blackpool to Jersey and the Isle of Man and Birmingham to the Isle of Man, and the DH.86 was sometimes used on these services, increasing the passenger capacity until Dakotas came on the scene. Reliable as ever, the Rapides and DH.86 continued to fly the dwindling number of scheduled services, but when the company was bought by British Aviation Services Group in December 1956 only the DH.86 was still in its ownership.

Aircraft: DH.86   G-ACZP

DH.89   G-AGOJ, G-AGUG, G-AHAG, G-AHEA, G-AHGD,
G-AJKW, G-AJKX, G-AJKY, G-AJMY, G-AKLA,
G-AKNN, G-AKNV, G-AKNW, G-AKOD, G-AKOE,
G-AKOY, G-AKRO, G-ALEJ, G-ALPK, G-ALZF

A posed line-up of Rapides of Lancashire Aircraft Corporation at Newcastle (Woolsington) in 1950, with G-AGOJ nearest the camera
[MAP via P H T Green]

LEES-HILL AVIATION (BIRMINGHAM) Ltd

Formed in January 1947 by E G Lees and F A Hill, this company started operations with Austers and an Aerovan before three Rapides replaced them in 1948. They were put into service on charter flights to the Isle of Wight, Isle of Man and Channel Islands and also carried out some pleasure flying. This continued until, on 5th September 1951, the company became part of Don Everall Aviation Ltd.

Aircraft: DH.89   G-AGLR, G-AHGF

LUTON AIRWAYS Ltd

Registered as an airline on 13th December 1957 by A M Fisher and F A Jarvis, Luton Airways initially leased a Rapide for charter work and pleasure flying. Three similar aircraft were purchased in 1958 and worked for the company until December 1959, when it ceased trading.

Aircraft: DH.89   G-AHLF, G-AIBB, G-ALBC, G-ALGC

G-AIBB of Luton Airways being ignored by spectators at an air show!
[via A. Chivers]

LUXURY AIR TOURS Ltd

Formed on 14th July 1932 by the Hon Mrs Victor Bruce, Mrs M M Bruce, Flt Lt J B Pugh and L T Griffin, this company was based at Hanworth, then in June 1933 at Hook and finally in May 1936 at Croydon. The Thames Valley Flying Club, formed in August 1933 at Hook, also came under the company's control. An air taxi service using four-seat cabin aircraft was advertised in October 1933, but little is known of the company's day-to-day activities. By November 1936 the company was dormant and was then bought by L J Petre and A W Morgan to carry out Army co-operation work and charter flights, particularly carrying sports teams. This new venture began in January 1937, but no information on the fate of the company is available.

Aircraft: DH.84 G-ACDL

MACSMITH AIR CHARTER Ltd

Based at Newcastle (Woolsington), this company operated one Rapide, delivered in November 1959. Extensively used for pleasure flying, and for many charter flights within Scotland, the Hebrides, Orkneys and Shetlands. However, at the end of the 1960 season operations ended, and the Rapide was later sold.

Aircraft: DH.89 G-ALGE

G-ALGE of Mac Smith Air Charter Ltd was sold subsequently in the Irish Republic, France and the USA, where it had been scrapped by 1990
[G M Simons collection]

MANNIN AIRWAYS Ltd

Three Rapides were put into service by this company in 1948 from Isle of Man (Ronaldsway). They were used on passenger and freight charters and some ambulance work, and one was lost in tragic circumstances on 11th November 1948, when it came down in the River Mersey. Early in 1949, the company went into partnership with Ulster Aviation to create a new company, North-West Airlines (Isle of Man) Ltd which would set up a network of scheduled services. Mannin Airways was to concentrate on charter flying, but in the event all activities were taken over by North-West Airlines early in 1950.

Aircraft: DH.89 G-AKOF, G-AKOH, G-AKOK, G-ALET

MANX AIR CHARTERS Ltd
MANX AIRLINES Ltd

A subsidiary of Air Charter Experts Ltd of the Isle of Man, Manx Air Charters acquired two Rapides in 1947 and was soon busily engaged in charter flights from the mainland to Ronaldsway, particularly when the TT races were staged and also for conferences held on the island. Air Charter Experts ceased trading in the summer of 1948, transferring its workload to Manx Air Charters, and five Rapides were now in use. In May 1950 an application for a BEA Associate agreement was successful, and Manx began flying on the route, between Carlisle and Ronaldsway. The cessation of flying by certain competitors encouraged Manx Air Charter to apply for more scheduled services, including routes from the Isle of Man to Newcastle and Glasgow (Renfrew), to be flown not by Rapides but by newly-acquired Dakotas. To present a more appropriate image, the company changed its name in February 1953 to Manx Airlines Ltd. The Rapides were then restricted to the Carlisle service.

In May 1956 Manx Airlines Ltd became part of the British Aviation Services group, but continued to operate under its own name. In the spring of 1958, however, the company's interests were merged into the Northern Division of Silver City Airways Ltd.

Aircraft: DH.89 G-AEMH, G-AJGV, G-AKGY, G-AKIF, G-AKSE

G-AKIF when in use by Manx Airlines Ltd *[G M Simons collection]*

MARSHALL'S FLYING SERVICES Ltd

A pioneering organisation based at Cambridge (Teversham) since 1937 and at nearby Fen Ditton before that, Marshall's took delivery of a Rapide in April 1946. Three more were added in the next two years or so, and were used on charter work, particularly for the movement of newspapermen and camera crews. Newmarket racecourse was a frequent destination for the Rapides on race days. Eventually, however, this type of operation declined, and in 1962 all the Rapides were sold.

Aircraft: DH.89 G-AGZO, G-AHED, G-AHLM, G-AKNN

Marshall's of Cambridge used G-AKNN, seen here at Liverpool (Speke) on 21.4.58 *[P H Butler]*

MAYFAIR AIR SERVICES Ltd

During 1948 a fleet of Rapides was acquired by this company to operate passenger and freight charter flights from Croydon and other London area airfields, often to continental destinations. Before long, airfields in the Middle East and north Africa were being visited, and a subsidiary company, Mediterranean Air Services Ltd, was established to further this type of business. However, this scheme appears to have been unsuccessful, as the aircraft were disposed of in May 1950 when flying ceased.

Aircraft: DH.89 G-AIUN, G-AKMF, G-AKTX, G-AKUS,
G-AKZI, G-AKZJ, G-AKZW

The short-lived Mayfair Air Services Ltd operated Rapide G-AKMF, seen here at a Mediterranean location, guarded by British troops *[Denis Fox collection]*

MAYFLOWER AIR SERVICES Ltd

Founded by Sqn Ldr P Cleife in January 1961, this company applied for permission to operate scheduled services from the Scilly Isles to Exeter and Plymouth. Although permission had not been received, a proving flight in Rapide G-AHLM was made on 13th June and another one on 8th July. From that point, services were flown on an ad-hoc basis, and a number of charter flights were also carried out. It was not until 5th December 1961 that the long-awaited approval was received. On 26th February 1962 the service from Plymouth (Roborough) to the Scilly Isles opened officially, and before long Mayflower's Rapide was operating the Land's End to the Scillies route on behalf of BEA when that airline's aircraft was out of service. In addition, Dan-Air's Gatwick to Plymouth service was sometimes flown by Mayflower.

A second Rapide was acquired in 1963, and expanded the company's operations. On 21st June a new scheduled service from Cardiff (Rhoose) to the Scillies was inaugurated, followed next day by a service from Newquay (St Mawgan) to the Scillies. Unfortunately, on 20th July Rapide G-AHLM was written off in a take-off accident at St Mary's in which Capt Cleife was seriously injured. Services continued, and in December 1963 the company's operations and sole Rapide were bought by Scillonian Air Services, although the Mayflower name was retained. Another Rapide was bought in May 1964 and was used on a service from Bristol (Lulsgate) to the Scillies, but later that month Mayflower Air Services was bought by British Westpoint Airlines Ltd, which allowed the Mayflower name to continue until the end of that summer season.

Aircraft: DH.89 G-AHLM, G-AIUL, G-ASKO

Mayflower Air Services Ltd owned G-AIUL between April 1963 and May 1964, when the company became part of British Westpoint Airlines Ltd
[Denis Fox collection]

McALPINE AVIATION Ltd

A subsidiary of the old-established construction company, McAlpine Aviation was formed in 1947 at Fairoaks with a Gemini aircraft. In September 1948 a Rapide was added, and carried out most of the company's executive flying for several years. Other types were gradually added to the fleet, and the Rapide was sold in 1962, by which time the company had moved to Luton.

Aircraft: DH.89 G-ALBC

G-ALBC at Fairoaks in 1956, when it was registered to K McAlpine
[G M Simons collection]

MELBA AIRWAYS Ltd

An associate company of Melba Motors Ltd, Melba Airways Ltd was registered on 28th August 1948 as an airline operator, based at Manchester (Barton). Passenger and freight charter flights, including trips to the Isle of Wight and Isle of Man, were carried out, using a small fleet of Rapides and other types. Pleasure flying also formed an important part of the company's operations. In 1951 the company began operating scheduled services from Manchester to Bournemouth (Hurn) and from there to the Isle of Wight and Land's End, all under a BEA Associate agreement. However, after a winter of little activity Melba Airways went into voluntary liquidation in February 1952.

Aircraft: DH.89 G-AJMY, G-ALGC, G-ALGE

G-ALGE in use with Melba Airways Ltd and seen here at Newcastle (Woolsington)
[E Taylor via R C Sturtivant]

METROPOLITAN AIR MOVEMENTS Ltd

One of the few UK companies to operate the DH.90 on charter work, Metropolitan Air Movements was formed in June 1960 by ACM Sir Guy Garrod as an executive air charter operator. Its first aircraft was DH.90A G-ANYK, which was acquired in December of that year and based at Biggin Hill, where it was used mainly for aerial photographic purposes, although not intensively. It was damaged beyond repair at La Baule in France in June 1961, ending the use of members of the Dragon family by this company.

Aircraft: DH.90 G-ANYK

MID-FLY Ltd

Based at Birmingham (Elmdon), Midfly Ltd was formed in April 1964 by M J Webb, E A Bott and Capt C C Holloway. A Rapide was acquired in 1965 and devoted its time to charter flights, pleasure flying, aerial photography and training. However it was disposed of a year later.

Aircraft: DH.89 G-AHKV

MIDLAND & SCOTTISH AIR FERRIES Ltd

Founded on 10th March 1933 by John Sword, at the time a manager with Scottish Motor Traction, this company opened a route from Glasgow (Renfrew) to Campbeltown (The Strath) on 18th April, using a Dragon, and this was soon extended to Islay (Bridgend Sands). A M&SAF Dragon carried out the first air ambulance flight in Scotland when on 14th May 1933 it picked up a patient at Islay for Glasgow. Surveys of possible landing grounds were carried out, including Barra on 14th June and North Uist (Sollas) in the same month. Ten thousand passengers were carried in 1933 and the aim was to handle fifty thousand in 1934. A route from Glasgow via Liverpool (Speke) to Romford (Maylands) with connections from Belfast and the Isle of Man was established on 9th April 1934 but lasted only until 14th July. On 29th September that year the company closed down after John Sword was warned by the directors of SMT that his airline activities had to cease or he would be obliged to leave that company's employ. This was mainly because he would have become a serious competitor to Railway Air Services Ltd, then being formed by, among others, directors of SMT. M&SAF's final flight was on 17th November 1934.

Aircraft: DH.84 G-ACCZ, G-ACDL, G-ACDM,
G-ACDN, G-ACET, G-ACJS

MODERN TRANSPORT (WOLVERHAMPTON) Ltd

Formed in 1946 by Don Everall, this company bought a Rapide in 1949 for use on summer holiday flights from Wolverhampton to the Channel Islands and the Isle of Man and for general charter work and pleasure flights. In September 1951 the company took over Lees-Hill Aviation and the combined companies were retitled Don Everall (Aviation) Ltd.

Aircraft: DH.89 G-AGPP

MORTON AIR SERVICES Ltd

One of the first new airline companies to be formed after the end of the Second World War was Morton Air Services Ltd, based at Croydon, with Capt T W Morton as its founder. Two Rapides were purchased, and on 21st January 1946 the company's first charter, to Zurich, was flown, with the benefit of extra fuel tanks to allow longer endurance. By that summer three Rapides and two Consuls were being used, and holiday charters to the Channel Islands and other destinations were being flown. 1947 saw a steady increase in the number of charter flights to race meetings, a task which would continue for many years. Two more Rapides were obtained in 1948 to replace Consuls which had gone to Palestine under the auspices of the United Nations.

In April 1949 an office was opened at Bristol (Whitchurch), initially for pleasure-flying operations, but in 1950 a scheduled service from there to the Channel Islands was begun. A BEA Associate agreement was entered into in 1951, allowing Morton Air Services to fly from Croydon to Innsbruck and to Knocke (Le Zoute) and from Bristol to the Isle of Man and Channel Islands.

At the end of 1953 Morton Air Services bought Olley Air Service Ltd, although the latter continued to trade under its own name. By this time the Rapides had been replaced on scheduled services by Doves and the few remaining examples were used on short-range charters until December 1962, when the last one was sold.

Aircraft: DH.89 G-AGUG, G-AGWP, G-AGWR, G-AHIA, G-AJXX,
G-AKOR, G-AKUS, G-AKTZ, G-AKZW, G-ALBH

G-AGUG of Morton Air Services Ltd at Liverpool (Speke) on 23rd March 1961, with Dove 6 G-ANPH in the background
[P H Butler]

MURRAY CHOWN AVIATION Ltd

Based at Gloucester/Cheltenham (Staverton), this company was registered on 26th March 1949 by C M Chown and G Hansen, and continued the operations begun two years earlier by Mr Chown with two Cessna aircraft. A Rapide was leased from Inter-City Air Services in 1950, and in October the company was awarded a number of BEA Associate agreements. The first to open was between Staverton and Newquay (Perranporth) and on to the Scilly Isles, and in 1951 a service between Staverton and Jersey was opened, a second Rapide having been obtained to supplement Proctors. At the end of the 1952 season the services were suspended, and the company was sold to Cambrian Air Services, which took over the Jersey route. The Rapide which belonged to Murray Chown Aviation did not pass to Cambrian, but was leased to Dragon Airways.

Aircraft: DH.89 G-AIYP

NATIONAL AIR COMMUNICATIONS

National Air Communications was the title of the short-lived organisation which controlled 257 civil transport aircraft and placed them at the disposal of the RAF at the outbreak of the Second World War. Managed by Lt Col Sir Francis Shelmerdine, the Director General of Civil Aviation, the organisation came into operation on 1st September 1939, by which time hostilities were seen to be inevitable, and most of the aircraft were flown to prearranged airfields. DH types were distributed as follows:

Bristol (Whitchurch) –
one DH.86 of Imperial Airways; three DH.86s and one DH.89 of Railway Air Services.

Cardiff (Pengam Moors) –
nine DH.84s, three DH.89s and six DH.90s of Air Dispatch.

Glasgow (Renfrew) –
three DH.84s and six DH.89s of Scottish Airways.

Jersey –
six DH.86s of Jersey Airways.

Liverpool (Speke) –
one DH.90 of Birkett Air Service; one DH.89 of British-American Air Services; two DH.84s and three DH.89s of Great Western & Southern Air Lines; seven DH.89s of North Eastern Airways.

Manchester (Barton) –
one DH.84 and one DH.90 of Air Taxis; one DH.89 of Personal Airways; two DH.86s and three DH.89s of Wrightways.

Isle of Man (Ronaldsway) –
two DH.89s and one DH.90 of Air Commerce; one DH.84 and four DH.89s of Isle of Man Air Services.

Weston-super-Mare –
one DH.84 of Surrey Flying Services; six DH.84s, one DH.86, four DH.89s and two DH.90s of 1Western Airways.

Many of these aircraft joined in the task of carrying blood plasma and other important medical products to France from RAF Stations in the south of England, as well as signals equipment, top-secret messages and key personnel. Later in September, Army co-operation flights were begun again, and a letter service became a regular feature, eight DH.89s being among the aircraft allocated to perform this service between York (Clifton), Hendon and France. Eight other DH.89s were fitted out to carry a total of 29 stretchers and their attendants, and a host of other functions were tackled.

One DH.84 and three DH.89s of Allied Airways (Gandar Dower) were added to the organisation in December 1939, and the general commitment to NAC continued. Several NAC aircraft were lost in accidents in England and France (see aircraft listings for details) before, on 27th March 1940, the decision was made to transfer all aircraft flying in support of the RAF to them, the aircraft involved generally being impressed for military service. Control of scheduled passenger services of strategic value which still continued were transferred to a new body, the Associated Airways Joint Committee, on 5th May 1940.

NEWMAN AIRWAYS Ltd

One of the earliest postwar charter companies, Newman Airways was founded at Panshanger in 1945 by W W Lyle and J F Perren. Proctors were used at first, but a Rapide was added in June 1948 and was employed on holiday charter flights to the Isle of Wight and the Channel Islands. Approval was gained for several scheduled routes to be opened, but no services were flown before the company ceased operations in 1951.

Aircraft: DH.89 G-AKPA

Newman Aircraft Co Ltd operated G-AKPA from Croydon under the title Newman Airways between 1948 and 1951. This aircraft still exists in 2003 in the United States as N89DH *[Denis Fox collection]*

NORMAN EDGAR (WESTERN AIRWAYS) Ltd
WESTERN AIRWAYS Ltd

Originally known as Norman Edgar & Co, this company began operating a route between Bristol (Whitchurch) and Cardiff (Splott/Pengam Moors) on 26th September 1932, using a Puss Moth. This was extended on 17th May 1934, using a DH.84, to Christchurch to provide connections to Portsmouth, Shoreham and the Isle of Wight. The service had become so well-patronised that four DH.84s came to be employed. Further development came on 1st June 1936, when the company began to include the new airport at Weston-super-Mare in its scheduled service, moving there entirely in August. Three DH.89s were acquired in the summer of 1937, and remained in service until the outbreak of war. In January 1938 the company came under control of the Straight Corporation, and on 27th July the Cardiff route was extended to the new airfield at Swansea (Jersey Marine), using a DH.86.

The newly-opened Manchester airport at Ringway was the starting point of a service to Weston-super-Mare which began on 17th June 1939, flown by DH.89s and DH.90s. Yet another route was flown three times daily via Barnstaple and Newquay to Penzance. Like so many other small airlines, Western Airways closed its operations on the outbreak of war in 1939 and came under the control of National Air Communications. Later, most of its aircraft were impressed for military service. After the war, operations began again, but did not employ DH aircraft types.

Aircraft: DH.84 G-ACAO, G-ACCZ, G-ACJT, G-ACLE, G-ACMJ, G-ACMP, G-ACPX, G-AECZ
DH.86 G-AETM
DH.89 G-ACTU, G-ADBV, G-ADDD, G-AFSO
DH.90 G-ADNA, G-AEDH

G-ACMJ while in service with Western Airways, probably seen here at Barnstaple's small airfield *[MAP via P H T Green]*

Loading passengers onto a Dragon of Western Airways for the short hop from Bristol to Cardiff *[G M Simons collection]*

NORTH DEVON FLYING CLUB

An unusual type of owner for aircraft of the Dragon family, North Devon Flying Club at RAF Chivenor acquired a Rapide in March 1952 and used it and two Austers on a daily service to Lundy Island. Pleasure flying at Chivenor and elsewhere was also undertaken. In December 1952 the Club became part of Devonair Ltd.

Aircraft: DH.89 G-AKNY

NORTH EASTERN AIRWAYS Ltd

Registered in 1935, North Eastern Airways opened a service from Heston to Leeds/Bradford (Yeadon) and Newcastle on 8th April that year. A service between Croydon and Perth began on 14th September 1936, using a DH.86.

The company's fleet of six DH.89s was taken over by National Air Communications at the outbreak of war and apart from two which were abandoned in France while carrying out urgent military duties they were impressed for RAF service in 1940.

Aircraft: DH.84 G-ACFG, G-ACLE

DH.89 G-ADDE, G-ADWZ, G-AEMH, G-AEXO, G-AEXP, G-AFEO, G-AFEP

Two DH.89s of North Eastern Airways at Southend in 1937/38, G-ADDE in the foreground and G-ADFX behind it [A J Hallams via GMS]

NORTHERN AIRWAYS Ltd

Formed on 1st July 1934 and wholly owned by George Nicholson, this company operated a service from Newcastle (Cramlington) to Carlisle (Kingstown) and the Isle of Man, using DH.84 G-ACFG, between 1st August and 29th October 1934. Three daily flights were scheduled on this route, which was extended on 17th August to Belfast (Newtownards). However, on 23rd August the service was reduced to three return flights per week due to a poor response, and on 3rd September it was reduced further to Mondays and Saturdays only. The last flight was on 29th October 1934, after which the company became known as Northern & Scottish Airways Ltd.

Aircraft: DH.84 G-ACFG

NORTHERN & SCOTTISH AIRWAYS Ltd

Developed from Northern Airways Ltd, this company was registered by George Nicholson on 21st November 1934, with an office at Exchange Buildings, Quayside, Newcastle and an office and town terminal at 153 Hope St, Glasgow. At the end of the month Dragon G-ACFG positioned at Renfrew, and on 1st December Northern & Scottish reopened the former Midland & Scottish Air Ferries route between there and the Isle of Islay (Duich Farm), via Campbeltown, with a single-way fare of £1-10-0 (£1.50).

On 1st January 1935 the company assumed responsibility for the air ambulance service which John Sword had established at Renfrew in May 1933, and almost immediately an emergency flight from the Western Isles was made. A second Dragon, G-ACJS, complete with toilet and radio, was purchased from John Sword in January 1935 so that services could be expanded. Using the small airfield at Hall Caine as its Isle of Man terminus, the company began a three or four times per week service from Glasgow (Renfrew) on 11th May 1935, the return fare being £3-5-0 (£3.25). This route proved popular and the frequency was soon increased to two flights each day.

On 23rd May 1935 the company was merged with Highland Airways and United Airways under the financial control of Whitehall Securities Ltd, but existing titles were retained. Two more Dragons were purchased in July, from Jersey Airways, which was then re-equipping, and a third arrived in August. Another route in the Hebrides opened on 5th December 1935 between Glasgow and Skye (Glen Brittle), still using DH.84s, and this route was extended on 21st January 1936 to South Uist (Askernish), on 27th February 1936 to North Uist (Sollas) and finally, on 2nd July 1936, to Benbecula. The original route to Islay

was extended to Tiree (Reef) at the same time, and five Rapides soon followed, augmenting the four Dragons.

Other services were from Glasgow to Belfast (Newtownards) and Liverpool, Belfast to the Isle of Man, and Carlisle to the Isle of Man, all of which were taken over from British Airways on 1st July 1936. However, on 20th May 1937 several routes were handed to Railway Air Services. Northern & Scottish Airways was now flying the Glasgow to Islay route, Western Isles services and Glasgow to the Isle of Man, but on 12th August 1937 merged with Highland Airways to form Scottish Airways Ltd.

Aircraft: DH.84 G-ACFG, G-ACJS, G-ACMC, G-ACMO, G-ACNG, G-ACNH, G-ACOR

DH.89 G-ADAE, G-ADAG, G-ADAH, G-ADBU, G-ADDF

Northern & Scottish Airways' G-ADDF at Belfast (Newtownards) [J Stroud via GMS]

NORTH SEA AIR TRANSPORT Ltd

Following some success with early charter operations using single-engined aircraft, this company, a subsidiary of Blackburn Aircraft Co, acquired three Rapides in 1946 to expand the operation. Many flights were made to holiday destinations in the UK, including the Channel Islands. By 1950 all flying was based on Hull (Brough) airfield, but after that date the charter side of the group business was allowed to decline, and by 1952 only one Rapide remained, used as a communications aircraft by Blackburn Aircraft Company. Surprisingly, it lasted for many years in this role, flying from Holme-on-Spalding Moor and Brough, and eventually became part of the Hawker Siddeley Group's assets.

Aircraft: DH.89 G-AHAG, G-AHGD, G-AHLU, G-AHTY, G-AIWG, G-AIWZ

Seen here at Croydon, G-AHLU was in use by North Sea Air Transport Ltd, but eventually found its way to Australia as VH-AHI

NORTH-WEST AIRLINES (ISLE OF MAN) Ltd

This company was the result of a merger between Mannin Airways Ltd and Ulster Aviation Ltd in 1948. In the process, a fleet of four Rapides was created, based at Ronaldsway. The new airline soon applied for BEA Associate agreements, and was awarded routes from Ronaldsway to Birmingham, Blackpool, Glasgow, Leeds/Bradford, Manchester and Newcastle, and these were flown by the Rapides, although Dakotas soon began to replace them due to passenger demand exceeding the capacity that Rapides could handle. Ulster Aviation's former base at Belfast (Nutts Corner) was taken over, and from there the Rapides flew charter operations, particularly in the winter 'close season'.

During the summer of 1950 the company was taken over by Lancashire Aircraft Corporation Ltd, although the North-West title was retained. At the end of the 1951 summer season the new owners decided to end this arrangement, took over the routes and sold most of the aircraft.

Aircraft: DH.89 G-AGIF, G-AHLN, G-AKOH, G-AKOK

OCEAN AIRWAYS

This concern was the brainchild of L E Gisborne and D J Hayles, to whom the sole Rapide was registered. It flew from Portsmouth in March and April 1948 before being sold.

Aircraft: DH.89 G-AKTY

OLDSTEAD AIRCRAFT Ltd

Formed by ship owner J W Adamson in May 1948, this company acquired a Rapide in April 1950 and used it for Army co-operation work from its Newcastle (Woolsington) base. Charter flights and pleasure flying were also carried out until February 1954, when the Rapide was written off and the company ceased flying.

Aircraft: DH.89 G-AFMF

OLLEY AIR SERVICE Ltd

A major user of aircraft of the Dragon family, Olley Air Service Ltd was established by Capt Gordon Olley at Croydon on 10th January 1934, with capital of £6015 and with important backers, among them Sir Hugo Cunliffe-Owen and Sir James Dunn. Charter flights formed the mainstay of Olley's business in the early days, for which DH.84s and later, DH.89s were used. From 1st May 1934 the new company operated a service from Croydon to Luxembourg using DH.84s.

In 1935 Gordon Olley formed Isle of Man Air Services Ltd (which see), took over Blackpool & West Coast Air Services Ltd and acquired the assets of Cobham Air Routes. Never letting the grass grow under his feet, he formed Channel Air Ferries in May 1936, and placed the shares of all his companies under a holding company, British & Foreign Aviation Ltd.

On the outbreak of war in September 1939 Olley Air Service became part of National Air Communications, and in April 1940 transferred to AAJC, of which Capt Olley was appointed General Manager.

The company survived the war and in January 1946 recommenced charter flights from Croydon, using two Rapides. In December that year Olley took over Air Commerce Ltd and its two Rapides, although the Air Commerce title was retained for the time being. Many charters to France and the Channel Islands were flown in 1947, when the number of Rapides in the fleet was still growing although an order had been placed for the DH.104 Dove. Race meetings seem to have been favourite destinations for Olley aircraft at this time. Several scheduled services under BEA Associate agreements were developed, but appear to have been the province of the three Doves bought by the company. Towards the end of 1953 the share capital of Olley Air Service Ltd was bought by Morton Air Services Ltd, and many of the aircraft were sold, including the last remaining Rapide.

An evocative picture of G-ACYR of Olley Air Service at Deauville, its passengers deplaning after the 45-minute flight from Croydon

Two Rapides of Olley Air Service   *[G M Simons collection]*

Aircraft: DH.84 G-ACAN, G-ACEK, G-ACNA, G-ACPY

DH.89 G-ACTT, G-ACYM, G-ACYR, G-AENN, G-AEPE, G-AEPF, G-AEPW, G-AFEP, G-AGSI, G-AHGG, G-AIUL, G-AIYE, G-AKSB, G-AKSC, G-AKSD

PATRICK-DUVAL AVIATION Ltd
PATRICK AVIATION Ltd

Established in 1946 by J A Patrick and Capt Duval, this company was a subsidiary of Patrick Motors Ltd of Birmingham, to which most of the aircraft were registered. Flying began in January 1947, but Rapides did not join the small fleet until June 1948, when two of them inaugurated a scheduled service between Birmingham and the Isle of Man under the BEA Associate scheme. After Capt Duval left the company, its name was altered to Patrick Aviation in January 1949, and three more Rapides were then acquired. For the 1949 season, more BEA Associate routes were set up, this time from Birmingham to Blackpool, Jersey, Southampton and Croydon, the last from Castle Bromwich rather than Elmdon, for the British Industries Fair. The company lost the Jersey route in 1950 because it had proved so popular that BEA wanted to fly it itself! The Isle of Man service was the only one flown that year, and at the end of the summer when it closed all scheduled flying came to an end. Small-scale charter work continued, but in 1953 this also ended and the aircraft were sold.

Aircraft: DH.89 G-AHGH, G-AHGI, G-AIBB, G-AKNX, G-AKNY, G-AKOA, G-AKVU, G-ALRW

G-AKNX of Patrick Aviation Ltd of Birmingham (Elmdon), who operated it between 1949 and 1952   *[G M Simons collection]*

PERSONAL AIRWAYS Ltd

Croydon was the base of this company, founded on 9th March 1936 by Capt W Ledlie, the Hon P R L Beatty and the Hon P Pleydell-Bouverie. Regular services on behalf of Radio Luxembourg and later Radio Normandie seem to have been the company's main activity, for which the aircraft fleet in October 1937 included four DH.89s. By the outbreak of war, when the company's six aircraft were taken over by National Air Communications, only one DH.89 was in service, and this was later impressed into the RAF.

Aircraft: DH.89 G-ACTU, G-ADWZ, G-AEMH, G-AEOV, G-AEPE, G-AFAH

DH.90 G-AEHC

PORTSMOUTH AVIATION Ltd

Having survived as an aircraft maintenance company, Portsmouth, Southsea & Isle of Wight Aviation Ltd changed its name to Portsmouth Aviation Ltd on 8th February 1943. The only further use of DH aircraft came about in 1946/47, when a certain amount of charter work was undertaken.

Aircraft: DH.89 G-AFMG, G-AHEB

PORTSMOUTH, SOUTHSEA
& ISLE OF WIGHT AVIATION Ltd

Known as Wight Aviation Ltd until 11th May 1932, this company was capitalised at £17,500 and had L M J Balfour, Flt Lt F L Luxmoore DFC, Capt F S Symondson MC and A G Murray as directors. The original equipment consisted of Fox Moths, Monospars and a Wessex, but a DH.84 fitted with Marconi radio was delivered on 18th May 1934 and was put into service on a new route from Heston to Ryde and Shanklin. This service came to an end at the end of the 1935 summer season after considerable pressure from the Southern Railway. In March 1935 Sir Alan Cobham became a director, but the company's use of the DH.84 ended in June 1936.

Aircraft: DH.84 G-ACAO, G-ACRF

PRIVATE AIR HIRE SERVICE Ltd

Charter flights by this company began from Croydon in December 1946, using a Proctor aircraft. A Rapide was added in August 1947, and destinations on the continent were frequently visited. The Rapide was, however, sold at the end of the 1948 season.

Aircraft: DH.89 G-AJKE

PROVINCIAL AIRWAYS Ltd

Provincial Airways appears to have begun life as Western Air Express with a route from Croydon to Plymouth (Roborough) via Portsmouth, Southampton and Haldon opened in November 1933, using a Dragon and a Fox Moth. From 19th March 1934 a 'request' stop at Christchurch was available and other places called at from time to time were Dorchester, Newquay and Hayle.

On 4th March 1935 Provincial Airways opened a route from Hull (Hedon) to Plymouth (Roborough) via Nottingham (Tollerton), Leicester (Braunstone) and Southampton (Eastleigh), using Dragons. At the opening of Denbury (Torbay Airport) on 6th April three of Provincial's DH.84s were on display. This was followed on 1st July by the inauguration of a route from Nottingham to Paris via Leicester, but by October the company was in financial difficulties.

Aircraft: DH.84 G-ACBW, G-ACDL, G-ACKD

A striking picture of DH.84 G-ACKD "Saturn" of Provincial Airways ready to taxy at Croydon *[R C Sturtivant]*

RAILWAY AIR SERVICES Ltd

Royal assent was given on 10th May 1929 for railway companies to operate air services in their own regions and in Europe as far as 20 degrees east. It was 1933, however, before domestic air services began to make any serious impact, and in March 1933 the GWR had discussions with Imperial Airways on the subject of co-operation. As a result, a small-scale service was established from Cardiff (Pengam Moors) to Plymouth via Haldon, from where the Torbay resorts could be serviced by bus. This route was inaugurated on 11th April, flown by a Westland Wessex of Imperial Airways, painted in the GWR's cream and brown livery. On 23rd May the route was extended to Birmingham (Castle Bromwich) but was closed on 30th September for the winter.

By the end of 1933 ideas for an airline owned jointly by the four main-line railway companies and Imperial Airways were being discussed. Final plans for the setting-up of Railway Air Services Ltd were agreed in January 1934 and the company was duly registered on 21st January at Imperial Airways' terminus, Hudson House, next to Victoria Station. Nominal capital was £50,000, of which £502 was in £1 shares. Each railway company nominated a Director and paid for his 100 shares.

Railway Air Services routes were the final responsibility of the company in whose area the route was established. All revenue was paid to the railway companies and Railway Air Services then charged them with full direct and overhead costs.

The first aircraft to be used by Railway Air Services was DH.84 Dragon G-ACPX, which arrived at Croydon on 3rd May 1934 for use on SR and GWR routes. Two DH.86 Express aircraft were ordered for a LMS Glasgow to Croydon service, as well as several DH.89 Dragon Rapides. On 7th May the original GWR Birmingham to Plymouth route reopened, extended now to Liverpool and flown by G-ACPX. A joint GWR/SR service from Birmingham to Cowes via Bristol (Whitchurch) and Southampton (Eastleigh) opened on 30th July and was operated by a second Dragon, G-ACPY. In August the first single-pilot DH.86, G-ACVY, was delivered for use on the new route from Glasgow (Renfrew) to Belfast (Aldergrove), Manchester (Barton), Birmingham (Castle Bromwich) and Croydon, which opened on 20th August, calling at Stoke-on-Trent (Meir) on demand.

Passengers boarding G-ACPX of Railway Air Services; note the 'plus fours' worn by the gentleman nearest the fuselage *[P H T Green collection]*

In February 1935 two new Dragons, G-ADDI and G-ADDJ, were bought for use on a route from Nottingham (Tollerton) to Plymouth (Roborough) via Cardiff (Pengam Moors) and Torbay (Denbury) which opened on 27th May. Another route operated by the DH.84s was from Liverpool to Castle Bromwich, Bristol (Whitchurch), Southampton (Eastleigh), Portsmouth and Shoreham. For this service two new DH.89s had been delivered on 18th May. That summer one of the DH.84s was chartered to Spartan Air Lines for use on their very short ferry route from Sandown, Isle of Wight, to Cowes (Somerton) and Southampton. The final new service that year was Railway Air Services' first venture into overseas flying, a Sunday excursion from Shoreham to Le Touquet in a DH.89. The 'Manx Airway' trade mark was used by Railway Air Services from the summer of 1935, when new DH.84s G-ADED and G-ADEE were put into service in June.

1936 was a very active year for Railway Air Services, effectively opening on 14th March, when the first of six new DH.89s was delivered, the others following within ten weeks. New routes to be operated by these aircraft were between Leeds/Bradford (Yeadon) and the Isle of Man via Manchester (Barton) and Blackpool (Squires Gate) and from Carlisle to the Isle of Man. On 25th May Portsmouth was deleted from the Liverpool to Shoreham route and a call at Ryde substituted, and a revised route from Plymouth to Bristol via Haldon, Cardiff and Weston-super-Mare was established. On 4th July Railway Air Services became a partner with Spartan Air Lines on a route from newly-reopened Gatwick to Ryde and Cowes, using DH.84 G-ACNI.

Major action to reorganise the Isle of Man services began on 21st May 1937, when Railway Air Services took over four Northern & Scottish Airways routes from the Isle of Man: to Glasgow, Blackpool and Liverpool, Carlisle and Belfast. In addition, the same airline's service from Liverpool to Belfast and Glasgow was absorbed. On 1st June the Blackpool terminal was moved from Squires Gate to Stanley Park airfield. 'Manx Airway' ceased to be used as a trade mark on 26th September, and all the services now under the RAS banner were transferred to Isle of Man Air Services Ltd. Two DH.84s, two DH.86s and five DH.89s were handed over to the new company.

This move left Railway Air Services with just two routes: the Croydon – Belfast – Glasgow mail service and the separate Belfast to Glasgow service. However, on 2nd May 1938 a new direct Croydon to Glasgow service was inaugurated, and on the same day Belfast flights were transferred from Newtownards airport to Belfast Harbour, otherwise known as Sydenham. Later in the month a new Shoreham – Ryde – Bournemouth (Christchurch) route was established in conjunction with Portsmouth, Southsea & Isle of Wight Aviation and was flown by a RAS DH.84. Another move was the transfer of Manchester operations from the small Barton airfield to the new Ringway airport on 27th June 1938.

In the summer of 1938 a reorganisation of routes in the south and south-west of England took place, and a company which had been formed in 1936, Channel Air Ferries Ltd, was activated to control them. Dragon G-ADDI was transferred from RAS for use on the Land's End to Scilly Isles service. Another newcomer in southern England was Great Western & Southern Airlines Ltd, to which RAS also handed over a number of aircraft.

1939 began with a move of operation from Castle Bromwich to the new Birmingham airport at Elmdon on 1st May, and the last peacetime schedules came into force on 22nd May. These were flown by DH.86s and DH.89s, and were given 'line numbers' (flight numbers) as follows: Line No 650 from Croydon to Belfast via Birmingham, Manchester and Liverpool; Line No 651 from Croydon to Glasgow via Birmingham, Manchester, Liverpool and the Isle of Man; Line No 652 from Croydon to Glasgow via Manchester and Liverpool; Line No 653 from Glasgow to Belfast; and Line No 654 from Croydon to Liverpool.

When war was declared three DH.86s and a DH.89 of Railway Air Services were sent to Exeter to join parts of the Imperial Airways and

British Airways fleets as part of the government's National Air Communications organisation. As such, the aircraft were employed intensively in ferrying supplies and personnel to France, and this went on until May 1940, when the RAF, which was in the process of impressing many civilian aircraft, took over the task. At that point, a new organisation, the Associated Airways Joint Committee, was set up to co-ordinate the operation of a number of vital scheduled services. Railway Air Services then reopened its Liverpool – Belfast – Glasgow route on 6th May 1940, but nine days later all AAJC aircraft were once more sent to Exeter and thence to France to take part in the evacuation of service personnel. During this frantic operation two DH.86s of Railway Air Services had to be abandoned at Bordeaux. After about six weeks, the Railway Air Services aircraft and crews once more found themselves on the Liverpool – Belfast – Glasgow service, and two replacement DH.86s were acquired from Jersey Airways. This service continued, and in addition, on 1st September 1941, a Rapide of Railway Air Services began to operate a much-needed mail service between Liverpool and Belfast. Aircraft were used as and when they were available by any member of AAJC, and in particular those of Scottish Airways were often seen on the Railway Air Services routes.

With the end of the war in Europe in sight, Railway Air Services extended its 'main line' route to Croydon on 13th November 1944, and this service soon became very busy. Following this, a service direct from Croydon to Prestwick was opened on 9th April 1945, designed to connect with the transatlantic aircraft of Trans-Canada Air Lines. However, this venture was closed on 18th May and a route from Croydon to Renfrew with a fuel stop at Liverpool was substituted. Immediately after the Channel Islands were liberated, two Rapides of Railway Air Services were lent to Jersey Airways to help in the re-establishment of their services.

During the winter of 1945/46 these routes were maintained, two DH.86s and two DH.89s being employed on the Croydon – Liverpool – Belfast route and one DH.89 on the Croydon to Glasgow service. In the summer of 1946 Dakotas and Ansons began to replace the DH.86s and some of the older DH.89s, although more of the latter type were still being acquired. On 1st August British European Airways was established under the Civil Aviation Act to effectively nationalise the internal airlines, but for the time being they continued being operated by the original companies on behalf of BEA. However, on 1st February 1947 BEA formally took over the services, aircraft and personnel of AAJC, including, of course, Railway Air Services Ltd, including some DH.89s.

Aircraft: DH.84   G-ACHV, G-ACNI, G-ACPX, G-ACPY, G-ACVD, G-ACXI, G-ADDI, G-ADDJ, G-ADED, G-ADEE

DH.86   G-ACVY, G-ACVZ, G-ACZP, G-AEFH, G-AENR, G-AEWR

DH.89   G-ACPP, G-ACPR, G-AEAJ, G-AEAK, G-AEAL, G-AEAM, G-AEBW, G-AEBX, G-AFFF, G-AGLE, G-AGLP, G-AGLR, G-AGUU, G-AHGF, G-AHGG, G-AHGH, G-AHGI, G-AHKS, G-AIHN

Rapide G-ACPR "City of Birmingham" in the livery of Railway Air Services, its first owner   *[P H T Green collection]*

RAMSGATE AIRPORT Ltd (see Southern Airways Ltd)

RINGWAY AIR CHARTER SERVICES Ltd

This company's primary function was to provide pleasure flights at Manchester (Ringway), for which two Rapides were used. Founded in 1953 by Capt D L Lancaster and N Baxter, the company was registered as an airline on 10th March 1954, and carried out some charter flights, but at the end of 1955 both aircraft were disposed of and flying ceased.

Aircraft: DH.89   G-AKZP, G-ALBA

G-AKZP of Ringway Air Charter Services Ltd   *[G M Simons collection]*

ROCHESTER AIR CHARTER SERVICE Ltd
SHORT BROS & HARLAND Ltd
SHORT'S AIR CHARTER SERVICE Ltd

A subsidiary of Short Bros & Harland Ltd, Rochester Air Charter Service began operating in June 1947, its small fleet including a DH.90 Dragonfly. In 1948 the procurement of a number of Rapides began, and these were used for general charter flying and as communications aircraft for the parent company. During 1949 scaling-down of Short Bros' facilities at Rochester began, work being transferred to Belfast, and most of the Rapides moved there. Renamed Short's Air Charter Service Ltd, the Rochester operation continued on a reduced scale until the last Rapide was disposed of in 1958.

Aircraft: DH.89   G-AGDP, G-AKDW, G-AKRP, G-AKRR, G-ALOV, G-ALWI, G-ALWJ, G-AMCT

DH.90   G-AEWZ

Rapide G-AKRP was first owned by Short Bros & Harland Ltd at Rochester in 1948, since when it has seen many other owners   *[Denis Fox collection]*

ST CHRISTOPHER TRAVEL-WAYS Ltd

Based at Croydon, this small company was established in 1946, and in January 1947 a Rapide was acquired to join the original Proctor. Charter flights to the continent, particularly to Monte Carlo, proved popular. In February 1948, however, following a fatal accident to a recently-acquired Gemini, the company ceased flying and the Rapide was sold.

Aircraft: DH.89   G-AIYP

SCILLONIA AIRWAYS Ltd

Founded in 1965 by Capt K B Neely, this company soon acquired five Rapides and based them at Land's End (St Just) for use on scheduled services from Newquay (St Mawgan) and Lands's End to the Scilly Isles which had been flown previously by British Westpoint. In addition, many charter flights were made, as well as the inevitable pleasure flying, the latter using Rapides with 'Scenic Flights' markings. The charter flights soon included regular trips to northern France carrying crayfish.

By 1968 Scillonia was almost the last commercial operator of the Dragon Rapide in Europe. Replacement was becoming urgent, and two Twin Pioneers were purchased in the Middle East, but legal difficulties forced the company into liquidation before they could be put to use. At auction, one Rapide fetched £125 and another one £250, an ignominious end to a promising company.

Aircraft: DH.89   G-AHAG, G-AHGC, G-AHKU, G-AJCL, G-ALGC

SCOTTISH AIRWAYS Ltd

Scottish Airways Ltd. was registered on 1st August 1937, with shares owned by Northern & Scottish Airways (31.9%), Highland Airways (18.1%), the London, Midland & Scottish Railway Company (40%) and David MacBrayne Ltd (10%). The new airline operated former Highland Airways routes from Aberdeen, Inverness and other northern Scottish airfields to the

Orkneys and Shetlands as well as a new service from Glasgow (Renfrew) to Perth and Inverness (Longman) which opened on 15th April 1938. That day, new Dragon Rapide G-AFEY continued from Inverness to Wick (Hillhead), Kirkwall (Wideford) and Lerwick (Sumburgh). Fares were £4-5-0 (£4.25) return between Glasgow and Inverness and £10.00 from Glasgow to Lerwick. Under the banner of Western Isles Airways, routes from Glasgow to the Western Isles and Hebrides were also operated.

During the summer of 1938 the Scottish Airways fleet consisted of Dragons G-ACIT, G-ACNG and G-ADCT, and Dragon Rapides G-ADAJ, G-AEWL and G-AFEY, all based at Inverness (Longman) except CNG and FEY. Services flown that year comprised the Glasgow – Campbeltown – Islay (Duich Farm) – Glasgow triangular route; the Glasgow – Barra – South Uist – Benbecula – North Uist – Glasgow route; Inverness (Longman) – Wick (Hillhead) – Kirkwall (Wideford) – Lerwick (Sumburgh); Thurso – Kirkwall; and the Orkney Islands routes between Longhope, Westray, Sanday, Stronsay and North Ronaldsay, all of which were flown on a 'request' basis.

From 15th May 1939, the start of the summer season, the long-distance route from Glasgow to Perth, Inverness, Wick and Kirkwall was extended to Lerwick three times each week. The Scottish Airways fleet now consisted of six Rapides: G-ADAJ, G-AFEY, G-AEOV (acquired on 1st May 1939), G-AFFF (acquired 26th May 1939), G-AFRK (acquired 19th July 1939) and G-AEWL. In addition, three Dragons, G-ACIT, G-ACNG and G-ADCT, were still in service.

G-AFRK of Scottish Airways resting on the sands at Barra one sunny morning. Salty atmospheres caused severe corrosion of metal components
[G M Simons collection]

On the outbreak of war on 3rd September 1939 all services were suspended, although some restarted a week later. All aircraft were then taken over by National Air Communications for emergency work. Scottish Airways played a significant role in those early days of war, beginning on 1st September, when Dragon G-ACNG flew to RAF Harwell in Berkshire. From there it flew service personnel and equipment to France almost every day until it was replaced by Rapide G-AFEY on 14th September. Dragon G-ACIT joined CNG at Harwell on 2nd September but returned to Renfrew four days later. Rapide G-AFRK replaced it at Harwell and apart from a short trip back to Glasgow stayed there until 14th November. All these aircraft were camouflaged while at Harwell.

Early in May 1940 the airline's Glasgow – Tiree – Barra – Benbecula – North Uist service was reopened under the control of AAJC, as was the Campbeltown – Islay triangular route to and from Glasgow. A new service from Glasgow to Stornoway was opened at the same time. However, on 22nd May all pilots and aircraft were ordered to fly to Croydon to prepare to take part in an inevitable evacuation from France. The destination was soon altered to Heston, where the aircraft remained unused until 1st June, when they returned to Glasgow. Two weeks later, on 14th June, they went back to Heston, from where they flew to evacuate personnel from western France.

During the winter of 1940/41 the Western Isles and Islay triangular routes from Glasgow and services from Inverness to the Orkneys and Shetlands were maintained. Services in the summer of 1941 were given numbers: Service No 1 was from Inverness northwards; No 2 was from Kirkwall to the outer islands of the Orkneys; No 3 was the Campbeltown – Islay triangular route; No 4 was the Western Isles service; and No 5 was between Glasgow and Stornoway. In service that summer were seven Rapides and solitary Dragon G-ACIT. From that point until the end of the war Scottish Airways provided a steady and, as far as possible, reliable service with few alterations, although Service No 2 was suspended and in the summer of 1944 became the Inverness to Stornoway route. Dragon G-ACIT was still in service, with eight Rapides, increased by four in 1945.

Services immediately after the end of the war in Europe were the Western Isles service, flown nine times per week; Inverness to Kirkwall three times daily; Inverness to Stornoway three times per week; Glasgow to Croydon daily; Inverness to Sumburgh six times per week; Glasgow to Islay daily; Glasgow to Campbeltown six times per week; and Glasgow to Isle of Man (Ronaldsway) three times per day. On 1st February 1947, however,

Scottish Airways, which had continued to operate under its own name since nominal nationalisation on 2nd August 1946, became part of British European Airways, and its staff and equipment, including some Rapides, were absorbed into the State airline.

Aircraft: DH.84 G-ACIT, G-ACNG, G-ACOR, G-ADCT

DH.89 G-ACPP, G-ACYR, G-ADAJ, G-AEOV, G-AEPE, G-AERN, G-AERZ, G-AEWL, G-AFEY, G-AFFF, G-AFOI, G-AFRK, G-AGDG, G-AGDH, G-AGED, G-AGEE, G-AGIC, G-AGIF, G-AGJF, G-AGJG, G-AGLE, G-AGLP, G-AGLR, G-AGOJ, G-AGUR, G-AHGI, G-AHLL, G-AHLM, G-AHLN, G-AIHN

A DH.89 of Scottish Airways, possibly G-AGJG, takes on board passengers and their produce for market; the scene is somewhere in the Orkneys or Shetlands during the Second World War *[via C N Dodds]*

SCOTTISH AVIATION Ltd

Three Rapides were acquired in June 1948 by this company for charter operations too small for the Dakotas already in service. Apart from one which was written off in 1949, they lasted until 1953/54.

Aircraft: DH.89 G-ALBH, G-ALBI, G-AKSF

Rapide G-AKSF of Scottish Aviation Ltd at Prestwick, with a Lockheed Constellation in the background *[Denis Fox collection]*

SCOTTISH MOTOR TRACTION Ltd

An Aviation Division of this large bus company was formed at Edinburgh on 1st July 1932 to operate private charter services, using initially DH.83 aircraft. The first directors were Bailie (later Sir) William J Thomson, the Lord Provost of the City of Edinburgh, and Sqn Ldr H G Malet. The manager was John C Sword, who previously had managed the combined bus fleet in the Glasgow/Ayr area. Originally flying took place from Glasgow (Renfrew) but in May 1933 a move was made to Edinburgh (Turnhouse) and in June 1934 to Macmerry. On 30th May the 'Irish Scot' service between Renfrew and Belfast (Aldergrove) was inaugurated, using a Dragon and an Avro Ten, and a week later Dragon G-ACDM flew to Sumburgh in the Shetlands on a survey mission.

However, SMT's foray into aviation did not last long, partly due to John Sword's involvement in Midland & Scottish Air Ferries Ltd, which clashed with the interests of SMT. By January 1934 SMT had reverted to running its bus fleet.

Aircraft: DH.84 G-ACDM, G-ACDN, G-ACET

SHORT BROS & HARLAND Ltd
SHORT'S AIR CHARTER SERVICE Ltd
(see Rochester Air Charter Service Ltd)

SIVEWRIGHT AIRWAYS Ltd

This company was established in June 1946 by W C Bacon and N M Bacon to carry out charter flights from Manchester (Ringway and Barton). Initial equipment was Avro 19s, but in March 1948 two Rapides joined the fleet and began work on holiday flights from Manchester to the Isle of Man and Channel Islands. However, political considerations made the directors decide that there was little future in their type of business and the company ceased flying.

Aircraft: DH.89 G-AGDM, G-AJMY, G-AKMG

G-AKMG of Sivewright Airways Ltd, Manchester   [G M Simons collection]

SKEGNESS AIR TAXI SERVICES Ltd

When Bond Air Services went out of business, this company was formed to continue pleasure flying at Skegness (Ingoldmells) airfield. A Rapide was added to the fleet of Austers in September 1951 and worked faithfully until being sold in 1954.

Aircraft: DH.89 G-ALBA

SKYTRAVEL Ltd

Based at Liverpool (Speke) and Blackpool (Squires Gate), this company, registered in June 1946, operated a fleet of single-engined aircraft until two DH.86s joined them in October of that year. These were put into use, with Consuls also recently bought, on charter flights to the Isle of Man, but in September the company went into liquidation and the aircraft were auctioned at Blackpool.

Aircraft: DH.86 G-ACZP, G-ADYH

SKYWAYS Ltd

This very significant company used many aircraft much larger and more sophisticated than the Rapide, but nonetheless one Rapide was bought in March 1946 and three more in 1950. They were used on ad-hoc charter work until the last one was sold in May 1952. A further Rapide was acquired in 1955 as a company 'hack' for Skyways Coach-Air Ltd, but this was written off in May 1961.

Aircraft: DH.89 G-AGOJ, G-AHIA, G-AHFJ, G-AKNW, G-AKOR

G-AGOJ was the Skyways Ltd company 'hack' from 1955 to 1961
[Denis Fox collection]

SOLAIR FLYING SERVICES Ltd

Formed at Coventry (Baginton) in 1962, this charter company began flying in May of that year using a Rapide. The work consisted of charter flights and pleasure flying, and a second Rapide joined the company in July 1963. In June 1964, by which time the original Rapide had been written off, Solair was awarded a licence to fly scheduled services from Birmingham and Coventry to the Scilly Isles via Exeter and from Gloucester/Cheltenham (Staverton) to the Scillies, with certain weekday restrictions. In the event, most of the services were flown by a Cessna 172, and all flying ceased on 12th October 1964.

Aircraft: DH.89 G-AHKV, G-ALBC

SOLENT AIRWAYS Ltd

The operator of one Rapide, Solent Airways was formed at Southampton (Eastleigh) in 1948 and used its aircraft on charter flying for about a year before going into liquidation.

Aircraft: DH.89 G-AHGF

SOMERTON AIRWAYS (COWES) Ltd

Among other types, this company operated two Rapides from Cowes (Somerton), originally for pleasure flying, from July 1948. In 1949 the company was granted a BEA Associate agreement, under which two routes, from Cowes to Portsmouth and Southampton, were to be flown. This duly began in May and continued until April 1951, when the agreement expired and the company ceased flying.

Aircraft: DH.89 G-AGPI, G-ALBA

SOUTHAMPTON AIR SERVICES Ltd

Based at Southampton (Eastleigh), this company operated a mixed fleet of aircraft, including a Rapide owned by Stewart Smith & Co Ltd, which was in use in 1946.

Aircraft: DH.89 G-ADAE

G-ADAE, owned by Stewart Smith & Co Ltd but operated by Southampton Air Services, seen here in July 1946, had seen service in Denmark before returning to the UK   [via C N Dodds]

SOUTHERN AIRCRAFT (GATWICK) Ltd

Before the Second World War this company had traded as a general aircraft dealer and maintenance organisation. Many aircraft were purchased and sold, but at the end of 1946 examples of several types were put to use on ad-hoc charter work, including six Rapides. This operation, however, came to an end in 1952.

Aircraft: DH.89 G-AIUM, G-AJTU, G-AKFO, G-AKOB,
G-AKOM, G-AKON

SOUTHERN AIRWAYS Ltd

A subsidiary of the Straight Corporation, which operated Ramsgate airport, this company began flying a route from Ramsgate to Ilford [sic] on 26th July 1938, using DH.84 G-AECZ, previously registered to Ramsgate Airport Ltd. It is unclear how long this service lasted. Western Airways was closely associated with this company, as was Plymouth Airport.

Aircraft: DH.84 G-ACJT, G-AECZ
DH.90 G-ADNA

SPALDING AIRWAYS Ltd

Formed in 1947 by G Clifton at Spalding, this company established itself as a charter operator. A Rapide was purchased in January 1949 and the company soon set up a base at Peterborough (Westwood) in order to further its business prospects. The Rapide was sold in 1952 but another one was acquired in 1954, remaining in service until being replaced by a DH.104 Dove in 1957.

Aircraft: DH.89 G-AEMH

SPARTAN AIR LINES Ltd

Working under the British Airways banner, Spartan Air Lines operated DH.84 aircraft on the Sandown — Cowes (Somerton) — Southampton ferry service from June 1935 and on a route from Gatwick to Ryde and Cowes which opened on 25th May 1936.

Aircraft: DH.84 G-ACNG, G-ACNI

STANLEY SPENCER'S TOURS Ltd

Set up at Manchester (Ringway) in 1952, this company owned one Rapide which was used for charter flights and pleasure flying for one season.

Aircraft: DH.89 G-ALBA

STARWAYS Ltd

Among the considerable number of aircraft used by this postwar Blackpool-based company was one Rapide, which was presumably used on those charters for which a larger aircraft would have been uneconomic.

Aircraft: DH.89 G-AIBB

STEINER'S AIR AND TRAVEL SERVICES Ltd

Registered on 1st November 1946 by Mr and Mrs D L Steiner, this company was based at Liverpool (Speke). Holiday flights to the Isle of Man and to the continent began at once, using a DH.86 and a Proctor, which were soon joined by a fleet of Consuls and two Rapides. This did not last long, unfortunately, and several of the aircraft were disposed of in October 1947, before all flying ceased at the end of the year.

Aircraft: DH.86 G-ADUH

DH.89 G-AFMF, G-AIUN

STRAMSWAY Ltd

Formed in 1963 at Shoreham, this company began operations on 12th July with one Rapide. The normal task for this aircraft was providing pleasure flights, but it was grounded a year later and replaced by other types.

Aircraft: DH.89 G-APSD

SURREY FLYING SERVICES Ltd

Basically a 'heavy' aircraft operator, Surrey Flying Services acquired a Rapide in 1952 and used it for about four years.

Aircraft: DH.89 G-AJSL

SWANSEA AIRWAYS Ltd

Originally known as Valley Motor Aero Services Ltd, this company acquired two Rapides in September 1960 to join a Prentice already in use for charter work. This enterprise lasted just a few months, however, before the operation was allowed to decline early in 1961 and the Rapides were disposed of.

Aircraft: DH.89 G-AGJG, G-AHJA

THORNE AVIATION Ltd

From a base at Blackpool (Squires Gate), Thorne Aviation Ltd began pleasure flying in 1947. Before the company was absorbed by Air Navigation & Trading Ltd in 1951, a Rapide was used to augment the small fleet of aircraft.

Aircraft: DH.89 G-ALXJ

TIPPERS AIR TRANSPORT Ltd

Charter operations from Coventry (Baginton) were commenced by the company in November 1964, using an Avro 19 and a Rapide. The latter was sold in August 1965, although the company continued to fly its Avro 19s until 1968.

Aircraft: DH.89 G-AKRS

TRAK AIR Ltd

One of the last companies to be formed to use the Rapide, this was established at Dunkeswell in 1968 for charter operations with one of the type. A Dove and two light aircraft were added later but the company ceased flying early in 1970.

Aircraft: DH.89 G-AKNN

TRANSAIR Ltd

Among the large fleet of aircraft operated by this company, which had been established at Croydon in 1947 by G H Freeman, were six Rapides acquired in April 1952 to join nine Ansons, but as they were sold again almost at once it seems doubtful if they saw much service.

Aircraft: DH.89 G-AKMG, G-AKSL, G-AKVU, G-ALWI, G-ALWL, G-ALWN

TRANS EUROPEAN AVIATION Ltd

Established at Swansea (Fairwood Common) early in 1959 by Capt A M Ross, Capt A C Stauber, E D Kayton and L Perez, this company began charter operations at once with two Rapides. In April 1960 a move to Coventry (Baginton) was made, and the Rapides continued to fly charters until 1961/62, by which time the company had developed into a more significant organisation flying Constellations.

Aircraft: DH.89 G-AFFB, G-ALBA

G-ALBA at Coventry on 11.7.59, when in service with Trans-European Airways *[P H Butler]*

TRENT VALLEY AVIATION Ltd

This company, based at Nottingham (Tollerton) was founded in 1948 by S W Wigley, A Christian and Capt F J Cronk, and had already put a Dakota into service by the time the first of two Rapides was acquired in September 1948. This was used for charters over shorter ranges than the Dakota covered, and on holiday flights to the Channel Islands. It was, however, sold in December 1949 but replaced by a similar aircraft in June 1950. On 1st September 1950, Trent Valley Aviation was absorbed by Eagle Aviation Ltd, although the name was allowed to continue in use. For the 1951 season, the Rapide flew regularly to Jersey under a BEA Associate agreement, but after that the Trent Valley name lapsed.

Early in 1966, the Trent Valley Aviation title reappeared when a Rapide began flying charters from East Midlands airport, as well as being used as a parachuting platform and for pleasure flights. A similar aircraft was added in March 1968 and another in November, by which time most of the flying was being carried out from Halfpenny Green. However, after two of the Rapides had been damaged in separate accidents, the company ceased flying in the summer of 1969.

Aircraft: DH.89 G-AGSJ, G-AHGC, G-AHJA, G-AJSL, G-AKRS

TYNE TAXIS Ltd

A development of a city taxi company, Tyne Taxis was formed at Newcastle (Woolsington) in 1947 and was equipped originally with Messenger aircraft. In May 1948 a Rapide was added, and was used on holiday charters to the Isle of Man and other centres. Another Rapide joined in April 1949, but early in 1950 all flying came to an end and the aircraft were sold.

Aircraft: DH.89 G-AKME, G-ALEJ

TYNE TEES AIR CHARTER Ltd
TYNE TEES AIRWAYS Ltd

Registered as an airline on 21st December 1960, this company already owned a DH.104 Dove when a Rapide was delivered in April 1961. Both were used for ad-hoc charter work, the Rapide lasting until July 1964 and the company itself not much longer.

Aircraft: DH.89 G-ALPK

G-ALPK at Newcastle (Woolsington) in 1961, when owned by Tyne Tees Air Charter   *[E Taylor via R C Sturtivant]*

ULSTER AVIATION Ltd

Two Rapides which arrived in April 1948 were the last aircraft to join this company, which already used a variety of other types, including Aerovans. The newcomers were put into service on summer holiday flights from Newtownards to Blackpool and the Isle of Man, but later in the year Ulster Aviation merged with Mannin Airways to form North-West Airlines (Isle of Man) Ltd, which took over all the assets.

Aircraft: DH.89 G-AGIF, G-AHLN

UNION AIR SERVICES Ltd

Founded by Capt C Treen and R A Treen at Gatwick in 1946, this charter operator acquired a DH.86 by the end of the year, flying their comparatively large aircraft to race meetings and on ad-hoc charters within the UK and Europe. On 22nd October 1947 the company made a reverse take-over of Bond Air Services Ltd and the DH.86 was included in the Bond fleet.

Aircraft: DH.86 G-ADUH

UNITED AIRWAYS Ltd

Owned by Whitehall Securities Ltd, United Airways came into being on 4th April 1935, and in May began operating a route from Heston to Blackpool (Stanley Park), with connection to the Isle of Man (Hall Caine) and Carlisle (Kingstown). At first Dragons were used, but they were superceded by Spartan Cruisers. A service from Heston to Blackpool began on 30th April using DH.86s borrowed from Jersey Airways. During that summer the company was operating two Dragons and two Rapides among other types., but United Airways and Spartan Airways amalgamated on 30th September 1935 to form Allied British Airways Ltd.

Aircraft: DH.84 G-ACMC, G-ACMJ, G-ACNI

DH.89 G-ADAE, G-ADBU, G-ADBV, G-ADBW, G-ADBX

UNIVERSAL FLYING SERVICES Ltd

Between August and October 1946 this company, based at Fairoaks, acquired three Rapides and put them into service on charter work from there and sometimes from Hanworth and Kidlington. Two years later, the company's charter operations were merged with North Sea Air Transport's similar functions, both companies being owned by Blackburn & General Aircraft Ltd, and by the end of 1949 the transition was complete. The Universal name was then no longer used.

Aircraft: DH.89 G-AHAG, G-AHGD, G-AHTY

After a short time with Lancashire Aircraft Corporation Ltd, Universal Flying Services Ltd operated G-AHAG from Kidlington and Fairoaks from 1946 to 1949   *[Denis Fox collection]*

WESTAIR FLYING SERVICES Ltd

Westair Flying Services Ltd had been set up at Blackpool (Squires Gate) in 1947 by the Westoby family, who initially used Austers for pleasure flying. In 1948 they acquired a Dragon Rapide and employed it on charter flights, mainly in the north of England and Northern Ireland, and during the next few years three similar aircraft were added to the fleet. At any one time two of them continued to operate the Company's charters until the last example was disposed of in 1963, by which time Westair was concentrating on other business.

Aircraft: DH.89 G-AJKW, G-AKMH, G-AKRS, G-ALGI

G-AKRS in the markings of Westair Flying Services of Blackpool (Squires Gate)   *[G M Simons collection]*

WEST COAST AIR SERVICES Ltd

When war was declared in September 1939 this company, based at Croydon, was using an Express Air Liner and a Dragon Rapide on scheduled services between Dublin (Baldonnel), Bristol (Whitchurch), Croydon, the Isle of Man and Liverpool (Speke). All these routes were then suspended, but the Liverpool service was reopened in October, flown by the DH.86, which had to be abandoned at Jersey in June 1940 as the Germans occupied the island. The service was maintained, however, using aircraft borrowed from other airlines, including Aer Lingus. Manchester (Barton) became the English terminal in August 1940.

In September 1941, LMSR, GWR and Coast Lines Ltd joined with British & Foreign Aviation Ltd to form West Coast Air Services (Holdings) Ltd, which controlled WCAS. The Dublin route, terminating at Liverpool again from November 1942, was flown throughout the war under the control of AAJC.

Aircraft: DH.86 G-ADYH

DH.89 G-AERN

In service with West Coast Air Services from December 1937, G-ADYH was operated by AAJC throughout the Second World War   *[via R C Sturtivant]*

WEST CUMBERLAND AIR SERVICES Ltd

One Rapide used by this company, which had been founded early in 1947, was acquired in December of that year and the other one in March 1948. A base at Carlisle (Kingstown) was established, and in June 1948 a scheduled service to the Isle of Man under a BEA Associate agreement began. However, in June 1949 the route and the surviving Rapide were taken over by Astral Aviation Ltd.

Aircraft: DH.89 G-AKNN, G-AKOC

WESTERN AIRWAYS Ltd (see NORMAN EDGAR Ltd)

WESTERN ISLES AIRWAYS Ltd

A subsidiary of Scottish Airways Ltd, Western Isles Airways' capital was held by Scottish Airways Ltd and David MacBrayne Ltd in equal shares.

WESTWARD AIRWAYS (LAND'S END) Ltd

Founded by V H Bellamy at Land's End (St Just) in August 1971, this company acquired a Rapide for a scheduled service to the Scilly Isles, replacing a leased Islander. Between flights, the Rapide flew pleasure flights and carried sky-divers.

Aircraft: DH.89 G-AIYR

WILLIAM DEMPSTER Ltd

Charter operations with one Rapide began at Blackbushe late in 1948, and the company acquired a second Rapide in January 1949. However, the company had greater ambitions, and after two Avro Tudors arrived in April 1950 the Rapides were sold.

Aircraft: DH.89 G-AFMA, G-AKGV

WINDMILL THEATRE TRANSPORT Co Ltd

To supplement a Proctor, this company purchased a Rapide in November 1948 to expand charter operations from Gatwick and Croydon. The Rapide soldiered on until 1960, when the company ceased trading.

Aircraft: DH.89 G-AKSD

WINGS AND WHEELS Ltd
HARGREAVES AIRWAYS Ltd

A charter operator established at Birmingham (Elmdon) in 1947, this company used several single-engined aircraft before the advent of a Rapide in May 1947. The company's name was altered to Hargreaves Airways Ltd in September 1947, and the Rapide continued its charter work. However, in June 1948 the Rapide was destroyed in a fatal crash on the Isle of Man, which brought the company's flying to an end.

Aircraft: DH.89 G-AIUI

Rapide G-AIUI of Hargreaves Airways Ltd was named "City of Birmingham I"
[Denis Fox collection]

WOLVERHAMPTON AVIATION Ltd

Previously the Wolverhampton Flying School, this company was formed in June 1949, and with its sister company, Derby Aviation Ltd, operated charter flights and scheduled summer services with Rapides in the early 1950s.

Aircraft: DH.89 G-AIUK, G-AKOV, G-ALGE

WRIGHT AVIATION Ltd

Although founded at Hooton Park in 1946, this company used single-engined aircraft for several years before acquiring a Rapide in 1952 for charter work and Army co-operation contracts. This continued only until the end of 1953, when the company's financial backer withdrew his support and the company ceased trading.

Aircraft: DH.89 G-AHPT, G-AIBB

G-AIBB and G-AHPT, both of Wright Aviation, parked at Liverpool (Speke) on 25.7.53 with Proctor G-AIAA   *[P H Butler]*

WRIGHTSON & PEARCE Ltd

Based at Heston, Wrightson and Pearce Ltd was formed in August 1933 by R V Wrightson and R C Pearce to carry out charter and air taxi work. A tragic accident to DH.84 G-ACHX on 15th September 1933 in which the pilot, G A Pennington, was killed, did not help the company's fortunes, and in April 1934 the hire department was transferred to Wrightson Air Hire Ltd and aircraft sales and brokerage interests to Wrightson Aircraft Sales Ltd. From May 1934 a service from Heston to Berck and Le Touquet was operated, but in December residual business was transferred to a new company, Wrightways Ltd.

Aircraft: DH.84 G-ACHX, G-ACKU

WRIGHTWAYS Ltd

Formed on 17th December 1934 to acquire the assets of Wrightson & Pearce Ltd, Wrightways Ltd carried on the business of an air charter operator. Its original directors included the Hon J D Kemp, G P McGiveney (the former manager of Wrightson & Pearce Ltd) and J W Duggan. Regular newspaper flights from Croydon to Paris began on 14th May 1935. By January 1936 the company's fleet included two DH.84s, while in March 1937 a DH.86, two DH.89s and a DH.84 comprised the whole fleet. Another DH.86 was added by March 1938. At the outbreak of war, however, remaining aircraft were taken over by National Air Communications and later were impressed for military service, bringing the activities of Wrightways Ltd to an end.

Aircraft: DH.84 G-ACHX, G-ACKU
          DH.86 G-ADYI, G-AEJM
          DH.89 G-ADAL, G-AEML, G-AFEZ

G-AEJM was the last DH.86A, and is seen here in the hands of Wrightways after conversion to DH.86B standard in 1937. Note the ADF loop aerial
[via C N Dodds]

Rapide G-ADAL in early wartime service with Wrightways Ltd
[MAP via P H T Green]

YELLOW AIR TAXI Co Ltd

Registered in January 1948, this company began charter operations from Birmingham airport with a Percival Q6 and other types. A Rapide replaced the Q6 in June 1948 and was in service until September 1951, soon after which the company stopped flying.

Aircraft: DH.89 G-ACPP

YORKSHIRE AEROPLANE CLUB Ltd

Based at Sherburn-in-Elmet, the club acquired a Rapide in 1949 and used it for pleasure flying and a few charters until May 1954.

Aircraft: DH.89 G-ALGB

Appendix 2

BRITISH MILITARY SERIALS, CONSTRUCTION AND CONTRACT NUMBERS

Military serials allocated to DH.84s, all impressed aircraft

Serial	c/n	Formerly	Qty
X9379	6035	(ex G-ACHV)	1
X9395	6041	(ex G-ACIU)	1
X9396	6058	(ex G-ACMJ)	1
X9397	6044	(ex G-ACLE)	1
X9398	6001	(ex G-ACAO)	1
X9399	6075	(exc G-ACPX)	1
X9440	6092	(ex G-ADCP)	1
AV982	6105	(ex G-AECZ)	1
AW154	6015	(ex G-ACCZ)	1
AW163	6028	(ex G-AEKZ)	1
AW170	6018	(ex G-ACDN)	1
AW171	6021	(ex G-ACET)	1
AW172	6066	(ex G-ACKU)	1
AW173	6110	(ex G-AEMI)	1
AX863	6055	(ex G-ACKB)	1
AX867	6019	(ex G-ACEK)	1
BS816	6009	(ex G-ACBW)	1
HM569	6103	(ex G-ADOS)	1

Military serials allocated to DH.86s, including impressed aircraft

Serial	c/n	Contract No.	Qty
L7596	2348	435442/35 + 670941/37	1
L8037	2340	686051/37 (ex G-ADYC)	1
L8040	2341	686051/37 (ex G-ADYD)	1
N6246	2343	773287/38 (ex G-ADYG)	1
X9441	2351	(ex G-AEJM)	1
X9442	2327	(ex G-ADMY)	1
AX760	2328	(ex G-ADFF)	1
AX762	2333	(ex G-ADUE)	1
AX800	2308	(ex VT-AKZ)	1
AX840	2314	(ex BD105 ntu)	1
AX841	2318	(ex BD106 ntu)	1
AX842	2352	(ex G-AENR)	1
AX843	2321	(ex G-ACZP)	1
AX844	2322	(ex BD104 ntu)	1
BD104	2322	(NTU)	
BD105	2314	(NTU)	
BD106	2318	(NTU)	
HK828	2334	(ex G-ADUF)	1
HK829	2305	(ex G-ACWD)	1
HK830	2337	(ex G-ADUI)	1
HK831	2335	(ex G-ADUG)	1
HK843	2349	(ex G-AEAP)	1
HK844	2300	(ex G-ACPL)	1
HX789	2306	(ex VT-AKM)	1

Military serials allocated to DH.89s, including impressed aircraft

Note: Dominies ordered under contracts 6/Acft/2580/C20a and 6/Acft/5072/C20c were built by Brush Coachworks Ltd at Loughborough, and all others by de Havilland at Hatfield.

Serials	c/n	Mk.	Contract No.	Qty.
DH.89M				
K4772	6271		35284/38	1
DH.89 Dragon Rapide				
K5070	6267		362793/34	1
DH.89A Dragon Rapides				
P1764-1765	6421-6422		808642/38	2
P9588-9589	6455-6456		9859/39	2
R2485-2487	6446-6448		981944/39	3
Dominies				
R5921-5925	6457-6461	I	B21547/39	5
R5926-5934	6463-6471	I	ditto	9
R9545-9564	6473-6492	I	B26448/39	20
DH.89A Dragon Rapides				
V4724	6442		(ex G-AFNC)	1
V4725	6443		(ex G-AFND)	1
W6423	6300		(ex G-ADNH)	1
W6424	6326		(ex G-AEAM)	1
W6425	6320		(ex G-AEAJ)	1
W6455	6340		(ex G-AENN)	1
W6456	6342		(ex G-AEOV)	1
W6457	6445		(ex G-AFSO)	1
W9365	6301		(ex G-ADNI)	1
Dominies				
X7320-7354	6493-6527	I	B104592/40	35
X7368-7417	6528-6577	I	ditto	50
X7437-7442	6578-6583	I	ditto	6
X7443-7456	6585-6598	I	ditto	14
X7482-7525	6599-6642	I	ditto	44
DH.89 and DH.89A Dragon Rapides				
X8505	6369		(ex G-AEXP)	1
X8506	6405		(ex G-AFEO)	1
X8507	6368		(ex G-AEXO)	1
X8508	6377		(ex G-AFAH)	1
X8509	6257		(ex G-ACTT)	1
X8510	6350		(ex G-AEPW)	1
X8511	6286		(ex G-ADBV)	1
X9320	6269		(ex G-ACYM)	1
X9386	6282		(ex G-ADDE)	1
X9387	6336		(ex G-AEMH)	1
X9388	6406		(ex G-AFEP)	1
X9448	6263		(ex G-ADAL)	1
X9449	6309		(ex G-ADWZ)	1
X9450	6337		(ex G-AEML)	1
X9451	6408		(ex G-ADFX)	1
Z7188	6399		(ex VQ-PAC but not used)	1
Z7253	6426		(ex G-AFLY)	1
Z7254	6429		(ex G-AFLZ)	1
Z7255	6430		(ex G-AFMA)	1
Z7256	6432		(ex G-AFMF)	1
Z7257	6431		(ex G-AFME)	1
Z7258	6434		(ex G-AFMH)	1
Z7259	6433		(ex G-AFMG)	1
Z7260	6435		(ex G-AFMI)	1
Z7261	6436		(ex G-AFMJ)	1

Z7262	6287		(ex G-ADAI)	1
Z7263	6293		(ex G-ADIM)	1
Z7264	6266		(ex G-ADAG)	1
Z7265	6288		(ex G-ADBW)	1
Z7266	6264		(ex G-ACZE)	1
AW115	6258		(ex G-ACTU)	1
AW116	6283		(ex G-ADDD)	1
AW155	6281		(ex G-ADAK)	1
AX806	6378		(ex VT-AIZ)	1
BD143	6344		(ex G-AEPE)	1

Dominies

HG644-674	6643-6673	I	6/Acft/2580/C20a	31
HG689-732	6674-6717	I	ditto	44

DH.89A Dragon Rapides

HK862	6410	(ex G-AFFC)	1
HK864	6399	(ex G-AFEN)	1
HK915	6323	(ex EP-AAC)	1
HK916	6322	(ex EP-AAB)	1
HK917	6321	(ex EP-AAA)	1
HX790	6381	(ex VT-AJB)	1
HX791	6454	(ex VT-ALO)	1
MA961	?	(ex ?)	1

Dominies

NF847-896	6718-6767	I	6/Acft/2580/C20a	50
NR669-701	6768-6800	I	ditto	33
NR713-756	6801-6844	I	ditto	44
NR769-815	6845-6891	I	ditto	47
NR828-853	6892-6917	I	ditto	26
RL936-946	6918-6928	I	ditto	11
RL947-968	6929-6950	II	ditto	22
RL980-986	6951-6957	II	ditto	7
TX300-319	6958-6977	II	6/Acft/5072/C20c	20

Dominies renumbered

MA963	6652	I	(ex HG653)
MA964	6649	I	(ex HG650)
MA965	6650	I	(ex HG651)
MA966	6651	I	(ex HG652)
VG764	6803	I	(ex NR715)

Cancelled Dominies:

JM617-630		I	B104592/40
JN702-743		I	ditto
JN775-807		I	ditto
RL987-999		II	6/Acft/2580/C20a
RM112-158		II	ditto
TX320-339		II	6/Acft/5072/C20c
TX361-370		II	ditto

Note: JN serials were later reallocated to Tempests

Military serials allocated to DH.90s, all impressed aircraft

Serial	c/n	Formerly	Qty
V4734	7540	(ex VT-AHY)	1
X9327	7509	(ex G-ADXM)	1
X9337	7521	(ex G-AFVJ)	1
X9389	7524	(ex G-AEDV)	1
X9390	7507	(ex G-AEFN)	1
X9452	7500	(ex G-ADNA)	1
AV976	7544	(ex G-AESW)	1
AV987	7510	(ex G-AEDH)	1
AV992	7515	(ex G-AEDJ)	1
AV993	7519	(ex G-AFRF)	1
AV994	7536	(ex G-AFRI)	1
AW164	7517	(ex G-AEDK)	1
AX797	7527	(ex VT-AHW)	1
AX855	7505	(ex G-AECX)	1
BD149	7533	(ex G-AFTF)	1
DJ716	7555	(ex G-AEWZ)	1
HX792	7545	(ex VT-AIE)	1

In pristine silver finish, Dominie X7396 stands in the sun; its last service operator was a detachment of ATDU at St Mawgan   *[Denis Fox collection]*

Appendix 3

REGISTRATION, SERIAL NUMBER AND CONSTRUCTION NUMBER CROSS-REFERENCE INDEX

Military Serials

Serial	Type	c/n

Royal Air Force and **Fleet Air Arm**

Serial	Type	c/n
K4772	DH.89M	6271
K5070	DH.89	6267
L7596	DH.86A	2348
L8037	DH.86A	2340
L8040	DH.86A	2341
N6246	DH.86A	2343
P1764	DH.89A	6421
P1765	DH.89A	6422
P9588	DH.89A	6455
P9589	DH.89A	6456
R2485	DH.89A	6446
R2486	DH.89A	6447
R2487	DH.89A	6448
R5921-5925	Dominie I	6457-6461
R5926-5934	Dominie I	6463-6471
R9545-9564	Dominie I	6473-6492
V4724	DH.89A	6442
V4725	DH.89A	6443
V4734	DH.90	7540
W6423	DH.89A	6300
W6424	DH.89A	6326
W6425	DH.89A	6320
W6455	DH.89A	6340
W6456	DH.89A	6342
W6457	DH.89A	6445
W9365	DH.89A	6301
X7320-7354	Dominie I	6493-6527
X7368-7417	Dominie I	6528-6577
X7437-7442	Dominie I	6578-6583
X7443-7456	Dominie I	6585-6598
X7482-7525	Dominie I	6599-6642
X8505	DH.89A	6369
X8506	DH.89A	6405
X8507	DH.89A	6368

Serial	Type	c/n
X8508	DH.89A	6377
X8509	DH.89A	6257
X8510	DH.89A	6350
X8511	DH.89A	6286
X9320	DH.89A	6269
X9327	DH.90	7509
X9337	DH.90	7521
X9379	DH.84	6035
X9386	DH.89A	6282
X9387	DH.89A	6336
X9388	DH.89A	6406
X9389	DH.90	7524
X9390	DH.90	7507
X9395	DH.84	6041
X9396	DH.84	6058
X9397	DH.84	6044
X9398	DH.84	6001
X9399	DH.84	6075
X9440	DH.84	6092
X9441	DH.86A	2351
X9442	DH.86	2327
X9448	DH.89A	6263
X9449	DH.89A	6309
X9450	DH.89A	6337
X9451	DH.89A	6408
X9452	DH.90	7500
X9457	DH.89A	6290
Z7188	DH.89A	6399
Z7253	DH.89A	6426
Z7254	DH.89A	6429
Z7255	DH.89A	6430
Z7256	DH.89A	6432
Z7257	DH.89A	6431
Z7258	DH.89A	6434
Z7259	DH.89A	6433
Z7260	DH.89A	6435
Z7261	DH.89A	6436
Z7262	DH.89A	6287
Z7263	DH.89A	6293

Serial	Type	c/n
Z7264	DH.89A	6266
Z7265	DH.89A	6288
Z7266	DH.89A	6264
AV976	DH.90	7544
AV982	DH.84	6105
AV987	DH.90	7510
AV992	DH.90	7515
AV993	DH.90	7519
AV994	DH.90	7536
AW115	DH.89A	6258
AW116	DH.89A	6283
AW154	DH.84	6015
AW155	DH.89A	6281
AW163	DH.84	6028
AW164	DH.90	7517
AW170	DH.84	6018
AW171	DH.84	6021
AW172	DH.84	6066
AW173	DH.84	6110
AX760	DH.86A	2328
AX762	DH.86A	2333
AX795	DH.86A	2345
AX797	DH.90	7527
AX800	DH.86	2308
AX806	DH.89A	6378
AX840	DH.86	2314
AX841	DH.86	2318
AX842	DH.86	2352
AX843	DH.86	2321
AX844	DH.86	2322
AX855	DH.90	7505
AX863	DH.84	6055
AX867	DH.84	6019
BD104	DH.86	2322
BD105	DH.86	2314
BD106	DH.86	2318
BD143	DH.89A	6344
BD149	DH.90	7533
BS816	DH.84	6009

R5921 had a varied service history, and is seen here taxying past Mustangs at an unrecorded location   *[FAA Museum via R C Sturtivant]*

At Farnborough the ETPS used Dominie HG715, coded 5, as a 'hack'

DJ716	DH.90	7555	NR669-701	Dominie I	6768-6800	A31-5	DH.86	2307
HG644-674	Dominie I	6643-6673	NR713-756	Dominie I	6801-6844	A31-6	DH.86	2310
HG689-732	Dominie I	6674-6717	NR769-815	Dominie I	6845-6891	A31-7	DH.86	2323
HK828	DH.86A	2334	NR828-853	Dominie I	6892-6917	A31-8	DH.86	2359
HK829	DH.86	2305	RL936-946	Dominie I	6918-6928	A33-1	DH.89A	6259
HK830	DH.86A	2337	RL947-968	Dominie II	6929-6950	A33-2	DH.89A	6318
HK831	DH.86A	2335	RL980-986	Dominie II	6951-6957	A33-3	DH.89A	6270
HK843	DH.86A	2349	TX300-319	Dominie II	6958-6977	A33-4	DH.89A	6346
HK844	DH.86	2300	VG764	Dominie I	6803	A33-5	DH.89A	6253
HK862	DH.89A	6410				A33-6	DH.89A	6384
HK864	DH.89A	6399	**British military**			A33-7	DH.89A	6341
HK915	DH.89A	6323	**ground instructional airframes**			A34-1	DH.84	6081
HK916	DH.89A	6322				A34-2	DH.84	6088
HK917	DH.89A	6321	2779M	DH.84	6021	A34-3	DH.84	6097
HM569	DH.84	6103	2780M	DH.84	6009	A34-4	DH.84	6062
HX789	DH.86	2306	2820M	DH.84	6015	A34-5	DH.84	6112
HX790	DH.89A	6381				A34-6	DH.84	6082
HX791	DH.89A	6454				A34-7	DH.84	6037
HX792	DH.90	7545	**Royal Australian Air Force**			A34-8	DH.84	6065
MA961	DH.89A	?	A3-1	DH.89A	6270	A34-9	DH.84	6045
MA963	Dominie I	6652	A3-2	DH.89A	6314	A34-10	DH.84	6025
MA964	Dominie I	6649	A31-1	DH.86	2360	A34-11	DH.84	6104
MA965	Dominie I	6650	A31-2	DH.86	2313	A34-12 to	DH.84	2001-2087
MA966	Dominie I	6651	A31-3	DH.86	2326	A34-98		
NF847-896	Dominie I	6718-6767	A31-4	DH.86	2315	A43-1	DH.90	7546

NF855 of the Fleet Air Arm, probably of 782 Squadron at Donibristle

Arab Legion Air Force

R300	DH.89B	6958
R301	DH.89A	6443

Belgian Air Force

D-1	Dominie I	6881
D-2	Dominie I	6745
D-3	Dominie I	6739
D-4	Dominie I	6785
D-5	Dominie I	6787
D-6	Dominie I	6852
D-7	Dominie I	6853

Brazilian Navy

D4H-178	DH.84	6085

Royal Canadian Air Force

7623	DH.90	7543
7624	DH.90	7557
7625	DH.90	7558
7626	DH.90	7530
7627	DH.90	7531
7628	DH.90	7522

Chinese military

?	DH.89A	6385
?	DH.89A	6388
?	DH.89A	6389
?	DH.89A	6390
?	DH.89A	6391
?	DH.89A	6392

Danish Army Air Force

S.21	DH.84M	6060
S.22	DH.84M	6061
S.23	DH.90	7551
S.24	DH.90	7552

Finnish Air Force

DH-1	DH.86	2353

Free French Air Force

HG664	Dominie I	6663
HG670	Dominie I	6669
HG672	Dominie I	6671
HG689	Dominie I	6674
HG720	Dominie I	6705

French Air Force (l'Armée de l'Air)

NF860	Dominie I	6731
NR670	Dominie I	6769

German Air Force (Luftwaffe)

RP+MY	DH.90	?
SB+AH	DH.89A	6351 or 6352
?	DH.89	6332
?	DH.89M	6348
?	DH.89M	6349

Kenya Auxiliary Air Unit

K4	DH.89A	6366
K8	DH.89	6413
K10	DH.89A	6394
K11	DH.89	?
K13 or K14	DH.90	7554 & 7528
K15	DH.84	6059
K16	?	?

Indonesian Air Force

RI-008	DH.86	2344

Iraqi Air Force

16-21	DH.84M	6003-6008
22	DH.84M	6012
23	DH.84M	6013

Iranian Air Force

?	DH.89M	6321
?	DH.89M	6322
?	DH.89M	6323

Irish Air Corps

DH-18	DH.84	6071
18	DH.84	6071

Israeli Air Force, later Israeli Defence Force Air Force (IDFAF)

S-71	DH.89B	6806 ?
S-72	DH.89B	6639
S-73	DH.89B	6834 ?
S-74	DH.89B	6617
S-75	DH.89B	6602
S-76	DH.89B	6536
S-77	DH.89B	6805
1301	DH.89B	6806
1302	DH.89B	6639
1303	DH.89B	?
1304	DH.89B	6617
1305	DH.89B	6602
1306	DH.89B	6805
1307	DH.89B	?
1308	DH.89B	?
1309	DH.89B	?
1310	DH.89B	6496
1311	DH.89B	?
1312	DH.89B	?
1313	DH.89B	?

Lithuanian Air Force

701	DH.89M	6348 ?
702	DH.89M	6349 ?

Royal Netherlands Air Force

LVA962	DH.90	7539
V-1	Dominie I	6748

The two DH.90s, S.23 and S.24, for the Danish Army before delivery from Hatfield in April 1937 [BAe via K Ellis]

RNeth AF V-3 in the RNethAF Museum at Soesterberg in April 1982   *[G M Simons collection]*

V-2	Dominie I	6872
V-3	Dominie I	6740
V-4	Dominie I	6819

Royal New Zealand Air Force

NZ523	Dominie I	6647
NZ524	Dominie I	6648
NZ525	Dominie I	6653
NZ526	Dominie I	6654
NZ527	Dominie I	6655
NZ528	Dominie I	6662
NZ529	Dominie I	6664
NZ530	Dominie I	6673
NZ531	Dominie I	6668
NZ550	DH.84	6091
NZ551	DH.84	6090
NZ552	DH.86	2330
NZ553	DH.86	2331
NZ554	DH.86	2332
NZ555	DH.89A	6334
NZ556	DH.89A	6305
NZ557	DH.89A	6306
NZ558	DH.89A	6423
NZ559	DH.89A	6343

Peruvian Air Force

438	DH.89B (floats)?	

Portuguese Air Force

504	DH.84M	6111
505	DH.84M	6113
506	DH.84M	6114
2304	DH.84M	6111
2305	DH.84M	6113
2306	DH.84M	6114

South African Air Force

1353	Dominie I	6507
1354	Dominie I	6508
1355	Dominie I	6512
1356	Dominie I	6510
1357	Dominie I	6619
1358	Dominie I	6626
1359	Dominie I	6627
1360	Dominie I	6637
1361	Dominie I	6628
1362	Dominie I	6564
1363	Dominie I	6477
1364	Dominie I	6680
1365	Dominie I	6761
1366	Dominie I	6788
1401	DH.89A	6411
1402	DH.89A	6387
1403	DH.90	7523
1404	DH.90	7564
1408	DH.90	7535
1414	DH.84	6054
1560	DH.89	6380
1570	DH.84	6017
IS13	DH.84	6017

Southern Rhodesian Air Force

SR8	DH.89A	6412
SR9	?	?
SR23	DH.89A	6412
SR24	DH.89B	6678
SR57	DH.89B	6666

Southern Rhodesia Air Services

260	DH.84	6030
300	DH.89A	6412
301	DH.89	6285
302	DH.89	6256
303	DH.89A	6358
304	DH.89A	6359
305	DH.89A	6404

<u>Note:</u> the SRAS was a combined airline and military communications squadron which gave serial numbers to its aircraft from 9.39 to 4.42, after which they reverted to civil registrations.

The three DH.86s of the RNZAF, NZ552, 554 and 553, formerly ZK-AEF, ZK-AEH and ZK-AEG   *[via C N Dodds]*

One of three DH.90s impressed into the SAAF, this one appears to be carrying the badge of 61 Air School [via K Smy]

Spanish Air Force (Aviación Militar)

(See Notes below; both pre- and post-Civil War serials are included here.)

22-1	DH.89M	6310
22-2	DH.89M	6311
22-3	DH.89M	6312
40-3 ?	DH.90	7501
40-4 ?	DH.90A	7529
756	DH.90A	7529
L9-	DH.89A	6424
L9-	DH.89A	6425
L9-	DH.89A	6427

Spanish Nationalist Forces

40-1	DH.89	6275 ?
40-2	DH.89	6277
40-3	DH.89	6291
40-4	DH.89	6252
40-5	DH.89M	6312
40-6	DH.89A	6420
40-4 ?	DH.90A	7529

Note: a substantial number of DH.89s and at least one DH.90 were used by the Nationalist side in the Spanish civil war, but positive information on them remains hard to find. The details given above are believed to be correct but should be treated with caution.

Spanish Republican Forces

22-1	DH.89M	6310
22-2	DH.89M	6311
?	DH.84	6016
?	DH.84	6023
?	DH.84	6056
?	DH.84	6067
?	DH.89A	6383
?	DH.89A	6420
?	DH.89A	6424
?	DH.89A	6425
?	DH.89A	6427
?	DH.89A	6428
?	DH.90	7556 ?

Note: as with the Nationalist aircraft, little information on the subject can be confirmed. It is known that eleven 'Dragons' were recovered from the Republicans by the victorious Nationalists at the end of the civil war, including six which fled to north Africa in March 1939; all six were then absorbed into the Spanish Air Force's Grupo 40, but most remain unidentified.

Swedish Air Force

6-3	DH.90	7550
Fv.906	DH.90	7550

Turkish Air Force

?	DH.84	6087
?	DH.84	6107
?	DH.84	6108
?	DH.84	6109

Civil Registrations

Serial	Type	c/n

United Kingdom

G-ACAN	DH.84	6000
G-ACAO	DH.84	6001
G-ACAP	DH.84	6002
G-ACBW	DH.84	6009
G-ACCE	DH.84	6010
G-ACCR	DH.84	6011
G-ACCV	DH.84	6014
G-ACCZ	DH.84	6015
G-ACDL	DH.84	6016
G-ACDM	DH.84	6017
G-ACDN	DH.84	6018
G-ACEK	DH.84	6019
G-ACET	DH.84	6021
G-ACEU	DH.84	6022
G-ACEV	DH.84	6023
G-ACFG	DH.84	6027
G-ACGG	DH.84	6025
G-ACGK	DH.84	6033
G-ACGU	DH.84	6034
G-ACHV	DH.84	6035
G-ACHX	DH.84	6036
G-ACIE	DH.84	6032
G-ACIT	DH.84	6039
G-ACIU	DH.84	6041
G-ACIW	DH.84	6038
G-ACJH	DH.84	6040
G-ACJM	DH.84	6049
G-ACJS	DH.84	6042
G-ACJT	DH.84	6043
G-ACKB	DH.84	6055
G-ACKC	DH.84	6056
G-ACKD	DH.84	6052
G-ACKU	DH.84/2	6066
G-ACLE	DH.84	6044
G-ACLP	DH.84	6057

G-ACMC	DH.84	6053
G-ACMJ	DH.84	6058
G-ACMO	DH.84/2	6062
G-ACMP	DH.84/2	6063
G-ACNA	DH.84/2	6067
G-ACNG	DH.84/2	6069
G-ACNH	DH.84/2	6070
G-ACNI	DH.84/2	6071
G-ACNJ	DH.84/2	6072
G-ACOR	DH.84/2	6073
G-ACPL	DH.86	2300
G-ACPM	DH.89	6251
G-ACPN	DH.89	6252
G-ACPO	DH.89	6253
G-ACPP	DH.89	6254
G-ACPR	DH.89	6255
G-ACPX	DH.84/2	6075
G-ACPY	DH.84/2	6076
G-ACRF	DH.84/2	6077
G-ACRH	DH.84/2	6078
G-ACRO	DH.84/2	6079
G-ACTT	DH.89	6257
G-ACTU	DH.89	6258
G-ACVD	DH.84/2	6084
G-ACVY	DH.86	2302
G-ACVZ	DH.86	2303
G-ACWC	DH.86	2304
G-ACWD	DH.86	2305
G-ACWE	DH.86	2306
G-ACXI	DH.84/2	6087
G-ACYF	DH.86	2313
G-ACYG	DH.86	2314
G-ACYM	DH.89	6269
G-ACYR	DH.89	6261
G-ACZE	DH.89	6264
G-ACZF	DH.89	6268
G-ACZN	DH.86	2316
G-ACZO	DH.86	2318
G-ACZP	DH.86	2321
G-ACZR	DH.86	2322
G-ACZU	DH.89	6274
G-ADAE	DH.89	6272
G-ADAG	DH.89	6266
G-ADAH	DH.89	6278
G-ADAI	DH.89	6287
G-ADAJ	DH.89	6276
G-ADAK	DH.89	6281
G-ADAL	DH.89	6263
G-ADAO	DH.89	6275
G-ADBU	DH.89	6280
G-ADBV	DH.89	6286
G-ADBW	DH.89	6288
G-ADBX	DH.89	6289
G-ADCL	DH.89	6277
G-ADCM	DH.86	2317
G-ADCN	DH.86	2319

Reg.	Type	c/n	Reg.	Type	c/n	Reg.	Type	c/n
G-ADCP	DH.84/2	6092	G-AEIS	DH.84/2	6107	G-AGED	DH.89B	6621
G-ADCR	DH.84/2	6094	G-AEIT	DH.84/2	6108	G-AGEE	DH.89B	6622
G-ADCT	DH.84/2	6095	G-AEIU	DH.84/2	6109	G-AGFU	DH.89B	6463
G-ADDD	DH.89	6283	G-AEJM	DH.86	2351	G-AGHI	DH.89A	6455
G-ADDE	DH.89	6282	G-AEKF	DH.89	6332	G-AGIC	DH.89B	6522
G-ADDF	DH.89	6284	G-AEKZ	DH.84	6028	G-AGIF	DH.89B	6509
G-ADDI	DH.84/2	6096	G-AEMH	DH.89	6336	G-AGJF	DH.89B	6499
G-ADDJ	DH.84/2	6097	G-AEML	DH.89	6337	G-AGJG	DH.89B	6517
G-ADEA	DH.86	2323	G-AEMM	DH.89	6339	G-AGLE	DH.89B	6784
G-ADEB	DH.86	2324	G-AEMX	DH.92	6400	G-AGLN	DH.89B	6795
G-ADEC	DH.86	2325	G-AENN	DH.89	6340	G-AGLO	DH.89B	?
G-ADED	DH.84/2	6098	G-AENO	DH.89	6341	G-AGLP	DH.89B	6780
G-ADEE	DH.84/2	6099	G-AENR	DH.86	2352	G-AGLR	DH.89B	6781
G-ADFF	DH.86	2328	G-AEOV	DH.89A	6342	G-AGNH	DH.89B	6803
G-ADFI	DH.84/2	6100	G-AEPE	DH.89A	6344	G-AGOJ	DH.89B	6850
G-ADFX	DH.89	6290	G-AEPF	DH.89A	6353	G-AGOP	DH.89B	6873
G-ADFY	DH.89	6291	G-AEPW	DH.89A	6350	G-AGOR	DH.89B	6877
G-ADIM	DH.89	6293	G-AERE	DH.89A	6355	G-AGOT	DH.89B	6876
G-ADMY	DH.86	2327	G-AERN	DH.89A	6345	G-AGOU	DH.89B	6875
G-ADNA	DH.90	7500	G-AERZ	DH.89A	6356	G-AGOV	DH.89B	6874
G-ADNG	DH.89	6297	G-AESR	DH.89A	6363	G-AGOW	DH.89B	6849
G-ADNH	DH.89	6300	G-AESW	DH.90	7544	G-AGOX	DH.89B	6848
G-ADNI	DH.89	6301	G-AETM	DH.86	2353	G-AGPH	DH.89B	6889
G-ADOS	DH.84/2	6103	G-AEWL	DH.89A	6367	G-AGPI	DH.89B	6885
G-ADUE	DH.86	2333	G-AEWR	DH.86	2354	G-AGSH	DH.89B	6884
G-ADUF	DH.86	2334	G-AEWZ	DH.90	7555	G-AGSI	DH.89B	6886
G-ADUG	DH.86	2335	G-AEXI	DH.90	7554	G-AGSJ	DH.89B	6888
G-ADUH	DH.86	2336	G-AEXN	DH.90	7559	G-AGSK	DH.89B	6887
G-ADUI	DH.86	2337	G-AEXO	DH.89A	6368	G-AGTM	DH.89B	6746
G-ADUM	DH.89	6315	G-AEXP	DH.89A	6369	G-AGTN	DH.89B	6749
G-ADUN	DH.89	6316	G-AEIS	DH.84	6107	G-AGUF	DH.89B	6855
G-ADUO	DH.89	6317	G-AEIT	DH.84	6108	G-AGUG	DH.89B	6859
G-ADUP	DH.89	6319	G-AEIU	DH.84	6109	G-AGUP	DH.89B	6911
G-ADVJ	DH.86	2338	G-AEKZ	DH.84	6028	G-AGUR	DH.89B	6910
G-ADVK	DH.86	2339	G-AEMI	DH.84/2	6110	G-AGUU	DH.89B	6908
G-ADWZ	DH.89	6309	G-AEMJ	DH.84/2	6111	G-AGUV	DH.89B	6912
G-ADXM	DH.90	7509	G-AEMK	DH.84/2	6112	G-AGWC	DH.89B	6916
G-ADYC	DH.86	2340	G-AFAH	DH.89A	6377	G-AGWP	DH.89B	6918
G-ADYD	DH.86	2341	G-AFAJ	DH.86	2355	G-AGWR	DH.89B	6917
G-ADYE	DH.86	2346	G-AFAK	DH.86	2356	G-AGZJ	DH.89B	6936
G-ADYF	DH.86	2347	G-AFAL	DH.86	2357	G-AGZK	DH.89B	6937
G-ADYG	DH.86	2343	G-AFAM	DH.86	2358	G-AGZO	DH.89B	6913
G-ADYH	DH.86	2344	G-AFAN	DH.90	7556	G-AGZU	DH.89B	6773
G-ADYI	DH.86	2345	G-AFAO	DH.89A	6372	G-AHAG	DH.89B	6926
G-ADYJ	DH.86	2348	G-AFEN	DH.89A	6399	G-AHEA	DH.89B	6946
G-ADYK	DH.89	6310	G-AFEO	DH.89A	6405	G-AHEB	DH.89B	6945
G-ADYL (1)	DH.89	6311	G-AFEP	DH.89A	6406	G-AHED	DH.89B	6944
G-ADYL (2)	DH.89B	6895	G-AFEY	DH.89A	6402	G-AHFJ	DH.89B	6545
G-ADYM	DH.89	6312	G-AFEZ	DH.89A	6408	G-AHGC	DH.89B	6583
G-AEAJ	DH.89	6320	G-AFFB	DH.89A	6409	G-AHGD	DH.89B	6862
G-AEAK	DH.89	6324	G-AFFC	DH.89A	6410	G-AHGF	DH.89B	6903
G-AEAL	DH.89	6325	G-AFFF	DH.89A	6386	G-AHGG	DH.89B	6902
G-AEAM	DH.89	6326	G-AFHY	DH.89A	6417	G-AHGH	DH.89B	6934
G-AEAP	DH.86	2349	G-AFHZ	DH.89A	6418	G-AHGI	DH.89B	6935
G-AEBU	DH.90	7501	G-AFIA	DH.89A	6419	G-AHIA	DH.89B	6948
G-AEBW	DH.89	6327	G-AFLY	DH.89A	6426	G-AHJA	DH.89B	6486
G-AEBX	DH.89	6328	G-AFLZ	DH.89A	6429	G-AHJS	DH.89B	6967
G-AECW	DH.90	7504	G-AFMA	DH.89A	6430	G-AHKA	DH.89B	6839
G-AECX	DH.90	7505	G-AFME	DH.89A	6431	G-AHKB	DH.89B	6596
G-AECZ	DH.84/2	6105	G-AFMF	DH.89A	6432	G-AHKR	DH.89B	6824
G-AEDG	DH.90	7516	G-AFMG	DH.89A	6433	G-AHKS	DH.89B	6812
G-AEDH	DH.90	7510	G-AFMH	DH.89A	6434	G-AHKT	DH.89B	6811
G-AEDI	DH.90	7511	G-AFMI	DH.89A	6435	G-AHKU	DH.89B	6810
G-AEDJ	DH.90	7515	G-AFMJ	DH.89A	6436	G-AHKV	DH.89B	6792
G-AEDK	DH.90	7517	G-AFNC	DH.89A	6442	G-AHLF	DH.89B	6494
G-AEDT	DH.90	7508	G-AFND	DH.89A	6443	G-AHLL	DH.89B	6576
G-AEDU (1)	DH.90	7509	G-AFOI	DH.89A	6450	G-AHLM	DH.89B	6708
G-AEDU (2)	DH.90	7526	G-AFRF	DH.90	7519	G-AHLN	DH.89B	6754
G-AEDV	DH.90	7524	G-AFRI	DH.90	7536	G-AHLU	DH.89B	6633
G-AEDW	DH.90	7503	G-AFRK	DH.89A	6441	G-AHPT	DH.89B	6478
G-AEEK	DH.90	7518	G-AFSO	DH.89A	6445	G-AHPU	DH.89B	6963
G-AEFH	DH.86	2350	G-AFTF	DH.90	7533	G-AHPV	DH.89B	6759
G-AEFN	DH.90	7507	G-AFVJ	DH.90	7521	G-AHPW	DH.89B	6678
G-AEFX	DH.84/2	6106	G-AGDG	DH.89B	6547	G-AHPX	DH.89A	6429
'G-AEGK'	DH.84	6035	G-AGDH	DH.89B	6548	G-AHPY	DH.89B	6561
G-AEGS	DH.89	6335	G-AGDM	DH.89B	6584	G-AHRH	DH.89B	6823
G-AEHC	DH.90	7514	G-AGDP	DH.89A	6403	G-AHTR	DH.89B	6964

Reg	Type	No	Reg	Type	No	Reg	Type	No
G-AHTS	DH.89B	6962	G-AKND	DH.89B	6515	G-ALGC	DH.89B	6906
G-AHTT	DH.89B	6966	G-AKNE	DH.89B	6591	G-ALGE	DH.89B	6907
G-AHTY	DH.89B	6608	G-AKNF	DH.89B	6518	G-ALGI	DH.89B	6909
G-AHWF	DH.89B	6965	G-AKNN	DH.89B	6598	G-ALGM	DH.89B	6559
G-AHXV	DH.89B	6747	G-AKNV	DH.89B	6458	G-ALGN	DH.89B	6943
G-AHXW	DH.89B	6782	G-AKNW	DH.89B	6469	G-ALGO	DH.89B	6830
G-AHXX	DH.89B	6800	G-AKNX	DH.89B	6629	G-ALNS	DH.89B	6778
G-AHXY	DH.89B	6808	G-AKNY	DH.89B	6470	G-ALNT	DH.89B	6713
G-AHXZ	DH.89B	6825	G-AKNZ	DH.89B	6550	G-ALOV	DH.89B	6638
G-AIBB	DH.89B	6813	G-AKOA	DH.89B	6618	G-ALPK	DH.89B	6757
G-AIDL	DH.89B	6968	G-AKOB	DH.89B	6492	G-ALRW	DH.89B	6941
G-AIHN	DH.89B	6498	G-AKOC	DH.89B	6814	G-ALVU	DH.89B	6526
G-AIUI	DH.89B	6675	G-AKOD	DH.89B	6566	G-ALWI	DH.89B	6703
G-AIUJ	DH.89B	6724	G-AKOE	DH.89B	6601	G-ALWJ	DH.89B	6777
G-AIUK	DH.89B	6640	G-AKOF	DH.89B	6538	G-ALWK	DH.89B	6856
G-AIUL	DH.89B	6837	G-AKOG	DH.89B	6878	G-ALWL	DH.89B	6845
G-AIUM	DH.89B	6519	G-AKOH	DH.89B	6582	G-ALWM	DH.89B	6755
G-AIUN	DH.89B	6602	G-AKOI	DH.89B	6546	G-ALWN	DH.89B	6729
G-AIUO	DH.89B	6467	G-AKOJ	DH.89B	6580	G-ALWO	DH.89B	6840
G-AIWG	DH.89B	6497	G-AKOK	DH.89B	6474	G-ALWP	DH.89B	6707
G-AIWY	DH.89B	6775	G-AKOM	DH.89B	6758	G-ALWY	DH.89B	6741
G-AIWZ	DH.89B	6867	G-AKON	DH.89B	6620	G-ALXA	DH.89B	6727
G-AIYE	DH.89B	6815	G-AKOO	DH.89B	6468	G-ALXI	DH.89B	6690
G-AIYJ	DH.90	7553	G-AKOP	DH.89B	6636	G-ALXJ	DH.89B	6863
G-AIYP	DH.89B	6456	G-AKOR	DH.89B	6577	G-ALXS	DH.89B	6715
G-AIYR	DH.89B	6676	G-AKOV	DH.89B	6612	G-ALXT	DH.89B	6736
G-AIYY	DH.89B	6854	G-AKOY	DH.89B	6504	G-ALXU	DH.89B	6797
G-AIZI	DH.89B	6861	G-AKPA	DH.89B	6709	G-ALZF	DH.89B	6541
G-AJBJ	DH.89B	6765	G-AKRE	DH.89B	6606	G-ALZH	DH.89A	6448
G-AJCL	DH.89B	6722	G-AKRN	DH.89B	6513	G-ALZJ	DH.89B	6573
G-AJDN	DH.89B	6860	G-AKRO	DH.89B	6480	G-AMAI	DH.89B	6879
G-AJFJ	DH.89B	6587	G-AKRP	DH.89B	6940	G-AMAM	DH.89B	6571
G-AJFK	DH.89B	6552	G-AKRR	DH.89B	6950	G-AMCT	DH.89B	6714
G-AJFL	DH.89B	6631	G-AKRS	DH.89B	6952	G-AMDG	DH.89B	6818
G-AJFM	DH.89B	6496	G-AKSB	DH.89B	6951	G-AMJK	DH.89B	6657
G-AJFN	DH.89B	6520	G-AKSC	DH.89B	6779	G-ANAH	DH.89B	6786
G-AJFO	DH.89B	6756	G-AKSD	DH.89B	6949	G-ANET	DH.89B	6700
G-AJGS	DH.89	W1001	G-AKSE	DH.89B	6870	G-ANEU	DH.89B	6836
G-AJGV	DH.89B	6589	G-AKSF	DH.89B	6490	G-ANJR	DH.89B	6816
G-AJGZ	DH.89B	6883	G-AKSG	DH.89B	6931	G-ANYK	DH.90	7529
G-AJHO	DH.89B	6835	G-AKSH	DH.89B	6471	G-ANZP	DH.89B	6682
G-AJHP	DH.89B	6770	G-AKSL	DH.89B	6865	G-AOAO	DH.89B	6844
G-AJKE	DH.89B	6555	G-AKTD	DH.89B	6791	G-AOZG	DH.89B	6603
G-AJKF	DH.84	2081	G-AKTX	DH.89B	6639	G-APBJ	DH.89B	6872
G-AJKH	DH.89B	6763	G-AKTY	DH.89B	6563	G-APBM	DH.89B	6748
G-AJKI	DH.89B	6868	G-AKTZ	DH.89B	6482	G-APBN	DH.89B	6787
G-AJKW	DH.89B	6539	G-AKUB	DH.89B	6488	G-APJW	DH.89B	6578
G-AJKX	DH.89B	6457	G-AKUC	DH.89B	6565	G-APKA	DH.89B	6827
G-AJKY	DH.89B	6553	G-AKUS	DH.89B	6805	G-APSD	DH.89B	6556
G-AJMY	DH.89B	6511	G-AKVU	DH.89B	6476	G-ASFC	DH.89B	6679
G-AJNA	DH.89B	6516	G-AKYW	DH.89B	6581	G-ASIA	DH.89B	6718
G-AJNB	DH.86	2342	G-AKYX	DH.89B	6864	G-ASKI	DH.89B	6858
G-AJSJ	DH.89B	6826	G-AKYY	DH.89B	6822	G-ASKO	DH.89B	6735
G-AJSK	DH.89B	6500	G-AKYZ	DH.89B	6789	G-ASRJ	DH.89B	6959
G-AJSL	DH.89B	6801	G-AKZA	DH.89B	6892	G-ASRM	DH.89B	6961
G-AJTU	DH.89B	6558	G-AKZB	DH.89B	6790	'G-RCYR'	DH.89B	6879
G-AJVA	DH.89B	6600	G-AKZH	DH.89B	6529	G-ECAN	DH.84	2048
G-AJVB	DH.89B	6753	G-AKZI	DH.89B	6536			
G-AJXB	DH.89B	6530	G-AKZJ	DH.89B	6549			
G-AKBW	DH.89B	6585	G-AKZO	DH.89B	6575	**United Kingdom Class B registrations**		
G-AKDW	DH.89B	6897	G-AKZP	DH.89B	6882			
G-AKDX	DH.89B	6898	G-AKZT	DH.89B	6894	E.2	DH.90	7500
G-AKED	DH.89B	6487	G-AKZV	DH.89B	6843	E.2	DH.86	2300
G-AKEU	DH.89B	6672	G-AKZW	DH.89B	6896	E.2	DH.86	2342
G-AKFO	DH.89B	6460	G-ALAT	DH.89B	6851	E.3	DH.92	6400
G-AKGV	DH.89B	6796	G-ALAU	DH.89B	6609	E.4	DH.84	6103
G-AKGY	DH.89B	6723	G-ALAX	DH.89B	6930	E.4	DH.89	6250
G-AKIF	DH.89B	6838	G-ALAY	DH.89B	6942	E.4	DH.89A	6342
G-AKJS	DH.89	W1002	G-ALAZ	DH.89B	6932	E.9	DH.84	6000
G-AKJY	DH.89A	6447	G-ALBA	DH.89B	6821	E.9	DH.89A	6420
G-AKJZ	DH.89B	6880	G-ALBB	DH.89B	6829	E.0228	DH.89	?
G-AKLA	DH.89B	6764	G-ALBC	DH.89B	6572			
G-AKMD	DH.89B	6802	G-ALBH	DH.89B	6607			
G-AKME	DH.89B	6767	G-ALBI	DH.89B	6525	**Aden**		
G-AKMF	DH.89B	6617	G-ALEJ	DH.89B	6484			
G-AKMG	DH.89B	6635	G-ALET	DH.89B	6832	VR-AAL	DH.89B	6700
G-AKMH	DH.89B	6704	G-ALGB	DH.89B	6706	VR-AAP	DH.89B	6803

Angola

CR-LAT	DH.89A	6453
CR-LAU	DH.89A	6452
CR-LAV	DH.89A	6451
CR-LAX	DH.89	?
CR-LBG	DH.89B	6847
CR-LBH	DH.89B	6846
CR-LBN	DH.89B	6904
CR-LBO	DH.89B	6905
CR-LCK	DH.89B	6932
CR-LCO	DH.89A	6430
CR-LKR	DH.89B	6900
CR-LKS	DH.89B	6901

Argentina

R326	DH.90	7537
LV-AEN	DH.89B	6864
LV-AEO	DH.89B	6789
LV-AEP	DH.89B	6892
LV-AER	DH.89B	6609
LV-AES	DH.89B	6822
LV-AES (2)	DH.89B	6942
LV-AGR	DH.89B	6581
LV-AGV	DH.89A	6399
LV-AGW	DH.89B	6843
LV-AGX	DH.89B	6942
LV-AGY	DH.89B	6550
LV-FEP	DH.89B	6550
LV-FET	DH.89B	6942
LV-FFO	DH.89B	6864
LV-KAB	DH.90	7563
LV-RDA	DH.90	7537

Australia

VH-AAC	DH.84	6025
VH-AAD	DH.90	7508
VH-AAG	DH.89B	6668
VH-AAO	DH.84	6112
VH-ABI	DH.84	?
VH-ABK	DH.84	6062
VH-ADE	DH.89	6341
VH-ADG	DH.90	7516
VH-ADN	DH.86	2313
VH-AEF	DH.84	2057
VH-AFH	DH.84	2085
VH-AFK	DH.84	2024
VH-AGC	DH.84	2045
VH-AGI	DH.84	2017
VH-AGJ	DH.84	2046
VH-AGM	DH.84	2082
VH-AHI	DH.89B	6633
VH-AHY	DH.84	2073
VH-AIA	DH.84	2086
VH-AIC	DH.89	ntu
VH-AIK	DH.89B	6497
VH-AJS	DH.89	ntu
VH-AKX	DH.84	2061
VH-ALL	DH.84	2022
VH-AMB	DH.84	2023
VH-AML	DH.84	2081
VH-AMN	DH.84	2059
VH-AMO	DH.84	2067
VH-AOE	DH.84	2058
VH-AOK	DH.84	2056
VH-AOL	DH.84	2084
VH-AOM	DH.84	2066
VH-AON	DH.84	2019
VH-AOP	DH.84	2010
VH-AOQ	DH.84	2011
VH-AOR	DH.84	2042
VH-AOS	DH.84	2006
VH-AOT	DH.84	2050
VH-APJ	DH.84	2064

VH-APK	DH.84	2079
VH-APL	DH.84	2051
VH-APP	DH.84	2072
VH-AQU	DH.84	2048
VH-AQW	DH.84	2068
VH-ARI	DH.84	2028
VH-ARJ	DH.84	2080
VH-ASK	DH.84	2002
VH-ASL	DH.84	2020
VH-ASN	DH.84	2039
VH-ASO	DH.84	2045
VH-ASU	DH.84	2079
VH-ASX	DH.84	2039
VH-AVU	DH.84	2074
VH-AWG	DH.89B	6903
VH-AXL	DH.84	2071
VH-AYB	DH.84	2065
VH-AYM	DH.84	2031
VH-AYZ	DH.84	2053
VH-BAF	DH.84	2027
VH-BAH	DH.84	2055
VH-BDB	DH.84	2063
VH-BDC	DH.84	2083
VH-BDS	DH.84	2081
VH-BFS	DH.89B	6886
VH-BGP	DH.89B	6648
VH-BIF	DH.89B	6903
VH-BJH	DH.84	2044
VH-BKM	DH.89B	6543
VH-BKR	DH.89B	6929
VH-BMX	DH.84	2049
VH-CBU	DH.89B	6530
VH-CFA (1)	DH.89B	6814
VH-CFA (2)	DH.89B	6713
VH-CLH	DH.89B	6929
VH-CPP	DH.84	2072
VH-CRP	DH.89	6270
VH-CSL	DH.84	2034
VH-DHX	DH.84	2048
VH-DMA	DH.84	6029
VH-DMB	DH.84	2072
VH-ECW	DH.89B	6530
VH-FDA	DH.84	2045
VH-FDB	DH.84	6029
VH-GAU	DH.84	2049
VH-IAN	DH.89B	6655
VH-PSZ	DH.84	2064
VH-RSZ	DH.84	2064
VH-SJW	DH.84	2020
VH-SNB	DH.84	2002
VH-UBN	DH.89	6253
VH-UFF	DH.89	6270
VH-URD	DH.84	6037
VH-URE	DH.84	6029
VH-URF	DH.84	6045
VH-URG	DH.84	6046
VH-URN	DH.86	2301
VH-URO	DH.84	6068
VH-URT	DH.86	2312
VH-URU	DH.84	6088
VH-URV	DH.84	6089
VH-URW	DH.84	6080
VH-URX	DH.84	6081
VH-URY	DH.84	6082
VH-USA	DH.84	6074
VH-USC	DH.86	2307
VH-USD	DH.86	2308
VH-USE	DH.86	2309
VH-USF	DH.86	2310
VH-USG	DH.86	2311
VH-USW	DH.86	2315
VH-UTJ	DH.90	7562
VH-UTV	DH.89B	6655
VH-UTX	DH.84	6104
VH-UUA	DH.86	2306
VH-UUB	DH.86	2326

VH-UUO	DH.89	6259
VH-UVB	DH.84	6102
VH-UVG	DH.89	6314
VH-UVI	DH.89	6318
VH-UVN	DH.84	6106
VH-UVS	DH.89	6265
VH-UVT	DH.89	6319
VH-UXA	DH.90	7533
VH-UXB	DH.90	7513
VH-UXG	DH.84	6077
VH-UXK	DH.84	6053
VH-UXS	DH.90	7546
VH-UXT	DH.89	6346
VH-UXZ	DH.89	6365
VH-UXZ (2)	DH.89B	6801
VH-UYU	DH.86	2359
VH-UYV	DH.86	2360
VH-UYW	DH.86	2361
VH-UZF	DH.84	6065
VH-UZG	DH.84	6027
VH-UZX (1)	DH.84	6084
VH-UZX (2)	DH.86	2323
VH-UZY	DH.89	6384
VH-UZZ	DH.84	6097

Austria

OE-FAA	DH.89B	6690
OE-FKD	DH.84	6101

Belgium & Belgian Congo

OO-AFG	DH.89B	6458
OO-APO	DH.89	6273
OO-ARI	DH.89B	6787
OO-ARN	DH.89B	6785
OO-CCD	DH.89A	6442
OO-CDE	DH.89B	6520
OO-CDF	DH.89B	6756
OO-CFI	DH.89B	6932
OO-CJD	DH.89B	6607
OO-CJE	DH.89B	6918
OO-CJS	DH.89A	6429
OO-CJT	DH.89B	6925
OO-CJU	DH.89A	6380
OO-CJW	DH.89B	6508
OO-CJX	DH.89B	6658
OO-CMS	DH.89B	6902
OO-CNP	DH.89B	6458
OO-CRS	DH.89B	6559
OO-CYE	DH.89	?
OO-DCB	DH.89B	6758
OO-ITI	DH.89B	6913
OO-JFN	DH.89	6273
OO-JFN	DH.90	7561
OO-PET	DH.90	7529

Brazil

PP-AIA	DH.89B	6920
PP-AIB	DH.89B	6922
PP-AIC	DH.89B	6923
PP-AID	DH.89B	6921
PP-AIE	DH.89B	6970
PP-AIF	DH.89B	6971
PP-AIG	DH.89B	6972
PP-DPH	DH.89B	6807
PP-LAA	DH.89A	6449
PP-OMA	DH.89A	6449
PP-OMB	DH.89B	6927
PP-OMC	DH.89B	6960
PP-OMD	DH.89B	6774
PP-SPC	DH.84	6085
PP-VAN (1)	DH.89A	6449
PP-VAN (2)	DH.89B	6900

Canada

CF-AEO	DH.89	6279
CF-APJ	DH.84	6024
CF-AVD	DH.84	6086
CF-AVI	DH.84	6093
CF-AVJ	DH.89	6295
CF-AYE	DH.89	6304
C-FAYE	DH.89B	6796
CF-AYF	DH.90	7506
CF-BBC	DH.89	6307
CF-BBD	DH.90	7522
CF-BBG	DH.89A	6354
CF-BBH	DH.89A	6370
CF-BFF	DH.90	7543
CF-BFL	DH.89A	6373
CF-BFM	DH.89A	6371
CF-BFP	DH.89A	6374
CF-BND	DH.89A	6375
CF-BNE	DH.89A	6376
CF-BNG	DH.89B	6472
CF-BNJ	DH.89	'89232'
CF-BPD	DH.90	7538
CF-BXU	DH.90	7522
CF-BXV	DH.90	7557
CF-BZA	DH.90	7531
CF-DIM	DH.89B	6928
CF-DIN	DH.89B	6938
CF-MPA	DH.90	7530
CF-MPB	DH.90	7531
CF-MPC	DH.90	7522
CF-MPD	DH.90	7538
CF-PTK	DH.89	6254
C-GXFJ	DH.89B	6796

Cape Verde Islands

CR-CAA	DH.89B	6905

Ceylon

CY-AAI	DH.89B	6736
CY-AAK	DH.89B	6894

Chile

CC-CIC-0034	DH.89B	6468 ?

China

?	DH.89A	6444

Congo, Democratic Republic

9O-CJD	DH.89B	6607
9O-CJE	DH.89B	6918
9O-CJT	DH.89B	6925

9O-CJU	DH.89A	6380
9O-CJW	DH.89B	6508
9O-CJX	DH.89B	6658
9Q-CJD	DH.89B	6607
9Q-CJE	DH.89B	6918
9Q-CJK	DH.89B	6667
9Q-CJU	DH.89A	6380
9Q-CJW	DH.89B	6508
9Q-CJX	DH.89B	6658
9Q-CPF	DH.89B	6961
9Q-C..	DH.89B	6704

Czechoslovakia

OK-ATO	DH.84	6032

Denmark

OY-AAO	DH.89B	6775
OY-ACV	DH.89B	6467
OY-ACZ	DH.89B	6888
OY-DAS	DH.89A	6347
OY-DIN	DH.89	6272
OY-DYA	DH.89B	6917
OY-DZY	DH.89B	6956

Dutch East Indies

PK-AKU	DH.89	6296
PK-AKV	DH.89	6292
PK-AKW	DH.89	6294

Egypt

SU-ABH	DH.84	6028
SU-ABI	DH.84	6031
SU-ABJ	DH.84	6051
SU-ABN	DH.86	2320
SU-ABO	DH.86	2329
SU-ABP	DH.89	6298
SU-ABQ	DH.89	6299
SU-ABR	DH.89	6302
SU-ABS	DH.89	6303
SU-ABU	DH.89	6313
SU-ABV	DH.86	2342
SU-ABW	DH.90	7553
SU-ABZ	DH.84	6032
SU-ACR	DH.86	2334
SU-ACS (1)	DH.89B	6641
SU-ACS (2)	DH.89B	6544
SU-ACT (1)	DH.89B	6642
SU-ACT (2)	DH.89B	6551

Ethiopia

ET-P-16	DH.89B	6950
ET-P-22	DH.89B	6700

Fiji

VQ-FAL	DH.89B	6707
VQ-FAM	DH.89B	6471
VQ-FAN	DH.89B	6577
VQ-FAZ	DH.89B	6886

Finland

OH-BLA	DH.89A	6347
OH-BLB	DH.89A	6401
OH-DHA	DH.89A	6347
OH-DHB	DH.89A	6401
OH-IPA	DH.86	2353
OH-SLA	DH.86	2353
OH-VKH	DH.89A	6347
OH-VKI	DH.89A	6401

France and dependencies

F-AMTM	DH.84	6040
F-AMTR	DH.84	6057
F-AMUZ	DH.84	6064
F-ANES	DH.84	6083
F-ANGE	DH.84	6038
F-AOYK	DH.90	7521
F-AOZC	DH.90	7519
F-APAX	DH.90	7536
F-APDE	DH.90	7529
F-APES	DH.89	6309
F-APFK	DH.90	7542
F-AQEU	DH.90	7501
F-AQIL	DH.89A	6382
F-AQIM	DH.89A	6383
F-AQIN	DH.89A	6393
F-AQJH	DH.89A	6395
F-AQJI	DH.89A	6396
F-AQOH	DH.89A	6403
F-AQOI	DH.89A	6407
F-ARII	DH.89A	6420
F-ARIJ	DH.89A	6424
F-ARIK	DH.89A	6425
F-ARIL	DH.89A	6427
F-ARIM	DH.89A	6428
F-AZCA	DH.89B	6541
F-BAHX	DH.89B	6547
F-BAHY	DH.89	6276
F-BAHZ	DH.89B	6522
F-BCDB	DH.89B	6897
F-BDJX	DH.89B	6769
F-BEDI	DH.89B	6516
F-BEDX	DH.89B	6547
F-BEDY	DH.89	6276
F-BEDZ	DH.89B	6522
F-BEFU	DH.89B	6555
F-BEKB	DH.89B	6596
F-BEPE	DH.89B	6845
F-BFEH	DH.89B	6723

Three Rapides, F-BEDY, F-BEDZ and F-BEDX ready for delivery from Witney to Air France in 1948   *[via P. Davis]*

Reg	Type	c/n
F-BFPU	DH.89B	6796
F-BFVM	DH.89B	6791
F-BFVR	DH.89B	6563
F-BGIS	DH.89B	6608
F-BGOL	DH.89B	6559
F-BGON	DH.89B	6541
F-BGOQ	DH.89B	6754
F-BGPG	DH.89B	6729
F-BGPH	DH.89B	6845
F-BGPI	DH.89B	6635
F-BGPJ	DH.89B	6703
F-BGPK	DH.89B	6474
F-BGPL	DH.89B	6865
F-BGPM	DH.89B	6476
F-BGXH	DH.89B	6582
F-BGXT	DH.89B	6769
F-BGZT	DH.89B	6913
F-BHAF	DH.89B	6931
F-BHCD	DH.89B	6706
F-BHCE	DH.89B	6851
F-BHCF	DH.89B	6946
F-BHDY	DH.89B	6753
F-BHFM	DH.89B	6575
F-BHGR	DH.89B	6844
F-BHOB	DH.89B	6578
F-BHTH	DH.89B	6714
F-BHVQ	DH.89B	6945
F-BJUY	DH.89A	6367
F-BJUZ	DH.89B	6911
F-BLHE	DH.89B	6870
F-BLHZ	DH.89B	6709
F-BLXX	DH.89B	6907
F-DABY	DH.89B	6487
F-DAFS	DH.89B	6940
F-LAAB	DH.89B	6724
F-LAAC	DH.89B	6729
F-LAAE	DH.89B	6845
F-LAAF	DH.89B	6935
F-LAAL	DH.89A	6408
F-OABH	DH.89B	6606
F-OADX	DH.89B	6547
F-OADY	DH.89	6276
F-OADZ	DH.89B	6522
F-OAGP	DH.89B	6755
F-OAHL	DH.89B	6957
F-OAIH	DH.89B	6715
F-OAIL	DH.89B	6724
F-OAIR	DH.89B	6818
F-OAJI	DH.89	?
F-OAKD	DH.89B	6802
F-OAKE	DH.89B	6943
F-OAKF	DH.89A	6448
F-OAKX	DH.89B	6816
F-OALD	DH.89B	6832
F-OAME	DH.89B	6573
F-OAMS	DH.90	7529
F-OAND	DH.89B	6909
F-OANF	DH.89B	6935
F-OANU	DH.89B	6671
F-OAOS	DH.89B	6620
F-OAOY	DH.89B	6480
F-OAPS	DH.89B	6638
F-OAPT	DH.89A	6447
F-OAQL	DH.89B	6839
F-OAQU	DH.89B	6836
F-OAQY	DH.89B	6566
F-OAQZ	DH.89B	6553
F-OARH	DH.89B	6580
F-OASC	DH.89B	6797
F-OATC	DH.89B	6779
F-OATD	DH.89B	6629
F-OATT	DH.89A	6367
F-OAUE	DH.89	6325
F-OAUG	DH.89B	6811
F-OAUH	DH.89B	6612
F-OAVG	DH.89	6270
F-OAVZ	DH.89A	6453
F-OAXK	DH.89B	6584
F-AOYN	DH.89B	6504
F-OAYS	DH.89B	6815
F-OAZT	DH.89B	6577
F-OBAL	DH.89B	6856
F-OBAQ	DH.89A	6424
F-OBDV	DH.89B	6591
F-OBGE	DH.89B	6872
F-OBGU	DH.89B	6715
F-OBGY	DH.89B	6911
F-OBHH	DH.89B	6487
F-OBHI	DH.89A	6408
F-OBIA	DH.89B	6787
F-OBIO	DH.89B	6507
F-OBIV	DH.89B	6860
F-OBKH	DH.89B	6477
F-OBMQ	DH.89B	6878
F-OBOD	DH.89A	6412
F-OBOH	DH.89B	6823
F-OBOI	DH.89B	6770
F-OBRU	DH.89B	6748
F-OBRV	DH.89B	6525
F-OBRX	DH.89B	6470
F-OBVI	DH.89B	6949
F-OBVJ	DH.89B	6813
F-OBVL	DH.89B	6657
F-OCAG	DH.89B	6859
F-OCBX	DH.89B	6563
F-OCHF	DH.89B	6735
F-OGAU	DH.89B	6758

Note: F-OAJI was an unidentified Rapide operated by Cie Laotienne de Commerce et Transport, Hanoi; it crashed due to engine failure on 15.8.51 and was subsequently DBF at Nghia Lo, 150 mls NW of Hanoi.

Gabon

Reg	Type	c/n
TR-LKQ	DH.89B	6715

Germany (West)

Reg	Type	c/n
D-IDAK	DH.89B	6467
D-IGEL	DH.89A	6347
D-IGUN	DH.89A	6437
D-ILIT	DH.89B	6879

Gold Coast

Reg	Type	c/n
VP-AAA	DH.89B	6951

Iceland

Reg	Type	c/n
TF-ISM	DH.89B	6670
TF-ISO	DH.89B	6730
TF-KAA	DH.89B	6622

India

Reg	Type	c/n
VT-AEK	DH.84	6050
VT-AEL	DH.84	6048
VT-AES	DH.84	6065
VT-AFF	DH.84	6074
VT-AHB	DH.89	6308
VT-AHW	DH.90	7527
VT-AHY	DH.90	7540
VT-AIE	DH.90	7545
VT-AIZ	DH.89A	6378
VT-AJA	DH.89A	6379
VT-AJB	DH.89A	6381
VT-AKC	DH.90	7505
VT-AKM	DH.86	2306
VT-AKZ	DH.86	2308
VT-ALO	DH.89A	6454
VT-ARF	DH.89B	6569
VT-ARK	DH.89B	6652
VT-ARL	DH.89B	6649
VT-ARM	DH.89B	6650
VT-ARN	DH.89B	6651
VT-ARR	DH.89B	6503
VT-ART	DH.89B	6656
VT-ARV	DH.89B	6657
VT-ARW	DH.89B	6661
VT-ARY	DH.89B	6681
VT-ARZ	DH.89B	6717
VT-ASA	DH.89B	6588
VT-ASC	DH.89B	6762
VT-ASJ	DH.89B	6793
VT-ASQ	DH.89B	6794
VT-AVW	DH.89B	6947
VT-AVX	DH.89B	6953
VT-AXG	DH.89B	6957
VT-CBY	DH.89B	6869
VT-CHZ	DH.89B	6724

Iraq

Reg	Type	c/n
YI-AAC	DH.84	6044
YI-ABD	DH.89B	6897
YI-ABE	DH.89B	6898
YI-ABF	DH.89B	6906
YI-ABG	DH.89B	6907
YI-ABH	DH.89B	6909
YI-FYA	DH.89A	6416
YI-HDA	DH.89A	6415
YI-HMK	DH.90	7502
YI-OSD	DH.90	7525
YI-ZWA	DH.89A	6414

Iran

Reg	Type	c/n
EP-AAA	DH.89	6321
EP-AAB	DH.89	6322
EP-AAC	DH.89	6323
EP-AAD	DH.89B	6692
EP-AAE	DH.89B	6695
EP-AAN	DH.89	?
EP-AAT	DH.89B	6696
EP-AAU	DH.89	?
EP-AAV	DH.89B	6763
EP-AAW	DH.89B	6965
EP-AAX	DH.89B	6966
EP-AAY	DH.89B	6868
EP-ADM	DH.89B	6565
EP-ADN	DH.89B	6488
EP-ADO	DH.89B	6618
EP-ADP	DH.89B	6518

Irish Republic

Reg	Type	c/n
EI-ABI (1)	DH.84	6076
EI-ABI (2)	DH.84	6105
EI-ABK	DH.86	2338
EI-ABP	DH.89	6341
EI-ABT	DH.86	2336
EI-ADP	DH.89B	6945
EI-AEA	DH.89A	6433
EI-AFK	DH.84	6105
EI-AGK	DH.89B	6458
EI-AJO	DH.89B	6884
EI-AKH	DH.89B	6870
EI-AML	DH.89B	6709
EI-AMN	DH.89B	6907

Israel

Reg	Type	c/n
4X-ACN	DH.89	?
4X-ACU	DH.89B	6549
4X-AEI	DH.89B	6895
4X-970	DH.89B	6952

JY-ACE, c/n 6959, airborne in the Middle East   [Denis Fox collection]

Italy

I-BOBJ	DH.89B	6858
I-DRAG (1)	DH.89	6260
I-DRAG (2)	DH.90	7541

Jordan

JY-AAE	DH.89B	6961
JY-AAJ	DH.89B	6580
JY-AAV	DH.89B	6797
JY-AAZ	DH.89B	6753
JY-ABP	DH.89B	6887
JY-ACE	DH.89B	6959
JY-ACF	DH.89B	6961
JY-ACG	DH.89B	6959
JY-ACL	DH.89B	6746

Kenya

VP-KAW	DH.84	6047
VP-KBA	DH.84	6059

VP-KBG	DH.84	6079
VP-KCA	DH.90	7528
VP-KCG	DH.89A	6357
VP-KCJ	DH.89A	6366
VP-KCK	DH.89	6267
VP-KCL	DH.89A	6394
VP-KCR	DH.89A	6413
VP-KCS	DH.90	7554
VP-KCT	DH.89B	6803
VP-KCU	DH.89B	6848
VP-KCV	DH.89B	6849
VP-KCW	DH.89B	6875
VP-KCX	DH.89B	6876
VP-KCY	DH.89B	6874
VP-KEA	DH.89B	6890
VP-KEB	DH.89B	6891
VP-KEC	DH.89B	6893
VP-KED	DH.89B	6895
VP-KEE	DH.89B	6496
VP-KEF	DH.89B	6831
VP-KFH	DH.89A	6418
VP-KFI	DH.89B	6619

VP-KFV	DH.89B	6406
VP-KFW	DH.89B	6545
VP-KFX	DH.89B	6620
VP-KGE	DH.89B	6515
VP-KGS	DH.89B	6558
VP-KHF	DH.89B	6627
VP-KHJ	DH.89A	6387
VP-KIO	DH.89B	6898
VP-KJB	DH.89	ntu
VP-KLB	DH.89B	6877
VP-KLL	DH.89B	6777
VP-KMD	DH.89B	6500
VP-KNC	DH.89B	6612
VP-KND	DH.89B	6640
VP-KNS	DH.89B	6492
5Y-KLB	DH.89B	6877
5Y-KLL	DH.89B	6777

Laos

XW-TAB	DH.89B	6832
XW-TBI	DH.89B	?

XW-TA? in sorry condition in Laos; if this was indeed XW-TAB it may never have been put into service   [G M Simons collection]

Part of the fleet of Divisao de Exploracao des Transportes Aereos (DETA), Lourenco Marques: three Rapides, a Dragonfly and a Hornet Moth [via C N Dodds]

Latvia

| YL-ABC | DH.89A | 6351 |
| YL-ABD | DH.89A | 6352 |

Lebanon

LR-AAD	DH.89B	6843
LR-AAE	DH.89B	6894
LR-AAF	DH.89B	6896
LR-ABH	DH.89B	6469
OD-ABH	DH.89B	6469
OD-ABL	DH.89B	6672
OD-ABP	DH.89B	6746

Liberia

| EL-AAA | DH.89B | 6902 |

Luxembourg

| LX-LAC | DH.89B | 6607 |
| LX-LAD | DH.89B | 6525 |

Madagascar

5R-MAM	DH.89B	6563
5R-MAN	DH.89B	6591
5R-MAO	DH.89B	6507
5R-MAP	DH.89B	6620

Malaya

VR-OAA	DH.89B	6908
VR-OAB	DH.89B	6800
VR-OAC	DH.89B	6812

Morocco

| CN-TTO | DH.89B | 6940 |

**Mozambique
(Portuguese East Africa)**

CR-AAB	DH.90	7526
CR-AAD	DH.89A	6361
CR-AAE	DH.89A	6362
CR-AAM	DH.89A	6397
CR-AAN	DH.89A	6398
CR-AAT	DH.89A	6439
CR-AAU	DH.89A	6440
CR-ABT	DH.84	?
CR-ADH	DH.89A	6387
CR-ADM	DH.89B	6840
CR-ADT	DH.89B	6564
CR-AEQ	DH.89B	6969

Netherlands

PH-AKU	DH.89	6296
PH-AKV	DH.89	6292
PH-AKW	DH.89	6294
PH-ATK	DH.90	7539
PH-KOK	DH.90	7539
PH-OTA	DH.89B	6740
PH-RAA	DH.89B	6890
PH-RAB	DH.89B	6891
PH-RAC	DH.89B	6893
PH-RAD	DH.89B	6895
PH-RAE	DH.89B	6740
PH-RAF	DH.89B	6819
PH-TGC	DH.89B	6740
PH-VNA	DH.89B	6748
PH-VNB	DH.89B	6872
PH-VNC	DH.89B	6740
PH-VND	DH.89B	6819

New Zealand

ZK-ACO	DH.89	6259
ZK-ADR	DH.84	6090
ZK-ADS	DH.84	6091
ZK-AEC	DH.89	6334
ZK-AED	DH.89	6305
ZK-AEE	DH.89	6306
ZK-AEF	DH.86	2330
ZK-AEG	DH.86	2331
ZK-AEH	DH.86	2332
ZK-AER	DH.84	6090
ZK-AEW	DH.89A	6343
ZK-AFB	DH.90	7560
ZK-AGP	DH.90	7566
ZK-AGT	DH.89A	6423
ZK-AHS	DH.89A	6423
ZK-AHT	DH.84	6090

The five Rapides which formed the original post-war fleet of KLM. PH-RAC was c/n 6893

[G M Simons collection]

ZK-AHS in the colours of Tourist Air Travel Ltd [G M Simons collection]

ZK-AHW	DH.86	2331
ZK-AKS	DH.89B	6647
ZK-AKT	DH.89B	6673
ZK-AKU	DH.89B	6662
ZK-AKY	DH.89B	6653
ZK-ALB	DH.89B	6655
ZK-ALC	DH.89B	6664
ZK-AXI	DH.84	2057
ZK-AYR	DH.90	7508
ZK-BAU	DH.89B	6654
ZK-BBP	DH.89B	6668
ZK-BCP	DH.89B	6648
ZK-BFK	DH.89B	6903
ZK-SWR	DH.89B	6853

Nigeria

VR-NAA	DH.90	7565

Northern Rhodesia

VP-RBT	DH.89B	6665
VP-RBU	DH.89B	6924
VP-RCH	DH.89B	6878
VP-RCI	DH.89B	6660
VP-RCP	DH.89B	6659

Norway

LN-BEZ	DH.89B	6838
LN-BFB	DH.89A	6401

Nyasaland

VP-NAK	DH.89B	6659

Pakistan

AP-ADM	DH.89B	6916
AP-AFN	DH.89B	6552
AP-AGI	DH.89B	6457
AP-AGL	DH.89B	6859
AP-AGM	DH.89B	6504

Palestine

VQ-PAC	DH.89A	6399
VQ-PAR	DH.89B	6806

Paraguay

ZP-TDH	DH.89A	6436
?	DH.89B	6589

Peru

OB-RAA-156	DH.89B	6973
OB-RAB-157	DH.89B	6974
OB-RAC-158	DH.89B	6975
OB-RAD-159	DH.89B	6976
OB-RAE-160	DH.89B	6977
OB-RAF-195	DH.89B	6804
OB-RAG-196	DH.89B	6798
OB-RAH-197	DH.89B	6783

Portugal

CS-ADI	DH.89B	6899
CS-ADJ	DH.89B	6900
CS-ADK	DH.89B	6901
CS-AEB	DH.89A	6430

Portuguese Guinea

CR-GAI	DH.89B	6896
CR-GAJ	DH.89B	6529
CR-GAK	DH.89B	6511

LN-BFB at Eggemoen in 1964, after it was withdrawn from use [G M Simons collection]

Three Rapides, CS-ADK, CS-ADJ and CS-ADI for Portugal ready for delivery from Witney

[via P. Davis]

Rumania

YR-DNC	DH.89	6338
YR-DRA	DH.89	6329
YR-DRI	DH.89	6330
YR-DRO	DH.89	6331
YR-FLO	DH.90	7548
YR-FLU	DH.90	7549
YR-FLY	DH.90	7547

São Tomé e Príncipe

CR-SAD	DH.89B	6900
CR-SAE	DH.89B	6901

Senegal

6V-AAC	DH.89B	6470

Seychelles

VQ-SAD	DH.89B	6831

Sierra Leone

VR-LAC	DH.89B	6603
VR-LAD	DH.89B	6963
VR-LAE	DH.89B	6827

Singapore

VR-SAV	DH.89A	6360
VR-SAW	DH.89A	6364
VR-SAX	DH.90	7511
VR-SBC	DH.86	2323
VR-SBD	DH.86	2313

South Africa

ZS-AEF	DH.84	6026
ZS-AEG	DH.84	6030
ZS-AEH	DH.84	6054
ZS-AEI	DH.84	6017
ZS-AES	DH.89	6256
ZS-AHV	DH.90	7523
ZS-AIK	DH.90	7535
ZS-AKT	DH.89A	6380
ZS-AME	DH.89A	6387
ZS-ANM	DH.90	7564
ZS-AOM	DH.89A	6411
ZS-ATV	DH.89B	6914
ZS-ATW	DH.89B	6915
ZS-AXS	DH.89B	6969
ZS-AYF	DH.89A	6429
ZS-AYG	DH.89B	6759
ZS-BCD	DH.89B	6477
ZS-BCI	DH.89B	6510
ZS-BCO	DH.89B	6678
ZS-BCP	DH.89B	6561
ZS-BCR	DH.89B	6564
ZS-BCS	DH.89B	6508
ZS-BCT	DH.89B	6627
ZS-BEA	DH.89B	6626
ZS-BEF	DH.89B	6507
ZS-BMV	DH.89B	6619
ZS-BMW	DH.89B	6637
ZS-BYT	DH.89B	6834
ZS-BZC	DH.89B	6788
ZS-BZV	DH.89B	6925
ZS-CAB	DH.89A	6411
ZS-CAC	DH.89B	6788
ZS-CTR	DH.90	7526
ZS-DDH	DH.89B	6833
ZS-DDI	DH.89B	6658
ZS-DDX	DH.89A	6411

ZS-DFG	DH.89B	6667
ZS-DFL	DH.89A	6387
ZS-DJT	DH.89B	6498
ZS-DLS	DH.89B	6773
ZS-JGV	DH.89B	6831

Southern Rhodesia

VP-YAU	DH.89	6285
VP-YAX	DH.90	7512
VP-YBB	DH.90	7520
VP-YBJ	DH.89A	6358
VP-YBK	DH.89A	6359
VP-YBR	DH.90	7503
VP-YBT	DH.89A	6404
VP-YBU	DH.89A	6412
VP-YBY	DH.84	6030
VP-YBZ	DH.89	6256
VP-YCI	DH.89B	6658
VP-YCJ	DH.89B	6659
VP-YCK	DH.89B	6660
VP-YCL	DH.89B	6665
VP-YCM	DH.89B	6666
VP-YCN	DH.89B	6667
VP-YCO	DH.89B	6833
VP-YCP	DH.89B	6834
VP-YDE	DH.89B	6925
VP-YDF	DH.89B	6924
VP-YEZ	DH.89B	6680
VP-YFA	DH.89B	6761
VP-YHE	DH.89B	6840
VP-YIU	DH.89B	6969
VP-YKJ	DH.89B	6477
VP-YLF	DH.89B	6878
VP-YLV	DH.89B	6660
VP-YMW	DH.89B	6667
VP-YNJ	DH.89A	6412

Rapide VP-YAU with sister aircraft VP-YBK and Dragonfly VP-YAX, all of Rhodesia & Nyasaland Airways, await their next scheduled trips

[Denis Fox collection]

Page 231

VP-YNN	DH.89B	6875
VP-YNU	DH.89B	6508
VP-YOE	DH.89B	6500
VP-YOL	DH.89B	6666
VP-YOY	DH.89B	6678

Spain

(See Notes in Military Index.)

Second register series 1929-39
EC-AZZ	DH.89	6262
EC-TAT	DH.84	6020
EC-W14	DH.84	6020
EC-W27	DH.89	6262

Third register series 1939-45
EC-AAV	DH.89A	6425
EC-AAY	DH.89	6277
EC-AGO	DH.89	6262 ?
EC-AGP	DH.89	6262 ?
EC-BAA	DH.90	7529
EC-BAC	DH.89A	6420
EC-CAQ	DH.89A	6275 ?

Fourth register series from 1945
EC-AAQ	DH.90	7529
EC-AAR	DH.89A	6420
EC-AAS	DH.89A	6424
EC-AAV	DH.89A	6425
EC-AAY	DH.89A	6277 or 6427
EC-ABG	DH.89	6275 ?
EC-AGP	DH.89B	6879
EC-AKO	DH.89A	6345

Sri Lanka
4R-AAI	DH.89B	6736
4R-AAK	DH.89B	6894

Sudan
SN-ABB	DH.89B	6950

Sweden
SE-APH	DH.89B	6919
SE-APS	DH.89	ntu
SE-AYA	DH.89	ntu
SE-AYB	DH.89	ntu
SE-BTA	DH.89B	6519
SE-BTT	DH.89B	6467
SE-BXZ	DH.89B	6934
SE-CBU	DH.89B	6530
SE-CDI	DH.89B	6917

Switzerland
CH-287	DH.89	6250
HB-AME	DH.89A	6437
HB-AMU	DH.89A	6438
HB-APA	DH.89	6250
HB-APE	DH.89A	6437
HB-APU	DH.89A	6438
HB-ARA	DH.89	6250

Tanzania
5H-AAM	DH.89B	6492
5H-AAN	DH.89B	6831

Transjordan
TJ-AAA	DH.89B	6954
TJ-AAB	DH.89B	6955
TJ-AAC	DH.89B	6958
TJ-AAD	DH.89B	6959
TJ-AAE	DH.89B	6961
TJ-AAI	DH.89A	6399
TJ-AAJ	DH.89B	6580
TJ-AAP	DH.89A	6443
TJ-AAQ	DH.89B	6546
TJ-AAU	DH.89B	6715
TJ-AAV	DH.89B	6797
TJ-AAZ	DH.89B	6753
TJ-ABJ	DH.89B	6749
TJ-ABM	DH.89B	6600
TJ-ABP	DH.89B	6887
TJ-ACE	DH.89B	6959

Tunisia
TS-BME	DH.89B	6573

Turkey
TC-AGA	DH.89B	6686
TC-ALI	DH.89	6315
TC-ARI	DH.89	6315
TC-BAY	DH.89	6316
TC-CAN	DH.89	6317
TC-DAG	DH.89A	6372
TC-ERK (1)	DH.86	2355
TC-ERK (2)	DH.89	?
TC-FER	DH.86	2356
TC-GEN	DH.86	2357
TC-HAD	DH.89B	6687
TC-HEP	DH.86	2358
TC-IDE	DH.90	7556
TC-LAV	DH.89B	6643
TC-MUT	DH.89B	6644
TC-NUR	DH.89B	6645
TC-PER	DH.89B	6688
TC-VUR	DH.89B	6689
TC-ZOR	DH.89B	6646

Uganda
VP-UAW	DH.89B	6631
VP-UAX	DH.89A	6418
VP-UBB	DH.89B	6619

United Nations
1	DH.89B	6917
2	DH.89B	6918
3	DH.89A	6436
4	DH.89B	6492
5	DH.89B	6629
6	DH.89B	6748
7	DH.89B	6740
8	DH.89B	6872
9	DH.89B	6819

United States
N34DH	DH.84	6096
N89DH	DH.89B	6709
N190DH	DH.90	7526
N683DH	DH.89B	6782
N2034	DH.90	7508
N2290B	DH.89B	6588
N2290F	DH.89B	6794
N8053	DH.89B	6907

Uruguay
CX-AAH	DH.86	2325
CX-AAR	DH.90	7532
CX-AAS	DH.90	7534
CX-ABG	DH.86	2346
CX-ABI	DH.89A	6371
CX-ABL	DH.89	6333
CX-API	DH.89B	6786

USSR
CCCP-L20	DH.89M	6351
CCCP-L21	DH.89M	6352

Venezuela
YV-P-BPE	DH.89B	6938

Yugoslavia
YU-SAS	DH.89	6332

Three Dragon Rapides about to leave on their ferry fight to Turkey for delivery to Devlet Hava Yollari in July 1943, with TC-LAV nearest to the camera, then TC-MUT and TC-NUR; note the space left on the fuselage side for the ferry registrations   *[G M Simons collection]*

Appendix 4

TABLE 1 : REGISTRATIONS OF NEW CIVIL AIRCRAFT

	DH.84 / 1	DH.84 / 2	DH.86	DH.86 A	DH.86 B	DH.89	DH.89 A	DH.90	DH.90 A	DH.92
1932	3	-	-	-	-	-	-	-	-	-
1933	49	3	-	-	-	-	-	-	-	-
1934	-	25	15	-	-	13	-	-	-	-
1935	-	14	17	6	-	46	-	1	-	-
1936	-	9	-	15	-	27	4	37	-	1
1937	-	-	-	-	9	-	35	9	10	-
1938	-	-	-	-	-	-	42	-	5	-
1939	-	-	-	-	-	-	17	-	-	-
1940	-	-	-	-	-	-	1	-	-	-
1941	-	-	-	-	-	-	1	-	-	-
1942	-	-	-	-	-	-	1 ◊	-	-	-
1947	-	-	-	-	-	-	2 ◊	-	-	-
TOTALS	**52**	**51**	**32**	**21**	**9**	**86**	**103**	**47**	**15**	**1**
	103		62			189 ◊◊		62		1

Notes:	◊	Built from spares
	◊◊	Plus 1 static airframe

Carrying its original registration CH-287 is the protoype DH.89, c/n 6250   [G M Simons collection]

TABLE 2 : DISTRIBUTION OF NEW CIVIL AIRCRAFT BY COUNTRY

	DH.84	DH.86	DH.89	DH.90	DH.92	TOTALS
United Kingdom	68	44	95	21	1	**229**
Argentina	-	-	-	2	-	**2**
Australia	13	12	7	4	-	**36**
Austria	1	-	-	-	-	**1**
Belgium	-	-	1	1	-	**2**
Brazil	1	-	1	-	-	**2**
Canada	3	-	13	6	-	**22**
China	-	-	1	-	-	**1**
Dutch E Indies	-	-	3	-	-	**3**
Egypt	3	3	5	1	-	**12**
Finland	-	-	2	-	-	**2**
France	2	-	12	5	-	**19**
Holland	-	-	-	1	-	**1**
India	3	-	5	3	-	**11**
Iraq	1	-	3	2	-	**6**
Italy	-	-	1	1	-	**2**
Kenya	2	-	6	1	-	**9**
Latvia	-	-	2	-	-	**2**
New Zealand	2	3	6	2	-	**13**
Nigeria	-	-	-	1	-	**1**
Portuguese E Africa	-	-	9	1	-	**10**
Rumania	-	-	4	3	-	**7**
Singapore	-	-	2	-	-	**2**
South Africa	3	-	4	3	-	**10**
Southern Rhodesia	-	-	2	2	-	**4**
Spain	1	-	1	-	-	**2**
Switzerland	-	-	3	-	-	**3**
Uruguay	-	-	1	2	-	**3**
TOTALS	103	62	189	62	1	417

TABLE 3 : MILITARY AIRCRAFT DELIVERIES (EXCLUDING IMPRESSMENTS)

	DH.84				DH.89						DH.90		
	RAAF	Iraqi AF	DAAF	Port AF	RAF	RAAF	IIr AF	Lith AF	China	SRAF	RCAF	DAAF	SwedAF
1932	-	-	-	-	-	-	-	-	-	-	-	-	-
1933	-	8	1	-	-	-	-	-	-	-	-	-	-
1934	-	-	1	-	-	-	-	-	-	-	-	-	-
1935	-	-	-	-	2	1	-	-	-	-	-	-	-
1936	-	-	-	-	-	-	3	-	-	-	-	-	-
1937	-	-	-	2	-	-	-	2	6	-	-	-	-
1938	-	-	-	-	2	-	-	-	-	1	-	2	1
1939	-	-	-	-	20	-	-	-	-	-	-	-	-
1940	-	-	-	-	30	-	-	-	-	-	2	-	-
1941	-	-	-	-	92	-	-	-	-	-	-	-	-
1942	25	-	-	-	47	-	-	-	-	-	-	-	-
1943	62	-	-	-	35	-	-	-	-	-	-	-	-
1944	-	-	-	-	150	-	-	-	-	-	-	-	-
1945	-	-	-	-	101	-	-	-	-	-	-	-	-
1946	-	-	-	-	49	-	-	-	-	-	-	-	-
TOTALS	87	8	2	2	528 ◊	1	3	2	6	1	2	2	1
	99				541						5		

Notes: ◊   Including 23 diverted from RAF contract
(9 to RNAAF, 14 to SAAF)

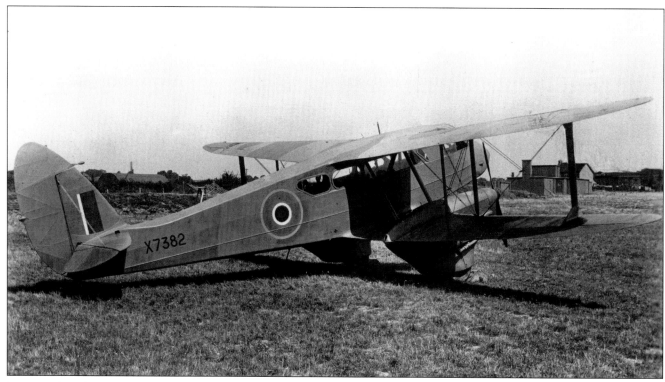

Dominie X7382, c/n 6542, of the Air Transport Auxiliary in August 1942   *[RTP 10949 via P H T Green]*

TABLE 4 : FORMER RAF OR FAA DOMINIES SOLD FOR CIVILIAN USE, EITHER AFTER MILITARY USE OR 'AS NEW' (DATES GIVEN ARE THE YEARS OF REGISTRATION)

	1941	1942	1943	1944	1945	1946	1947	1948	1949	1950	1953	1955	1957	1958	1959	1963	TOTALS
United Kingdom	2	3	5	4	26	64	61	56	9	21	5	2	1	1	1	3	264
Australia	-	-	-	-	-	-	-	2	-	-	-	-	-	-	-	-	2
Angola	-	-	-	-	-	4	-	-	-	-	-	-	-	-	-	-	4
Brazil	-	-	-	-	-	6	3	-	1	-	-	-	-	-	-	-	10
Canada	-	-	-	-	-	2	-	-	-	-	-	-	-	-	-	-	2
Denmark	-	-	-	-	-	1	-	-	-	-	-	-	-	-	-	-	1
Ecuador	-	-	-	-	-	-	1	-	-	-	-	-	-	-	-	-	1
Egypt	-	2	2	-	-	-	-	-	-	-	-	-	-	-	-	-	4
Holland	-	-	-	-	4	-	-	-	-	-	-	-	-	-	-	-	4
Iceland	-	-	-	-	2	-	-	-	-	-	-	-	-	-	-	-	2
India	-	-	5	7	1	3	1	-	-	-	-	-	-	-	-	-	17
Iran	-	-	-	3	-	-	-	-	-	-	-	-	-	-	-	-	3
Iraq	-	-	-	-	-	5	-	-	-	-	-	-	-	-	-	-	5
Kenya	-	-	-	-	-	-	1	-	-	-	-	-	-	-	-	-	1
Lebanon	-	-	-	-	3	-	-	-	-	-	-	-	-	-	-	-	3
Palestine	-	-	-	-	-	-	1	-	-	-	-	-	-	-	-	-	1
Peru	-	-	-	-	-	5	2	-	-	-	-	-	-	-	-	-	7
Portugal	-	-	-	-	3	-	-	-	-	-	-	-	-	-	-	-	3
South Africa	-	-	-	-	-	3	-	-	-	-	-	-	-	-	-	-	3
Southern Rhodesia	-	-	-	6	2	2	-	-	-	-	-	-	-	-	-	-	10
Sweden	-	-	-	-	-	1	-	-	-	-	-	-	-	-	-	-	1
Transjordan	-	-	-	-	-	3	2	-	-	-	-	-	-	-	-	-	5
Turkey	-	-	-	8	-	-	-	-	-	-	-	-	-	-	-	-	8
Yugoslavia	-	-	-	-	-	1	-	-	-	-	-	-	-	-	-	-	1
TOTALS	2	5	12	28	41	100	72	58	10	21	5	2	1	1	1	3	362

Dominie X7381, c/n 6541, was still in wartime camouflage when photographed at White Waltham on 8th May 1949, when still in use by A&AEE, Boscombe Down. It is still extant after over fifty years as a civil aircraft in Britain and France [Denis Fox collection]

Survivors

DH.84 : 6021, 6039, 6062, 6096, 6105, 2002, 2019, 2048, 2057, 2081

DH.89 : 6254, 6261, 6278, 6336 ?, 6337, 6345, 6375 ?, 6423, 6430 ?, 6458, 6517, 6588, 6601, 6647, 6648, 6653, 6655, 6662, 6676, 6706, 6709, 6736, 6740, 6746, 6782, 6794, 6796, 6801, 6831, 6837, 6838, 6853, 6879, 6884, 6897, 6899, 6900, 6926, 6940, 6944, 6952, 6968, W.1001

DH.90 : 7508, 7526

Abbreviations

AAC	Anti-Aircraft Co-operation		CANS	Civil Air Navigation School
AACU	Anti-Aircraft Co-operation Unit		Capt	Captain
A&AEE	Aircraft & Armament Experimental Establishment		CAS	Chief of the Air Staff
AAJC	Associated Airways Joint Committee		Cat	Category
AAU	Air Ambulance Unit (RAAF)		CCCF	Coastal Command Communications Flight
ACCCF	Army Co-operation Command Communications Flight		Cdr(E)	Commander (Engineer)
ACM	Air Chief Marshal		Cdte	Commandante
ACSEA	Air Command South East Asia		CF	Communications Flight
AC2	Aircraftsman Second Class		CFS	Central Flying School
AD	Air Depot (RAAF)		Cie	Compagnie
ADF	Aircraft Delivery Flight		CIGS	Chief of the Imperial General Staff
ADGB	Air Defence of Great Britain		Cld	Cancelled
AF	Air Force		Cmd	Command
AFC	Air Force Cross		c/n	construction number
AG	Air Gunner(y)		Co	Company
AG&AOS	Air Gunners & Air Observers School		CoA	Certificate of Airworthiness
AGS	Air Gunnery School		Comms	Communications
AHQ	Air Headquarters		CoR	Certificate of Registration
AHS	Aircraft Holding Section		Corp	Corporation
AHU	Aircraft Holding Unit		CPO	Chief Petty Officer
Alb	Alberta		CRD	Civilian Repair Depot
AM(A)	Airman (Air Fitter)		CS	Communications Squadron
AM(O)	Airman (Ordnance)		CSE	Central Signals Establishment
ANA	Australian National Airways		CT	Connecticut
AONS	Air Observers' Navigation School		CU	Communications Unit
AOS	Air Observers' School			
AP	Aircraft Park (RAAF)			
APC	Armament Practice Camp		DAAF	Danish Army Air Force
ARD	Aircraft Repair Depot (RAAF)		DBF	Destroyed by fire
arr	arrived or arriving		DBR	Damaged beyond repair
AS	Air School (SAAF)		DCA	Director of Civil Aviation
asl	above sea level		DCAS	Deputy Chief of the Air Staff
ATA	Air Transport Auxiliary		Def Flt	Defence Flight
ATC	Air Training Corps		del	delivered
ATDU	Air Torpedo Development Unit		det	detached or detachment
ATG	Air Transport Group (USAAF)		DF	Delivery Flight
ATS	Armament Training Station		DGRD	Director General of Research & Development
attd	attached		DH	de Havilland
AURI	Indonesian Air Force		DH of SA	de Havilland of South Africa
AVM	Air Vice-Marshal		DH RU	de Havilland Repair Unit
			DSM	Distinguished Service Medal
			DSO	Distinguished Service Order
BA	British Airways			
BAS	Beam Approach School			
BBOC	Brought back on charge		E	East
BC	British Columbia		EA	East African
BEA	British European Airways		EAAC	East African Airways Corporation
BER	Beyond economic repair		EFS	Empire Flying School
Bf	Bayerische Flugzeugbau		EFTS	Elementary Flying Training School
B&GS	Bombing & Gunnery School		ENE	East-North-East
BLEU	Blind Landing Experimental Unit		ERS	Empire Radio School
BOAC	British Overseas Airways Corporation		ETPS	Empire Test Pilots School
Bt	Baronet		E&WF	Electrical & Wireless Flight
BW Flt	Bristol Wireless Flight		E&WS	Electrical & Wireless School
(C)	Coastal		FAA	Fleet Air Arm
CA	California		FCCF/S	Fighter Command Communications Flight/Squadron
Cal Flt	Calibration Flight		FFAF	Free French Air Force
Cam	Camouflage		FL	Florida

Flg Off	Flying Officer
Flt	Flight
Flt Sgt	Flight Sergeant
Flt Lt	Flight Lieutenant
FOFT	Flag Officer Flying Training
FORA	Flag Officer Reserve Aircraft
FPP	Ferry Pilots Pool
FTS	Flying Training School
FU	Ferry Unit
gall	gallons
Gen	General
GI	Ground instructional
GM	George Medal
GOC	General Officer Commanding
Govt	Government
GP	General Purpose
Gp CF	Group Communications Flight
GR	General Reconnaissance
GW&SA	Great Western & Southern Airlines
HQ	Headquarters
HRH	His Royal Highness
(I)	India
IAF	Indian Air Force
IAL	Imperial Airways Ltd
IDFAF	Israel Defence Force Air Force
IFTU	Intensive Flying Trials Unit
IN	Indiana
KAAU	Kenya Auxiliary Air Unit
kg	kilograms
KNILM	Koninlijke Nederlandsch-Indische Luchvaart Maatschappij
KY	Kentucky
LAC	Leading Aircraftman
lb	pounds
LG	Landing Ground
Lt	Lieutenant
Lt Col	Lieutenant Colonel
Lt(E)	Lieutenant (Engineer)
Ltd	Limited (Company)
Maj	Major
Man	Manitoba
MARU	Mobile Aircraft Repair Unit
MC	Military Cross
MCCS	Maintenance Command Communications Squadron
MCS	Metropolitan Communications Squadron
MD	Managing Director
ME	Maine
Mk	Mark
mls	miles
MN	Minnesota
MO	Miissouri
MoAP	Ministry of Aircraft Production
MoCA	Ministry of Civil Aviation
MoS	Ministry of Supply
MoT&CA	Ministry of Transport & Civil Aviation
MoTaT	Ministry of Transport & Technology
MPRD	Military Produce Reduction Depot ?
MU	Maintenance Unit
MVAF	Malayan Volunteer Air Force
N	North
NAC	National Air Communications
NARIU	Naval Air Radio Installation Unit
NB	New Brunswick

NFT	No further trace
NG	Ne∆w Guinea
NGTE	National Gas Turbine Establishment
NI	Northern Ireland
NJ	New Jersey
no	number
NSW	New South Wales
NT	Northern Territory (of Australia)
NTU	Not taken up
NWT	North-West Territory
NY	New York
NZNAC	New Zealand National Airways Corporation
(O)AFU	(Observers) Advanced Flying Unit
OAPU	Overseas Aircraft Preparation Unit
Off	Officer
OFS	Orange Free State
OH	Ohio
OK	Oklahoma
OR	Oregon
OTU	Operational Training Unit
P&GTS	Parachute & Glider Training School
Plt Off	Pilot Officer
PO	Petty Officer
PO(A)	Petty Officer (Air)
PQ	Province of Quebec
PS&IoW	Portsmouth, Southsea & Isle of Wight
PSOC	Presumed Struck Off Charge
Ptnrs	Partners
PTS	Parachute Training School
PTU	Parachute Training Unit
Pty	Proprietary
Pvt	Private
PWFU	Permanently withdrawn from use
QANTAS	Queensland & Northern Territory Aerial Service Ltd
QEA	Qantas Empire Airways
Qld	Queensland
RAAF	Royal Australian Air Force
RAE	Royal Aircraft Establishment
RARA	Rear Admiral, Reserve Aircraft
RAS	Railway Air Services td
R&CF	Rescue & Communications Flight (RAAF)
RCMP	Royal Canadian Mounted Police
RDAF	Royal Danish Air Force
RDU	Receipt & Despatch Unit
redes	redesignated
regd	registered
regn	registration
Regt	Regiment
retd	returned
RFDS	Royal Flying Doctor Service
RIrAF	Royal Iranian Air Force
RMA	Royal Mail Aircraft
RN	Royal Navy
RNARY	Royal Naval Aircraft Repair Yard
RNAY	Royal Naval Aircraft Yard
RNEC	Royal Naval Engineering College
RNethAF	Royal Netherlands Air Force
RNZAF	Royal New Zealand Air Force
ROS	Repaired on site
Rt Hon	Right Honourable
RPE	Rocket Projectile Establishment
RRAF	Royal Rhodesian Air Force
RRE	Royal Radar Establishment
RS	Radio School
R&SU	Repair & Salvage Unit
RTP	Reduced to produce
RU	Repair Unit
RWE	Radio Warfare Establishment

S	South	t/a	trading as
SA	Société Anonyme	Tas	Tasmania
	South Africa	TCCF	Transport Command Communications Flight
	South Australia	TEU	Tactical Exercise Unit
SAAF	South African Air Force	TFU	Telecommunications Flying Unit
SAC	Senior Aircraftman	TOC	Taken on charge
SAS	Special Air Squadron	TrAG	Training Air Group
SBA	Standard Beam Approach	TTCCF	Technical Training Command Communications Flight
SF	Station Flight		
	Survey Flight (RAAF)		
SFC	School of Flying Control	UK	United Kingdom
SFPP	Service Ferry Pilots' Pool	US	United States (of America)
SFS	Service Ferry Squadron	USAAC	United States Army Air Corps
SFTS	Service Flying Training School	USAAF	United States Army Air Force
Sgt	Sergeant		
SHAEF	Supreme Headquarters Allied Expeditionary Force		
Sigs	Signals	Vic	Victoria
SLAW	School of Land-Air Warfare		
SoAT	School of Air Transport		
SOC	Struck off charge	W	West
SoGR	School of General Reconnaissance	WA	Washington
SoS	Secretary of State		Western Australia
Sqn	Squadron	wef	with effect from
Sqn Ldr	Squadron Leader	W&GS	Wireless and Gunnery School (RAAF)
SRAF	Southern Rhodesian Air Force	WFU	Withdrawn from use
SS	Signals School (RAF context)	Wg	Wing
	Storage Section (FAA context)	Wg Cdr	Wing Commander
	Straits Settlements (geographical context)	WI	Wisconsin
SoTT	School of Technical Training	WOp	Wireless Operator
stbd	starboard	W/T	Wireless Telegraphy
Sté	Société	WW2	Second World War
Sub Lt	Sub Lieutenant		
Surg Cdr	Surgeon Commander		
SW	South-West	ZG	Zerstörergeschwader (Destroyer [Heavy Fighter] Wing)
SWA	South West Africa		
		2nd TAF	Second Tactical Air Force

Bibliography

In preparing this Volume, the author has made reference to a number of different publications, many of which are worthy of further reference.

Air Crash (Vol 1) by Macarthur Job (Aerospace Publications Pty Ltd, 1991) ISBN 0 9587978 9 7

Journal of the Aviation Historical Society of Australia, Vol 18, No 2

Wings Over the Glens by Peter Clegg (GMS Enterprises, 1995) ISBN 1 870384 35 0

de Havilland Aircraft Since 1915 by A J Jackson (Putnam & Co Ltd, 1962) no ISBN

British Civil Aircraft 1919-1972 by A J Jackson (Putnam & Co Ltd, 1973) ISBN 0 85177 813 5

British Independent Airlines 1946-1976 by A C Merton-Jones (The Aviation Hobby Shop, 2000) ISBN 0 907178 82 0

The Squadrons of the Royal Air Force and Commonwealth 1918-1988 by J J Halley
    (Air-Britain [Historians] Ltd, 1988) ISBN 0 85130 164 9

Royal Air Force Flying Training and Support Units by R C Sturtivant, J F Hamlin and J J Halley
    (Air-Britain [Historians] Ltd, 1997) ISBN 0 85130 252 1

Railway Air Services by John Stroud (Ian Allan Ltd, 1987) ISBN 0 7110 1743 3

Merchant Airmen (anon) (HMSO, 1946) no ISBN

Nine Lives Plus by the Hon Mrs Victor Bruce (Pelham Books Ltd, 1977) ISBN 0 7207 0974 1

Aircraft of the Spanish Civil War by Gerald Howson (Putnam & Co Ltd, 1990) ISBN 0 85177 842 9

Imperial Airways and the First British Airlines 1919-40 by A S Jackson (Terence Dalton Ltd, 1995) ISBN 0 86138 098 3

The Vectis Connection by Peter Newberry (Waterfront, 2000) ISBN 0 946184 90 9

The Triple Alliance by Neville Doyle (Air-Britain [Historians] Ltd, 2001) ISBN 0 85130 286 6

AIR-BRITAIN SALES

This publication and companion volumes are available by post-free mail order from

Air-Britain Sales Department (Dept DRF)
41 Penshurst Road, Leigh,
Tonbridge, Kent TN11 8HL

For a full list of current titles and details of how to order, visit our e-commerce site at www.air-britain.co.uk
Visa / Mastercard / Delta / Switch accepted - please give full details of card number and expiry date.

THE TRIPLE ALLIANCE - The Predecessors of the first British Airways
By Neville Doyle   £18.00 (Members) £22.50 (Non-members)
The story of Hillman's Airways Ltd, Spartan Air Lines and United Airways Ltd, and other operators involved through mergers and take-overs, who amalgamated on 1st October 1935 to form British Airways Ltd. Fully illustrated with contemporary photos, timetables and advertising, and describing the personalities, routes flown and aircraft used. Hardback A4, 128 pages with 8 in colour.

THOSE FABULOUS FLYING YEARS - Joy-Riding and Flying Circuses between the Wars
By Colin Cruddas   £19.95 (Members) £29.95 (Non-members)
First tracing the history of 'barnstorming' in the United States, this book then covers the history of British companies that attempted to bring aviation to every corner of the country, either through pleasure flying or aerial displays. While Cobham's extensive tours at home and abroad are covered, so too are the smaller companies, their fleet lists and the personalities who provided the thrills for the public. Profusely illustrated. Hardback A4, 128 pages.

THE SOPWITH PUP
By J M Bruce, Gordon Page and Ray Sturtivant   £24.00 (Members) £30.00 (Non-members)
The definite work on the Sopwith Pup, covering in detail the aircraft's development, service history and units in a narrative account supported by all known details of individual aircraft histories, survivors and replicas. Hardback A4, 320 pages containing over 400 photographs and numerous colour and black-and-white scale drawings.

THE DH.4/DH.9 FILE
By Ray Sturtivant and Gordon Page   £24.00 (Members) £30.00 (Non-members)
The story of the development of these types built in large numbers for the RFS, RNAS, RAF and USAAC. Another definitive work which includes details of widespread use overseas. Hardback A4, 300 pages including 450 photos and 16 pages of colour drawings.

SPITFIRE INTERNATIONAL
By Helmut Terbeck, Harry van der Meer and Ray Sturtivant   £32.50 (Members) £39.50 (Non-members)
Well over 6000 Spitfires served with overseas air and naval forces during and after the Second World War. All known details of these, together with background information about their operators and the units to which they belonged, and of the Spitfires known to have flown outside the UK with civil registrations, are included in this 480 page A4 hardback book which contains many colour photos, drawings, maps and insignia.

THE DH.106 COMET An Illustrated History
By Martin Painter   £29.50 (Members) £37.00 (Non-members)
The story of the development of Britain's pioneering jet airliner, its operators, routes, detailed individual histories, fates and survivors. Contains over 600 illustrations, 242 in colour. Hardback A4, 368 pages.

For civil aircraft enthusiasts Air-Britain publishes annually a series of titles covering UK and European Registers, worldwide Airline Fleets, Business Jets and a series of low-priced "Quick Reference" books on these topics.
Air-Britain also publishes a comprehensive range of military titles, please check for latest details of RAF Serial Registers, detailed RAF aircraft type "Files", Squadron Histories and Royal Navy Aircraft Histories.

IMPORTANT NOTE – Members receive substantial discounts on prices of all the above Air-Britain publications.
For details of membership see the following page or visit our website at http://www.air-britain.co.uk

AIR-BRITAIN MEMBERSHIP

Join on-line at www.air-britain.co.uk

If you are not currently a member of Air-Britain, the publishers of this book, you may be interested in what we have on offer to provide for your interest in aviation.

About Air-Britain

Formed over 50 years ago, we are the world's most progressive aviation society, and exist to bring together aviation enthusiasts with every type of interest. Our members include aircraft historians, aviation writers, spotters and pilots – and those who just have a fascination with aircraft and aviation. Air-Britain is a non-profit organisation, which is independently audited, and any financial surpluses are used to provide services to the ever-growing membership. In the last 7 years, our membership has increased annually, and our current membership now stands at over 4,200.

Membership of Air-Britain

Membership is open to all. A basic membership fee is charged and every member receives a copy of the quarterly house magazine, Air-Britain Aviation World, and is entitled to use all the Air-Britain specialist services and buy **Air-Britain publications at discounted prices**. A membership subscription includes the choice to add any or all of our other 3 magazines, News &/or Archive &/or Aeromilitaria. Air-Britain also publishes 10-20 books per annum (around 70 titles in stock at any one time). Membership runs January – December each year, but new members have a choice of options periods to get their initial subscription started.

Air-Britain Aviation World is the quarterly 48-page house magazine containing not only news of Air-Britain activities, but also a wealth of features, often illustrated in colour, on many different aviation subjects, contemporary and historical, contributed by our 4,200 members.

Air-Britain News is the world aviation news monthly, containing data on aircraft registrations worldwide and news of Airlines and Airliners, Business Jets, Local Airfield News, Civil and Military Air Show Reports, and International Military Aviation News. An average 160 pages of lavishly–illustrated information for the dedicated enthusiast.

Air-Britain Archive is the quarterly 48-page specialist journal of civil aviation history. Packed with the results of historical research by Air-Britain specialists into aircraft types, overseas registers and previously unpublished facts about the rich heritage of civil aviation. Up to 100 photographs per issue, some in colour.

Air-Britain Aeromilitaria is the quarterly 48-page unique source for meticulously researched details of military aviation history edited by the acclaimed authors of Air-Britain's military monographs featuring British, Commonwealth, European and U.S. Military aviation articles. Illustrated in colour and black & white.

Other Benefits

Additional to the above, members have exclusive access to the Air-Britain e-mail Information Exchange Service (ab-ix) where they can exchange information and solve each other's queries, and to an on-line UK airfield residents database. Other benefits include numerous Branches, use of the Specialists Information Service; Air-Britain trips; and access to black & white and colour photograph libraries. During the summer we also host our own popular FLY-IN. Each autumn, we host an Aircraft Recognition Contest.

Membership Subscription Rates – from £10 per annum.

Membership subscription rates start from as little as £10 per annum, and this amount provides a copy of 'Air-Britain Aviation World' quarterly as well as all the other benefits covered above. Subscriptions to include any or all of our other three magazines vary between £18 and £50 per annum (slightly higher to overseas).

Join on-line at www.air-britain.co.uk. Or, write to 'Air-Britain' at 1 Rose Cottages, 179 Penn Road, Hazlemere, High Wycombe, Bucks HP15 7NE, UK, or telephone/fax on 01394 450767 (+44 1394 450767) e-mail: Barry.Collman@air-britain.co.uk, and ask for a membership pack containing the full details of subscription rates, samples of our magazines and a book list.